I0605650

Let the Oppressed Go Free

EARLY AMERICAN STUDIES

Series editors: Kathleen M. Brown, Roquinaldo Ferreira, Emma Hart, and Daniel K. Richter

Exploring neglected aspects of our colonial, revolutionary, and early national history and culture, Early American Studies reinterprets familiar themes and events in fresh ways. Interdisciplinary in character, and with a special emphasis on the period from about 1600 to 1850, the series is published in partnership with the McNeil Center for Early American Studies.

A complete list of books in the series is available from the publisher.

Let the Oppressed Go Free

Abolitionism in Colonial and Revolutionary America

Nicholas P. Wood

PENN

UNIVERSITY OF PENNSYLVANIA PRESS

PHILADELPHIA

Published with the generous support of the National Endowment for the Humanities. Any views, findings, conclusions, or recommendations expressed in this book do not necessarily reflect those of the National Endowment for the Humanities.

Published with the generous support of the Fellowship in Memory of Kenneth R. LaVoy Jr., established by the Society of Colonial Wars in the State of Florida and administered by Florida Atlantic University.

Published with the generous support of the Friends Historical Association.

Copyright © 2025 University of Pennsylvania Press

All rights reserved. Except for brief quotations used for purposes of review or scholarly citation, none of this book may be reproduced in any form by any means without written permission from the publisher.

Published by
University of Pennsylvania Press
Philadelphia, Pennsylvania 19104 USA
www.pennpress.org

EU Authorized Representative:
Easy Access System Europe—Mustamäe tee 50,
10621 Tallinn, Estonia, gpsr.requests@easproject.com

Printed in the United States of America on acid-free paper
10 9 8 7 6 5 4 3 2 1

A Cataloging-in-Publication record for this book is available from the Library of Congress.

Hardback ISBN 978-1-5128-2832-0
Ebook ISBN 978-1-5128-2833-7

For Alison

1 Cry aloud, spare not, lift up thy voice like a trumpet, and
shew my people their transgression, and the house of Jacob
their sins. 2 Yet they seek me daily, and delight to know my
ways, as a nation that did righteousness, and forsook not
the ordinance of their God: they ask of me the ordinances of
justice; they take delight in approaching to God. 3 Wherefore
have we fasted, say they, and thou seest not? wherefore have
we afflicted our soul, and thou takest no knowledge? Behold,
in the day of your fast ye find pleasure, and exact all your
labours. 4 Behold, ye fast for strife and debate, and to smite
with the fist of wickedness: ye shall not fast as ye do this day,
to make your voice to be heard on high. 5 Is it such a fast that
I have chosen? a day for a man to afflict his soul? is it to bow
down his head as a bulrush, and to spread sackcloth and
ashes under him? wilt thou call this a fast, and an acceptable
day to the LORD?

6 Is not this the fast that I have chosen? to loose the bands
of wickedness, to undo the heavy burdens, and to let the
oppressed go free, and that ye break every yoke? 7 Is it not
to deal thy bread to the hungry, and that thou bring the
poor that are cast out to thy house? when thou seest the
naked, that thou cover him; and that thou hide not thyself
from thine own flesh? 8 Then shall thy light break forth as
the morning, and thine health shall spring forth speedily:
and thy righteousness shall go before thee; the glory of the
LORD shall be thy reward.

—Isaiah 58:1–8 (King James Version)

CONTENTS

Introduction

At the close of the Revolutionary War in 1783, David Cooper of New Jersey anonymously published an antislavery pamphlet, *A Serious Address to the Rulers of America*, which he sent to General George Washington and every member of the Confederation Congress. The pamphlet (Figure 1) called on politicians to demonstrate "that America was in earnest, and meant what she said . . . that *all mankind* came from the hand of their Creator *equally free*" by enacting a national program of gradual emancipation. Cooper proposed liberating every person of color who was "brought into, or born within any of the United States, after the Declaration of Independence." His efforts to link the Revolution to abolitionism have led one scholar to describe Cooper as a "typical example" of patriots whose antislavery zeal was inspired "by their own struggle for independence." However, such characterizations distort both chronology and causality while exaggerating the link between the patriot movement and abolitionism. Cooper was a Quaker who had remained neutral during the Revolutionary War on account of his commitment to pacifism. He supported the Quaker practice of disowning members who supported the war—which included his own brother, John, with whom he never again spoke. Clearly, Cooper was hardly a typical patriot. When Cooper quoted patriots' natural rights rhetoric, he did so reveal to the hypocrisy of "ye cruel taskmasters, ye petty tyrants" and "mock patriots" who cared only about "the *rights* of *whitemen* not of *all men*." Patriots' rhetoric did not inspire Cooper's antislavery sentiments; rather, it provoked his derision.[1]

Cooper's own antislavery conversion had occurred decades earlier. Born in 1724, he had come of age at a time when the Society of Friends was engaged in contentious scriptural debates over whether slaveholding was a divinely sanctioned institution or a sinful form of oppression. In *A Serious Address*, Cooper alluded to the fact that many Quakers had tolerated slaveholding

A
SERIOUS ADDRESS
TO THE
RULERS OF AMERICA,
On the Inconſiſtency of their Conduct reſpecting
SLAVERY:
FORMING A CONTRAST
Between the ENCROACHMENTS of England on American LIBERTY,
AND,
American INJUSTICE in tolerating SLAVERY.

As for me, I will aſſuredly contend for full and impartial liberty, whether my labour may be ſucceſsful or vain.

TRENTON:
Printed by ISAAC COLLINS,
M.DCC.LXXXIII.

Figure 1. George Washington's copy of David Cooper's *A Serious Address.* Courtesy of the Boston Athenaeum.

"until the difficulties attending the late French and Indian war brought the rights of men into a more close inspection." Like many of their contemporaries, Quakers believed that God's providence shaped earthly events, often punishing or rewarding nations for their sinfulness or righteousness. The brutality of the French and Indian War—and especially the captivity of white settlers taken prisoner by Native Americans—appeared to many Quakers as a fitting form of divine retaliation for the sin of enslaving Africans. As a delegate in 1758 to the Philadelphia Yearly Meeting (PYM, which established policy for Quakers in the surrounding colonies), Cooper had supported a new "minute" (policy statement) that described the French and Indian War as evidence of

God's "Judgments" against the sin of slavery. The new policy instructed any Friends "who have any Slaves to sett them at Liberty." Cooper then helped oversee manumissions during the 1760s and published his first antislavery pamphlet, *A Mite Cast Into the Treasury: Or, Observations on Slave-Keeping*, in 1772, seeking to promote emancipation beyond the Society of Friends.[2]

Religion was central to both of Cooper's pamphlets, as was also true with the handful of antislavery pamphlets that had been published in North America since 1693. Cooper began *A Mite Cast Into the Treasury* by copying the text of Proverbs 31:8–9: "Open thy mouth for the dumb, and all such as appointed to destruction, and plead the cause of the poor and needy." He felt compelled by God to promote emancipation for the oppressed. Cooper approached slavery from a biblicist perspective, meaning that he believed the Bible was divinely inspired and should be interpreted in a literal manner to determine what God viewed as sinful and righteous. Echoing earlier Quaker abolitionists such as Ralph Sandiford and Benjamin Lay, Cooper argued that although the Lord had tolerated some forms of slavery in the Old Testament, Christ's teaching and sacrifice had rendered slaveholding sinful. Cooper also warned that God would "avenge" the cause of the enslaved, subjecting slaveholders to "retribution," either in this life or the next. Quoting from Isaiah 58:6, Cooper instructed slaveholders: "Do the best the present circumstances will admit of, 'Loose the bands of wickedness, and let the oppressed go free,' and thereby atone for what cannot be recalled." Eleven years later, Cooper repeated many of these same arguments—and again repeated Isaiah's call for liberation—in his *Serious Address*. He cited the Bible dozens of times and described slavery as a "crying transgression" that was "opposite to every precept of christianity." Like other abolitionists, Cooper interpreted the series of crises during the previous decades—the French and Indian War, the imperial crisis over parliamentary taxation, and the Revolutionary War—as God's means of chastising the British Empire for the sin of slavery. He hoped that the Revolutionary War would awaken patriots to slavery's sinful nature, as the French and Indian War had done among Quakers. Yet he bemoaned that in most of the new nation there had been "no effectual advance yet made towards loosing the bands of wickedness, and letting the oppressed go free." Cooper warned that God would punish America if it failed to extend liberty to the enslaved.[3]

Most white patriots did not embrace abolitionism, but those who did generally shared Cooper's belief that slaveholding was a God-provoking sin. Religion was the dominant theme in virtually all the antislavery pamphlets published during the revolutionary era. Indeed, British historian John Coffey notes that by the late eighteenth century, the prophet Isaiah's injunction to "let the oppressed go free" became "the motto of abolitionists on both sides of the Atlantic." American historians, however, tend to underestimate the crucial link between religion and antislavery in the revolutionary era. Instead, they often maintain a false dichotomy between religion and natural rights ideology (treated as a secular concept), assuming that the former gave way to the latter as the source of antislavery inspiration during the American Revolution. Patrick Rael illustrates this common tendency in *Eighty-Eight Years: The Long Death of Slavery in the United States*, writing: "Arguments based on Christian principles faced considerable hurdles, not least of which was the Bible's apparent sanction of servitude in many instances. . . . But more compelling in the last quarter of the eighteenth century was the notion that slavery violated the transcendent principles upon which the new nation had been established. . . . The ideology of the Revolution thus created the antislavery cause."[4] This widely held view neglects the continued centrality of religion within the antislavery movement from the colonial period through the revolutionary era.

* * *

Revisiting the role of religion can provide a new answer to an old question: *Why did the American Revolution—which began as a dispute regarding taxes and property rights—coincide with antislavery reforms, especially in the northern states?* Slavery was tolerated throughout the entire British Empire in 1764, when Parliament passed the first of the tax reforms that eventually led thirteen of the North American colonies to rebel. Twenty years later, four of the newly independent states (five counting Vermont, which was not formally admitted to statehood until 1791) had abolished hereditary slavery while many southern states had passed laws facilitating voluntary emancipations. *Why?* From the late nineteenth century into the mid-twentieth century, many scholars portrayed this timing as largely coincidental rather than causal. They asserted that northerners had ended slavery simply because "slavery was not suited to the climate" and "unprofitable." This view was advanced by both "Lost Cause" adherents (Confederate apologists who sought to downplay slavery's role as the motive for southern secession) and "Progressive" historians (who tended to view economic self-interest as the driving force in history). Such views were thoroughly refuted by the mid-1960s, with historians demonstrating that slavery had remained profitable in the North (albeit less so than in the South) and crediting its abolition to ideological changes wrought by the Revolution.[5]

According to this still standard view, natural rights rhetoric and republican ideology forced patriots to recognize that slaveholding was antithetical to their cause. Ideological consistency thus demanded abolition. As Winthrop Jordan states in *White Over Black*: "It was perfectly clear that the principles for which the Americans had fought required the complete abolition of slavery; the question was not *if*, but *when* and *how*."[6] Yet only the northern states had actually abolished slavery during the revolutionary era, and they did so in a gradual manner that often took decades and allowed other forms of racial oppression to persist. By the time Jordan published *White Over Black* in 1968, the driving question was already shifting to *Why did the American Revolution—which was based on natural rights ideology—fail to fully abolish slavery and establish racial equality throughout the nation?* Of course, slavery was more economically important in the South (where enslaved people generally made up more than 30 percent of each colony's population) and, thus, far harder to abolish there than in the North (where enslaved people were typically less than 10 percent of the population).[7] Despite the greater obstacles in the South, many historians have nonetheless argued that the Revolution presented a missed opportunity "when slavery might have been abolished peacefully without dismembering the Union."[8] They often operate under the assumption that the Revolution's egalitarian ideology would have led to national emancipation had some new trend or event not emerged to stall progress.

Scholars have offered various explanations for the "failure of abolitionism" in the South along with the shortcomings of emancipation and the persistence of racial discrimination in the North. Some, like Jordan, highlight the gradual hardening of nascent racial prejudice into full-blown racism, alleging that by the early nineteenth century, many white Americans had concluded that Black people were innately inferior and did not possess natural rights. Other historians emphasize a more concerted political effort to counter the Revolution's antislavery impulse, culminating with the United States Constitution of 1787, which contained numerous provisions serving the interests of slaveholders. Recently, some scholars have pushed back the date of antislavery's decline. For example, Robert Parkinson argues that the antislavery sentiment inspired by patriot protests peaked in the early 1770s and quickly collapsed in 1775, "when the American Revolution became the Revolutionary War." He documents how patriot newspaper editors "weaponized prejudice" to mobilize white support for the war after British commanders began enlisting Black and Indian allies. Parkinson argues that such practices "foreclosed" the Revolution's antislavery potential. Other writers go further, arguing that proslavery had actually been a central motive for independence from the start. This view has reached a large audience through Nikole Hannah-Jones's *1619 Project*, which argues that slaveholders supported the Revolution because they "believed that independence was required in order to ensure that the institution [of slavery] would continue unmolested."[9] Thus, a growing number of scholars argue that the Revolution either reflected proslavery sentiment from the beginning or became increasingly racist as it unfolded.

Meanwhile, some historians have steadfastly defended the Founding Fathers' reputation regarding slavery. In a series of books, Gordon Wood has claimed that the founders enthusiastically embraced antislavery reform and sincerely (if mistakenly) believed they had taken sufficient steps to put slavery on the road to extinction in spite of the Constitution's compromises. In his telling, it was unforeseen developments, such as the 1793 invention of the cotton gin, that reversed the South's supposed antislavery progress. And whereas scholars such as Gary Nash, Douglas Egerton, Manisha Sinha, and Patrick Rael have prominently featured African Americans' antislavery activism, Gordon Wood suggests that revolts and conspiracies by impatient Black people were counterproductive, alienating previously sympathetic white southerners. He asserts that the 1791 slave revolt in St. Domingue (present-day Haiti) and an 1800 conspiracy in Virginia "guaranteed that the state's earlier anti-slave [*sic*] liberalism would never be revived." Although Wood is somewhat unusual in shifting some of the blame for slavery onto its victims, Sean Wilentz and other scholars similarly assert that many Americans in the founding generation naively imagined that slavery would wither away once the new nation stopped importing additional African captives.[10]

In sum, after 250 years, the American Revolution's connection to slavery and abolitionism remains a subject of intense dispute. Scholars cannot agree whether the Revolution was motivated by proslavery or if it inspired widespread antislavery sentiment, whether Black people expedited or hindered antislavery progress, or whether the start of the war in 1775, the Constitutional Convention of 1787, the invention of the cotton gin in 1793, or a more gradual process of hardening racism was most decisive in curtailing any antislavery potential the Revolution may or may not have had.

Given slavery's economic importance and scholars' increased emphasis on racial prejudice and proslavery sentiment among white patriots, the persistence of slavery in the South and racial inequality in the North are hardly surprising. Indeed, aspects of Christopher Brown's analysis of Britain also applies to the United States: "In the end, what is remarkable about abolitionism in Britain is not that it took so long to emerge, that it was politically ineffective for many years, or that it was limited in its ambition and selective in its scope. Such movements often are. What is truly surprising about British abolitionism is that such a campaign ever should have developed at all." In the American context, it is the extent of antislavery gains in the revolutionary era—rather than the persistence of slavery—that is surprising and warrants further exploration. Nothing about abolitionism in America was inevitable; the Revolution played a crucial role but was insufficient alone to inspire political reform.[11]

* * *

Let the Oppressed Go Free seeks to move beyond the common tendencies of being overly celebratory or overly cynical, thereby revealing the contingency and complexity of the Revolution's connection to abolitionism. Patriots' natural rights rhetoric may have made politicians more sensitive to charges of hypocrisy, but antislavery reforms depended on tenacious activism by a dedicated corps of abolitionists, most of whom came from marginalized backgrounds and were inspired by religious zeal. In order to explain the extent as well as limitations of antislavery progress during the revolutionary era, *Let the Oppressed Go Free* examines how abolitionists' ideology, activism, and influence evolved over time and were shaped by war from the colonial era through the 1780s.

In terms of ideology, I highlight the importance of biblicism and providentialism within antislavery thought. During the last quarter of the seventeenth century, a handful of Quakers and Puritans articulated antislavery arguments grounded in scripture. Of course, these early abolitionists did not inspire widespread emancipation, nor did they prevent slaveholders from continuing to twist the Bible to justify slavery. Nonetheless, their early biblicist antislavery arguments were more sophisticated and consequential than historians have realized. These arguments gained adherents throughout the eighteenth century, especially among Quakers during the French and Indian War and then among a significant portion of the broader white public during the American Revolution. Antislavery patriots generally viewed slavery as a sin that threatened to bring God's wrath down upon the land.

My emphasis on religious concepts is not to claim that natural rights ideology was unimportant; rather, I argue that it was the crucial interplay between religious conviction and natural rights ideology that inspired antislavery *activism*. Natural rights rhetoric and a supposed desire for ideological consistency were rarely enough to inspire antislavery action on behalf of others, even when they aroused a level of antislavery sympathy. As Christopher Brown has observed, "There was an important difference, and often a significant distance, between antislavery sympathies and antislavery commitments."[12] Most white patriots embraced natural rights ideology in defense of their own rights, but only a small minority felt compelled to actively support the liberty of enslaved Black people. Some whites, especially slaveholders, insisted that Black people lacked natural rights because they were racially inferior and cursed by God. Others lamented slavery's existence but accepted its persistence. Historian François Furstenberg has demonstrated the ease with which many white patriots could reconcile the defense of their own natural rights with the persistence of slavery through the concept of virtue. For example, Samuel Adams declared in the *Boston Gazette* in 1771: "I Believe that no people ever yet groan'd under the heavy yoke of slavery, but when they deserv'd it . . . if they have not *virtue* enough to maintain their liberty against a presumptuous invader, they deserve no pity." Furstenburg notes that although this rhetoric was "not racially specific," it still "provided an insidious new legitimation of slavery, which placed the onus of freedom on slaves themselves." In this view, even if Black people possessed God-given natural rights, it was their own responsibility to defend them. This type of thinking soothed the consciences of many white Americans who celebrated their own virtuous resistance to tyranny while imagining that Black people had tacitly submitted to enslavement.[13]

By contrast, the minority of white people who actively supported abolitionism were generally inspired by the conviction that God required them to restore enslaved Black people to the enjoyment of their natural rights. The process of antislavery awakening occurred first among a majority of Quakers during the French and Indian War and then among a minority of white patriots during the Revolution. These groups of inspired activists viewed slavery as a sinful violation of Black people's God-given natural rights that was provoking rounds of divine chastisement. They feared that God would punish slaveholding societies with increasing severity until they reformed. These providentialist beliefs created a sense of urgency and self-interest (the desire to avoid God's wrath) that was crucial in converting antislavery sentiment into action. Antislavery patriots believed that by promoting abolition, they also ensured that God would aid them in their struggle for their own liberty.[14]

Scholars' tendency to treat antislavery as resulting from the "contagion of liberty" has often led them to portray reforms as largely inevitable, thereby underestimating the extent and impact of organized antislavery activism between the 1750s and 1780s. Historians have acknowledged the role of individual activists, such as Quakers John Woolman and Anthony Benezet, before the Revolutionary War, but they have generally assumed there was little concerted activism until the rise of secular antislavery groups such as the Pennsylvania Abolition Society (initially established in 1775 but quickly disbanded until a postwar resurrection in 1784) and the New-York Manumission Society (established in 1785). Thus, studies of organized abolitionism tend to begin in the postwar period. Historian Paul Polgar, for example, considers the 1780s as the start of "first movement abolitionism" (in contrast to the "second wave" or "immediatist" abolitionists after 1830, who have received the bulk of scholarly attention). Polgar acknowledges colonial-era Quaker abolitionists as "important precursors" but does not consider them part of a coherent "movement" because they "lacked the same level of systematic and institutionally organized activism of the abolition societies."[15] However, such a characterization underappreciates the extent to which Friends gave institutional support to antislavery through groups known as "meetings for sufferings" and "standing committees." Woolman, Benezet, David Cooper, and many other early abolitionists were active members of the Philadelphia Meeting for Sufferings (PMS, which included Quaker delegates from Pennsylvania, New Jersey, Delaware, and Maryland) and used it to advance the antislavery cause before, during, and after the Revolution. Similar Quaker groups in North Carolina, Virginia, New York, and New England were also important and helped coordinate antislavery activities across colonial and state lines. Some of the era's most active and influential abolitionists—such as Warner Mifflin and John Parrish—remain largely unknown because they primarily acted through Quaker groups rather than formal abolition societies. Moreover, it seems that in Massachusetts during the 1770s, Black activists and a handful of white allies (who did not leave detailed records) organized a sophisticated campaign of antislavery petitioning and publishing while bringing lawsuits against enslavers. As historian Christopher Cameron argues, these Black-initiated efforts should be recognized as "antislavery committees" that helped establish a movement. In sum, abolitionists developed sophisticated organizing techniques in the 1760s and 1770s, decades earlier than scholars have generally realized.[16]

The influence of organized abolitionism increased during the imperial crisis and Revolutionary War, though this growth was not steady. Moments of crisis heightened the power of antislavery rhetoric while easing tensions made it less salient. Public days of fasting and prayer provided important opportunities for abolitionists to promote their cause but have been overlooked by scholars. Throughout the colonial era, it was common for legislatures and governors to respond to crises—whether caused by war, disease, or natural disasters—by appointing fast days on which the colonists would refrain from eating from sunup to sundown, repent of their sins, and attend special sermons calling for reformation. The inspiration for fast days came from the Old Testament, such as Jonah 3:1–10, in which God spares the city of Nineveh from destruction after the king declares a day of fasting, repentance, and prayer. From the 1750s through the 1780s, colonial, state, and national authorities routinely appointed fast days in response to warfare and political disputes, hoping that God would grant them victory in battle or inspire Parliament to repeal obnoxious taxes. Most ministers' fast-day sermons focused on the need to refrain from personal sins, such as drunkenness or sabbath-breaking.[17] However, an important minority of ministers and writers used the fast days as an opportunity to call for antislavery reform. In sermons and publications, they argued that God would continue chastising slaveholding societies—in the form of war or other calamities—until they abolished slavery. Most of these antislavery voices invoked the prophet Isaiah, who repeatedly condemns superficial fasts and prayers among the Israelites, calling instead for the end of oppression. For example, in Isaiah 58:5–6, God dismisses performative fasting and proclaims, "wilt thou call this a fast, and an acceptable day to the LORD? Is not this the fast that I have chosen? to loose the bands of wickedness, to undo the heavy burdens, and to let the oppressed go free, and that ye break every yoke?" Abolitionists maintained that God viewed slaveholders' hypocritical prayers for the preservation of their own liberty with utter disdain. If the Americans expected the Lord to help them—whether by ending Parliament's attempts to tax them or by granting victory on the field of battle—they must first release their oppressed slaves.

* * *

The seven chronological chapters of *Let the Oppressed Go Free* demonstrate the growing receptivity of many white Americans to antislavery arguments during the colonial and revolutionary eras. The first two chapters examine the articulation of antislavery theology, beginning in the late seventeenth century and culminating with Quakers reaching an antislavery consensus during the French and Indian War. I dub the wartime Quaker reformers the "Generation of 1758," as they convinced the PYM to adopt an antislavery policy that year and then continued to promote the antislavery cause for decades. Chapters 3 and 4 focus on the imperial crisis of 1764 to 1775, showing that a growing number of white patriots, especially evangelicals (those committed to spreading Christianity), came to embrace antislavery. These patriots interpreted Parliament's oppressive tax policies as God's means of chastising them for the sin of slavery. "We have been loudly complaining of the heavy burdens cast upon us, and, that by the infringement of our natural rights, we are like to be reduced to a state of slavery," a writer in the *Boston Evening-Post* noted in 1768. The author believed actual slaveholding was the cause, explaining that "God in his *righteous providence*, has manifested the tokens of his displeasure in the troubles brought upon us *at this day*; and causes us to read our enormous *guilt*, in the *nature* and severity of the *punishment*." Having enslaved Africans, "we are like to be reduced to a state of slavery." In order to regain the Lord's favor, the colonists must follow Isaiah and "let the oppressed go free." Not surprisingly, African Americans embraced and promoted such interpretations of events. In 1773, a Black writer in the *Boston Gazette* proposed, "May not the late Troubles be esteemd as Ordered by Heaven to open Men's Eyes, and bring them to a Sense of their Duty towards us? and if they regard not this Providence, may they not look for more Distressing Judgments?"[18] Meanwhile, Quaker groups were increasingly active in promoting emancipation on both sides of the Atlantic.

The outbreak of war in 1775 interrupted antislavery efforts and altered the context of abolitionism, as shown in Chapters 5 and 6. Patriot politicians often persecuted Quakers for their pacifism and alleged loyalty to Britain, hindering their antislavery organizing and activism at times. Despite being skeptical of the patriot cause, Quaker abolitionists strategically embraced elements of patriots' rhetoric to advance their antislavery agenda. Insisting that wartime destruction was another example of divine punishment, they argued that the patriots must fulfill the antislavery promise of their natural rights rhetoric if they hoped to escape the Lord's further wrath.[19]

A significant contingent of white patriots also interpreted political and military developments in this manner. In 1776, Rhode Island minister Samuel Hopkins asserted in *A Dialogue Concerning Slavery* that slavery was "a very great and public sin . . . which God is now testifying against in the calamities he has brought upon us." He believed abolition was necessary "before we can reasonably expect deliverance, or even sincerely ask for it." In *A Discourse on the Times,* which went through three editions in 1776–1777, Jabez Huntington of Connecticut predicted that God would continue chastising the Americans with increasing severity until they "set at liberty those vast numbers of *Africans,* which have so long been inslaved by us."[20] Over time, the war's brutality and destruction increasingly appeared to fulfill abolitionists' prophetic warnings. Some patriot politicians embraced this antislavery logic. For example, Pennsylvania's 1780 gradual abolition law was explicitly framed as a means of expressing public gratitude to God for rescuing Philadelphia from the British and as a means of ensuring the Lord's continued blessing. Meanwhile, a series of court cases between 1772 and 1783 ended hereditary slavery in Massachusetts, with enslaved people and their allies routinely arguing that slavery was a God-provoking sin. Rather than stalling antislavery momentum, the war accelerated antislavery progress by magnifying the power of religious arguments.

Even Quaker pacifists appreciated that the war had aided the antislavery cause. Indeed, David Cooper feared that the "sunshine of peace" would lead to complacency and slow antislavery progress.[21] His concerns proved prescient, as Chapter 7 demonstrates. Although Connecticut, Rhode Island, and New Hampshire adopted gradual abolition measures in 1784, in part to express gratitude to God for their military triumph, momentum then slowed. Without the wartime sense of urgency, many white patriots who had espoused antislavery ideals lost their zeal. Legislative efforts to end slavery in New Jersey and New York failed while South Carolina and Georgia imported record numbers of enslaved Africans. Quakers and Black Americans remained the dedicated core of the abolitionist movement who continued the struggle against slavery in the new nation, exerting significantly more influence than scholars have generally appreciated. While the Founding Fathers were making concessions to slaveholders at the Constitutional Convention of 1787, abolitionists throughout the nation were engaged in a coordinated effort to strengthen and expand antislavery reform at the state level. Their activism helped ensure the antislavery gains made during the Revolution would not be undone and would instead be the basis of pushing for more progress.

CHAPTER 1

The Biblical Basis of Slavery and Antislavery in Colonial North America

Whereas Black people resisted their enslavement from the outset, few white colonists challenged slavery before the second half of the eighteenth century. In New England, where colonists were known for their piety, leading Puritans defended African slavery as part of God's plan to spread the Gospel. Even Quakers, later famous for their antislavery activism, initially engaged in slave trading and slaveholding, beginning in the 1650s in Barbados and subsequently in the North American colonies. Quakers would not adopt significant antislavery reforms until a century later, during the French and Indian War (1754–1763). Nonetheless, a small coterie of white Quakers began condemning slavery during the 1670s, followed by a smaller number of white Puritans. These early critics of slaveholding have been aptly described as "Voices crying in the wilderness" and "prophets without honor," as their efforts did not lead to policy changes during their lifetimes.[1]

The slow start of the American abolitionist movement is hardly surprising given it was attacking a practice that was thousands of years old. Slavery was widespread in virtually all ancient civilizations, but the precedents set in Israel and the Roman Empire were most important for the development and justification of slavery in the American colonies. Understanding the development of antislavery ideas in colonial America requires first examining the ways previous generations had used the Bible to justify slavery and the ways the Bible informed the development of slave law in the colonies. White Christians' perception of race and the legitimacy of enslaving certain peoples was shaped by religion, though such perceptions changed over time. During the first thousand years or so of Christianity, church leaders accepted that enslavement was a legitimate status, even for fellow Christians. By the fifteenth century,

Christians widely believed that only people of other religions could be legitimately enslaved, especially if they had dark skin. Slaveholders and theologians developed sophisticated scriptural justifications for subjecting Black people to hereditary bondage even after they converted to Christianity. The challenge for abolitionists was to develop an antislavery theology asserting that God forbade the arbitrary enslavement of anyone.

The core of abolitionists' argument was that any Old Testament sanction for slaveholding had been rendered void by the New Testament and that hereditary slavery was therefore sinful. Of course, most slaveholders and many religious leaders ignored this argument or responded with proslavery interpretations of scripture. Slaveholders' espousal of proslavery biblicism has led historians to question the efficacy of abolitionists' attempts to enlist the Bible against slavery. As Eran Shalev notes, "Historians tend to agree that the proslavery advocates developed a sounder scriptural argument in the debate on slavery and the Bible."[2] However, such characterizations reflect slaveholders' economic and political influence rather than the rhetorical power of their proslavery arguments. Evaluating biblicist debates on their own terms—treating the Bible as literally true and as the proper basis of morality—shows that abolitionists had the stronger arguments. The limits of their immediate influence is hardly surprising given that they were up against the wealthiest class of colonists and powerful imperial interests. Still, these early abolitionists are more significant than scholars often assume, and their importance lies not just in their status as forerunners to a more successful later movement. They developed an antislavery ideology grounded in the Bible that was sophisticated, coherent, and seemingly irrefutable. By the early 1700s, antislavery colonists had articulated the biblicist arguments against slavery that remained central to the abolitionist movement through the American Civil War, although they had few white adherents until the second half of the eighteenth century. The religious logic and scriptural basis of these debates provide essential context for understanding abolitionism during the American Revolution.

The Bible and the Development of New World Slavery

The Bible was the single most important source for both the defenders and opponents of American slavery. For the slaveholders, the most important parts were contained in the Torah (the first five books of the Hebrew Bible or Old Testament). Slavery is mentioned several times in Genesis, and the

Mosaic law codes—laid out in Exodus, Leviticus, and Deuteronomy—regulated both temporary servitude and permanent enslavement. The Hebrew prophets, such as Jeremiah and Isaiah, often railed against oppression, so slaveholders tended to ignore them. The New Testament did not address slavery as explicitly as did the Old Testament, but slaveholders emphasized passages that instruct servants to be obedient to their masters.[3]

Theologians who justified slavery generally accepted that slavery had not been part of God's initial design of the world. Genesis 1:26 asserts that God made men and women in his own "image" and "likeness," and granted them "dominion over the fish of the sea, and over the fowl of the air, and over the cattle, and over all the earth, and over every creeping thing that creepeth upon the earth." Early antislavery theologians, such as Saint Gregory of Nyzza (or Nyssa) writing around 385 C.E., used this passage to insist that God only granted humans control over "brute animals." He denounced slaveholders: "You condemn a person to slavery whose nature is free and independent, and you make laws opposed to God and contrary to his natural law."[4] By contrast, proslavery theologians—who were more influential, especially after Christianity became the official religion of the Roman Empire in the fourth century—insisted that God accepted slavery as an inevitable result of humanity's sinful nature following Adam and Eve's expulsion from the Garden of Eden. They assumed that slavery quickly arose in the post-Edenic world and that God directly sanctioned its revival following the great flood that wiped out all people except for Noah and his family, who were safe aboard the ark God had instructed them to build.

The first biblical reference to bondage appears in chapter 9 of Genesis and is often dubbed "Noah's Curse," "the Curse of Canaan," or "the Curse of Ham." The passage recounts a confusing and likely garbled tale full of innuendo set sometime after Noah and his family have survived the flood. While Noah is passed out drunk, his son Ham commits an offense for which Noah later punishes Ham's son Canaan:

> And Noah began to be an husbandman, and he planted a vineyard: And he drank of the wine, and was drunken; and he was uncovered within his tent. And Ham, the father of Canaan, saw the nakedness of his father, and told his two brethren without. And Shem and Japheth took a garment, and laid it upon both their shoulders, and went backward, and covered the nakedness of their father; and their faces were backward, and they saw not their father's nakedness. *And Noah awoke*

> *from his wine, and knew what his younger son had done unto him. And he said, Cursed be Canaan; a servant of servants shall he be unto his brethren.* And he said, Blessed be the LORD God of Shem; and Canaan shall be his servant. God shall enlarge Japheth, and he shall dwell in the tents of Shem; and Canaan shall be his servant. (Genesis 9:20–27, emphasis added)

The exact nature of what supposedly happened—and why Canaan rather than Ham is cursed—is less important than the fact that slaveholders used this story to justify slavery for millennia. First, the Hebrews used the story to further justify their conquest of the Canaanites, whose land the Lord later grants to Abraham and his descendants (Genesis 17:8). Thousands of years later, light-skinned people claimed that dark-skinned people from sub-Saharan Africa were uniquely suited to slavery based on their alleged descent from Ham's cursed lineage. In 1860, for example, Jefferson Davis of Mississippi told the United States Senate that African Americans were descended from the "vulgar son of Noah." The future president of the Confederate States of America thus claimed that the "inequality of the white and black races" was "stamped from the beginning, marked in decree and prophecy."[5] By that time, centuries of proslavery theology claimed that Noah's Curse was the origin of both slavery and Black skin.

Although Noah's Curse became racialized, Christians initially used it to justify slaveholding in general as a divinely sanctioned practice. In *The City of God* (ca. 426 C.E.), Saint Augustine of Hippo used the example of "righteous Noah" to argue that slavery was legitimate in a world tainted by "original sin" (a concept he popularized). Augustine developed a proslavery theology to refute Saint Gregory's criticism of slavery and to justify the Roman Empire's longstanding practice of enslaving prisoners of war (who included people of various religions and skin colors).[6] Through the Middle Ages, Europeans used the story of Ham's sin and Canaan's servitude to justify slavery and serfdom without reference to color or ideas about race.

Christian slaveholders also claimed authority from other parts of the Old Testament dealing with Abraham and Moses. In Genesis, Abraham becomes a wealthy slaveholder after God blesses him with a covenant. Abraham's slaves include both those "bought with money" and "born in the house" (Genesis 17:12), which was later interpreted as further evidence that God sanctioned hereditary enslavement. And although Moses leads the Hebrews out of Egyptian bondage in the book of Exodus, he is also credited with establishing some of the earliest slave codes. Mosaic law placed limits on the servitude of fellow Hebrews, most significantly by establishing the rule that they could not typically be subjected to periods of bondage exceeding six or seven years (Exodus 21:2 and Deuteronomy 15:12). In Leviticus 25:42–43, God reiterates that Hebrews could be temporary servants but not permanently enslaved, explaining, "For they are my servants, which I brought forth out of the land of Egypt: they shall not be sold as bondmen. Thou shalt not rule over him with rigour." But whereas Hebrew servants must be released on the year of "jubilee," God permits the Hebrews to permanently enslave outsiders of other religions:

> Both thy bondmen, and thy bondmaids, which thou shalt have, shall be of the heathen that are round about you; of them shall ye buy bondmen and bondmaids. Moreover of the children of the strangers that do sojourn among you, of them shall ye buy, and of their families that are with you, which they begat in your land: and they shall be your possession. And ye shall take them as an inheritance for your children after you, to inherit them for a possession. (Leviticus 25:44–46)

In addition to acquiring "heathen" slaves through purchase, the ancient Israelites also claimed divine permission to enslave enemy prisoners of war, including women and children, whom the Lord "delivered" into their hands (Deuteronomy 20:10–14).

Christian slaveholders claimed that Jesus had also approved of slavery, for there is no record that he ever explicitly condemned the practice by name. Indeed, as slaveholders liked to point out, Jesus praised the faith of a Roman centurion who boasted of his authority over his "servant," who was likely an enslaved prisoner of war (Matthew 8:5–13 and Luke 7:1–10). Moreover, Christian slaveholders could cite numerous letters by the Apostle Paul that seemed to sanction servitude. For instance, Ephesians 6:5–8 instructs:

> Servants, be obedient to them that are your masters according to the flesh, with fear and trembling, in singleness of your heart, as unto Christ; Not with eyeservice, as menpleasers; but as the servants of Christ, doing the will of God from the heart; With good will doing service, as to the Lord, and not to men: Knowing that whatsoever good thing any man doeth, the same shall he receive of the Lord, whether he be bond or free.

According to slaveholders, the instructions for servants indicated that Christian slaves should accept their earthly status and be obedient in the hopes of salvation in the afterlife. Ephesians 6:9 adds, "And, ye masters, do the same things unto them, forbearing threatening: knowing that your Master also is in heaven; neither is there respect of persons with him." Slaveholders understood this as evidence that slaveholding and Christianity were compatible (while ignoring the injunction against mistreatment). And whereas Jews believed they were forbidden from enslaving one another (a policy Muslims would also adopt), it seems that some early Christians simply followed Roman law and saw no problem with subjecting fellow Christians to lifelong—sometimes even hereditary—bondage. Still, it is important to note that the boundary between freedom and slavery during this early period was much more "fluid" than later race-based forms of slavery; enslavement was often only temporary, manumissions (individual emancipations) were common, and freed people could become full members of society.[7]

Various forms of slavery and servitude (such as serfdom and villenage) continued in Europe through the Middle Ages. In the thirteenth century, for example, the Italian priest Saint Thomas Aquinas cited the Old Testament and Roman law when discussing slavery in his *Summa Theologica*. Aquinas justified the practice of treating slavery as hereditary through the mother, regardless of the father's status, because the "mother provides the substance of the body, and it is to this that the condition of slavery attaches." Around the same time, the Spanish law compilation *Las Siete Partidas* stated, "There are three kinds of slaves, the first is those taken captive of wars who are enemies of the faith; the second, those born of female slaves; the third, when a person is free and allows himself to be sold." Clarifying the second form of enslavement, the law code added, "Persons born of a father who is free and a mother who is a slave are slaves, because they follow the condition of the mother, as respects both slavery and freedom." Thus, although Christians could not be enslaved against their will (in contrast to Muslims and other "enemies of the faith" captured in war), they could still voluntarily sell themselves into slavery (most commonly because of debt), which would pass to their descendants in the case of enslaved women. Although Europeans eventually ended the enslavement of fellow Christians, the longstanding practice of treating enslavement as hereditary through the mother, known by the Latin phrase *partus sequiter ventrem* (the birth follows the womb), was subsequently applied to the children of enslaved Black women in the American colonies.[8]

Although never formally abolished, Christian slavery died out in most of Europe, especially Western Europe, between the eleventh and fifteenth centuries. Historians have identified various reasons for this decline. For instance, the rapid population growth facilitated by agricultural advances led to a sizeable landless class that could be compelled to work for minimal compensation rather than through outright enslavement. Moreover, Christians gradually adopted the view that they should not enslave people of their own religion. Historian Robin Blackburn argues that it was the "struggles with Islam"—especially the Crusades in the Middle East and the efforts to expel Muslim invaders from the Iberian Peninsula (Portugal and Spain)—that led Europeans to end the practice of holding fellow Christians in slavery. By the fifteenth century, it seems Christians had generally adopted the Old Testament's provisions against enslaving one's coreligionists.[9]

The decline of slavery was soon reversed, however, during the "Age of Discovery." Under the patronage of Prince Henry "the Navigator," the Portuguese began exploring the West African coast and enslaving Black captives in the 1440s. In 1452, Pope Nicholas V issued the "Dum Diversas," the first of several papal bulls legitimizing and promoting the African slave trade. The pope implicitly relied on Old Testament precedents for enslaving heathens when authorizing the Portuguese to subjugate "pagans and any other unbelievers" in Africa and "to reduce their persons into perpetual servitude." The Portuguese quickly discovered it was easier and safer to purchase captives from other Africans rather than attempting to conquer them. They still used religion to justify slave trading and slaveholding, with the blessing of numerous popes.[10]

In the 1450s, Prince Henry commissioned Gomes Eannes de Azurara (or Zurara) to write an account celebrating the prince's role in promoting the African slave trade. In *The Chronicle of the Discovery and Conquest of Guinea*, Azurara touted the religious aspect, claiming that the traffic would help save the "lost souls of the heathen" by exposing Africans to Christianity. Thus, while Prince Henry profited handsomely from slaving voyages, Azurara claimed, "yet the greater benefit was theirs [the Africans], for though their bodies were now brought into some subjection, that was a small matter in comparison of their souls, which would now possess true freedom for evermore." In other words, it was the Africans who truly benefited from being enslaved, as a lifetime of brutal forced labor was a small price to pay for the opportunity of Christian salvation. This rationalization for European greed depended on the assumption that all non-Christians were destined to suffer an eternity in Hell. Historians estimate that by the end of the fifteenth century, Portuguese slave traders had purchased more than one hundred thousand enslaved Africans, bringing some into port cities such as Lisbon and sending more to raise sugar and other crops on the Azores and other islands off of Portugal's coast.[11]

The basic justifications that would later be used for racial slavery in the Americas were already in place by the time Christopher Columbus reached the "New World" in 1492. Based on the Old Testament as well as legal traditions going back to ancient Rome, European imperialists believed that heathen Africans could be enslaved through war or purchase. They already assumed enslavement to be hereditary through the mother. However, the growing conviction that Christians should not hold fellow Christians in bondage led some to question whether African converts—and especially their children—could be legitimately enslaved. It was in this context that Noah's Curse became so important. By the end of the fifteenth century, Iberian Christians were interpreting the curse as applying singularly to Black Africans, asserting that conversion did not affect *their* enslaveability. As several historians have demonstrated, the Portuguese followed the lead of North African Muslims in this regard. Indeed, Azurara's *Chronicle* explained that although Muslims did not normally enslave one another, the light-skinned North Africans made an exception for dark-skinned sub-Saharan Africans "in accordance with ancient custom, which I believe to have been because of the curse which, after the Deluge, Noah laid upon his son Cain [Canaan], cursing him in this way:—that his race should be subject to all the other races of the world." Numerous publications during the sixteenth century used versions of Noah's Curse to explain the skin color of sub-Saharan Africans and justify their perpetual enslavement. Richard Hakluyt, the English advocate of colonization, reprinted some of these accounts in the late sixteenth and early seventeenth centuries, boosting their influence on English thinking. The racist claim that Black people were especially suited for slavery—based on biblical rather than biological (mis)understandings of race—was already circulating before the English established the colonies that would later become the United States.[12]

By 1607, when the English established Jamestown, Virginia, slave traders had already taken more than three hundred thousand African captives to Spain and Portugal's New World colonies, supplementing and replacing the labor of conquered Indigenous peoples.[13] Given that hereditary Black slavery was the economic basis of most New World colonies, it is hardly surprising that white colonists in Virginia bought as many African captives as they could afford following the arrival of the *White Lion* slave ship in 1619. Although older scholarship emphasized that some of the early Africans in Virginia were treated like white indentured servants and released after several years of unpaid labor, it is now clear that many white Virginians immediately followed the well-known Spanish and Portuguese custom of subjecting Black people to lifelong and hereditary enslavement.[14]

The principal legal controversies over Black slavery in Virginia dealt with the issues of religious conversion and sexual relations between white Christian men and enslaved Black women. In 1662, the Virginia legislature codified "that all children borne in this country shal be held bond or free only according to the condition of the mother." The law's preamble makes clear that the only previous "doubts" about heritability were "whether children got by any Englishman upon a negro woman should be slave or free." Enslavement had always been the assumed status when both parents were Black slaves.[15] The Virginia legislature's policy that the mother's status alone determined whether a child was free or enslaved was no innovation; rather, it followed custom going back to ancient Rome, which the Spanish had codified in the thirteenth-century *Siete Partidas* and subsequently applied to the New World. In 1667, another Virginia law addressed the issue of conversion. The preamble stated that "some doubts have risen whether children that are slaves by birth, and by the charity and piety of their owners made pertakers of the blessed sacrament of baptisme, should by vertue of their baptisme be made ffree." Even though converting heathens into Christians was ostensibly a chief rationale for the African slave trade, many English slaveholders were often reluctant to baptize their slaves' children out of concern that they would have to liberate their Black coreligionists. In response, the legislation pronounced that "the conferring of baptisme doth not alter the condition of the person as to his bondage or freedome." The legislators hoped that resolving this ambiguity would encourage the "propagation of christianity" among the enslaved. The logic of law, which responded to the common English assumption that Christians should not enslave one another, rested implicitly on the view that Noah's Curse exempted Black people from the privileges typically associated with conversion. Again, the law was not an innovation in the context of New World slavery; the Spanish and Portuguese had long maintained that conversion did not lead to emancipation. A series of additional Virginia laws further strengthened the association between Blackness and enslavement, culminating with a 1723 statute prohibiting masters from manumitting any slave "except for some meritorious services, to be adjudged and allowed by the governor and council." This regulation was intended to curtail the free Black population while still preserving manumission as a reward for enslaved people who provided "meritorious services," such as informing on slave conspiracies. Most of the other English colonies in North America and the Caribbean adopted similar laws, clarifying that slavery was hereditary through the mother and unaffected by conversion while also placing limits on manumissions.[16]

New England was somewhat of an outlier in English America, as the region never adopted the level of detail common in slave codes elsewhere. By 1638, Massachusetts settlers began exchanging Native Americans they captured during the Pequot War for enslaved Africans from the Caribbean colonies. The Massachusetts legislature codified such practices in the 1641 law compilation known as the Body of Liberties. The Puritans in Massachusetts envisioned themselves as establishing a "new Israel," and much of their law code was taken directly from Mosaic law. For instance, the provisions imposing the death penalty for crimes such as witchcraft or fornicating with animals cited Leviticus 20:15–27. The Body of Liberty's provisions related to servitude and slavery were clearly based on the Bible as well, though usually without specific citations.

Articles 85–88 of the Body of Liberties codified the "Liberties of servants." Typically, indentured servants would be released after "seaven years, [and] shall not be sent away emptie." This provision was based on Deuteronomy 21:12–14, which described the treatment of Hebrew servants: "In the seventh year thou shalt let him go free from thee. And when thou sendest him out free from thee, thou shalt not let him go away empty: Thou shalt furnish him liberally out of thy flock, and out of thy floor, and out of thy winepress." Following Exodus 21:26–27, the Massachusetts code limited the corporal punishment of servants; if "any man smite out the eye or tooth" or "otherwise mayme or much disfigure" their servants, the servant would "goe free from his service." The colonists also modified Deuteronomy 23:16, offering a level of protection and arbitration for servants who "shall flee from the Tiranny and crueltie of their masters." In sum, Massachusetts's servants (presumed to be white and Christian) received protections similar to those the ancient Israelites had extended to their brethren.[17]

The Body of Liberties permitted the enslavement of outsiders in certain circumstances. Article 91—part of a section titled "Liberties of Forreigners and Strangers"—codified this practice: "There shall never be any bond slaverie, villinage or Captivitie amongst us unless it be lawfull Captives taken in just warres, and such strangers as willingly selle themselves or are sold to us. And these shall have all the liberties and Christian Usages which the law of god established in Israell concerning such persons doeth morally require. This exempts none from servitude who shall be Judged thereto by Authoritie." The first sentence sanctioned existing practices regarding Native Americans captured in war and African "strangers" imported from abroad. The second was somewhat contradictory, as it described Israelite practices in the Old Testament as "Christian." Still, it clearly indicates that Puritan lawmakers viewed their involvement in slavery as conforming to biblical standards. The final provision most likely refers to slavery as a legitimate punishment for certain crimes, again reflecting preexisting practices. For example, Massachusetts authorities had previously enslaved a white rapist for life and sentenced a white arsonist to twenty-one years of bondage.[18] A final reference to slavery was contained in Article 94, which listed capital offenses and quoted Exodus 21:16: "If any man stealeth a man or mankinde, he shall surely be put to death." Abolitionists would later claim this Bible passage reflected a universal condemnation of slavery, but neither the Puritan colonists nor the ancient Israelites understood it that way. In the Hebrew Bible, the assumed meaning of Exodus 21:16 can be discerned from the phrasing of a parallel text: "If a man be found stealing any of his *brethren of the children of Israel*, and maketh merchandise of him, or selleth him; then that thief shall die" (Deuteronomy 24:7, emphasis added). Rather than a blanket condemnation of enslaving people, the passages forbade the enslavement only of one's own religious "brethren." Thus, in the eyes of the Massachusetts legislators, the biblical condemnation of "manstealing" did not apply to their practice of enslaving Indigenous heathens captured in "just" wars or buying Black strangers who were already enslaved.

The central ambiguities of the 1641 rules regulating slavery revolved around the issues of heritability and conversion. Unlike colonies such as Virginia, Massachusetts never clarified these issues with additional statutes. Many Massachusetts slaveholders nonetheless followed the New World custom of treating Black slavery as hereditary. For instance, in 1638—before *any* English colony had codified slavery—Massachusetts colonist Samuel Maverick commanded a "Negro young man he had" to rape his "Negro Woman" so that he could "have a breed of Negroes." Meanwhile, biblical commentaries authored by English Puritans affirmed that the children of enslaved

"Blackamores" were "borne the slaves of their Masters." Most of the New England colonies therefore treated Black slavery as legitimate and hereditary, even in the absence of specific legislation. There was, however, discomfort among some white New Englanders regarding the practice of keeping Black Christian converts enslaved. In 1653, for example, members of one Massachusetts church voted to redeem a member of their congregation, "Dorcas ye blackmore," from slavery. Dorcas may have been among the first Africans purchased by Massachusetts colonists in 1638, for she joined the church in 1641, and it seems that her conversion and church membership eventually helped her escape permanent enslavement. This was not an isolated incident, and there were a modest number of free Black New Englanders by the end of the century.[19]

More commonly, masters sought to avoid the issue altogether by denying their slaves access to baptism and religious instruction. This practice might have made it easier to justify the hereditary nature of colonial slavery, but it upset missionaries and religious leaders. The Reverend Cotton Mather, the most famous minister in North America at the turn of the eighteenth century, framed the issue in providentialist terms. He suggested that if the colonists worked to save Black souls, God would bless the colonies with "prosperity." But he also warned slaveholders not to neglect this obligation, "lest the God of Heaven out of meer Pity, if not Justice, to those unhappy *Blacks*, be provoked unto a Vengeance." In other words, Mather warned that God would punish New England if colonists neglected their slaves' souls. Yet Mather did not view slaveholding itself as sinful; he repeatedly sought to reassure slaveholders that allowing their slaves to be baptized and attend church would not jeopardize their property rights. Moreover, he argued that religious instruction would encourage slaves to be more obedient in the hopes of achieving salvation.[20]

Eventually, Quakers would take the lead among white abolitionists, but they also focused initially on promoting conversion rather than emancipation. George Fox, who established the Society of Friends in England during the 1640s, became increasingly critical of slaveholders but never advocated abolition. He first addressed the subject of slavery in a 1657 epistle, "To Friends beyond the Sea, that have Blacks and Indian Slaves." Fox reminded slaveholding Quaker colonists that God "hath made all *Nations of one Blood*" (Acts 17:26) and that Christ had destroyed the old division between Hebrews and heathen, offering "*Salvation to the Ends of the Earth*." Slaveholders thus had an obligation to facilitate their slaves' salvation through religious instruction. In

1671, Fox visited Barbados—the English colony with the largest slave population and many Quakers—and was disturbed by what he saw. Still, he refrained from calling for outright emancipation. Speaking before a group of Friends on the island, Fox proclaimed that Christ had "dyed for the *Tawnes* and for the *Blacks*, as well as for you that are called *whites*." Fox clearly believed that Christ's "new Covenant" had altered the Old Testament's distinction between temporary Hebrew servants and perpetual heathen slaves, for he then quoted Deuteronomy 15:12–15, which requires Hebrew masters to liberate their Hebrew servants in the seventh year. Still, instead of limiting Black servitude to seven years, Fox equivocated; manuscript accounts of his initial sermon in Barbados indicate that he suggested Black servitude last "30 yeares after or more or less." He may later have regretted such a lengthy period, as the version of his sermon published as *The Gospel Family-Order* (printed in London in 1676 and Philadelphia in 1701) simply encouraged manumission after "a term of years." In any case, Fox spent more time highlighting masters' duties to suppress vice among their slaves and "teach Christ" to them. He predicted that doing so would earn "the Blessing and Favour of God," while also warning that slaveholders must otherwise expect God's "Judgments and Curse upon you and your Families and your plantations." He reiterated the emphasis on religious education and suppression of vice, without any reference to manumission, in several subsequent epistles to Quakers in Barbados, Maryland, and other colonies. Ultimately, Fox was concerned that the sins of slaveholders (such as failing to care for their slaves' souls) and of enslaved people (such as fornication outside of marriage) might provoke divine retribution, but he did not characterize slaveholding itself as a sin.[21]

The situation was similar among religious reformers and policymakers in England. During the 1680s, ministers such as the Anglican Morgan Godwyn and the Puritan Richard Baxter published books that warned that failure to convert enslaved heathens to Christianity would provoke God's wrath. Still, they stopped short of calling for abolition.[22] In 1670, a prominent Englishman suggested that once enslaved Black people demonstrated sufficient knowledge of Christianity, "they be baptized; and after that time to serve Seaven Years and no longer, and then to be free." This proposal reflected the common notion that Christian servitude should be limited to the biblical seven years. However, English advocates of conversion soon reversed course. Realizing that equating conversion with manumission would discourage planters from permitting the enslaved to receive religious instructions, reformers disavowed any link. Parliamentary legislation drafted shortly after the Glorious

Revolution of 1688 would have encouraged the conversion of slaves—warning that failure to do so "may provoke some severe judgment of God"—while clarifying that conversion did not lead to emancipation. Several similar bills were drafted during the following decades but never passed.[23]

In the absence of a formal English law, the Society for the Propagation of the Gospel in Foreign Parts (SPG) and similar groups sought to reassure slaveholders that missionaries posed no threat to the value of their human property. In 1727, the Bishop of London assured slaveholders: "The Freedom which Christianity gives is a Freedom from the Bondage of Sin and Satan . . . but as to their *outward* Condition, whatever that was before, whether bond or free; their being baptized and becoming Christians makes no manner of Change in it." The SPG publicized this letter and solicited a written statement from England's leading jurists to resolve the question of conversion's effect on the legal status of enslaved people. The resulting "Yorke-Talbot Opinion," by Attorney General Philip Yorke and Solicitor General Charles Talbot, declared in part: "Baptism doth not bestow freedom on him, nor make any alteration in his temporal Condition." In 1730, this opinion was quickly published in the *Boston Gazette* and elsewhere in the hope of permanently settling the legal debate in the colonies, thereby facilitating evangelizing efforts.[24]

Clearly, religion was central to how the English understood the enslavement of Black people in the colonies. The advocates of slavery used the Bible to justify it, even as they routinely neglected—or even opposed—religious instruction for the enslaved. The writings of people like Cotton Mather and George Fox, and the efforts of groups like the SPG, indicate their sincere commitment to saving Black souls yet also show their unwillingness to challenge the religious legitimacy of slavery itself. Throughout the colonial period, most Christian reformers prioritized saving slaves' souls over liberating their bodies from bondage.

The Development of Antislavery Theology

During the last quarter of the seventeenth century, a handful of antislavery reformers in North America began attacking slavery itself as a sinful form of oppression. These early abolitionists exerted little influence, at least in the short term. Scholars often assume that their lack of influence derived in large part from their reliance on religion. Historian Mark Noll, for example, has repeatedly asserted that the proslavery biblicists had the advantage because they could draw on the "letter" of the Bible—such as Leviticus 25:44, which explicitly allowed the purchase of heathen slaves—whereas abolitionists had to rely more on its general liberationist "spirit."[25] However, such characterizations underestimate the strength of antislavery biblicism during the colonial period. By 1700, abolitionists such as Quaker William Edmundson and Puritan Samuel Sewall developed compelling biblicist arguments that slaveholders chose to either dodge or misrepresent. Scholars who have not been sufficiently attuned to abolitionists' scriptural logic have often been misled by proslavery polemicists' misrepresentations of antislavery biblicism. The weakness of the abolitionists' position lay not in their arguments but rather in that they were fighting against broad economic and political trends that encouraged the expansion of slavery in the colonies.

Antislavery biblicism relied on distinctions between God's different covenants and dispensations. God's covenant with Abraham had implicitly allowed slaveholding, while the dispensation at the time of Moses had done so explicitly. Slaveholders insisted that Christ's "New Covenant of Grace" or "Gospel Dispensation" preserved and expanded divine sanction for slaveholding. By contrast, abolitionists argued that Christ's covenant had revoked previous dispensations permitting perpetual slavery. They grounded these claims directly in scripture, albeit often by paraphrasing without citations. It seems their lack of citations has prevented scholars from appreciating the power of antislavery biblical exegesis. Historians routinely note that slaveholders used Ephesians 6:5—"Servants, be obedient to them that are your masters according to the flesh"—to defend hereditary slavery without recognizing the ways abolitionists used Ephesians 2:11–19 to attack slavery.

Because Ephesians 2:11–19 was so central to abolitionist thought, it is worth considering at length. In the Epistle to the Ephesians, the Apostle Paul—a Jewish convert to Christianity—addresses a group of former "Gentiles" (or "heathens") who had embraced Christianity. Paul tells them:

> Wherefore remember, that ye being in time past Gentiles . . . being aliens from the commonwealth of Israel, and strangers from the covenants of promise, having no hope, and without God in the world: But now in Christ Jesus ye who sometimes were far off are made nigh by the blood of Christ. For he is our peace, who hath made both one, and hath broken down the middle wall of partition between us. . . . Now therefore ye are no more strangers and foreigners, but fellow citizens with the saints, and of the household of God. (Ephesians 2:11–19)

This passage has various layers of meaning. Matthew Poole, whose bible commentary was popular in the colonies, explained that it meant Christ had brought Gentiles "into a state of communion with God, and his People, and participation of their Privileges." It also indicated Christ had ended the "Ceremonial Laws" that were peculiar to the Hebrews (such as circumcision and dietary restrictions) while preserving the Old Testament's "Moral Law."[26] Based on this logic, abolitionists claimed that Christ's death and New Covenant had also ended the past dispensations distinguishing Hebrew servitude and heathen slavery. In the Old Testament, Hebrews were forbidden from enslaving each other because God had "redeemed" them from Egyptian bondage and established a covenant with them (Leviticus 25:42 and Deuteronomy 15:15) but were permitted to enslave "heathens" and "strangers" (Leviticus 25:44–45). When Christ established the New Covenant and died for Jew and Gentile alike, abolitionists argued, he destroyed the "wall of partition" (Ephesians 2:14) that had previously determined who could be enslaved. In doing so, he universalized the protection against enslavement that had previously been limited to the Hebrews. Moreover, in Luke 10:25–37, Jesus tells his followers to "love thy neighbour as thyself." When a "certain lawyer" asks, "And who is my neighbour?" Jesus responds with the parable of the Good Samaritan—about a Gentile who helps a presumably Jewish man who was injured—and then says, "Go and do thou likewise." Abolitionists understood Jesus as calling on Christians to treat *all* people as brethren and neighbors (even if they came from different faiths or nations), thereby nullifying the Old Testament dispensations that had permitted the ancient Israelites to oppress heathen outsiders.[27]

This antislavery argument was first advanced in the English colonies by William Edmundson, an Irish Quaker who traveled extensively. He had been one of George Fox's traveling companions to Barbados in 1671 and returned in 1675. During Edmundson's second visit, a local Anglican priest accused the Quaker of spreading religious ideas that would inspire the enslaved to "rise and cut their Throats." In 1676–1677, Edmundson traveled throughout North America, visiting Quakers from New England to North Carolina and witnessing the destruction caused by King Philip's War and Bacon's Rebellion. Before returning to Ireland, he wrote two circular letters that were distributed in manuscript form among North American Quakers. Although not well known, Edmundson's letters are among the earliest extant antislavery statements written in North America. Like Fox, Edmundson stressed masters' obligations to provide religious instruction for their servants, but he also developed a stronger critique of "perpetuall slavery." In his first letter, composed in Rhode Island in the summer of 1676, Edmundson reminded Quakers that Christ died for "all Men" and asked them to evaluate enslavement based on the Golden Rule: "Consider their Condition of perpetuall Slavery, and make their Conditions your own, and soo fulfill the Law of Christ."[28]

The following February, Edmundson elaborated the biblicist case against slavery in a circular letter "For Friends in Maryland, Virginia & other parts of America" (Figure 2). Responding to those who drew on Leviticus to justify the enslavement of "Negroes" with "no year of Jubile," Edmundson asked rhetorically, "Did not Jesus Christ shed his blood for us all?" He then dismissed the relevance of Noah's Curse, asserting that even if Africans "were of Ham's stock, and was to be the Servants of Servants," the curse had been "fulfilled" long ago. More importantly, paraphrasing Ephesians 2:14 and Acts 10:34, Edmundson added: "And doth not Christ take away ye wall of partition y^{t} made a difference between people & people? And is it not now that God is no respecter of Persons, but of every Nation, Tongue, & People y^{t} fears God & works Righteousness shall find mercy?" In other words, if Noah's Curse had ever applied to Africans, it—like the old dispensation allowing the perpetual enslavement of the heathen—had been ended by Christ's New Covenant. Because the Lord was "no respecter of persons," God would judge white slaveholders and Black slaves alike based on their "righteousness," not their skin color.[29]

Edmundson also warned of God's judgment against slaveholding societies: "Y^{e} Lords righteous Sceptre y^{t} must sway all nations, & bring down all injustice & oppression, & undo ye heavy burdens wch is bound upon ye shoulders of People by others (who will not touch y^{m} y^{m}selves, having cast ye Law of Christ behind their backs) & must root out all unrighteous dealings wch cryes to the Lord; & he doth hear, & is ready to visit the Nations." In other words, societies that violated the Golden Rule and oppressed others must expect divine retribution. Paraphrasing Isaiah 58:6, Edmundson proclaimed that the testimony of "ye Prophets, Apostles, & Christ Jesus" demanded that Christians "reform all abuses, & remove all Oppression, and break ye yoke of ye heavy burthens by wch ye Creation hath been burthened & bondaged." He therefore demanded political reform against slavery in the colonies. Friends who served as "Assembly Men, or other Offices of Authority" should use their influence "to undo ye heavy Burdens, & ease ye Oppression." Edmundson closed his letter with a warning that paraphrased Proverbs 14:34: "Righteousness exalts a nation . . . for God so loves Righteousness & Truth, Justice, & Mercy, but hates Iniquity

21

Judge it: The Prayers of ye Wicked are an Abomination to ye Lord, & he he hears not Hypocrites (This is for ye Service of this day) but ye Prayers of ye Righteous are heard. And this is to go abroad in ye World.

G. F.

All Friends heed nothing but ye Life & Power of ye Lord God: for all yt is out is & will be confounded; Therefore dwell in yt wch Condemns it: in wch will be your peace.

G. F.

For Friends in Maryland, Virginia & other parts of America

The God of all Truth who hath called us to be a People; & made known to us his Everlasting Truth, wch leads out of ye ways of Untruth (wch ye World is in) into all Truth in Words, & Deeds; every one to speak Truth & to do Truth in all things; yt God who hath called & gathered us to be a People may have ye glory, & we appear to all Men wth whom we have to do to be his Workmanship, Created anew in Christ Jesus to good works; by wch our Faith may appear unto all Men to be ye Faith once delivered to ye Saints, wch Jesus is ye Author of, wch overcomes ye World, & ye Spirit of it; in wch ye Saints Judges ye World & out lives ym in ye Life of Righteousness, & Truth in Justness & equity uprightness, purity & cleanness, in all holy conversation in words & deeds as a City set upon a Hill, ye Holy Mountain of Gods House set a top of all Mountains, & no oppression must be here; But ye Royall Law of Christ must be kept to do to others as we would have ym to do to us: & this Answers ye Just Answers ye Just principle in all where your Light shines before all men, wch Christ hath enlightened you wth; & is a sweet savor to God, & to his Principle in all, & ye Salt of ye Earth, seasoned wth ye Spirit of Grace & Truth in words & Deeds, & conversations in ye fear of God, walking blameless, doing Justly, dealing faithfully wth all as in ye sight of God; keeping your words promises, & engagements wth all Men: and let yor Yea be your yea as Christ commanded, & now by his Spirit is renewing; and this was it wch Christ established wn he ended swearing: & how can yu keep up the Testimony of Jesus against taking Oaths if yu be not punctuall, Just, & Faithfull in your promises, words & engagements; & let your yea be your yea, & your nay be your nay wth all men. And thus we received Truth at first who received it in ye Love of God: & Truth changeth not, neither is Truth yea & nay, but yea & Amen. So sell not Truth, nor your birthright in it, but keep it blameless in all things; & keep yor Habitation in it; for a day is coming yt no other place will shelter; & blessed are they yt keep their garments unspotted, & their Hearts & hands undefiled: And if you be not carefull to keep Truth clear in yor Lives & deportments; & true & faithfull in all yor dealings to keep yor words & engagements yu will forfeit your interest in ye Truth, yt is ye word of Truth to you all; and will be like ye Salt yt hath lost its Savor good for nothing but to be trodden under foot: for wt are they good for yt keeps not Truth in words & deeds? & wt is their confession worth who is in Words & not in Works: and wt is their holding worth, who holds Truth in unrighteousness? And if all would keep wth in ye bounds & limits of ye Lords good Spirit, & learn to be contented wth ~~[illegible]~~ food & rayment, & in ye State & Condition they are in, & not will, & run, strive, plot, contrive

&

Figure 2. William Edmundson's circular letters from 1676–1677, which were copied in this volume along with letters by George Fox, are the earliest known antislavery writings produced in North America. Courtesy of Haverford College, Quaker & Special Collections Library.

& oppression."[30] This letter offered a powerful condemnation of slavery and a call for reform within and beyond the Society of Friends.

Edmundson's circular letters likely spurred extensive conversation and debate over slavery, but the next extant antislavery document produced in North America is not dated until 1688. At that time, four Quakers in Germantown, in the newly established colony of Pennsylvania (founded by Quaker William Penn in 1681), submitted an antislavery petition to their monthly meeting. They denounced slavery as unchristian and insisted that enslaved Black people "ought to be delivered out of ye hands of ye robbers, and set free." The petition troubled other Quakers who recognized that it raised "weighty" questions and referred it to the Philadelphia Yearly Meeting, but it declined to take a formal stance on slavery.[31] Five years later, in 1693, a group of schismatic Pennsylvania Quakers led by George Keith published the first antislavery pamphlet in North America. The six-page *Exhortation & Caution to Friends Concerning Buying or Keeping Negroes* expanded some of the biblicist arguments that Edmundson had made. White Christians could not justify slavery based on race, for "*Negroes, Blacks* and *Taunies* are a real part of Mankind, for whom Christ hath shed his precious Blood." Because Christ had ended dispensations specific to the Israelites while universalizing the Old Testament's moral teachings, the Keithians denounced slavery as "Man-stealing" based on Exodus 21:16 and the Golden Rule. The pamphlet also drew on the book of Revelation to warn of divine retribution against slaveholders and slaveholding societies. God had punished the Babylonians for selling "Slaves and Souls of Men" (Revelations 18:13), and the Keithians warned that slaveholding colonists might also "draw Gods Judgments upon them." The final line, taken from Revelations 13:10, indicated the form such judgment might take: "*He that leads into Captivity shall go into Captivity*." Publishing their piece during King William's War, the authors may have been implicitly referring to cases of white colonists captured by Native Americans. The Keithians' pamphlet represented another important step in developing antislavery biblicism and providentialism but did not lead to any policy change among the Friends. A generation later, abolitionist John Hepburn complained that copies of the pamphlet were "almost as scarce to be found as the *Phenix* egg" because they had been "destroyed by *Negro-Masters*."[32]

Nevertheless, antislavery Quakers continued agitating for reform. William Southeby, a former Catholic turned Quaker who had lived in Maryland (where he had hosted William Edmundson in 1676) before settling in Philadelphia, submitted an antislavery address to his monthly meeting in the spring of 1696. Viewing slaveholding as sinful, Southeby warned that if nothing was done for the slaves, "God will heare their Cry, and also avenge it on their Oppressors." In order to escape God's wrath, Southeby hoped slaveholders would liberate their bondspeople once their labor had made "reasonable Satisfaction for what they cost."[33] While Southeby focused on God's wrath, other Quakers worried about slave resistance. In 1696, Cadwallader Morgan wondered what he could do, as a pacifist, if a slave "would Run away" or "Committ Wickedness." Two years later, Robert Piles expressed concern about the danger that enslaved people "might rise in rebellion." He advocated giving enslaved people religious education and then suggested "setting them free." Quaker concerns about slave resistance reflected both fear of and empathy for Black people. The Germantown petitioners had asked in 1688: "Have these negers not as much right to fight for their freedom, as you have to keep them slaves?"[34] Quaker writings thus indicate how Black resistance encouraged some white colonists to contemplate emancipation.

During this time, Quaker slaveholders continued relying on traditional proslavery biblicism as well as racism to defend the institution. They often claimed to support amelioration and conversion while opposing emancipation. Examples of these arguments survive in a manuscript by George Gray, a slaveholding Quaker who moved to Philadelphia from Barbados in 1692. He likely prepared his manuscript to serve as his notes when he was a delegate at the 1696 PYM, which discussed the antislavery addresses submitted by Southeby and Morgan (neither of whom was chosen as a delegate). Gray drew selectively on the writings of Fox and Edmundson to advocate religious instruction for slaves but without acknowledging their criticism of slavery. To justify colonial slavery, Gray copied the text of Leviticus 25:44–46, which allowed Hebrews to purchase heathen slaves. He also employed racist rhetoric, describing Black people as "Heathens by Nature" while suggesting that freeing them would only lead them "into greater bondage to Sin and Satan."[35] It is noteworthy that Gray's proslavery biblicism failed to directly address the argument—advanced most clearly by Edmundson and the Keithians but also alluded to by Southeby—that Christ's sacrifice had nullified the Old Testament dispensations permitting slavery when he destroyed the partition wall between Jew and Gentile.[36] Gray's resort to racist appeals suggests the limitations of Christian proslavery biblicism

Delegates at the 1696 PYM took a compromise position regarding slavery, issuing the following advice to Quakers in the mid-Atlantic colonies: "that Friends be careful not to Encourage the bringing in of any more Negroes, &

that such that have Negroes be careful of them, bring them to Meetings, or have Meetings with them in their Families, & Restrain from Loose & Lewd Living as much as in them lies, & from Rambling abroad on First Days [i.e., Sundays] or other Times." Scholars recognize this advice as "the first institutional attempt to limit slave trading in America" but also acknowledge its limitations. Rather than forbidding the slave trade and disciplining violators, the PYM simply advised Quakers "not to Encourage" the practice. The advice said nothing about emancipation, settling instead on the type of ameliorative—and controlling—practices that Gray had encouraged. Collectively, Quakers sought to reconcile slaveholding with Christianity by advocating religious instruction while also calling for greater surveillance of Black people on the Sabbath, the one day they traditionally enjoyed a modicum of freedom. A few Quakers, such as Southeby, Pentecost Teague, and Christopher Hill, continued arguing that slavery should be abolished rather than reformed, but they had only limited influence.[37]

Despite abolitionists' efforts and the PYM's 1696 advice, slaveholding increased among Quaker colonists during the early eighteenth century. The growth of slaveholding among Quakers at this time reflected larger trends throughout the Americas. One major factor in the expansion of slavery was Parliament's decision to end the Royal African Company's monopoly on African trade in 1696. This policy change increased the scale of the Atlantic slave trade and reduced the price of African captives throughout the colonies. As the price of slaves dropped, they became increasingly more desirable compared to white indentured servants or wage laborers. Economic calculations routinely trumped moral and religious qualms.[38]

Outside of the Society of Friends, the most extensive literary debate over slavery in North America occurred among Puritans in Massachusetts. Although New England's short growing season rendered plantation slavery less profitable than in southern colonies, small-scale slavery was common, especially in urban areas. Enslaved Black New Englanders worked on farms, as urban laborers and skilled artisans, and as household domestics. Indeed, they helped make the cold New England winters more bearable for their white masters by chopping wood and tending fires. The growth of the Black population and instances of slave resistance—often through arson—raised concerns. As with Quakers, white Puritans were divided over whether slavery was itself sinful or if the problem was masters who neglected their slaves' spiritual well-being.[39] Puritans differed with Quakers regarding many doctrinal concerns, but similar assumptions about divine providence and biblicist reasoning shaped their respective debates over slavery. Samuel Sewall, a Boston merchant and judge, came to embrace antislavery based on the same scriptural passages and reasoning as William Edmundson.

In the summer of 1700, Sewall felt "call'd of *God*" to publish an antislavery essay. Part of the inspiration came from his reading of Paul Baynes's 1645 tome, *An Entire Commentary upon the Whole Epistle of the Apostle Paul to the Ephesians*. In his diary, Sewall recorded that after reading Baynes's discussion of "Blackamoors, I began to be uneasy that I had so long neglected doing any thing." Sewall was referring to the section on Ephesians 6:5–8 (about God rewarding obedient servants), which Baynes portrayed as evidence that Christianity was compatible with the hereditary enslavement of "Blackamores." Sewall rejected this claim and set out to prove his point through biblical analysis, publishing *The Selling of Joseph* in June 1700.[40]

Although only three pages long, Sewall's pamphlet is dense, and parts require careful explication to fully comprehend. Some of his arguments were based on white self-interest and revealed the limits of his racial egalitarianism. Sewall began by commenting on the "Numerousness of Slaves at this day in the Province, and the Uneasiness of them under their Slavery"; he thereby acknowledged that Black people's own resistance was part of his inspiration to write. Still, the bulk of Sewall's arguments were drawn from the Bible. In response to the claim that the African slave trade was justifiable as a means of spreading the Gospel, Sewall paraphrased Romans 3:8: "Evil must not be done, that good may come of it." One of Sewall's most important contributions to antislavery biblicism was refuting the claim that Black people were the "*Posterity of Cham* [the Latin spelling of Ham], *and therefore are under the Curse of Slavery*." He began by noting that the "extent and duration" of the Noah's Curse are not specified in the biblical text (Genesis 9:25–27). The curse thus could be "long since out of date," already fulfilled "in the Extirpation of the *Canaanites*, and the Servitude of the *Gibeonites*." Moreover, Sewall noted that the text only applied the curse to Ham's son Canaan, whereas "Ethiopians" were "descended not of Canaan, but of Cush [his brother]" (based on the genealogy contained in Genesis 10). In sum, any hereditary curse by Noah upon Canaan had *never* applied to Africans.[41]

Sewall also drew on several other passages and stories from the Old Testament; this aspect of his pamphlet was subsequently attacked by a proslavery opponent and has confused many scholars. Sewall took his title from Genesis 37, in which Joseph's jealous brothers sell him to an Ishmaelite slave trader and he ends up enslaved in Egypt. Sewall used this story to represent the injustice of slavery. He also quoted Exodus 21:16 ("*He that Stealeth a Man and Selleth him, or if he be found in his hand, he shall surely be put to death*") to claim that slaveholding was sinful. Sewall also cited Leviticus 25:39 to show "that the *Israelites* were strictly forbidden the buying, or selling one another as slaves."[42] Criticism of Sewall's pamphlet has focused on these Old Testament examples.

In 1701, John Saffin, another Boston judge, published *A Brief and Candid Answer to . . . the Selling of Joseph*, which historians recognize as the first proslavery pamphlet published in North America. Saffin began *A Brief and Candid Answer* by summarizing Sewall's pamphlet:

> *The Selling of Joseph, A Memorial*, seems . . . to draw this conclusion, that because the Sons of Jacob did very ill in selling their Brother Joseph to the Ishmaelites, who were Heathens, therefore it is utterly unlawful to Buy and Sell Negroes, though among Christians; which Conclusion I presume is not well drawn from the Premises, nor is the case parallel; for it was unlawful for the Israelites to Sell their Brethren upon any account, or pretence whatsoever during life. But it was not unlawful for the Seed of *Abraham* to have Bond Men, and Bond women either born in their House or bought with their Money.

Saffin then provided numerous Old Testament passages, such as Leviticus 25:44, showing that the Israelites were authorized to have heathen slaves, which he interpreted as proof that Christians had divine sanction to enslave Africans. As for Sewall's exegesis showing that Noah's curse on Canaan had no connection to Africans, Saffin responded that "not only the seed of Cham or Canaan, but any lawful Captives of other Heathen Nations may be made Bond men as hath been proved."[43] In sum, Saffin's proslavery biblicism relied on the Levitical law allowing the enslavement of heathens.

Although historians sympathize with Sewall's antislavery sentiments, they have almost uniformly concluded that Saffin had the stronger biblical argument. In *The Problem of Slavery in Western Culture*, David Brion Davis asserts that "by ignoring Biblical sanctions for perpetual slavery and by falsely invoking Hebrews' rules against selling their own children, Sewall had, in effect, undermined the authority of Scripture." Mark Noll states that in his rebuttal, Saffin "seized the biblical high ground" and "pointed out that the Old Testament had clearly allowed Israelites to perpetually enslave non-Hebrews, along with their children." Other scholars have similarly assumed that Saffin made the stronger biblical argument.[44] These conclusions, however, fail to understand that Saffin had distorted and misrepresented *The Selling of Joseph* and that Sewall actually based his argument on the New Testament.

Like William Edmundson, Sewall used Ephesians 2:14 (about Jesus destroying the partition wall) to argue that Christ's New Covenant had nullified all Old Testament dispensations permitting slaveholding. He acknowledged that Genesis 17:12 described Abraham as having servants "*bought with his Money, and born in his House*," and conceded: "Charity obliges us to conclude, that He knew it was lawful and good." Yet Sewall also insisted that because the biblical text did not explain the justification, "no Argument can be drawn from it." In other words, the example of Abraham thousands of years earlier was insufficient to justify slavery in the colonies. More relevant were the Mosaic laws forbidding the enslavement of each other. Implicitly acknowledging that Leviticus authorized the Hebrews to have heathen slaves, Sewall added that "since the partition Wall is broken down, inordinate Self love should likewise be demolished. *God* expects that Christians should . . . carry it [love] to all the World, as the *Israelites* were to carry it toward one another." In other words, whereas God's covenants with Abraham and Moses had only applied to the Hebrews, Christ's New Covenant implicitly extended the prohibition on enslaving one's brethren to all people. Africans "black as they are" were "the Sons and Daughters of the First *Adam* [i.e., Adam and Eve], the Brethren and Sister of the Last *Adam* [i.e., Jesus]." Therefore, Christians could not "persist in holding their Neighbours and Brethren under the Rigor of perpetual Bondage." Christian slaveholders were thus guilty of the type of manstealing punishable by death in Exodus 21:16. In sum, Sewall's pamphlet was a forceful condemnation of Black slavery based on interpreting the Old Testament in light of the New Testament. Scholars, however, have not appreciated the sophistication and extent of Sewall's analysis, likely because they missed his reference to Ephesians 2:14 (which Sewall, like Edmundson, only paraphrased without citation).[45]

It cannot be known whether Saffin truly misunderstood Sewall's argument or cynically chose to misrepresent it in his *Brief and Candid Answer*. More important is that Saffin—contrary to historians' typical portrayals—could not refute Sewall's biblicist logic. Saffin invoked "the Command of God, Lev. 25, 44" (about enslaving heathen) without acknowledging Sewall's point that Ephesians 2:14 indicated Christ had destroyed the distinction upon which that dispensation was based. The only New Testament passage regarding slavery that Saffin cited was 1 Corinthians 12:13, indicating that Christians could achieve salvation regardless of whether they were "bond or free." But this verse had little relevance. Sewall never questioned whether enslaved people could be Christians; the issue was whether Christians could keep others in perpetual slavery. Saffin buttressed his weak scriptural logic with racism. He appended a poem on "The Negroes Character," in which he listed many negative attributes that he claimed were "*Innate*" in Black people: "*Cowardly and cruel . . . Libidinous, Deceitful, False, and Rude.*" Saffin also insisted that if Black slaves were freed, they "must all be sent out of the Country, or else the remedy would be worse than the disease." Saffin's evasions and his reliance on racism underscore the weakness of proslavery biblicism, just as had been the case with Quaker George Gray. Sewall viewed Saffin's arguments as so weak that they were unworthy of reply.[46]

Although *The Selling of Joseph* did not lead to emancipation, historians have likely underestimated Sewall's influence. Many contemporaries, better versed in the Bible than the typical modern American, would have understood how Sewall used Ephesians 2:14 to argue that the New Testament had amended the Hebrew Bible in ways that nullified past dispensations permitting slavery. Judge William Atwood, who would soon be appointed chief justice of New York, praised *The Selling of Joseph* as "an ingenious Discourse." Sewall circulated *The Selling of Joseph* among "the Council and Assembly" in hopes of inspiring legislative reform. This was likely the impetus for a 1701 proposal by Boston's selectmen to curtail slave importations and "put a period to the Negroes being slaves." Although this bill did not pass, it suggests that some politicians sought to gradually abolish slavery in the colony by ending slave importations and limiting the length of Black people's servitude.[47]

Moreover, an enslaved man named Adam recruited Sewall to help him win his freedom from John Saffin, who had reneged on a 1694 promise to manumit him after seven years. (Indeed, it was this legal controversy that provoked Saffin to publish his proslavery pamphlet.) The lawsuit took several years and multiple appeals, but Adam ultimately won his freedom. Scholars have offered little explanation for Adam's eventual legal success, aside from an observation made in the late nineteenth century that it was an example of the "flexibility of the common law" and "a leaning in favor of liberty." Sewall was one of the three judges overseeing Adam's final appeal in 1703 and likely helped shape the outcome, which was determined by a jury. It was customary for judges to give jurors guidance on the law. Although the substance of any jury charge does not survive, it is easy to imagine what Sewall might have reiterated the arguments from *The Selling of Joseph*. Or perhaps he stressed the sanctity of manumission agreements as a form of contract. Whatever its basis, this ruling only applied to Adam and did not undermine the legal status of slavery itself. Saffin, enraged by the loss of his human property and the obligation to pay two years' worth of court costs, unsuccessfully petitioned the Massachusetts legislature to overturn the verdict.[48]

Although legislators declined to grant Saffin's request, they were also far from supporting abolition during this time. In the summer of 1703, they passed "An Act Relating to Molato and Negro Slaves," which required anyone manumitting an enslaved person to post a bond for £50. Localities could then call for this money if the liberated Black person became "uncapable to support him- or herself."[49] A similar law had been enacted in Connecticut the year before, and most colonies adopted comparable regulations regarding manumissions. These laws served both racist and humanitarian ends: reducing the number of free people of color and also preventing masters from abandoning elderly slaves who were no longer profitable laborers.[50] Sewall left no comment on either law, but he was outraged in December 1705 when he learned the legislature was considering a harsh new bill against interracial unions. Sewall feared the bill "would be an Oppression provoking to God," and he lobbied legislators to amend it.[51]

As part of his lobbying efforts, Sewall distributed additional copies of *The Selling of Joseph* and reprinted an antislavery essay from an English newspaper. The four-page extract from John Dunston's *The Athenian Oracle* argued that slavery was a "sin against the very Laws of *Nature*" and "*especially contrary to the great Law of Christianity*." The Old Testament dispensations that had allowed the Hebrews to enslave heathen were "made void" by Christ's New Covenant. In addition to bolstering Sewall's antislavery biblicism, *The Athenian Oracle* indicated metropolitan disgust at colonial slavery. The essay insisted that Black Christians in England were "under the same Law with other Christians," and it condemned colonial slavery as "a Disgrace to Christianity." Furthermore, *The Athenian Oracle* argued that the slave trade "hinders the Propagation of the Christian Faith" and would provoke God's wrath.[52]

Sewall's lobbying accomplished a partial "mitigation" of the 1705 bill. The final law still included harsh punishments for interracial fornication and marriage (including for anyone who officiated such a marriage), but it also protected the sanctity of slave marriages and imposed a £4 duty on slave importations into Massachusetts. The extent to which Sewall's religious arguments might have inspired the effort to limit the slave trade is difficult to discern. Racist ideas about political economy could also encourage anti-slave trade sentiment, as demonstrated by an essay in the *Boston News-Letter* the following summer. The essay complained that Black people were "addicted to Stealing, Lying and Purloining," whereas white indentured servants were a better investment and could be enlisted in defense of the colony during wars.[53]

Meanwhile, Cotton Mather had rejoined the public debate over slavery with his tract *The Negro Christianized*, in the summer of 1706. Parts of *The Negro Christianized* make Mather sound like an abolitionist as he defended the spiritual equality of Black people. Likely influenced by Sewall, Mather observed that the old claim that Black people were the cursed "Offspring of Ham" was "not so very certain." Arguing that Black people could be among God's "elect" (i.e., predestined for Heaven), Mather warned slaveholders that the Lord would punish them if they denied their slaves access to the Gospel and salvation. Still, Mather sought only to Christianize rather than to liberate enslaved Black people. He tempered his threats of eternal damnation for cruel slaveholders with assurances that Christianity "allows of *Slavery*" and that conversion did nothing to alter a slave's legal status.[54] Mather believed appeasing slaveholders was necessary to achieve the greater good of spreading the gospel among enslaved heathens.

Over time, however, Mather became increasingly critical of slaveholders as it became clear that few of them shared his commitment to evangelization. In a sermon published in 1710 as *Theopolis Americana* and dedicated to Samuel Sewall, Mather railed against greed and materialism, which he believed were subverting New England's providential mission. He pointed to the colonists' enslavement of Africans and Native Americans as especially heinous expressions of greed. He quoted Richard Baxter, the English Puritan who had pronounced that slaveholders who "neglect[ed] their [slaves'] Souls, are fitter to be called *Incarnate Devils* than *Christians*." Moreover, Mather suggested that slaveholders' behavior was among the sins provoking God's chastisement in the form of "*Indian* Depredations" and attacks by "*Popish Idolaters*."[55] He thus came very close to articulating the type of antislavery providentialism that Quaker abolitionists would promote during the French and Indian War. Still, Mather called only for slavery's amelioration rather than abolition.

During the 1710s, the most extensive debates over slavery occurred within the Society of Friends, although the minority of slaveholding Quakers effectively used their disproportionate influence to suppress antislavery agitation and limit reform. Historian Jean Soderlund has calculated that slaveholding

Quakers occupied more than two-thirds of leadership roles (serving as officers or on committees) in the PYM at the start of the eighteenth century.[56] Antislavery Quakers were generally from a lower social class and had less influence. Needless to say, Black people remained firmly opposed to slavery, and their persistent resistance was not without effect. Following episodes of slave unrest, Quaker activists such as William Southeby worked to promote antislavery reform by appealing to both religious ideals and white fears.

In April 1712, several dozen enslaved Black New Yorkers rose in rebellion, reportedly "having conspired to murder all the Christians [i.e., white people]." The militia managed to suppress the insurrection, and the New York authorities executed twenty-one Black men and women through hanging, burning, and other forms of torture.[57] After hearing the news, Southeby organized antislavery petitions to the Pennsylvania legislature. One calling for a ban on slave importations was signed by "many of the Inhabitants," but Southeby was the only signer of a second petition calling for the liberation of the Black people already enslaved in the colony. Neither petition survives, but Southeby likely reiterated his humanitarian and biblical arguments from 1696. The legislature, which included many wealthy Quakers, quickly dismissed Southeby's second petition, declaring "it is neither just nor convenient to set them at Liberty." Legislators responded more favorably to the other petition, raising the forty-shilling revenue tax on imported African captives to a prohibitive £20 duty. The law's preamble made clear the concern that inspired the legislators (and likely the petitioners): the "Plots and Insurrections" by enslaved people in both the Caribbean and "our Neighboring Colony of *New York*." Whereas religious and humanitarian concerns had proved insufficient, Black resistance finally inspired legislative attempts to limit slavery's growth. However, Pennsylvania's prohibitive duty was soon annulled by the Crown, as trade regulation was considered beyond the authority of colonial legislatures. Many white Pennsylvanians, including Quakers, then resumed buying enslaved Africans. Greed again trumped both fear and moral scruples.[58]

The only surviving abolitionist pamphlet written in the colonies during the 1710s is John Hepburn's *The American Defence of the Christian Golden Rule*, published in New York in 1715. Hepburn (or Hebron), who lived in northern New Jersey and identified as a Quaker, consciously wrote as part of an abolitionist minority. He cited and built on antislavery writings by the Keithians, Cotton Mather, and others. As indicated by the title, Hepburn condemned slaveholding based on the Golden Rule, labeling it an "Anti-christian Practice." He warned slaveholders that they would face God's punishment if they did not "make Restitution to the Negroes for the wrong they have done them." Referring to both written and oral debates over slavery, he noted that those who used the Bible to defend slavery generally drew on the Old Testament but "meddle not with the *New*." Hepburn reinforced his biblicist arguments by appending two other antislavery texts: Samuel Sewall's 1705 extract of *The Athenian Oracle* and an essay titled "Arguments against making Slaves of Men." The latter was signed "by a Native of America, Sept. 14, 1713," suggesting it was not written by a Quaker (as Friends numbered months instead of using their "pagan" name). The anonymous author refuted the common tenets of proslavery biblicism, insisting that Old Testament dispensations for slavery were "peculiar to the *Jewish Nation*." The most unique part of the essay was a proposal that after enslaved Africans were liberated, they should be sent to Africa to spread the Gospel among "their Country-Men," an idea that gained popularity in later decades.[59]

Meanwhile, slaveholding Pennsylvania Quakers were working to silence Southeby and other antislavery voices. Uncowed, Southeby declared that he would continue promoting abolition, for he was "not much concerned for ye frownes or displeasures of Any that may Apose it." In response to his antislavery agitation in 1715, the Philadelphia Yearly Meeting instructed Quakers to "avoid judging one another in this matter publickly or otherwise." After Southeby printed an antislavery pamphlet (now lost) without permission, the Philadelphia Monthly Meeting repeatedly condemned him as "disorderly" in 1716. Later that year, after Chester County (Pennsylvania) Quakers renewed calls for a stronger antislavery stance, the PYM grudgingly reiterated the advice from 1696 against buying slaves. However, it explained that it did so only "in Condescention to such Friends as are streightened in their minds against the holding them," and it emphasized that the advice was "only a caution and not Censure." PYM leaders thus made it clear that slaveholding Friends could ignore the troublesome reformers' antislavery admonitions. Southeby, meanwhile, persisted in his efforts despite the censure of powerful Quakers. Shortly before his death in 1722, Southeby submitted a final petition "about Negroes" to the Pennsylvania legislature. The legislators read it but declined to act.[60]

* * *

By the 1730s, individual white colonists had been denouncing the enslavement of Black people for half a century. The extant antislavery publications and manuscript writings must reflect "only the tip of the iceberg of antislavery sentiment," as historian Jon Kershner states.[61] Most white people, even in the southern colonies, did not own slaves. Of course, many of them were poor people who aspired to become slaveholders, but there still must have been many others who held antislavery convictions without leaving records of them. Nonetheless, the fact remains that antislavery activists—the vast majority of whom were Quakers—were not able to attract sufficient followers to create any sort of movement. But if abolitionists had not yet developed the organizational tactics needed for a social movement, they had articulated a powerful critique of slavery.

Indeed, colonial abolitionists' biblicist case against slavery was stronger than historians have generally understood. By the start of the eighteenth century, William Edmundson, Samuel Sewall, and others had composed decisive refutations of slaveholders' two most important biblical defenses: Noah's Curse in Genesis and the Levitical permission to enslave the heathen. Biblical exegesis demonstrated that any curse on the descendants of Ham's son Canaan would not have applied to Africans. Moreover, abolitionists cited Ephesians 2:14 and other New Testament passages to argue that Christ's New Covenant had nullified the past dispensations permitting slaveholding among the ancient Israelites. Although historians do not typically associate Ephesians with antislavery, arguments based on Jesus's destruction of the "wall of partition" remained common in abolitionist writings from the seventeenth through nineteenth centuries.[62]

Slaveholders proved unable to come up with compelling responses to biblicist antislavery arguments. In general, they simply ignored them or repeated the discredited claims about Noah's Curse and Levitical slave codes. Quaker slaveholders used leadership positions within the Society of Friends to suppress debate and ostracize agitators. Because slaveholders benefited from the status quo, they did not need to change public opinion or inspire activism; they simply needed to discourage reform. Abolitionists had a much harder task; they needed to change opinions and inspire activism.

CHAPTER 2

Antislavery Providentialism During the French and Indian War

Providentialism became an increasingly prominent theme in antislavery discourse during the eighteenth century. From the 1650s into the 1740s, advocates of slave conversion—such as George Fox, Cotton Mather, and George Whitefield—repeatedly warned that God would punish the colonies if they neglected the souls of enslaved people. Yet they continued to prioritize conversion over liberation, often even claiming that slaveholding was compatible with Christianity as long as masters cared for their slaves' souls. By contrast, abolitionists insisted that slavery was inherently sinful and could not be sufficiently reformed. Based on their view that national sins provoked national punishments, they believed that emancipation was necessary to prevent God's wrath. William Edmundson had warned in 1677 that God would "visit nations" for the sin of slavery, and this view became widespread among Quakers by the end of the 1750s.[1] This shift must be understood within the larger context of providentialist thought and the French and Indian War (1754–1763), which spawned the global Seven Years' War of 1756–1763.

As historian Nicholas Guyatt and others have shown, providentialist beliefs were widespread during the early modern era and persisted through the Enlightenment. Guyatt divides providentialist thinking into several types, with the most common being "historical providentialism" and "judicial providentialism." Guyatt defines historical providentialism as the "belief that God imagined a special role for certain nations in improving the world and tailored history to prepare them for the achievement of this mission." For instance, many British Protestants (throughout the empire) imagined their nation was chosen by God to reform Christianity and civilize the world. Meanwhile, Guyatt defines judicial providentialism as the belief that "God judged nations solely on the virtues of their people and leaders and then rewarded or punished them without reference to any grand plan for humanity."[2] Aspects of this second variety were compatible with the first. British Protestants could imagine that they were God's chosen people but that the Lord would nevertheless punish them for their sins. Abolitionists' biblicist convictions about slavery's inherent sinfulness often led them to believe that God would punish the British (and other slaveholding empires) until they abolished slavery. This aspect of their theology can be termed *antislavery providentialism.*

Quakers such as Ralph Sandiford and Benjamin Lay published lengthy biblicist and providentialist attacks on slavery during the 1730s, but elite slaveholding Quakers continued to suppress antislavery voices within the Society of Friends. The critical change came in the 1750s, when a "perfect storm" of broad trends and contingent events enabled antislavery Quakers to gain influence in the Philadelphia Yearly Meeting and elsewhere in the colonies. A broader reform movement begun during the late 1740s encouraged increased sectarian discipline and uniformity among Quakers. These reforms enforced such policies as temperance, plainness of dress, and the requirement to marry within the Society of Friends.[3] Whereas Quaker reformers' antislavery position conforms to modern sensibilities, some of their other concerns can appear silly in the twenty-first century. For instance, Quaker women lamented "that so many of our Youth are getting Into the Superfluous use of Ribbons" while future-abolitionist John Pemberton described theaters and dance halls as evidence that "wickedness seems greatly to be let loose."[4] Still, growing numbers of middling Friends—small farmers, artisans, and merchants—came to view slavery as sinful while wealthy slaveholders lost their earlier dominance within the PYM hierarchy. In 1753, the PYM authorized the publication of an antislavery pamphlet for the first time. Five years later, the PYM issued a new policy that forbade buying or selling slaves and called for emancipation.

The rapidity of these changes depended on the outbreak of the French and Indian War in May 1754. A new generation of Quaker abolitionists, most notably John Woolman and Anthony Benezet, portrayed the war as divine punishment for slaveholding. The war helped fuel Quakers' embrace of antislavery theology and activism. Inspired by biblicist and providentialist beliefs, the antislavery members of the Quaker "Generation of 1758" promoted abolitionism within and beyond the Society of Friends. Although Britain triumphed militarily over France, Quaker abolitionists insisted the empire must eradicate slavery to avoid worse divine chastisement in the future. By 1763, a nascent abolitionist movement was emerging, even if it consisted almost entirely of Quakers.

Persistent Antislavery Agitation

Quaker slaveholders' respite from antislavery agitation following William Southeby's death in 1722 did not last long. By the end of the decade, Ralph Sandiford, a Philadelphia merchant, had emerged as a new thorn in their side. In 1729, he published *A Brief Examination of the Practice of the Times, by the Foregoing and the Present Dispensation* (expanded and retitled *The Mystery of Iniquity* in 1730). Repeating standard biblicist arguments, Sandiford showed that Noah's curse on Canaan would never have applied to Africans and argued that Christ's New Covenant had nullified the Old Testament dispensations permitting slaveholding. Moreover, he argued that God had spoken through the Hebrew prophets to discourage slaveholding in Israel even before the coming of Christ. Sandiford cited numerous passages from Isaiah, including 58:6 and 61:2, about letting the oppressed go free and proclaiming liberty to the captives. The problem, he believed, was that too many slaveholders—especially those in positions of influence and authority—ignored the biblical prophets in favor of their own "Profits." Sandiford also drew on Jeremiah and the book of Revelation to warn that God would punish slaveholding societies. Emancipation was thus necessary to avoid God's wrath, he argued.[5]

In an emancipation plan appended to his book, Sandiford called on slaveholders to provide their slaves with "*a humane and a Christian Education*" and then "*set them free, being furnished with a Trade and Necessaries*." It is worth noting that although he was especially concerned with slaveholding among Quakers, Sandiford sought the complete abolition of slavery throughout Pennsylvania and the other British colonies. He addressed his arguments to Quakers as well as legislators in Pennsylvania and Parliament, arguing that abolition would make the colonies a better place in which Britain's poor could settle. Sandiford also called on voters to reject slaveholding candidates.[6]

Sandiford's book, along with new antislavery statements from Chester County Friends, compelled the Philadelphia Yearly Meeting to discuss the issue of slavery in 1729. Again, slaveholding delegates blocked the adoption of any definitive policy. After postponing the issue in 1729, the 1730 PYM simply stated: "Friends ought to be very Cautious of making any such Purchases [of enslaved Africans] for the Future, it being Disagreeable to the Sense of this Meeting." As with earlier compromises, this statement indicated growing discomfort with slave trading but did not actually prevent Quakers from purchasing additional slaves. Moreover, slaveholding Friends ostracized Sandiford, leading him to seek refuge in a farm outside of Philadelphia, where he soon died at age forty in 1733.[7]

New England Quakers were more tolerant of abolitionism. In the early 1730s, the Nantucket Monthly Meeting and the Newport Quarterly Meeting granted Elihu Coleman of Nantucket permission to issue an antislavery pamphlet. Coleman published *A Testimony Against That Antichristian Practice of Making Slaves of Men: Wherein it is Shewed to be Contrary to the Dispensation of the Law and Time of the Gospel* in 1733. As the subtitle indicates, he made the traditional biblicist argument that Christ's New Covenant ended the past dispensations that had allowed slavery. He also drew from the Old Testament to show that God "would not allow of Sin" to "go unpunished," even among his chosen people. Coleman did not predict what form punishment for slaveholding would take, but he trusted that God "best knows the Rod that is suitable to chastise with."[8]

Antislavery Quakers in Pennsylvania, meanwhile, continued facing opposition and censure. In 1738, Benjamin Lay took his predecessors' arguments up a notch in *All Slave-Keepers That Keep the Innocent in Bondage, Apostates*. He warned that slaveholders who "pervert, misconstrue, and misapply Scripture to serve their covetous ends" would end up "in the hottest Place in Hell." It was clear to Lay—who reprinted Samuel Sewall's *Selling of Joseph* in his book—that slavery had been rendered a crying sin in the era of Christ's Gospel dispensation, and he repeatedly warned of divine retribution. Quoting from Isaiah 28:15–19, Lay warned slaveholders that "*your covenant with Death, and Hell shall be broken when the over-flowing Scourge shall pass through, then ye shall be trodden down by it.*" (A century later, William Lloyd Garrison and others would use the same biblical passage to condemn the U.S. Constitution's compromises with slavery.) Lay also quoted Revelation 13:10 (which Sandiford had used as an epigraph), warning: "*He that leadeth into Captivity, shall go into Captivity.*" Lay believed the only way to forestall "*the Day of Vengeance*" was to follow Isaiah 61:1 and "*proclaim Liberty to the Captives.*" He called on Quakers to educate their bondspeople and then "let them go free in a very reasonable time."[9]

Lay advertised his book "particularly for my true inwardly beloved Friends called Quakers, and likewise for a general service." Yet Lay was already an outcast when he published his book, having been disowned by both the Philadelphia and Abington monthly meetings. The PYM subsequently published a newspaper announcement disavowing his book. Nonetheless, Quaker abolitionists' persistent agitation helped keep the issue alive and seems to have gradually increased antislavery sentiment among the younger generation who would assume leadership positions by the 1750s.[10]

Outside of the Society of Friends, it seems that many evangelical Christians—the type who were later most likely to become abolitionists—recognized slavery's injustice but simply did not prioritize emancipation. The Reverend George Whitefield, the leading itinerant minister in the religious revival known as the Great Awakening, was in this camp. "Whether it be lawful for Christians to buy slaves," Whitefield wrote, "I shall not take upon me to determine; but sure I am it is sinful, when bought, to use them as bad as, nay worse than brutes." Like Cotton Mather, Whitefield was primarily concerned with conversion. As he explained: "Enslaving or misusing their Bodies would, comparatively speaking, be an inconsiderable Evil, was proper Care taken of their Souls." Whether or not slaveholding could be biblically justified, Whitefield accepted it as part of God's mysterious plan to spread the Gospel throughout the world, saving souls that otherwise would have been lost.[11]

Enslaved people's own resistance sometimes had the power to inspire antislavery reform when religious arguments proved inadequate. For example, repeated instances of slave unrest in South Carolina led imperial planners in London to ban slavery in the new colony of Georgia, established in 1733. Georgia was to serve in part as a destination for English paupers and convicts while creating a buffer between South Carolina and Spanish Florida, where Catholic colonists welcomed and protected runaways from Protestant masters (although slavery remained otherwise legal in the Spanish colonies). However, by the end of the 1730s, some elite Georgians were petitioning to legalize Black slavery in their colony. This effort, in turn, spurred an antislavery petition signed by "eighteen Freeholders" in Darien, Georgia. They concluded their petition by denouncing the immorality and danger of slaveholding: "It is shocking to human Nature, that any Race of Mankind and their Posterity should be sentenc'd to perpetual Slavery; nor in Justice can we think otherwise of it, than that they are thrown amongst us to be our Scourge one Day or other for our Sins: And as Freedom must be as dear to them as to us, what a Scene of Horror must it bring about!"[12] In other words, they knew that slavery would inevitably lead to revolts and also feared that God would use slave resistance as a means of chastising white colonists for their sins.

Several months later, in September 1739, the Stono Rebellion slave revolt in South Carolina seemed to fulfill such fears.

Reverend Whitefield interpreted the Stono Rebellion, along with a smallpox outbreak and some unexplained fires, as divine retribution. "God has a quarrel with you, for your abuse of and cruelty to the poor Negroes," he declared in a public letter, *To the Inhabitants of Maryland, Virginia, North and South-Carolina, Concerning Their Negroes*. Drawing on Isaiah 26:9 and 2 Chronicles 10:11, Whitefield proclaimed: "These Judgments are undoubtedly sent abroad, not only that the Inhabitants of that [i.e., South Carolina], but that of other Provinces, should learn Righteousness: And unless you all repent, you all must in like Manner expect to perish.—God first generally corrects with Whips; if that will not do, he must chastise us with Scorpions." Whitefield even raised the specter of a successful slave insurrection in which the Black rebels gained "the upper Hand," asserting that "should such a Thing be permitted by Providence, all good Men must acknowledge the Judgment would be just." In other words, a just God might permit enslaved people to murder their oppressors. In these parts of Whitefield's letter, he sounded as militant as any abolitionist. He sounded similarly radical when discussing race. Responding to white people who imagined they were "better by Nature than the poor Negroes," Whitefield retorted: "No, in no wise." Black and white people were equally "conceived and born in Sin" and "are naturally capable of the same Improvement." Whitefield's apparent belief in racial equality and his anger at slaveholders did not, however, lead him to call for abolition. He remained convinced that religious instruction for enslaved people was more important than their liberation.[13]

Indeed, Whitefield soon joined the ongoing effort to legalize slavery in Georgia. In 1740, he established an orphanage near Savannah that was to be the center of his missionary activities, but it, like much of the colony, struggled financially. By 1742, he was advocating for the introduction of slavery. "Georgia never can be a flourishing province unless negroes are employed," he wrote, referring implicitly to the fact that enslaved people could be forced to work harder and longer than free people would be willing to labor in Georgia's hot climate. After the trustees of Georgia legalized slavery in 1749, Whitefield predicted that "many negro children will be brought up for the sake of Christ."[14] Whitefield avoided biblicist questions about whether slavery was divinely sanctioned, believing that God at least tolerated the institution as long as masters sought to convert their bondspeople to Christianity.

Although Whitefield never became an abolitionist, his commitment to evangelization and his providentialist beliefs both held latent antislavery potential. The emphasis that Whitefield and other advocates of slave conversion placed on Black people's spiritual equality and capacity for uplift undermined racist assumptions. Moreover, his belief that God would punish slaveholding societies if they neglected the souls of the enslaved was not far removed from the view that God might simply punish societies for allowing slavery.[15]

Another of the Great Awakening's leading figures, the Reverend Jonathan Edwards Sr., also had complex views on slavery and spiritual equality. Believing in the equality of souls, he allowed enslaved Black people to become full members of his church in Northampton, Massachusetts. He celebrated the expanding Gospel fold, predicting a glorious future in which "many of the Negroes and Indians will be divines, and . . . excellent books will be published in Africa." Yet Edwards also purchased his first of several slaves in 1731 and penned a defense of slavery a decade later.[16]

In 1741, Edwards was tasked with defending a fellow minister, Benjamin Doolittle, from complaints from several deacons and other disgruntled members of Doolittle's congregation in Northfield. This incident is an unusual example of grassroots antislavery among white New Englanders. It also reveals the difficulty that Doolittle and Edwards had articulating a coherent Christian defense of slaveholding. Although Edwards's rough notes are frustratingly incomplete and disorganized, they give a sense of the controversy's basic contours. Edwards noted that Northfield dissidents were "Reproaching their Pastor as tho he lived in notorious iniquity & Indulgence of his Lusts" (in this case, lusts might refer to greed rather than sexual impropriety). Doolittle's critics also boasted that when they compared slavery to "Robbery in the high way," the minister "was not able to vindicate [slavery] & had nothing to say for worth the mentioning."[17] It seems it was Doolittle's inability to overcome his congregants' antislavery criticism that led Edwards to intervene.

Although Edwards was one of the most learned Americans of his era, he (like Cotton Mather before him) clearly had great difficulty organizing a biblicist defense of slavery. His notes are disorganized, with fragments of arguments that were revised, reordered, or abandoned. It seems the antislavery Congregationalists believed that Christ's new covenant had nullified earlier dispensations allowing slavery. In response, Edwards repeatedly referred to the "Law for Jews" while indicating that slavery was "not made unlawful by any new positive Law." Moreover, he argued, it was impossible that slavery was sinful "in its own nature," because God had given the Israelites permission to enslave the Canaanites and other heathen peoples. Edwards charged that anyone claiming slavery was inherently sinful implied that God was guilty of "Encourag[ing] iniq[uity] . . . which would be a blasphemous way of talking." He claimed that because God had tolerated slavery in ancient Israel, it was also legitimate in colonial America.[18]

By the mid-1750s, a growing number of Quakers had come to believe that God demanded the entire abolition of slavery. John Woolman of New Jersey played a key role in this development, aided by contingent events such as the outbreak of war with France. He had been deeply troubled by slavery since traveling through Virginia and North Carolina in 1746. Woolman felt "a dark gloominess hanging over the land" and feared "in future the consequences will be grievous to posterity!" Back in New Jersey, where he worked as a tailor and shop clerk, he began refusing to draft legal documents that included enslaved people as property.[19] In 1753, the PYM's committee on publications granted Woolman permission to print an antislavery pamphlet, *Some Considerations on the Keeping of Negroes*, which appeared early the following year. The PYM's decision to let Woolman publish this pamphlet marked a shift from previous practice, which had suppressed antislavery. The decision reveals the growth of antislavery sentiment since the 1730s and the fact that slaveholders no longer dominated Quaker leadership positions. Although the permission to print the pamphlet did not establish any formal policy change, the PYM also permitted Woolman to "distribute [it] to the several Quarterly Meetings," indicating that the PYM expected Friends to read and reflect on the pamphlet before the next yearly meeting.[20]

In his pamphlet, Woolman admonished slaveholding Christians of "Every Denomination" in gentle yet firm terms. Instead of denouncing their greed outright, he acknowledged their natural desire to provide for their own families. Yet he warned that "*as the judgments of God are without Partiality*," slaveholders' pursuit of "*earthly Treasures . . . will rather be injurious than of any real Advantage to them*." In other words, the slaveholders were risking eternal damnation for themselves and their children. Woolman also reiterated many themes that had been part of Quaker antislavery biblicism since the seventeenth century. Implicitly responding to Christians who claimed a right to enslave Black people based on dispensations granted to the ancient Israelites, Woolman pronounced: "To consider Mankind otherwise than

Brethren, to think Favours are peculiar to one nation, and excludes others, plainly supposed a Darkness in the understanding: For God's Love is universal." Woolman also emphasized that slaveholding violated the general spirit of the Old Testament and the New. Whereas slaveholders claimed authority to enslave the heathen based on Leviticus 25:44, Woolman quoted passages such as Leviticus 19:33, which declared, "the Stranger that dwelleth with you, shall be as One born amongst you." He also used natural rights language a decade before the imperial crisis made such rhetoric ubiquitous. Enslaved people had "never forfeited [their] Liberty, and the natural Right of Freedom is in [them]." In Woolman's view, natural rights and religious principles were intimately linked, for rights came from God. People who violated the rights of others would face the Lord's judgment and "incur his heavy Displeasure." While warning of divine wrath, Woolman also promised that God would aid righteous work and help reformers overcome "the most exquisite Difficulties."[21] This conviction that God would punish slaveholding societies but assist antislavery efforts helped persuade Woolman and his followers of both the necessity and feasibility of ending slavery.

As Woolman and his allies hoped, the next yearly meeting, in September 1754, issued a new antislavery statement. A year later the PYM adopted new restrictions on slaveholders that were further tightened in 1758.[22] The French and Indian War, which had begun in May 1754 as a series of frontier conflicts, contributed to the speed of these reforms. The Quakers' collective embrace of antislavery providentialism is thus best understood in the broader religious context of the French and Indian War.

British Providentialism During the French and Indian War

Many people in the British Empire described the war with France as divine punishment. Throughout the conflict, government authorities in Britain and the colonies called for public days of "fasting, humiliation, and prayer." On these days, inhabitants were supposed to fast from sunup to sundown, attend special church services, repent for their sins, and pray for God's aid in the military conflict. In 1755, for instance, King George II issued a proclamation lamenting that "the manifold sins and wickedness of these kingdoms have most justly deserved heavy and severe punishments from the hand of heaven." He called on the people to humble themselves and implore God's "protection and blessing, upon our fleets and armies."[23] Although the British viewed the war as indicative of divine anger at them, they did not presume that God was on the side of their enemies. The Old Testament provided numerous examples of when the Lord used heathen nations, such as the Assyrians, as the "rod of mine anger" with which to chastise the Israelites (Isaiah 10:5). In the Judeo-Christian tradition, these instances of divine chastisement did not mean that God had turned against his chosen people; rather, the Lord was behaving as a stern but loving father, disciplining his children to put them back on the path of righteousness.

Thus, although government officials and ministers emphasized Britons' need for repentance, they also stressed their confidence that God would ultimately favor British Protestants over French Catholics and their "heathen" Native American allies. For example, the Reverend Samuel Davies told Virginians "that a provoked God intends to scourge us with the Rod of *France*" but added: "When God has finished his Work of Correction with this Rod, he will break it, or burn it in the fire."[24] In other words, the Lord was using the French merely as tools and would welcome the British back into his embrace once they had been sufficiently chastened. Fast days continued throughout the war, concluding with a day of thanksgiving celebrating victory in 1763.[25] Wartime sermons provide a window into the colonists' providentialist views and help explain why some, especially Quakers, came to embrace antislavery reform.

Ministers routinely used "slavery" as a metaphor to describe the Catholic threat. The Reverend John Lowell of Newbury, Massachusetts, warned that France would "spare no Cost or Pains to fix and rivet *Shackles* upon the rest of Mankind. *Their* People are *already* Slaves, and their absolute Monarch would make *them* their Instruments of enslaving *all others*."[26] In Boston, the Reverend Samuel Webster warned that the king of France was "an *arbitrary tyrant*, who will strip us of all our liberties at once, and make us like *French slaves*."[27] There is no record that either minister spoke out against the actual enslavement of Black people during the French and Indian War, though Webster subsequently called for abolition during the imperial crisis and Lowell's son (also named John) helped dismantle slavery in Massachusetts during the 1770s as a lawyer representing enslaved plaintiffs.

Meanwhile, other ministers during the French and Indian War used the slavery metaphor in ways that appealed to a sense of British superiority while ignoring actual slavery. For instance, the Reverend Matthias Harris of Delaware proclaimed: "Let us remember from whom we are sprung, and often reflect, that we are the descendants of those brave *Britons*, who have for many ages been the assertors of the common rights of mankind and the glorious vindicators of the liberties of a free people; *who* have scorned to be slaves and *who* have ever resolved to live, or at least to die free." Of course, the British, who trafficked unprecedented numbers of enslaved Africans during the eighteenth century, hardly promoted the "common rights of mankind." Harris ignored the enslavement of thousands of Black people in the colonies when discussing the "crying sins and iniquities" that must have provoked the Lord's anger. Instead, he identified debauchery and impiety as the colonists' primary offenses.[28]

Aside from Quakers, the white colonists most likely to criticize slavery were missionaries who sought to convert the enslaved. Missionaries sent by the Society for the Propagation of the Gospel (SPG) and similar groups, such as the Associates of Dr. Bray, had grown increasingly frustrated with opposition from slaveholders. In 1748, a missionary in Delaware complained that many slaveholders opposed religious instruction because they were "destitute of common humanity . . . their hearts set upon nothing but gain." A missionary in Georgia lamented in 1753 that slaveholders "call themselves by the glorious name of Christians, & yet are a Scandal not only to human Nature but to our Holy Profession."[29] During the French and Indian War, the Reverend Davies blamed slaveholders for bringing God's wrath down upon the British Empire.[30] In addition to citing standard sins—"drunkenness, swearing, lying, defrauding, whoredom, sabbath-breaking"—the Presbyterian minister gave special attention to the "general neglect of the souls of the poor negroes." He claimed these sins had provoked God to use the French and Indians "as his rod to scourge us."[31] In a series of letters published in London in 1757, Davies called for greater efforts to spread the Gospel among enslaved Africans in the colonies. Saving the souls of "*Heathen Slaves*" would be an "acceptable offering to God" and reduce the "burden of guilt under which my country groans, on this account." He also argued that enslaved people should be taught to read in order to facilitate conversion and religious comprehension.[32]

Amid the war, the Associates of Dr. Bray decided to establish schools that would educate enslaved Black children in the colonies in hopes that literacy would boost conversion. The group worked with Benjamin Franklin and other colonists to open a series of schools, beginning with one in Philadelphia in November 1758. Franklin, who had been working in London as a lobbyist on behalf of the Pennsylvania legislature, first visited the Bray School in 1763. He was impressed, telling the school's English patrons: "From what I then saw, [I] have conceiv'd a higher Opinion of the natural Capacities of the black Race, than I had ever before entertained. Their Apprehension seems as quick, their Memory as strong, and their Docility in every Respect equal to that of white Children." He added: "You will wonder perhaps that I should ever doubt it, and I will not undertake to justify all my Prejudices, nor to account for them." Apparently, educating Black people could open white minds and help dispel prejudice. Other supporters of Philadelphia's Bray School included the Reverend Jacob Duché, the Anglican minister at Christ Church. But while the Philadelphia school maintained a steady enrollment of a few dozen Black students (most of whom were enslaved), a similar school in Virginia collapsed within a few years due to slaveholders' reluctance to support Black education. The Reverend John Waring, secretary of the Associates of Dr. Bray, fumed: "& how will the Masters be able to stand before the Son of Man at the Last Day, when all rich & poor bond & free will [be] on a level, when a strict account will be demanded for refusing to have his Slave instructed in the word of Life, when the involuntary Ignorance of the Slave will be pardoned but the hard hearted Master will be severly punished?"[33] Despite such frustrations, most religious reformers still advocated for conversion rather than emancipation.

Most white Americans, it seems, ignored the issue of Black slavery as much as they could. The vast majority of wartime sermons focused on the need to reform personal sins rather than institutionalized evils. As had been the case for decades, the only antislavery pamphlets published in North America during the French and Indian War were written by Quakers.

Quakers and Antislavery Providentialism

The Philadelphia Yearly Meeting began the steps that led to its new abolitionist stance before the outbreak of the French and Indian War, but warfare undoubtedly helped galvanize support and accelerated the rate of antislavery reform. In September 1754, after Quakers had had time to read and consider John Woolman's pamphlet but before the recent frontier hostilities had become a full-fledged war, the PYM issued *An Epistle of Caution and Advice Concerning the Buying and Keeping of Slaves*. The pamphlet was principally authored by Anthony Benezet, a Quaker school teacher who had been born in France.[34] The subsequent expansion of the war—especially the capture of frontier settlers by Native Americans allied with the French—seemed to fulfill Benezet's warnings that slaveholding would provoke divine wrath. By 1758, a new generation of Quaker leaders was committed to abolishing slavery.

Scholars often emphasize the centrality of Matthew 7:12 (the Golden Rule) to Quaker antislavery sentiment, but Matthew 7:2 (on retaliatory justice) was the crucially important corollary text. Benezet linked them in *An Epistle of Caution and Advice*: "Remember our blessed Redeemer's positive Command, *To do unto others, as we would have them do unto us*, and that, *with what Measure we mete, it shall be measured out to us again*." By joining the verses together, he asserted that God would punish those who violated the Golden Rule. Benezet reminded readers that Mosaic law punished manstealing with death (Exodus 21:16) and that "*Christ* died for all Men, without respect of person." Christians thus had no right to enslave anyone. Benezet hoped slaveholders would "think it your Duty to set them free."[35]

The part of *An Epistle of Caution and Advice* that came to seem most prescient in light of Benezet's warning of retaliatory justice was his reference to the African wars that slave traders provoked. "What dreadful Scenes of Murther and Cruelty those barbarous rampages must occasion in these unhappy People's Country," he lamented. In 1754, Benezet had called on readers to use their imaginations: "Let us make their Case our own, and consider what we should think, and how we should feel, were we in their circumstances . . . stolen away, Parents from Children, and Children from Parents." By the time of the 1755 PYM, less imagination was required as the conflict with the French and their Indigenous allies had escalated into full-scale war. Newspapers described Indian raids with "Families butchered in their Beds; or carried into Captivity, often more intolerable than Death itself." Benezet's warning that slaveholding "draws down the displeasure of Heaven" must have seemed to ring true. At the 1755 PYM, Quakers adopted a new policy (or "discipline query"), calling on slaveholders to treat their enslaved people "well" and "to train them up in the Principles of the Christian Religion." They also forbade the purchase (or sale) of additional slaves. Although these injunctions lacked enforcement provisions and did not require emancipation, they indicated an emerging antislavery consensus—or "sense of the meeting" in Quaker parlance—within the PYM.[36]

During their 1756 and 1757 sessions, PYM delegates directed most of their attention to issues related to their peace testimony. The Pennsylvania government had established a militia law and was paying bounties for the scalps of Delaware Indian men and women.[37] Quakers had long refused military service and adopted a stronger stance against paying wartime taxes during this new conflict. Quaker politicians were also pressured to withdraw from the government so as not to be complicit in the violence. As some scholars have emphasized, their withdrawal from the government may have encouraged Quakers to embrace antislavery as a means of reasserting moral authority despite losing formal political influence. Still, the Quakers' turn against slavery had preceded their withdrawal from the government, and theology was likely more influential than status anxiety.[38]

The Quaker reformers who left records of the impulse behind their antislavery sentiment emphasized their providentialist worldview. John Churchman, from Chester County, is an instructive example. During the 1740s, he had focused on suppressing personal vices such as drunkenness and swearing. He interpreted the outbreak of war with France as divine retribution but did not initially show any interest in the antislavery reforms that Woolman and Benezet were promoting. This changed in September 1756, when Churchman witnessed a wagon carrying the corpses of settlers who had been "murdered and scalped" by Native Americans on Pennsylvania's frontier. At first Churchman imagined "that the sins of the inhabitants, pride, profane swearing, drunkenness with other wickedness were the cause, that the Lord had suffered this calamity and scourge to come upon them." But he recorded that after further reflection, "mine eyes turned to the case of the poor enslaved Negroes . . . it then appeared plain to me, that [slaveholders] were partakers in iniquity, encouragers of war and the shedding of innocent blood, which is often the case, where those unhappy people are or have been captivated and brought away for slaves."[39] After concluding that the enslavement of Black people and the mistreatment of Native Americans were the greatest sins in the land, Churchman became a leading advocate for antislavery reform.

Individual activism was also important in spreading antislavery sentiment among Quakers. John Woolman personally persuaded several Quakers to add manumission clauses to their wills, freeing their slaves upon their deaths. As a "Public Friend" appointed by his monthly meeting, he also continued visiting Quaker meetings throughout the colonies despite the war. During a southern visit in the spring of 1757, Woolman promoted his antislavery views in North Carolina and Virginia. When staying at the homes of slaveholders, he feared partaking in "the gain of oppression" and insisted on paying his hosts' enslaved servants for their services. When attending the Virginia Yearly Meeting (VYM) in May 1757, Woolman pressed them to adopt the PYM's 1755 discipline query against buying or selling slaves. He was disappointed that they modified the language to only prohibit "importing" slaves or buying them "to trade in." These changes meant that while Virginia Friends were forbidden from participating in the Atlantic slave trade, they could still buy enslaved people born in the colonies for their personal use (but not for resale). Still, Woolman celebrated that it was at least "one step further than they have heretofore gone."[40]

Woolman also recorded encountering Friends who still defended slavery on biblical grounds. One unnamed Virginian claimed Africans were "the offspring of Cain, their blackness being the mark God set upon him after he murdered Abel his brother, that it was the design of providence they should be slaves." Woolman responded by pointing out that such claims contradicted the Bible, which indicated that the great flood had wiped out all life except for the people and animals on Noah's ark. Another slaveholder interjected with the claim that Cain's cursed descendants had survived in the Land of Nod, which "the flood did not reach." He further claimed that after Ham was cursed by Noah, he went to the Land of Nod, where he married one of Cain's descendants. With "these two families being thus joined," Africans were a doubly cursed race and "undoubtedly fit only for slaves." In response, Woolman again tried pointing out that this claim lacked scriptural support and was illogical. If God intended the flood to punish humanity's wickedness "and it was granted that Cain's stock was the most wicked," it was "therefore unreasonable to suppose they were spared." However, Woolman's scriptural analysis and reasoning were no match for the slaveholders' "love of gain." He ended the conversation by insisting that the enslaved had a right to liberty and warning that "he who is a refuge for the oppressed will in his own time plead their cause." In other words, God would intervene on behalf of the enslaved if their oppressors did not voluntarily manumit them.[41]As the war continued, more and more Quakers came to see it as God's means of punishing the colonies for slavery and other sins.

Institutional changes within the Society of Friends also facilitated the spread of antislavery sentiment and policies during and after the French and Indian War. Based on its members' commitment to pacifism, the PYM encouraged them to withdraw from government positions and refuse to pay taxes during the war. Without politics as a venue, ambitious and socially prominent Quakers such as the Pemberton brothers—Israel, James, and John—directed their energies toward reform and humanitarian concerns, especially antislavery. They drew on religious networks and business connections in other colonies and England to spread the reform impulse geographically.[42] American Quakers also established regional meetings for sufferings or standing committees during the war, following the earlier precedent of their English brethren. Beginning in May 1755, the Philadelphia Meeting for Sufferings (PMS) met monthly (or as needed) to address the "sufferings" caused by the French and Indian War. These sufferings included not only wartime violence but also the persecution of Quakers by colonial assemblies on account of their refusal to serve in militias or pay wartime taxes. The Quaker committees routinely petitioned colonial legislatures to request that Quakers' rights of conscience be respected during the war.[43]

Antislavery pioneers such as Woolman and Benezet served in the PMS, as did more recent converts such as John Churchman, David Cooper, and the three Pemberton brothers. Dominated by reformers, the PMS as a whole soon became a vehicle for advancing Quaker testimony against slavery as well as war. The situation was similar in other colonies. In 1756, several Virginia Friends formed an ad hoc committee to petition the legislature to seek exemption from wartime taxes and militia duty, and the VYM formalized its standing committee the following year. This committee routinely corresponded with the PMS, and some of its founding members, such as Robert Pleasants and Edward Stabler, later emerged as the colony's leading abolitionists. Thomas Nicholson, who became North Carolina's most active Quaker abolitionist, helped establish the North Carolina Standing Committee (NCSC) in 1757 after attending the PYM and meeting with Anthony Benezet and other PMS members. In 1758, Nicholson helped convince the North Carolina Yearly Meeting (NCYM) to adopt a discipline query admonishing members to treat their slaves well and encourage their religious instruction.[44] Although southern Quakers lagged behind their northern brethren, standing committees facilitated the spread of antislavery activism.

Wartime fast days further encouraged Quakers' growing antislavery commitments. Shortly after offering bounties for Indian scalps, Pennsylvania's lieutenant governor designated May 21, 1756, as "a day of public fasting, humiliation, and prayer" (Figure 3). Many Quakers undoubtedly agreed with his conclusion that the land was full of sin and that the war, especially the "barbarous Captivity" among Indians, was "the Method of God's Providence . . . to visit His People for their Sins, and . . . call them to Repentance." Yet Quakers differed regarding the type of sins that had provoked "the Judgments of the Lord." Based on Matthew 7:2, Indian captivity seemed to them a fitting form of retaliatory justice for the sin of enslaving Black people. Moreover, Quaker abolitionists had routinely quoted Revelation 13:10 to warn, "He that leadeth into Captivity, shall go into Captivity."[45] In sum, fast-day proclamations and the capture of colonists by Native Americans strengthened providentialist antislavery convictions among Quakers.

PHILADELPHIA, May 6.
By the HONOURABLE
ROBERT HUNTER MORRIS, Eſq;
Lieutenant Governor and Commander in Chief of the Province of Pennſylvania, *and Counties of* New-Caſtle, Kent *and* Suſſex, *upon* Delaware,

A PROCLAMATION.

WHEREAS it is often the Method of GOD's Providence, for the Glory of His Name, and the Maintainance of true Holineſs, graciouſly to viſit His People for their Sins, and in a more ſolemn Manner to call them to Repentance by awakening Judgments from Heaven, which, if neglected or contemned, render ſuch a People ſtill more obnoxious to the Divine Diſpleaſure: AND WHEREAS, at this preſent time, the Judgments of the Lord ſeem viſibly to be abroad upon the Earth, whoſe habitable Parts have been almoſt univerſally agitated with frequent and moſt dreadful *Earthquakes*, great Cities, in divers Places, being overturned to their Foundations, many Thouſands of their Inhabitants whelmed in the Ruins, and Wars, and Rumours of Wars, with Sin and Wickedneſs, neverthele ſs extenſively prevailing: AND WHEREAS Our Gracious Sovereign on the *Britiſh* Throne, touched with a deep Senſe of theſe Things, and a thorough Concern for the Glory of GOD, and the Proſperity of His Dominions, was pleaſed to appoint and command a Day of publick *Faſting*, *Prayer* and *Supplication*, and to hallow that Day by His Royal Example, riſing from the Throne like the King of *Nineveh*, and humbling himſelf in the Duſt, together with his good Subjects, in one grand and ſolemn Act of Devotion before the LORD of LORDS, and KING of KINGS, moſt fervently imploring the adorable Majeſty of Heaven "to avert juſt "Judgments from us, to continue His Mercies towards us, to per-"petuate the Enjoyment of the *Proteſtant Religion*, and to protect "and bleſs our Fleets and Armies." AND WHEREAS the Imitation of ſuch an illuſtrious Pattern of *Humiliation* and *Devotion*, is not only our indiſpenſable Duty, on ſo awful and intereſting an Occaſion, as we are Subjects to the beſt of Kings, and equally concerned with others of his faithful Subjects in the general Safety and Proſperity of his Dominions, but eſpecially as the Province which we inhabit is at this time particularly viſited with the murdering Sword of a ſavage Enemy, a conſiderable Part of it being already laid waſte by their bloody Ravages; great Numbers of our unhappy Fellow Subjects cruelly murdered, or carried into barbarous Captivity, and the enſuing Summer opening a Proſpect that ſeems big with the Fate of theſe Colonies, and more nearly intereſting their future Safety than any Period which they have ever yet beheld.

WHEREFORE, upon mature and weighty Conſideration of theſe Matters, I have thought fit, by the Advice of the Council, to appoint and ſet apart *Friday*, the Twenty-firſt Day of *May*, to be obſerved throughout this Province and Counties, under my Government, as a Day of publick *Faſting* and general *Humiliation* before the LORD OUR GOD, that we may, with one Heart and Voice, in the moſt ſolemn and devout Manner, ſend up our united Prayers and Supplications to the Throne of Grace and Mercy, through the unſpeakable Merits and Interceſſion of our

Figure 3. Fast-day proclamations, printed as broadsides and in newspapers, were common throughout the French and Indian War, the imperial crisis, and the Revolutionary War, and provided important context for religious and political debates over slavery. This proclamation explicitly described frontier violence committed by Native Americans against white settlers as reflecting God's means of chastising the colonists for their sins. Detail from *Pennsylvania Gazette* (Philadelphia), 6 May 1756, 3. Courtesy of the American Antiquarian Society.

Quakers, however, declined to participate in fast days based on longstanding theological traditions. The biblical inspiration for fast days went back to Leviticus 16:29 (in which the Lord commands an annual fast on the tenth day of the seventh month), while the most famous example—routinely cited in colonial fast-day proclamations and sermons—occurred in Jonah 3:4–10. In this story, after Jonah warns the people of Nineveh of their impending destruction, God decides to spare the city when the inhabitants perform a public day of fasting, repentance, and prayer. However, Quakers noted that other Hebrew prophets had routinely condemned fasts and that nothing in the New Testament supported the tradition's continuance. Moreover, they asserted that repentance and prayer (if not fasting) should be daily practices rather than special occasions. Beginning in the 1650s, following the English Civil War, George Fox had published several pamphlets explaining why Friends would not participate in the fast days proclaimed by Lord Protector Oliver Cromwell. For instance, in 1654, Fox published *A Warning from the Lord, to All Such as Hang Down the Head for a Day, and Pretend to Keep a Fast unto God, When They Smite with the Fist of Wickedness, and Suffers the Innocent to Lie Oppressed.* He denounced Cromwell's fast day as superficial and insulting to God. Fox based his pamphlet on Isaiah 58, in which the Lord rebukes the Israelites and explains that he has ignored their fasts and prayers because they are superficial and self-serving. In Isaiah 58:6, God outlines the actions that would actually earn his blessing: "Is not this the Fast that I have chosen? to loose the bands of wickedness, to undo the heavy burdens, and to let the oppressed go free, and to break every yoke?" Based on this scriptural passage, Fox argued that England needed true repentance and reform, including an end to political and religious persecution.[46] When he spoke of "letting the oppressed go free," Fox was primarily referring to oppression within England, especially Cromwell's attempts to suppress the Society of Friends as religious dissidents. A century later, Quaker reformers would increasingly put an antislavery spin on Isaiah 58:6.

In the summer of 1757, Pennsylvania Friends published a seven-page *Apology for the People Called Quakers,* explaining their refusal to participate in public fast days. The pamphlet was authored by a committee including Anthony Benezet along with Israel and James Pemberton. Reminding readers that Friends had established Pennsylvania as a province where they could enjoy religious toleration, they quoted William Penn (the colony's founder) to demonstrate that participating in public days of fasting and prayer violated Quaker beliefs. The committee also copied the text of Isaiah 58:4–9 and argued that superficial fast days offended God unless accompanied by sincere "Repentance and Amendment of Life." The pamphlet described the ongoing war as "the just Judgments of the Lord" and argued that only with permanent righteous reform could the colonists "have some well-grounded Reason to hope that the Scourge which hangs over us, will in due Time be removed."[47] Quakers therefore sought to please the Lord not by observing public days of fasting but through actual reform. Antislavery

Quakers wanted to follow the prophet Isaiah's command and literally let the oppressed go free.

However, Quakers were still far from united in favor of emancipation. Indeed, in February 1758, the Philadelphia Quarterly Meeting (PQM) complained of an "Increase of the unjust Practice of Purchasing & Selling Slaves, notwithstanding their care & Endeavours to prevent it." (One of the offenders, James Logan, explained that he was obliged "to buy a Negro" after several white servants had left him to enlist in the army.) In May, a committee proposed pressing for further reform at the next PYM, but the PQM ultimately decided to postpone the matter. John Woolman learned of this and made sure to be in Philadelphia on the date of the next quarterly meeting, in August. Although he was not a delegate to the meeting, he "was admitted . . . and had a weighty conference on the subject." In the end, the PQM endorsed the report calling for more reform. Woolman also traveled farther west to attend the Chester County Quarterly Meeting. One of his antislavery allies there, John Churchman, reported to John Pemberton (the third of three reform-minded brothers) that several topics, "particularly about Negroes," provoked contentious discussion at the meeting.[48] Clearly, Woolman and other abolitionists were planning a coordinated strategy to push for more reform at the upcoming yearly meeting, in September.

The 1758 PYM was held in John Woolman's hometown of Burlington, New Jersey (as was typical on alternating years). He played an unusually active role, starting with announcing that Israel Pemberton had been chosen as clerk. Spurred by the PQM's report, the PYM soon began discussing calls for further antislavery reform.[49] Woolman recorded in his diary that "several faithful Friends" endorsed emancipation while no delegates would "openly justify the practice of slavekeeping." Still, many called to delay further action, arguing that "the Lord in time to come might open a way for the deliverance of these people." Woolman rejected this form of passive providentialism, which would shift the responsibility to God. He believed it was time for human action, retorting that "many slaves on this continent are oppressed, and their cries have reached the ears of the Most High!" His Quaker audience, well versed in the Bible, would have recognized his implicit reference to Exodus 2:23 ("and the children of Israel sighed by reason of the bondage, and they cried, and their cry came up unto God"). They also would have realized that in this biblical analogy, their position was akin to that of the Egyptians who came to suffer God's wrath. Continuing the Exodus metaphor, Woolman insisted that God was calling on them to liberate their slaves and warned that if "[we] neglect to do our duty . . . still waiting for some extraordinary means to bring about their deliverance, it may be that by terrible things in righteousness God may answer us in this matter." In other words, Quakers could choose to support emancipation with God's blessing or provoke further divine wrath through inaction. "Such is the purity and certainty of his judgments that he cannot be partial in our favour . . . it is not a time for delay," Woolman warned. Ultimately, "many Friends declared that they believed liberty was the Negro's right, to which at length no opposition was made publicly." Clearly, there were still some Quakers who were opposed to the reform, but the "sense of the meeting" had shifted to embrace emancipation.[50]

As clerk of the PYM, Israel Pemberton drafted its new policy minute. Likely paraphrasing the speeches of other delegates, he described their wartime decision in providentialist terms. By "permission of divine Providence," the colonies were "visited with ye desolating Calamities of Warr and bloodshed, so that many of our fellow Subjects are now suffering in Captivity [among the Indians]." The Quakers were thankful "for the peculiar favour extended & continued to our Friends and Brethren in profession, none of whom as we have yet heard [have] been Slain or carried into Captivity." It seems they attributed the particular mercy that God had shown to Quakers as evidence that the Lord was pleased with their 1754 antislavery statement and 1755 policy. In order to "manifest an humbling sense of these Judgments and in Thankfullness," the PYM declared that its members should "steadily observe The Injunction of our Lord and Master, 'To Do unto others as we would they should do unto us,' which it now appears to this Meeting would induce such Friends who have any Slaves to sett them at Liberty."[51] In sum, the war had convinced Quakers that God required them to support not only enslaved people's conversion but also their freedom.

The PYM's call for manumission was not (yet) accompanied by coercive power, but it did adopt disciplinary sanctions against Quakers who bought or sold slaves. The delegates instructed the monthly meetings to "testify their disunion with such persons" by forbidding them to serve in any formal capacity within local meetings or even donate money to Quaker charities. Sixty-two years after the PYM's 1696 toothless (and ineffective) statement discouraging the slave trade, Quakers were finally backing up antislavery advice with disciplinary action (albeit not yet complete disownment). Upon hearing the news, Benjamin Lay, the elderly antislavery agitator who had been disowned by Friends two decades earlier, reportedly exclaimed: "*Thanksgiving and praise be rendered unto the Lord God . . . I can now die in peace.*" He did so the following year.[52] Whereas Lay had been an outcast, the new generation of reformers was able to combine antislavery theology with the power of Quakers' collective authority and organizational structure.

The 1758 PYM also created a committee to visit slaveholding Friends and encourage manumissions. The most active members of the committee were John Woolman and John Churchman. In 1759 they reported "some progress" but apparently had not yet inspired any manumissions. The committee had a difficult task, partly because the French and Indian War set in motion demographic trends that undermined the push for manumissions. European immigration declined while many white servants left their masters to enlist in the army, creating more demand for enslaved labor. In this context, many slaveholding Friends resisted the pressure to manumit their slaves, and some even bought more of them.[53]

Frustrated by the intransigence of some slaveholding Friends, reformers kept warning that God would continue afflicting the colonies until they abolished slavery. Benezet published *Observations on the Inslaving, Importing and Purchasing of Negroes* in early 1759, arguing that God subjected colonists to war and captivity as punishment for slaveholding and "to teach us to feel for others." The 1759 PYM echoed these sentiments in an epistle sent to the monthly and quarterly meetings. The Quakers described the war as God's punishment of sin "in a national capacity," and they hoped that the public would sufficiently reform so that "heavier chastisement may not become necessary!"[54] When Benezet reprinted his *Observations* the following year (Figure 4), he added two quotes from the book of Isaiah as an epigraph, reflecting his view that God would ignore the colonists' prayers for peace until they "let the Oppressed go free." Still, not all Quakers shared Benezet's sense of divine mandate and urgency. After representatives at the 1760 PYM reviewed the "discipline reports" from the local meetings (about efforts to enforce Quaker policies), they simply expressed "some hopes, that the testimony of truth against the importation & keeping of Negroes, seems rather to gain ground." Progress was steady but slow. Woolman's committee that visited slaveholders was also cautiously optimistic, reporting further "progress" each year until the group disbanded in 1762. After that point, the monthly meetings were expected to "continue the necessary care in this matter."[55]

A growing number of Friends began liberating their bondspeople outright or via their wills during this time. Jean Soderlund and Gary Nash have calculated that the proportion of slaveholding Quakers who manumitted slaves in their wills increased from 18 percent in the 1740s to 30 percent in the

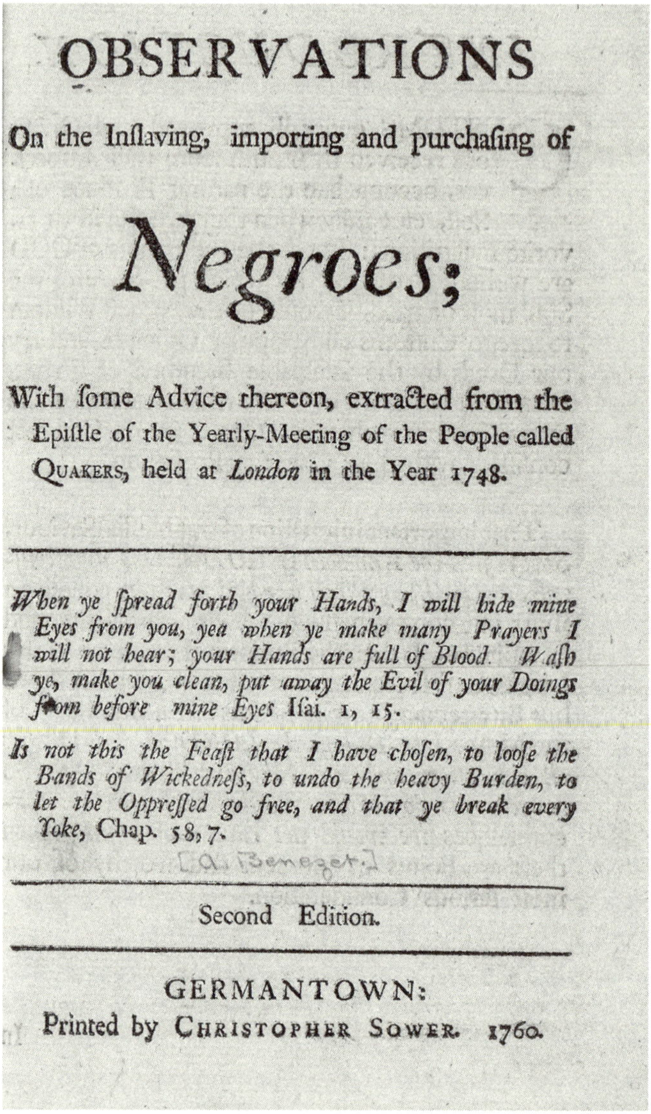

OBSERVATIONS

On the Inſlaving, importing and purchaſing of

Negroes;

With ſome Advice thereon, extracted from the Epiſtle of the Yearly-Meeting of the People called QUAKERS, held at *London* in the Year 1748.

When ye ſpread forth your Hands, I will hide mine Eyes from you, yea when ye make many Prayers I will not hear; your Hands are full of Blood. Waſh ye, make you clean, put away the Evil of your Doings from before mine Eyes Iſai. 1, 15.

Is not this the Feaſt that I have choſen, to looſe the Bands of Wickedneſs, to undo the heavy Burden, to let the Oppreſſed go free, and that ye break every Yoke, Chap. 58, 7.

[A. Benezet.]

Second Edition.

GERMANTOWN:
Printed by CHRISTOPHER SOWER. 1760.

Figure 4. The second edition of Anthony Benezet's pamphlet included epigraphs taken from Isaiah, reflecting his belief that the French and Indian War represented divine punishment and that the Lord would not answer the colonists' prayers while they participated in the sin of slavery. (Note that the printer erroneously dated the advice from the 1758 London Yearly Meeting as 1748 and misidentified the second Isaiah passages as 58:7 instead of 58:6.) Courtesy of the American Antiquarian Society.

1750s. After 1758, outright manumissions became more common, but the rate is difficult to determine because Quakers did not begin keeping systematic records of manumissions until 1776, when they made slaveholding a disownable offense. Before then, Quaker committees only recorded manumissions if they occurred under unusual circumstances.[56] Take, for instance, the 1764 case of Isaac Andrews of Haddonfield, New Jersey, and a "Negro lad" named Cato. When Andrews's aunt died, she willed Cato to another heir "forever" unless Andrews would pay the estate £30 (presumably because Andrews, who was a PMS activist, had previously expressed concern about the boy's enslavement). He wanted to help Cato but was afraid of violating the PYM's policies against purchasing slaves. Andrews brought his dilemma to the Haddonfield Monthly Meeting, which referred the matter to a committee (which included David Cooper, the future antislavery pamphleteer). The committee determined to exempt Andrews from the PYM's policy against buying slaves so that he could purchase Cato in order to free him. The agreement they worked out required Cato to serve Andrews "faithfully as a good Servent" until age twenty-four. This arrangement was presumably intended to repay Andrews for Cato's purchase price.[57] While Andrews purchased Cato to liberate him, other Quakers had to be pressured to liberate slaves whom they had purchased in violation of the 1758 policy. In 1765, for example, Daniel Walton of Philadelphia County was compelled to sign a five-year indenture and manumission agreement with "a certain Negro Man Slave Named James" whom he had purchased "some time ago." Not all Friends who violated the 1758 policy agreed to make amends. Between 1758 and 1774, the Philadelphia Monthly Meeting (PMM) investigated forty-four members who violated the prohibition of buying or selling slaves, disciplining two dozen of them.[58]

Meanwhile, the progress of abolitionism among British Quakers largely paralleled developments in the North American colonies, facilitated by the exchange of epistles from the respective yearly meetings and the meetings for sufferings. The London Yearly Meeting condemned the slave trade in 1758 and began disowning slave traders in 1761.[59] Thus the seeds of a transatlantic abolitionist movement were planted during the Seven Years' War.

An Expanding Movement

By the start of the 1760s, the Quaker antislavery movement had greater coherence and a broader agenda than scholars have often appreciated. It is common for historians to overemphasize the limitations of Quaker reform. Christopher Brown asserts that "the Quaker antislavery ethic of the 1750s and 1760s aimed at separatism rather than abolitionism . . . with the important exception of Anthony Benezet." Instead of "pushing for wholesale challenges to the slave system throughout the empire," Quakers sought primarily to "cleanse the religious society of sin."[60] It is true that some Friends resisted emancipation, that many more were unenthusiastic, and that Benezet was exceptional (as was John Woolman). But Benezet and Woolman were far from alone. A majority of PYM delegates agreed that enslaved Black people deserved their freedom. The Generation of 1758 who pressed the PYM to adopt its antislavery stance contained many reformers who made abolition a lifelong vocation from that point on. It is natural that Quaker reformers initially prioritized ending slaveholding within their own ranks, but they quickly began pushing for broader reform. Indeed, their belief that national sins provoked national punishments made it imperative to end slavery throughout the British Empire. Practical considerations also necessitated that Quakers simultaneously press for antislavery reform within their denomination and for political change. Manumissions were almost entirely forbidden in North Carolina and Virginia, while manumitters in northern colonies had to post bonds in case their former slaves became indigent and required poverty relief. This type of law made legislative reform a prerequisite for ending slaveholding among Friends. Quaker abolitionists began working to expand the antislavery movement politically in the early 1760s, amid the ongoing war. The Philadelphia Meeting for Sufferings lent crucial institutional and organizational support to these efforts.

In 1760, PMS activists promoted reform up and down the coast. Considering the entrenched economic and political opposition that abolitionists faced, it is hardly surprising that they made only slow progress. Yet the extent of activism by the PMS and its allies in other regions challenges the common assumption that antislavery sentiment in this era "lacked political organization and was largely inconsequential."[61] When Woolman attended the New England Yearly Meeting (NEYM) in 1760, he not only supported its adoption of a discipline query against buying or selling slaves but also drafted a petition calling on the Rhode Island legislature to ban all involvement in the Atlantic slave trade. From his home in Philadelphia, PMS clerk James Pemberton sent letters as far south as South Carolina, encouraging southern Quakers to reflect on the war's providential significance. "The case of your Neighbours & Fellow Subjects forcibly taken away and carried into Captivity," he wrote, "will lead you to consider by what means the Slaves among you were first deprived of their Liberty." He hoped they would follow northern Quakers in enacting antislavery reforms.[62]

The South Carolina legislature did ban slave importations in 1760, but this decision preceded Pemberton's letter and reflected more pragmatic concerns. In his 1759 pamphlet, Anthony Benezet had noted that slavery endangered society by increasing "the number of natural enemies." Few, if any, of South Carolina's legislators read Benezet's pamphlet, but they undoubtedly heard about a massive uprising, known as Tacky's Revolt, that began in Jamaica in April 1760. There, Black freedom fighters killed more than one hundred white colonists and caused an estimated £100,000 in property damage. News of the revolt likely inspired South Carolina's ban on further imports, as the legislators observed that their own growing slave population "may prove of the most dangerous consequence." Thus, even people with few moral qualms about slaveholding could agree that slavery might be dangerous, especially amid war. However, King George II's Privy Council eventually overruled the legislation so that British slavers could continue serving the South Carolina market.[63]

Quakers played a larger role in a push to ban the slave trade to Pennsylvania. In February 1761, a "great Number" of Philadelphians petitioned against the trade. The petition's text does not survive, but the legislature described it as "setting forth the mischievous Consequences attending the Practice" while the PMS described it as based on both "Religious & Civil Considerations." In response, local slave dealers—including future Founding Father Robert Morris, the "Financier of the American Revolution"—organized a counter-petition defending human trafficking. The merchants argued that enslaved Africans were necessary to replace white servants who had joined the army. Ultimately, the Pennsylvania assembly imposed a modest duty of £10 per slave, discouraging importations into the colony. The PMS celebrated the law and supported a similar petitioning effort in New Jersey, which also proved successful by 1763.[64]

In early 1762, both Woolman and Benezet published new pamphlets, hoping to maintain antislavery momentum. In *Some Considerations on the Keeping of Negroes . . . Part Second*, Woolman reiterated many of the arguments from his first volume, condemning slaveholding as sinful and unjust. He also recounted the biblical story of the Israelites facing a Babylonian invasion, as recorded in Jeremiah 34:1–22. After the Israelites renege on a "solemn Covenant" to free their servants, God retorts ironically: "*Behold, I proclaim Liberty to you . . . to the Sword, to the Pestilence, and to the Famine.*"

The Babylonians then sack Jerusalem. Earlier antislavery Quakers had used this passage as evidence of God's disapproval of slavery and oppression, but Woolman used it as an allegory for contemporary events. His message was clear: God would punish the Quakers if they did not fulfill the PYM's 1758 call for emancipation. Woolman also hoped his influence would extend beyond the Society of Friends. Although the PYM formally approved his essay and offered to fund its printing, Woolman chose to publish it privately and advertise its sale in newspapers to people of "every Denomination."[65]

Benezet similarly sought to reach a broader audience with *A Short Account of That Part of Africa, Inhabited by the Negroes*, which he published anonymously and without reference to Quakerism. In addition to his traditional focus on the "Iniquity and Danger" of slavery, Benezet provided lengthy extracts from travel writers to demonstrate the slave trade's harmful effects on Africa. He also rejected racist justifications for enslaving Africans, writing that "their Capacity is as good, and as capable of Improvement as that of the *Whites.*" Benezet also quoted from British authors who challenged the legal basis of slavery. For example, Scottish jurist George Wallace portrayed liberty as inalienable and dismissed the idea that humans could be property, stating that "every one of those unfortunate Men, who are pretended to be Slaves, has a Right to be declared to be free, for he never lost his Liberty; he could not lose it." In addition, Benezet included lengthy extracts from *Two Dialogues on the Man-Trade*, a pioneering antislavery tract published in England in 1760. "No Legislature on Earth," Benezet quoted, "can alter the Nature of Things, or make that to be lawful which is contrary to the Law of God." In the second edition of his pamphlet, published in September 1762, Benezet added more quotations from well-known philosophers such as Francis Hutcheson, portraying slavery as an illegitimate violation of "Natural right." Providentialist language also remained prominent in the pamphlet; Benezet insisted that emancipation was "the best Means to avert the Judgments of God." In his view, these claims were all linked. He believed that natural rights and equality came from God, and that slavery provoked divine retribution.[66]

Perhaps the most important addition to Benezet's second edition was his proposed emancipation plan for British North America. Noting that generations of slaves had been born in the colonies, he quickly dismissed the idea of sending them to Africa, which many of them would perceive as "a strange Land." Instead, Benezet believed freed people of color should remain in the American colonies. He conceded that setting all the slaves "suddenly free" would involve great "Difficulty," and therefore he proposed a plan of staggered emancipation. Ending all further importations of enslaved Africans was the first step. Second, enslaved people already in the colonies would be freed "after serving so long as shall be adequate to the Money paid, or Charge of bringing them up." During that period, the Black people would be educated to ensure that they would "make proper Use of their Liberty" and become "useful Members of the Community." Finally, the freed people would receive twenty-five-acre plots of land in some "uncultivated" region of the "Southern Colonies." Although staggered and paternalistic, aspects of Benezet's plan are significantly more progressive than scholars traditionally associate with the idea of "gradual" emancipation. He wanted emancipation to begin immediately and eventually free all enslaved people (instead of being restricted to future generations, like later gradual abolition laws). Moreover, his proposal included land grants as a form of reparations that would encourage self-sufficiency. Benezet knew his plan was ambitious but believed that, once initiated, "doubtless the Almighty would bless this good Intention" and overcome any difficulties.[67] This faith in divine aid counterbalanced abolitionists' fear of divine wrath.

Despite believing God would aid their righteous cause, Quaker abolitionists did not suffer from any naïve optimism. They understood that many Friends—let alone other white colonists—remained ambivalent or opposed abolitionism. Their celebrations of antislavery victories were generally tinged with caution and doubts. For example, when James Pemberton lauded the potential of Pennsylvania's 1761 slave trade duty to reduce the traffic, he added, "tho' we fear not so effectually as we desire." He suspected that American slave traders would find ways to evade it, and he also feared that slave traders in England would lobby Parliament "to obtain a Repeal of the Law." In one of the earliest examples of transatlantic antislavery coordination, Pemberton called on the London Meeting for Sufferings (LMS) to counter such lobbying efforts by meeting with members of Parliament.[68] The Generation of 1758 expected God to aid their cause, but they also understood economic self-interest and power dynamics, and they engaged in political lobbying from the outset.

Pemberton's concerns about the effectiveness of colonial slave trade laws proved prescient. Philadelphia slave traders circumvented the duty by unloading and selling their cargoes of African captives outside of Pennsylvania's jurisdiction. For example, in May 1762, Robert Morris advertised to his Philadelphia customers that he had 179 enslaved Africans from the Gold Coast—known for "their good Dispositions, and being capable of hard Labour"—for sale duty-free just down the river in Wilmington, Delaware.

Meanwhile in London, the Board of Trade disallowed several colonial laws restricting slave importations, including those passed by South Carolina and New Jersey. These imperial vetoes further underscored the necessity of coordinating antislavery activities on both sides of the Atlantic.[69]

American abolitionists were also paying close attention to Britain's territorial conquests during the war, examining their potential implications for the future of slavery within the empire. In his 1762 pamphlet, Benezet noted with apprehension that forts along the Senegal River, "lately taken by the *English* from the *French*," were among the largest exporters of enslaved Africans. By the war's end, Britain also acquired Dominica and several other "Ceded Islands" in the Caribbean. In North America, the British solidified their control over the contested Ohio Valley and gained Canada from France, along with East and West Florida from Spain, France's ally. (Meanwhile, France transferred Louisiana to Spain.) The British acquisitions represented both perils and possibilities for abolitionists. Benezet complained in 1763 that slavery was "greatly encreasing in these Northern [i.e., North American] Colonies, and likely still more to encrease, by the New Acquisitions the English have lately made." On the other hand, he hoped that the North American territorial acquisitions might "provide the Government an advantageous opportunity" as a source of land on which to settle freed people.[70]

Although a few British policymakers also imagined antislavery reform as a means of strengthening the postwar empire, there was more support for using the slave trade to expedite British settlement in new territories. Before the war, British slave traders had operated several forts in West Africa with the permission of local chiefs, but Britain had not possessed any African colonies. After the war, Parliament established Senegambia as a royal colony, strengthening Britain's position in the Atlantic slave trade. Meanwhile, metropolitan authorities adopted plans to rapidly develop the Ceded Islands by selling large plantation plots and encouraging the importation of enslaved Africans. They also hoped to develop slaveholding settlements in West Florida, particularly around Pensacola and Mobile (in present-day Alabama). However, the strength of local Native American tribes hindered their ambitions.[71]

During this period, many within the Church of England were also promoting proslavery interpretations of the Bible to justify the expansion of hereditary Black slavery within the empire. The ideology of Christian slaveholding had long contained inherent tensions: on the one hand, slavery was justified as a means of spreading the Gospel among the African heathens, while on the other hand, conversion did not lead to freedom—even for Black Christians' children. The only way to theologically justify hereditary slavery for Black Christians that would not also legitimize the enslavement of white Christians was to claim that Africans were somehow excluded from typical God-given rights. That was precisely why Noah's Curse had been so important since the start of European involvement in the African slave trade in the mid-fifteenth century. However, since the late seventeenth century, numerous writers—in both the colonies and in England—had thoroughly refuted the notion that the Noah's Curse applied to Africans. For instance, Morgan Godwyn, a seventeenth-century English missionary, had shown that slaveholders' use of the so-called Curse of Ham depended on "five *Falsehoods*." Among other objections, Godwyn pointed out that in the text of the curse (Genesis 9:25–27), "none besides *Canaan*, his [Ham's] youngest Son was *mentioned*," whereas Africans were presumed to be descended from Canaan's brother Cush (who was not cursed). As a result of such arguments, references to the curse had declined during the first half of the eighteenth century. The Reverend Thomas Newton reversed this trend with his 1754 *Dissertations on the Prophecies, Which Have Remarkably Been Fulfilled, and at This Time Are Fulfilling in the World.*[72]

Newton began his book by discussing Noah's Curse and rejecting the argument that it applied only to Canaan and not Ham's other children. He acknowledged that "the present copies of our bible" portrayed Canaan as the recipient of the curse, but he suggested this was an ancient "corruption of the text." Newton theorized that long ago, "a copyist by mistake wrote only *Canaan* instead of *Ham the father of Canaan*." Among his arguments in support of this hypothesis, Newton noted that the "Arabic version in these three verses [Genesis 9:25–27] hath *the father of Canaan* instead of *Canaan*." This is true, but it reflects the way that Muslims had begun distorting the text of the Old Testament to justify the enslavement of Black Africans during the ninth century. Treating Arabic translations as more authoritative than much older Hebrew and Greek versions violated the academic standards of Newton's own time, as scholars such as David Whitford have emphasized. Newton buttressed his problematic methodology with circular logic. He described the fact that Africans were the chief victims of enslavement in the eighteenth century as further evidence that Noah's Curse applied to them. "It is both wonderful and instructive," Newton exclaimed: "a prophecy that was delivered near four thousand years ago, and yet hath been fulfilling thro' the several periods of time to this day!"[73] Based on this proslavery logic, the hereditary enslavement of Africans within the British Empire was fulfilling God's providential design of perpetually punishing Black people for the supposed sin of their alleged ancestor.

Newton's 1754 book, which he dedicated to the bishop of Canterbury, apparently helped him climb the career ladder within the Church of England. He was appointed chaplain to King George II in 1757, and King George III made him bishop of Bristol in 1761. By that time, Bishop Newton's book was regularly advertised for sale in North America.[74] Other English Bible commentaries soon began repeating Bishop Newton's claim that Africans were subject to the Curse of Ham.[75] Thus, while Quakers embraced antislavery theology and activism, proslavery biblicism gained renewed strength throughout the British Empire.

* * *

The Generation of 1758 viewed ending slavery among Quakers as merely the first step, for they believed that God punished entire nations for their sins. By the early 1760s, Quaker reformers were using the Philadelphia Meeting for Sufferings and similar groups to amplify and expand their antislavery activism, supporting lobbying throughout the colonies and in London. It is impossible to know what level of influence Quaker abolitionists might have had if the postwar period had been characterized by political tranquility throughout the empire. Still, most trends went against abolitionism. The British Empire's acquisition of new territory—including its first African colony—and the embrace of proslavery biblicism by officials in the Church of England made it unlikely that the metropole would support antislavery reforms. Indeed, British officials would continue vetoing colonial attempts to curb slave importations. In any case, the next phases of the antislavery movement would be shaped by the imperial crisis caused by Parliament's decision to impose unprecedented taxes on the colonies, beginning with the Stamp Act in 1764.

CHAPTER 3

Abolitionism and the Imperial Crisis, Part I: 1764–1772

Colonial protests against Parliament's postwar reforms—led by those dubbed Whigs (after an English political faction) or patriots—altered the context of abolitionism. Patriots claimed that being taxed by Parliament without representation violated their rights as Englishmen and even their natural rights. Drawing on traditional political rhetoric, they routinely described parliamentary oppression as "slavery." In *Letters from a Farmer in Pennsylvania*, one of the era's most popular political pamphlets, John Dickinson asserted, "*We are taxed* without our own consent, expressed by ourselves or our representatives. *We* are therefore SLAVES." Some white patriots also criticized the actual enslavement of Black people. "The Colonists are by the law of nature free born, as indeed all men are, white or black," declared James Otis of Boston in his 1764 pamphlet, *The Rights of the British Colonies Asserted and Proved*.[1] A couple of other white patriots, such as Nathaniel Appleton Jr. of Massachusetts and Arthur Lee of Virginia, published antislavery essays and pamphlets between 1767 and 1772.

Lumped together, these publications might seem to indicate that the growth of antislavery sentiment was the "inevitable" consequence of the patriots' rhetoric. Scholars often argue that the imperial crisis over taxation initiated a decisive secular shift in antislavery inspiration and rhetoric, with the patriots' natural rights ideology supplanting the earlier emphasis on religion.[2] However, reconsidering the content, context, and extent of antislavery publications underscores the relatively limited influence of natural rights rhetoric on its own. In general, white patriots found it easy to focus on preserving their own liberties without questioning the continued enslavement of Black people. Some, like John Adams—a proslavery lawyer from Massachusetts who later helped write the Declaration of the Independence—even explicitly appealed to racism when defending white rights. Other white patriots conceded that Black people had abstract claims to natural rights but felt no imperative to act on their behalf.

Still, a small but meaningful number of white patriots joined Quakers and people of color in calling for antislavery reform. Most of these antislavery patriots were inspired by the same biblicist and providentialist beliefs as their Quaker counterparts. For example, the Reverend Samuel Webster of Massachusetts wrote in 1769: "God forbid the Jews to enslave their brethren; Christ has taught us to look upon all Mankind as our brethren in as full a sense as the Jews were to esteem one another such; therefore so far as we can argue from this [scriptural] law, we are forbid to enslave any of mankind." This was essentially the same biblicist argument made many decades earlier by Quaker William Edmundson and Puritan Samuel Sewall, among others. Referring to the controversy over taxation, Webster suggested that the "design of providence in permitting the gloom of the present day, may be to awaken in us a sense of this great evil, which is so common in our land, and to cure it."[3] This was akin to the way Quakers had understood the French and Indian War. These biblicist and providentialist themes were typical of patriot antislavery but have been largely overlooked in scholars' greater focus on natural rights ideology.

As during the French and Indian War, colonial authorities repeatedly called for days of fasting and prayer in reaction to the imperial tensions. For example, the governor of Connecticut responded to the "*dark Aspects of Divine Providence, with regard to our most dear and valuable rights*" by appointing a fast day in December 1765. Fast-day proclamations cataloged a litany of vices—"*Profaneness, Impiety, neglect of Gospel-Grace . . . and other Immoralities*"—that had provoked God "to visit us with the Rod of his Anger." The colonists hoped that through "sincere Repentance and Amendment of life," they could convince a merciful God to "avert deserved and impending judgments."[4] Over the course of the imperial crisis, some colonists—especially Congregationalists and Presbyterians in New England—joined Quaker abolitionists in warning that divine chastisement would continue until they purged the sin of slavery from the land. Yet each time Parliament repealed a tax, many white colonists interpreted it as evidence that they were back in God's favor. Whenever imperial tensions eased, antislavery patriots' sense of urgency declined. As a result, antislavery sentiment ebbed and flowed in an uneven pattern, in contrast to the sense of linear progression common in traditional scholarly accounts.

Throughout this period, Quakers and people of color remained the most consistent and active opponents of slavery. At the start of the disputes over parliamentary taxation, some Quaker merchants signed nonimportation agreements and supported boycotts as a form of peaceful protest; however, they grew progressively wary of the patriot movement as mob violence against tax collectors and other officials increased. A 1766 publication by the Philadelphia Meeting for Sufferings condemned the "violent ferment reigning at this time in the Colonies."[5] Although Friends increasingly sought to remain aloof from the imperial disputes, Quaker abolitionists nonetheless welcomed any opportunity to promote antislavery ideas. Anthony Benezet published new pamphlets in 1766 and 1771, portraying the imperial crisis as further evidence of God's opposition to slaveholding. Throughout the 1760s and 1770s, he continued working with the PMS and similar regional groups to promote antislavery reform within and beyond the Society of Friends.

Meanwhile, individual Black people increasingly looked to the judicial system, especially in Massachusetts, as an avenue to freedom. Initially, Black plaintiffs were only likely to win their freedom if they could demonstrate descent from a free mother in the colonies. After 1772, however, white juries were increasingly sympathetic to antislavery arguments that had little legal precedent.[6] News of the 1772 *Somerset v. Steuart* decision (often rendered *Somerset v. Stewart*), which undermined slavery's legal status in England, increased this trend but also led some slaveholders to double down on the claim that Black people were the cursed descendants of Ham. These assertions provoked extensive rebuttals, demonstrating the growth of antislavery sentiment, even though legislators remained largely apathetic.

Antislavery and the Stamp Act Crisis

Patriots' natural rights rhetoric did not inspire much optimism among Quaker abolitionists. In 1766, Anthony Benezet expressed his dismay that "many of those who distinguish themselves as the Advocates of Liberty, remain insensible and inattentive to the treatment of thousands and tens of thousands of our fellow-men" held in actual slavery.[7] James Otis's famous statement about Black natural rights was an outlier; few patriot leaders linked their cause to antislavery during the early years of the imperial crisis. Reconsidering the public discussions of slavery during the mid-1760s underscores the limitations of patriot politicians' egalitarianism.

Indeed, Otis's positive reference to Black rights was counterbalanced by racist statements made by other patriot leaders, like John Adams. In October 1765, the month before the Stamp Act was set to go into effect, Adams pseudonymously encouraged opposition to Parliament, proclaiming, "We won't be their negroes. Providence never designed us for negroes, I know, for if it had it wou'd have given us black hides, and thick lips, and flat noses, and short woolly hair, which it han't done, and therefore never intended us for slaves."[8] At best, this essay indicated Adams's callous disregard for Black people's oppression; at worst, it implied he believed that God intended Africans for bondage. This type of racist rhetoric enabled white patriots to decry their own political oppression even as they subjected Black people to far greater exploitation. As a lawyer, Adams routinely defended slaveholders and justified the Atlantic slave trade. (The common assertion that Adams "represented several bondsmen" in freedom suits is mistaken; he always served on the side of slaveholders.) Adams had purchased the 1758 edition of Dr. Thomas Newton's *Dissertations on the Prophecies*, and the section on the Curse of Ham seems to have assuaged any moral qualms he might have had about Black slavery.[9]

Some New England ministers also condemned metaphorical slavery in ways that implicitly excused actual slavery, even as they interpreted the imperial crisis in providential terms. In a fast-day sermon from December 1765, the Reverend Stephen Johnson of Connecticut ignored the oppression of Black people while using the story of Exodus to interpret the imperial crisis. In his analogy, (white) New Englanders were the "covenant people of God" while Parliament and the king's ministers played the role of their Egyptian taskmasters. The colonists were threatened with "slavery and ruin," but Johnson prophesized that if they prayed with "piety and virtue, repentance and reformation . . . the Lord God of Israel will see our affliction, hear our groaning cries, (through his eternal Son) and appear to deliver us." Consciously or not, Johnson's characterization of white New Englanders as a virtuous people whom God would "never forsake," implied that enslaved Black people were forsaken or even cursed by God.[10]

Anthony Benezet, of course, understood divine providence differently. During the Stamp Act crisis, he composed *A Caution and Warning to Great Britain and Her Colonies* (though by the time it was printed, in September 1766, Parliament had repealed the offensive law). Assuming that colonial slavery was only tolerated because "both of the Clergy and Laity" were ignorant of the violence, fraud, and greed involved, Benezet drew on travel narratives to catalog the horrors of slavery and the Atlantic slave trade. He warned of providential punishment for these sins: "Will not the groans of this deeply afflicted and oppressed people reach heaven, and when the cup of iniquity is full, must not the inevitable consequence be pouring forth of the judgments of God upon their oppressors." He interpreted the imperial crisis, like the French and Indian War before it, as chastisement intended by God to inspire abolitionism. In an implicit reference to the patriots who described parliamentary taxation as "slavery," Benezet quoted from a twelfth-century archdeacon who noted that the Lord sometimes punished slaveholding peoples "by way of just retaliation, to leave them to be reduced . . . to the same state of slavery." Benezet admonished his readers to avoid this fate by becoming "sensible of your guilt, and repent in time."[11] Increased piety alone was insufficient; Benezet believed antislavery reform was necessary to establish permanent harmony and prosperity for the British Empire.

The reach of Benezet's pamphlet was boosted by his connection to the Philadelphia Meeting for Sufferings. John Pemberton and other members of a PMS committee printed 2,000 copies of *A Caution and Warning* and distributed it widely, from North Carolina through New England. The PMS also funded another 1,500 copies printed in England. American Quakers gave copies to local politicians while the London Meeting for Sufferings distributed six hundred copies among members of Parliament. Thus, while American patriots denounced Parliament's infringement of American rights, colonial Quakers sought to convince it to pass antislavery legislation for the entire British Empire.[12]

Some patriots did advocate for antislavery reform at the local level. During the Stamp Act crisis, a town hall meeting in Worcester, Massachusetts, had proposed abolishing the "unchristian and impolitic practice of making slaves of the human species." Residents in Boston issued a similar statement after learning of the Stamp Act's repeal by Parliament. In June 1766, the Massachusetts legislature created a committee to draft an antislavery bill, but the effort quickly fizzled out that fall.[13] It was in this context that Nathaniel Appleton Jr., who worked as a chandler in Boston, published *Considerations on Slavery in a Letter to a Friend* in February 1767. Scholars often highlight his later involvement in the Sons of Liberty and use his pamphlet to illustrate the growth of secular antislavery inspired by patriot rhetoric. Yet his book was clearly influenced by the works of Benezet, from which Appleton likely took statistics (such as the estimated ten thousand Africans who died each year on slave ships) and descriptions of Africa. Moreover, his family's Congregationalist faith undoubtedly informed his views as well.[14]

Appleton's father, the Reverend Nathaniel Appleton, was among the most eminent ministers in the colony. In the summer of 1766, Reverend Appleton was among the dozens of ministers who gave thanksgiving sermons celebrating the Stamp Act's repeal. He drew on Isaiah 59:2 to explain the entire Stamp Act crisis in providentialist terms: "By the divine permission that oppressive act was pass'd, by which God hid his face from us, testified his anger, and let us see what our sins deserved: and that it is of his undeserved mercy, and thro' his all governing influence, that it is now repealed." The colonists should learn from their chastisement and be forever grateful for the Lord's mercy, the elder Appleton insisted.[15] The residents of Worcester and Boston who issued antislavery resolutions apparently felt that such reform would help earn the Lord's continued favor. This religious context (and the legislature's slothfulness) provided the backdrop for the younger Appleton's pamphlet.

The bulk of *Considerations on Slavery* comprised two letters, and religion was central to the first and longer of them. Appleton attributed slavery and the slave trade to human greed while dismissing the "specious argument" that slavery was an effective means of spreading the Gospel. Few slaveholders actually promoted conversion; moreover, Appleton reminded readers that "we are not to do evil that good may come" (Romans 3:8). The Bible provided the central frameworks through which Appleton evaluated slavery; indeed, his antislavery biblicism shared much in common with Samuel Sewall's *Selling of Joseph* from the turn of the century. Appleton cited Exodus 21:6 and Deuteronomy 24:7 to show that while Jews had been permitted to enslave heathens, they were absolutely forbidden—upon pain of death—to enslave "*brethren*" of "their own nation." God's toleration of slavery in the ancient world had long ceased, for Christ had taught his followers "to esteem all men, our brethren," thereby destroying the old "wall of partition" (Ephesians 2:14) that had allowed Israelites to enslave heathen strangers. Christians were instead taught, "*Do Unto others, as ye would that they should do to you*" (Matthew 7:12). In sum, the minister's son portrayed contemporary slavery as fundamentally incompatible with the New Testament, asking, "Can any who are concerned in this black hellish business, pretend to the character of Christians?"[16] Far from reflecting a secular shift, Appleton's pamphlet shared a great deal with those penned by Quaker and Puritan abolitionists during the previous ninety years. His antislavery biblicism was especially poignant in Massachusetts, where the law of slavery had been explicitly linked to the Bible since 1641 (as discussed in Chapter 1).

Appleton supplemented his religious arguments with appeals based on political economy and natural rights rhetoric. He argued that the presence of enslaved people hindered job opportunities for poor white colonists, undermined "domestic security," and led to "haughty and imperious" manners. Appleton then connected antislavery to the Stamp Act controversy in his brief second letter. After celebrating the colonists' opposition to Parliament, Appleton called for consistency: "Oh! ye sons of liberty . . . can you review our late struggles for liberty, and think of the slave-trade at the same time, and not blush?" Abolishing slavery would demonstrate that their opposition to Parliament was based on noble sentiments rather than economic self-interest. Appleton had copies of his pamphlet delivered to every member of the legislature.[17]

Appleton's efforts helped revive antislavery momentum; the Massachusetts legislature began considering antislavery reform in early March 1767. Committees proposed two bills, one that focused only on slave importations and another entitled, "A Bill to prevent the unwarrantable and unusual Practice or Custom of inslaving Mankind in this Province, and the importation of Slaves into the same." Unfortunately, no draft of the latter bill appears to be extant, but the title indicates that the committee sought to end hereditary slavery. However, the full legislature quickly killed this bill in favor of the one focused solely on slave importations. Moreover, they revised it so that it only curtailed slave importations for a single year. Even this conservative bill failed to become law when the bicameral legislature could not agree on specific details before the session ended. A few writers in local newspapers praised the bill or expressed their disappointment that it "miscarried," but the legislature would not revisit the issue for several years.[18] Antislavery reformers faced significant apathy and opposition even in New England, where the patriot movement was strongest and slaveholding was of marginal direct economic significance.

During this time, some New England ministers continued using the Bible to defend slavery. The Reverend Jonathan Edwards had defended slavery during the 1740s, and his son did the same in the 1760s. In the spring and summer of 1767, Jonathan Edwards Jr. repeatedly delivered a sermon defending slavery. Edwards titled the sermon "Question" and began by querying "whether it be lawful to buy & keep negro-slaves." His choice of topic certainly reflected an awareness that slaveholding was coming under increased scrutiny. Edwards insisted that God did not merely tolerate or "wink at" slavery but "did positively & in express terms consent & give leave for it." As with most biblicist defenders of slavery, Edwards relied primarily on Leviticus 25:44–46, in which God permits the Israelites to enslave heathen strangers. (He ignored the argument that Christ's death had erased the previous distinction between Jew and Gentile upon which Leviticus 25 was based.) He defended not only slaveholding but also the Atlantic slave trade, dismissing concerns (expressed by Benezet, Appleton, and others) that it was based on fraud and aggressive wars. Because heathens could be enslaved based on divine law, Edwards maintained that "it is not necessary y[t] we sho'd know the negroes to be first lawfully captive." In his view, heathenism was a sufficient basis for enslavement. At this point in his career, Edwards was only recently ordained and in search of a permanent position; it seems that he sought to please the slaveholders and slave traders among his prospective employers. He would, however, reverse his position within six years and become a leading antislavery voice.[19]

Meanwhile, one of the most famous "antislavery" essays of the era was written by Arthur Lee, a slaveholder from Virginia, the North American colony with the largest enslaved population (over two hundred thousand). Under the pseudonym Philanthropos, the first installment of Lee's two-part essay, "The Abolition of Slavery and the Retrieval of Specie," was published in the *Virginia Gazette* on March 19, 1767. In it, Lee attacked slavery as "a Violation of both Justice and Religion" that endangered the "safety of the Community," discouraged the "growth of arts & Sciences," and produced a "very fatal train of Vices, both in the Slave and his Master." Lee's Philanthropos essay can seem to embody a natural connection between the imperial crisis and the growth of antislavery sentiment, even among some slaveholders. Although the *Virginia Gazette* "suppressed" the second installment, scholars often indicate that an extract of Lee's Philanthropos essay was immediately printed in pamphlet form in Virginia and other colonies, suggesting its widespread popularity. Indeed, it has been cited as evidence that "the Chesapeake leadership was much infected by natural rights ideology and saw clearly the necessity of abolishing slavery."[20]

A closer look, however, suggests that Lee's essay was not reprinted in pamphlet form until 1771 and that its historical reputation reflects its popularity among Quaker abolitionists rather than patriots. Moreover, historian Eva Sheppard Wolf's recent rediscovery of Lee's second installment mandates a fundamental reconsideration of Lee's supposed concern for Black natural rights. After the editor of the *Virginia Gazette* refused to publish the second installment, Lee had it printed in Philadelphia's *Pennsylvania Gazette*, where it attracted only limited attention and has been almost entirely overlooked by historians. In this second essay, Lee elaborated on his criticism of slavery based on economic and cultural considerations, and then outlined a gradual abolition plan for Virginia. Yet his solution to the dilemma of slavery showed a callous disregard for enslaved people themselves and was antithetical to the forms of emancipation imagined by abolitionists and Black people. Under Lee's plan, each year one-tenth of Virginia's enslaved population would be turned over to the government and then "sent to the *West-India* islands, and sold." The gold and silver ("specie") from sales would then be distributed as compensation to the white Virginians who had turned over their slaves. They could use some of the proceeds to import "white servants on indentures." This plan thus addressed the joint concerns of the essay's title "The Abolition of Slavery and the Retrieval of Specie."[21] It did not, however, liberate any enslaved people; it merely sold them out of the continent.

Moreover, Lee's plan would ship Black Virginians to a region where the climate, Caribbean diseases, and working conditions shortened life expectancy to the point that deaths outnumbered births. Thus, unlike North America, constant slave importations were necessary to preserve the enslaved population. Acknowledging the brutal conditions of Caribbean slavery, Lee anticipated that humanitarians would object "that this plan, instead of being humane toward the slaves, will plunge them into miseries still more dreadful than those they now suffer." In response, he wrote that his plan was the best that could be done given the circumstances. Referring to enslaved Virginians who would be sold to Caribbean planters, Lee added: "By such of them, as have yet retained the least spark of virtue, some consolation will be drawn from considering, that this sacrifice of themselves will put a quicker period to a miserable life, will leave fewer children to heir the wretchedness of their parents."[22] Technically, Lee's proposal was "abolitionist" in the sense that he wanted to abolish slavery in Virginia (for the benefit of white people), but it hardly indicated an egalitarian commitment to natural rights.

In any case, in April 1767 the Virginia legislature voted merely to increase the existing duty on slave importations, using the revenue to pay down the colony's wartime debts. Four years later, Anthony Benezet gave Lee's first Philanthropos installment a new life when he appended a lengthy extract from it to his *Some Historical Account of Guinea*.[23] The Philadelphia Quaker's propaganda efforts have given some historians an exaggerated impression of the extent of abolitionist sentiment held by Lee and other white Virginia patriots.

Throughout the 1760s, public expressions of antislavery sentiment among white southerners were confined mainly to Friends. From 1764 through 1768, the Virginia Yearly Meeting engaged in contentious debates about slavery. Edward Stabler, clerk of the VYM, led the push for emancipation, supported by other reformers such as Robert Pleasants and his brother Samuel, who sought to "cleans[e] the Camp from this Leprosy." Knowing they faced "strong opposition" from local Friends, Virginia reformers even tried recruiting some Pennsylvania Quakers to attend their yearly meeting in 1767. However, nobody from Pennsylvania made the journey, and the 1767 VYM failed to reach a consensus on a formal policy change. Nonetheless, the meeting discouraged any future slave purchases and encouraged members who held slaves "to pay them as servants or permit them to hire themselves . . . so it may be a means of proving and fitting them for freedom if way should be opened for that purpose." The following year, Stabler's faction triumphed and the VYM prohibited its members from purchasing or selling enslaved people.[24] Friends in neighboring North Carolina lagged behind, to the chagrin of local reformers such as Thomas Nicholson. In a 1767 open letter to his Quaker brethren, Nicholson denounced slavery as "a very wicked and abominable Practice, contrary to the natural Rights and Privileges of all mankind, and against the Golden Rule." Although North Carolina law (as in Virginia) forbade private manumissions, Nicholson hoped Friends would prohibit buying or selling slaves and give their bondspeople as much freedom as they could. Instead, the 1768 North Carolina Yearly Meeting merely banned the purchase of slaves for resale.[25] Although this step was small and compromised, it nonetheless indicated some progress.

The first phase of the imperial crisis, revolving around opposition to the Stamp Act, did not significantly change the character of abolitionism. A few white patriots espoused antislavery ideas in print, but only Nathaniel Appleton, the minister's son, followed Quakers by actually proposing emancipation. If the repeal of the Stamp Act had ended Parliament's attempts to tax the colonies, the abolitionist movement might have long remained confined almost entirely to Quakers and people of color.

Rising Antislavery in New England, 1767–1772

Patriot protests revived in the late summer of 1767 when the colonies received news of the Townshend Duties, which taxed various imported goods (such as tea). Colonial patriots—who remained most active in New England—again responded with prayers, pamphlets, petitions, boycotts, and mob action. In order to quell protests and enforce tax collection, the British government sent General Thomas Gage and two regiments of troops to Boston the following year.[26] As during the Stamp Act crisis, most publications denouncing "slavery" continued to refer to Parliament's treatment of white colonists rather than the actual enslavement of Black people. But the new taxes could also appear to fulfill Anthony Benezet's prophecy in *A Caution and Warning* that God would continue chastising the colonists until they abolished slavery. Indeed, the Quaker used the renewed tensions as an opportunity to promote a second edition of his pamphlet, advertising it for sale in Boston, the hotbed of patriot resistance.[27] During the controversy over the Townshend Duties, more and more writers in the mid-Atlantic and, especially, New England colonies began echoing the providentialist language of Benezet and the Generation of 1758 who had embraced abolitionism during the French and Indian War.

White New Englanders had long imagined they possessed a special covenant relationship with God, and this belief primed some of them to embrace antislavery providentialism. In January 1768, a "True Son of Liberty" in Rhode Island wrote that patriots had to take action against domestic slavery before they could "*with a well grounded confidence implore Heaven*" to protect their own rights from parliamentary tyranny. A writer in the *Boston Evening-Post* belittled a public day of fasting, arguing that the colonists' prayers would "only serve to enhance our guilt, and inflame our reckoning, unless we *undo the heavy burdens*, break every yoke, *and let the oppressed go free*." This was essentially the argument—based on Isaiah 58:6—that Quaker abolitionists had made a decade before about the French and Indian War. The Reverend Samuel Webster similarly drew on Isaiah 58:6—indeed, he quoted it three times—in a lengthy essay published in the *Boston Chronicle* in March 1769. Webster refuted Biblical justifications for slavery and argued that colonists must "let the oppressed go free" to forestall God's further wrath.[28] Acting consistently in favor of natural rights was important not only for the sake of appearance but also to regain God's favor, according to antislavery writers.

A series of sermons given in the spring of 1770, following the "Boston Massacre" of March 5, reveal the providentialist mentality of New Englanders and the way it had the potential to inspire antislavery sentiment. On the Sunday after the clash—which left five protestors dead, including the Black sailor Crispus Attucks—the Reverend John Lathrop gave a sermon that was subsequently published in London and Boston as *Innocent Blood Crying to God from the Streets of Boston*. Lathrop celebrated "*that Liberty which the God of nature*" granted to "*his rational creatures*" and based most of his sermon on two verses of Genesis that condemned murder. After Cain kills his brother Abel, God declares, "What hast thou done? the voice of thy brother's blood crieth unto me from the ground. And now *art* thou cursed" (4:10–11). Later, God instructs Noah, "Whoso sheddeth man's blood, by man shall his blood be shed: for in the image of God made he man" (9:6). In Lathrop's sermon, the British soldiers played the role of Cain, and the "blood of the innocent [i.e., the Boston protestors], like that of Abel, cry unto God for vengeance." He also warned that if society failed to impose justice, God would punish "the *government* and *land*."[29] Lathrop's purpose was to condemn the British policies that had led to the deaths of five colonists, not to promote antislavery. Nonetheless, the notion that God would punish societies for killing or oppressing people made in his image had antislavery implications that other ministers developed.

The Reverend Nathaniel Appleton Sr., who had been appointed chaplain to the Massachusetts legislature, gave a fast-day sermon on April 5, 1770 commemorating the Boston Massacre. He sought to make sense of the previous five years in providentialist terms. Parliament's repeal of the Stamp Act had suggested that the colonists were back in God's favor, but this blessing had been followed by the Townshend Duties, the presence of troops in Boston, and finally the "shedding of blood." Appleton explained and cautioned that "God does sometimes remove (as we may suppose) some present judgment or calamity, even although there not be a sincere repenting and turning to God: But whenever this is the case, the consequence will be, that sorer and heavier judgments will come upon them afterwards." In other words, the Townshend Duties and the Boston Massacre indicated that God remained angry, and there might be worse yet to come if the "backsliding" colonists did not offer sincere prayers to the Lord and reform their sinful ways. Given his son's antislavery sentiments, it is likely that Reverend Appleton was thinking of Black bondage when he listed "oppression" among the "provoking evils."[30] Still, the fact that the minister did not specifically call for antislavery action may suggest that he sensed there would be little legislative support for such measures.

The Reverend Samuel Cooke was more direct, in a sermon marking the start of Massachusetts's new legislative session on May 30, 1770. Near the close of his sermon, which stressed the importance of rulers being just and God-fearing, he called on legislators to turn their attention to "the cause of our African slaves." Cooke combined Psalm 68:31, Revelation 18:13, Exodus 4:21, and Job 31:4 in a brief paragraph: "Ethiopia has long stretched out her hands to us—Let not sordid gain, acquired by the merchandize of slaves, and the souls of men—harden our hearts against her piteous moans. When God ariseth, and when he visitith, what shall we answer!" Whereas Christians should be spreading the Gospel in Africa, they instead engaged in the sinful practice of slavery, for which God had punished the Babylonians and Egyptians. Although Cooke disavowed complete emancipation, which faced "insuperable" difficulties, he called on the legislature to promote "the cause of the oppressed" and thereby "avert the impending vengeance of heaven." Cooke hoped the legislature would take action "this session," but legislators did not view antislavery as a priority.[31]

In the winter of 1770–1771, Deacon Timothy Pickering Sr. of Salem sought to spur action by repeatedly publishing an antislavery letter in the *Massachusetts Spy*. Along with sabbath-breaking, pride, and luxury, he identified slavery as a "publick Sin" that rendered the patriots' prayers "hypocritical." In a subtle biblicist argument, he condemned the practice of "American Gentiles enslave[ing] African Gentiles." His implicit point, it seems, was to refute those who justified slavery by citing Leviticus 25, which had permitted the Hebrews to enslave the "heathen" or Gentiles. As Pickering indicated, it was absurd for white Christians—Gentiles in the eyes of Jews—to claim a right to enslave Africans based on a dispensation given to the ancient Israelites. He argued that God would not grant the patriots' prayers until they acted against slavery: "No Reformation, no Salvation."[32]

The Massachusetts legislature did pass a slave trade bill in April 1771, but it was only superficially antislavery and never became law. It simply forbade the further importation of enslaved people into the colony. This trade had never been large and had mostly ceased by the 1760s. On the other hand, Massachusetts slave traders were actively involved in trafficking human cargo from West Africa to Britain's southern and Caribbean colonies, and this more considerable trade remained legal under the 1771 bill. The bill also would have done nothing for the five thousand or so enslaved people then living in Massachusetts. In any case, the bill was vetoed by Governor Thomas Hutchinson, a royal appointee who had a contentious relationship with the legislature. Hutchinson had royal instructions against authorizing "any Laws of a new and unusual nature," and he decided to send the bill to England so that he "might know his Majesty's pleasure." Moreover, he doubted that legislators' alleged moral scruples were truly the "chief motive" behind the bill. Given the bill's superficial and conservative character, Hutchinson may have had a point.[33]

Some scholars have cited Cooke's 1770 sermon and the 1771 slave trade bill (which they often conflate with an emancipation bill from 1777) as evidence of the antislavery momentum inspired by the patriots' natural rights rhetoric. Yet the events, like Pickering's letter, are more indicative of abolitionists' religious inspiration, along with most politicians' unwillingness to support meaningful reform of slavery itself. Moreover, the broader context suggests that while imperial controversies could encourage antislavery proposals, easing tensions undercut momentum. Like the earlier Stamp Act, the Townshend Duties inspired a small wave of antislavery rhetoric, often framed in providentialist terms. However, several weeks before Cooke's sermon, the colonists learned that Parliament had repealed most of the Townshend Duties, preserving only the tax on tea. Colonists continued grumbling about the tea tax or sought to evade it through smuggling, but imperial tensions cooled for several years after May 1770.[34] New Englanders no longer perceived God's chastising rod upon their backs, and their customary spring fasts and fall thanksgivings became less politicized. In this context, New England's white antislavery advocates (temporarily) lost their platform and their sense of urgency.

The decline in antislavery momentum can be seen in the publishing history of one of the era's most famous antislavery pamphlets. In November 1771, James Swan, a young Boston merchant from England, proposed publishing an antislavery pamphlet by subscription. He recruited Isaiah Thomas, editor of the prominent patriot newspaper, the *Massachusetts Spy*, to print his pamphlet. However, it seems Swan and Thomas were still struggling to find subscribers the following spring, when they began advertising the proposal in other cities and colonies. Despite a promise in April 1772 that it would be printed "in a fortnight," the pamphlet failed to appear, and Swan and Thomas soon parted ways. Swan's pamphlet was finally published by printer Ezekiel Russell—who was emerging as a leading ally of Black writers and activists—in November 1772. By that time, the *Somerset v. Steuart* decision in England had revived public interest in slavery.[35]

Beginning in the mid-1760s, unprecedented numbers of Black people turned to the legal system to assert their freedom. Sometimes, enslaved plaintiffs were supported by Quaker patrons such as Israel Pemberton and other PMS members in New Jersey and Pennsylvania, cousins Matthew and Thomas Robinson in Rhode Island, and William Rotch in Massachusetts.[36] Yet the bulk of freedom suits occurred without Quaker involvement and took place in Massachusetts, where the law of slavery was unusually ambiguous and Black people had relatively easy access to the courts. The resulting freedom suits of the 1760s and 1770s reveal shifts in how contemporaries thought about slavery. It is clear that slavery was customarily treated as hereditary through the mother, even though this had never been formally codified in Massachusetts law. It is also clear that in practice, many people of color who were supposed to be freed after a term of years—such as those born out of wedlock to free but impoverished mothers in violation of the 1705 law against interracial sex—ended up being treated as slaves for life. Such practices came under increased scrutiny beginning in 1766, when Jenny Slew, the daughter of a white mother and a Black father, successfully won freedom and £4 in damages from her enslaver, John Whipple Jr.[37] Over time, enslaved people and their lawyers began making broader attacks on the entire system of slavery.

The limited records of lawyers' arguments (which were not typically preserved) suggest that antislavery sentiment merging religious and natural rights principles became increasingly prominent in freedom suits, especially in cases where the enslaved plaintiff could not claim freedom based on maternal descent. Many lawyers who served enslaved plaintiffs were former ministers or the sons of ministers, which may have influenced their willingness to accept such cases (often pro bono, it seems). Freedom suits were apparently most common in Essex County, which included towns located north of Boston such as Andover, Newbury, Newburyport, and Salem. Perhaps not coincidentally, some ministers from this region were among the most outspoken critics of slavery during the imperial crisis.[38]

Churches played essential roles in facilitating some of these freedom suits. For example, a Black woman named Violet, the daughter of an enslaved father and a free Black mother, found an ally in the Reverend John Lowell of Newburyport. In 1766, thirty years after Reverend Lowell had baptized Violet, he arranged for his son, also named John, to serve as the Black woman's attorney. With the younger John Lowell's help, Violet received her freedom and payment for damages through a negotiated settlement. Violet's son, Edward Lewis, was eventually similarly successful with the younger Lowell's help in a 1769 case that went to the Superior Court of Judicature. Lowell subsequently served as Lewis's guardian until he reached adulthood; he also aided at least two other enslaved plaintiffs during the 1770s. According to later family tradition, Lowell offered his "services as a lawyer gratis to any slave suing for [their] freedom."[39] It is likely that the lawyer's decision to advocate for Black people reflected the influence of his father, who ministered to a mixed-race congregation. In turn, the younger Lowell's resulting reputation and connection to Lewis may have encouraged other Black colonists to seek Lowell as an ally.

John Adams, on the other hand, earned a reputation for defending the rights of enslavers (albeit not always effectively). Hiller B. Zobel, editor of the *Legal Papers of John Adams*, notes that a lawyer's decision to take a client does not necessarily indicate their own opinions related to the legal matter. Yet Zobel also observes that Adams's friend and competitor Jonathan Sewall (grandnephew of Judge Samuel Sewall and a future loyalist) was involved in at least three freedom suits, always on behalf of the enslaved plaintiffs, whereas "Adams appeared for the owner in four, never for the slave." In 1768, the two lawyers squared off in the case of *Margaret v. Muzzy*, in Middlesex County. There is no record of Adams's arguments, but Sewall prevailed after producing depositions asserting that Margaret's mother, a "Spanish Indian woman," had been indentured for a term of years but was "not a slave for life."[40]

While Margaret's freedom suit went through its final appeal, her son James sued his own master, Richard Lechmere, in May 1769. Sewall also served as James's attorney and must have based his case on the same evidence that liberated Margaret, conforming to the legal custom that a child born in the colony to a free (or indentured) woman could not be enslaved. (Some antebellum politicians as well as modern scholars, unaware of James's connection to Margaret, have mistakenly asserted that his victory broke with precedent and represented the jury's embrace of "the principle of emancipation.")[41] Successful freedom suits based on maternal descent must have had great significance for the individual Black plaintiffs and their children. Yet because these suits relied on narrow grounds, they did not challenge the institution of slavery itself.

Some enslaved plaintiffs and their lawyers offered more direct challenges to hereditary slavery itself, though initially with little success. For instance, Amos Newport had no apparent legal precedent on his side when he sued to recover his "Lawfull Liberty" from his master, Joseph Billings, in November 1766. Newport had been legally imported from Africa in his youth and had worked as a slave in Hampshire County for decades. He was represented in the Court of Common Pleas by Moses Bliss, a former minister who had become a lawyer. The substance of Bliss's argument is not preserved, but the jury ruled in the slaveholder's favor in the spring of 1767.[42] When Newport appealed, with Jonathan Sewall and James Putnam as co-counsel, Billings added John Adams to his legal team. Adams took brief notes during the appeal, providing a sense of the courtroom debates.

Adams and his co-counsel Simeon Strong helped the slaveholder win again during the appeal by providing a 1728 bill of sale for Newport and by making proslavery and racist arguments. They emphasized that the laws of Massachusetts and Parliament recognized the slave trade, and asserted that victors in a just war had the "Right to enslave them [enemy captives] to repay the Expences of defending ones self." It seems they were repeating the common fiction that all captives imported from Africa had legally forfeited their liberty through their bad conduct (rather than being kidnapped or taken in an unprovoked slave raid). Newport's lawyers responded with wide-ranging attacks on slavery and sought to shift the burden of proof onto slaveholders. Putnam argued that many slaves were actually "stolen in Affrica" rather than enslaved through just wars or as punishment for crimes, an argument likely informed by Anthony Benezet's publications. Putnam demanded proof that Newport "has forfeited his Liberty, by the Laws of his Country," while Sewall buttressed their position with references to "Humanity, common Justice, and eternal Morality." Adams and Strong dismissed these moral qualms and relied on racist assumptions. "Presumption here is that an African black is a slave," they declared. In other words, Blackness was considered prima facie evidence of enslavement in Massachusetts. Adams also recorded that they discussed "Noah's Curse. Dr. Newton."[43] Apparently, Adams and Strong bolstered their case by citing Dr. Thomas Newton's claim, in *Dissertations on the Prophecies*, that Noah's curse on Canaan applied also to Ham's other children and included all people of African descent. The jury again ruled in favor of the slaveholder. During the next few years, the only successful freedom suits in Massachusetts were those with evidence that the plaintiffs had been born in the colony to a mother who was not enslaved.

More significant was the case of *Caesar v. Taylor*, a successful Essex County freedom suit argued over the course of three court sessions between September 1771 and June 1772. Caesar and his lawyers based his claim to freedom on his specific circumstances as well as broad attacks on the legitimacy of slavery and the Atlantic slave trade. Caesar, who worked as a tanner in Andover, had been enslaved in Africa and brought to Massachusetts as a youth. In 1763 he was baptized and "owned the covenant" (admitted as full church member). In 1768, Caesar had convinced Samuel Taylor to purchase him from his former master (Edward Hircom) and then permit him to live on his own and work for others while paying installments to purchase his freedom over the course of six years (with a £20 profit going to Taylor). But when a series of unforeseen events hindered Caesar's ability to make some of the scheduled payments, Taylor sold Caesar before the conclusion of the six-year period (pocketing all the payments Caesar had already made). Caesar resisted the sale and sued Taylor for trespass (a common means of asserting one's freedom). For legal counsel, Caesar hired John Lowell (the minister's son) and Nathaniel Peaslee Sargeant (the son of another minister). Jurors at the lower court in Newburyport ruled in Caesar's favor, liberating him and awarding damages. Taylor immediately appealed and recruited John Adams as his new legal counsel. Adams sought to overturn the verdict and re-enslave Caesar using arguments that had succeeded in *Newport v. Billings*, insisting "that negroes are presumed to be slaves and must make their freedom appear."[44] Nonetheless, the appeal ended with another jury confirming Caesar's freedom. This antislavery victory had little precedent, for most successful freedom suits in the past had been based on claiming freedom through maternal descent and birth within the colony, whereas Caesar had been enslaved in Africa.

The limited records related to *Caesar v. Taylor* do not conclusively indicate the arguments that inspired the juries' rulings, but they enable fruitful speculation. Caesar's lawyers apparently made both a narrow argument focused on Taylor's abrogation of his contract with Caesar and a larger argument attacking the legitimacy of slavery itself. During the trials, more than twenty witnesses testified or gave depositions related to the contract between Caesar and Taylor. There is no record of how Lowell and Sargeant used this testimony, but they may have connected it to John Locke's *Second Treatise of Government* (1690), which experienced a resurgence of popularity during the imperial crisis. Locke accepted enslavement as a legitimate form of punishment and fate for some prisoners of war but asserted that "Slavery ceases" once a slaveholder "enters into conditions with his Captive."[45] If Lowell and Sargeant used this logic, they could have argued that once Taylor established a contract with Caesar, the Black man could no longer be sold as chattel property.

Lowell and Sergeant also attacked the legitimacy of slavery itself. After Taylor's lawyers cited the colony's laws regarding slavery and manumission, Lowell and Sergeant retorted: "The Province law doth not make any negroes slaves if it did it being contra[ry] to Laws of God and reason must be void."[46] It seems Lowell and Sergeant argued that slavery—or at least the slavery of a Christian convert—was not supported by Massachusetts law and that such laws would be sinful and invalid in any case. Adams's brief trial notes also indicate that Lowell "made difference between property in matter and moral beings."[47] The possible substance of Lowell's argument is suggested in an antislavery essay printed in the *Essex Gazette* several months later. The newspaper essay was taken, without attribution, from George Wallace's 1760 legal treatise, *A System of the Principles of the Law of Scotland*. Wallace's book on Scottish jurisprudence was far from casual reading, suggesting that whoever excerpted it in the *Essex Gazette* was a lawyer, perhaps Lowell or Sargeant. In the excerpted passage, Wallace attacked slavery and the Atlantic slave trade by refuting the notion that African princes had the right to sell their subjects as commodities: "Men and their liberty are not *in commercio*; they are not either saleable or purchasable." Lowell could have employed Wallace's language directly to Caesar's case: "His Prince had no right to dispose of him; of course, the sale was ipso jure void." During the trial, Lowell or Sargeant could have quoted Wallace in regard to Taylor's position: "One, therefore, has no body but himself to blame, in case he shall find himself deprived of a man, whom he thought he had, by buying for a price, made his own; for he dealt in a trade which was illicit, and was prohibited by the most obvious dictates of humanity."[48] It is impossible to know if Lowell and Sargeant drew on either Locke or Wallace, but they somehow persuaded two sets of jurors to break with precedent and liberate Caesar.

Although the outcome of *Caesar v. Taylor*, like other freedom suits, did not establish any *formal* legal precedent for other suits, Caesar's victory must have inspired other enslaved people in Massachusetts. Moreover, other passages from Wallace printed in the *Essex Gazette* practically invited additional freedom suits:

> Every one of these unfortunate men, who are pretended to be slaves, has a right to be declared free, for he never lost his liberty, he could not lose it. . . . This right he carries about with him, and is entitled every where to get it declared; as soon therefore as he comes into a country, in which the judges are not forgetful of their own humanity, it is their duty to remember that he is a man, and to declare him to be free.

Other freedom suits soon followed, and Massachusetts juries became increasingly sympathetic. In hindsight, *Caesar v. Taylor* marks the beginning of an era—at least in Essex County—in which juries would almost always side with enslaved plaintiffs in freedom suits, even without evidence of freedom based on maternal descent and birth in Massachusetts.[49] Although legislators—who were often drawn from the wealthy elite and were thus more likely to be slaveholders—remained unwilling to support any antislavery reform beyond curtailing slave importations, jury verdicts indicate that many ordinary white New Englanders were turning against slavery itself.

Meanwhile, other Black New Englanders challenged slavery in new ways. In Boston, Phillis Wheatley was becoming the "founding mother of African American literature." Born in Africa, Wheatley had been enslaved and transported to Boston in 1761, when she was about nine years old. By her own account, her mistress, Susannah Wheatley, treated her "more like her child than her Servant," educating her and encouraging her writing of poetry. New evidence also indicates that Phillis Wheatley was employed in 1767 by the Rotches, a prominent Quaker family on Nantucket who employed Black sailors on their whaling vessels. The Rotches apparently encouraged Wheatley's literary pursuits—she wrote at least two poems or elegies about family members—and she may in turn have encouraged their commitment to Black rights. Wheatley's poetry focused mainly on religious themes but also addressed slavery, both directly and indirectly.[50]

Wheatley first explicitly touched on slavery in her poem "On Being Brought from Africa to America," which she composed around 1768 and initially circulated in manuscript form. The opening lines of the poem can at first glance seem to justify the Atlantic slave trade, for she expressed her gratitude for being brought from her "*Pagan* land" and taught about Jesus. However, these verses are better understood as reflecting her belief that God "alone can bring good out of Evil" (as she wrote in a later letter). If Wheatley accepted the slave trade as part of God's mysterious plan, this did not absolve its human perpetrators from sin. At the end of the poem, she refuted racist justifications for enslaving "our sable race," concluding: "Remember, *Christians, Negros*, black as *Cain*, / May be refin'd and join th' angelic train." She thus highlighted Black people's capacity for salvation while questioning the sincerity of some white Christians. Two years later, Wheatley again emphasized Black salvation in a poetic elegy for the Reverend George Whitefield. This poem, printed and sold in Boston by Ezekiel Russell, brought Wheatley transatlantic fame and transformed her into a public example of Africans' intellectual potential.[51]

Wheatley gained more attention in February 1772 when she and Russell advertised their intention to publish a book of her poetry. The advertisement described her as having arrived in Boston as "an uncultivated Barbarian from Africa" but who nonetheless composed her poetry "from the strength

Figure 5. This portrait of Phillis Wheatley appeared as the frontispiece of her *Poems on Various Subjects, Religious and Moral* (London: A Bell, 1773). Courtesy of the Library Company of Philadelphia.

of her own Genius." However, Wheatley and Russell could not attract the three hundred subscribers they desired. She eventually had greater success attracting patrons in London, where she published her book in 1773 (Figure 5).[52] Meanwhile, Wheatley's growing fame may have emboldened other Black writers. A poem by "A Negro" published in a Connecticut newspaper in May 1772 critiqued hypocritical patriots who prayed for "A partial god to vindicate their cause, / And plead their freedom, while they break its laws."[53] Black New Englanders would increasingly invoke providentialist antislavery rhetoric to critique white patriots' hypocrisy.

During the period of relative imperial calm from the spring of 1770 to the summer of 1772, enslaved activists and Black writers kept the antislavery flame burning in New England. Through their writings and freedom suits, they challenged white colonists' view of themselves as God's chosen people as well as their complacent acceptance of slaveholding. Black activists found individual white allies, such as the printer Ezekiel Russell and lawyers such as John Lowell, who were willing to attack slavery itself. Moreover, the decisions of jurors in *Caesar v. Taylor* suggest that a growing number of white New Englanders were also becoming uncomfortable with slavery.

Quakers' Intercolonial Antislavery Activism

Quakers remained the most active white abolitionists during the early 1770s. They continued advancing their antislavery testimony both within and beyond the Society of Friends. By the end of 1773, Quakers in North Carolina, Virginia, Maryland, Pennsylvania, New Jersey, New York, and Rhode Island had also urged their local legislatures to discourage the slave trade or facilitate private manumissions. The resulting legislative discussions of slavery can seem to be the predictable result of the patriots' use of natural rights rhetoric to defend their own political privileges. Yet few if any legislatures would have considered antislavery reform without instigation from Quakers. Continuing the previous decade's trend, members of Quakers' regional meetings for sufferings and standings committees acted as an intercolonial antislavery network, with Anthony Benezet serving as the central node.[54]

Regional yearly meetings continued purging slavery from within their ranks at varying speeds. There were relatively few Quakers in New England, but they surpassed those in the mid-Atlantic in pushing for manumission. The New England Yearly Meeting instructed its members (concentrated mainly in Rhode Island along with pockets in Massachusetts, especially on Nantucket) to liberate all healthy adult slaves in 1769 and began enforcing the policy with the penalty of disownment in 1772 (four years before such disownments became standard for the Philadelphia Yearly Meeting). The speed with which New England Quakers increased sanctions against slaveholding likely reflects their greater proximity to the epicenter of the imperial crisis and the fact that slavery was less important economically there compared to the rest of America.[55] Quaker reformers in the southern colonies, meanwhile, faced more legal restrictions on manumissions and more opposition from slaveholding Friends. In 1772, the Virginia Yearly Meeting advised monthly meetings to disown members who bought or sold slaves, but it avoided the question of emancipation due to the province's ban on private manumissions.

The North Carolina Yearly Meeting was a bit more conservative; by 1772, members could only buy or sell slaves from other Quakers (ideally to unite or preserve families) and were advised to "use them well in every respect." In the mid-Atlantic colonies, local committees continued visiting slaveholding members and admonishing them "against a Practice manifestly repugnant to the Doctrine and Precepts of the Gospel."[56] However, the PYM did not yet disown members who refused to liberate their bondspeople.

Perhaps the most important development within the PYM during this time was the creation of the Philadelphia Monthly Meeting's Negro School, which helped lay the foundations for the interracial activism of the following decades. Established in 1770, the school educated people of color who were already free as well as enslaved children scheduled to be manumitted upon reaching adulthood. As Quakers explained, the school reflected "our Concern for these oppressed People obtaining Liberty . . . by endeavouring to prepare their Posterity for the making a right use of it." Anthony Benezet served on the school's committee of overseers (like a board of trustees), as did the Pemberton brothers and several other members of the Generation of 1758. Other Friends who became prominent abolitionists, including John Parrish and Nicholas Waln, soon joined the committee as well. After observing Black students at the school, the overseers proclaimed their "Capacity for Learning, to be equal to other Children." Simply by embracing educational opportunities, Black students reinforced white Quakers' commitment to emancipation. The Negro School also helped educate a generation of Black abolitionists; its students later included Absalom Jones and James Forten, who became leading religious and civic leaders in the Black community.[57] (During this time, Anglicans in Philadelphia also continued educating Black youth at the Bray School.)

Benezet remained North America's most prominent abolitionist in terms of both publishing and organizing. In October 1771 he released his magnum opus, *Some Historical Account of Guinea*, which was actually several books in one. The first 148 pages covered slavery's history dating back to the ancient world, along with descriptions of the slave trade's destructive effects on Africa. This portion incorporated many quotations from travel narratives and other antislavery tracts. Benezet used these sources to advance an argument about Christian duty and divine providence. He credited the demise of slavery in Europe to the "gentle spirit" of Christianity and insisted that the enslavement of Africans violated "every Christian and moral virtue." The Quaker repeatedly warned that the cries of enslaved Africans would reach heaven and provoke divine vengeance. This section concluded with an emancipation proposal that was essentially the same as Benezet had included in the second edition of his *Short Account of Africa* in 1762. He again called for the immediate abolition of the slave trade, the staggered emancipation of enslaved people in the colonies, and land grants for freedpeople in the uncultivated lands to the south and west. Although such a massive undertaking would pose challenges, Benezet assured readers: "Doubtless the Almighty would bless this good intention."[58] He thus reiterated the view, central to the Generation of 1758, that an interventionist God would punish the perpetuation of slavery but aid emancipation.

The second part of *Some Historical Account of Guinea* was essentially a lengthy appendix of extracts from other antislavery writers. It consisted primarily of a condensed version of *A Representation of the Injustice and Dangerous Tendency of Tolerating Slavery*, published in England by Granville Sharp in 1769. Sharp, an evangelical Anglican emerging as Britain's leading abolitionist, had authored his text as part of a successful effort to prevent the re-enslavement of a Black man named Jonathan Strong in London. Much of Sharp's book involved legal precedents and arguments designed to refute the 1729 Yorke-Talbot opinion, which had asserted that slaveholders' control over human property extended throughout the empire and was unaffected by religious conversion. Some aspects of Sharp's book were heavily influenced by Benezet's 1766 *Caution and Warning* (which Sharp had republished in London in 1768, unbeknownst to Benezet). The Anglican shared the Quaker's providentialist beliefs, writing that Britain was "loaded with the horrid guilt of tolerating such abominable wickedness," and warning that the cries of slaves "certainly reach to Heaven." Quoting from Benezet, Sharp argued that emancipation was "the best means to avert the judgments of God." He also denounced slaveholding American patriots for their "theatrical bombast and ranting expressions in praise of liberty." The Englishman concluded: "It too plainly appears, that they have no real regard for liberty, farther than their own private interests are concerned." Indeed, Sharp used the North American colonies as an example of how slaveholding threatened the basis of British liberty by destroying the morals and manners of (white) British subjects. When Benezet abridged Sharp's book, he preserved the Englishman's warnings of divine retribution as well as his criticism of hypocritical American patriots.[59]

Benezet concluded *Some Historical Account of Guinea* by appending shorter extracts of antislavery writings by the Bishop of Gloucester and several European intellectuals and jurists, including George Wallace, Francis Hutcheson, and James Foster. He had used these extracts in previous publications, but Benezet now added an extract of the first antislavery essay by "Philanthropos" (Arthur Lee), which had appeared in the *Virginia Gazette* in 1767. By quoting from European intellectuals and American patriots, Benezet clearly sought to show that antislavery sentiment was not limited to Quakers. He advertised his book in newspapers in Philadelphia and Boston, and sent copies to Quakers and public officials throughout the colonies and in London for further distribution.[60]

Benezet hoped *Some Historical Account of Guinea* would inspire or strengthen antislavery political activism in the form of petitions to colonial legislatures and Parliament. During the early 1770s, these petitions focused on modest goals, such as banning slave importations and easing private manumissions, as attainable steps toward the larger goal of eradicating slavery throughout the empire. Concentrating initially on the slave trade also allowed abolitionists to attract a broader coalition. Benezet reported that many southern slaveholders were at least "convinced of the inexpediency, if not all of the iniquity of any further importation of negroes."[61] He and other Quaker reformers worked to promote antislavery (or at least anti-slave trade) petitioning efforts throughout the colonies.

Some Virginia Quakers, including Robert Pleasants, had been lobbying individual politicians against slavery since 1769, asserting that the patriots' arguments in defense of their natural rights applied "with equal justice" to "the Negroes." At the 1770 Virginia Yearly Meeting, the Quaker activists reported that although many legislators "acknowledge the inconsistence and injustice" of slavery, there was little chance for reform. Unfortunately, the records of the VYM from 1771 (and several other years) were destroyed in a fire, but it seems the activists continued their lobbying efforts. Records for Maryland Quakers are even more sparse for this period, but Benezet reported that they were mobilizing against the slave trade as well. In November the Maryland legislature quickly "Read and Rejected" a slave trade petition from Quakers.[62] Despite such setbacks, they persisted in their efforts.

Quakers may have provided the catalyst behind an anti-slave trade address from the Virginia House of Burgesses to King George III. In January 1772, Benezet reported that the Virginia Quakers had a slave trade petition "under their consideration." The House of Burgesses left no record of receiving an antislavery petition, but in March the legislators began drafting a bill to raise the duty on slave importations. This impulse reflected various motives and considerations, including the fact that the natural growth of the colony's large slave population rendered slave importations unnecessary and potentially dangerous. The legislative committee drafting the petition included Richard Bland, who had previously received antislavery publications from Robert Pleasants. The House of Burgesses' petition, dated April 1, 1772, focused primarily on matters of expediency, asking for the king's "paternal Assistance in averting a Calamity of most alarming Nature." The slave trade endangered the colony and discouraged "the settlement of the Colonies with more useful inhabitants." The Virginians also lamented the slave trade's "great inhumanity." This moral posturing was likely intended to make their repeated complaints about parliamentary tyranny appear more principled. Since the 1760s, British pamphlets had sarcastically belittled the "upright, humane and virtuous" pretensions of colonial "negro-whippers" who complained about imperial taxation.[63]

Whether or not they had instigated the Virginia petition, Quakers celebrated it and helped publicize it from South Carolina through New England and across the Atlantic. A committee from the VYM sent news of the petition to the London Meeting for Sufferings, encouraging it to lobby the Board of Trade.[64] Quakers in other colonies used Virginia's example to press their local legislatures to take a stand against the slave trade as well. In July 1772, Thomas Nicholson and other members of the North Carolina Standing Committee called on their legislature "to Joyn heartily with their Prudent Brethren, the Burgesses of the Colony of Virginia," in opposing slave importations. The Quakers also distributed copies of Benezet's antislavery books "to the leading Men" in North Carolina. Like the Virginia Quakers, those in North Carolina also requested that the LMS support their antislavery efforts by lobbying Parliament and imperial officials.[65] The North Carolina legislature, however, declined to act.

Abolitionists found even less encouragement farther south, where Benezet sent additional copies of *Some Historical Account of Guinea*. Thomas Knox Gordon, the chief justice in South Carolina, praised Benezet's "pious endeavours" but lamented: "One Argument drawn from worldly interest, and advantage, will outweigh a thousand supported by every principle of Religion, Reason, Justice and sound Policy." Slavery was the source of South Carolina's prosperity, and Gordon could not imagine any reformation. Benezet was undoubtedly disappointed but probably not surprised. A year later, he wrote that South Carolina and Georgia planters had "hearts so hardened, by the love of gain" that "nothing less than a blow from heaven, will rouse them from their lethargy."[66] Benezet remained confident that God would deliver the Africans from bondage, but he feared that it would not be a peaceful process.

The *Somerset* Decision and Massachusetts Reactions

Some Historical Account of Guinea likely proved even more consequential in England than Anthony Benezet had hoped. The Quaker mailed a copy of his book to Granville Sharp in May 1772, introducing himself to the British abolitionist and explaining that he had "taken the freedom to republish" part of Sharp's earlier pamphlet. Benezet reported that antislavery sentiment was growing in America and that Quakers and other reformers in several colonies were organizing petitions against the slave trade. He hoped Sharp could help mobilize antislavery sentiment in England to pressure the king and Parliament to take action.[67] Unbeknownst to Benezet, Sharp had already received a copy of his book back in February from Dr. John Fothergill, one of Benezet's correspondents in the LMS. Indeed, Sharp had already used *Some Historical Account* in ways Benezet could not have foreseen.

Benezet's book reached London at a fortuitous moment: when Sharp was scrambling to prepare for the court case that would ultimately end slavery in England. On January 13, 1772, Sharp had been contacted by James Somerset, an African-born man who had been held enslaved in Virginia and Massachusetts before being brought to London by his master, Charles Steuart (commonly rendered as Stewart). Somerset had absconded, but Steuart recaptured him and arranged to sell him to a planter who intended to send him from London to Jamaica. Somerset recruited Sharp, who was known as an ally to Black Londoners, to fight the sale. Within two weeks, Sharp had hired lawyers on Somerset's behalf and hastily printed *An Appendix*, a pamphlet meant as an update to his 1769 *Representation of the Injustice and Dangerous Tendency of Tolerating Slavery*. He included additional legal arguments he had compiled in 1770 while working to liberate another enslaved man, Thomas Lewis. Sharp concluded *An Appendix* by warning that tolerating slavery within England would "certainly cause our measure of Iniquity to overflow, and, in all probability, draw down upon us some dreadful and speedy *national* calamity."[68] He hoped for a judicial ruling that would not simply liberate another enslaved individual but end slavery throughout England.

Sharp received Benezet's book amid this activity, and he immediately requested additional copies from Fothergill before Somerset's trial began.

Sharp identified Benezet's appendix as especially useful, writing that "the extracts (from Mr. Wallis [*Wallace*], Dr. Foster, &c.) are so concise, and yet so full and unanswerable, especially on some points where our lawyers stick." Sharp's deep religious faith may have inspired his abolitionism, but he knew Somerset's case would depend on legal reasoning, and he saw Benezet's extracts from European jurists and philosophers as a great resource. Fothergill and the LMS were able to provide five more copies, which Sharp then distributed to Somerset's four lawyers. Somerset himself acted as courier between Sharp and Fothergill, and personally delivered the fifth copy of Benezet's book to Chief Justice Lord Mansfield, who was overseeing the trial.[69]

After hearing preliminary arguments in early February, Mansfield determined to postpone further proceedings until May. During the interim, Sharp arranged for Benezet's book to be reprinted in London so that he could distribute it to other English judges and statesmen. For instance, he sent copies of Benezet's book and his own *Representation of the Injustice* to Lord Frederick North, the prime minister. Assuming that Lord North would be too busy to read the entire books, Sharp took the liberty of using bookmarks and red ink to highlight a few pages of each. From his own book, Sharp highlighted passages on divine retribution, such as his warning "that the cries of these much-injured people will certainly reach to Heaven." Whereas Sharp focused on legal arguments in court, he hoped the fear of God would inspire statesmen. In order to avoid God's wrath, Sharp pointed North to Benezet's "sensible propositions for *abolishing Slavery in the Colonies*."[70] Although North declined to take any action, Mansfield did rule in James Somerset's favor, undermining slavery throughout England.

Mansfield's ruling, issued in June 1772, asserted that because slavery contradicts natural law, it could only legally exist where established by "positive law" (e.g., written statute law in contrast to custom). Local laws established slavery in the colonies, but England itself lacked such statutes. In the absence of positive law, the common law of England favored natural rights. Therefore, Charles Steuart had no right to treat James Somerset as his property while they were in England. In hindsight, historians recognize this ruling as effectively (though not immediately) ending slavery in England, but its antislavery significance was not initially apparent. Sharp reported to Benezet that the verdict "would have done Lord Mansfield honour, had he not all along seemed inclined to the other side of the question." Mansfield shared neither Sharp's commitment to natural rights nor his fear of divine retribution; he based his ruling on legal grounds that could be altered through legislation. Indeed, the chief justice encouraged Steuart and other slaveholders to lobby Parliament to legalize slavery in England (where about sixteen thousand Black people were enslaved). In August 1772, Sharp warned Benezet that slaveholders might "carry their point at the next session [of Parliament]," thereby reversing the judgment and increasing the nation's collective guilt.[71]

Parliament ultimately chose not to act, and the tensions with the American colonies may have shaped this decision. For more than five years, colonial protestors had been accusing Parliament of trying to metaphorically "enslave" them, and Mansfield's ruling allowed the mother country to claim the moral high ground regarding actual slavery. Essays in British periodicals praised the ruling for doing "more honour to the law of England than any that has been made since the [Glorious] Revolution."[72] By declining to formally legalize slavery in England, Parliament ensured that slavery remained an aberrant institution associated with the colonial periphery rather than the metropolitan center of the British Empire. Of course, Parliament and the king had actively sanctioned and supported the Atlantic slave trade, as some American critics pointed out. Benjamin Franklin, stationed in London as a colonial lobbyist, critiqued metropolitan notions of moral superiority in the *London Chronicle.* He noted that the English congratulated themselves on "setting free *a single Slave* that happens to land on thy coasts, while thy Merchants in all thy ports are encouraged by thy laws to continue a commerce whereby so many *hundreds of thousands* are dragged into a slavery that can scarce be said to end with their lives, since it is entailed on their posterity!" In Boston, someone writing as "Ben Scotus" later suggested that Mansfield should do something about the millions of white colonists whom Parliament held "in chains" (metaphorically speaking).[73] Whereas abolitionists such as Benezet sought to use patriot rhetoric to advance antislavery goals, patriots like Franklin and "Ben Scotus" used antislavery rhetoric to critique the metropole for partisan advantage.

The *Somerset* trial and decision provoked more extensive newspaper coverage in Massachusetts than in any other North American colony. The extent of controversy has struck some scholars as curious, given the colony's small number of enslaved people. Yet the logic of the *Somerset* decision had great potential influence in Massachusetts. Mansfield had declared that "slavery is of such a nature, that it . . . must take its rise from positive law."[74] The "*Somerset* principle"—that slavery could only exist where supported by statue law—posed little threat to colonies like Virginia, where slavery was legally codified in great detail, but Massachusetts was different. Although some forms of enslavement-for-life had been legally codified in the colony since 1641, the practice of treating enslavement as hereditary and unaffected by conversion to Christianity rested on the type of informal custom that Mansfield had dismissed as an insufficient basis for slaveholders' rights in England.

The Massachusetts newspaper controversy started in September 1772 in the *Boston Evening-Post*, when a "John Marsham" denounced the *Somerset* decision and defended slavery using the Bible. The pseudonymous writer adopted the name of an English antiquarian who had published a history of Egypt a century earlier, and his essays must be understood in the context of the preexisting debate over hereditary slavery's biblical basis. Drawing on the Bible and various historical accounts, Boston's "John Marsham" claimed:

> Slavery for wise-Reasons is of *divine* Institution, that God Almighty has *expressly* and by solemn Repetition separated a particular Part of Humankind to be in that Condition, and that this People (wherever they be, and whoever they are) have been, are now, and ever will be under that Curse, a Curse as *absolute* and *irrevocable* as any in the Bible . . . The Curse related to Ham, the second Son of Noah, and all his Posterity forever . . . as we have in the Account of Genesis ix. 25, 26.

The author then used the Bible and other sources to claim "that Africa was settled by Ham and his Descendants" and thus all Black people remained subject to Noah's Curse.[75] Although Marsham did not cite Thomas Newton's *Dissertations on the Prophecies*, he echoed its claims.

If "Marsham" hoped his arguments would silence abolitionists, his effort backfired. By the end of October, three antislavery writers published at least six newspaper essays in response. Marsham's opponents dismissed his "false Reasonings and Perversions of holy Scripture." In the *Boston Evening-Post*, "Commiserator Africanorum" emphasized that Africans were "made of the same *one blood*" (Acts 17:26). They charged Marsham with having "grossly perverted" the text of Genesis 9:25, which showed the curse only applied to Canaan and the Canaanites, not to Ham's other descendants who settled in Africa. In the *Massachusetts Spy*, "Manetho" (the name of an Egyptian historian) further demonstrated that Marsham had misrepresented the text of Genesis. An "M. Cato," warned that slavery provoked "Divine displeasure" and hoped the "glorious precedent" of the *Somerset* decision would eventually extend to the colonies. Marsham tried defending his position using additional references to scripture, but he was outnumbered and eventually abandoned his defense of slavery, which his critics said could only have reflected his "secular interest" (i.e., greed).[76]

Several weeks later, in mid-November 1772, Ezekiel Russell finally published James Swan's long-delayed pamphlet, *A Dissuasion to Great-Britain and the Colonies, from the Slave-Trade to Africa*. Although he was neither a Quaker nor a minister, Swan made religion central to his text, which he consciously composed "after the form of a sermon." Exodus taught Swan that manstealers "justly deserved death," and Leviticus, Deuteronomy, and Jeremiah all placed limits on slavery and servitude. Moreover, the New Testament erased the distinctions that had allowed Israelites to enslave heathens and strangers. Swan frequently cited Anthony Benezet's work and echoed his antislavery providentialism. The Bostonian suggested the current tensions with Parliament indicated "divine anger" at the sin of slavery. Reflecting on days of fasting and prayer, Swan asked: "Can you think that God will hear your prayers, receive your supplications, or grant your desires, while you act this grossly and openly against his divine will and pleasure?" He focused primarily on the slave trade to the Caribbean but also called for the emancipation of "every Negro throughout . . . North America." Swan told readers that Black people are "your Brethren who have the same capacities, understandings and souls." He concluded with the hope that the colonists would end the "accursed Trade" and earn the Lord's mercy through repentance.[77] Swan's pamphlet hardly reflected a secular shift in abolitionist ideology; religious arguments remained central to abolitionism.

* * *

At the end of 1772, the most active opponents of slavery remained Quakers and Black people, but more white colonists were beginning to espouse antislavery views. The antislavery pamphlets, sermons, and newspaper essays published in New England had much in common with the antislavery biblicism and providentialism that had been central to abolitionist thought since the late seventeenth century. As colonists sought to make sense of the imperial crisis, a meaningful minority concluded that it reflected God's anger over slavery. They essentially reached the same conclusion that the Quakers had made during the French and Indian War. Benezet and other Quaker abolitionists encouraged this trend, disseminating antislavery publications throughout the colonies.

Although these developments failed to inspire successful legislative reform, they likely primed white jurors in Massachusetts to be sympathetic to freedom suits brought by Black plaintiffs, as indicated by the outcome of *Caesar v. Taylor*. Meanwhile, slavery's defenders continued using the Bible, especially the Old Testament, to justify the institution. Yet, the reactions to the "John Marsham" essays indicate that antislavery biblicism—which Anthony Benezet, Nathaniel Appleton, and others had worked to spread—was gaining ground.

CHAPTER 4

Abolitionism and the Imperial Crisis, Part II: 1772–1775

Between 1764 and 1772, imperial tensions had repeatedly risen and relaxed in response to policy changes in the metropole. However, colonial relations with the mother country steadily worsened after the fall of 1772, when Massachusetts colonists learned that the royal governor and superior court justices would henceforth receive their salaries using money collected from the tax on tea. This change reduced the colonial legislature's influence and incentivized royal officials to enforce imperial taxes. Tensions rose further in the summer of 1773 following Parliament's passage of the East India Tea Act, which led to the Boston Tea Party in December. In response, Parliament passed the Coercive Acts—dubbed the "Intolerable Acts" by patriots—closing Boston Harbor and curtailing representative government in Massachusetts. Instead of isolating Massachusetts, these actions caused patriots in the other colonies to rally against imperial policies.[1]

Throughout this time, an unprecedent number of white and Black antislavery writers and activists demanded reform through newspapers, sermons, pamphlets, and lawsuits. This movement built on the groundwork Quakers had laid since the 1750s but was clearly accelerated by the imperial crisis. Historians have made much of the continued rise in antislavery publications during the early 1770s, attributing it to patriot rhetoric. They routinely assert that by the end of 1774, American patriots were optimistic that slaveholding would soon be abolished or die out on its own.[2] However, such characterizations oversimplify the inspiration for antislavery and exaggerate the naivete of abolitionists on the eve of the Revolutionary War. Far from being inevitable or spontaneous, most expressions of antislavery sentiment were carefully orchestrated by a dedicated core of activists.

As during the earlier phases of the imperial crisis, much of the antislavery impulse reflected providentialist and biblicist beliefs. Parliament's efforts to tax the colonies and punish protestors reinforced abolitionists' perception that God was chastising the colonies and the empire as a whole for the sin of slavery. Anthony Benezet conceded that the previous generations of colonists who established slaveholding did so "in times of Ignorance," but he argued that it was "criminal to Continue such laws now [that] the rights of Humanity have come more Particularly under Consideration." He warned that "National offences may procure National Calamites" and predicted that the colonists would continue suffering until they abolished slavery.[3] Nonetheless, abolitionism remained a fringe movement among patriots, and the most dedicated activists were still Black people, Quakers, and a few other white allies. Benezet and other Quaker abolitionists expanded their earlier efforts to coordinate antislavery petitions and lobbying campaigns in several colonies from Maryland through New York. Despite relatively small numbers, abolitionists managed to push debates over slavery into the public sphere and pressure some legislatures to consider reform.

New England was largely disconnected from Quaker organizing but also experienced a surge in antislavery activity. Enslaved people in Massachusetts continued struggling for freedom using the court system; they also began petitioning the legislature and publishing antislavery newspaper essays and pamphlets. They found a handful of white allies, including the Reverend John Allen, Ezekiel Russell, James Swan, John Lowell, and a host of unidentified newspaper essayists. Although Quakers played a less direct role in New England, Benezet's publications influenced the antislavery movement there. Black and white abolitionists in New England often used both biblicist and providentialist language to condemn slavery and call for reform, arguing that the imperial crisis reflected divine chastisement for the sin of slaveholding. Their efforts were most successful in the judicial system, where juries began routinely liberating Black plaintiffs even when their enslavement conformed to legal custom. Massachusetts legislators, however, still resisted calls for substantive reform. Other New England colonies also experienced growing antislavery agitation by both enslaved activists and a handful of clergymen who employed providentialist antislavery rhetoric.

The Quaker-Led Abolitionist Campaign of 1772–1774

In the fall of 1772, Anthony Benezet persisted in his attempt to organize antislavery petitions addressed to the imperial government. He had announced this plan in his May letter to Granville Sharp and asked for the Englishman's advice. Sharp responded by explaining that any petitions against the slave trade itself should be directed to Parliament, which had passed laws sanctioning and supporting the trade, but that petitions "*with respect to the toleration of slavery in the colonies . . . should be addressed only to the King*." He based this distinction on the view that Parliament "had no right to interfere" with internal colonial legislation (a view shared by American patriots) but that the monarch did possess such powers (a view not shared by patriots). Although Sharp had no expectation that King George III would actually abolish slavery, he hoped a petition "might at least occasion the setting on foot some wholesome regulations by way of restraint of the masters." He then described Spanish regulations that allowed slaves to gradually purchase their freedom. Sharp suggested that the British Empire adopt this policy as a step toward the "*total abolition of slavery*." Benezet circulated manuscript copies of Sharp's letter among his allies, who published extracts in newspapers throughout the northern colonies and promoted local petitioning efforts.[4]

In November 1772, Benezet worked with James Pemberton and other members of the Philadelphia Meeting for Sufferings to create three petitions addressed to the king and both houses of Parliament. The initial drafts were prepared by Samuel Allinson, a PMS member and prominent attorney and politician from New Jersey who had supported various freedom suits since the mid-1760s. Allinson explained to collaborators in New Jersey, Pennsylvania, Maryland, and Virginia that the petitions "should be engrossed on skin of parchment for signing with columns for the names."[5] At some point between late November and January, however, Benezet and the PMS altered their strategy. Instead of having colonists at large directly petition the king and Parliament, they determined to work through the colonial legislatures, hoping these bodies would then address the king, as the Virginia legislature had done in 1772. The Quakers also decided to focus solely on the Atlantic slave trade rather than directly attacking colonial slaveholding itself. These decisions likely reflected an awareness that patriots were concerned with preserving the power of colonial legislatures and that there was little political support for emancipation. Nonetheless, the petitions to the colonial legislatures broke new ground because they called for abolishing the Atlantic slave trade within the entire British Empire, rather than simply focusing on importations into individual colonies.

The petition to the Pennsylvania legislature was completed by January 1773 and was reportedly signed by "about two hundred Persons," including Philadelphia's four "clergymen of the church of England, five Presbyterian

Clergymen, and four other ministers." The petition condemned the slave trade "on account of its inconsistency with the whole tenor of the Christian religion . . . and the dreadful consequences which it is to be feared, will one day attend in those parts where it prevails." In other words, they feared retribution at the hands of either enslaved people or God. They called on the legislature to send an address to the king and Parliament asking them to take action against this "mighty evil" throughout the "provinces and islands of the British dominions."[6] Abolitionists hoped that similar petitions would inspire legislatures throughout the continent to unite in calling on the imperial government to end the British slave trade.

The Pennsylvania legislature, however, was only prepared to support limited reform. Instead of addressing the king and Parliament in favor of antislavery reform throughout the empire, it simply raised the duty on slaves imported into Pennsylvania to the prohibitive level of £20. Benezet had hoped for more but accepted this law, enacted in February 1773, as a "preliminary" step. Knowing that prohibitively high duties had been disallowed in the past, the PMS sent a letter to the London Meeting for Sufferings, soliciting the aid of English Quakers who "have an Interest with the Council or Lords of Trade." In response, the LMS's John Fothergill met with Pennsylvania proprietor John Penn, who expressed "his Inclination to countenance them on every proper Occasion."[7] American abolitionists were developing sophisticated strategies that combined antislavery propaganda, petitions, and lobbying on both sides of the Atlantic.

During this time, Quaker abolitionists also promoted emancipation at the colony level, especially in New Jersey and Pennsylvania. In December 1772, PMS member David Cooper published *A Mite Cast into the Treasury: Or, Observations on Slave-Keeping*. Cooper (who was Samuel Allinson's father-in-law), felt compelled by the Bible to "plead the cause of the poor and needy" (Proverbs 21:8–9), and his pamphlet reflected the biblicist and providentialist basis of his antislavery sentiments. He quoted the prohibition on manstealing from Exodus 21:16 and argued it was a moral law that had been universalized by Christ rather than "part of the ceremonial law intended only for the Jewish nation." Cooper warned that slavery would provoke divine punishment, citing Matthew 7:2: "Such measures as you mete, shall be measured to you again." He instructed slaveholders to "set your negroes free at the same age as your own children are [i.e., eighteen for women and twenty-one for men]." If slaveholders refused "to let the oppressed go free," the Almighty would surely "avenge their cause," Cooper warned. In a postscript, he buttressed his religious arguments with excerpts from John Locke's *Second Treatise of Government*. Locke described the "law of nature" as synonymous with "the will of God" and declared that "no human sanction can be good or valid against it." Cooper also used Locke to reinforce his argument against hereditary slavery. The English philosopher had accepted that aggressors in a just war could be legitimately enslaved for life, but he also emphasized that slavery "dies with them." The slaveholder "has no such right over their children." Both Cooper and Locke believed that hereditary slavery violated God-given natural rights.[8]

A month later, in January 1773, Benjamin Rush published *An Address to the Inhabitants of the British Settlements in America, Upon Slave-Keeping*. He was a prominent Philadelphia physician and devout Presbyterian whom Benezet had recruited to the abolitionist cause. Rush refuted racist and religious justifications for slavery (insisting that the Old Testament's tolerations of slavery had ended with Christ), and referred to the *Somerset v. Steuart* decision in order to encourage a sense of antislavery competition among American patriots. Claiming (exaggeratingly) that in England, "the Clamors of the whole nation" were raised against the slave trade, Rush called on his fellow colonists to abolish not only the slave trade but also slavery itself (albeit gradually, by freeing "young Negroes"). In the pamphlet's conclusion, which reached a broad audience via newspaper extracts, Rush described the providential significance of the imperial crisis. He told readers to reflect on "the Rod which was held over them a few years ago in the Stamp, and Revenue Acts." The colonists should expect worse to come unless they embraced antislavery reform, because "national crimes require national punishments." This belief in antislavery providentialism, already shared by many Quakers and some New England Congregationalists, would become increasingly common in the mid-Atlantic colonies, thanks in part to the efforts of Rush and his Quaker allies. Rush's supporters also reprinted his pamphlet in New York, Massachusetts, and Connecticut.[9]

Yet abolitionists faced opposition on both sides of the Atlantic. In the spring of 1773, Benezet received a shipment from Granville Sharp, containing copies of proslavery pamphlets that their activism had provoked. *A Treatise upon the Trade from Great-Britain to Africa . . . by an African Merchant* mockingly dismissed "the formidable Anthony Benezet" for producing a pamphlet notable for its "thickness" but based on "defective reasoning." The proslavery pamphlet described Black people in racist terms and claimed that those enslaved in the colonies were better off than those in Africa. Moreover, it insisted that the slave trade was essential for the prosperity and power of the British Empire. Benezet vented his frustration in a letter to Sharp, writing that the "assertions are shamefully and even foolishly contrary to plain truths." Perhaps even more offensive was the Reverend Thomas Thompson's *The African Trade for Negro Slaves, Shewn to be Consistent with Principles of Humanity, and with the Laws of Revealed Religion.* The Anglican clergyman used scripture—especially Leviticus 25—to defend slavery and argued that nothing permitted in the Bible could be "contrary to the law of nature." Noting favorably that Parliament had long "encouraged and promoted" the slave trade, Thompson dismissed abolitionists' claims that slavery violated the spirit of Christianity, for in that case "it must be deemed a national sin." This comment exasperated Benezet, who scribbled in the margins of his copy: "Certainly a *national Sin!* so that we have great reason to dread the consequences."[10]

Abolitionists also had opponents in Philadelphia. In the summer of 1773, Richard Nisbet, a colonist who had moved from the Caribbean to Philadelphia, published *Slavery Not Forbidden by Scripture* as a challenge to Rush's pamphlet. The Old Testament clearly permitted slaveholding, and Nisbet insisted that "if the custom had been held in abhorrence by Christ and his disciples, they would, no doubt have preached against it in direct terms." He also defended slavery based on its economic importance and by using allegations of racial inferiority. Whereas Rush had praised Phillis Wheatley as an example of Black potential, Nisbet dismissed her "silly poems." He claimed that most Caribbean slaves lived in such "ease and plenty" that "they ought to be envied, rather than pitied."[11] His proslavery pamphlet prompted both serious and satirical responses.

Rush answered Nisbet with an enlarged second edition of his own pamphlet in September 1773. He reiterated that Christianity had annulled the Old Testament's limited sanction of slaveholding. Pointing to recent news of large slave revolts in Surinam and Brazil, Rush warned, "Are not these Insurrections the beginnings of universal Retribution and Vengeance upon European Tyranny, in America?" His antislavery views were echoed in newspapers. In the *Pennsylvania Packet*, "Onesimus" (named after the Christian slave discussed in Paul's letter to Philemon) also refuted scriptural defenses of slavery.[12]

Another writer in the *Pennsylvania Packet* took a different approach, ridiculing Nisbet through parody. The paper published a fake Bible verse, purportedly from Genesis, asserting that God had granted Adam authority over not only animals but also "the beasts of Ethiopia . . . even they whose figures and speech are like unto thine own, and whose heads are covered with a covering like unto fine wool."[13] The point was that slavery's defenders inevitably distorted the word of God. A full-length pamphlet, *Personal Slavery Established*, further satirized Nisbet. The author dedicated the volume to the Royal African Company of slave traders, in honor of their "generous disinterested exertion of benevolence and philanthropy." After parodying proslavery arguments, the author concluded with a Swiftian proposal to end food shortages in the colonies: The corpses of the thousands of Africans who died each year on slave ships could be "cured in pickle or smoak" and then fed to the "lower class whites."[14] Benezet wrote that he could not fully approve of this satire because "serious subjects, should be treated with seriousness," but he nonetheless circulated copies in Pennsylvania and Virginia.[15] He endorsed neither colonial resistance against Parliament nor satire, but he hoped both would advance abolitionism.

A pragmatist as well as a pacifist, Benezet was also willing to engage in fearmongering to promote abolition. He believed that accounts of slave insurrection could be an effective form of antislavery propaganda, especially in the southern colonies, where they might "open the Eyes of people to see the iniquity and danger of any farther import of Slaves." Benezet began copying newspaper reports of slave revolts into his letters and encouraged his correspondents to reprint them in local newspapers. He justified this tactic in letters to his Quaker allies in Virginia and Maryland. "I know it is the general opinion, that nothing ought to be published whereby the Negroes may be acquainted with their own strength . . . but I am persuaded this fear may be carried too far, for it is certainly yet more dangerous to withhold from the generality of the people the knowledge of the danger they will be in, thro' a continued importation of Negro Slaves."[16] In essence, he hoped that fear would succeed where arguments based on religion and compassion had failed.

It appears that Benezet and his Quaker allies used this fearmongering tactic effectively in Maryland. In March 1773, Benezet told Sharp that Maryland Quakers planned to insert some materials in the *Maryland Gazette* in conjunction with a new antislavery petition to the legislature. The materials to which Benezet referred likely included a brief account of slave revolt in Surinam that he had appended to his letter and that soon appeared in the *Gazette*. The article described the danger that the white colonists faced from the "rebellious negroes." The same newspaper issue also reported that a recent slave ship revolt had killed "every soul on board." Additional accounts of slave resistance continued appearing in the *Gazette* throughout the year, and the Maryland assembly discouraged slave importations with a higher duty in December 1773. Scholars have noted that "the leaders of Virginia and Maryland worried that they had more than enough [slaves] for their economy and too many for security from revolt" without realizing the role abolitionists played in amplifying such fears.[17]

During this time, Quakers also continued pushing for antislavery reform in New Jersey. Samuel Allinson organized at least nineteen petitions to the New Jersey legislature between November 1773 and February 1774. One from Salem County, home to many Quakers, asserted that liberty was an "inherent and universal Right of Man" based on "the Laws of God and Nature." Recognizing that total emancipation had no chance of success, the petitioners simply called for a ban on slave importations and the repeal of the law requiring slaveholders to post a £200 bond before manumitting a slave. Allinson recruited some prominent patriot allies, including Elias Boudinot, a devout Presbyterian, to help circulate petitions and lobby legislators.[18]

Quakers supplemented the petition drive with several new pamphlets. William Dillwyn, a former pupil of Benezet's, published *Brief Considerations on Slavery* in November 1773. Linking religious arguments against slavery to the imperial crisis, Dillwyn argued that antislavery reform would demonstrate that colonial opposition to Parliament came "not merely from selfish motives . . . but from a disinterested generous love to liberty, founded on principle." It was not simply a matter of convincing the British of the sincerity of their motives, but also of earning the "divine blessing" that seemed "necessary to ensure us success in asserting our rights." Like other Quaker abolitionists, Dillwyn did not personally support the patriot cause—indeed, he subsequently moved to England—but he opportunistically combined patriot rhetoric with antislavery providentialism to promote emancipation.[19]

In December 1773, Samuel Allinson arranged for the publication of *An Essay on Slavery: Proving from Scripture Its Inconsistency with Humanity and Religion.* Granville Sharp had penned the manuscript in response to the Reverend Thompson's proslavery pamphlet and sent it to Benezet. Sharp explained that God's toleration of the Israelites' enslavement of heathens had ceased with Christ, who taught "that *all strangers* . . . are to be esteemed our *neighbours* or *brethren*." Slavery was a "*national sin*," and Sharp prayed, "May God give us grace to repent of this abominable national oppression, before it is too late!" Allinson published Sharp's pamphlet in Burlington, NJ, after adding a lengthy preface that used the *Somerset* decision to shame American slaveholders. Noting that the English refused to tolerate slavery in England because they understood it violated natural rights and English common law,

Allinson observed: "Why it should be revived and continued in the colonies, peopled by the descendants of Britain, and blessed with sentiments as truly noble and free as any of their fellow subjects in the mother country, is not easily conceived." He warned of divine punishment while promising that antislavery reform would benefit from "the approbation of Divine Providence."[20] New Jersey abolitionists also used newspapers to promote their reform effort, publishing further biblicist arguments as well as calculations showing that the manumission bonds required in the colony were unnecessarily high.[21]

In response to this antislavery pressure, the New Jersey legislature drafted a bill prohibiting slave importations and reforming manumission procedures. It should be emphasized that the legislature's bill would not have compelled emancipation; it simply made voluntary manumissions easier. Still, Allinson reported that the bill faced "many enemies." Slavery was an important economic institution in parts of New Jersey, especially the eastern region, and many slaveholders and other whites feared any measure that might undermine slavery and increase the population of free Black people. After slaveholders organized petitions against reform, the legislature repeatedly postponed voting on the bill and failed to act before the start of the war. The bill's fate thus also illustrates the obstacles facing even modest antislavery reforms in the northern colonies.[22]

Abolitionists' hopes also came up short in neighboring New York. In February 1773, Benezet told Sharp that he had "sent an extract of thy letter, the Virginia Petition, &c, to some weighty members of three different counties in New-York." One of these recipients, writing as "Eleutheros" (Greek for "freeborn"), published the materials in the *New-York Journal*. Eleutheros's introductory letter disavowed immediate emancipation but proposed banning slave importations into North America as the first step toward abolishing slavery. Eleutheros called on the colonial legislature to encourage the king and Parliament to take action against the slave trade. The New York legislature, like that in Pennsylvania, declined to appeal to the imperial authorities but did pass a prohibitive duty of £20 on slaves imported into the colony. However, the governor and his council vetoed the measure.[23]

Despite mixed results, the Quakers' antislavery campaigns of 1772 to early 1774 demonstrated the development of a coherent—if still only loosely connected—abolitionist movement that spanned from Virginia to New York. Quakers' regional standing committees and meetings for sufferings were the backbone of this movement, coordinating their petitions and lobbying efforts with each other and with London Meeting for Sufferings across the Atlantic.

This approach of simultaneously lobbying the colonial and imperial governments later evolved into a bifurcated approach targeting state and federal governments after American independence.[24]

Moreover, Quaker abolitionists continued developing interdenominational and transatlantic connections during the 1770s. John Woolman was promoting antislavery in England at the time of his death in October 1772. The English Quaker Mary Hinde posthumously published his *Serious Considerations on Various Subjects of Importance*, which included several antislavery passages. Woolman denounced the slave trade and warned that God would punish Britain for its "great Load of Guilt."[25] American Quakers also promoted transatlantic cooperation through their correspondence, including with new contacts beyond the Society of Friends. For instance, Anthony Benezet had sent a copy of his *Some Historical Account of Guinea* to John Wesley, the English founder of Methodism, in late 1771. By early 1772, Wesley had become an antislavery convert and was collaborating with Benezet and Granville Sharp to insert antislavery essays in London newspapers. In 1774, Wesley published *Thoughts upon Slavery*, which drew heavily on Benezet's work. The American Quaker then reprinted the English Methodist's pamphlet in Philadelphia, more than doubling its length with additional commentary and supplementary extracts from other writers. This transatlantic collaboration undoubtedly contributed to the rise in antislavery sentiment among Methodists on both sides of the Atlantic in the ensuing years.[26]

Meanwhile, Benezet was further radicalized by his correspondence with Sharp. In January 1774, Sharp had railed against colonial laws that permitted sheriffs and jailors to arrest Black people whom they suspected were runaway slaves. Such practices, Sharp exclaimed, "are expressly contrary to the Divine Law!" He then included the text of Deuteronomy 23:16: "*Thou shalt not deliver unto his Master* the Servant *which is escaped* from his Master unto thee." Sharp insisted that this "Moral Law," unlike ceremonial laws and specific Old Testament privileges that were peculiar to the Jews, "must be *ever* binding." He believed this scripture justified the actions of "those persons who think it their Duty to *protect Slaves* that have escaped from their Masters." This biblicist argument in turn gave Benezet "uncommon satisfaction"; he promised it "will be made use of to profit in these parts." He later told Samuel Allinson, "I showed it to Dr. Rush; and inquiring whether we should publish it in the prints, he replied: 'They would knock us on the head if we did.'" Although Benezet agreed not to publicly encourage aiding runaways, he circulated manuscript copies of Sharp's Deuteronomy-based argument.

While early abolitionists did not publicly aid fugitives unless they had a legal claim to freedom, they were prepared to give clandestine support based on religious conviction.[27]

Interracial Activism in New England

Abolitionism in New England remained largely distinct from the Quaker-coordinated activism of the mid-Atlantic and Upper South, and involved African Americans playing a more prominent role. In 1773 and 1774, people of color produced several legislative petitions, public addresses, and other publications, making antislavery an unavoidable subject of political discussion. They modeled some of their tactics on those used by the Boston Committee of Correspondence, seeking to tie mobilization against imperial policies to calls for antislavery reform. Meanwhile, individual enslaved people continued suing for freedom through the courts. These various forms of activism involved greater coordination than has been previously realized. Printer Ezekiel Russel served an increasingly important role, linking the different strands of New England abolitionism together. He helped Black petitioners and writers reach white audiences, and disseminated the types of religious and legal arguments that helped sway juries in freedom suits.[28]

The timing of antislavery activism in New England was shaped by the imperial crisis and patriot resistance, which at times stifled abolitionism but ultimately helped inspire new forms of Black activism. In late November 1772, Samuel Adams and the Boston Committee of Correspondence published *The Votes and Proceedings of the Freeholders . . . of Boston*, designed to mobilize patriot opposition to Parliament. The pamphlet proclaimed, "All Persons born in the British American Colonies, are, by the Laws of GOD and Nature, and by the common Law of England . . . entitled, to all the natural, essential, inherent and inseparable Rights, Liberties and Privileges of Subjects born in Great-Britain." The authors then cataloged ways that Parliament was violating colonists' rights in order to "compleat our slavery." The Committee of Correspondence distributed six hundred copies of the pamphlet to town selectmen throughout Massachusetts, calling on them to join with Boston in resisting "the Iron Hand of Oppression." In December and January, town meetings throughout the colony issued resolutions endorsing the Boston pamphlet and instructing their representatives to defend their rights and liberties at the next legislative session. These resolutions often merged the rhetoric of natural rights with religious language. Parliament's revenue laws were "against the natural rights of man, and in open violation of the laws of God," according to the inhabitants of Petersham, in Worcester County.[29]

As during the earlier phases of the imperial crisis, New England patriots looked to the Lord for deliverance. They called on their fellow colonists to "humble themselves before almighty God" and pray "for those special and remarkable interpositions of divine providence, grace and mercy, which have so often saved New-England." The townspeople of Marlborough knew that Thomas Hutchinson, the royal governor, would refuse to authorize a public fast day, but they hoped the individual towns would "set apart a day of fasting to humble ourselves before Almighty God, and likewise to implore the assistance of the Ruler above the Skies." Sermons reinforced the link between patriot resistance and appeals to God. One of the most popular, *An Oration on the Beauties of Liberty, or the Essential Rights of the Americans*, based on a December sermon by the Baptist minister John Allen, quickly went through multiple printings.[30] When the next legislative session began, Massachusetts patriots were prepared to forcefully defend their God-given natural rights against imperial oppression.

Against this backdrop, Black people in Massachusetts organized an antislavery petitioning effort, the first of its kind directed at a colonial legislature. A Black man named Felix, on behalf of "many Slaves, living in the town of Boston, and other towns," submitted an antislavery petition to the legislature on the first day of its session, January 6, 1773. In later documents, Felix included the surname Holbrook, and he may have been enslaved or employed by Abia Holbrook, a Boston schoolmaster; such employment might account for his literacy. In any case, the text of the petition demonstrates the Black activists' awareness of both the local political controversies and the nascent transatlantic antislavery movement. Likely thinking of James Swan in Boston, Anthony Benezet in Philadelphia, and Granville Sharp in London, the petitioners thanked God for inspiring "the Hearts of Multitudes on both Sides of the Water . . . who have pleaded our Cause." Appealing to the legislators' sense of "Humanity and justice," they requested "such Relief as is consistent with your Wisdom, justice, and Goodness." The enslaved activists used religious language throughout the petition, noting for example that God was "no respecter of person" (Acts 10:34). They also emphasized their own "desire to bless God" and argued that they would be better able to perform their Christian duties as freemen. Although written in a deferential tone, the petition implicitly critiqued white Christian patriots' hypocritical behavior.[31]

An unidentified white ally using the pseudonym "Hume" endorsed the petition in a letter that was delivered to the legislature and published in the *Massachusetts Spy*. Hume explicitly connected the Black activists' petition to the imperial crisis and the *Somerset* decision. Noting that patriots routinely defended their colony's "charter rights" against imperial interference, Hume argued that hereditary slavery was "in direct opposition" to the Massachusetts Bay charter. According to the colony's charter, the children of all inhabitants "shall have and enjoy all the liberties and immunities of *free* and natural subjects of the realm of England." Hume then applied the logic of the *Somerset* ruling to the colony: "*No person can be held as slaves otherwise than by an express law of the country he lives in*, and that there is any such law in the province of the *Massachusetts Bay*, I absolutely deny." Moreover, slavery was "expressly against the laws of God" and "incompatible with the laws which Christ delivered." Noting that town meetings were "daily" issuing resolutions defending their own rights as English subjects, Hume called on the legislature to act consistently and recognize the Black colonists' God-given right to freedom, which he believed was also affirmed by the Massachusetts charter.[32]

The legislature spent most of January arguing with Governor Hutchinson, but it also took Felix Holbrook's petition under consideration at the end of the month. Within a week, the legislators drafted a new bill "to prevent the Importation of Negro Slaves."[33] As with similar bills in 1767 and 1771, this action was largely symbolic and provided no relief to those who were currently enslaved in the colony. Moreover, it would have permitted Massachusetts slave traders to continue their lucrative involvement in the slave trade between Africa and other British colonies (especially in the Caribbean). Nonetheless, the bill is significant as the first legislation in America drafted in response to Black petitioners.

The Black activists sought greater reform and worked with white allies to mobilize public support. In early February 1773, printer Ezekiel Russell advertised the sale of *The Appendix: Or, Some Observations on the Expediency of the Petition of the Africans*. Russell had printed James Swan's antislavery pamphlet the year before, and had also served as one of Phillis Wheatley's earliest publishers. The new pamphlet reflected the progression of his involvement in the antislavery cause and seems to have been intended as a sequel or appendix to Swan's *Dissuasion to Great-Britain and the Colonies*. The new pamphlet included Felix Holbrook's petition, the letter by "Hume," and several new antislavery pieces. The pamphlet's introduction began by denouncing the hypocrisy of colonists "who *call* themselves Christians" yet enslaved others while "*talking* of *Liberty*." An essay by "The Sons of Africa" used providentialist language to demand reform. Slavery violated the Golden Rule, "and for such Iniquity we have the utmost Reason to expect that God will visit us with his righteous Judgments," the author(s) warned. In order to "avert those deserved Judgments," the legislature needed to not only end slave importations but also "relieve those who are now in *Bondage* in this Province." Such rhetoric, however, inspired only tepid support in the legislature. The Massachusetts House of Representatives passed its slave trade bill at the end of February but still did nothing to address the plight of those already enslaved in the colony. Even this narrow bill again amounted to nothing, as the legislative session ended in March without the Council Board (the upper house of the legislature) agreeing to it.[34] The following month, Felix Holbrook and three other Black men—Peter Bestes, Sambo Freeman, and Chester Joie—convinced James Swan to issue an abridged version of his 1772 antislavery pamphlet so that they could send "a copy to each town." On April 20, 1773, they also printed a circular letter addressed to legislators and town hall meetings throughout the state, distributing them along with Swan's pamphlet.[35]

The April circular illustrates the ways that Black abolitionists took advantage of the imperial crisis, drew on the transatlantic antislavery movement, and appropriated the tactics and rhetoric of the Boston Committee of Correspondence. Referring to the town hall resolutions from December and January, they used ironic flattery to press patriots to live up to their natural rights rhetoric: "We expect great things from men who have made such a noble stand against the designs of their fellow-men to enslave them." The Black men also noted that "even the Spaniards, who have not those sublime ideas of freedom that English men have," allowed their slaves to earn money one day each week, which they could use to gradually "purchase the residue of their time." The Black activists' detailed knowledge of this Spanish policy almost certainly came from Granville Sharp via Anthony Benezet's antislavery network. Sharp had discussed the policy in his first letter to Benezet, extracts of which had recently appeared in several Massachusetts newspapers. The Black activists, some of whom had likely been born in Africa, also expressed a desire "to transport ourselves to some part of the coast of Africa, where we propose a settlement." They concluded the circular by asking the representatives to share it with their constituents so that the individual towns could then issue "instructions relative to us." One sympathetic legislator, Samuel Dexter, later recalled that a Black man—"Newton Prince, lemon merchant"—had approached him outside of the legislative chamber and "very politely presented the pamphlet."[36] Dexter's reference to Prince makes it clear that although only four names appeared on the circular letter, other Black activists were involved as well.

The Reverend John Allen reinforced the Black abolitionists' call for patriot consistency, in an expanded fourth edition of his popular pamphlet, *An Oration on the Beauties of Liberty*, which Ezekiel Russell printed in May 1773. In several short antislavery essays appended to the pamphlet, Allen denounced hypocritical patriots who complained of political slavery while ignoring the plight of Black people "held in REAL *Slavery*." Allen warned that slavery would "ruin *America*" unless "every Christian and Son of Liberty" followed the demand of Isaiah 58:6: "*Loose the bands of wickedness, undo the heavy burdens, let the oppressed go free, that ye break every yoke.*" The pamphlet then concluded by reprinting the Black petitioners' circular letter.[37] The pamphlets by Allen and Swan, along with the Black activists' circular, helped mobilize antislavery public opinion.

At least five of the town meetings held during the second half of May 1773 instructed their representatives in the legislature to support abolition in some form. Residents of Salem denounced the slave trade as "repugnant to the natural rights of mankind" while those of Medford referred to it as "that most cruel, inhuman, and unchristian practice." Residents of Leicester described slavery as an institution that was "illegally" tolerated by the "custom of the country." They proposed legislation recognizing that the children of slaves "should be free at the same age that the children of white people are." Sandwich residents similarly believed that slaves' children should be "free at 21 years of age." Residents of Pembroke wrote: "We think the Negro Petition Reasonable—agreeable to natural Justice and the precepts of the Gospel." They hoped the legislature would devise a plan for the "total abolition of Slavery." Massachusetts patriots could then "with humble confidence look up to the Great Arbiter of Heaven and Earth" to deliver them from parliamentary oppression. The instructions from the Pembroke town meeting illustrate the leading antislavery impulses of the era: providentialist interpretations of events and Black activism.[38]

Yet these impulses remained insufficient, and most town meetings left no record of their reactions to the antislavery petitions. At the end of May, the legislature did establish a new committee to draft another antislavery bill, but it again limited the bill's focus to slave importations without addressing either the plight of enslaved people within Massachusetts or the role of local slave traders supplying African captives to other colonies. Felix Holbrook and the other Black activists desired broader reforms, and soon reprinted their April circular letter in local newspapers and submitted a second petition to the legislature on June 25, 1773.[39]

This petition—which also appeared in Boston's *Massachusetts Spy* and Salem's *Essex Gazette*—was Black activists' most assertive statement yet. They began by expressing their conviction that they had "in common with all other men a natural right to be free." Then they challenged the legality of hereditary slavery in Massachusetts: "We are informed, there is no law of this province, whereby our masters can claim our services; mere custom is the tyrant that keeps us in bondage." This statement clearly alluded to recent freedom suits in Massachusetts as well as the *Somerset* decision in England. The enslaved petitioners called on the legislature to pass a law "enabling all the slaves throughout this province, to demand and obtain their freedom from their masters." They had apparently rethought their embrace of African emigration since writing their circular letter in April. Once freed, they expected to be "made free-men of this community, and be entitled to all the privileges and immunities of its free and natural born subjects." Furthermore, they hoped the legislature would "give and grant to us some part of the unimproved land, belonging to the province" as "some compensation for our toils and sufferings." Nonetheless, they closed by saying they would accept transportation to their "native country" if the government could not provide them with land in Massachusetts. The Massachusetts legislature referred the petition to a committee but delayed further consideration until the next session, in January 1774.[40]

In the meantime, abolition remained a subject of public interest, likely due to the petitions and publications by Black activists and their white allies. In July 1773, Harvard College's commencement ceremonies included a public debate between two graduates over whether slavery in Massachusetts was "agreeable to the law of nature." The antislavery side was taken by Theodore Parsons, whose father, Moses, was a Congregationalist minister in Newbury (Essex County) and whose brother, Theophilus, would serve as legal counsel for at least five enslaved plaintiffs in freedom suits during the Revolutionary War. Unsurprisingly, Theodore merged natural rights ideology and religious rhetoric during the 1773 debate. Insisting that Black and white people shared the "same common parent," Parsons expressed his "painful astonishment, that in this enlightened age and land, where the principles of natural and civil Liberty, and consequently the natural rights of mankind are so generally understood, the case of these unhappy *Africans* should gain no more attention." His opponent (and close friend), Eliphalet Pearson, defended slavery primarily by arguing that Black people enslaved in Massachusetts were better off than those who remained in the "savage barbarity" of Africa. In response, Parsons drew extensively on Anthony Benezet's *Some Historical Account*, attributing African wars to the influence of European slave traders. The debate ended without a clear winner, but with the focus having shifted away from abstract principles to disagreement over the relative "misery" of Africans in their native land and in Massachusetts. Reflecting the growing level of public interest in the subject, the debate was soon published in pamphlet form.[41]

In August 1773, an unidentified Black man joined the print debate via an essay in the *Boston Gazette*. Using the New Testament as a counter to Old Testament dispensations regarding slavery, he reminded readers that "Jesus the indiscriminate Saviour of Jew and Gentile, of White and Black, has Commanded that all men do unto others as they would have others do to them." After condemning hypocritical slaveholding "Sons of Liberty," he warned: "May not the late Troubles be esteem'd as Ordered by Heaven to open Men's Eyes, and bring them to a Sense of their Duty towards us? and if they regard not this Providence, may they not look for more Distressing Judgments?"[42] This essay thus reflected the biblicist and providentialist arguments that were central to abolitionism.

Black activists also continued attacking slavery through the courts, where they achieved a new level of success in the post-*Somerset* era. Traditional accounts of the abolition of slavery in Massachusetts have long pointed to a series of freedom suits in 1781–1783 that reportedly established the view that the state constitution of 1780 had rendered slavery unconstitutional.[43] Recent scholarship, however, suggests the process of abolition was already underway before 1780. Based on Jeanne Pickering's research on freedom suits in Essex County, it appears that 1772–1773 was the turning point. The 1772 case of *Caesar v. Taylor* (discussed in Chapter 3) may have been anomalous and likely hinged on Caesar's contract with Samuel Taylor, but the next year another enslaved man named Caesar struck a lasting blow against hereditary slavery in the case of *Caesar [Hendrick] v. Greenleaf*.[44] This case and subsequent victories appear to have relied on the "*Somerset* principle" (that slavery depended on positive law) in conjunction with religious arguments that gained salience during the imperial crisis.

Caesar Hendrick, who was born in Massachusetts around 1738, sued his enslaver, Richard Greenleaf, in March 1773, seeking liberty and £50 in damages. For his legal counsel, he recruited John Lowell Jr., the minister's son who had successfully argued *Caesar v. Taylor*. At the trial, in September

1773, Greenleaf produced a bill of sale from 1754 showing that he had paid £36 for the "molatto slave Casar of about sixteen years of age." Greenleaf's attorney (Daniel Farnham) also cited Massachusetts laws tolerating slavery, and he noted that slavery was common throughout history and sanctioned in the Old Testament. Although records of arguments in *Caesar* [*Hendrick*] *v. Greenleaf* are limited, they give a sense of the antislavery legal reasoning Lowell employed. He was clearly familiar with the *Somerset* decision, as reported in local newspapers along with *An Argument in the Case of James Sommersett*, a pamphlet authored by Francis Hargrave, one of James Somerset's lawyers.[45]

The crux of Lowell's argument was that *hereditary* slavery lacked a statutory basis in Massachusetts and was thus illegal because it violated English common law. Drawing on the precedent of the *Somerset* decision, Lowell claimed that the colony's laws "establish Slavery only by implication if it does at all." He emphasized that the 1641 law permitted "no slaves but those made by their own consent or by taking in lawful war." Neither description applied to Hendrick, who was born in Massachusetts. Citing the "Somersett case," Lowell argued that "liberty is not to be taken from him by implication of law. There must be express law for it." Knowing that the Massachusetts custom of treating Black slavery as hereditary was commonly justified by reference to Leviticus and Noah's Curse, Lowell also invoked the Bible and echoed common antislavery arguments that had appeared in pamphlets and newspapers: "The precepts of revealed law, golden rule of the gospel are that we are not to sell our brethren, that we are to do as we would be done unto." Additionally, Lowell produced documents showing that Hendrick had been baptized and was "a member of Mr. Parson's church." (Lowell was likely referring to the Newbury church led by the Reverend Jonathan Parsons, brother of Moses and uncle of Theodore and Theophilus.) In sum, Lowell argued that hereditary slavery was illegitimate under the laws of Massachusetts and of God, especially when imposed by Christians on other Christians.[46] Jurors apparently found this argument convincing; they liberated Hendrick and awarded him £18 in damages.

Although this ruling did not establish a formal legal precedent that courts were bound to follow, it was nonetheless a watershed moment in hindsight, and some contemporaries also recognized its significance. It seems that Anthony Benezet heard about the case while it was still ongoing. In August 1773 he informed Granville Sharp: "I am told a certain Lawyer, there [i.e. Massachusetts], has undertaken to answer on behalf of such Negroes as have applied to him for their freedom. He puts the Masters upon the proof, what legal right they have to their Negroes service. This will, I trust, prove a favourable opening on behalf of freedom." After Hendrick won his freedom, at least two Massachusetts newspapers published brief accounts of this "novel case," something that had not been done for earlier freedom suits.[47] This coverage helped spread the emerging conviction that *hereditary* slavery was illegal in Massachusetts. In 1795, the Reverend Jeremy Belknap emphasized the role of "*publick opinion*" in abolishing Massachusetts slavery. He stated that by the mid-1770s, sympathetic juries routinely ruled that "though the slavery of the parents be admitted, yet no disability of the kind could descend to the children."[48] In other words, even before the 1780 state constitution (often portrayed as laying the foundation for judicial abolition), jurors in the Bay Colony were determining that slavery was not hereditary. The shift in public opinion and jury behavior was not the inevitable result of the patriots' natural rights rhetoric. Rather, it was a process heavily shaped by Black activism, abolitionists' efforts to publicize the *Somerset* decision, and religious arguments pioneered by Quakers about slavery and the providential meaning of the imperial crisis.[49]

Antislavery sentiment grounded in providentialism increased during the fall of 1773 as the new East India Tea Act appeared to indicate that God was still using Parliament as a rod with which to chastise the colonists. An essay by "Justin" (likely the Reverend Samuel Webster) in the *Essex Journal* denounced slavery as unchristian and asked, "How can we look up to Heaven for the removal of those judgements with which we are afflicted, whilst we continue plagues and scourges to others?" Paraphrasing Isaiah 26:9, he added, "Happy would it be for us if, whilst God's judgments are abroad in the earth, we might learn justice and righteousness towards our fellow-creatures!"[50] In other words, the colonists should embrace antislavery reform lest God's chastisement become even worse. The Massachusetts legislature was not prepared to act on such sentiments, but it appears these ideas influenced juries in freedom suits.

During this time, Phillis Wheatley had been busy advancing the cause of Black freedom in her own way. She had spent the summer of 1773 in England, arranging the publication of her book, *Poems on Various Subjects, Religious and Moral*, with the support of her patron, Selina Hastings, the Countess of Huntingdon. Phillis also toured London with Granville Sharp, met with Benjamin Franklin and other statesmen, and formally received her freedom from the Wheatleys. When she returned to Boston in September, newspapers announced the return of "Phillis, the extraordinary poetical genius." Copies of her book arrived in December and were on sale by January 1774. The volume, which included a portrait of Wheatley and a biographical sketch, had antislavery implications simply as a demonstration of Africans' intellectual potential. Moreover, Wheatley included poems alluding to her personal experience of being "snatch'd from Afric's fancy'd happy seat," and of imagining the "sorrows" and "misery" her parents must have felt.[51]

Wheatley worked with other Black New Englanders and white allies to promote her book and other forms of activism. Her correspondents and collaborators included Obour Tanner, a Black woman from Newport, Rhode Island, and the Reverend Samuel Hopkins, Tanner's minister. Tanner and Hopkins helped distribute Wheatley's book in Rhode Island while Wheatley helped promote a missionary venture Hopkins was organizing with the Reverends Ezra Stiles and Levi Hart of Connecticut. The white ministers hoped to send at least two African-born former slaves back to Africa as missionaries. In a fundraising appeal from August 1773, they described spreading the Gospel in Africa as the "best compensation" that could be made to Africa for the "iniquity of the *slave trade*." Wheatley praised their "laudable design" and quoted Psalm 68:31: "Ethiopia Shall Soon Stretch forth her hands unto God." She also used the opportunity to point out the hypocrisy of many professed white Christians, writing that "Europe and America have long been fed with the heavenly provision, and I fear they loathe it, while Africa is perishing with a Spiritual Famine."[52]

Wheatley was even more critical of white patriots in a letter to the Reverend Samson Occom, a Mohegan Indian and Presbyterian minister in Connecticut. The letter subverted white New Englanders' conception of themselves as God's chosen people being oppressed by a tyrannical Parliament. Comparing Africans to the Israelites and referring to slaveholding Americans as "our modern Egyptians," Wheatley predicted that "God [will] grant Deliverance in his own Way and Time, and get him honour upon all those whose Avarice impels them to countenance and help forward the Calamities of their fellow Creatures." Whereas white patriots hoped for divine aid, Wheatley imagined righteous retribution that would liberate their Black captives. Occom decided to publish the letter, which appeared in at least eleven newspapers and thus reached a large audience.[53]

Felix Holbrook and his collaborators also remained active. In early January 1774, Samuel Adams, who had recently helped organize the Boston Tea Party, reported that "the Negroes" were "very solicitous" as the new legislative session approached. On January 26, the first day of the session, Felix Holbrook and the other Black petitioners presented a memorial intended to spur renewed discussion on their petition from June 1773. They called on the legislators to restore their "freedom, which we as men, and by nature, have a right to demand." Comparing their cause to the patriots' own petitions to King George III complaining of parliamentary usurpations, the Black petitioners hoped "that his Majesty would hear your prayers, and that you would hear ours." In response, the legislature instructed a committee to resume considering their antislavery requests.[54]

In February, the *Massachusetts Spy* published an essay by "A Son of Africa" designed to encourage legislative action. The author refuted biblical justifications for slavery and dismissed slaveholders' claim that slavery was an effective means of conversion, retorting that "christianity is made a cloak to fill their coffers and to screen their villainy." Implicitly referring to freedom suits in the colony and the *Somerset* decision in England, he argued that the "custom" of slavery was actually illegal: "I am informed there is no law in the kingdom of Great-Britain, nor in this province, to hold a man in perpetual slavery. Whatever is contrary to the law of God and the English constitution must be deemed unlawful."[55] Whereas Felix Holbrook's first petition from a year earlier had deferentially requested relief, he and other Black activists were now insisting that slavery was already illegal in Massachusetts.

Even as abolitionists pressed the legislature to act against slavery, they continued pursuing judicial abolition as well. The same issue of the *Massachusetts Spy* that included the essay by "A Son of Africa" also advertised that Ezekiel Russell had just reprinted an American version of Francis Hargrave's pamphlet about the *Somerset* decision. The advertisement was unusual in its scope and detail, taking up more than half a column of newspaper text to promote a single pamphlet. It indicates that Russell also viewed his work as directly supporting the efforts of enslaved plaintiffs and their lawyers in freedom suits. The advertisement recommended the pamphlet especially "to the perusal of the gentlemen of the law," while also boasting that Russell was selling the pamphlet for a single shilling—half the price of the English version—so that it would be affordable to all.[56]

Although Massachusetts freedom suits are often seen by scholars as ad hoc and disconnected, their proponents viewed them as part of a concerted campaign. Russel's advertisement openly espoused the goal of "abolishing [the] iniquitous and disgraceful practice of *enslaving* our fellow men." Indeed, the advertisement for Hargrave's pamphlet pointed specifically to an ongoing freedom suit initiated by a Black man named Abraham Colden against his enslaver, Dr. Benjamin Stockbridge. Russell prayed that "such a set of Jurors may be found, on the trial of *Abraham*, who uninfluenced either by interest or party, will venture to give a verdict in favour of liberty, justice, and humanity." He hoped this case would serve as an American equivalent of *Somerset*, proclaiming that "perhaps on these two important and decisive trials may depend the future happiness of millions yet unborn." In the end, Abraham Colden's case was repeatedly delayed until he won his freedom in 1777 when Stockbridge failed to show up at court, rendering it less climactic than abolitionists had initially hoped.[57] However, in the summer of 1774, Russell was able to help the Reverend John Allen publicize the result of another freedom suit in *The Watchman's Alarm*, a pamphlet that combined patriot critique of British policy with antislavery arguments. Allen included a footnote praising the "*referrees*" in an Essex County freedom suit who had liberated a "negro servant," Sampson, from his enslaver, Caleb Dodge. According to *The Watchman's Alarm*, the case's outcome indicated there was "no law in the province to hold a man to serve for life."[58] Like other freedom suits from the era, Sampson's case did not have any formal legal implications beyond the specific parties involved, but abolitionists magnified the informal power of freedom suits by disseminating news of them. The knowledge that some juries believed that slaveholding (or at least *hereditary* slavery) was both unchristian and unsupported by positive law in Massachusetts could encourage other potential jurors to rule the same way in similar cases. This trend could also convince slaveholders to acquiesce when their bondspeople threatened to sue if they were not liberated or paid wages, for the slaveholders might expect juries to sympathize with enslaved plaintiffs.

Abolitionists also continued pressing the legislature to take formal action against slavery. In early March 1774, with imperial relations deteriorating, "The Preacher" warned in the *Massachusetts Spy* that slaveholding was the "*Achan* in the camp," undermining their struggle against parliamentary tyranny. Contemporary readers would have understood the reference to chapters 6 and 7 of the book of Joshua, in which God temporarily abandons the Israelites after a warrior named Achan covetously takes some forbidden plunder from Jericho. The Israelites do not regain the Lord's favor until they stone Achan to death and destroy the "accursed things" he had taken. Based on this analogy, until the colonists abolished slavery, their prayers to heaven "must be abominable in the sight of *Him* who hateth all iniquity."[59] Some legislators apparently shared this sentiment, proposing legislation that would have not only banned slave importations but also made "provision for the relief of children of such as are already subject to slavery." In other words, they sought to end the custom of treating enslavement as hereditary. However, legislators subsequently struck out this section, and the final bill only prohibited slave importations. Thus the majority of legislators continued denying calls for emancipation from Black petitioners and their white allies. On March 9, the outgoing governor, Thomas Hutchinson, dismissed the legislature without signing the slave trade bill into law.[60] His successor, General Thomas Gage, arrived in mid-May, charged by Parliament with suppressing the rebellious spirit of Massachusetts patriots.

Although white patriots greeted Governor Gage with disdain, some Black colonists apparently hoped he would support their cause. On May 25, 1774, the day the legislature reconvened, the Black activists tried submitting another petition to the legislature and new governor. This petition, based partly on the one from the previous June, called on Gage and the legislature to restore "our Natural right our freedoms." The Black activists continued insisting that slavery was illegitimate, especially as a hereditary status. Even if Massachusetts laws had tolerated the purchase of enslaved foreigners, they argued "there never was aney [law] to inslave our children for life when Born in a free Countrey." They hoped Black people born in Massachusetts would "be set at liberty at the yeare of Twenty one." It is important to note that they were not calling for a gradual abolition law that would apply only to children born *after* its passage; rather, they were demanding the legislature recognize that hereditary slavery had *never* been legal in Massachusetts, and that all people born in the colony—white or Black—were entitled to full liberty at adulthood. The legislature made no record of receiving the petition, focusing instead on rallying the rest of the colonies against the Boston Port Act (one of the Coercive Acts or "Intolerable Acts"), which Parliament had passed to punish the city for the Tea Party.[61] Gage then adjourned the session and had the legislature relocate to Salem.

Felix Holbrook or one of his allies followed the legislature to Salem and succeeded in submitting a newly revised version of the petition. In it, the Black activists requested "relief" from their bondage and thanked the "honourable gentlemen who spoke so much in our favour last sessions."[62] This time, the legislature responded by passing a bill on June 16 that banned slave importations but again offered no relief to the colony's current slaves or their posterity. In any case, Gage dissolved the legislature the next day without signing the bill into law.[63]

Most white patriots remained preoccupied with their own metaphorical enslavement. On June 17, 1774—the day that Gage dissolved the legislature—the legislators adopted resolutions condemning Parliament's effort to "establish arbitrary Governments and reduce the inhabitants to Slavery." They proposed that a congress of delegates from the various colonies meet in Philadelphia to collectively defend "their Just Rights and Liberties." Seeking divine aid, they also called for another day of fasting and prayer. On the July 14 fast day, ministers throughout Massachusetts condemned Parliament's efforts to "enslave" the colonists and called on patriots to earn God's favor through repentance and reform. Their sermons repeated the notion that New Englanders had a special covenant with God but that the Lord was nonetheless chastising them for their sins.[64]

At least a few white colonists pointed to slaveholding as their worst sin and argued that God would not answer their prayers until they embraced antislavery reform. In his fast-day sermon, the Reverend Jeremy Belknap lamented that the colonies contained thousands of people "detained in bondage and slavery for no other crimes than that their skin is of a darker color than our own." He described parliamentary oppression as retaliatory justice for white colonists' oppression of Black people: "As we have made them slaves without their consent and without any crime, so it is just in God to permit other men to make slaves of us." Others advanced antislavery ideas in print. Writing in the *Essex Journal*, Benjamin Colman employed Ephesians 2:14 (about Christ destroying the wall of partition between Jew and Gentile) to refute slaveholders' use of Leviticus 25:45 to justify enslaving African heathens. Colman, a church deacon and son of a minister, also invoked Joshua 6–7 to describe slaveholding as the "accursed thing that is the trouble of our land, and for which God is at this day contending with us." Given that God was punishing the colonists for the sin of slavery, Colman exclaimed, "I confess I blush, when I hear a proposal for a provincial fast, (although I am as desirous of it as others) when I read the 58th chapter of Isaiah." He believed that white Americans could not expect God's favor until they "let the oppressed go free." The Reverend John Allen also quoted Isaiah 58:6 and mocked the "fasting, praying, non-importing, non-exporting, remonstrating, resolving, and pleading" of patriots who refused to support emancipation.[65]

Similar points were made in the *Essex Journal* (Figure 6) in August 1774 by Caesar Sarter, a formerly enslaved African-born man living in Newburyport. He was perhaps the same Caesar who had been liberated in *Caesar v. Taylor* in 1772 and was apparently connected to Felix Holbrook and the other

THE Essex Journal AND Merimack Packet: OR The Massachusetts and New-Hampshire General Advertiser.

Vol. I. WEDNESDAY, August 17, 1774. No. 35.

Messrs. PRINTERS,

... from an African.

CÆSAR SARTER.

Newbury Port, August 12th, 1774.

A writer in the London Advertiser, who takes the signature of Moderator, concludes an ingenious and spirited essay on American affairs, as follows:

SHOULD it happen, and that it may is not beyond the bounds of possibility that a coalition of all the provinces of America should be formed into one unanimous alliance to oppose the measures of our government, and join in a determined resolution to cut off all intercourse under *dependant circumstances* with Great Britain; should the mystic roll of fate bring to pass this, which yet exists but in supposition, how fruitless then would be all our attempts to assert a sovereign right to America, or regain its loss: We might then remain envious spectators of her flourishing situation, and in that situation perceive the visible traces of ill policy and misguided administration. It has been advanced, with a view perhaps to future contingencies, that Great-Britain could suffer no loss, but, on the contrary, be a gainer by the independence of her American acquisitions. This assertion, considering the late [illegible] ready compliance with what is foreseen to be inevitable, for without a revolution in nature, or the supernatural aid of miracles, America may (and the belief is not singular) in future times have the seat of empire within herself, and instead of receiving laws from the island of Great Britain, may enforce a code of her own through her almost boundless continent. This conjecture is far from beyond probability; the present appearance of things carry with them an evident tendency towards its completion; the present perhaps is the important crisis, on which depends the continuance of our possession of the American colonies, or their total independence; they know their strength, and will if incensed, call it forth; our policy, therefore, should be to bind them by ties of affection to the mother country, by gentle, by persuasive measures, but on no account to harbour the most distant idea of adopting compulsatory ones; palliative means may possess them with gratitude, coercive ones will fill them with vindictive rage. Great-Britain may retain the con-

Figure 6. Caesar Sarter's antislavery essay on the front page of the *Essex Journal* (17 August 1774). Courtesy of the American Antiquarian Society.

Black petitioners. Sarter used providentialist arguments to encourage white support for "*our humble petition*." If white patriots sought to protect their own liberties, he instructed them: "*As the first step let the oppressed Africans be liberated; then, and not till then, may you with confidence and consistency of conduct, look to Heaven for a blessing on your endeavours.*" He cautioned that legislators who "*harden your hearts, and turn a deaf ear to our complaints*," might suffer the same fate as the Egyptian pharaoh.[66] The same issue of the *Essex Journal* advertised the publication of a recent sermon by the Reverend Nathaniel Niles, also of Newburyport. In the sermon's conclusion, Niles cautioned that "God gave us liberty, and we have enslaved our fellow-men. May we not fear that the law of retaliation is about to be executed on us?" The colonists could not expect God to protect their own liberty unless they would "grant it to others."[67] Black and white abolitionists in Massachusetts clearly hoped that biblicist and providentialist rhetoric would galvanize more white patriots to support antislavery reform.

Following Governor Gage's dissolution of the legislature, patriot politicians began meeting as the Provincial Congress of Massachusetts in October 1774. The insurgent legislators forbade residents from consuming tea, which they denounced as "the baneful vehicle of a corrupt and venal administration, for the purpose of introducing despotism and slavery into this once happy country." They also called for another day of fasting and prayer. On October 26, two days after these proclamations appeared in newspapers, the Provincial Congress received a letter addressed to its chaplain, the Reverend Nathaniel Appleton Sr. (whose son, the author of *Brief Considerations on Slavery* in 1767, was now serving in the congress). The letter, as summarized in the legislative journal, suggested "the propriety, that while we are attempting to free ourselves from our present embarrassments, and preserve ourselves from slavery, that we also take into consideration the state and circumstances of the negro slaves in this province." In response, someone—perhaps the younger Appleton, though the records do not show—proposed creating a committee to consider the matter, but this proposal was rejected after a brief unrecorded debate. Massachusetts's patriot politicians would not consider antislavery legislation again until 1777.[68]

Legislative progress thus remained stalled despite the growing public support for antislavery reform. Black activists had submitted numerous petitions and addresses to the legislature while publicly distributing other antislavery writings. A growing number of white colonists supported antislavery efforts, often inspired by their conviction that oppressive imperial taxes and laws reflected divine chastisement for slavery. They expressed their antislavery views in sermons, newspapers, and jury verdicts but had little influence in the legislature. Of course, the legislature had passed bans on the slave trade only to be thwarted by royal governors. Yet the Black petitioners had always focused on slavery itself, which the legislature had largely ignored. The legislators' focus on slave importations allowed them to take a nominally antislavery stance with very little sacrifice, as their bills always allowed slaveholders to keep their property and permitted slave traders to continue servicing the lucrative markets in other colonies. Antislavery reform in Massachusetts was a grassroots movement that most politicians refused to support in any meaningful way.

As imperial tensions escalated, some Black New Englanders welcomed the prospect of war. In September 1774, Abigail Adams warned her husband John, who was attending the (first) Continental Congress in Philadelphia, of a "conspiracy of the Negroes." She reported: "They conducted in this way—got an Irishman to draw up a petition to the Governor telling him they would fight for him provided he would arm them and engage to liberate them." The accuracy of this rumor is unknown, but it clearly alarmed Abigail. Nonetheless, she also indicated a level of empathy for the slaves, adding: "It allways appear a most iniquitious Scheme to me—fight ourselfs for what we are daily robbing and plundering from those who have as good a right to freedom as we have. You know my mind upon this Subject."[69] Abigail's final remark perhaps indicated her earlier disappointment at John's role as a regular defender of slaveholders in Massachusetts freedom suits.

While Massachusetts experienced the highest level of abolitionist activity, especially by Black people, similar forms of agitation occurred in other New England colonies. Particularly in Connecticut, antislavery essays (and proslavery responses) became increasingly common in newspapers. In May 1773, the Connecticut legislature received a "Negro's memorial" that apparently included a proposed gradual emancipation bill. Legislators, however, voted to postpone any discussion until their October session and then let the matter drop.[70] Abolitionists coordinated the publication of antislavery newspaper essays throughout the colony in hopes of shaping public opinion and spurring legislative action.

Connecticut's antislavery movement was coordinated in large part by two ministers, Ebenezer Baldwin of Danbury and Jonathan Edwards Jr. of New Haven, the colonial capital. Edwards's involvement indicated a reversal since 1767, when he had repeatedly given sermons defending slavery and the Atlantic slave trade.[71] There are probably numerous reasons for his change of heart. By 1773, Edwards had spent four years ministering to a mixed-race congregation in New Haven, and it is possible that his Black parishioners led him to feel more empathy for enslaved people. The writings of Anthony Benezet and others may have led Edwards to reevaluate his thinking about the Bible and slavery. Years later, in 1791, he posed the question, "How is it possible, that our fathers and men now alive, universally reputed pious, should hold Negro slaves, and yet be the subjects of real piety?" Paraphrasing Acts 17:30, he answered that "our fathers lived in a *time of ignorance which God winked at; but now he commandeth all men every where to repent* of this wickedness, and *to break off this sin by righteousness.*" God's chastisement of the colonists had revealed slaveholding's sinful nature to them, and thus the revolutionary generation could no longer "sin at so cheap a rate as our fathers." By the winter of 1773–1774, Edwards had dismissed his old rationalizations for slavery and instead proclaimed that God was calling on the colonists to "*let the oppressed go free.*"[72] Along with Baldwin, Edwards published dozens of antislavery pieces in Connecticut newspapers.

Despite the barrage of antislavery publications, the legislature declined to revive discussion of the antislavery petition and bill. Moreover, slaveholders organized a counterattack. Lieutenant Governor Matthew Griswold published six proslavery essays under the pseudonym "Philemon" in the *Connecticut Journal* during January and February 1774. He drew on John Locke to justify the purchase of enslaved African prisoners of war and used Noah's Curse as well as Leviticus 25 to justify their hereditary enslavement, largely ignoring the facts that Locke had opposed hereditary slavery and that other antislavery writers had refuted Old Testament justification for modern slavery. Although Griswold's position was rhetorically weak, Edwards complained to Baldwin that "such is the propensity of many people to y^{t} side of the question, y^{t} they are disposed to embrace every thing written upon y^{t} side, as demonstration."[73] In other words, Edwards had come to recognize that proslavery biblicism—which he had himself previously espoused—distorted scripture but was attractive because it supported slaveholders' self-interest.

In the fall of 1774, Black and white Connecticut abolitionists ramped up their efforts, likely in collaboration with one another. A group of Black activists, led by Bristol Lambee "*in behalf of many others,*" submitted a petition to the local Sons of Liberty in the fall of 1774. The Black abolitionists hoped "that whilst you are consulting, asserting and maintaining your own natural rights against the arbitrary designs of those who would subject you to slavery, that you would think on our unhappy case." Like their brethren in Massachusetts, the Black petitioners also insisted that hereditary slavery was already illegal in Connecticut, "unless mere *custom*, however ill-founded, be deemed *law.*"[74] A writer using the pseudonym "Liberty" in the *Connecticut Gazette* praised the Black petitioners and argued that their request should be granted based on the "principle of justice." Moreover, emancipation would help regain the Lord's favor, for slavery was "the *crying sin* of this land, and the principal cause of all the evils we are threatened with." Edwards and Baldwin also rejoined the fray, drawing heavily on Anthony Benezet's books to attack the slave trade and slaveholding. In October 1774, the Connecticut legislature finally agreed to ban slave importations but did nothing more about slaveholding in the colony.[75] The Reverend Levi Hart of Preston circulated a manuscript asserting that "no just good reason can be given why the Negro Slaves should not be immediately made free, & the accursed thing [Joshua 6:18 . . .] put away from among us."[76] Connecticut legislators, however, showed no interest in further antislavery reform.

Rhode Island also forbade slave importations in 1774, with a law that might give the superficial appearance of strong antislavery commitment among patriot politicians. The law's preamble proclaimed: "Whereas the inhabitants of America are generally engaged in the preservation of their own rights and liberties . . . those who are desirous of enjoying all the advantages of liberty themselves, should be willing to extend personal liberty to others." Some historians have therefore concluded that the law "was prompted by the new equalitarian ideas" and reflected the "secular argument that the slave trade (and, by implication, slavery itself) contradicted the natural rights ideology."[77] Yet such an interpretation obscures the religious impulse behind the law's creation as well as the way patriot politicians had diluted its principles.

The Rhode Island slave trade law was a watered-down version of a proposal by a local Quaker, Moses Brown. The Society of Friends was more prominent in Rhode Island than in the rest of New England, and Quakers had begun petitioning against slavery in 1773. Brown, a former Baptist who had converted to Quakerism and liberated his slaves, corresponded with Anthony Benezet and inserted antislavery essays in local newspapers. He also authored an antislavery resolution at a Providence town meeting in May 1774 that became the preamble of Rhode Island's slave trade law. The legislature, however, ignored the part of the initial resolution that had prposed that "all negroes born in the colony, should be free, after attaining to a certain age." Moreover, Rhode Island legislators framed the law to explicitly permit local slave traders to continue transporting African captives to other colonies. Although slave traders from Rhode Island (like those from Massachusetts) brought few slaves into their own colony, they were heavily involved in the traffic from Africa to the Caribbean. Rhode Island's ban on slave importations thus sacrificed little while protecting the largest and most lucrative part of the trade. Although the law's preamble can give the impression of widespread abolitionist sentiment grounded in natural rights ideology, the actual provisions reveal the limits of antislavery commitments among patriot politicians.[78]

The conservative nature of the Rhode Island law must have frustrated the colony's abolitionists and people of color. The Reverend Samuel Hopkins regretted that many who opposed further slave importations ignored the injustice of slavery within the colonies. In his private correspondence, he insisted that "*all* owners of slaves are under indispensable obligation to free them, whether the public will compensate them, or not; as the slaves have of a just demand for their liberty, and the masters have no right to refuse to set them free one day longer." Hopkins essentially believed that justice warranted immediate emancipation.[79]

Antislavery Prospects on the Eve of War

In September 1774, delegates from twelve colonies attended the (first) Continental Congress in Philadelphia to plan a united response to Parliament's Coercive Acts. They issued a series of resolutions in October, asserting that Parliament's actions during the past decade indicated a "system formed to enslave America." They also planned new boycotts and petitions, tactics that patriots had been employing for years. Some white colonists outside the convention suggested that antislavery reform would be an even more effective means of preserving their own liberty, by winning God to their side. For example, Richard Wells, a Philadelphia Quaker, argued that if the colonies united in opposition to the slave trade, it would "so corroborate our own claims, that I should dare to hope for an intervening arm of Providence to be extended in our favour."[80] Anthony Benezet also lobbied delegates against the slave trade. On October 20, the Continental Congress adopted the Articles of Association, establishing a boycott of English trade, including the importation of slaves. This slave trade ban, in conjunction with antislavery statements by Thomas Jefferson and Benjamin Rush, have led some historians to imagine that patriots were on the verge of embracing more comprehensive antislavery reforms. Such assessments, however, appear unwarranted.

Jefferson's antislavery statements appeared in *A Summary View of the Rights of British America*, written in July 1774. In it, the Virginia slaveholder claimed: "The abolition of domestic slavery is the great object of desire in those colonies, where it was unhappily introduced in their infant state. But previous to the enfranchisement [i.e., liberation] of the slaves we have, it is necessary to exclude all further importations from Africa; yet our repeated attempts to effect this by prohibitions, and by imposing duties which might amount to a prohibition, have been hitherto defeated by his majesty's negative."[81] In response to Jefferson's statement and to antislavery efforts by Virginia Quakers, scholar Gordon Wood claims that "some Virginians hoped that the impending break from Great Britain would allow them not only to end the slave trade but to end the colony's prohibition against manumission."[82] Although Jefferson may have sincerely wished slavery could be abolished, there are numerous reasons to be skeptical of the notion that there was widespread support in Virginia—outside of Quakers and Black people—for abolition or even manumission reform. It is true that Virginian politicians had repeatedly tried to ban slave importations and that the king had prevented such measures, based on the notion that trade regulations should be determined by metropolitan rather than colonial authority. But the laws restricting manumissions—from 1723 and 1741—were local municipal laws that the Virginia legislature could have repealed or amended at any time if it had so chosen. Although a majority of Virginia politicians believed that the continued importations of enslaved Africans were unnecessary and perhaps dangerous, they had no intention of ending slavery itself.

Jefferson's exaggerated claims about abolition were likely designed to "deflect antislavery critiques of the Americans in English pamphlets," as Staughton Lynd and David Waldstreicher suggest.[83] Earlier in 1774, for instance, one English pamphlet had denounced the patriots' natural rights rhetoric as "the most impudent Prostitution of Words that ever was, or can be," for "no People ever so cruelly enslaved their Fellow-Creatures as the *Americans*." And Granville Sharp, the English abolitionist, had just published a pamphlet sympathetic to the colonists but charging that "the toleration of domestic slavery in the Colonies greatly weakens the claim or natural right of our American brethren. Let them put away that accursed thing, that horrible oppression! from among them, before they presume to implore the interposition of divine justice."[84] Jefferson's pamphlet, like the Continental Congress's slave trade ban, allowed white patriots to counter English charges of hypocrisy by shirking moral responsibility for slavery without actually embracing emancipation.

Benjamin Rush was a sincere abolitionist, but he also exaggerated patriots' antislavery sentiment for political reasons. In a letter to Sharp, he touted the congressional slave trade ban, adding: "I venture to predict there will be not a Negro slave in North America in 40 years." Gordon Wood and other scholars cite Rush's letter as evidence of widespread patriot antislavery and optimism.

Wood claims contemporaries believed "that slavery was on its last legs and was dying a natural death." Robert Parkinson reports Rush was "sanguine that the rhetoric of liberty would sweep away all obstacles ahead of it."[85] However, the context of Rush's letter, and the qualifications it contained, indicate that historians have often exaggerated both patriots' commitment to antislavery and abolitionists' naïve optimism. Rush was a patriot first and an abolitionist second, and he clearly hoped that the slave trade ban would impress Sharp, who had had repeatedly lamented the hypocrisy of slaveholding patriots.[86] Like Jefferson, Rush sought to counter British allegations of patriot hypocrisy.

Several of Rush's statements to Sharp were misleading, either reflecting ignorance or conscious duplicity. Rush claimed that the Continental Congress "agreed *never* to import more slaves," without acknowledging that the ban was part of a larger—and temporary—boycott. It would have looked very bad for Congress to specifically exempt the slave trade from the general trade embargo. He also asserted that the ban "was proposed and defended entirely upon *moral* and not political [i.e., expedient] principles."[87] There are no extant records of the actual congressional debate, but Rush's claim is contradicted by Anthony Benezet's description of his own lobbying activities. The Quaker wrote that he frequently warned delegates of the "dreadful situation" created by large numbers of enslaved Africans in the southernmost colonies. As in the past, Benezet pragmatically appealed to white fear of slave revolt in the service of his righteous cause.[88] Rush must also have realized that southern politicians remained committed to preserving slavery itself even as they opposed further slave importations for practical reasons.

Other abolitionists fully recognized the limitations of the Continental Congress's position. Benezet noted that the Articles of Association only applied to twelve colonies (Georgia did not participate in the First Continental Congress), and he complained to Sharp of "no mention being made of ceasing the imports to the West Indies and on the long & extensive river Mississippi, I expect but little good to be done." Moreover, Benezet was already aware of the growing domestic slave trade, through which slaveholders in the mid-Atlantic colonies sold slaves to planters farther south. As he had explained to Sharp in 1773: "Indeed Agents from the Southern Provinces have, for some years past, been employed even in this City and Province [i.e., Philadelphia and Pennsylvania] and given out publick Advertisements for the purchase of all the Slaves, that are to be disposed of, of all ages which they generally purchase at a cheaper rate than from on board the Guinea Vessels."[89] Abolitionists already understood that merely curbing slave importations from abroad would end neither slave trading nor slaveholding. For his part, Sharp praised the Continental Congress's slave importation ban as an initial step but emphasized that "the business is but half done." In a published letter, he called on Americans to adopt a plan of abolition that would liberate the current generation of slaves as well as their offspring.[90]

Antislavery essays in American newspapers also complained that the Continental Congress had not done enough. A writer in the *Pennsylvania Packet* argued that the patriots should "turn their attention towards the Negro Captives, which may be a means (under the all-commanding hand of Providence) to avert the impending scourge." The author concluded by copying the text of Isaiah 58:6, calling on the colonists to "let the oppressed go free."[91] New England newspapers reprinted this piece and published similar sentiments. A writer in the *Essex Gazette* wished the Continental Congress "had taken one Step farther" and "resolved to set at Liberty all those that are now under the cruel Yoke of Oppression and Slavery among us." Doing so would have ended "the very Crime for which God is contending with us." They, too, closed with the text of Isaiah 58:6.[92] Clearly, more and more white colonists were interpreting the imperial crisis the way the Quaker Generation of 1758 had interpreted the French and Indian War: as God's method of awakening white colonists to the injustice of their actions toward Black people. In order to regain the Lord's blessing and protect their own liberty, these antislavery colonists believed that they would need to let the oppressed go free.

The dominant themes of antislavery sentiment are illustrated in an essay, "African Slavery in America," published anonymously in the *Pennsylvania Journal* in March 1775. Since the 1890s, this essay has often been mistakenly attributed to Thomas Paine, who published *Common Sense* in 1776. Due to this attribution, the 1775 essay is sometimes cited as evidence that abolitionism grew out of patriots' rhetoric and "was not confined to Quakers and others on the political margin."[93] However, specialists now conclude that the essay was authored by the Reverend Samuel Hopkins, the Congregationalist minister from Rhode Island. This attribution makes sense, as the substance and style of the essay conform to that of a minister and share little in common with the other writings of Paine (an avowed atheist).[94] "African Slavery in America" centered around the type of biblicist and providentialist arguments that had been the mainstays of antislavery rhetoric for decades. Refuting proslavery claims, Hopkins argued that Old Testament dispensations permitting ancient Israelites to enslave heathens had ended with Christ's sacrifice, which destroyed "distinctions of nations, and privileges of one above others." After demonstrating the sinful nature of slaveholding, Hopkins suggested that the imperial crisis was God's means of chastising the colonists: "How just, how suitable to our crime is the punishment with which providence threatens us? We have enslaved multitudes, and shed much innocent blood in doing it; and now we are threatened with the same." Referring to public fast days, he added: "And while other evils are confessed and bewailed, why not this [i.e., slaveholding] especially . . . which . . . has brought so much guilt on the land?" Hopkins argued that emancipation was necessary to regain the Lord's favor. His emancipation plan was apparently modeled on Anthony Benezet's earlier proposals, with freedpeople receiving land grants "on the frontiers." Hopkin's essay was inserted into the *Pennsylvania Journal* at the request of "A.B." who may have been Benezet himself.[95]

Shortly thereafter, on April 14, Benezet was involved behind the scenes in the creation of the world's first formal antislavery society, the "Society for the Relief of Negroes &c," known later as the Pennsylvania Abolition Society (PAS). Because of the timing—less than a week before the Battles of Lexington and Concord, the PAS is sometimes used to demonstrate that "the Revolution created the first antislavery movement in the history of the world." Yet the group formed in 1775 was not "the first antislavery convention known to humanity," for Quaker committees—not to mention groups of enslaved Black rebels—had long organized against slavery.[96] Indeed, the PAS grew out of one of the legal disputes in which the Philadelphia Meeting for Sufferings occasionally intervened. Beginning in the 1760s, Israel Pemberton, Samuel Allinson, and other PMS members provided legal aid to help several enslaved families gain their freedom.[97] In September 1773, Pemberton, Allinson, and several others interceded on behalf of an enslaved Indian woman named Dinah Nevil, who "asserted she & her children were Free People." The resulting lengthy legal wrangling led another Quaker, Thomas Harrison, to establish the Society for Relief of Free Negroes &c. in 1775 and file a suit against Benjamin Bannerman, a Virginia slaveholder who had purchased the Nevil family. (The lawsuit was unsuccessful, but Harrison eventually purchased and freed the family.) Although the group was ostensibly nondenominational, most early members were Quakers. Moreover, contrary to common belief, Thomas Paine was never involved. The PAS is thus better understood in the context of traditional Quakerism rather than of patriot ideology. In any case, its members only met a few times before the war disrupted their proceedings for eight years.[98] During the war, the PMS remained the most important abolitionist organization in North America.

* * *

By early 1775, there was far greater antislavery sentiment in North America than ever before. Still, there was little support among politicians for substantive antislavery reform. Not even in New England. The abolitionist movement on the eve of war thus consisted of the same types of people as before: Black people who had opposed slavery from the beginning, a significant number of white Quakers since the 1750s, and a small (if growing) number of other evangelical white Christians since the 1760s. African Americans had obvious motives for opposing slavery while white abolitionists were largely inspired by religious ideas centered around biblicism and providentialism. The imperial crisis contributed to the growth of antislavery sentiment, but its influence was strongest among those who interpreted it as a form of divine chastisement. Religious beliefs provided the sense of urgency that compelled white abolitionists to act. Few patriot legislators shared this impulse. With the possible exception of Massachusetts, where legal ambiguities rendered slavery uniquely vulnerable through the courts, abolitionists had little reason to expect additional antislavery reform in the foreseeable future.[99]

The ubiquity of patriots' references to natural rights did not inspire naive optimism that emancipation was on the horizon. Rather, slaveholding patriots' insincere and self-serving professions inspired dread of further divine retribution against the colonies. Abolitionists feared that if white colonists ignored God's chastisements and instead hardened their hearts like the pharaoh, there would be worse plagues to come. As the itinerant minister Elhanan Winchester warned an audience in Virginia at the end of 1774: "God knows how to deliver these poor oppressed creatures, and to render sevenfold to those who have so long and unjustly detained them in slavery."[100] A Quaker minister in New Jersey similarly warned that the colonists could not escape the "overflowing scourge" of divine wrath provoked by their "cruel oppression of the negroes." This type of apocalyptic language was much more common than were optimistic predictions about slavery's inevitable decline.[101]

CHAPTER 5

Wartime Antislavery Ideology and Activism, 1775–1779

On April 19, 1775, a decade of imperial tension finally erupted into violence between Massachusetts patriots and British regulars at Lexington and Concord. Events unfolded rapidly thereafter as the rebellion spread. Within two months, the Continental Congress had established an army and appointed George Washington as commander in chief. In November 1775, Lord Dunmore, Virginia's royal governor, fulfilled his earlier threat of offering freedom to patriots' servants and slaves who would join the British army to fight against their former masters. Ultimately, about fifteen thousand "Black loyalists" would aid the British side (about three times the number who served with the patriots). In January 1776, Thomas Paine published *Common Sense*, attacking the idea of monarchy and calling for the creation of an independent republic. On July 4, 1776, the Continental Congress issued the Declaration of Independence, turning the rebellion into a revolution justified by reference to "unalienable Rights." France allied with the United States in February 1778, but American victory remained in doubt until the Battle of Yorktown in October 1781. Even then, fighting continued on a smaller scale until the Treaty of Paris was signed two years later.[1]

The transition from imperial tensions to an eight-year war had a profound influence on slavery and abolitionism. By 1783, Massachusetts and Pennsylvania (along with the breakaway region of Vermont) had taken steps to end hereditary slavery while others, including Virginia, had liberalized manumission policies. Scholars such as Patrick Rael have increasingly recognized that Black people were not passive beneficiaries of abolitionism but rather "integral players in this process," whether by petitioning for abolition, suing for freedom, negotiating freedom in return for service in the Continental Army, or simply running away (sometimes to join the British and fight against their former masters).[2] However, historians have been unable to agree on how to characterize the American Revolution's overall effect on slavery, and how to explain the extent and limitations of antislavery reforms.

Celebratory accounts of the Revolution and the Founding Fathers often portray antislavery reform as the inevitable result of patriots' natural rights ideology and republicanism—the "contagion of liberty," as Bernard Bailyn dubbed it. Gordon Wood has pushed this view even further than Bailyn, asserting that during the war "nearly all the newly independent states, including Virginia, began moving against slavery." He adds: "The desire to abolish slavery was not an incidental offshoot of the Revolution; it was not an unintended consequence of the contagion of liberty. It was part and parcel of the many enlightened reforms that were integral to the republican revolutions taking place in the new states." In this view, antislavery reform was largely the work of elite politicians inspired by natural rights and republican ideology.[3] Others disagree. "No 'contagion of liberty' flowed inexorably according to its own logic," Manisha Sinha writes. Rather it was Black Americans and their allies who "transformed revolutionary currents into a call for African liberty."[4] A detailed examination of antislavery agitation confirms its bottom-up nature.

Still, scholars disagree on whether the Revolutionary War itself accelerated or hindered antislavery progress. Robert Parkinson persuasively argues that after the war began—and especially once Lord Dunmore offered freedom to Black runaways—patriot leaders and newspaper editors "weaponized prejudice about African Americans and Indians to unite the [white] American colonists and hammer home the idea that the British were treacherous and dangerous enemies." Parkinson demonstrates that wartime newspapers were full of sensational accounts of atrocities allegedly committed by Britain's nonwhite allies. He asserts that racial fear helped create the "common cause" that united white patriots against Britain and in favor of independence. Parkinson also asserts that this type of racist propaganda reversed antislavery momentum: "As powerful as that 1770s antislavery wave became, it crested in 1774 and receded even faster." He notes, for example, that none of the original thirteen colonies passed antislavery legislation before 1780, and he argues that the patriots' racist propaganda "had an effect of closing off possibilities during the war, limiting the radical scope of the Revolution."[5] Thus, whereas Gordon Wood sees persistent elite antislavery sentiment and Manisha Sinha stresses Black activism, Parkinson argues that patriots' wartime propaganda undercut momentum and reduced the extent of reform that would have otherwise occurred.

Despite drawing different conclusions, both Wood and Parkinson share mistaken assumptions that are common in much of the scholarship on the Revolution and antislavery. Both scholars view earlier antislavery agitation by Quakers and evangelicals during the mid-eighteenth century as insignificant compared to the "wave of antislavery fever" inspired by patriots' republican and natural rights rhetoric during the early 1770s. Indeed, Parkinson's conclusion that the war hurt abolitionism rests on the assumption that patriots were on the verge of major antislavery reforms in 1774, a misperception based on giving too much credence to transatlantic political posturing by Thomas Jefferson and Benjamin Rush (as discussed in Chapter 4). And while Wood exaggerates patriots' support for antislavery reform throughout the Revolution, Parkinson overstates the decline in abolitionist sentiment once the shooting began. A temporary lull in antislavery publishing by Quakers (who were often persecuted for their pacificism during the war) was more than made up for by other writers.[6] Parkinson is undoubtedly correct that racist propaganda discouraged abolitionism, but the overall trend of the Revolutionary War nonetheless encouraged antislavery sentiment and activism. If only a minority of white Americans actively promoted abolition during the Revolutionary War, it was still a larger and more dedicated minority than had ever done so previously. Moreover, religious beliefs remained the dominant impulse for the growing number of white abolitionists.

The outbreak of war increased antislavery sentiment and inspired activism because abolitionists' arguments meshed not only with the patriots' natural rights language but also—and crucially—with widely held providentialist beliefs. As during the earlier stages of the imperial crisis, many Americans interpreted earthly events in providentialist terms. White patriots often confidently imagined that God had a special plan for America and would deliver them from British bondage. As John Coffey has noted, even "so-called Deists" such as Thomas Jefferson and Benjamin Franklin proposed that the official seal of the United States feature an image of Moses parting the Red Sea, using the story of Exodus as an allegory for the Revolutionary War. Although patriots often assumed that they were God's chosen people, many also acknowledged that the Lord might be chastising them in the process, just as he had repeatedly done with the ancient Israelites. From the beginning of the war, a vocal minority connected this chastisement to the sin of slavery.[7] For example, in *A Poem upon the Bloody Engagement That Was Fought on Bunker's-Hill*, Baptist minister Elisha Rich celebrated patriots' valor while also describing the war in terms of antislavery providentialism. The second half of the poem, which went through multiple editions, instructed:

> New England search and know the cause,
> Hast thou not broke God's blessed laws,
> For which God doth thee chastise,
> And turn thy Friends to Enemies.
> Would thou obtain thy Liberty,
> Then break all bands of slavery.
> And do thou Liberty proclaim,
> To all that have a human frame;
> But if oppression here is found,
> Can you with victory be crown'd[?];
> No no, be sure this cannot be,
> Whilst thou thy neighbours do not free.[8]

In other words, the outbreak of war reflected divine chastisement for the sin of slavery, and God would not grant the patriots victory until they liberated the enslaved. Throughout the conflict, similar religious arguments remained predominant in antislavery discourse, even after the Declaration of Independence, belying historians' typical focus on secular ideology.

Of course, providentialist beliefs did not automatically lead to antislavery sentiments. Many Americans, including many ministers, called on God to protect them from Britain's attempt to "enslave" them while still assuming their own enslavement of Black people was legitimate. For instance, the Reverend William Foster, the slaveholding minister of the Upper Octorara Presbyterian Church in Chester County, Pennsylvania, described Americans as facing the choice between "Liberty or Slavery." And although he believed God was using the British army as "the rod of his anger" to chastise the colonists for their sins, he was confident that as long as patriot soldiers placed their faith in God and avoided such vices as "cursing and swearing," they could expect the "interposition of God" on their behalf. It seems Foster assumed that Black people's enslavement must have been just or else God would not have allowed it, and he resisted antislavery activism.[9]

Nonetheless, the war initiated or increased discomfort with Black slavery among many other patriots. Americans who had expressed antislavery sentiment in providentialist terms during the early 1770s often described the outbreak of war as fulfilling their prophetic warnings that God would increase the severity of his chastisement until the colonists eradicated the sin of slavery. One of the clearest examples of this view came from Jabez Huntington. Since 1773, he had argued in the *Connecticut Gazette* that "God has a controversy with us, and his demand on us is to let the Africans so long inslaved, go free." In *A Discourse on the Times* (which went through three editions in 1776–1777), Huntington asserted that the war reflected the escalation of divine punishment for the sin of slavery:

> And here lies that controversy between the great God and us—just as when a kind father corrects a rebellious child, his aim is to bring him to obedience, and do his duty; now if the child is regardless of his father's corrections, and will not turn for the stripes his father gives him, there is an absolute necessity of a more severe correction. . . . Just so the blessed God has been dealing with *America*—he has been manifesting his sore displeasure against us—he has been most severely correcting us—his stripes have been most severely laid upon us.—Now, if we still go on, and will not remove the cause of his controversy, there is a necessity of his stripes being laid on more severe; for God never began a controversy with any people, that ever ended in any thing short of their reformation or final ruin.[10]

Huntington lamented that God's chastisement in the form of oppressive parliamentary taxes and laws had not inspired emancipation, and he hoped that the war would soon compel reform. He was confident that emancipation would restore God's favor and ensure patriot victory, but he also feared slaveholders' obstinance would provoke further chastisement, causing the Revolution to end in failure. Other wartime antislavery essays—by Congregationalist ministers such as Samuel Hopkins and Isaac Foster, Quakers such as Anthony Benezet, and Black activists such as Lemuel Haynes—advanced similar arguments grounded in biblicism and providentialism.

Although the war energized abolitionists and galvanized more public antislavery support, they faced great obstacles and achieved few legislative victories during the first four years of war. Initially, very few patriot leaders supported significant antislavery reform. To be sure, a majority of white Americans probably agreed that slavery was wrong in the abstract; but it is important to remember Christopher Brown's point that there is a "wide gulf that divides the mere perception of moral wrong from decisions to seek remedies."[11] Even whites who regretted slavery's existence worried that abolition would threaten economic prosperity, destabilize social hierarchies, and undermine the sanctity of property rights. And patriots' concern about property rights was, after all, a primary reason they had mobilized against taxation without representation in the first place. Moreover, legislators tended to be wealthier and thus were more likely to own slaves than the typical white American. The minority of white Americans who felt compelled to prioritize Black liberation over these other concerns were generally inspired by a sense of providential dread. Most patriot legislators, however, did not share such fears and they blocked or delayed antislavery reform efforts in the thirteen original colonies during the first half of the Revolutionary War.

Antislavery and the Appeal to Heaven

Wartime antislavery rhetoric must be understood within the context of widespread providentialist beliefs. Many patriots conceived of the war as an "Appeal to Heaven," even emblazoning the motto on the Continental Army's first flag (featuring a pine tree) in early July 1775. When the flag was unveiled, military chaplain Abiel Leonard instructed soldiers to pray that the Lord would "protect and deliver them from all dangers" just as he had "preserve[d] the children of Israel from the hand of the Pharoah and his host." Americans' conception of the relationship between war and divine providence was also shaped by John Locke's *Second Treatise of Government*, which asserted the right of an oppressed people to follow biblical examples and "appeal to Heaven" by rising in revolt after peaceful means had proved ineffective. Although Locke recognized that just causes did not always prevail on the battlefield, he wrote that anyone who hoped God would aid their side "must be sure he has Right on his side." Even before the war began, some patriots worried that the sin of slaveholding would undermine their military prospects by alienating God. One Connecticut patriot wrote in February 1775: "As our cause is good, I think we need not fear success; except on the account of our sins . . . particularly the guilt we lay under on account of our enslaving the poor Africans." He believed that the colonists had to release their slaves before they could confidently "appeal to heaven, and gird on the sword."[12] Such concerns would grow during the war as a quick victory eluded the patriots.

Patriots' desire for providential aid led them to expand the practice of designating public days of fasting and prayer during the war (Figure 7), inspiring

IN CONGRESS,

MONDAY, *JUNE* 12, 1775.

AS the GREAT GOVERNOR OF THE WORLD, by his ſupreme and univerſal Providence, not only conducts the courſe of nature with unerring wiſdom and rectitude, but frequently influences the minds of men to ſerve the wiſe and gracious purpoſes of His providencial Government; and it being, at all times, our indiſpenſible duty, devoutly to acknowledge His ſuperintending Providence, eſpecially in times of impending danger, and public calamity, to reverence and adore his immutable Juſtice, as well as to implore his merciful Interpoſition for our deliverance.

THIS CONGRESS, therefore, conſidering the preſent critical, alarming and calamitous ſtate of theſe Colonies, do earneſtly recommend, that THURSDAY, the *Twentieth* day of *July* next, be obſerved by the INHABITANTS of all the Engliſh Colonies on this Continent, as a day of public HUMILIATION, FASTING, and PRAYER, that we may, with united hearts and voices, unfeignedly confeſs and deplore our many ſins, and offer up our joint ſupplications to the All-wiſe, Omnipotent and Merciful Diſpoſer of all Events, humbly beſeeching Him to forgive our iniquities, to remove our preſent calamities, to avert thoſe deſolating judgments with which we are threatened, and to bleſs our rightful Sovereign King GEORGE the IIId. and inſpire him with wiſdom to diſcern and purſue the true intereſt of all his ſubjects,---that a ſpeedy end may be put to the civil diſcord between Great-Britain and the American Colonies, without further effuſion of blood,---and that the Britiſh nation may be influenced to regard *the things that belong to her peace, before they are hid from her eyes*,---that theſe Colonies may be ever under the care and protection of a kind Providence, and be proſpered in all their intereſts,---that the divine Bleſſing may deſcend and reſt upon all our civil Rulers, and upon the Repreſentatives of the people in their ſeveral Aſſemblies and Conventions, that they may be directed to wiſe and effectual meaſures for preſerving the Union and ſecuring the juſt rights and privileges of the Colonies,---that virtue and true religion may revive and flouriſh throughout our land,---and that America may ſoon behold a gracious interpoſition of Heaven for the redreſs of her many grievances, the reſtoration of her invaded rights, a reconciliation with the parent State, on terms conſtitutional and honourable to both,---and that her civil and religious Privileges may be ſecured to the lateſt poſterity. And it is recommended to Chriſtians of all Denominations to aſſemble for public worſhip, and to abſtain from ſervile Labour and Recreations on ſaid day.

By Order of the Congreſs,

JOHN HANCOCK, Preſident.

(*A true Copy*,)

CHARLES THOMPSON, Secretary.

WATERTOWN: Printed by BENJAMIN EDES.

Figure 7. Beginning on June 12, 1775, the Continental Congress and Confederation Congress appointed seven days of fasting and prayer (and four of thanksgiving) during the Revolutionary War, calling on God to aid their cause. Courtesy of the American Antiquarian Society.

more antislavery discussions as a result. In June 1775, as the patriots sought to expel the British army from Boston, the Continental Congress designated the first continental "day of public humiliation, fasting and prayer."[13] As with earlier fast days, most American ministers lamented common sins such as sabbath-breaking and drunkenness but insisted that God was nonetheless on the patriots' side. An important minority, however, put an antislavery spin on wartime fast-day sermons.[14]

This antislavery minority included some prominent clergy. The Continental Congress's own chaplain, the Reverend Jacob Duché, repeatedly combined patriotism with unease about slavery's implications for the war effort. In a sermon delivered to a battalion of troops leaving Philadelphia on July 7, 1775, the Anglican minister justified the patriots' efforts to resist a tyrannical government that sought to "injure, oppress, and enslave" them. When he published the sermon a few weeks later, dedicating it to George Washington, he added a footnote addressing the apparent hypocrisy of slaveholding colonists fighting for liberty. He blamed England for originating the slave trade and for opposing the efforts by "the legislatures of some of the colonies . . . to put a stop to the importation of African slaves." Duché also included an implicitly antislavery statement in his sermon on July 20, 1775, the first continental fast day. He began by reminding the congressional delegates that God inflicted "*national punishments upon national guilt!*" He further cautioned. "*Our* fastings and humiliations, therefore, will stand us in no stead, unless . . . we endeavour likewise *to undo the heavy burdens of others, and to let the oppressed go free*." Duché sounded much like Quaker abolitionists had during the last war, which is somewhat ironic because he had been a harsh critic of Quaker pacifism during the French and Indian War.[15] On the other hand, he had long been a supporter of the Bray School for Black students, which may have increased his antislavery sentiments. Moreover, during the imperial crisis, growing numbers of patriots had begun using Isaiah 58:6 to call for antislavery reform, and the war increased this trend.

Several other ministers are known to have included antislavery sentiment in their sermons on the first continental fast day. In Maryland, Thomas Rankin, a Methodist missionary from Britain, told a crowd that "the sins of Great Britain and her colonies had long called aloud for vengeance; and in a peculiar manner, the dreadful sin of buying and selling the souls and bodies of the poor Africans." By paraphrasing Revelation 18:13, Rankin indicated that God might punish the British Empire as he had ancient Babylon. In Connecticut, the Reverend Samuel Andrews suggested that slavery was among the "capital sins which have bro't the judgments of God upon us." After citing Isaiah 58:6, he asked, "How can we expect, God will work that deliverance for us, which we refuse to give others?"[16] It is impossible to know how common antislavery expressions were during fast days, for only a tiny fraction of sermons were published. But some prominent patriots shared providentialist concerns about American slavery. In October 1775, following the destruction of several Massachusetts towns by British troops, Abigail Adams lamented: "We have done Evil or our Enimies would be at peace with us. The Sin of Slavery as well as many others is not washed away."[17] Her husband may not have shared her antislavery sentiments, but many ordinary white Americans likely did.

Freeborn Garrettson, a slaveholder from Maryland who was a "professed friend to the American cause," experienced an antislavery awakening in the summer of 1775, shortly after his conversion to Methodism. Believing that he was called by God but also tempted by the Devil, Garrettson undertook a regiment of intensive biblical study along with fasting and praying, until he "was almost reduced to a skeleton." The words of Isaiah 58:6 stuck in his mind, and he reported that one night while leading his family in prayer, God spoke directly to him, proclaiming: "It is not right for you to keep your fellow-creatures in bondage; you must let the oppressed go free." Until that moment, Garrettson later wrote, he had "never suspected that the practice of slave-keeping was wrong," but after a minute's reflection he responded: "Lord the oppressed shall go free." He manumitted his own slaves and became an itinerant Methodist minister. Garrettson's antislavery convictions must have been further strengthened by his subsequent readings of John Wesley's *Thoughts upon Slavery*. However, Wesley's opposition to the patriot cause, espoused in his *Calm Address to the American Colonies* of 1775, increased the hostility that Methodist ministers such as Garrettson faced in America. Garrettson reported that his preaching to Black people and his attempts "to inculcate the doctrine of freedom" among their owners often provoked "ill will" from slaveholding patriots.[18] Nonetheless, Garrettson did inspire some slaveholders to reevaluate bondage. Most notably, a young Delaware slave known as Negro Richard successfully recruited Garrettson in 1779 to persuade his master, Stokely Sturgis, that slaveholding was sinful. Sturgis subsequently allowed Richard to purchase his freedom over time. After being manumitted, Richard adopted the surname Allen and settled in Philadelphia, where he later established the first African Methodist Episcopal (AME) Church.[19]

Although relatively few prominent patriots expressed antislavery sentiments, Thomas Paine was a partial exception. In October 1775, the soon-to-be-famous writer (who had emigrated from England the previous year) apparently penned a short antislavery piece in the *Pennsylvania Journal* using the pseudonym "Humanus." Paine criticized the Atlantic slave trade as "the most horrid of all traffics" but did so primarily to condemn George III. He also used providentialist rhetoric but was more concerned with promoting independence than abolition. In his telling, God would separate the colonies from Britain in order to punish the king for his sins. Paine advocated antislavery reform, but only after the war: "And when the Almighty shall have blest us, and made us a people dependent only upon Him, then may our first gratitude be shown by an act of continental legislation, which shall put a stop to the importation of Negroes for sale, soften the hard fate of those already here, and in time procure their freedom."[20] It is possible that Paine, whose father was Quaker, hoped that such rhetoric would attract Pennsylvania Friends into the patriot fold. It did not, however, reflect much actual commitment to antislavery reform on Paine's part.

Antislavery Quakers, meanwhile, emphasized Americans' shared guilt for slavery and argued that emancipation was an urgent duty. When some Virginia Quakers proposed deferring antislavery action based on the "publick confusion & distress of the Times," the Philadelphia Yearly Meeting responded by arguing that the outbreak of war was cause for expediting rather than delaying reform. The PYM interpreted the war as "the Judgments of the Lord," designed to give the British Empire a taste of the type of "intestine War" (i.e., civil war) that Africans experienced as a result of the Atlantic slave trade. It seems that the start of war accelerated the rate of manumissions by Quakers and inspired the PYM to strengthen its stance against buying, selling, or holding enslaved people. By September 1775 the PYM was able to report that "since the last Year, a considerable number has been restored to liberty." In September 1776, the PYM instructed local meetings to "testify their disunion with" (i.e., disown) members who still refused to liberate their slaves. When justifying this policy, it reiterated the biblicist and providentialist basis of the PYM's views: "Christ died for all Men without distinction," while the war was an "awful, & alarming dispensation" reflecting God's wrath.[21] The Revolutionary War thus played an important—perhaps essential—role in ensuring that Quakers followed through with their 1758 call for manumissions.

The number of manumissions by Quakers appears to have increased significantly during the war, though no systematic efforts were made to preserve manumission records in central locations until September 1776. At that point, Quakers gathered records of recent manumissions and preserved new ones, but these centralized records are far from comprehensive for the previous decades. Scholars have located additional manumissions in wills and probate records, but the data remain incomplete. Records compiled for the city of Philadelphia indicate that thirty-four Quakers had manumitted slaves between 1751 and 1774 while seventy-four did so between 1775 and 1780. Although these statistics probably undercount the number of manumissions before 1775, it is nonetheless clear the new war and the threat of disownment convinced many recalcitrant slaveholding Quakers to finally release their bondspeople. It also seems that some slaveholding Quakers had freed their adult slaves during the 1760s and early 1770s (at times hiring them to stay on as paid workers) while keeping their former bondspeople's children on as uncompensated laborers into adulthood. To ensure the freedom of these Black minors, the monthly meeting committees pressed slaveholders to sign conditional manumissions for them. By June of 1776, these committees were providing printed forms for delayed manumissions that slaveholders completed by hand, usually promising to liberate Black girls when they turned age eighteen and boys at twenty-one.[22]

Some of the Quakers who were most active in facilitating manumissions included prominent members of the Generation of 1758 who rededicated themselves to the antislavery cause during the new war. Anthony Benezet along with Israel, James, and John Pemberton routinely signed manumission forms as witnesses, at times likely after coaxing reluctant manumitters. Their efforts were surpassed by John Parrish and Nicholas Waln, who were emerging as prominent activists also involved in both the Philadelphia Monthly Meeting's Negro School and the Philadelphia Meeting for Sufferings. Parrish witnessed a dozen manumissions in Philadelphia (e.g., Figure 8) while Waln witnessed twenty-nine (often joined by his wife, Sarah). Waln and Parrish also routinely traveled outside of Philadelphia to witness dozens of additional manumissions.[23] These two Quakers would remain among the nation's most active abolitionists long after the war.

Quaker abolitionists also embraced the war as an opportunity to promote antislavery legislation, albeit with little initial success. In November 1775, Quakers from Burlington County used providentialist arguments in an antislavery petition to the New Jersey legislature. Linking Matthew 7:2 and

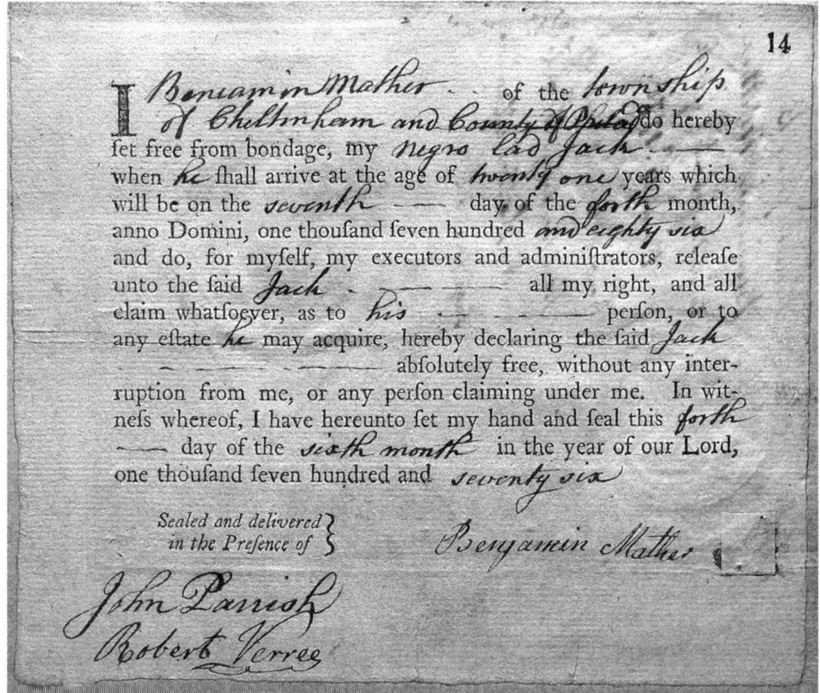

14

I Beniamin Mather of the township of Cheltenham and County of Phila do hereby ſet free from bondage, my negro lad Jack when he ſhall arrive at the age of twenty one years which will be on the seventh day of the forth month, anno Domini, one thouſand ſeven hundred and eighty six and do, for myſelf, my executors and adminiſtrators, releaſe unto the ſaid Jack all my right, and all claim whatſoever, as to his perſon, or to any eſtate he may acquire, hereby declaring the ſaid Jack abſolutely free, without any interruption from me, or any perſon claiming under me. In witneſs whereof, I have hereunto ſet my hand and ſeal this forth day of the sixth month in the year of our Lord, one thouſand ſeven hundred and seventy six

Sealed and delivered in the Preſence of

Benjamin Mather

John Parrish
Robert Verree

Figure 8. In 1776, Quakers started printing manumission forms for immediately liberating enslaved adults and establishing indentured servitude agreements for children. John Parrish was especially active in arranging for manumissions and serving as a witness to the process. Original Papers of Manumission, Philadelphia Quarterly Meeting. Courtesy of Haverford College, Quaker & Special Collections Library.

7:12, the petitioners argued that slavery violated the Golden Rule, and they suggested the war was fulfilling God's warning that "the Measure ye Mete to others shall be Measured to you again." The petitioners called on the legislature to "pass an Act of Freedom" for New Jersey's slaves in order "to avert the further judgment of God from our heads." Thus, Quakers who had turned against slavery during the French and Indian War hoped the new war would have a similar influence on colonists at large. However, they were unable to inspire a majority of the legislature, which declined even to pass a bill easing voluntary manumissions by reducing the security bond in case freed people became indigent. The following January, the PMS included antislavery statements in *The Ancient Testimony and Principles of the People Called Quakers*, a short leaflet defending their pacifistic principles. It described the war as divine punishment for the "sins and iniquities of the people," and called on readers to "prevent the slavery and oppression of our fellow-men, and to restore them to their natural rights." Doing so, the PMS predicted, would help restore peace and prosperity through God's blessing.[24] Pennsylvania Quakers may also have been involved in a petition "respecting the setting Negro Slaves at Liberty" that was submitted to the Pennsylvania legislature in April 1776. However, its substance was not recorded, and the legislature took no action.[25]

Abolitionists of various denominations in New England were similarly disappointed in their legislatures, underscoring the limits of antislavery sentiments among elite patriots. In September 1775, Deacon Benjamin Colman of Newbury called on the Massachusetts legislature to support emancipation, reiterating his view that slavery was an unchristian sin provoking "the Judgments of God." Noting that some colonists imagined that the British troops were "near taking their departure," and that peace and prosperity would soon return, Colman cautioned: "But stop my friends, your rejoycing;—God's arm is strong, he has many arrows in his quiver . . . and did he ever take up his rod of correction, and exercise it upon any people, and lay it down without accomplishing his design?" The war would continue, he predicted, until the colonists fulfilled the Lord's command to "let the oppressed go free." The legislature ignored Colman's letter, so he published it in the *Essex Journal* the following spring, after events confirmed his prediction that the war would not be short.[26] Still, the legislature refused to act.

In neighboring Rhode Island, Moses Brown, a Quaker convert, also proposed an abolition bill in September 1775. The bill would have freed the next generation born to enslaved parents when the children reached age twenty-one, while also making it easier for slaveholders to manumit their other slaves. Many abolitionists believed that true justice demanded total emancipation, but they accepted gradual abolition as a necessary compromise. An essay in the *Providence Gazette* by "A Friend to America," who was likely Brown, defended the bill from conservative opposition. Although there could never be legitimate "property in our fellow man," the bill respected claims of "private property" by only applying to the as-yet unborn children of those who were legally enslaved. Moreover, only after taking steps to end slavery could the patriots "plead our rights with confidence." In the *Newport Mercury*, "A Sincere Friend to the Community," likely the Reverend Samuel Hopkins, made the case for abolition in more explicitly providentialist terms.

He dismissed wartime fast day as "solemn mockery" and called for the emancipation of slaves "throughout this whole continent" in order to fulfil the Lord's command in Isaiah 58:6. He dismissed arguments for delaying abolition until times of peace, arguing that the war reflected "national judgments" that indicated the necessity of immediate reform. If legislators delayed, they would be playing the part of the pharaoh "and may, as on Egypt of old, bring down judgment after judgment upon our heads." The Rhode Island legislature, however, refused to take action.[27]

Hopkins also called on delegates to the Continental Congress to take antislavery action. In a letter from December 1775, he praised the congress's 1774 slave trade ban and credited it for the patriots' early military successes, such as having driven the British troops from Boston. These victories, he claimed, reflected the Lord's "approbation of our resolving to put a stop to the slave trade." But Hopkins warned that God "will take his protection from us, and give us up to the power of oppression and tyranny, when he sees we stop short of what might be reasonably expected . . . by refusing to let the oppressed go free." In other words, ending slave importations was an important first step, but the colonists needed to emancipate their own slaves if they desired God's continued blessing. By this point, Lord Dunmore had begun enlisting Black Virginians in his Ethiopian Regiment, and Hopkins also argued that emancipation was the best way to undercut Dunmore's tactic. Hopkins concluded by asking the Continental Congress to fund his plan to send Black missionaries to Africa, which he argued would further please God. His letter was passed along to John Adams, who, predictably, declined to support any antislavery measures.[28] Nonetheless, Hopkins's warning that God might withdraw his protection from the Americans soon appeared prophetic, when the Continental Army suffered an embarrassing defeat at the Battle of Quebec on the last day of 1775.

In 1776, Jabez Huntington published *A Discourse on the Times*, expanding on antislavery arguments he had previously made in the *Connecticut Gazette*. Although he viewed the war as divine punishment for the sin of slavery, he believed the patriots could gain God's blessing through reform: "As we would have the Lord on our side, we must set at liberty those vast numbers of *Africans*, which have so long time been enslaved by us, and who have as good a right to liberty as we have." Huntington argued that abolishing slavery would do more than anything else for the war effort, even rendering the search for earthly allies unnecessary. "Surely, if *God* be for us, we need not apply to *France*, *Spain*, or *Prussia*, for protection; for the blessed *God* will protect us," he promised his readers. Yet, like so many abolitionists of the revolutionary generation, Huntington was inspired as much by fear as optimism. He closed the second edition of his pamphlet by referring to the defeat at Quebec and alluding to the story of Achan (from Joshua 6–7), warning that slavery was the "accursed thing which may provoke him [i.e., God] finally to forsake us."[29] Huntington's pamphlet apparently sold well, as it went through three editions, but legislators remained slow to act.

Although neither the Continental Congress nor colonial legislatures were prepared to support antislavery reform, pragmatic considerations eventually led them to allow people of color to enlist in the army. Some New England militias had already allowed such enlistments, and militiamen of color had seen action during early battles including Lexington, Concord, and Bunker Hill. But many white southerners were uncomfortable with the notion of Black men with guns, and Congress had initially forbade their enlistment in the Continental Army. General George Washington agreed that slaves should not serve in the army, but he supported permitting free men of color, especially those who had already served, to enlist. Congress eventually relented in February 1776 due to a shortage of white military volunteers and a desire to forestall British recruitment of African Americans. Ultimately, more than five thousand people of color—many of whom served in exchange for freedom—fought for the patriot side. Meanwhile, two or three times as many enslaved Black people escaped from patriot masters and allied with the British.[30]

Black loyalists and rebel slaves (along with Native Americans) were seen as so worrisome that the Continental Congress even referred to them in their next fast-day proclamation, issued in March 1776. The Congress asked God to bless "our strenuous efforts in the cause of Freedom" against the attempts "of the British Ministry to subvert our invaluable rights and privileges, and to reduce us by fire and sword, by the savages of the wilderness and *our own domestics*, to the most abject and ignominious bondage." Thus, whereas the Reverend Hopkins had urged Congress to emancipate slaves in order to gain the Lord's blessing, Congress essentially asked God to help white Americans preserve their control over enslaved Black people. The Philadelphia Meeting for Sufferings responded to the new fast-day proclamation by appointing John Parrish to reprint and distribute two thousand copies of *An Apology for the People Called Quakers*, which critiqued government-appointed fast days. Originally published during the French and Indian War, the pamphlet quoted Isaiah 58 to demonstrate that superficial fasts unaccompanied by "Repentance and Amendment of Life" merely angered the Lord. The pamphlet was apparently not fully persuasive, for patriot mobs pelted Quaker businesses with stones when they refused to close on the appointed fast day in May.[31]

Meanwhile in Rhode Island, the Reverend Samuel Hopkins increased his efforts to link abolitionism to the patriot cause through several publications and sermons. In April 1776, he and Ezra Stiles issued a new fundraising call for their effort to send Black missionaries to Africa, describing it as a "likely method" to preserve God's favor in the struggle with Britain.[32] (The war, however, eventually forced them to put the African venture on hiatus.) Hopkins next composed *A Dialogue Concerning the Slavery of the Africans*, which combined biblicist and providentialist antislavery arguments. He began the pamphlet with a prefatory letter to the Continental Congress, commending its slave trade ban and reiterating his belief that the ban was already paying dividends in the form of providential support for Americans on the battlefield. But he also insisted God demanded the "total abolition of slavery." The subsequent sixty-three pages, written in the form of a dialogue, argued that slavery was "in open violation of the law of God." Hopkins asserted that the patriots "cannot expect deliverance from present calamities, and success in our struggle for Liberty," until they followed the mandate of Isaiah 58:6—which he quoted six times—and "let the oppressed go free."[33]

Throughout his *Dialogue*, Hopkins repeated the standard biblicist refutations of common proslavery arguments. He dismissed Old Testament sanctions for slaveholding, arguing that Christ "has taken down the wall of separation, [and] taught us to look on all nations as our neighbors and brethren . . . by which he has most effectually abolished the permission given to the *Jews*." He thus paraphrased the same verse—Ephesians 2:14—that Quaker William Edmundson had used for the same purpose a full century before and that Samuel Sewall had used in *The Selling of Joseph* in 1700. Responding to slaveholders who cited other passages of Paul's writing in which the apostle seemed to tolerate slavery, Hopkins differentiated between ancient enslavement as a fluid status and hereditary chattel slavery as practiced in the colonies. An individual's enslavement could at times be "consistent with justice" if they had "forfeited their liberty" through their own actions. By contrast, the Atlantic slave trade was based on fraud and violence; Hopkins estimated that only one in a thousand African captives was an actual criminal. Moreover, *hereditary* slavery could never be reconciled with justice or the New Testament. It was impossible, Hopkins maintained, for people to be "born slaves." If the colonists did not abolish slavery, he warned, "God will yet withdraw his kind protection from us, and punish us as yet seven times more."[34] Although

Hopkins hoped that patriots would embrace emancipation, he clearly feared they would instead play the part of the pharaoh and suffer God's wrath.

The first year of war altered the context of abolitionism without significantly changing the form of antislavery discourses; biblicism and providentialism remained central. If anything, the war simply made these twinned religious concepts more relevant as Americans sought to make sense of the wartime destruction and losses. Still, few patriot leaders embraced abolitionism. Enslaved Black people, naturally, remained the most committed to freedom, seeking it through lawsuits, negotiated manumission (often in exchange for military service), or running away (perhaps joining the British to fight against their former masters). Among white abolitionists, there was little correlation between supporting Black freedom and supporting the patriot cause. Reverend Hopkins embraced both, but abolitionist sentiment was more common among those who were skeptical of the patriot cause, such as Quakers. It is also noteworthy that several ministers who were known to include antislavery sentiments in their fast-day sermons—including Jacob Duché, Samuel Andrews, and Thomas Rankin—either never supported the patriot cause or abandoned it.[35] Other writers who expressed antislavery principles were also skeptical of the patriot movement. Take, for instance, *An Affectionate Address to the Inhabitants of the British Colonies in America*, anonymously published in Philadelphia in early 1776. Its author had little sympathy for patriot complaints against Britain and declared, "Sin alone is the moral and procuring cause of all those evils we either feel or fear." The author traced the "declension of vital religion" since the early colonial days and added that "the monstrous sin of the slave-trade is one of those great evils that has so highly provoked Almighty God." One of the only good things they had to say about the Continental Congress was that it had prohibited the Atlantic slave trade, but the author clearly felt more should be done.[36]

In sum, antislavery agitation persisted and grew after the war began, but abolitionism remained marginal within patriot leadership. Nor would the Declaration of Independence significantly alter this state of affairs.

Antislavery Ideology After the Declaration of Independence

Although later generations of antislavery activists would celebrate the Declaration of Independence, it inspired little confidence among contemporary abolitionists. Indeed, many viewed it as a provocation to God. The most famous passages from the Declaration, which are also the most pertinent to abolitionism, come from the second paragraph of its preamble:

> We hold these truths to be self-evident, that all men are created equal, that they are endowed by their Creator with certain unalienable Rights, that among these are Life, Liberty and the pursuit of Happiness.—That to secure these rights, Governments are instituted among Men, deriving their just powers from the consent of the governed,—That whenever any Form of Government becomes destructive of these ends, it is the Right of the People to alter or to abolish it, and to institute new Government, laying its foundation on such principles and organizing its powers in such form, as to them shall seem most likely to effect their Safety and Happiness.

Despite its lofty language, the Declaration of Independence reveals the limited potential of secular natural rights ideology alone to inspire abolitionism.[37]

The problem is not, as modern Americans sometimes imagine, that the Founding Fathers all considered Black people as less than fully human and therefore excluded from the self-evident truths of equality and unalienable rights. Jefferson's rough draft makes it clear that he considered Africans as "MEN" possessing the "most sacred rights of life & liberty." (This assertion was part of a passage blaming King George III for the existence of the Atlantic slave trade, which was removed at the insistence of Lower South delegates.) Rather, the bigger problem is that the logic and purpose of the Declaration of Independence was premised on the *limitations* of natural rights. Drawing on John Locke and other philosophers, the founders recognized that natural rights were only "unalienable" in the abstract. In the "state of nature" (e.g., outside of society and government), rights were liable to be abused and trampled upon because each individual was responsible for enforcing their own rights. The insecurity of life, liberty, and property in the state of nature compelled people to form societies with governments that could effectively protect the rights of its members. The Declaration of Independence asserted that the Americans were creating a new nation to enforce their rights because the British government had begun violating instead of protecting them. In practical terms, the Declaration did not extend rights to anyone; it was primarily a diplomatic document justifying a colonial rebellion and seeking to attract foreign allies that could help the patriots win independence and secure their rights.[38]

White patriots often found it easy to reconcile their efforts to secure their own rights while violating the rights of Black people. For instance, the Declaration of Rights in Virginia's state constitution, adopted in June 1776, proclaimed "That all men are by nature equally free and independent, and have certain inherent rights, of which, *when they enter into a state of society*, they cannot, by any compact, deprive or divest their posterity."[39] In other words, membership in society was necessary to convert abstract rights into enforceable ones. Black people did not necessarily lack natural rights in the eyes of white Virginians, but elite white politicians created the new government to better secure their own rights (especially their property rights), not to undermine the basis of their prosperity by recognizing the abstract rights of others. Moreover, patriots throughout the nation used rhetoric about fighting against metaphorical slavery in ways that could implicitly justify actual slavery. For example, the New Jersey legislature appealed to potential military recruits by declaring: "On you, our friends and brethren, it depends, this day, to determine—Whether you, your wives, your children, and millions of your descendants, yet unborn, shall wear the galling, the ignominious yoke of slavery; or nobly inherit the generous, the inestimable blessings of freedom. . . . Say!—will you be slaves? . . . Will you, of choice, become hewers of wood and drawers of water?"[40] Of course, the legislators hoped this rhetoric about the choice between submitting to slavery and defending one's freedom would inspire military enlistments. But, as François Furstenberg has noted, framing enslavement as a "choice" also implied (intentionally or not) that enslaved Black people had chosen to submit to their fate, "thereby legitimating slavery on principles consistent with the American Revolution."[41] The Declaration of Independence could thus energize white patriots to fight for their own liberty while inspiring little concern for the liberties of others. The fact that the Declaration failed to inspire American slaveholders to liberate their slaves is hardly more surprising than that the document did not convince the British to peacefully relinquish the rebellious colonies.

Of course, the principles of the Declaration of Independence could justify slaves' attempts to assert their natural rights through revolt, but Jefferson and his editors worked to discourage such an interpretation. The final draft of the Declaration removed Jefferson's condemnation of the Atlantic slave trade while preserving an implicit denunciation of the British tactic of recruiting patriots' slaves (along with Native Americans) into the army. The culminating grievance against the king charged that "He has excited domestic insurrections [i.e., slave revolt] amongst us, and has endeavoured to bring on the inhabitants of our frontiers, the merciless Indian Savages, whose known rule of warfare, is an undistinguished destruction of all ages, sexes and conditions." As scholars such as Woody Holton and Robert Parkinson have increasingly emphasized, this accusation exploited and encouraged white colonists' racialized fears of the king's non-white allies. It also served to strip Black people of their agency, suggesting that they resisted their enslavement because of outside instigation rather than their own innate desire for liberty. The patriots' "common cause" rhetoric thus simultaneously emphasized natural rights ideology while also undercutting its universal application.[42]

The creation of Pennsylvania's 1776 state constitution provides an illustration of the contradictory elements of the common cause. John Dickinson, a lapsed Quaker who reluctantly supported independence, included a gradual emancipation proposal in his anonymous *Essay of a Frame of Government for Pennsylvania*. His plan would have facilitated the voluntary manumission of the state's existing slaves while mandating the emancipation of those "hereafter coming into, or born in this country."[43] However, the framers of the state's constitution ignored Dickinson's abolition proposal. Instead, the constitution's preamble echoed the Declaration of Independence's final grievance, justifying independence by pointing to the king's use of "foreign mercenaries, savages and slaves." Pennsylvania politicians thus ingrained racialized fear into the state's founding document. And although the state constitution's Declaration of Rights referred to equality and "inalienable rights," the government was only charged with protecting the rights of "member[s] of society," which implicitly excluded enslaved people. In many ways, Pennsylvania's constitution was the most radical in the new nation—it consisted of a unicameral legislature and plural executive council while allowing all taxpaying adult men to vote—but it left slaveholding untouched even as it endorsed the idea of inalienable rights.[44]

Dickinson was similarly unsuccessful in pressing the Continental Congress to take a stronger stance against slavery. In April 1776, the Congress had reaffirmed its 1774 ban on slave importations, but this resolution was not permanent and could be repealed at any time.[45] On July 12, 1776, as the Congress was drafting the Articles of Confederation, Dickinson suggested a provision "to prevent those who are hereafter brought into these Colonies, from being held in Slavery." Nothing came of this proposal, because some delegates were already—barely a week after declaring independence—looking forward to resuming slave importations once the war ended.[46]

The elements of the Declaration of Independence that were most relevant to the contemporary antislavery movement were its religious references, most of which were added by Jefferson's congressional editors. Whereas Jefferson had grounded people's rights in an ambiguous "creation," the final draft portrayed them as coming from "their Creator." Moreover, the editors amended the Declaration's final sentence to record their "reliance on divine Providence."[47] It was this type of religious language that made the Declaration of Independence appear so hypocritical to abolitionists. White patriots were asking God to help them protect their own rights even as they trampled the God-given rights of others. Rather than inspiring contemporary abolitionists, the Declaration appeared to them as a hypocritical document that would likely further provoke God's anger.

The first occasion on which legislators discussed the Declaration of Independence in relation to slavery was probably in Massachusetts in September 1776. The controversy dealt with the fate of two Black men whom patriot privateers were planning to sell (as slaves) as part of the cargo captured from a British ship. On September 13, the state House of Representatives proposed a resolution prohibiting the sale and declaring "That the selling and enslaving the human species is a direct violation of the natural rights alike vested in all men by their Creator, and utterly inconsistent with the avowed principles on which this and the other United States have carried their struggle for liberty, even to the last appeal." This powerful antislavery statement, which merged natural rights and religious language, was supported by the Reverend John Murray, a representative from Maine (then a province of Massachusetts), who pressed the legislative council (forerunner to the state senate) to concur in the lower house's resolution. However, the resolution's final text dropped the religious reference to the "Creator" and the "last appeal," and simply stated that Black captives taken during the war should be treated "as Prisoners" rather than as slaves. Murray and several other antislavery legislators, including the lawyer John Lowell and the pamphleteer Nathaniel Appleton, nonetheless used the opportunity to form a committee to consider the larger issue of slavery within Massachusetts.[48]

The legislature's chaplain, the Reverend William Gordon, also encouraged this antislavery effort. In a newspaper essay published in October, Gordon warned that the Declaration of Independence would "provok[e] the Deity, by acting hypocritically," unless the legislature abolished "slavery from among ourselves." He argued that all servitude should be limited to "seven or eight years" and that Black children should be freed at adulthood. A pseudonymous "Son of Liberty" (who may also have been Gordon) described the war as divine punishment and prayed, "May our legislative authority hear the cries of the oppressed, brake every yoke, and cause the prisoners to leap, by loosing the chains."[49] However, neither this providentialist rhetoric nor the Declaration of Independence's natural rights ideals proved sufficient to inspire the legislature to take further action. Antislavery legislators like Appleton and Lowell remained in the minority.

The Reverend Samuel Hopkins was also among the earliest ministers to discuss the Declaration of Independence in the context of slavery, in a sermon he likely delivered on November 28, 1776. This day was designated by the Rhode Island government as a day of fasting and prayer in hopes that God would "crown their Arms with Success." Hopkins began his sermon by quoting Isaiah 1:15, which Anthony Benezet had used as an epigraph in one of his antislavery pamphlets during the French and Indian War. In the passage God declares, "And when ye Spread forth your hands, I will hide mine Eyes from you: Yea, when ye make many prayers, I will not hear: *Your hands are full of blood*." Hopkins explained that during the time of Isaiah, God ignored the Israelites' sacrifices and prayers because they were superficial offerings by a sinful people who engaged in "extortion and oppression." He then evaluated "our own character as a people" and concluded that "this whole country have their hands full of Blood" on account of slaveholding, the worst form of oppression. The Lord might "overlook sins of ignorance," but the Declaration of Independence showed that white Americans understood God-given natural rights and were thus morally culpable for the sin of slavery. Combining language from Jeremiah 34 and Isaiah 58, Hopkins warned of the providential wrath to come: "God . . . will by Sword and pestilence Execute Judgment for all the oppressed. Don't think that fasting and praying will do—no *God almighty* will never be bribed by this, to withdraw his Judgments and Let us go on in Sin. But we may Expect that now he has begun, he will Soon make a full End with us unless this iniquity be put away by breaking the Yoke and Let[t]ing the oppressed go free."[50] Although this sermon is among the earliest antislavery texts to invoke the Declaration of Independence, it is important to recognize that the Declaration neither inspired Hopkins's antislavery sentiment nor filled him with optimism. Rather, it increased his fear that the slaveholding patriots were provoking God's wrath through their superficial rhetoric.

The situation was similar for Lemuel Haynes, a self-described "young Mollato." In 1775, while serving in the Massachusetts militia, he penned a patriotic ballad, "The Battle of Lexington." Although he celebrated American valor, Haynes closed the ballad by suggesting that an "angry God . . . Armed with an awefull Rod" was chastising the colonists for their "Sin."[51] A year later, he identified the specific sin in an essay draft titled "Liberty Further Extended: Or Free Thoughts on the Illegality of Slave-Keeping." Haynes quoted the Declaration of Independence in an epitaph, but he drew his arguments primarily from the Bible and antislavery publications. Like Hopkins's *Dialogue* (and Sewall's *Selling of Joseph*), Haynes paraphrased Ephesians 2:14 to refute slaveholders' use of the Old Testament, arguing Christ had destroyed the "wall of partition" that had allowed Israelites to enslave the Canaanites and other Gentiles. Moreover, he pointed out the absurdity of modern slaveholders claiming a privilege granted to ancient Israelites given that white Americans were themselves descended from the "Gentiles [who] were then Subject to Slavery." Haynes also reiterated his belief that the conflict itself was a form of divine chastisement. Noting that God often punished sinners "by retaliating Back upon men the Same Evils they unjustly Bring upon others," he suggested that the colonists' enslavement of Black people "may be the procuring cause of this very Judgment that now impends, which so much portends *Slavery*." If Americans desired God's blessing in their struggle against British tyranny, it was "hygh time to undo these heavy Burdens, and Let the Oppressed go free."[52] Although Haynes did not publish his manuscript, other antislavery patriots propagated similar sentiments in print.

Abolitionists also continued distributing and reprinting antislavery pamphlets that had been written before the Declaration of Independence but had gained increased salience because the start or persistence of the war seemed to fulfill their providentialist warnings. Anthony Benezet, for instance, believed his 1766 *Caution and Warning* was as relevant as ever, and sent copies to Henry Laurens and other members of the Continental Congress. Judah P. Spooner, the Connecticut printer who published two editions of Jabez Huntington's *Discourse on the Times*, reprinted Benjamin Rush's 1773 *Address to the Inhabitants of the British Colonies in America, Upon Slave-Keeping*. Rush's closing warning, "that national crimes require national punishments," must have appeared prophetic in hindsight. In late 1776, Ezekiel Russell (now operating out of Salem) printed *The Strange and Remarkable Swansey Vision*, an account of a prophetic vision allegedly from years earlier by an unnamed person—apparently a Quaker—who seemed to predict the current sufferings. Paraphrasing Revelation 18:13, the author identified the "making Slaves of the Souls of Men" as among the land's "crying sins" provoking God's anger.[53] In early 1777, Huntington issued (still anonymously) a third edition of his *Discourse on the Times*, printed by the prominent patriot publisher Jonathan Trumbull. It reiterated Huntington's belief that the "*Liberties of these American States*" depended on earning God's favor by abolishing slavery.[54] Another Connecticutian, the Reverend Elam Potter, concluded a 1777 pamphlet inspired by the book of Revelation, and entitled *A Second Warning to America*, by calling on the new nation to "put away Negro slavery" in order to regain the Lord's "favour."[55] These pamphlets, like the writings of Hopkins and Haynes, reflect the dominant religious impulse behind revolutionary-era antislavery.

The Declaration of Independence was hardly a watershed moment in the supposed transition from a religious basis of abolitionism to a secular one; it merely heightened existing concerns about God's judgment. The potential power of such arguments increased as the war dragged on and hopes of a quick victory faded. In 1777, several other antislavery writers used the biblical story of Achan to explain the patriots' military failures by identifying slaveholding as the "accursed thing that inflames divine anger." The war itself, according to this view, was designed by God "to bring us into a more thorough obedience to him."[56] Clearly, the antislavery patriots' "spirit of 1776" had much in common with the Quakers' "spirit of 1758," with biblicist and providentialist beliefs remaining preeminent.

Across the Atlantic, Granville Sharp similarly interpreted the escalating war as God's means of promoting abolition throughout the British Empire. Indicating his sense of urgency, Sharp published four antislavery books in 1776 alone. The first three—*The Law of Liberty*, *The Just Limitation of Slavery*, and *The Law of Passive Obedience*—provided biblicist analysis refuting proslavery arguments. He reiterated that Old Testament dispensations regarding slavery had been nullified by Christ's new covenant, and that the Apostle Paul's instructions for slaves to be obedient in no way established the legitimacy of slaveholding, especially not the hereditary form practiced in the colonies.[57] Sharp followed these biblicist discussions with providentialist arguments in *The Law of Retribution: Or, a Serious Warning to Great Britain and Her Colonies, Founded on Unquestionable Examples of God's Temporal Vengeance Against Tyrants, Slave-Holders, and Oppressors*. This book contained more than three hundred pages of examples and warnings of divine retribution. Many of Sharp's examples came from the Old Testament and involved instances in which God punished the Israelites for subjecting "*their Brethren*" to servitude that was either overly rigorous or exceeded the seven-year limit permitted by Mosaic law. Referring back to his earlier publications, Sharp argued that Christians were obliged to view all men as brethren and thus could not justify subjecting Black people to periods of bondage exceeding seven years. The British Empire, therefore, should expect the type of "severe *National Judgements* which the Jews brought upon themselves principally by *exceeding these very limitations*." Sharp interpreted the transition from imperial tension to war through this framework, suggesting the "present Civil Dissentions and horrid *mutual* Slaughters of *National Brethren*" were God's retaliatory justice for the sins of slaveholding and slave trading. Sharp also invoked Isaiah 58:6 in reference to contemporary debates about whether King George III should proclaim a national fast day. This biblical passage showed that the Israelites' "public Fasts and outward Humiliations were not only vain, but even offensive to God, while *such notorious Oppressions* continued among them." Britain's fast days would be similarly offensive until it "*let the oppress go free*."[58]

Seeking to promote a sense of transatlantic antislavery competition, Sharp appended various colonial petitions against the Atlantic slave trade in lengthy footnotes. He was not, however, naive about the extent of antislavery sentiment in America. He concluded that hypocritical guilt was shared throughout the empire, noting: "The *Colonies protest* against the Iniquity of the *Slave-trade*; but, nevertheless, continue to hold the poor wretched *Slaves* in a most *detestable Bondage! Great-Britain*, indeed, keeps *no Slaves*, but publicly encourages the *Slave-trade*." Warning against superficial rhetoric unaccompanied by true reform, he repeatedly drew on Jeremiah 34, in which God punishes the Israelites for failing to fulfill wartime promises of manumission.[59] In sum, Sharp hoped both Britons and the American rebels would embrace abolition in order to escape God's further wrath.

Some other prominent Englishmen shared Sharp's providentialist views regarding slavery and the war. James Oglethorpe, who had fought a losing battle to keep slavery out of Georgia in the 1740s, agreed that the "unnatural war" between Britain and the colonies was divine punishment for slaveholding. He hoped Sharp's *Law of Retribution* would inspire Parliament to embrace antislavery reforms and thereby save the nation "from the justly-menaced destruction." John Fletcher, a Methodist vicar, had little sympathy for slaveholding American rebels who "absurdly complain that *they* are enslaved." Still, he conceded that Parliament was complicit in the slave trade and other sins that had "provoked God to permit the Colonists to rise against us." In *The Bible and Sword*, published in late 1776, Fletcher expressed his hope that the "American controversy" would lead to a moral reformation in which the British would embrace antislavery policies. Such measures, in conjunction with the national fast day, would ensure God's aid in suppressing the colonial rebellion, he promised. These arguments, however, had little influence on Parliament. British antislavery policies instituted during the war years were confined to the military's expansion of Lord Dunmore's practice of enlisting Black men who escaped from patriot masters.[60]

In America, abolitionists had similarly little influence on the Continental Congress. The Reverend Isaac Foster of Connecticut appended an antislavery address to Congress in his 1777 pamphlet, *A Discourse Upon Extortion: Wherein It Is Shewn . . . That by Enslaving the Negroes, the American States are Become Guilty of the Worst Kind of Extortion*. The minister drew on the Bible as well as John Locke's *Second Treatise of Government* to condemn hereditary slavery as a sinful violation of natural rights. Invoking Matthew 7:2, Foster described the war, especially British mistreatment of American prisoners of war (POWs), as evidence that "a holy God is measuring to us as we have measured to our neighbours." He called on the Continental Congress and state legislatures to live up to the ideals of the Declaration of Independence and abolish slavery in order to regain the Lord's favor.[61] Meanwhile in Philadelphia, a pseudonymous "Antibiastes" encouraged Congress to expand the use of Black troops as a means to promote emancipation. Such an act of "joint piety" would not only be militarily advantageous but also help make "atonement" and "expiate the crimes" of slavery and slave trading.[62]

Instead of embracing antislavery reform, the Continental Congress and the Pennsylvania government cracked down on Quakers, whose pacifism rendered them increasingly unpopular. Many patriots vilified the Quakers as traitors, at times threatening them with imprisonment for refusing to swear loyalty oaths, serve in the military, or pay wartime taxes. In 1777, patriot mobs began a Fourth of July tradition of throwing stones at the homes of Quakers who failed to indicate support for the war by illuminating their windows with candles. For instance, Nicholas Waln, the wealthy Philadelphia Meeting for Sufferings activist, had to replace fourteen broken windows.[63] The situation worsened the next month when a forged document allegedly issued by Quakers from "Spanktown" (a pejorative nickname for Rahway, New Jersey) implied they were conspiring with the British army. On September 1, Pennsylvania officials arrested more than two dozen prominent Friends "deemed inimical to the cause of *American* liberty," including Henry Drinker and the three Pemberton brothers, and also seized the "records and papers of the Meeting for Sufferings." A week later, Pennsylvania's patriot government exiled seventeen of the Quakers (and five others) to be imprisoned in Virginia because they refused to swear loyalty oaths.[64]

Many white Pennsylvania patriots were happy to see the Quakers go. The Reverend Henry M. Muhlenberg, a Lutheran pastor, dismissed the Quakers' claims of conscience, writing in his journal that "they did not suffer for Christ's sake but on account of their transgressions as traitors, etc." On the other hand, John Pemberton recorded that as he and the other exiles were being transported out of Philadelphia, "many poor blacks . . . shook me by the hand, being affected with our hard treatment." Incidentally, Muhlenberg also claimed around this time that almost all Black Pennsylvanians "secretly wished that the British army might win." Thus it seems that many Black people believed Quakers and the British were more likely than white patriots to act as their allies. Eventually, Pennsylvania's patriot government would in fact embrace emancipation (albeit through a very gradual process), but there was little reason in 1777 to expect this outcome.[65]

Meanwhile, the PMS members held under house arrest in Virginia developed low opinions of southern patriots. Henry Drinker accused Virginia legislators of "talking much & making a shew of promoting the cause of Liberty & Virtue, while they . . . merely prostitute those terms to serve their base & wicked purposes." Referring to the Virginia legislators, whom the Quakers had petitioned for relief, he wrote: "Surely these are not the Men to let the Oppressed go free & loose the Bonds of Wickedness, have they not for many years been wantoning in Blood, & holding in a severe, merciless captivity, thousands of their fellow Men, whose Cases are deplorable beyond description, & bear no comparison. . . . Can Righteousness be expected from men so depraved & corrupt? verily nay."[66] In sum, Drinker doubted that the patriots would liberate the wrongfully imprisoned white Quakers, let alone their Black slaves.

Limited Antislavery Gains and Legislative Rebuffs

As the war continued, abolitionists in various states persisted in demanding reform but with only limited influence. The most significant antislavery progress during the early years of the war occurred in New England. Several factors helped facilitate antislavery reform in the region, including the fact that enslaved people made up less than 3 percent of the population. Biblicist and providentialist arguments also had special resonance due to the influence of the region's Puritan heritage and the tradition of fast days. In Massachusetts, moreover, the legal ambiguities related to hereditary slavery rendered it vulnerable to legal challenges. Still, although antislavery sentiment was apparently more widespread in New England than among whites in other regions, legislatures generally resisted reform.

In Massachusetts, individual slaves continued to win their freedom with the help of sympathetic lawyers and juries. In her recent study of Essex County freedom suits, Jeanne Pickering demonstrates a shift in slaveholding defendants' tactics following the 1773 case of *Caesar [Hendrick] v. Greenleaf* (in which John Lowell had argued that hereditary slavery was sinful and unsupported by statute law). Expecting juries to rule against them, some slaveholders negotiated freedom agreements with their bondspeople while others simply stopped contesting freedom suits. For instance, Richard Greenleaf apparently chose the latter route when he was sued by another one of his enslaved laborers in the fall of 1776. The Black man, who called himself Pomp Somersett (a significant choice of surname in itself), hired Theophilus Parsons (brother of the antislavery speaker at Harvard College's 1773 debate) as his attorney and sought £30 in damages. Greenleaf, having previously been forced to pay damages and court costs to Caesar Hendrick, did not bother to hire a lawyer or even show up to court. Somersett thus won his freedom by default and voluntarily chose to forego pursuing damages against his former master (likely as part of an informal arrangement). He was one of at least a dozen enslaved people in Essex County who won their freedom through similar means during the war (four of them with Parsons's aid).[67]

It also appears that some slaveholders were inspired to formally manumit their slaves while others simply acquiesced when their slaves asserted their freedom. When asked about the process of abolition in 1795, Thomas Pemberton of Boston (no relation to the Pembertons of Philadelphia) recalled that "in some of the country towns they voted to have no slaves among them, and to indeminifie their masters (after they have given them freedom) from any expence that might arise by means of their age, infirmities, or inability to support themselves."[68] In other words, towns chose to ignore, either formally or informally, the 1703 law that required posting a bond when manumitting an enslaved person. Pemberton also reported that many Black people simply "took the liberty to free themselves, and left their masters (these were not considered as runaways and apprehended as formerly)." Some of these former masters likely assumed that courts would no longer enforce their property rights over fellow human beings, especially given the ambiguous status of hereditary slavery based on the *Somerset* principle and the biblicist arguments common in antislavery publications. It is no surprise that scholars' analyses of probate records from Suffolk County confirm a "drastic reduction" of human property during the 1770s.[69]

Black activists also sought to revive the state-wide push for emancipation in early 1777, submitting another petition to the legislature. It seems that this petition was organized through a lodge of Black Freemasons recently established by Prince Hall. At least three of the eight petitioners were Freemasons, including Hall as well as Peter Bestes, who had been involved in the petitioning efforts since 1773. They drew heavily on the text of the petitions submitted in 1773 and 1774 but updated the language based on the context of the war. Referring to the many petitions that white patriots had sent to Parliament and the king, the Black men wrote: "In imitation of the laudable example of the good People of these States, your Petitioners have long and patiently waited the event of Petition after Petition . . . and can not but with grief reflect that their success has been but too similar." Unstated but perhaps implicit was the fact that white patriots had resorted to violence when their petitions went unanswered; perhaps enslaved Blacks would do the same. The petitioners described freedom as "the natural right of all Men" and called for complete emancipation, with enslaved children serving until age twenty-one. They closed by invoking the patriots' frequent prayers for providential aid. Once white patriots were "no longer chargeable with the inconsistency" of slavery, they could expect to "be prospered in their present glorious struggles for liberty; and have those blessings secured to them by Heaven."[70]

Several white religious leaders soon echoed the Black petitioners' providentialist language. The Reverend Samuel Webster, who in 1767 and 1773 had described Parliament's oppressive policies as divine punishment for the sin of slavery, gave a sermon before the legislature on May 28 in which he called on the body to abolish all forms of oppression. Paraphrasing Isaiah 26:9 to interpret the war, he declared that "God's *judgments* are now *abroad* in all the land, and he justly expects that we learn righteousness." In public letters to newspaper editors, the Reverend William Gordon also encouraged abolition while bemoaning the fact that newspapers continued to advertise slaves for sale. Deacon Timothy Pickering Sr. drafted a public letter invoking Matthew 7:2 to describe the war as retaliatory justice for having "*Oppressed* Africans with Slavery." He also cited Isaiah 58:6 as well as Jeremiah 22:13, which warns, "Woe unto him that buildeth his house by unrighteousness . . . that useth his neighbour's service without wages, and giveth him not for his work." To atone for slavery, Pickering called for not only emancipation but reparations: "Our Slavers are advised to pay their Africans for their Past Services and to

Let them Goe free." This letter, which also declared America was more sinful than Sodom, was deemed too provocative for publication.[71]

In June 1777, a legislative committee including Nathaniel Appleton and Nathaniel Peaslee Sargeant (who, with John Lowell, had helped Caesar win his freedom in *Caesar v. Taylor* in 1772) drafted an antislavery bill. The committee asserted that slaveholding violated the principles of Christianity and natural rights, and was especially disgraceful when the state was "struggling against Oppression." The initial draft proposed freeing only slaves' children "hereafter born" but was soon revised to liberate the current generation of slaves as well. The bill also explicitly granted Black residents the same "privileges and immunities" as other citizens of Massachusetts.[72] It was the most radical abolition bill of the era.

The state House of Representatives began considering the bill on June 9, but conservative legislators effectively killed it four days later by insisting that they consult the Continental Congress. One legislator explained to John Adams that he had "divert[ed]" the effort, "supposing it would Embarrass." Adams in turn was happy to let the matter "sleep for a Time," noting that "We have Causes enough of Jealousy Discord and Division, and this Bill will certainly add to the Number." The concern that liberating Black people in Massachusetts could upset the South underscores the limits of many patriot politicians' support for the natural rights ideals they frequently espoused.[73] By contrast, the minority of legislators who actively promoted abolition generally had religious inspiration and believed that it would aid the war effort by pleasing God.

Meanwhile, some Black people in Massachusetts asserted their own freedom based on rumors "that all Negros were made Free." In September 1777, Joseph Prout petitioned the legislature for help after his "Two Negro Men" abandoned him for paid employment elsewhere. The petition was "Read and dismissed" by the legislators. Although they would not endorse emancipation, neither would they intervene to prop up slaveholders' power.[74]

The only significant antislavery legislative reform adopted by politicians during the first four years of the war was Vermonters' decision to forbid slavery in the state constitution they adopted in July 1777. The breakaway state—which would not be formally admitted into the union until 1791—consisted of land claimed at various times by New Hampshire, New York, and Massachusetts. The Vermont Constitution was directly modeled on Pennsylvania's 1776 constitution, including the preamble's condemnation of King George III for enlisting "foreign mercenaries, savages and slaves." Yet, anger at George III for arming Black loyalists did not prevent Vermont from embracing antislavery. After copying the Pennsylvania Constitution's assertion of "inalienable rights," the Vermonters added: "Therefore, no male person, born in this country, or brought from over sea, ought to be holden by law, to serve any person, as a servant, slave or apprentice, after he arrives to the age of twenty-one years, nor female, in like manner, after she arrives to the age of eighteen years, unless they are bound by their own consent, after they arrive to such age, or bound by law, for the payment of debts, damages, fines, costs, or the like." There were only a few hundred enslaved people living in Vermont, and the antislavery clause theoretically liberated adults immediately and children at the age of adulthood. However, within a decade the legislature would determine that further laws were needed to prevent the sale of Black children out of the state as hereditary slaves. Despite the ambiguities and imperfections of the 1777 antislavery clause, Vermont is recognized as "the first sovereign polity in the New World to have legally ended slavery." Vermonters' antislavery stance was of course facilitated by the fact that the region contained far fewer slaves than any other state, and they were likely inspired in part by the Declaration of Independence. Religious beliefs undoubtedly also played a role. Most of the region's settlers were from New England, especially Connecticut (indeed, Vermont was initially known as New Connecticut), where for years ministers such as Samuel Andrews, Ebenezer Baldwin, Isaac Foster, Jonathan Edwards Jr., and Levi Hart had been arguing that slaveholding was a God-provoking sin. Settlers in Vermont, it seems, wanted their new state to be free of this sin.[75]

Events in the fall of 1777 seemed to reveal God's chastising hand and as well as his mercy. In September, the British captured Philadelphia, causing the Continental Congress to flee west to Lancaster County. This embarrassment was partially offset by a patriot victory at the Battle of Saratoga in early October, inspiring Congress to proclaim the first national day of thanksgiving. On December 18, the patriots expressed their gratitude that the Lord "hath been pleased in so great a measure . . . to crown our arms with most signal success." In sermons, patriot ministers commonly compared the Battle of Saratoga to Old Testament battles in which God intervened to help the Israelites triumph over their adversaries. Nonetheless, the ministers stressed that God's continued aid depended on Americans' gratitude, piety, and righteousness. Some could not help but worry that divine chastisement for slavery would soon resume. In Connecticut, the Reverend David Avery used his thanksgiving sermon to warn, "*Our enslaving* NEGROES *is not the smallest of our crying sins. Doth not this sin cry to heaven for retaliation?*"[76] The Connecticut legislature had passed a bill facilitating voluntary manumissions in October (in large part to help recruit Black men into the army), but Avery still felt greater reform was necessary.[77]

The winter of 1777–1778, which General Washington's army spent at Valley Forge, Pennsylvania, was a difficult and disheartening time. A shortage of recruits led Washington to endorse a Rhode Island proposal to reward slaves with freedom in exchange for a pledge to serve for the duration of the war. With Washington's blessing, the Rhode Island assembly passed the Act to Enlist Slaves in February 1778. Under the law, masters would receive compensation from the state government, but their permission was not required for the enslaved men to enlist and receive their freedom. In the face of slaveholders' opposition, the Rhode Assembly repealed the law in May, but not before the First Rhode Island Regiment acquired a Black majority. The Continental Army continued to welcome free people of color along with slaves who were manumitted and enlisted by their former masters (sometimes as draft substitutes).[78]

Meanwhile, the patriots also continued praying for divine aid. The Continental Congress's call for a fast day in the spring of 1778 was its most somber proclamation yet, describing the "cruel and desolating war" as "evident tokens of [God's] displeasure." Since 1775, all congressional fast-day proclamations had lamented the people's sins and viewed the war in providentialist terms, but this was the first one that suggested the Americans might *deserve* the Lord's chastisements (as was common in New England proclamations). Congress did not, however, explicitly identify slaveholding among the sins angering the Lord. The proclamation instructed Americans to "implore the mercy and forgiveness of God; and to beseech him that vice, prophaneness, extortion, and every evil, may be done away; and that we may be a reformed and happy people."[79] Antislavery ministers felt this type of supplication remained insufficient.

The Reverend Jacob Green of New Jersey advocated for emancipation on the spring 1778 fast day. Green, a Presbyterian minister who served in the state legislature, had been an early advocate of independence. But he believed that God was using the imperial crisis and war as retaliatory justice to awaken white Christians to the sin of slavery. In his fast-day sermon, Green identified slavery as "the most crying sin in our land" and argued "that on this account, more than any one particular thing, God maintains his controversy against us." Quoting Isaiah 58:6, he proclaimed: "These American

States must, and will groan under the afflicting hand of God, till we reform in this matter . . . *to let the oppressed go free*." When Green published his sermon the following year (its publication had been delayed due to the "Scarcity of Paper"), he appended an emancipation plan. Enslaved adults and their children would continue serving for various lengths of time based on their ages. For example, children under five (and those born in the future) would receive their freedom at the age of majority (eighteen for women and twenty-one for men), those aged thirty to thirty-five would be freed in five years, and those between fifty and sixty would be freed after a single year of additional service. Green's plan, like the form of abolition adopted by Quakers, was gradual but complete (aside for elderly slaves, who would be cared for by their masters).[80]

New Jersey's governor, William Livingston, shared some of Green's antislavery sentiments but did not prioritize them, especially as America's military prospects improved. France had formed an alliance with the United States in February 1778, and the arrival of French troops in New Jersey led the British forces to abandon Philadelphia in June. In a message to the New Jersey legislature, Governor Livingston celebrated the French alliance and described the war as God's means of punishing the British Empire for its sins. He was confident that Americans would soon be victorious because the "Hand of Providence" was on their side. Livingston also advocated harsh measures against loyalists and those who maintained a "shameful and most disingenuous Neutrality."[81] The governor's assumption that God supported the war, along with his criticism of neutral Americans, offended Quakers.

Samuel Allinson, the PMS activist from Burlington who had served in New Jersey's colonial government, addressed a polite but stern letter to Livingston in July 1778, complaining about his "late Message to the Assembly." Allinson emphasized that Christ favored love and mercy, and he explained that Quakers' religious principles prevented them from supporting the war. He agreed that the war was the will of providence but argued that it was designed to punish the Americans as well as the British for their sins, especially slavery. "The same measure that ye mete, shall be measured to you again," he reminded Livingston, quoting Matthew 7:2. Invoking the story of Joshua and Achan, Allinson argued that God would continue punishing America as long as "the 'accursed thing' remaineth in her possession." Merging Isaiah 58:6 and 61:1, he predicted that "America never can or will prosper in a right manner; or receive & enjoy true peace & its delightful fruits; until she 'proclaims liberty to the captives, & lets the oppressed go free.'" In his response, Livingston claimed that he had previously submitted a proposal "to lay the foundation for their Manumission" but that the legislature had determined the state was in "too critical a Situation to enter on the consideration of it at that time." Allinson encouraged the governor to persist in promoting emancipation, noting that Pennsylvania had recently begun considering an abolition bill (discussed in Chapter 6).[82] Livingston, however, lacked the Quaker's sense of urgency. Whereas abolitionists such as Allinson and Green were inspired to act by their belief that the war was divine punishment, Livingston's faith in providential military aid led to complacency even though he shared antislavery sentiments.

Most delegates in the Continental Congress were also complacent regarding Black slavery. They celebrated the French alliance and their own return to Philadelphia following the British evacuation by calling for another national day of thanksgiving in late 1778. The proclamation thanked God for "disposing the heart of a powerful monarch to enter into alliance with us, and aid our cause."[83] Abolitionists, however, felt that the patriots owed God more than a simple thanks; they needed to demonstrate their gratitude by letting the oppressed go free.

Anthony Benezet argued as much in "Observations on Slavery," the centerpiece of his 1778 pamphlet, *Serious Considerations on Several Important Subjects*. He interpreted the war as evidence that "the good and just father of mankind is now arisen to plead the cause of the oppressed Africans." He emphasized that God's purpose was not simply to punish white Americans, but to inspire reform. "Perhaps nothing will so sensibly teach us to feel for the affliction of the oppressed Africans," he proposed, "as that ourselves partake of the same cup of distress, we have so long been instrumental in causing them to drink." Benezet quoted natural rights references from the Declaration of Independence and the Virginia Constitution, but these documents did not inspire optimism for the Quaker. Instead, Benezet described them as "a great aggravation of that guilt which has so long laid upon America," for they illustrated white patriots' hypocrisy. Hoping to inspire actual antislavery reform, Benezet sent copies of *Serious Considerations* to prominent politicians including Governor Livingston and John Jay, president of the Continental Congress.[84]

The Continental Congress, of course, would not satisfy Benezet's wishes; but the Quaker's pamphlet and letter may have influenced the next continental fast-day proclamation, issued by Jay on March 20, 1779. The proclamation described the war as "just Punishment of our manifold Transgressions" and lamented that "notwithstanding the Chastisements received and Benefits bestowed, too few have been sufficiently awakened to a Sense of their Guilt, or warmed with Gratitude, or taught to amend their Lives and turn from their Sins, that so he might turn from his Wrath." Congress instructed the colonists to repent and reform, praying that God would "grant the Blessings of Peace to all contending Nations, Freedom to those who are in Bondage, and Comfort to the Afflicted." Many white patriots likely considered themselves as the ones needing deliverance from bondage, but Jay, who signed and likely helped write the proclamation, probably considered it partly as a prayer for the end of Black slavery. Jay was deeply religious and increasingly opposed to slavery; he had been disappointed in 1777 that New York's state constitution had tolerated slaveholding, and he would later join the New-York Manumission Society.[85] In 1780, when Pennsylvania passed a gradual abolition law, Jay expressed his hope that other states would emulate it: "Till America comes into this measure, her prayers to Heaven for liberty will be impious."[86] He clearly shared some of Benezet's antislavery providentialism.

At least one minister used the spring 1779 fast day as an opportunity to encourage abolition. The Reverend James Francis Armstrong had served in active duty in 1776 before being appointed an army chaplain in December 1777. The Presbyterian based his 1779 fast-day sermon on Proverbs 14:34: "Righteousness exalteth a nation: but sin is a reproach to any people." Although the sermon was not published during Armstrong's life, the audience included General George Washington and some of his troops stationed in Middlebrook, New Jersey. Armstrong described the war as a "heaven-commissioned scourge" that would continue until the Americans reformed their sinful ways. He focused mostly on individual sins that soldiers might be guilty of, such as drunkenness and swearing, but he also condemned slave trading and slaveholding at the end of his sermon, when denouncing greed. He described the slave trade as tearing Africans from their "heavenly inheritance—fair freedom," and consigning them to a "worse than Egyptian bondage." Two years later, when celebrating the victory at Yorktown, Armstrong would credit divine aid while still indicating Americans' duty to end the sin of slavery.[87]

Meanwhile, in March 1779, John Jay and the Continental Congress endorsed a proposal encouraging South Carolina and Georgia to recruit slaves into the army. Under this plan, slaveholders would be compensated up to one thousand dollars for each enslaved recruit, and Black soldiers who survived the war would receive freedom and fifty dollars. Military desperation—the fact that General Washington could not spare troops to defend the Lower South—was a primary impulse behind the proposal. But religion and antislavery sentiments played roles as well. The plan was developed by South Carolina delegate Henry Laurens and his son John. Although a wealthy slaveholder (and former slave trader), Henry had told John in 1776 that he was "not one of those who . . . dare trust in Providence for defence & security of their own Liberty while they enslave and wish to continue in Slavery, thousands who are as well entitled to freedom as themselves." A British acquaintance of John's, the poet Thomas Day, was even more dismissive of "a solemn appeal to heaven" made by slaveholding patriots. "If there be an object truly ridiculous in nature, it is an American patriot, signing resolutions of independency with the one hand, and with the other brandishing a whip over his affrighted slaves," he quipped in 1776.[88] Within two years, John Laurens began advocating the use of Black troops in South Carolina as a means to promote emancipation, routinely mixing arguments about natural rights, religion, and military advantage. When the plan reached Congress, most of its supporters likely focused on its ability to alleviate manpower shortages. But in addition to Jay, at least one other congressional delegate, William Whipple of New Hampshire, hoped the plan would "lay a foundation for the Abolition of Slavery in America."[89] Legislators in South Carolina and Georgia, however, overwhelmingly rejected Congress's proposal. Rather than promoting Black freedom, South Carolina later adopted a system of confiscating loyalists' slaves and then offering them as bounties to white army recruits. Northern states, on the other hand, continued enlisting growing numbers of free Blacks in the army. (Though some northern states, including New Jersey, also redistributed loyalists' slaves as bounties or sold them to raise funds.)[90]

The British army responded to the growing number of Black patriots by threatening to enslave them if they were captured in battle. In late June 1779, General Henry Clinton issued a proclamation from his headquarters in Philipsburg, New York, directed at African Americans and published repeatedly in the *Royal Gazette*. It warned Black patriots that "all *Negroes* taken in Arms, or upon any military duty" would be treated as enslaved laborers, with a bounty "paid to the Captor." In other words, he was incentivizing British troops to target, capture, and enslave free Black patriots. Clinton also reiterated that runaway Black loyalists who voluntarily came to British lines would be protected; moreover, they could work in "any Occupation" that supported the British army. These two provisions make clear that military strategy, not humanitarianism, determined British policy regarding Black people. Still, historians believe that Clinton's clarification that Black loyalists need not necessarily serve in a military capacity increased the number of enslaved Black families with women and children fleeing to British lines.[91]

White patriots' reactions to Clinton's Philipsburg Proclamation were complex and are difficult to interpret at times. One widely reprinted newspaper poem critical of Clinton contained the following sonnet:

> A proclamation oft of late he sends
> To thieves and rogues, who are his only friends;
> Those he invites; all colours he attacks,
> But deference pays to *Ethiopean Blacks.*

This sonnet could be interpreted as criticizing Clinton either for stealing patriots' enslaved property or, more likely, for preferring to attack free Black patriots whom he could enslave. The latter view was more clearly advanced in another widely reprinted piece that condemned "Clinton's proclamation, to sell Negroes captured from the enemy," as a dishonorable "disgrace."[92]

The Reverend John Murray, the legislator who had worked to ensure that Massachusetts treated captured Black loyalists as POWs rather than as slaves, similarly viewed Clinton's practice of enslaving Black patriots as disgraceful. But he also regarded Clinton's policy of arming Black loyalists in providentialist terms. During a Massachusetts fast day in November 1779, Murray told a Newburyport congregation that God was using the British army to chastise the Americans for their sins, just as God had used the Babylonians and Egyptians to discipline the Israelites. Noting that God often "adapt[ed] the punishment to the crime," Murray believed it was fitting that the British were "bribing the Savages of the wood" and "hiring the negroes of our families to embrue their hands in . . . blood." Although such rhetoric could reflect and encourage racial prejudice, Murray hoped to promote emancipation. He argued that the Lord would consider the patriots' fast days "as a repetition of a deliberate mockery" until they ended "the practice of enslaving the human species."[93] Murray's stance exemplifies the complexity of the Revolution's connection to antislavery. He believed slaveholding was a sin that had provoked God to punish the colonists and the British Empire, but he also had faith that the patriots would prevail with God's blessing if they embraced antislavery reform.

* * *

After several years of war, with independence still far from inevitable, the aspiring new nation had made little antislavery progress. None of the original thirteen colonies passed legislation ending slavery before 1780. Far from leading the antislavery charge, patriot politicians often worked to thwart the movement, even in the North. Unsurprisingly, the language of the Declaration of Independence had not inspired slaveholders to abandon the source of their wealth and status. Natural rights rhetoric and a desire to appear consistent were insufficient to inspire much antislavery commitment. Nonetheless, it is a mistake to imagine that the transition from imperial tension to open warfare had weakened the antislavery movement.

Abolitionists had been marginal figures to begin with, notwithstanding occasional lip service by a few prominent politicians. During the war, the backbone of the antislavery movement remained Black people along with white allies drawn principally from the ranks of Quakers and evangelicals. The war created new opportunities for Black people to claim their freedom, especially through military service or flight. Wartime destruction also reinforced the persuasive power of abolitionists' providentialist arguments. This rhetoric appeared not only in antislavery pamphlets and newspapers essays, but also in religious sermons, especially during fast days. The war thus helped publicize and spread antislavery ideas, even if many white Americans remained insufficiently moved during the early years of the conflict.

The Revolution's complex and contradictory effects on abolitionism are perhaps best illustrated through reference to the Society of Friends. On the one hand, the war caused Pennsylvania's Quaker-dominated Society for the Relief of Negroes (the future Pennsylvania Abolition Society) to temporarily disband, and caused the Philadelphia Meeting for Sufferings to focus its attention primarily on promoting Quaker pacifism and managing the patriot backlash it provoked. In this sense, the war hindered abolitionist activism. On the other hand, Quaker abolitionists celebrated the war's potential to spread antislavery even as they regretted the violence. Throughout the war, Quakers quoted Isaiah 26:9 to indicate their expectation that while the Lord's "judgments are in the earth, the inhabitants of the world will learn righteousness." They hoped the war would inspire reform in many aspects but especially in regard to slavery, which they identified as "among the grand Causes of the divine Wrath being manifestly poured out upon this Continent." British Quakers expressed similar sentiments, asserting that if the wartime suffering inspired abolition and other reforms, "happy will be the Exchange, & blessed the Day of our Chastisement." By September 1779, American Quakers could celebrate that nearly all members under the Philadelphia Yearly Meeting's jurisdiction "have let the oppressed go free." Moreover, they believed that the war had awakened antislavery sentiment "in the minds of many who are not in religious profession with us."[94] It seemed to them that God's chastisements were working, albeit more slowly among white Americans of other denominations. Antislavery Quakers were more optimistic about the prospects for reform during the war than they had been before.

If the Revolutionary War had somehow been avoided or had ended quickly, there is little reason to assume that any of the colonies or states (perhaps with the exception of Massachusetts) would have embraced abolition during the 1770s or 1780s.[95] But the longer the war lasted, the more reason Americans had to question why God had not yet granted them deliverance. Abolitionists offered a clear explanation that gained adherents over time. Additionally, as more and more African Americans served on the patriot side, they established a firmer basis from which to claim rights.[96] The prospects for antislavery reform thus increased as the war dragged on.

CHAPTER 6

Antislavery Reform During the Revolutionary War, 1778–1783

The providentialist aspect of antislavery increased as the war dragged on and a patriot military victory remained out of sight. Abolitionists insisted that the war reflected God's anger and that the divine chastisements would not end until patriots enacted antislavery reforms. For instance, Deacon Benjamin Colman of Newbury, Massachusetts, responded to the Continental Congress's 1780 fast day proclamation pessimistically:

> How can we with confidence, lift up our prayer . . . for deliverance from oppression, till we have loosed the bands of wickedness, proclaimed liberty to our captives, and let the oppressed go free? do not our crimes stare us in the face? and is not our God rising up out of his holy place, to retaliate our doings upon us? . . . Three, if not four, of our states are already fallen into the hands of our cruel enemies; and we have no reason to expect but that the rest will shortly fall a prey to them, if repentance and reformation don't prevent it. . . . God is now requiting blood for blood, oppression for oppression, according to his Word. Revelations 13, 10th, he that leadeth into captivity, shall go into captivity; he that killeth with the sword, must be killed with the sword.[1]

Although it is likely that only a minority of white patriots shared Colman's belief that slaveholding was the "*capital sin*" that had provoked the war, a substantial number came to agree that letting the oppressed go free could help curry divine favor. This providentialist belief inspired some patriots to transition from invoking natural rights rhetoric in defense of their own interests to implementing reforms extending liberty to others. It took several years to gain sufficient antislavery momentum—as had also been the case with Quakers during the French and Indian War—but the Revolutionary War ultimately facilitated and expedited antislavery reform.

Beginning with the passage of Pennsylvania's Gradual Abolition Act in March 1780, antislavery reformers achieved several important victories during the final years of the Revolutionary War. Slavery in Massachusetts was essentially defunct by the end of 1783, and New Hampshire also put the institution on the road to extinction that year. The Connecticut legislature debated emancipation during the war and would enact gradual abolition in 1784, as would Rhode Island. Several other states liberalized their manumission laws to enable slaveholders to manumit their bondspeople legally and easily, as Virginia—the largest slaveholding state—did in 1782. Of course, the antislavery movement also faced significant limitations and failures, as scholars have increasingly emphasized. Most of the northern states that legislated the end of slavery did so through *postnati* or "free womb" gradual abolition laws that in many ways privileged slaveholders' property rights over Black people's natural rights. They freed not the current generation of enslaved people but only their future children, and only after lengthy periods of indentured servitude. The states where slaveholding was most common and widespread—especially in the South as well as parts of the mid-Atlantic—preserved hereditary slavery. These unfortunate limitations are hardly surprising given the economic importance of enslaved labor, the political influence that slaveholders' wealth brought them, widespread prejudice among white Americans, and the fact that the Revolution originated in an effort to protect colonists' property rights. Given these realities, it is the extent rather than the limits of abolitionists' accomplishments that is most striking.

Examining the most significant antislavery reforms—those in Pennsylvania, Massachusetts, and Virginia—reveals the importance of religious ideology, abolitionist activism, and war as a catalyst for action. While ideological shifts grounded in religious responses to the Revolutionary War created favorable circumstances for abolitionism, actual reform still required persistent agitation by dedicated activists. None of the wartime antislavery reforms were inevitable or easy; they were hard-fought victories that contained concessions to slaveholders. Black and white abolitionists accepted compromises grudgingly and pragmatically as the best they could accomplish considering the obstacles they faced. The compromises, shortcomings, and limitations of wartime antislavery reforms should not obscure the fact that they nonetheless occurred with unprecedented rapidity and were almost certainly far more expansive than would have been the case if the Revolutionary War had been prevented or had ended quickly.

Legislative Abolition in Pennsylvania

Pennsylvania became the first state to abolish slavery through legislative action on March 1, 1780, fourteen months after the bill was first proposed. The bill was passed at a time when Quakers had little direct political influence (as they eschewed political participation during the war on account of their pacifism), and it is often portrayed as reflecting patriots' ideological consistency. "The Revolutionary generation was sincere in its espousal of the Rights of Man," Arthur Zilversmit writes in *The First Emancipation*, adding that the preamble to the Pennsylvania abolition law "appealed to the ideology of the Revolution to justify their actions." He highlights secular ideas while crediting Quakers' earlier religious arguments against slavery for having "prepared the way for the Whig-abolitionist arguments that it was irreconcilable with the Rights of Man." A reconsideration of the law and the arguments made in its favor, however, underscore the continued centrality of religion in the way white Pennsylvanians debated slavery. Providentialist interpretations of Pennsylvania's wartime experiences provided much of the impulse for the bill. Political opposition from slaveholders, however, nearly defeated the measure and rendered the final law more conservative. Black Pennsylvanians contributed indirectly to the law's creation by resisting their enslavement and joining the British army, highlighting the dangers slavery posed to society. After the law's passage, Black people mobilized politically to preserve and expand its liberationist potential.[2]

The person most directly responsible for Pennsylvania's Gradual Abolition Act was George Bryan, an Irish-born Presbyterian who had become a prominent politician in Philadelphia. His providentialist beliefs were central to his eventual embrace of abolitionism. In May 1778, Presbyterians at the Synod of New York and Philadelphia—held in New Jersey while the British remained in control of Philadelphia—prayed that the Lord would "prepare us for the deliverance from the chastenings he hath righteously afflicted upon us for our sins." They also asked God to bless the Continental Army and "our illustrious ally," the French. Their prayers seemed to be answered a month later, when the arrival of French troops prompted the British to abandon

Philadelphia. Bryan's public statements from 1778 to 1780 make it clear that he conceived of abolition as a means of expressing gratitude to God for delivering Philadelphia from British control.[3]

Although Bryan came to embrace an antislavery conception of divine providence akin to that held by many Quakers, he had previously been a leading persecutor of Friends. As a devout Presbyterian he disagreed with many Quaker doctrines, and as a patriot he despised their pacifism. As vice president of Pennsylvania's executive council in August 1777, Bryan had signed the orders arresting and exiling Quakers. Immediately following their initial arrest, the Quaker prisoners had begun submitting petitions—which they later published in pamphlet form—denouncing Bryan's "arbitrary" and "unjust" violation of their "religious and civil Liberty." The Quakers called on the patriot government to observe the Golden Rule and to reconcile its behavior with its "repeated declarations in favour of general Liberty." They warned that "the righteous judge of all the earth" would punish Pennsylvania patriots for their "unparalleled tyranny."[4] Such rhetoric did not sway the executive council at the time, but it may have gnawed on Bryan's conscience and irritated him. Moreover, as Bryan read through the papers confiscated from the Philadelphia Meeting for Sufferings, he would not have found any evidence that the Quakers had conspired with the British but he would have learned a great deal about Quaker pacificism and their belief that the war reflected divine chastisement for sins including slaveholding.[5]

Bryan was also likely among the politicians to whom Anthony Benezet gave a copy of his *Serious Considerations* in the summer of 1778. If Bryan bothered to read it, he may have been struck by Benezet's discussion of Jeremiah 34:14–22, which the Quaker believed "may produce a proper application for ourselves." This was the story—also recounted by John Woolman in his 1762 pamphlet and by Granville Sharp in *The Law of Retribution*—of the Israelites offering liberty to their servants when Jerusalem was facing attack by the Babylonians, only to renege after the enemy had retreated and thereby provoke God's wrath. In response to the Israelites' treachery, the Lord causes the Babylonians to resume their attack, subjecting his own chosen people to "the sword, the pestilence and the famine." The applicability of the story would have been obvious to Bryan and other Pennsylvanians. The Israelites' promise of manumission was akin to patriots' natural rights rhetoric while the Babylonians' retreat from Jerusalem was analogous to the recent British evacuation from Philadelphia. Benezet's point was clear: white Pennsylvanians should learn from the Israelites' mistake and follow through by manumitting their slaves. Otherwise, God might allow the British to recapture the city as punishment for the inhabitants' hypocritical sins and ingratitude.[6]

Whether influenced by Benezet or not, Bryan repeatedly described both the war and Pennsylvania's abolition bill in providentialist terms. The text of his initial legislative proposal, from August 1778, does not survive, but he chided the legislature for its inaction in an address published in November. Emancipation, he argued, would "offer to God one of the most proper and best returns of gratitude for his great deliverance of us and our posterity from enthraldom." Bryan also followed the advice of the Continental Congress and designated December 30 as a day of thanksgiving, expressing gratitude for God's "unmerited favours . . . by his over-ruling providence, to support us in a just and necessary war, for the defence of our rights and liberties."[7] But Bryan clearly felt that a day of thanksgiving was insufficient unless accompanied by righteous reform. In February 1779, the executive council again complained of legislative inaction regarding slavery in providentialist terms: "We would also again bring to your view a plan for the gradual abolition of slavery, so disgraceful to any people, and the more especially to those who have been contending in the great cause of liberty themselves, and upon whom providence has bestowed such eminent marks of its favour and protection. We think we are loudly called on to evince our gratitude, in making our fellowmen joint heirs with us of the same inestimable blessings." In response, the assembly finally appointed a committee to draft an abolition bill. It was based in part on the draft supplied by Bryan, and historians believe that William Lewis, a lapsed Quaker, was the primary author in the assembly.[8]

In March 1779, the bill appeared in the *Pennsylvania Packet* for public consideration. The preamble began by condemning slavery as an "invasion of the rights of mankind" that violated the "spirit of Christianity." It then explained the providentialist impulse behind abolition: "The most remarkable deliverance from the thraldom, which God, the great disposer of all events, has graciously vouchsafed to grant Pennsylvania . . . calleth for suitable returns of gratitude to the author of all salvation."[9] The preamble thus explicitly portrayed abolition as a way for white Pennsylvania patriots to demonstrate their gratitude to God for rescuing them (via the French) from the British army.

The bill's provisions adopted a gradual approach to abolition, balancing Black people's God-given natural rights with slaveholders' legally sanctioned property rights. The six thousand or so Black slaves in the state would remain enslaved for life while the next generation (born after the law's enactment) would be free upon reaching the age of majority (eighteen for women and twenty-one for men). This *postnati* version of gradual emancipation was thus not as complete as the form of abolition adopted by Quakers (or proposed by the Reverend Jacob Green in New Jersey), which included the current generation of enslaved people. Still, some white Pennsylvanians viewed the gradual abolition bill as too radical. In the *Pennsylvania Packet*, "A Citizen" proposed extending the labor of slaves' future children to age twenty-eight or thirty to better compensate their masters for the cost of raising them. Additionally, slaveholders mobilized against the bill during the legislature's summer recess, submitting petitions against it. The first of these petitions came from Chester County, where about 19 percent of families owned slaves. Meanwhile, Bryan stepped down from the executive council and was elected to the assembly, where he could more effectively oversee the bill's progress. In November, he introduced a revised abolition bill that sought to appease conservative critics by lengthening the period of unpaid labor for the slaves' children to age twenty-eight.[10]

The debate over slavery and abolition remained grounded in religion, as can be seen in Bryan's response to a proslavery petition from Chester County. The petition itself is no longer extant, but Bryan indicated that it came from a Presbyterian minister and other Presbyterians (a fact Bryan found "irksome" as a Presbyterian himself) in the western part of the county. Based on a 1780 census of slaveholders in Chester County, it seems that it was probably authored by the Reverend William Foster of Sadsbury, the minister of Upper Octorara Church. (The only other slaveholding minister in the area was Alexander Mitchell, also of Sadsbury, who took over as minister at Upper Octorara in 1785.)[11] The Chester County Presbyterians' proslavery petition had justified enslaving Black people based on Leviticus 25 (about "heathen" slaves); Bryan dedicated five columns of newspaper text to refuting this proslavery biblicism in two published letters. He argued that laws established for the ancient Israelites had little relevance for modern Christians, citing polygamy and other customs from Mosaic law that Christians deemed barbarous. Bryan conceded that neither Christ nor the apostles had explicitly condemned slavery, but he insisted that the apostles recognized the practice was "a gross departure from the great and golden rule of their master." Moreover, he asserted that history showed the practice of slaveholding "gradually gave way to the spirit of Christianity." Bryan regretted that Europeans had revived slavery in the New World, but he added that "the founding of a new empire in America seems to be designed by Providence, for the extinction of so savage a practice, inconsistent with civilization, morality, and the true spirit of Christianity."[12] He thus portrayed both the American Revolution and abolition as part of God's providential plan.

Bryan's second letter expanded on his biblical analysis while also drawing on political economy. He argued that "where labour depends upon slaves, art, invention and genius lie dormant." Furthermore, slaves were "internal enemies" who weakened society, as demonstrated by the "defection of negroes" to the British army. When justifying the liberation of slaves' children despite the government's obligation to protect private property, Bryan pointed to John Locke, Francis Hutcheson, and other philosophers who maintained that just enslavement could never be hereditary. (He likely pulled these examples from the excerpts that Benezet compiled in his many antislavery publications.) Bryan also dismissed concerns that abolishing slavery in Pennsylvania would somehow hurt or alienate the "Southern States," noting that the published bill had prompted "no objection" from southern delegates to the Continental Congress. "On the contrary," Bryan reported, "many gentlemen from the Southward tell us, that persons of generosity and liberality in that country, applauded the wisdom and benevolence of our Assembly." He ended by alluding to the religious and political tensions between Presbyterians and Quakers, exclaiming: "What! Shall Quakers, who we think have but clouded views of the gospel, have nearly cleared their society of the opprobrium of America [i.e., slaveholding], and shall any Presbyterian continue so void of charity and justice, as to wish and labour for the continuance of it[?]" This closing passage suggests that Bryan hoped his abolition law would help reclaim moral capital from the Quakers who had criticized his treatment of them in 1777. Bryan also referred to Quakers in a letter to Samuel Adams, writing: "Our bill astonishes and pleases the Quakers. They looked for no such benevolent issue of our new government exercised by Presbyterians."[13] The Presbyterian patriot was clearly happy to undermine Quaker pacifists' claim to moral superiority.

Quaker abolitionists may have been "astonished," but they were not entirely pleased with the gradual abolition bill. Samuel Allinson saw an early draft in August 1778 and commented, "I shall not animadvert on the form of the bill, tho I think several of the clauses rather improper or inconsistent with that liberality which is breathed in other parts."[14] Anthony Benezet was disappointed that the bill did not apply to the current generation of enslaved Black people. Apparently writing as "Phileleutheros" in the *Pennsylvania Gazette* in February 1780, he praised the bill's preamble but also reminded legislators that offerings to God must be "without blemish to be acceptable to him." He warned that failing to do full justice to the current generation of slaves "may bring down greater judgments upon us." The law should require masters to free all their slaves and support elderly freed people who were too old to earn a living, the Quaker argued. Benezet reportedly "had private interviews on the subject, with every member of the government," but the legislators declined to make the bill more progressive aside from removing a clause banning interracial marriage.[15]

Although the bill's compromises—such as the extension of labor requirements to age twenty-eight for slaves' children—disappointed Benezet, they were likely necessary to gain passage given the limits of antislavery sentiment among white politicians. While several petitions favored the bill, including another one from Chester County (likely from Quakers there), some inhabitants of Chester County and Lancaster County continued submitting proslavery petitions. The contents are lost, but the legislature dismissed the Lancaster petition "on account of its indecency." In the end, Pennsylvania's Gradual Abolition Act passed by a vote of 34 to 21 on March 1, 1780. The dissenting assemblymen issued a "Dissentient," subsequently printed in newspapers, listing their reasons for opposing abolition. They were concerned about property rights and feared abolition would increase slave unrest in other states, especially in the midst of war. Furthermore, they regretted that the law implicitly made free people of color full "citizens" with the same privileges as white people, including "the right of voting" and "intermarrying with white persons."[16] These concerns, endorsed by one-third of the legislature, reflect the contested and compromised nature of abolition in Pennsylvania.

The struggle to pass the Pennsylvania law was soon followed by a battle over implementing and revising it. A key provision of the law required slaveholders to register their slaves by November 1, 1780 or forfeit their human property. By early 1781, a "great number" of Black Pennsylvanians had already gained their freedom by suing owners who had failed to follow this provision. Anthony Benezet and William Lewis, the lapsed Quaker credited with drafting an early version of the bill, routinely aided Black Pennsylvanians in these proceedings. In response, slaveholders from Lancaster County repeatedly petitioned to repeal the entire law while many others requested additional time to register their slaves. In March 1781, the legislature drafted a bill extending the registration deadline and re-enslaving Black people who had already gained their freedom through the provision.[17]

A group of Black freedmen who faced the prospect of being re-enslaved petitioned against the proposed bill in April 1781. This was the first time that

Black Pennsylvanians petitioned their legislature, and they may have been inspired by knowledge of Black petitioning in New England. The Black Pennsylvanians were "fully sensible" that their petition was "wholly unprecedented" (at least in their state), but they proclaimed, "The grand question of slavery or liberty, is too important for us to be silent." Quoting from the 1780 law's preamble, they cautioned the legislators against undermining a law that had been enacted as "substantial proof" of the patriots' "gratitude" to God. The legislature delayed action until September, when Black activists submitted a second petition. At that time, a newspaper reprinted the petition from April along with an appeal by Cato, a Black man who had been freed as a result of his owner's failure to register him according to the abolition law. Cato also quoted from the 1780 law's preamble, and he warned that undermining the law would anger the Lord: "If we should be plunged back into slavery, what must we think of the meaning of all those words in the beginning of the said law . . . but what is most serious than all, what will our great father [i.e., God] think of such doings?" The following day, the legislature voted 30 to 20 against granting the proposed extension to slaveholders. Black Pennsylvanians' political activism and use of providentialist rhetoric thus helped preserve a crucial component of the 1780 Gradual Abolition Act. During the ensuing decades, hundreds of enslaved Pennsylvanians gained their freedom by showing that their masters had failed to follow the registration provision.[18]

Still, the provisions of the Gradual Abolition Act allowed slavery to linger in Pennsylvania for generations. For example, a female child born enslaved shortly before March 1780 would never receive her freedom under the law, and if she gave birth at age forty (in 1820), her child would not be free until 1848. Gary Nash and Jean Soderlund have aptly observed: "If the 1780 law was a death sentence for slavery in the state, it was a sentence with a two-generation grace period and one meant to avoid an abrupt or disruptive end to slavery and to accomplish abolition at little cost to those who claimed ownership over other human beings."[19] Contemporary abolitionists also understood the law's limitations and flaws; they criticized it as an inadequate halfway measure. New Jersey's John Cooper (the disowned brother of PMS member David) noted that by keeping the current generation of slaves in bondage, *postnati* abolition "save[d] that part of our tyranny and gain of oppression, which to us, the present generation, is of the most value." Instead of making a true sacrifice, he complained, patriots essentially told their slaves that "we will not do justice to you, but our posterity shall do justice to your posterity." Cooper warned that such covetousness would anger God.[20] Along with earlier complaints by Allinson and Benezet, John Cooper's criticism illustrates the problem with labeling all early abolitionists as "gradualists" in contrast to the "immediatists" of the antebellum era. When Quakers collectively turned against slavery, they acted gradually but were supposed to free all of their healthy slaves, not just the unborn future generations. A few white patriots proposed similar forms of emancipation, but the vast majority of patriot legislators would only accept gradual abolition that took generations to complete. The Pennsylvania Gradual Abolition Act was both unprecedently radical and deeply compromised. Its creation reflected contingent circumstances—including the British capture and evacuation of Philadelphia—along with providentialist conceptions of these events, and slaveholders likely would have succeeded in weakening the law if Black people had not mobilized to defend it.

Meanwhile, the wartime push for abolition in neighboring New Jersey proved unsuccessful. This failure is hardly surprising, as slaveholding was more prevalent there (especially in the southeastern part) than in Pennsylvania, and New Jersey legislators had previously declined even to revise policies regarding voluntary manumissions. Nonetheless, New Jersey's case further underscores the centrality of biblicism and providentialism to debates over slavery during the Revolution. In September 1780, the legislature received two antislavery petitions from Morris County and a third from Hunterdon County (both in the northern part of the state). The Reverend Jacob Green (who had called for emancipation in his 1778 fast-day sermon) lived in Morris County and may have initiated the effort; in any case, he subsequently supported it. The petitioners asserted that slavery violated the Golden Rule and cautioned that God would not allow the patriots to emerge victorious in the war "while we thus contravene his benevolent purposes to mankind in general." They called on the New Jersey legislature to earn God's blessing by following the example of Pennsylvania and passing an abolition law.[21] John Cooper immediately published (and signed) an essay in the *New-Jersey Gazette* that elaborated the petitioners' providentialist arguments. Noting that the war was lasting "far beyond" what the patriots had expected, Cooper referred to the biblical story of Joshua and Achan, identifying slaveholding as the "accursed thing" that was delaying the patriots' victory. "Can we imagine our prayers to Almighty God will meet with his approbation," he asked, "whilst the groans of our slaves are continually ascending mingled with them?" Revealing his frustration with the apathy of many patriots, Cooper implored: "If, therefore, neither the love of justice, nor the feelings of humanity are sufficient to induce us to release our slaves from bondage, let the dread of divine retribution—of national calamities—induce us to it."[22] He understood that fear of God's wrath was often a prerequisite for converting natural rights sentiment into antislavery action.

Cooper's essay provoked an extensive newspaper debate. Historians who have examined this debate tend to emphasize the racist rhetoric employed by slavery's apologists, but religion also remained a central theme. In the *New-Jersey Gazette*, "A Whig" insisted that slavery could not be an "accursed thing," for it was sanctioned by God in Leviticus 25:45–46. Soon "A Friend to Justice" came to Cooper's defense and challenged proslavery biblicism by asserting that Old Testament dispensations permitting slavery were peculiar to the ancient Hebrews and no longer applied. ("A Friend" also commented that a proslavery writer assuming the title of a "Whig" was akin to a "horse-turd" claiming to be an "apple.")[23] Most legislators, however, remained unswayed. In November 1780, the New Jersey General Assembly voted 20 to 8 to file the antislavery petitions without taking further action. Cooper, who had been recently elected to the legislative council, sought to introduce an abolition bill in December, but his motion was defeated in a 4 to 6 vote.[24] This effectively ended legislative debate regarding New Jersey slavery for the next five years.

The newspaper debate over slaveholding's compatibility with Christianity continued, however, into the summer of 1781. Slaveholders and their allies continued to defend slavery by citing the Old Testament. "A Lover of True Justice" cited not only Leviticus but also passages of Paul's writings in the New Testament that encouraged slaves to be obedient, such as Ephesians 6:5 and Philemon (in which Paul sends the fugitive Onesimus back to his master after converting him). This essay in turn drew a rebuttal from "E.," who asserted that "A Lover of True Justice" failed to recognize the distinction between enslavement for life and hereditary slavery. Moreover, "E." pointed to verses 16–17 of the letter to Philemon, in which Paul explicitly instructs him to welcome his former bondsman "not now as a servant, but above a servant, a brother beloved." This type of religious argument reportedly persuaded some slaveholders. "Homo Sum" stated that he had owned slaves for decades and initially declined when asked to sign the antislavery petition, which had been his first exposure to antislavery arguments. Afterward, however, he "could not get rid of the impression it made," and he embraced the cause. "Homo Sum" called on others to support Black freedom, using providentialist rhetoric: "The danger we have been in of losing our *own* liberty, may be a wise dispensation of Providence to awaken in us a juster sense of *theirs*. The national calamity of war, we cannot doubt, is sent as a punishment for national sins; because only in this life can states and kingdoms be punished." Of course, many slaveholders remained unpersuaded. "Truth et Justice" dismissed the notion that "the Almighty is offended with us for keeping slaves," and emphasized that slaves were "*legal property*." Another essay by "A Lover of True Justice" reiterated his proslavery biblicism, insisting that slavery "is not sin, and deserves no judgments of God."[25] The fact that slaveholders felt compelled to dispute abolitionists' biblicist and providentialist arguments indicates they feared the persuasive power of such rhetoric.

Although the effort to pass antislavery legislation miscarried in New Jersey (among other states) and was an arduous process in Pennsylvania, the Revolutionary War played a crucial role as a catalyst for action. First, in 1775 and 1776, the outbreak of war helped convince reluctant Quakers to conform to the antislavery stance adopted by the Philadelphia Yearly Meeting during the French and Indian War. Then, after 1777, the capture and liberation of Philadelphia convinced George Bryan and some other patriots that the war was God's means of awakening them to the sin of slavery. In other words, rather than hindering antislavery progress, the war strengthened the providentialist component of antislavery ideology. Moreover, the war also encouraged abolition by demonstrating the danger of "internal enemies" and facilitating self-emancipation, reducing slaveholders' investment in the institution. Pennsylvania politicians' embrace of abolition was a deeply contingent event; without the war, there is little reason to imagine that Pennsylvania would have taken any steps by 1780 (or in the near future) to end slavery. It is true that New Jersey would cling to slavery until finally passing a gradual abolition bill in 1804, but that date may well have been even later without the war.[26]

The Process of Emancipation in Massachusetts

The Revolutionary War also accelerated the process of emancipation in Massachusetts, where Black activists continued leading the push for abolition. In June 1775, after "negroes in the counties of Bristol and Worcester" petitioned the local committee of correspondence, the patriot committee published a statement proclaiming that they would support the "emancipation of the

Negroes" whenever "there shall be a door open."[27] The legislature, however, declined to deliver. Throughout the war, Black activists continued employing the tactics they had pioneered during the late 1760s and early 1770s, asserting their right to liberty through lawsuits, legislative petitions, newspaper essays, negotiations with masters, and simply running away. A handful of white allies, especially clergymen and their sons, continued lending support, arguing that hereditary slavery was an illegitimate and sinful custom that was provoking God's wrath. Although this interracial coalition never overcame legislative inertia, it influenced public opinion and chipped away at slavery through individual legal victories until the institution was all but defunct in the state by the end of the war.

Indeed, it has recently become clear to historians that slavery had been severely weakened even before the adoption of the 1780 state constitution, which was long cited as the basis of the freedom suits in 1781–1783 that are credited with ending slavery in Massachusetts.[28] While the 1780 constitution now appears less important than once assumed, scholars have not yet fully appreciated the role of religion in the abolition process in the Bay State. Patriots routinely asserted that they could only win if God was on their side, and many worried God would not answer their prayers until they let the oppressed go free. These beliefs help explain the decline of slavery in Massachusetts both before and after the state adopted its 1780 constitution.

Bay State abolitionists saw a new opportunity for political reform in the winter of 1777–1778, when the legislature drafted and debated a state constitution. But anyone who hoped Massachusetts would follow Vermont's lead and explicitly forbid perpetual slavery in its constitution was soon disappointed. By January 1778, a draft of the state constitution revealed that it contained no antislavery provision; indeed, it lacked a declaration of rights entirely. Moreover, Article V excluded "negroes, Indians and mulattoes" from the franchise.[29] In sum, Massachusetts legislators drafted a constitution that left slavery alone while making racial discrimination part of the state's fundamental law.

The draft constitution provoked antislavery criticism even before it was released to the public. The legislature's chaplain, the Reverend William Gordon, was the likely author of a newspaper essay addressed "To the Convention of the Massachusetts Bay" in January 1778. He condemned the racial restriction on voting as "ridiculous, inconsistent and unjust." Paraphrasing Acts 17:26, Gordon argued that the constitution should begin with a declaration of rights, "evidencing that the inhabitants are no respecters of persons and do *verily* believe that *God hath made of one blood all nations of man*, whether black, white, or otherwise coloured." In other words, the Congregationalist minister wanted a state constitution forbidding slavery and establishing racial equality before the law. Gordon's support for Black civil rights provoked a racist response in the form of a poem in the *Independent Chronicle* that described Blacks as "Cain's discolour'd seed." Phillis Wheatley, in turn, may have been the author of a poem defending Black capacity and suggesting that it was white racists who had the dark "*mental* hue."[30]

In the legislature, John Bacon, a former Presbyterian minister who represented Stockbridge (Berkshire County), unsuccessfully sought to remove the discrimination against voters of color. In a speech that he later published, Bacon asked: "Are they not Americans? Were they not (most of them at least) born in this country?" However, his effort to strike the racist exclusions failed, with "18 only out of 101 for the Question."[31] The vast majority of the Massachusetts legislators thus supported an explicitly racist constitution. After the legislature submitted the constitution to the people for ratification in March 1778, the Reverend Gordon again condemned it. He argued that Article V "will be an everlasting reproach upon the present inhabitants." Gordon's criticism ultimately cost him his job as the legislature's chaplain but likely helped persuade the public to reject the document.[32]

In May of 1778, the towns of Massachusetts overwhelmingly rejected the proposed constitution. Although most town meetings simply reported the number of voters who supported or opposed ratification, a substantial number included explanations in their returns. These reports complained about many aspects of the constitution, including its lack of a bill of rights and the level of overlap between the functions of the executive and legislative branches. Some also expressed antislavery sentiments. The towns of Essex County—which produced a disproportionate number of antislavery publications and freedom suits—published a pamphlet explaining their collective reasons for objecting to the constitution. The *Essex Result*, authored principally by Theophilus Parsons, the antislavery lawyer, complained that it lacked a bill of rights enumerating the "unalienable rights of mankind." Although the pamphlet did not call for any specific antislavery reform, it proclaimed that "would to God, the situation of America and the tempers of it's inhabitants were such, that the slaveholder could not be found in the land." Separately, at least ten towns explicitly complained about Article V's racist provisions.[33]

Some of the complaints about the racist language were phrased in both secular and religious terms. In Worcester County, the voters of Westminster complained that Article V "deprives a part of the humane Race of their Natural Rights, mearly on account of their Couler—Which in our opinion no power on Earth has a Just Right to Doe." Four other Worcester County towns appealed more explicitly to religious ideas. The people of Upton echoed the Reverend Gordon's biblicist complaints, arguing that suffrage should be "without regard to Nation or Colour, seeing all Nations are made of one blood." Those in Sutton condemned the racist provision as "manifestly adding to the already accumulated Load of guilt lying upon the Land in supporting the slave trade . . . this must be the bringing or incurring more Wrath upon us." Hardwick residents denounced slavery as a "Crying Sin which has Brought Gods Judgments upon the Land." They cited Jeremiah 34:14 as evidence that failing to follow through with the abolition of slavery would increase God's wrath against the patriots. They called on the legislature to liberate the enslaved Blacks who "have from time to time Humbly Petitioned to the General Court for their Liberty." Meanwhile in Boothbay, Maine, the townspeople warned that slaveholding "reflects dishonour and Endangers the curse of heaven on our public Struggles for our own rights."[34] These statements, expressing the views of collective town meetings rather than solitary antislavery writers, further demonstrate the centrality of providentialism within wartime antislavery sentiment.

People of color in Massachusetts must have been pleased by the defeat of the 1778 constitution, but they also hoped the state would take more decisive action against slavery. Phillis Wheatley was among them, subtly advancing antislavery in her own way. Throughout the war, she and her white allies such as the Reverend Samuel Hopkins in Rhode Island and the family of General David Wooster of Connecticut continued selling copies of her *Poems on Various Subjects*, which served as a demonstration that intellect was not limited by skin color. She also expressed her support for the patriot cause in October 1775, when she wrote a poem celebrating General George Washington and sent a copy directly to him. Washington's reply was far more gracious than might be expected from a slaveholder who had initially questioned the presence of Black troops in New England militias. He praised Wheatley's "genius" and "great poetical Talents" in a letter that one of his secretaries subsequently published in the *Virginian Gazette* (also republished in Thomas Paine's *Pennsylvania Magazine or Monthly American Museum*). Wheatley's bold move thus paid off with positive press for herself and, implicitly, Black intellectual potential in general. She hoped that the Revolutionary War, despite all the death and destruction (which she witnessed firsthand in New England), would lead to the creation of a more just society. "Let us leave the Event to him whose wisdom alone can bring good out of Evil," she wrote to her friend Obour Tanner. In July 1778, Wheatley made it clear that she hoped abolition would be one such result in a poem mourning the death of General Wooster, one of her patrons. The poem focused primarily on Wooster's virtue and patriotism but also contained a warning for the nation:

> But how, presumptuous shall we hope to find
> Divine acceptance with th' Almighty mind-
> While yet (O deed Ungenerous!) they disgrace
> And hold in bondage Afric's blameless race?
> Let Virtue reign—And thou accord our prayers
> Be victory our's, and generous freedom theirs.[35]

She thus asserted that the United States should earn God's favor through antislavery reform.

Antislavery ministers also encouraged the Massachusetts legislature and the public to support abolition following the defeat of the racist 1778 constitution. In an election sermon before the legislature in May 1779, the Reverend Samuel Stillman of Boston proclaimed that it "ought to banish from among us that cruel practice, which has long prevailed, of reducing to a state of slavery for life, the free-born Africans." Legislators declined to act on his suggestion, but they did authorize a separate convention to write a new state constitution. That November, the Reverend John Murray enjoined the constitutional convention delegates to purge the sin of slavery from the land, warning that failure to do so would "entail the curse of heaven." In addition to the published sermons by Stillman and Murray, it is likely that other ministers also expressed hope that the legislature or constitutional convention would formally abolish slavery. Moreover, the townspeople of Pittsfield (Berkshire County) told their delegate to the new convention that the bill of rights should ensure "that no man can be deprived of liberty, and subjected to perpetual bondage and servitude, unless he has forfeited his liberty as a malefactor."[36] Such a provision would have ended hereditary slavery.

The text of the 1780 Massachusetts Constitution (which was quickly ratified) did not explicitly forbid slavery, but it was easy to understand why many contemporaries interpreted it as doing so. Article I of its Declaration of Rights proclaimed: "All men are born free and equal, and have certain natural, essential, and unalienable rights; among which may be reckoned the right of enjoying and defending their lives and liberties." The suffrage clause also dropped the 1778 constitution's racial restriction, using the race-neutral phrase "Every male person." Together, these clauses suggested that the constitution did not differentiate rights based on color. Moreover, another clause nullified any colonial laws that were "repugnant to the rights and liberties contained in this constitution." Despite some ambiguity, it seems many Bay Staters believed that their constitution confirmed that anyone who had been born in Massachusetts—even if they had been born during the colonial era to an enslaved mother—could not be legally held in bondage past adulthood. Rather than initiating a transformation, the 1780 constitution broadened a preexisting antislavery trend. In Essex County at least, lawyers for years had been successfully arguing that that slavery was not legally hereditary under Massachusetts law. Still, some antislavery contemporaries worried the constitution's implicit antislavery stance was insufficient. Residents of Hardwick feared the Declaration of Rights could be "misconstrued hereafter, in such a manner as to exclude blacks," so they proposed amending it to read: "All men, whites and blacks, are born free and equal." The town of Rochester, in Plymouth County, wanted an explicit statement that no slaves would be "born or Imported into this Commonwealth." The people of Braintree (Suffolk County) and Petersham (Worcester County) had similar concerns. Their fears proved warranted, as some—perhaps many—slaveholders continued keeping Massachusetts-born Black people in bondage. In November 1780, Deacon Benjamin Colman of Essex County complained that the states' slaves were "not set free in a general way."[37]

The first known Black Bay Stater to sue for freedom after the adoption of the 1780 constitution was a thirty-one-year old mother named Elizabeth, or "Bett" for short (Figure 9). Her free Black husband had recently died fighting in the Continental Army for the nation's freedom, but Elizabeth and her daughter remained enslaved by Colonel John Ashley in Berkshire County. Elizabeth fled from the Ashleys following a beating in early 1781; she then recruited lawyer Theodore Sedgwick as an ally after Colonel Ashley tried to reclaim her. Years later, Sedgwick's children reported that Elizabeth had "heard gentlemen talking over the Bill of Rights and the new constitution," and that she had proposed suing for freedom based on its principle "that all people were born free and equal." Another of Ashley's slaves, a man named Brom, joined Elizabeth in the lawsuit, *Brom and Bett v. Ashley*, which they filed on May 28, 1781. In August, a jury in the Berkshire County Court of Common Pleas ruled that Brom and Elizabeth were not slaves and awarded

Figure 9. Although there had been numerous successful freedom suits before, Elizabeth Freeman ("Mum Bett") was the first to sue for her freedom after the ratification of the Massachusetts Constitution in 1780. This miniature portrait was painted twenty years later, in 1811, by Susan Anne Livingston Ridley Sedgwick. Courtesy of the Massachusetts Historical Society.

them thirty shillings in damages plus court costs.[38] After her liberation, Elizabeth adopted the surname Freeman and worked as a paid servant in the Sedgwick household before purchasing her own land and eventually bequeathing considerable property to her daughter and grandchildren. The Sedgwick children gave the aging Freeman the affectionate nickname Mum Bett (short for Mammy Elizabeth) and later credited her with inspiring them to become abolitionists. In a speech from 1831, two years after Freeman's death, Theodore Sedgwick Jr. recounted her life and virtues, concluding that "having known this woman as familiarly as I knew either of my parents, I *cannot* believe in the moral or physical inferiority of the race to which she belongs." Freeman, he said, was "a practical refutation of the imagined superiority of our race to hers."[39] Her antislavery legacy thus stretched into the antebellum era.

The immediate significance of *Brom and Bett v. Ashley*, however, is not entirely clear. The case did not establish a binding precedent that immediately led to freedom for all enslaved people in Massachusetts. The 1781 case is, however, the first successful freedom suit that historians have identified (so far) in Berkshire County (located along the state's western border). And although there are no contemporary accounts of the legal arguments Theodore Sedgwick employed at the trial, his son later claimed it was "the first instance (or among the first instances) of the practical application of the declaration in the Massachusetts Bill of Rights."[40] Perhaps the case hinged on constitutional arguments, though it is very possible the jurors would have ruled in favor of liberty regardless, as juries in Essex County had been doing routinely for nearly a decade. In any case, the legal activism of enslaved people such as Freeman and Brom accelerated the process of emancipation throughout Massachusetts by spreading the view that the colonial custom of hereditary slavery was no longer tolerated.

Following the August 1781 ruling, Colonel Ashley initiated an appeal but never followed through, perhaps because he learned about another slaveholder's unsuccessful appeal in a freedom suit in neighboring Worcester County. That freedom suit was initiated by Quock Walker against his enslaver, Nathaniel Jenison, in the town of Barre. Walker (whose first name was also rendered as Quaco, Quok, or Quork) based his claim to freedom in part on a promise of liberty at age twenty-one or twenty-eight from his deceased former master, James Caldwell. His lawyers also used broad antislavery arguments based on religion, natural rights, and the state constitution. Their victories, in conjunction with *Brom and Bett v. Ashley*, further solidified the perception that hereditary slavery was illegal in Massachusetts.[41]

Walker's effort to assert his freedom ultimately involved three separate cases and two appeals, which were "dizzyingly complicated," as Margot Minardi notes. He had been born in Massachusetts around 1753 to enslaved parents and was later transferred from the Caldwell family to Nathaniel Jenison (rendered as Jennison in court documents) as the result of a marriage. In 1781, when Walker turned twenty-eight (and had served the biblical maximum of seven years of servitude after adulthood), he left Jenison's farm and hired himself to John and Seth Caldwell, the sons of his former master. Jenison tried to reclaim Walker as a slave, leading to two lawsuits with initially contradictory rulings in the Worcester County Court of Common Pleas, both of which were then appealed to the Supreme Judicial Court.[42]

Although the collective "Quock Walker cases" are often remembered as establishing or confirming the view that the 1780 Massachusetts Constitution had abolished slavery, the jurors might have ruled in Walker's favor regardless of the constitution. Indeed, Levi Lincoln's trial notes suggest that most of his arguments were the types that antislavery lawyers had been successfully employing for a decade in Essex County, focusing on the limits of positive law and invoking religion. Implicitly referring to the *Somerset* principle and making the point that no Massachusetts law explicitly recognized slavery as a *hereditary* status, Lincoln rejected the applicability of "custom" and argued that laws regarding slavery must be "construed strictly." Jenison's lawyers, in turn, sought to overcome the limits of positive law by relying on proslavery biblicism. They paraphrased Exodus 21:21 to justify Jenison's right to beat "his servant, which was his money." They also cited Leviticus 25:44–46, in which God allowed the Israelites "to make slaves of the heathen round about them." Lincoln responded with the standard biblicist antislavery arguments that had become common in Massachusetts since the 1760s. Namely, Old Testament dispensations allowing slaveholding were "peculiar to the Jews" and had been nullified by Christ's teachings and death. Moreover, the Israelites had been strictly forbidden "to make slaves of their brothers" while the "Gospel dispensation" taught Christians to view all people as brethren. "Quork is our bother . . . [with] the same common Saviour," Lincoln told the jury. Paraphrasing Luke 4:18 (in which Jesus paraphrases Isaiah 61:1), the lawyer described emancipation as "glad tidings of great joy—it is opening the prison doors and letting the prisoners go free." Lincoln also used providentialist language to connect Black liberation to the Revolutionary War, asking: "Can we expect to triumph over G. Britain, to get free ourselves until we let those go free under us[?] Are we not acting as the Pharaoh and Egyptians[?]" He thus echoed countless sermons and newspaper essays insisting antislavery reform was necessary to win God's blessing during the war. Lincoln concluded his argument with another religious appeal, telling jurors to consider "your own souls." If they condemned Walker to a lifetime of slavery in violation of the "law of God," they could expect eternal damnation in Hell.[43]

In contrast to detailed comments on religious themes, Lincoln's notes on his own argument only included a two-word reference to "the constitution." Based on a later petition by Jenison, it seems Lincoln argued that the Declaration of Rights mandated the "total discharge & manumission of all Negro Servants whatsoever." Lincoln's notes provide greater insight into the response of William Stearns, one of Jenison's lawyers. Stearns conceded that the new constitution meant no one could be born enslaved in Massachusetts, but he argued that this only applied to "those that have been born since" ratification. In essence, Stearns argued that the Massachusetts Declaration of

Rights functioned like Pennsylvania's Gradual Abolition Law, leaving the status of current slaves untouched while freeing the next generation. Lincoln's principal argument, on the other hand, was that hereditary slavery had never been legally established in Massachusetts and was a God-provoking sin.[44]

After the lawyers wrapped up their arguments, the presiding judge, Nathaniel Peaslee Sargeant, would have issued a "charge" to the jury, advising them on points of law. Such charges were not typically recorded, so its substance is unknown. It is worth noting, however, that Sargeant had previously served as legal counsel for at least two enslaved plaintiffs, including with John Lowell in *Caesar v. Taylor* in 1771. At that time—before American independence and before the state constitution—Sargent and Lowell had argued that slavery "being contra[ry] to Laws of God and reason must be void."[45] Sargeant had also been a delegate at the 1779–1780 constitutional convention, and he apparently advanced an antislavery interpretation of the Declaration of Rights during the 1781 trial. A year later, Jenison described the judges as having "construed" the Bill of Rights to deprive him "of a great part of his property."[46] It is also worth remembering that Worcester's committee of correspondence had embraced emancipation in theory back in 1775 and that six towns in the county had expressed antislavery sentiments—primarily in religious terms—in response to the 1778 and 1780 constitutions. In the minds of the jurors, Lincoln's biblicist and providentialist rhetoric may well have been more decisive than any constitutional analysis. In any case, they confirmed Walker's freedom.

In a technical sense, the rulings liberated only Walker, and they were not printed or formally disseminated. Jenison, however, would not let the matter rest and unintentionally amplified Walker's influence by drawing political attention to the judicial proceedings. Jenison had much at stake, for he claimed to own "Ten Negro Servants" and was loath to release them. In early 1782, Jenison petitioned the legislature for permission to reenter an appeal in *Walker v. Jennison*. The legislature rejected his request after Walker submitted a counterpetition. Undeterred, Jenison submitted another petition in June, denouncing the judicial ruling as "repugnant & contradictory to the Revealed Word of God." He transcribed the text of Leviticus 25:44–46, which he claimed granted him permission "to hold the persons of the Heathen & Strangers in servitude from one Generation to another." Biblicism thus remained a central concern of both sides of the slavery debate, though it is noteworthy that Jenison chose to ignore (perhaps because he could not refute) Lincoln's assertion that Old Testament dispensations permitting slaveholding were granted only to the ancient Israelites and had been nullified by Christ's gospel dispensation. Jenison's final argument, which proved to be of the most interest to the legislature, dealt with the question of responsibility for freedpeople who became indigent. Jenison worried that under the provisions of the 1703 manumission law, he could be required to financially support Quock Walker and any other former slaves who might become indigent through infirmity or laziness. If the legislature would not reverse his former slaves' emancipation, Jenison hoped it would at least "repeal the Law which binds the master to support them."[47]

In response to this petition, the Massachusetts House of Representatives passed a bill in the spring of 1783 to repeal the 1703 manumission law, but the state senate rejected it. The text of the bill is lost, but an outline of its three provisions survives. Although the outline has often confused scholars, it helps illuminate shifting public opinion about the legitimacy of slavery in Massachusetts. It proposed the following:

> 1st. Declaring that there never were ~~Slaves~~ *legal* Slaves in this Government
> 2nd. Indemnifying all Masters who have held Slaves *in fact*
> 3rd. To make such a provision for the support of ~~such~~ Negro's & Molattos as the Committee may find most expedient[48]

Some scholars have long dismissed the first statement as a "contradiction" or a "legislative attempt to falsify history," because Massachusetts had explicitly legalized slavery in 1641. But rather than falsifying history, it seems the legislators were endorsing the type of argument that abolitionists and antislavery lawyers had long made—especially after the *Somerset v. Steuart* decision—distinguishing between enslavement for life (which was established by statute law in Massachusetts) and hereditary chattel slavery (a custom that lacked a statutory basis). In other words, although many people in colonial Massachusetts had been legally enslaved for life (because they were Indian POWs or imported African captives), they were not truly "slaves" in the sense of hereditary chattel status. The second provision acknowledged, however, that some slaveholders had "in fact" treated enslavement as hereditary. The main point of the second provision, about "indemnifying" masters, dealt with the 1703 manumission law. It did not, as some scholars have assumed, propose compensated emancipation, with masters receiving money for liberating their slaves.[49] Rather, it clarified—in response to Jenison's petition—that former slaveholders would not be held liable for the support of their former bondspeople if the latter ever became indigent. The third provision, providing "support" for freedpeople, would have established a formal process through which the state would fund poor relief for those who were unable to provide for themselves.[50]

The defeat of the 1783 bill may have reflected state senators' desire to preserve hereditary slavery in Massachusetts despite the 1780 constitution and the rulings in freedom suits. At least that is how it was interpreted—and celebrated—by a pseudonymous "Mentor" in the *Boston Evening-Post*. "Mentor" denounced the House's antislavery bill as a "retrospective" law that would "deprive citizens of their property, which they were legally possessed of under the sanction of former laws." Thanking "the honourable and sagacious Senate" for blocking the measure, "Mentor" called on voters to reject House members who had "supported such an obnoxious, execrable bill."[51] Clearly, some Bay State slaveholders would cling to slavery as long as possible.

Others in the Massachusetts government apparently decided to clarify that hereditary slavery was in fact illegal. In April 1783, a month after the Senate rejected the House's abolition bill, state Attorney General Robert Treat Paine revived a dormant criminal indictment against Nathaniel Jenison for assaulting Quock Walker. The lawyer's arguments from *Commonwealth v. Jennison* are lost, but notes from Chief Justice William Cushing's charge to the jury survive. Advising jurors on points of law, Cushing stated that although hereditary slavery had been a "usage" during the colonial era, "nowhere is it expressly enacted or established." This was an implicit reference to the *Somerset* principle. Moreover, he emphasized that public opinion had shifted against the practice: "Whatever Sentiments have formerly prevailed . . . a different Idea has taken place with ye people of America more favorable to ye natural rights of Mankind, & to that natural innate, desire of Liberty, with which Heaven (with[ou]t regard to Colors, complexion or Shapes of noses features) has inspired all ye human Race." Cushing likely meant the latter part as a rebuff to those who still justified hereditary Black slavery based on Noah's Curse and other Old Testament passages. He then connected this shift in public opinion to the 1780 constitution, which he described as "totally repugnant to ye Idea of being born Slaves." Cushing concluded by adding, "This being ye. Case I think ye Idea of Slavery is inconsistent with our own conduct & Constitution & there can be no such thing as perpetual servitude of a rational Creature, unless his Liberty is forfeited by

Some Criminal Conduct or given up by personal Consent or Contract." The jury then convicted Jenison of assault and fined him forty shillings.[52] Again, regardless of the 1780 constitution, the outcome might have been the same based solely on the *Somerset* principle and shifting biblical interpretations during the revolutionary era.

Scholars have sometimes differed on whether Chief Justice Cushing used judicial review to declare slavery unconstitutional or if he cited the constitution as evidence that shifts in public opinion had already delegitimized slavery.[53] Once again, distinguishing between enslavement for life and hereditary slavery helps clarify the matter. In his jury charge, Cushing did *not* argue that the 1780 constitution had fully nullified all colonial laws allowing slavery. Instead, he asserted more narrowly that *hereditary* slavery—"the idea of being born slaves"—had *never* been sanctioned by Massachusetts law and *also* violated the new constitution. His closing passage, referring to legitimate instances in which "Liberty is forfeited," could be interpreted as still approving of the types of enslavement-for-life specifically authorized in the 1641 Body of Liberties. It was therefore significant that Paine opened the prosecution by asserting Walker had been "Born in Caldwell's house." If Jenison had been able to claim that Walker was enslaved in Africa, the judges and juries might have considered the Black man as legitimately enslaved for life based on having forfeited his liberty in his native land.

In any case, the rulings of 1781–1783 left unexamined the legal status of African-born slaves who had supposedly been enslaved legitimately in their homeland. The position of Massachusetts-born Black people during the time of their minority also remained ambiguous. Some slaveholders seem to have believed that they could keep their slaves' children in bondage until at least adulthood and perhaps an additional seven years (the typical biblical limit on adult servitude). Thus, it is not surprising that scholars have found anecdotal evidence of Black individuals who remained in bondage in Massachusetts through the 1780s and even after the 1790 U.S. Census listed zero "Slaves" in the state.[54] (The 1790 Census returns for Barre also indicates that "Quoko Walke" headed a household of three people, presumably his wife, Elizabeth Harvey, whom he married in 1786, and their child.)[55]

Although the details of the freedom suits of 1781–1783 were not formally reported or published in newspapers, news of them spread via word of mouth and personal correspondence. In December 1783, the Reverend Samuel Hopkins explained to Anthony Benezet, "Slavery is wholly abolished in the State of Massachusetts—By virtue of their Constitution, every Slave is liberated:

And if their Masters refused to set them free, the Men in Authority will do it, whenever Application is made to them."[56] People who were paying attention to abolition believed the issue had been essentially settled in the Bay State by the final year of the war.

Although the process of emancipation in Massachusetts was hardly instantaneous, it occurred far more rapidly than the form of gradual abolition adopted by Pennsylvania, which established the model followed by most other northern states. The rapidity of Bay State abolition did not reflect a greater level of antislavery sentiment in the legislature, but rather the persistent activism of Black people and a handful of white allies. Through petitions, lawsuits, sermons, and other publications, this interracial movement destroyed the legitimacy of slavery in white public opinion. Although most white people never cared enough about slaveholding to petition against it or take other forms of antislavery action, when jurors were put in a position in which they had to determine whether an individual Black person deserved freedom or slavery, they routinely chose freedom after 1772. It is impossible to know what was in the hearts of those jurors, but biblicist and providentialist themes remained central in contemporary antislavery discourse. Regardless of what the framers of the state's 1780 constitution actually intended, it seems that public opinion had decisively shifted against hereditary slavery by the early 1780s. The war itself accelerated this trend by seeming to fulfil abolitionists' providentialist warnings.

The process of abolition in New Hampshire was similar to but slower than that in Massachusetts. The legality of hereditary slavery there had also been ambiguous under colonial law, and New Hampshire had only recorded 681 "negroes and slaves for life" in a 1773 census. In November 1779, twenty Black men led by Nero Brewster petitioned the state legislature to abolish slavery in the Granite State. The petitioners reported that they had been "born free" in Africa but then "seized, imprisoned, and transported from their native land." They challenged "those who claim us as their property," insisting that slavery was unjustifiable based on Christianity, state law, and natural law. The legislature read the petition in April 1780 and called for its publication in the *New Hampshire Gazette*.[57] It also scheduled a public discussion for June, instructing "all who may be concern'd in said Petition to appear at that time and show cause (if any they have) why the prayer thereof should not be granted." The slaves apparently had at least one white ally, as the legislative records refer to "counsel for the petitioners." But it seems the petitioners' masters (who included some of the legislators) and other slaveholders exerted more influence, for the legislature determined the time was "not ripe" to take action.[58]

A new state constitution adopted in 1783 was subsequently interpreted as ending hereditary slavery in New Hampshire, albeit through a more gradual process than had occurred in Massachusetts. Jeremy Belknap complained that New Hampshire slaveholders believed the constitution's declaration that "All men are born equally free and independent" meant those "who have been *born* since the constitution, are free; but that those who were in slavery before, are not liberated by it." Thus, the New Hampshire Constitution essentially functioned as a gradual abolition law, only freeing the next generation of slaves' children, and only when they reached adulthood. Many Black adults, however, managed to gain freedom during the war, often in exchange for military service. This was the case with Prince Whipple, who had signed the 1779 petition and been previously enslaved by politician and militia officer William Whipple. At least five others among the twenty Black petitioners gained their freedom before their deaths. (The rest were posthumously freed by the New Hampshire legislature in a symbolic act of atonement in 2013.)[59]

In Connecticut, Black activists repeatedly petitioned for their freedom, and the legislature considered several bills but ultimately declined to act. Although the Black activists were rebuffed, their petitions demonstrate the ways in which both natural rights and religious discourses shaped their activism. In May 1779, two enslaved men from Fairfield, Prime and Prince, worked with attorney Jonathan Sturges to submit a petition on behalf of themselves and others. They denounced slavery as a "flagrant injustice" that violated the "laws of Nature" and "the whole Tenor, of the Christian Religion." Religion was even more central in the next petition, submitted to Governor Jonathan Trumbull in October 1780. The petitioners—who did not include their names but referred back to their petition of "Last may"—cited the Bible more than a dozen times and made biblicist and providentialist arguments against slavery. The Black activists called on white patriots to do "your duty as the word of God says in the Book of Isaiah at the 58 Chapter 6 varse." If they did not "Leat the oppressed Go free," the patriots would "Bare the Sword in vain." In other words, the Black activists argued that God would oppose the patriots' prayers for victory until they proved their righteousness through abolition.[60] The legislature reportedly debated a gradual abolition bill, but nothing came of it. Connecticut's next group of Black petitioners, in 1783, would have greater success.

Manumission Reform in Virginia

Among the major slaveholding states, Virginia seemed to offer the best prospect for antislavery reform—at least based on political rhetoric. The colonial government had repeatedly sought to end slave importations, and Thomas Jefferson's 1774 *Summary View of the Rights of British America* had even claimed that it desired the "abolition of domestic slavery."[61] In reality, as many historians have shown, there was no political support for emancipation, and the slave trade was only vulnerable because Virginia slaveholders viewed it as unnecessary and potentially dangerous. A century and a half of slave importations and natural reproduction had given the Old Dominion an enslaved population of more than two hundred thousand by the start of the Revolutionary War. This large population, along with declining soil fertility and white fears of Black resistance, reduced the appeal of further slave importations. Yet the large Black population also discouraged emancipation, as the economic and societal impacts would have been much more disruptive than in the northern states.[62]

Nonetheless, Virginia did adopt an important antislavery reform during the Revolutionary War: the liberalization of its manumission policy, allowing slaveholders to voluntarily free their slaves for the first time since 1723. Some scholars have portrayed this reform and the ensuing surge of manumission as reflecting white Virginians' "dedication to revolutionary principles" and "commitment to the idea of natural equality."[63] Rather than indicating widespread white antislavery sentiment, however, the 1782 Manumission Act primarily reflected the persistence of Quaker activism, including intensive lobbying by Friends from other states. In fact, Quakers appear to have been more directly involved in the passage of Virginia's manumission law than in any of the other wartime antislavery reforms at the state level.[64]

The war reinforced many Virginia Quakers' belief that slavery was a "crying sin" provoking God's wrath. Some Friends had begun liberating their slaves illegally in the late 1760s, but their former bondspeople remained vulnerable to re-enslavement under the 1723 and 1741 laws restricting manumissions. In the midst of the war, Quaker Robert Pleasants complained to Governor Patrick Henry that "some busie medling people" were threatening to re-enslave Black people whom Quakers had manumitted. Pleasants argued that such actions violated the patriots' purported belief in natural rights, and he warned that the sin of slaveholding was the "principal cause of our present troubles." Implicitly dismissing the efficacy of the patriots' fast days, Pleasants suggested that "doing justice to the injured Africans would be an acceptable offering to him who 'Rules in the Kingdom of men.'" In response, Henry advised Quakers to keep their former bondsmen on their own land in order to protect them from being harassed or re-enslaved; he also assured them that he expected the legislature to reform the manumission law at the next session.[65]

In 1777 and 1778, the Virginia House of Delegates considered bills facilitating manumissions and prohibiting slave imports but only passed the latter, disappointing Quaker abolitionists. Edward Stabler, a prominent Virginia Friend, complained to Pennsylvania Quakers: "The work respecting the freedom of the negroes seems at present almost at a stand."[66] Friends at the 1779 Virginia Yearly Meeting applied God's condemnation of the Israelites in Ezekiel 22:29–31 to the plight of white Virginians: "Yea, they have oppressed the stranger wrongfully: therefore I have poured out mine indignation upon them: their own way have I recompensed them upon their own Heads." The Quakers reiterated their belief that members should liberate their bondspeople "when the females attain to the Age of 18 and the males to 21 Years." They also determined to "manifest our disunion" with members who bought, sold, or hired slaves. Some recalcitrant Virginia Friends, however, clung to their slaves, citing the fact that manumissions were still illegal.[67]

During this time, some Methodists also sought to purify their young denomination from the sin of slaveholding but faced even greater opposition. Francis Asbury, who became the first Methodist bishop in the United States, had been interested in antislavery since at least 1772 and was impressed by Quaker antislavery efforts during the war. "This is a very laudable design; and what the Methodists must come to, or, I fear, the Lord will depart from them," he wrote in 1778. Two years later, he and allies such as Freeborn Garrettson helped make antislavery part of Methodist identity (at least temporarily). The delegates at the Methodists' 1780 General Conference, held in Baltimore, adopted a resolution declaring "that slavery is contrary to the laws of God, man, and nature, and hurtful to society." They required "those travelling preachers who hold slaves to give promises to set them free" or face suspension. They advised other Methodists to do the same and expressed their "disapprobation" of those who refused. At this time, more than half of the nation's 8,500 Methodists lived in Virginia, but they had temporarily split with the General Conference over a disagreement about whether to remain connected to the Church of England. The 1780 antislavery instructions, therefore, carried less weight. Moreover, antislavery Methodists refrained from getting involved in politics.[68]

Meanwhile, antislavery Virginia Quakers increased their efforts in 1780, both within and without the Society of Friends. Edward Stabler and other activists visited the families of slaveholding Quakers, distributing copies of Anthony Benezet's antislavery writings and encouraging manumissions.[69] They also worked to remove the legal obstacles to manumission, submitting a petition to the state legislature in November 1780. The Quakers condemned slavery for violating the Golden Rule and "the natural Right of all Mankind." Recognizing that statewide emancipation was politically unattainable, they only asked the government to allow private manumissions and to protect Black freedpeople "in the enjoyment of their just Right to Liberty." The Quakers argued that doing so would please God, for "Righteousness exalteth a Nation" (Proverbs 14:34). Stabler and Pleasants reinforced the petition by distributing antislavery pamphlets to legislators. In response, the legislature formed a committee to draft a bill, but the bill's "enemies" prevented its passage, as Pleasants complained to Benezet. The British army, meanwhile, continued protecting and arming African Americans who ran away from patriot masters. Pleasants wryly noted that legislator Benjamin Harrison, who had been "the greatest enemy" to the manumission bill, lost forty slaves who escaped to the British.[70] Such episodes must have reinforced the Quakers' conviction that God would continue chastising the patriots until they let the oppressed go free.

Quakers had mixed feelings following General Washington's victory over General Cornwallis at the Battle of Yorktown in October 1781. As pacifists, they were pleased that the surrender of Cornwallis's army might herald the end of the war. Yet their pacifism also prevented them from joining in public celebrations of the victory, and the national day of thanksgiving and prayer proclaimed by Congress. This reluctance, in turn, provoked the ire of patriot mobs, especially in Philadelphia, where Quaker houses were vandalized because their windows were not illuminated with celebratory candles. Although Quaker abolitionists would not participate in the day of thanksgiving, they must have hoped that as patriots celebrated "the influence of divine Providence . . . in granting remarkable deliverances" (as Congress's thanksgiving proclamation described it), they would reflect on the plight of Black Americans who remained in bondage.[71] At least one minister made this connection publicly. The Reverend James Francis Armstrong, who had condemned Black slavery in a 1778 sermon, included another antislavery appeal in his unpublished 1781 thanksgiving sermon. After celebrating Washington as an instrument of divine providence, Armstrong concluded by stressing the need to demonstrate "gratitude" and asked: "How many of our fellow creatures are this moment trampled beneath the feet of cruel and capricious tyrants who will neither hear their cries nor relieve their distresses? America must have some idea of slavery. What a bitter draft it is, and how many are forced to drink it!"[72] No sermons published at the time, however, explicitly called for abolition. Quakers, meanwhile, remained the most persistent white advocates of emancipation.

In Virginia, antislavery Quakers finally achieved their legislative victory in June 1782, eight months after the Battle of Yorktown and a dozen years after Robert Pleasants had begun the campaign in favor of manumission reform. This victory reflected in part the support of outside allies. Benezet and members of the Philadelphia Meeting for Sufferings, such as John and James Pemberton (their brother Israel died in 1779), had long monitored the antislavery efforts of Virginia Quakers and aided them by sending antislavery pamphlets. In the spring of 1782, PMS activists John Parrish and Warner Mifflin traveled from Philadelphia and Delaware to lend direct support to their coreligionists in Virginia. Benezet subsequently described Parrish and Mifflin as among his staunchest antislavery allies (along with Nicholas Waln), and it may have been his idea to send them to Virginia. Parrish, who was fifty-one at the time, had been actively involved in the cause of emancipation and Black education for a decade. His traveling companion, Mifflin, was a generation younger. Born into a slaveholding Quaker family in Virginia's Eastern Shore in 1745, Mifflin had settled in Delaware after his first marriage in 1767. He had initially resisted antislavery pressure but began liberating his slaves following a moment of divine inspiration in 1774. He then dedicated much of his time to the antislavery cause. Mifflin's abolitionism as well as his pacifism made him unpopular among white patriots during the war. He later recounted that he was accused of "Toryism" and "insinuations were thrown out that my laboring for the freedom of the blacks, was in order to attach them to the British interest." Critics threatened to tear down his house and murder him. Experiencing threats and oppression at the hands of slaveholders further increased Mifflin's "sympathy with our African Brethren," he later wrote.[73] In preparation for his 1782 visit to Virginia, he collected copies of antislavery publications from the PMS. This expedition would be the first of many antislavery collaborations between Mifflin and Parrish.

Parrish kept a journal of the 1782 lobbying trip with Mifflin, and it reveals the deep religious convictions that motivated them as well as the extent of apathy and opposition they faced, even among some Quakers. Wartime devastation and economic depression were clearly visible as they traveled south, and the abolitionist duo encouraged people they met along the way to consider "whether the tyrany exercised over the Affricans was not one cause of the present Judgment." Whenever they lodged with slaveholders, Parrish and Mifflin did their best to persuade them to liberate their "Captives." Upon reaching Surry County, where they attended the Virginia Yearly Meeting in May, Mifflin began going on hunger strikes to protest Quaker hosts who still kept Black people enslaved. Parrish reported that while staying with Robert Hargrave, Mifflin "abstained from food so as to partake but once in 48 hours, but in the conclution Robert & 2 of his sisters executed manumistions for all they were posesd with." On other occasions, however, Mifflin "lost his supper" without inspiring any manumissions.[74] Strong antislavery sentiment was not universal among Virginia Quakers.

Slavery was a central issue at the 1782 VYM, though the Virginia Quakers were not willing to follow through with the threat of disownment while manumissions remained illegal. The most significant measure adopted by the VYM in 1782 was the creation of the Virginia Meeting for Sufferings (VMS), which they hoped would "hold up a standard of righteousness to the Nation."[75] Parrish and Mifflin may have inspired the group's creation; in any case they attended its first meeting. The VMS quickly drafted a new antislavery petition to the legislature.

The Quaker abolitionists framed their petition in providentialist terms, portraying the war as "the Judgment of an offended God." After quoting Matthew 7:2 and 7:12, they described the war as a fitting form of retaliatory punishment for slavery: "Britons and Americans heretofore united in ravaging the Coasts of Africa, promoting Wars among the different Nations, and captivating its Inhabitants: they have of late been killing and captivating each other, destroying Property, burning Towns and Houses, crowding into Jails and prison Ships." The Quakers cautioned the legislators against complacency following the patriot victory at Yorktown. If Americans failed to "learn Righteousness," the "present Prospect of Tranquility" would prove akin to "the respite of the Plagues . . . upon Pharoah, who refused to let Israel go from under his Bondage." In other words, God would resume and escalate his chastisements until America's slaves were delivered from bondage. As in 1780, the Quaker petitioners knew that the Virginia legislature would not embrace universal emancipation, so they focused their specific request around manumission reform. They explained that many Quakers had already released their slaves, and complained that some of their former bondspeople had been re-enslaved and sold by local authorities. Although Quaker manumitters had not followed the procedures of the colonial-era manumission law, they considered their actions "quite consistent with the Principles of the present [Virginia] Constitution, as set forth in the Declaration of Rights." The petitioners called on legislators to formally permit manumissions in order to avoid further angering the Lord.[76]

Parrish and Mifflin, feeling a "divine appointment," joined the VMS committee delivering the petition to the legislature in Richmond. The Quakers presented their petition on May 29 and watched the ensuing debates from the gallery. Parrish was cautiously optimistic of "something being done to good purpose for the relief of Negroes or at least to ripen matters for a futer day." He complained, however, that most VMS committee members proved "slack except E[dward] Stabler which made it the more necessary for us to give our close attention." (Robert Pleasants was ill and unable to attend.) Parrish, Mifflin, and Stabler spent nearly three weeks lobbying in Richmond, meeting with legislators "out of doors," circulating PMS publications, and taking every opportunity to "forward the Business." No formal record of the legislative debates survives, but Parrish's diary indicates that Patrick Henry supported the petition and overcame opposition in order to refer it to a committee and draft a bill.[77]

Slaveholders quickly mobilized and almost defeated the manumission bill. On June 3, the House of Delegates received a counterpetition from sixty-two inhabitants of Accomack County, where Warner Mifflin's father, Daniel, had previously (and illegally) liberated his ninety-one enslaved people. These petitioners strongly opposed any more manumissions, especially during wartime. They conceded that "universal Liberty" was "desirable" in the abstract but listed reasons why "the scale of sound policy and publick good" tilted against antislavery reform. For example, they argued that many freed people would end up requiring poor relief or would "subsist by pilfering." They also feared that free people of color would harbor runaways. A few days later another petition, from Henrico County, also complained about the results of private manumissions.[78] Many legislators apparently shared such concerns. Parrish recorded that even as the state senate read the bill for the third and final time, opponents endeavored to "lay waste and render abortive all that have been done." The Philadelphia Quaker and his companions believed that without their presence, the bill would have "been throne out of the house." But after nineteen days, their persistence paid off with a new law under which slaveholders could perform manumissions with a simple legal document.[79]

Although Virginia's 1782 manumission law was an important victory, its larger consequences for the future of slavery in the state were limited. Historians exaggerate its significance when they claim that Virginia, like northern states, "began moving against slavery" during the Revolution. Contemporary Quakers were more circumspect; they believed the law would help them purge slavery from their own religious society, but they had no illusions that it would end the institution throughout Virginia. Edward Stabler celebrated that the remaining Quaker slaveholders "will now be left without excuse," and two years later the VYM empowered monthly meetings to disown them. James Pemberton applauded the law as "one good step" but also conceded that the "Work of Righteousness is gradual, & eveil Customs cannot be broke at Once."[80] Quakers' assessments of the law were realistic rather than naively optimistic; they understood that the reform reflected intense lobbying by a religious minority rather than widespread antislavery sentiment among white Virginians at large.

Aside from Quakers, the white Virginians who were initially most likely to take advantage of the new manumission law were Methodists. Indeed, the Reverend Freeborn Garrettson had succeeded in persuading some slaveholders in Fluvanna County to emancipate their slaves back in March 1781, before manumissions were actually legal. More Virginia Methodists followed suit after 1782, though this trend proved short-lived. In 1785, the Methodists' General Conference decided that manumissions were unnecessary to remain in good standing.[81]

Between 1782 and 1806 (when the legislature reimposed restrictions on manumissions), around ten thousand Black Virginians were manumitted, mostly by Quakers, Methodists, and Baptists.[82] This surpassed the total number of slaves who had been emancipated in Pennsylvania and Massachusetts. But despite slaveholders' voluntary manumissions and enslaved people's self-emancipation during the war, Virginia's slave population grew throughout the revolutionary era, as enslaved births far exceeded liberations. Moreover, the 1782 manumission law would prove to be the peak of antislavery reform in the Old Dominion rather than the first step toward peaceful abolition.

Farther south, meanwhile, reformers could not persuade legislatures even to liberalize the colonial-era restrictions on manumissions. In October 1776, the North Carolina Yearly Meeting advised local Quakers who owned slaves to "cleanse their Hands of them as soon as they Possibly can," despite the law restricting manumissions. The following April, the state legislature revised its 1741 law banning manumissions, but only to specify that the proceeds of re-enslaving freedpeople would henceforth go to the state rather than the local Anglican parish. North Carolina subsequently re-enslaved and sold at least 134 Black men, women, and children whom Quakers had illegally freed, using the proceeds to help fund the war fought in the name of liberty. The Friends' North Carolina Standing Committee (their equivalent of a meeting for sufferings) hired lawyers on behalf of the Quakers' former slaves, and won a temporary victory for those who had been manumitted during the period of time between the Declaration of Independence (which ended North Carolina's connection to the Anglican Church) and the April 1777 manumission law. However, the legislature soon annulled this victory by passing a law confirming the legality of the re-enslavements and sales in question. Over the next two decades, North Carolina Quakers submitted at least ten petitions and repeatedly lobbied the legislature to allow voluntary manumissions, but to no avail.[83] South Carolina and Georgia lacked any sort of organized antislavery movement aside from the thousands of Black individuals who exploited the chaos of war to escape from bondage. Wartime destruction, Black resistance, and organized abolitionism disrupted slavery but did little lasting damage to the institution in the southern states.

* * *

The limitations of wartime antislavery gains are hardly surprising given that the war grew out of disputes over taxation and property rights. Indeed, it is the extent rather than limits of antislavery reform that is remarkable. The Revolutionary War, rather than discouraging antislavery reform, was a crucial ingredient that helped enable antislavery change, especially in the northern states. Moreover, religion was not supplanted by natural rights ideology but remained central to the ways in which white Americans considered slavery and abolition. War lent new salience and urgency to abolitionists' biblicist and providentialist rhetoric. A growing number of white Americans came to accept abolitionists' arguments that slaveholding was sinful and that God would not enable the patriots to successfully defend their own natural rights while they trampled on the rights of others.

Still, antislavery reform also depended on the activism of determined individuals. Since the late seventeenth century, a vocal minority had insisted that slavery was a sin and warned of divine retribution. The French and Indian War and then the American Revolution amplified these voices. In Massachusetts, hundreds of enslaved people took advantage of shifting public opinion and pressed their masters to recognize their freedom during the 1770s. Dozens of them took recalcitrant masters to court, where—with the help of sympathetic lawyers—they convinced juries that hereditary slavery was indefensible. It is possible that the cumulative power of such individual legal victories, which had begun in the aftermath of *Somerset v. Steuart*, might have eventually ended slavery in Massachusetts even without the American Revolution, but the war undoubtedly accelerated the process. The need for military recruits helped persuade some masters to liberate their slaves on the condition that they serve in the army, while the desire for God's mercy and blessing increased jurors' and legislators' fear that slavery was an "accursed thing" that was angering the Lord and hindering victory. Meanwhile, there is no reason to imagine that Pennsylvania would have passed an abolition law as early as it did if not for the war and George Bryan's persistence. And despite Bryan's disdain for Quaker pacifism, his providentialist antislavery convictions reflected the influence of decades of activism by Anthony Benezet and other abolitionists connected to the Philadelphia Meeting for Sufferings. Moreover, Benezet's protégés John Parrish and Warner Mifflin played indispensable roles in reforming Virginia's manumission laws. Thus, although the Revolutionary War did not naturally or inevitably lead to abolition, it created opportunities for dedicated reformers—whether elite politicians such as George Bryan or enslaved women such as Elizabeth Freeman—to take advantage of galvanized public sentiment to enact unprecedented political and legal change.

Quaker abolitionists recognized the war's role in promoting reform, for Isaiah 26:9 told them that the worlds' inhabitants would learn righteousness when the Lord's judgments were in the earth, as had been the case among many Friends during the French and Indian War. They therefore responded to the return of peace with mixed emotions. These views are perhaps best encapsulated in PMS activist David Cooper's 1783 *Serious Address to the Rulers of America, On the Inconsistency of Their Conduct Respecting Slavery*. Although Cooper was pleased that "two or three states" had taken steps to end slavery during the war, he added: "But I fear, that after the sunshine of peace takes place, we have little more to expect." He understood that the war had galvanized antislavery sentiment, enabling reform, but he worried that abolitionist momentum would become a casualty of peace and that the wartime reforms would prove insufficient to ward off a resumption of divine chastisement in the future. Hoping to maintain a sense of urgency, Cooper warned of a "gloomy" future in which "an *avenging God*" withdrew his blessing from America. He called on politicians to link the new nation's creation with the "entire *abolition* of *slavery*." Cooper argued that independence offered an opportunity to atone for their "accumulated guilt" by "letting the oppressed go free." Charles Crawford, a Philadelphia poet born in the Caribbean, praised Cooper's pamphlet and called on the rest of the union to follow Pennsylvania in ending slavery for the good of the nation. He warned that "the blood of the persecuted Africans, which has been shed by the merciless hand of oppression, cries also against this country (as well as against many others) to the throne of the Almighty for vengeance."[84]

Anthony Benezet also expressed concerns in his private and public writings. Referring to laws protecting slavery and slave trading, he told Benjamin Franklin that "we cannot expect peace will be of any long continuance whilst such wickedness of so deep a dye, is so publickly maintained." The Quaker developed this theme in his introduction to *Short Observations on Slavery*, which he published in May 1783. In the pamphlet, Benezet called for "a general abolition of Slavery on the continent" in order to earn "the blessing of Him who delights in Justice and Mercy; and has promised to reward every country, as well as individual, according to their deeds." Otherwise, he warned, the cries of the oppressed slaves would provoke the Lord to again visit the land with death and destruction.[85] In sum, many abolitionists—even pacifistic Quakers—worried that peace would end antislavery momentum, and they feared that the persistence of slaveholding would provoke future rounds of divine chastisement against the United States.

CHAPTER 7

The Critical Period of Abolitionism, 1783–1789

The years between the end of the Revolutionary War in 1783 and the implementation of the United States Constitution in 1789 are sometimes called the "Critical Period," as it was not clear whether the confederacy of newly independent states would remain united and establish a viable national government.[1] It was also a critical period for abolitionism, with many uncertainties. Would the abolitionist movement expand with the return of peace, or would it collapse? Would any additional states put slavery on the path to extinction? Would Congress maintain the ban on slave importations and enact further reform? Would any other denominations follow the Quakers in purging slaveholding from their ranks and promoting antislavery politics? Would free people of color be integrated into society, or would they be pressured to leave the new nation? None of these issues were completely resolved by the end of the 1780s, and progress was uneven.

Historians have tended to characterize the postwar period as one of sustained or even revived antislavery momentum, at least until the ratification of the U.S. Constitution (which many characterize as a proslavery backlash against the Revolution's antislavery thrust). The new nation's antislavery gains have been described as "a direct result of the Revolution," and it is true they would have otherwise been unlikely. Yet, scholars often exaggerate the extent and spontaneity of popular antislavery sentiment. "Petitions flooded northern state legislatures in the 1770s and 1780s, charging that slavery violated natural rights," we are told.[2] However, the flow was more like a gentle stream than a flood, and the majority of petitions were organized by Quakers who argued that slavery was a God-provoking sin.

A closer look at the Critical Period reveals several things: the highly contingent nature of antislavery progress in the face of significant obstacles and opposition, the contradictory effects of peace—including a declining sense of antislavery urgency among many patriots—and the continued centrality of Quakers within the movement. Indeed, Quaker members of the Generation of 1758 remained at the helm of the antislavery movement in both the United States and Great Britain. In 1783, Anthony Benezet and James Pemberton organized a petition to the Confederation Congress while John Pemberton and William Dillwyn helped the London Meeting for Sufferings petition Parliament. After Benezet's death the next year, James Pemberton served as the central coordinator of state-level antislavery campaigns from North Carolina through New England. Other Quakers who had joined the antislavery cause during the early 1770s, such as John Parrish, Warner Mifflin, Nicholas Waln, and Moses Brown, also remained steadfast in their commitment, as did a handful of white ministers from other denominations, including Samuel Hopkins, Jeremy Belknap, Francis Asbury, and Jonathan Edwards Jr., along with Black activists such as Prince Hall. Their persistent activism through the 1780s was essential in keeping the antislavery movement alive after the war ended.[3]

The centrality of the religious impulse and Quaker organizing among white abolitionists has been obscured by scholars' greater attention to the rise of secular antislavery societies, which is often conflated with an assumption of widespread antislavery sentiment among prominent patriots. In February 1784, Philadelphia Quaker Thomas Harrison revived what he now called the Society for the Relief of Freemen in Bondage. This group reorganized again in 1787 as the Pennsylvania Society for Promoting the Abolition of Slavery (better known as the Pennsylvania Abolition Society, or PAS). The group recruited prominent new members such as Benjamin Franklin, whom they honored with the presidency, and politician Tench Coxe, who served with Benjamin Rush as a secretary. Historian Kirsten Sword has shown that Quakers intentionally minimized their public role within the PAS in order to rebrand abolitionism as a nationalist and patriotic movement, even as Friends remained the most active members behind the scenes. Quaker abolitionists in other states also found prominent allies, as demonstrated by the membership of the New-York Society for Promoting the Manumission of Slaves (or New-York Manumission Society, N-YMS), established in 1785. More than half of the original members were Quakers, but their ranks also included leading patriots such as Alexander Hamilton and John Jay. Scholars such as Richard Newman, Paul Polgar, and Sarah Gronningsater have shown that the PAS and N-YMS did important legal work, helping individual enslaved people gain their freedom, but these groups' political activism remained limited during the 1780s.[4]

Much more important during the Critical Period were the antislavery petitioning and lobbying efforts by Quaker groups such as the Philadelphia Meeting for Sufferings and the New York Meeting for Sufferings. Quaker committees were responsible for every antislavery petition submitted to the Confederation Congress. The PAS became more active politically in 1787, but this also reflected the influence of Quakers. The group's most important new member was not Benjamin Franklin but rather James Pemberton, who agreed to serve as vice president. A member of the Quaker Generation of 1758 who had three decades of experience in the PMS and was also involved in the Philadelphia Monthly Meeting's Negro School, Pemberton was a natural choice for the PAS. Whereas Franklin treated his presidency of the group as an honorary position (and did not attend meetings), Pemberton attended and chaired virtually every PAS meeting. He also remained active in the Quaker organizations, often holding leadership roles simultaneously in the PAS and the PMS. Scholarship on the PAS and other secular abolition societies generally acknowledges the importance of Quaker members but ignores the continued relevance (or even existence) of the PMS and its counterparts in other regions. Pemberton's most important contribution to the PAS was his ability to link it to preexisting Quaker antislavery networks. Under PMS auspices, Pemberton had long corresponded with Quaker abolitionists such as Moses Brown, Robert Pleasants, and James Phillips in their roles as members of meetings for sufferings in New England, Virginia, and London, respectively. After 1787, these men continued corresponding in their old capacities as well as their new positions as members of the PAS, the Providence [Rhode Island] Abolition Society, the Virginia Abolition Society, and Britain's Society for Effecting the Abolition of the Slave Trade. James Pemberton occupied the central node of an interstate and international abolitionist network, coordinating strategies throughout the English-speaking world. The new secular antislavery organizations worked in tandem with the older sectarian groups rather than supplanting them. Yet despite increased organizational sophistication, the abolitionist movement still faced great challenges.[5]

In addition to the constant obstacles of economic interest, racial prejudice, and white public apathy, peace itself posed a challenge to abolitionism. Although it is true that peace facilitated the revival of the PAS and the creation of the N-YMS, it undermined one of abolitionists' central rhetorical positions. Military victory and the favorable terms of the Treaty of Paris contradicted abolitionists' wartime predictions that God would continue chastising the nation until slaveholding had been eradicated. The Reverend Samuel Hopkins, who had repeatedly made such assertions during the war, addressed this issue in an appendix to a second edition of his *Dialogue Concerning the Slavery of the Africans* (Figure 10), published by the N-YMS in 1785. Referring to the American success in the Revolutionary War, Hopkins wrote: "Thus we have had prosperity, and the smiles of Heaven, in our attempts, while the slavery of the Africans has not been wholly abolished by us. This may be considered by some, as evidence that this slavery, and even the slave-trade, are not so great and heaven-provoking sins, as they are represented to be in the dialogue; and that the repeated declarations there, that we could not reasonably expect prosperity, until this iniquity was reformed, were groundless and rash." In order to explain why God had favored the Americans despite the persistence of slavery in the new nation, Hopkins pointed to the progress that various states had made toward abolition. He argued that gradual emancipation in much of the North and manumission reforms in the Upper South were the reasons "why the omnipotent, long-suffering Governor of the world has spared and prospered us." But Hopkins warned that this respite from divine chastisement should not lead to complacency. He pointed to the story of Jerusalem's destruction, as recounted in Jeremiah 34, as a cautionary tale for the new nation. This was the account (used by several abolitionists before him) in which Israelites repulsed a Babylonian attack by liberating and arming their servants, only to return them to bondage after the siege, thereby provoking God to expose Jerusalem "to the sword, to the pestilence, and to the famine." If Americans hoped to "escape the destruction which came on the inhabitants of Jerusalem," Hopkins argued, they must complete their antislavery reformation throughout the nation.[6] Other abolitionists similarly adjusted their providentialist rhetoric, arguing that military victory reflected only a temporary cessation of God's chastisement, intended to give the patriots a chance to demonstrate their gratitude for unmerited mercy.

Fortunately for the antislavery cause, the Critical Period's economic and political problems lent credence to abolitionists' arguments that God was not yet satisfied with the new nation's efforts against slavery. Peace had brought economic depression as the British put restrictions on trade with their former colonies and the value of American paper money continued to depreciate. In terms of antislavery rhetoric, the most useful crisis was "Algerine slavery." American trade in the Mediterranean Sea was no longer protected by British

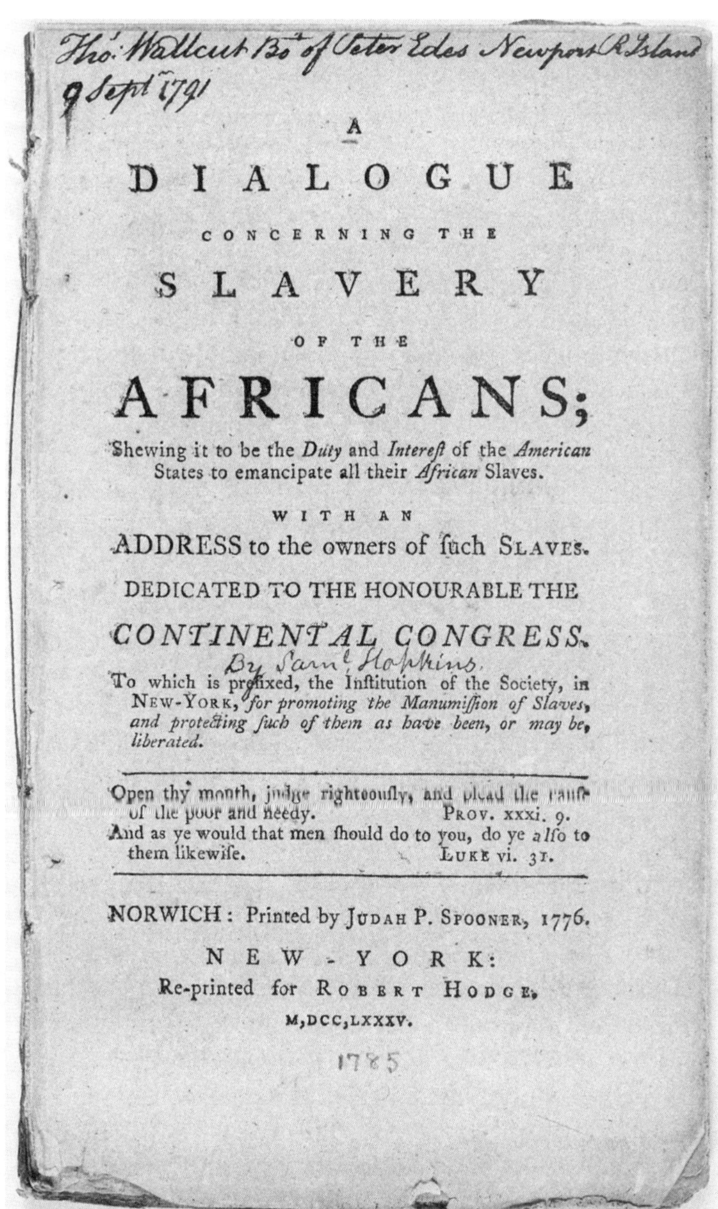

Tho: Wallcut Bo^t of Peter Edes Newport R Island
9 Sept 1791

A

DIALOGUE

CONCERNING THE

SLAVERY

OF THE

AFRICANS;

Shewing it to be the *Duty* and *Intereſt* of the *American* States to emancipate all their *African* Slaves.

WITH AN

ADDRESS to the owners of ſuch SLAVES.

DEDICATED TO THE HONOURABLE THE

CONTINENTAL CONGRESS.

By Saml Hopkins.

To which is prefixed, the Inſtitution of the Society, in NEW-YORK, *for promoting the Manumiſſion of Slaves, and protecting ſuch of them as have been, or may be, liberated.*

Open thy mouth, judge righteouſly, and plead the cauſe of the poor and needy. PROV. xxxi. 9.

And as ye would that men ſhould do to you, do ye alſo to them likewiſe. LUKE vi. 31.

NORWICH: Printed by JUDAH P. SPOONER, 1776.

NEW-YORK:

Re-printed for ROBERT HODGE,

M,DCC,LXXXV.

1785

Figure 10. When the Reverend Samuel Hopkins reprinted his *Dialogue Concerning the Slavery of the Africans* in 1785, he added an appendix explaining why God had allowed the Americans to win the war despite their not fully eradicating slavery. He argued that God would soon resume chastising the nation if it did not complete its antislavery reformation. Courtesy of the American Antiquarian Society.

treaties with the Barbary States of North Africa, and Algiers demanded ransom and tribute after capturing two American ships in 1785 and enslaving the crews. (It would take more than a decade to negotiate and finance the sailors' release.)[7] Abolitionists argued that this literal form of white slavery reflected God's retaliatory justice against the United States. They insisted that the new nation must complete the antislavery reform begun during the war if Americans expected God to bless them with permanent peace and prosperity.

Another impediment to antislavery reform was the weakness of the federal government under the Articles of Confederation (drafted in 1777 and formally approved in 1781). The Confederation Congress lacked the authority to regulate trade, which not only created financial problems for the new nation but also meant that it could not compel states to prohibit the Atlantic slave trade. In 1774 and 1776, the Continental Congress had agreed to abstain from this trade, but it was a wartime measure that depended on unanimity and the acquiescence of the individual colonies and states. After the war, abolitionists were disgusted but not surprised when Americans quickly renewed the "detestable Trade carried on to the Coast of Africa." South Carolinians and Georgians imported hundreds of African captives in 1783 and more than four thousand the following year as they sought to rebuild and expand their slave-based economies after independence.[8] Quakers repeatedly petitioned the Confederation Congress to discourage this trade but Lower South delegates blocked reform efforts.

While Quakers periodically petitioned Congress, state governments remained the locus of most antislavery lobbying. Quakers' antislavery campaigns, coordinated with white ministers of other denominations along with Black activists, were also crucial to many of the state-level victories during the Critical Period. Meanwhile, white abolitionists divided over the question of whether free people of color should remain in the United States or return to the land of their African ancestors. New Black organizations such as Philadelphia's Free African Society (FAS) and the Free African Union Society in Newport, Rhode Island, corresponded with each other about the practicality and desirability of emigration to Africa. Ultimately, most chose to work toward greater freedom and integration within the new nation. The antislavery activism of white allies, especially Quakers, informed these decisions.

In some ways, 1787 was a watershed year for antislavery. In July, the Confederation Congress agreed to ban slavery in the Northwest Territory at the same time that delegates at the Federal Convention were crafting constitutional compromises benefitting slaveholders and slave traders. Revisiting the genesis of the Northwest Ordinance's antislavery provision reveals that Quaker abolitionist played a significant role—perhaps a decisive though unheralded one—in its creation. And although abolitionists were disappointed by the U.S. Constitution's many concessions to slaveholders, they persisted in their state-level activism throughout the ratification process and vowed to ignore proslavery clauses that violated divine law. The PMS carefully tracked and coordinated local efforts, culminating in a confederacy-wide antislavery lobbying campaign in 1787–1789. In the face of concerted opposition and widespread apathy, abolitionists managed to preserve antislavery momentum after the war.

American Quakers and the British Parliament

Before writing their own antislavery petition to the Confederation Congress, American Quakers helped organize one to Parliament. In 1782, the Philadelphia Meeting for Sufferings had informed its counterpart in London about the progress of various antislavery efforts in America and chided British Friends for doing so little on their side of the Atlantic. Although England itself was largely free of slavery after the *Somerset* decision, the British Empire remained heavily invested in Caribbean slavery and annually trafficked tens of thousands of enslaved Africans to its own colonies and to foreign empires. The American Quakers used providentialist rhetoric to inspire action among their former countrymen. Quoting from Proverbs 14:34, they reminded English Quakers that "Righteousness exalteth a Nation, and Sin is shameful to any People." Britain's involvement in the Atlantic slave trade "must greatly encrease the Weight of national Guilt," they warned. American Quakers expected such arguments to carry extra weight following Britain's loss of the American colonies. Anthony Benezet described the war's aftermath as a "favourable Crissis" that British Quakers could exploit to "lay the foundation" of abolitionism. In other words, he hoped that military failure would facilitate antislavery efforts in a humbled Britain. As historians such as Christopher Brown and John Coffey have shown, the rise of an antislavery movement in Britain reflected in part a desire to regain "moral capital" and restore divine favor after the loss of the thirteen North American colonies.[9]

American Quakers not only encouraged British abolitionism through their writings—they were also intimately involved in the process on the ground. John Woolman had died while on a religious visit to England in

1772, and other abolitionist members of the Generation of 1758 continued to play important roles in British antislavery organizing after the war. When the London Meeting for Sufferings established a committee on the slave trade in April 1783 (in response to the PMS's 1782 epistle), one of the most active members was William Dillwyn. The New Jersey-born abolitionist and merchant had settled in London following his wife's death in 1774 (leaving behind his infant daughter Susanna, who would later marry Samuel Emlen Jr. from another New Jersey abolitionist family).[10] Dillwyn's old friends John Pemberton and Nicholas Waln of the PMS were also traveling through England in 1783, and they routinely attended local slave trade committee meetings as well as the London Yearly Meeting (LYM) in June. James Pemberton, who remained in Philadelphia, hoped that his brother and Waln could help overcome the "temerity & illgrounded fears" among some English Quakers regarding antislavery agitation.[11]

The American Friends' influence was important but not always welcome. In a letter about the yearly meeting, English Quaker David Barclay reported to James Pemberton: "I found with concern thy well meaning Countrymen are come here as *Reformers* with an Impetuousity that several of our most valuable Friends have termed *over driving*." He complained that the Americans had pressured the meeting to draft an antislavery petition to the king that was unduly provocative; he was relieved when this draft was replaced with a more moderate petition addressed to Parliament.[12] Although no copy of the draft addressed to the king is known to exist, it is easy to imagine that it might have denounced him for vetoing colonial efforts to ban slave importations and described the recent war as God's means of punishing the British Empire for the sin of slavery.

In its petition to Parliament, the LYM condemned slavery as inconsistent with "the Christian faith" and "the natural rights of mankind." The Quakers requested the "humane interposition of the Legislature" to abolish the Atlantic slave trade. When the petition was read in the House of Commons on June 17, 1783, Lord North regretfully asserted that it was "impossible to abolish the Slave Trade, against which the petition was so justly directed; for it was a trade which had, in some measure, become necessary to almost every nation in Europe; and as it would be next to impossible to induce them all to give it up." In other words, he conceded that the slave trade was immoral but could not imagine Britain withdrawing from the traffic as long as other empires continued reaping its economic advantages. Sir Cecil Wray, who presented the petition on behalf of the Friends, also praised the Quakers but suggested simply tabling the petition, ending discussion without calling for any further action.[13] Parliamentary discussion of the petition thus ended in a matter of minutes.

The unwillingness of Parliament to consider abolishing the slave trade is unsurprising given its economic importance to the British Empire. Indeed, in April the LMS had predicted that antislavery lobbying would "meet with the greatest Opposition from the Combination of interested parties." In contrast to North America, where the enslaved population grew through natural reproduction, constant importations of fresh captives was necessary to preserve labor forces in the Caribbean and Latin America due to the hot climate, the prevalence of disease, and the brutal working conditions imposed by enslavers to maximize the output of profitable tropical commodities such as sugar. Parliament's West India lobby, which consisted of absentee slaveholders (who lived in England while overseers ran their colonial plantations) and the commercial and banking firms that ran the African trade, held immense sway and made debating the slave trade almost politically unthinkable. Given this reality, the Quakers described the polite response to their petition as "more encouragement than was expected." David Barclay expressed his "hope" that the petition, which was published in British newspapers, had "laid a foundation for some relief to the poor oppressed Affricans."[14] It was only a modest start for political antislavery in Britain, but it was a start nonetheless.

Antislavery Quakers on both sides of the Atlantic recognized that much remained to be done in Britain. From Philadelphia, James Pemberton encouraged those in Britain to persist "with no relaxation of their Endeavours." Anthony Benezet continued coordinating tactics with English Quakers and with Granville Sharp, who himself was lobbying Anglican clergy to take a stand against the slave trade. Benezet also wrote a passionate letter to Queen Charlotte, in which he denounced the slave trade in providentialist terms. Implicitly referring to Britain's loss of the thirteen colonies, Benezet suggested that the Atlantic slave trade "has been, & till removed will continue to be, one of the principal Causes of drawing down the divine Displeasure upon the British Nation." During this time, the LYM and LMS each established standing committees on the slave trade (some members, such as William Dillwyn, served on both). These groups focused on "publishing extracts and Essays on this Subject, to open the Eyes of the public," as Dillwyn explained to James Pemberton. These publications included excerpts from the writings of Benezet and Benjamin Rush as well as new material.[15]

During the fall of 1783, Dillwyn worked with John Lloyd, another member of the LMS slave trade committee, to draft a short pamphlet, *The Case of Our Fellow-Creatures, the Oppressed Africans*. This pamphlet, of which they printed more than ten thousand copies, made the type of biblicist and providentialist arguments that had become standard among abolitionists during the preceding decades. The Quakers dismissed Old Testament sanctions for slaveholding as irrelevant, writing that "we now live under a dispensation essentially different from that of the [Mosaic] law; in which many things were permitted to the Jews, because of the hardness of their hearts. All distinctions of name and country, so far as they relate to the social duties, are now abolished." Slaveholding was thus sinful, and both scripture and history led the Quakers "to believe that the Righteous Judge of the whole earth chastiseth nations for their sins, as well as individuals." They catalogued the horrors of slavery and the slave trade, and argued that this cruel treatment made Africans less likely to embrace Christianity. The pamphlet also included several pages of extracts from John Woolman's antislavery writings, and concluded with more warnings of divine retribution taken from the prophets Amos and Jeremiah.[16]

This pamphlet, in conjunction with the petition to Parliament, ushered in a new era of abolitionism in England. The ensuing years witnessed more antislavery pamphlets by other Quakers as well as by Anglican allies such as James Ramsey, who began collaborating with Granville Sharp. English Quakers also reprinted Benezet's 1766 *A Caution and Warning to Great Britain*, assuming that it would appear prophetic following the loss of the thirteen colonies. Of the new English pamphlets, the most important was Thomas Clarkson's *Essay on the Slavery and Commerce of the Human Species*, published in 1786 and based on the publications of Sharp, Ramsey, Woolman, and especially Benezet. Clarkson traced the history of slavery and the slave trade, characterizing them as based on greed, fraud, and violence. He refuted allegations of racial inferiority and held up Phillis Wheatley and Ignatius Sancho (a Black British writer) as examples of Black people's intellectual potential. The lengthy pamphlet culminated with a chapter containing biblicist and providentialist arguments. Clarkson refuted attempts to justify slavery based on the Old Testament, arguing that Christ established the "law of *universal benevolence*, which was to take away those hateful distinctions of *Jew* and *Gentile*." Having established the sinful nature of slavery, Clarkson warned that God would not only condemn British slaveholders and slave traders to damnation but also punish the entire "body politick . . . in this world" for the empire's collective guilt. These antislavery publications helped inspire the creation of the Society for Effecting the Abolition of the Slave Trade in 1787. The origins of the antislavery movements in both Britain and the United States thus involved similar religious impulses and some of the same individual activists.[17]

Quaker Abolitionists and the Confederation Congress

In the United States, there was already widespread public opposition to the Atlantic slave trade—even among most slaveholders. Natural reproduction and the transition to wheat and other crops that were less labor-intensive than tobacco meant most slaveholders in the Upper South viewed slave importations as unnecessary. Only the states of Georgia and South Carolina revived slave importations after the war (though northern slave traders were involved in this traffic and also supplied foreign markets with African captives). As a result, the vast majority of delegates to the Confederation Congress were receptive to antislavery pressure regarding slave importations. The problem, abolitionists would soon learn, was the American structure of government. Quakers repeatedly petitioned Congress to discourage this trade but could accomplish little under the Articles of Confederation, which required a supermajority of states to agree to most legislation and could only regulate trade with a complete consensus. Nonetheless, their activism helped inspire the antislavery provision of the 1787 Northwest Ordinance.

In October 1783, more than five hundred delegates at the Philadelphia Yearly Meeting signed an antislavery petition to Congress. Signers included many prominent abolitionists from the area, such as Anthony Benezet, David Cooper, John Parrish, James Pemberton, and Warner Mifflin, as well as visitors from other regions, including Moses Brown of Rhode Island. In the petition, the Quakers continued linking the themes of natural rights and divine providence. The slave trade was not only "contrary to every righteous consideration" but also "in opposition to the solemn declarations often repeated in favour of universal liberty." Whereas the newly independent Americans should be expressing their "thankfulness to the all wise controller of human events," the revival of the slave trade instead threatened to provoke "future calamities."[18] Benezet led a delegation of fourteen members of the Philadelphia Meeting for Sufferings to deliver the petition to Congress, which was meeting in Princeton, New Jersey. The Quakers presented the petition on

October 8, 1783, but Congress quickly moved on to other matters. James Pemberton complained that the "unsettled State of Congress in respect to fixing on a place for their residence" prevented the legislators from addressing the petition before they moved from New Jersey to Annapolis, Maryland. Congress did, however, find time to proclaim "a day of Public Thanksgiving" to be held in December to celebrate the end of the war. Whereas the Quaker petitioners had called for antislavery reform in order to demonstrate their gratitude to God, the congressional proclamation simply prayed that God would "pardon all our offences."[19]

The Quakers' antislavery petition likely would have been lost in the shuffle without the intervention of David Howell, a congressional delegate from Rhode Island who was related to Moses Brown through marriage. Brown previously described Howell to James Pemberton as "a Man of Sense, a friend to Religious & Civil Liberty," and he hoped that his in-law's political position "may be of use" to the abolitionist cause. During the next few years, Howell proved to be the abolitionists' most important political ally. On December 18, Congress referred the Quakers' antislavery petition to a committee led by Howell, who issued a report in January. His report praised the Quakers' commitment to the "rights of mankind" and "the essential good of their Country" (although Congress subsequently struck out the latter phrase). The report then urged Congress to "recommend" that the state legislatures revive the slave trade ban of 1774.[20]

At this time, only South Carolina and Georgia permitted slave imports, while slaveholders in Virginia and Maryland were selling their surplus laborers via a growing interstate slave trade. Thus economic self-interest could lead Upper South slaveholders to support Howell's report condemning the Atlantic slave trade. The report's proposed recommendation, however, would have had no binding power, for Congress lacked authority under the Articles of Confederation to regulate trade or intervene in state matters. Lower South congressmen still blocked Congress from adopting Howell's report, killing the already-toothless recommendation.[21] Overall, Congress's response to the Quaker petition demonstrated both the disorganized state of government and the obstructionist power of sectional minorities under the Articles of Confederation.

Howell, however, continued working to promote an antislavery agenda in Congress. In the spring of 1784, he served with Thomas Jefferson on a committee tasked with establishing policy to deal with the western territories ceded by the states to the Confederation Congress. On March 1, they issued a draft of the 1784 Land Ordinance, the fifth article of which contained an antislavery provision: "That after the year 1800 of the Christian era, there shall be neither slavery nor involuntary servitude in any of the said States [created out of the western territory], otherwise than in punishment for crimes, whereof the party shall have been duly convicted to have been personally guilty."[22] Although the provision had important limitations—it delayed its implementation until 1800 and only applied to new states—it was nonetheless a powerful antislavery statement. It implicitly underscored the perception that slavery should not be tolerated in the "Christian era," subtly refuting slaveholders' continued tendency to invoke Old Testament passages in defense of human bondage. And while the provision still permitted forced labor as punishment for crimes, the clause about legal conviction for being "personally guilty" directly contradicted the logic of hereditary enslavement. Moses Brown commended Howell, writing: "I was glad to find you were so thoughtful of Liberty as to prevent Slavery in the new States 16 years hence." James Pemberton also praised Howell for being "hearty in promoting relief for the oppressed Africans" but told Brown he worried that the congressman's efforts would not overcome "obstruction from the Southern Slave holders." Brown responded: "I am sensible D. Howell is friendly to liberty & could wish he might have sufficient strength to join him, but I fear he will not."[23] The Quakers were right to be pessimistic.

On April 19, 1784—the ninth anniversary of the start of the Revolutionary War—Richard Dobbs Spaight of North Carolina and Jacob Read of South Carolina moved to strike the antislavery provision from the Land Ordinance. Howell insisted on a roll call vote, forcing congressmen to go on record regarding slavery's expansion in the federal territories. The vote was 16 delegates in favor of Howell's antislavery proposal and only 7 on the proslavery side. However, because the Articles of Confederations required a supermajority of states (rather than delegates), Spaight and Read's motion carried. Howell tried to reinsert the antislavery provision four days later but was unsuccessful. Pemberton complained that Congress showed little concern with "real Justice & Equity." His disgust at political hypocrisy must have increased in early August when Spaight and Read proposed another national day of thanksgiving to commemorate ratification of the Treaty of Paris. The resulting proclamation described the war as a contest over "the dearest and most essential rights of human nature," and appointed October 19 as a day for the public to offer "sincere praises and thanksgiving to the God of their deliverance."[24] Abolitionists, of course, felt that such displays of supposed piety were insulting if unaccompanied by righteous reformation, such as delivering the nation's Black slaves from bondage.

Two weeks later, the PMS initiated a new antislavery propaganda campaign. They began by printing five thousand copies of *The Case of Our Fellow-Creatures*, the British pamphlet compiled by William Dillwyn. The introduction to the American edition, authored by John Drinker, explained that Quakers in both Britain and the United States had submitted antislavery petitions to their respective governments, and that the publication was intended to raise awareness "of the enormity of the evil." In September, the Quakers sent excerpts of the pamphlet to the *Pennsylvania Mercury*, hoping "to see it reprinted in every Newspaper upon the continent." These extracts, which appeared in numerous northern papers, contained the standard biblicist and providentialist arguments against slavery, and must have been especially striking during the lead-up to the national day of thanksgiving. In October, the *Pennsylvania Mercury* also published a series of lengthy excerpts of the Reverend James Ramsey's *Essay on the Treatment and Conversion of African Slaves*, likely at James Pemberton's request.[25] On October 22, three days after the national day of thanksgiving, the *Pennsylvania Mercury* also reprinted the Declaration of Independence with a footnote asking, "Is it not inconsistent with the principles upon which America was declared independent, that negroes should be kept in slavery? Will not such a proceeding draw down a curse? Will not the land, or at least some part of it, tremble for this?" In other words, rather than merely offering prayers of thanksgiving for their deliverance from British tyranny, Americans should be working to please God by abolishing slavery. Meanwhile, someone paid the *New-York Journal* to print Thomas Day's antislavery letter from 1776, which had recently been published in England. New England newspapers also published an antislavery epistle from the London Yearly Meeting.[26] Rather than reflecting spontaneous examples of widespread antislavery enthusiasm, many of the era's antislavery publications were part of a concerted campaign by Quakers to shape public opinion and build political support in Congress.

During this time, David Howell strategized directly with James Pemberton and the PMS about how best to distribute antislavery literature and to "revive the Subject" in Congress. He assured the Quaker, "I am always pleased to be charged with every service in my power to render to the cause of personal liberty, in which your Society have taken so decidedly, & I may add successful a part."[27] In January 1785, Howell presented another address from the PMS calling on Congress to take action against the Atlantic slave trade. Congress, however, did not even acknowledge the event in its published proceedings. The Quaker abolitionists later learned that their address had prompted opposition from "some of the Southern States" on the grounds that "Congress had not the Power of Legislation" in regard to trade.[28] In March, Howell worked with Rufus King of Massachusetts and William Ellery of Rhode Island to revive the proposed ban on slavery in the western territories. In an attempt to make it more palatable to slaveholders, they added a fugitive slave clause specifying that runaways escaping to the territories could still be recaptured. Their committee issued a printed report, but Congress declined to adopt it.[29]

Quaker activists drafted another petition to the Confederation Congress in 1786. They acknowledged that Congress lacked the authority to prohibit the slave trade, but they hoped that a declaration of Congress's "sincere disapprobation of this public Wickedness . . . might not be void of Effect." Using providentialist language, they again argued that ending the "national iniquity" was the best means of ensuring "divine Blessing." In November, a delegation from the PMS traveled to New York, where Congress was then meeting. However, Congress lacked a quorum and had not yet chosen a member to preside over its proceedings. As James Pemberton complained to his brother, "[The Congress] being then without a head, we could not fully accomplish the business." The Pennsylvania Quakers left the petition with the New York Meeting for Sufferings; however, the New Yorkers found no "seasonable Opening" to present it. (The best news the New York Quakers could report was the death of Abner Nash, a delegate from North Carolina who had "expressed sentiments very unfavourable in respect to the poor Blacks.")[30] The weak and disorganized state of the Confederation Congress, along with concerted opposition from some quarters, hindered the development of antislavery politics at the national level.

In March 1787, with Congress again lacking a quorum, New York Quaker activist Edmund Prior encouraged abolitionists to focus on the upcoming Federal Convention in Philadelphia, which had been called to amend the Articles of Confederation. Prior reported that Massachusetts politician Rufus King had mentioned that the convention's focus on commerce powers could include the slave trade, and suggested that "some hints thrown before that body on that business might . . . be useful."[31] In response, the Pennsylvania Abolition Society and the New-York Manumission Society both wrote petitions for the Federal Convention. The decision to have these nominally nondenominational groups rather than the PMS and New York Meeting for Sufferings issue the petitions was almost certainly a calculated strategy intended to demonstrate that antislavery sentiment was not limited to Quakers, even though Quakers remained the nation's most important pool of white antislavery activists.

The PAS petition employed providentialist rhetoric and called on convention delegates "to make the Suppression of the African trade in the United States, a part of their important deliberations." The abolitionists praised the First Continental Congress's 1774 ban on slave importations but warned that the revival of "this inhuman traffic" threatened to bring down "the righteous vengeance of God in national judgments." Until the nation abolished the slave trade, any prayers for the good of the country "would only insult the majesty of heaven." The abolitionists described the recent capture and enslavement of American sailors by Algerian corsairs as "intended by Divine Providence to awaken us to a sense of the injustice and cruelty of dooming our African brethren to perpetual slavery."[32] This antislavery providentialism reflected the way abolitionists had interpreted Indian captivity during the French and Indian War, taxation without representation during the imperial crisis, and the sufferings of the Revolutionary War. Abolitionists were frustrated that greed still blinded so many white Americans to the necessity of reform, and they called on the convention to act in order to prevent further punishment from an angry God.

PAS members had hoped that Benjamin Franklin would present the petition to the Federal Convention, but the elderly statesmen declined to present a document he knew would exacerbate existing sectional tensions among the delegates. Alexander Hamilton apparently played a similar role in preventing the N-YMS from presenting an antislavery petition written by John Jay. (Ron Chernow, Hamilton's most prominent biographer, misrepresents the evidence, crediting Hamilton with initiating rather than suppressing the petition.)[33] Franklin and Hamilton, like most Founding Fathers who gave lip service to antislavery ideals, prioritized stabilizing the young republic and perceived (not inaccurately) abolitionist agitation as a threat to sectional harmony.

Nonetheless, antislavery advocates in Congress scored a major and unexpected victory in July 1787. The Confederation Congress (meeting in New York while the Federal Convention met in Philadelphia) adopted a new version of David Howell's 1784 slavery restriction. This version, Article VI of the 1787 Northwest Ordinance, declared: "There shall be neither Slavery nor involuntary Servitude in the said territory otherwise than in the punishment of crimes, whereof the party shall have been duly convicted; provided, always that any person escaping into the same, from whom labor or service is lawfully claimed in any one of the original States, such fugitive may be lawfully reclaimed and conveyed to the person claiming his or her labor or service as aforesaid."[34] This article had been proposed by Nathan Dane of Massachusetts, who expressed surprised when it passed. Writing to Rufus King (who had worked with Howell on the 1785 version), Dane explained, "I had no idea the States would agree to the sixth Art[icle] prohibiting Slavery . . . but finding the House favourably disposed on this subject, after we had completed the other parts I moved the art[icle]; which was agreed to without opposition."[35] In contrast to the proposal in 1784, the 1787 law only applied to the northern section of the western territories, specifically the area that eventually became Ohio, Indiana, Illinois, Michigan, and Wisconsin. Despite its limitations, it established the principle and practice of restricting slavery's expansion in the new nation.

During the nineteenth century, slavery's opponents highlighted Thomas Jefferson's involvement in drafting the 1784 proposal, making it appear to be the natural outgrowth of revolutionary republicanism. This tendency, adopted by most historians, has obscured the role that David Howell and Quaker petitioners played in the genesis of the Northwest Ordinance's antislavery provision. Without the sustained petitioning efforts of Quakers, and the support of Moses Brown's in-law, the Northwest Ordinance of 1787 likely would not have included an antislavery provision. American history would have unfolded very differently had slavery been permitted to spread without restriction in the new nation.[36]

Antislavery Activism in "These (dis)United States," 1783–1786

In between petitions to the Confederation Congress, Quaker abolitionists also pursued state-level campaigns throughout what James Pemberton liked calling "these (dis)united states."[37] Collectively, Quakers were the most important abolitionists, though some reformers and politicians of other faiths also endorsed antislavery after the war. This helped ensure that Rhode Island and Connecticut would follow the rest of New England in ending hereditary slavery. For a brief period, Methodists also followed the Quakers' lead, seeking to end slaveholding among their members and even engaging in antislavery political agitation in Virginia. Abolitionists achieved several victories but also encountered significant apathy and opposition, and the Quakers remained the only denomination that was firmly antislavery.

The most significant antislavery reforms occurred in New England, though these victories were still compromises shaped by the political power of slaveholders and slave traders. Moses Brown and the New England Meeting for Sufferings (NEMS) led an antislavery publishing and petitioning campaign in Rhode Island, also supported by the Reverend Samuel Hopkins. This Congregationalist minister continued to give antislavery sermons and coordinated the publication and republication of antislavery essays in different newspapers in order to obscure their authorships and give the sense of broader antislavery support. In 1784, the legislature rejected a bill designed by Brown by a 2-to-1 margin but eventually passed a more conservative version while also allowing Rhode Islanders to continue servicing the African slave trade to other states and countries. The New England Yearly Meeting celebrated this partial victory along with "considerable advances" in "several of the adjacent States."[38]

One of the nearby successes occurred in Connecticut, where about three thousand people remained enslaved. In May 1783, the legislature appointed Roger Sherman and Richard Law to compile all of the state's laws into a single volume "and make such Alterations Additions exclusions and Amendments as they shall Judge Proper and expedient." In July, seven Black men—Charles, Cato, Frank, Jack, Cuff, Yarrow, and Abel—submitted an antislavery petition on behalf of "themselves & the rest of the Negro servants in the state." They denounced slavery as an unjust violation of their "natural right to freedom." Moreover, they reported that while many enslaved people had been manumitted in exchange for military service, "many" others "had assurances from their Masters that if they would faithfully serve them during the War then they should be emancipated." The masters, however, had reneged on these promises, so the Black petitioners called on the legislature to abolish slavery in Connecticut.[39] The legislature's proceedings and debates were not preserved, but Sherman and Law decided to add a gradual abolition provision to their revised law code, perhaps prompted by the Black activists. Their revision to the "Act Concerning Indian, Molatto and Negro Servants and Slaves" did not grant any relief for those currently enslaved in the state, but their future children would be liberated at age twenty-five. The legislature adopted this provision as part of the larger law compilation in January 1784.[40]

Abolitionists were quick to celebrate the victory and spread the news. Moses Brown, for example, informed James Pemberton of it in March 1784, in the same letter in which he reported that Rhode Island had passed a similar law in response to antislavery petitions from Quakers. And while Connecticut's gradual abolition provision lacked a preamble and simply referred to "sound policy," abolitionists understood it in providentialist terms. A decade later, three Black petitioners (Harry, Cuff, and Cato) described the imperial crisis and Revolutionary War as "the judgments of God" that made the patriots "remember their faults." The patriots "in their distress made a solemn appeal to Heaven on the justice of their cause in regard to Britain, on which ground they drew swords, and the God of battles appeared for them and delivered them out of the hands of those who wished to enslave them." The Black petitioners described emancipation as a divine imperative, complained that Connecticut's gradual abolition policy was too slow, and argued that it should also apply to enslaved people born before 1784.[41] (Indeed, Cato and Cuff might have been involved in the 1783 petition and been disappointed that the resulting legislation had not included them.) Despite such shortcomings, the fact that all of New England as well as Pennsylvania had taken steps to end hereditary slavery by early 1784 is difficult to explain without both the Revolutionary War and concerted antislavery activism, especially by Quakers and people of color.

Abolitionists had only limited success in New York and New Jersey, the northern states with the greatest proportion of enslaved people. In February 1784, Ephraim Payne, a Baptist preacher and member of the New York legislature, proposed a gradual abolition law that would have liberated all enslaved people in the state who had been born since 1776, as David Cooper had proposed (for the nation) the year before in his *Serious Address to the Rulers of America*. Edmund Prior and other Quakers in the New York Meeting for Sufferings quickly mobilized to lobby in support of the bill, distributing additional copies of Cooper's pamphlet and submitting a petition calling for "the entire abolition of Slavery." After the bill was postponed, the New-York Manumission Society also submitted an antislavery petition. The final bill from 1785 only applied to those born after its passage (rather than since 1776), and failed when the assembly and council of revisions could not agree on certain details. The legislature did, at least, pass a law forbidding slave importations and easing the process of private manumissions. The New York Meeting for Sufferings viewed the law as "favourable yet . . . far short of giving effectual relief to that oppressed people." The group vowed to continue agitating for further reform.[42]

In December 1785, the New-York Manumission Society published the updated version of the Reverend Hopkins's *Dialogue on Slavery*, in which he warned that God would resume chastising the nation unless they completed their "reformation respecting slavery." A few months later, the Meeting for Sufferings sent another petition to the legislature, describing emancipation as necessary to avoid a reprisal of God's "righteous judgments." The more conservative Manumission Society petitioned more narrowly for "an act to prevent the further exportation of negro slaves from this state." The state senate passed a bill but the lower house adjourned without voting on it. In February 1787, Alexander Hamilton—who at times seems to have joined the N-YMS primarily in order to sabotage it—scuttled plans for another petition by claiming that it was unnecessary. The legislature then failed to pass the export ban at its ensuing session. Slaveholders who were nervous about the institution's future could thus sell their human property out of the state without consequence. Abolitionists later complained that Black New Yorkers were being exported "like cattle and other articles of commerce, to the West-Indies and the Southern States."[43] In New Jersey, meanwhile, David Cooper organized a petition campaign with the help of the PMS. Legislators resisted calls for emancipation but finally liberalized manumission requirements and prohibited slave importations in 1786.[44]

Abolitionists, of course, faced the greatest opposition in the South, where slaveholders sought not only to block new antislavery measures but also to repeal earlier reforms. For example, in November 1784, petitioners from Henrico and Hanover Counties asked the Virginia legislature to repeal the 1782 manumission law and require all free people of color to carry official documents proving their free status or face re-enslavement. Nonetheless, antislavery Methodist ministers such as Francis Asbury and Freeborn Garrettson began a concerted effort to advance the abolitionist cause in the South. The arrival of Dr. Thomas Coke, a British Methodist who had been appointed with Asbury as joint superintendents (later bishops) of the Methodist Episcopal Church in America, created an opportunity to push for a stronger antislavery policy within the denomination.[45]

The Methodists' 1784 "Christmas Conference," held in Baltimore and overseen by Asbury and Coke, took a bold stance against slavery. The Methodists vowed to "extirpate this Abomination from among us" through a process of gradual yet complete emancipation. The old policy, from 1780, had mandated that preachers arrange to manumit their slaves or face suspension, but it had not imposed any sanctions against slaveholding lay members. Under the new policy, Methodists had one year to sign delayed manumissions for all of their enslaved people, liberating them at different times based on their ages. There were, however, exemptions for Methodists living in states that still prohibited manumissions (such as the Carolinas), and Virginians were granted an additional year to comply with the new requirement (based on the assumption that they would require extra coaxing).[46] Coke and Asbury also began planning an antislavery petitioning campaign targeting southern legislatures. In sum, during the winter of 1784–1785, Coke and Asbury determined to follow Quaker precedents, purging slaveholders from their ranks and embracing antislavery political activism.

When Coke toured the South in the spring of 1785, he quickly learned that his antislavery zeal was often unpopular and even dangerous. His diary recounts a few occasions in which he inspired manumissions but also numerous instances in which his antislavery sermons were met with threats of violence. In the middle of one such sermon, a group of Methodists walked out, informing him that they would "flog" him when he exited. A "high-headed lady" encouraged them, proclaiming "that she would give fifty pounds, if they would give that little doctor one hundred lashes." Only the intervention of a local justice of the peace saved Coke's hide. Coke recorded that a few days later, another "mob came to meet me with staves and clubs," but he escaped uninjured when he left slavery out of his sermon.[47]

Coke and Asbury persisted in their plan to petition state legislatures, though this proved controversial among white southern Methodists. A petition signed on behalf of the North Carolina Methodist Conference in April 1785 called on the legislature to "pass an act to authorize those who are so disposed, to emancipate their slaves." Yet it is unclear if the petition was ever submitted. The legislative records from the ensuing session refer to another antislavery petition from Quakers but do not mention any such petition from Methodists.[48] It may be that North Carolina Methodists agreed to the petition proposal when Coke and Asbury were present but then failed to submit it, either by oversight or design.

In Virginia, antislavery Methodists succeeded in organizing a petition campaign, but it met with a hostile response from many Methodists as well as the legislature. The slavery issue proved so divisive at the Virginia Methodist Conference in early May 1785 that Asbury reported he and the other antislavery advocates felt lucky to escape "with whole bones." It seems that they worked out a compromise in which ministers could circulate antislavery petitions that individual Methodists (and others) could choose to sign, but it would not be signed "on behalf of the conference," as had been done in North Carolina. A few weeks after the conference, Coke and Asbury visited George Washington at Mount Vernon, hoping that he would lend his name and influence to the antislavery cause. The retired general told them that he shared their antislavery sentiments but "did not see it proper to sign the petition." Still, he promised that if the legislature took further antislavery reform into consideration, he "would signify his sentiments to the Assembly by a letter." Coke and Asbury were undoubtedly disappointed but at least happy that Washington conceded the immorality of slaveholding. The real frustration came from their fellow Methodists who continued calling for repeal of the 1784 policy against slaveholding. After one such encounter, Coke vented in his journal, "I could not beat into the head of that poor man the evil of keeping them in slavery."[49]

Eventually, opposition from slaveholders led Coke and Asbury to "suspend the execution" of the 1784 policy mandating manumissions. This retreat, made at the Baltimore Conference in June 1785, proved permanent. In all, the Methodists' attempt to purge slaveholding from their ranks had lasted barely six months. Coke lamented that the Methodist denomination was "in too infantile a state to push things to an extremity." In order to grow as a denomination, the Methodists chose to accommodate slavery.[50] But if antislavery Methodists backtracked on their internal policy, they refused to compromise on the text of their petition to the Virginia legislature, which they continued circulating during the summer of 1785.

Dozens of subscribers signed at least eight copies of the Methodists' antislavery petition. The petitioners attacked hereditary slavery as a "grand Abomination" that violated both Christianity and the spirit of the American Revolution. Indeed, they argued that the principles of the Revolution "plead with greater force for the Emancipation of our Slaves; in proportion as the Oppression exercised over them exceeds the Oppression formerly exercised by Great Britain over these States." They dismissed racist justifications for slavery, describing them as "beneath the Man of Sense, much more the Christian." Moreover, they argued that liberating the enslaved would facilitate conversion efforts and help establish "the Kingdom of Christ over all the world." They closed by entreating the legislature "to pursue the most Prudential, but effectual Method for the immediate or Gradual Exterpation of Slavery."[51] This foray into politics marked an important evolution of antislavery activism among Methodists but was undercut by the suspension of the denomination's internal policy regarding slaveholding.

Meanwhile, news that antislavery petitions were circulating inspired Virginia slaveholders to organize counterpetitions. More than eight hundred slaveholders signed at least six petitions advancing a proslavery conception of religion and the Revolution. The petitioners quoted Leviticus 25:44–46 and asserted that "under the Old Testament Dispensation, Slavery was permitted by the Deity himself." They insisted that Christ's teachings and death had given slaves spiritual liberty but did not affect their earthly bondage. Moreover, the slaveholding patriots described the American Revolution as about property rights for themselves rather than liberty for others. They claimed they had "risked our Lives and Fortunes, and waded through Seas of Blood" to protect their property rights, succeeding through the "favourable Interposition of Providence." In other words, the Virginians buttressed proslavery biblicism with the claim that divine providence supported their right to own human chattel.[52]

When the Virginia House of Delegates considered the opposing petitions, in November 1785, they found the proslavery ones more appealing. They voted "without dissent" to reject the Methodists' antislavery petition, with some members proposing "to throw it under the table." Moreover, the legislators voted (with the speaker breaking a tie) to draft a bill repealing the 1782 manumission law. James Madison, a member of the House of Delegates, opposed this "retrograde step with regard to an emancipation" and was pleased when the bill itself was abandoned in January 1786 (thus leaving the 1782 law intact). Still, Asbury and other antislavery Methodists felt stung by "the resentment of some of the members of the Virginia Legislature," and they ended their brief venture into antislavery politics.[53]

Meanwhile, Robert Pleasants, the Virginia Quaker, wrote a personal antislavery appeal to George Washington in November 1785. After describing the Revolution in providentialist terms, Pleasants insisted that the new nation had a sacred obligation to abolish slavery: "It is a Sacrifice which I fully believe the Lord is Requiring of this Generation." He also warned that "should we not submit to it, Is there not reason to fear, he will deal with us as he did with the Pharaoh on a similar occasion?" Washington did not respond to Pleasants, but he did feel increasingly troubled by slavery. In his personal correspondence with others, he routinely expressed his hope that slavery would eventually be abolished. Washington told David Humphreys, his former aide de camp, that his involvement with slavery "has been the only unavoidable subject of regret."

Perhaps hinting that he was already considering manumitting his slaves, Washington added that "to lay a foundation to prepare the rising generation [of enslaved people] for a destiny different from that in which they were born; afforded some satisfaction to my mind, & could not I hoped be displeasing to the Justice of the Creator." In other words, Washington recognized that slavery contradicted the ideals of the Revolution and agreed that letting the oppressed go free would please the Lord. While Washington would eventually follow through on this conviction (by including a manumission provision in his will), most Virginia slaveholders clung to their human property.[54] Between 1785 and 1788, a handful of antislavery Baptists in Virginia called for antislavery policies and petitions, but their efforts went nowhere.[55]

Slaveholders in other states also resisted calls for reform. Warner Mifflin submitted an antislavery petition to the Delaware legislature with the support of his local Duck Creek Monthly Meeting and the PMS in 1785. The petitioners hoped, ideally, that Delaware would follow northern precedents and enact a law for the "abolition of slavery," but they prioritized the modest request to simply liberalize manumission laws. However, the assembly refused to act at all. North Carolina's legislature also resisted Quakers' antislavery pressure, while slaveholders in South Carolina and Georgia imported over nine thousand African captives between 1783 and the end of 1786. South Carolina did, however, adopt a temporary ban on slave imports in April 1787. This ban was not inspired by humanitarian concern, but was instead part of a program to ensure the payment of preexisting debts and to limit the export of gold and silver.[56] Indeed, during the summer of 1787, South Carolinians and Georgians were the only delegates at the Federal Convention to defend the Atlantic slave trade.

The Antislavery Campaign of 1787–1789

The Federal Convention released its proposed U.S. Constitution to the public in September 1787. Although the framers had avoided using words such as "slave," "Black," or "Negro," the public saw through the euphemisms and realized that the Constitution contained numerous concessions to slaveholders. Quakers had hoped that it would immediately revive the 1774 Atlantic slave trade ban; instead, the Constitution forbade Congress from banning the "Importation of such Persons as any of the States now existing shall think proper to admit" until 1808. Meanwhile, the Constitution's three-fifths clause partially counted enslaved people ("other Persons") when calculating representation in the House of Representatives and Electoral College. In practice, this clause gave southern states one extra congressman per fifty thousand slaves (as the initial apportionment rate granted one representative per thirty thousand free inhabitants). Another clause reiterated masters' rights to reclaim fugitive laborers across state lines. Many other clauses indirectly protected slavery, as historians have increasingly emphasized. For example, the federal government would help suppress "domestic insurrections" (such as slave revolts) while a clause forbidding taxes on exports served slaveholders' economic interests (as slave-grown crops accounted for most exports). Furthermore, the federal division of powers implicitly left slavery as a domestic concern under the control of state governments, protecting the institution from federal regulation or interference (and the Fifth, Ninth, and Tenth Amendments soon strengthened this protection).[57]

Abolitionists worried that these concessions to slaveholders would anger God and provoke "additional judgments." William Rotch, the Massachusetts Quaker, pronounced that the Constitution's "cornerstone" was "founded on *Slavery* and that is on *Blood*." Many of Rotch's antislavery contemporaries shared this view of the Constitution, at least initially. A Philadelphia Friend described the slave trade clause as "one of the Grand reasons of our Objections" to the Constitution. One British Quaker wryly observed: "Your convention has not come up to what we expected from the Champions of Liberty—but it is liberty for *themselves* & not for mankind in general that noisy patriots brawl & fight for."[58] During the ratification debates, northern Anti-Federalists also appealed to antislavery conceptions of divine providence when critiquing the Constitution. One asked, "Is this the Way by which we are to demonstrate our Gratitude to Providence, for his divine Interposition in our Favor, when oppressed by Great Britain?" New York politician DeWitt Clinton warned that "it is a terrible thing to mock the almighty, for how can we expect to merit his favor, or escape his vengeance; if it should appear, that we were not serious in our professions [about natural rights], and that they were mere devices to gratify our pride and ambition." He cautioned that the slave trade provision threatened to "bring down a heavy judgment upon our land." It is likely that many Anti-Federalists used providentialist rhetoric opportunistically, but it nonetheless demonstrates their assumption that many people held such views.[59]

Despite their qualms, many abolitionists ultimately supported ratification. Benjamin Rush happily informed Boston's Jeremy Belknap that "the quakers in Pennsylvania" were almost unanimous in support of ratification and viewed the Constitution's slave trade clause as "a great point obtained from the Southern States." Rush exaggerated Quakers' enthusiasm, but abolitionists did view the Constitution's twenty-one-year delay as preferable to their current situation under the Articles of Confederation—in which there was no expectation that Congress would *ever* be able to abolish the slave trade. Moreover, James Pemberton was happy that the Constitution at least did not "restrain the Legislatures of the respective States from enacting such [antislavery] laws."[60] Thus, many of the nation's leading abolitionists supported ratification while redoubling their state-level antislavery efforts.

Abolitionists vowed to ignore the Constitution's fugitive slave clause and sought to end the slave trade even before 1808. A month after the Constitution was published, Moses Brown pronounced the fugitive clause "contrary to the Divine Law." He cited Deuteronomy 23:15–16, in which the Lord declares: "Thou shalt not deliver unto his master the servant which is escaped from his master unto thee: He shall dwell with thee, *even* among you . . . thou shalt not oppress him." The Quaker referred fellow abolitionists to a section of Granville Sharp's *The Just Limitation of Slavery in the Laws of God* (1776), which was "conclusive on the point." Sharp had argued that Christians should not be prosecuted for aiding runaways "because that would be punishing a man for doing *his indispensable duty* according *to the laws of God*." Any human law to the contrary "must necessarily be rejected as *null and void*." Quaker abolitionists throughout the United States agreed. Indeed, Pennsylvania and New Jersey abolitionists had been promoting Sharp's interpretation of Deuteronomy 23:15 since 1774, when he had shared a draft with Anthony Benezet. In 1783, Benezet had reiterated his belief that Deuteronomy 23:15 necessitated helping slaves "even if they had no legal claim."[61] Enslaved people, of course, did not need biblical analysis to convince them of their right to run away regardless of the Constitution.

Meanwhile, Quakers continued promoting antislavery reform throughout the confederacy.[62] Building on earlier experience, James Pemberton and the Philadelphia Meeting for Sufferings served as the de facto center of a national antislavery campaign in 1787–1789. While Pemberton limited his direct lobbying efforts to his own state, other Quaker activists including Warner Mifflin of Delaware, John Parrish of Philadelphia, and Moses Brown of Providence frequently traveled across state lines to instigate or reinforce local efforts. They also found important allies outside the Society of Friends, especially in

New England. Their coordinated efforts achieved significant victories but also revealed the extent of apathy and opposition often facing antislavery reform.

Abolitionists' goals varied in different states based on the level of progress they had already made, but efforts to suppress all forms of slave trading were a common thread. By 1787 most states had prohibited the importation of slaves, but their citizens were often free to engage in other branches of the traffic. New Englanders remained especially active as carriers, buying captives in Africa and "conveying them for sale to the Carolinas & the West Indias," as the PMS complained in late 1786. During the second half of the 1780s, more than three-quarters of slave-trading voyages undertaken by Americans supplied foreign markets. Meanwhile, a growing class of domestic traders transported slaves from states in the North and Upper South to the Lower South where there was a greater demand for enslaved labor. In states where gradual abolition laws were already in effect, like Pennsylvania and Connecticut, some slaveholders exploited loopholes to sell their slaves or their slaves' freeborn children into perpetual bondage in other states or the Caribbean. Some domestic traders simply kidnapped and enslaved free people of color. Tragically, these forms of human trafficking would only increase in the nineteenth century—and while the later era has received the bulk of scholarly attention, abolitionists led concerted efforts against these practices beginning in the 1780s.[63]

The confederacy-wide abolitionist campaign of 1787–1789 built on the previous efforts of local meetings for sufferings and individuals like Warner Mifflin. In early 1787, Mifflin witnessed one of his neighbors buy slaves from other Delaware planters and then hire a ship "to take a Cargoe of Negroes to [South] Carolina." After failing to dissuade his slave-trading neighbor, Mifflin spent "near four weeks" lobbying the legislature largely by himself. The Delaware assembly eventually passed a law that strengthened the state's ban on slave importations, guarded against kidnapping, eased manumission requirements, and curtailed the sale of slaves out of state by requiring the written permission of three justices of the peace. The Delaware law was a significant victory, but it had not come easily. Mifflin noted that there were "interested Individuals" who acted as a proslavery lobby against his efforts, and he believed that the legislature would have quietly abandoned the bill if he had not stayed and overseen its final passage.[64] Abolitionists could sometimes achieve antislavery reforms through firm pressure, but legislatures were unwilling to act on their own. Mifflin kept the PMS abreast of his actions, and it in turn expanded his one-man campaign into a coordinated effort throughout the confederacy.

The PMS sent members to the various yearly meetings held throughout the nation so they could aid local antislavery efforts. As abolitionists traveled south, they generally faced greater obstacles, including apathy among many Quakers. In June 1787, John Parrish and Warner Mifflin attended the Baltimore Yearly Meeting and gave it an antislavery petition drafted by the PMS, which they expected local Quakers to support. Although Maryland Quakers dutifully presented the petition to the legislature after Mifflin and Parrish left, they refrained from any direct lobbying—"either thro' a too timerous Disposition or for some other Cause." Predictably, the legislature took no action.[65] After next attending the yearly meeting in Virginia, Mifflin proceeded to the North Carolina Yearly Meeting, where he found Quakers still struggling against the anti-manumission laws that had re-enslaved scores of their former bondspeople. Mifflin accompanied an antislavery committee from the North Carolina Standing Committee to lobby the legislature. In response, the lower house passed a bill liberalizing manumissions, but one state senator "violently opposed" the bill, and it was defeated. Mifflin reported that many senators personally supported the bill, but because slaveholding was "spreading more among the People at Large, many are affraid to vote as they would like." The Revolution may have increased some white Americans' unease with human bondage, but many slaveholders and aspiring slaveholders were as committed as ever to protecting the institution from even the most moderate reforms. Indeed, in 1788 the North Carolina legislature tightened the ban on manumissions.[66]

Sarah Richards Harrison (wife of Pennsylvania Abolition Society founder Thomas Harrison) accompanied Mifflin on his visit to the southern yearly meetings, speaking out against slavery herself. She then continued even farther south, spending several weeks in Charleston. But whereas she had previously inspired several manumissions during her travels in Virginia and North Carolina, Harrison had little luck in South Carolina. She reported that her antislavery message was "repugnant to the minds of most of the inhabitants, who, like many others, love ease and do not wish their false rest disturbed." South Carolina Quakers conceded that slavery was wrong but resisted calls for emancipation.[67]

While Parrish, Mifflin, and Harrison traveled in the South during the summer of 1787, PMS members Samuel Emlen Jr. and William Savery went north. They visited Edmund Prior and attended the yearly meetings in New York and New England. During the latter, they stayed with Moses Brown and helped plan antislavery petitions. The petition to the Rhode Island legislature called for a law banning participation in the Atlantic slave trade and for expediting emancipation within the state in order to "avert from our land the judgments of Him, who has declared himself the avenger of the oppressed." Brown presented the petition in June, but the legislature delayed its consideration until October. The Quakers' Congregationalist ally, the Reverend Samuel Hopkins, doubted the legislature would act, but he helped circulate copies of his *Dialogue Concerning Slavery* and published other antislavery pieces in the press. Brown then personally lobbied legislators, distributing copies of a new antislavery essay Hopkins authored under the pseudonym "Crito."[68]

In the new essay, Hopkins described slavery as "a national sin, and a sin of the first magnitude—a sin which righteous Heaven has never suffered to pass unpunished in this world." As in his earlier writings, he praised the Continental Congress's 1774 slave trade ban and the principles of the Declaration of Independence but warned that God would punish the young republic if it failed to follow through and end slavery. Indeed, Hopkins believed the postwar economic slump was evidence that God was "frowning upon us now." He similarly suggested that the recent enslavement of American sailors by Algerian corsairs "may be considered as a small degree of retaliation for our enslaving the Africans." If Americans did not heed God's warning and reform, they could expect much worse to come. At the end of October—and after a decade of antislavery agitation, largely by Quakers—the Rhode Island assembly finally passed a law forbidding all participation in the Atlantic slave trade.[69]

Abolitionists hoped the victory in Rhode Island would revive stalled efforts in neighboring Massachusetts. In June 1787, Moses Brown had also delivered a petition from the NEYM to the Massachusetts legislature and received "assurances from many Members in both houses, that something shall be done." By September, however, it was clear that legislative momentum had died. In frustration, the Reverend Jeremy Belknap complained to the PAS's Benjamin Rush: "Can you believe that the State of Massachusetts whose first principle is that 'all men are by nature free & equal' still permits her Citizens to carry on the detestable traffic in 'slaves & souls of Men'?" Brown attempted to shame the Bay State legislature into action with a new petition in November.[70] The legislature still dragged its feet.

The final instigation for Massachusetts came after three Black Bostonians were kidnapped and shipped off as slaves in February 1788. Prince Hall, the Black Freemason, learned of the kidnapping and worked with Belknap to push the legislature to act. Twenty-three Black men signed a petition written by Hall while about ninety white people subscribed to another petition circulated by Congregationalist clergymen. The Black petitioners described their kidnapped brethren as "free citizens of the town of Boston" who had been carried "off from their wives and children, to be sold for slaves." They concluded by requesting that the legislature ban participation in the Atlantic slave trade. Moses Brown also returned to Boston for another ten days of lobbying.[71] The interracial group of antislavery petitioners and lobbyists faced considerable opposition but succeeded in the end. The legislature forbade participation in the slave trade and also sent letters to the governors of southern states and Caribbean islands, describing the kidnapped Bostonians. Fortunately, all three Black men eventually regained their freedom with the help of a sympathetic white Freemason in Saint Bartholomew. Accompanied by Hall, they later visited Belknap to express their gratitude, which the minister described as "a rich compensation for all the Curses of the whole Tribe of African Traders aided by the Distillers, which have been liberally bestowed on the Clergy of this town for their agency on the [antislavery] Petition." In Philadelphia, Rush and the PAS sought to aid Belknap and Hall by publishing accounts of their efforts in the newspapers, but these publications also inspired further threats by Massachusetts slave traders against Belknap. While much of the public shared Belknap's antislavery sentiments, there were still powerful interests invested in the traffic throughout New England. Members of the New England Meeting for Sufferings celebrated their local legislative victories but also worried that slave traders would simply relocate to New York and Philadelphia. They called on Quakers there to give their "united attention to this subject."[72]

James Pemberton and the PMS helped coordinate these various efforts while also working with the PAS to lobby their own government. Both the PAS and PMS authored petitions to the Pennsylvania legislature in January 1788, with Pemberton serving on committees for both groups. The PMS petition praised the 1780 Gradual Abolition Act but requested "supplementary amendments and additions" targeting slave traders who used the state's ports "for the iniquitous traffic to Africa for slaves." They also complained of kidnappers and slaveholders who transported Black Pennsylvanians out of the state, "where they have been sold into unconditional slavery." While the PMS petition spoke for the state's Quakers, nearly two thousand Pennsylvanians of various denominations signed the PAS's petition making similar demands. The delegations from the PMS and PAS presented their petitions in late February. According to the later recollections of an "aged member of the Abolition Society," abolitionists had previously worked "to have proper men elected." Among the newly elected members was William Lewis, a PAS lawyer who had served in the legislature in 1780 and had helped write the Gradual Abolition Act. Lewis introduced the petitions and led the committee charged with addressing them, which then consulted with PMS and PAS lobbyists. The committee report, issued in March 1788, endorsed the abolitionists' view of judicial providence: "If the whole race of men are created by one God for the same noble purposes & if he will as we are taught to believe 'Avenge the injuries of his people,' it appears to your committee, that the Petitioners speak but the divine Will in requesting, that the Evil be done away from the Land." PAS members arranged to publish the report in the newspapers and in pamphlet form.[73]

The resulting bill, also authored by Lewis, banned Pennsylvanians' involvement in the Atlantic slave trade and also forbade masters from separating the families of their slaves and servants or selling them out of the state. Under Pennsylvania's state constitution, the legislature was required to print bills for public consideration and wait until after a session break before voting them into law, "except in occasions of sudden necessity." When Lewis presented the bill, he called for an immediate vote, warning that slaveholders would take advantage of any delay to sell their slaves' freeborn children out of the state. William Finley, a prominent representative from western Pennsylvania who had also promised the PAS his support, gave a speech that reportedly "drew tears from every eye." The unicameral legislature quickly passed the bill into law with minor amendments on March 28, by a vote of 40–16. The PMS and PAS delegates "attended the House from day to day thro' the several stages of the bill's consideration," and celebrated the resulting "salutary Law." Moreover, African Americans and their allies in the PAS subsequently used the legal mechanisms of the 1788 law to pursue freedom suits, dismantling slavery in the Quaker State far more rapidly than the "gradual" process proscribed in the initial 1780 law.[74]

Despite this victory, PMS members understood the dilemma posed by American federalism: closing Pennsylvania's ports to slave traders was "likely to prove but a partial Remedy, unless like measures are adopted in the adjacent States." John Parrish and Warner Mifflin returned to Maryland with another antislavery petition in May 1788 but found most Quakers uncommitted to antislavery activism. They also encountered fierce criticism from some legislators who complained about the agitators "coming from another state." One alleged that Mifflin was notorious for giving false travel passes to runaway slaves (enabling them to claim they had permission to leave their plantation on an errand). Nonetheless, Mifflin believed they could have achieved something if the legislative session had not been so far advanced and if the local Quakers had been more supportive. He returned again in November and found a supportive legislative ally in William Pinkney, but opposition and preoccupation with national politics prevented legislators from taking action.[75]

In Delaware, Quakers had been optimistic that the legislature would act on a petition they submitted but, "being over confident of obtaining the end desired, left Dover unseasonably, by which the disappointment took place." James Pemberton hoped this failure would "be a lesson of Instruction on future occasions of a like nature." They had more success the next year when Pemberton undertook a letter-writing campaign and John Parrish reinforced Mifflin's lobbying efforts with a new petition from the PMS. In February 1789, through the "most strenuous endeavours," they secured passage of a law prohibiting involvement in the Atlantic slave trade and further regulating the domestic trade. Pemberton concluded that the legislation "so far as it goes is agreeable, but much remains yet necessary to be done." In hindsight, Delaware's law limiting the domestic slave trade was the peak of antislavery legislation south of Pennsylvania before the Civil War, but abolitionist contemporaries were frustrated by the limits of their success.[76]

Abolitionists also targeted New Jersey, another state where hereditary slavery remained legal. In October 1788, James Pemberton wrote to Governor William Livingston, encouraging him to support gradual emancipation and legislation banning any involvement in the Atlantic slave trade. Meanwhile, David Cooper delivered another PMS petition and proposed an abolition bill. In November, the assembly passed a version of Cooper's bill, but only after "it was pulled to pieces and the most essential parts left out." The legislators stripped gradual emancipation from the bill, but they did ban all participation in the Atlantic slave trade and required masters to obtain their slaves' consent before selling them out of the state. Governor Livingston apologized to Pemberton that the legislature did not do more but told him that "as *Rome was not built in a day*, slavery . . . requires *more than a day* to abolish." The halting progress of emancipation in New Jersey reflected the political influence of slaveholders rather than the conservatism or naivete of early national abolitionists.[77]

The push for abolition was also slow in New York, the only northern state with more slaves than New Jersey (21,324 compared to 11,423 according to the 1790 Census). In March 1788, the New York Meeting for Sufferings could finally report that the legislature had prohibited the sale of slaves out of the state. But the law still did nothing to prevent participation in the foreign slave trade, and the abolitionists' call for emancipation was defeated by "great opposition in many places."[78] The level of resistance facing abolitionists in the state should caution scholars against dismissing New York abolitionists as seeking "not to end the system [of slavery] itself but to reform it." Such a characterization might apply to Alexander Hamilton, but not to the more active members of the New-York Manumission Society and New York Meeting for Sufferings. These groups operated in a state where "a great number of Persons are violently opposed to the emancipation of their Slaves." Overall, the N-YMS demonstrated a firm commitment to emancipation and racial uplift. In 1787 it established the Free African School modeled in part after the one Quakers had previously established in Philadelphia.[79]

The interracial and interstate component of abolitionism can also be seen in a campaign to pass further reform in Connecticut, where Quakers hoped they had "some ground for success." In the spring of 1788, the New York Meeting for Sufferings gathered antislavery tracts "for distribution in Connecticut," and the *New-Haven Gazette* began publishing antislavery pieces with increased frequency.[80] The Quakers arrived in New Haven (then the state capital) in October 1788 and were soon visited by several Presbyterian activists with their own antislavery petition. Moses Brown, who came from the neighboring state of Rhode Island, was especially impressed by the Reverend Jonathan Edwards Jr., who proved "active, Zealous & very well acquainted with the subject." The petition from Quakers commended Connecticut for taking steps to gradually end slavery but warned that without additional legislation, slave traders would use the state's ports as base for the "Inhuman traffick" between Africa and the Caribbean.[81]

Meanwhile, the self-identified "Blacks of New Haven" submitted a more radical antislavery petition of their own. Their timing indicates they were attuned to white abolitionists' efforts, perhaps through attendance at Edwards's White-Haven Church. Apparently some of the petitioners had been born in Africa, for they complained of having been "Dragd from our native Country" and sold into "Cruil Slavirre Leving our mothers our fathers our Sisters and our Brothers." Clearly unsatisfied with the state's gradual abolition law (which applied only to children born after 1784), the Black activists asked the legislature to "grant us a Liberation." The legislators' reactions to this petition were not recorded, but they admitted the two groups of white petitioners "to the floor of the House to speak on the subject of Slavery." The lower house quickly drafted and passed a strong antislavery bill, and the Quakers from New York and Rhode Island returned home, confident that the Connecticut senate would soon pass the bill into law.[82]

But the Quakers left New Haven too soon. The state senate amended the bill in ways that weakened key provisions. Under the state's 1784 gradual abolition law, the children of slaves would serve as bound laborers until age twenty-five, and the initial bill from 1788 (like the new law in Pennsylvania) had closed a loophole through which some masters had been selling these children out of the state as slaves for life. But the Quaker activists later learned that in the final law, "that part which restrained the exportation of them [was] wholly left out." This type of legal loophole, allowing slaveholders to avoid virtually all the cost of gradual emancipation while condemning many freeborn Black children to hereditary enslavement in the South, revealed the callousness of many Connecticut legislators regarding the plight of Black people. Jonathan Edwards Jr. complained that "now the poor creatures will be carried out in ship-loads." He believed things might have turned out differently if the Quakers "had tarried a few days longer." James Pemberton lamented the outcome but viewed it as instructive. He enjoined abolitionists "not to place too much dependence on flattering prospects of success" and to persist in lobbying for legislation "thro' every stage of its progress to its final enaction." He blamed overconfidence in part for the failures and limited victories in North Carolina, Maryland, Delaware, New Jersey, and Connecticut. Pemberton summed up the lesson concisely to his brother: "Such business requires importunity and perseverance."[83]

The multiyear abolitionist campaign demonstrated the highly contingent nature of antislavery progress after the Revolution. Even in New England, antislavery progress depended on persistent agitation to overcome legislative apathy. Connecticut legislators turned a blind eye to masters who sold enslaved Blacks and their freeborn children out of the state as slaves, while New Jersey and New York still clung to hereditary slavery. Yet despite defeats and setbacks, the various antislavery campaigns at the state and federal levels during the Critical Period reveal a level of coordination that is absent from most studies of abolitionism, which treat progress as the natural result of the Revolution. Nowhere in the United States did the ideas of the Revolution (or economic interest) make slavery's death inevitable. Antislavery achievements resulted instead from persistent agitation by white abolitionists—most of them Quakers—in conjunction with Black protest and slave resistance.

Debating Black Emigration and Integration

Throughout this time, some activists debated whether the future of Black Americans lay within the United States or whether they should return to the land of their ancestors. The Reverend Samuel Hopkins, who had supported plans to send Black missionaries to Africa in the 1770s, promoted the idea of Black emigration to Africa after the war. In 1784, he outlined the multiple advantages of his program to some skeptical Quakers: "Such a settlement would not only be for the benefit of those who shall return to their native country, but it would be the most likely and powerful means of putting a stop to the slave trade, as well as of increasing Christian knowledge among those heathens." Hopkins appears to have found more enthusiasm among the local Black community, including members of the Free African Union Society in Newport. He remained frustrated, however, that most free people of color in Pennsylvania and New York showed little interest in emigration, and he complained that "so many Quakers . . . for some reason or other, are not disposed to support such a design." Indeed, Quaker abolitionists generally supported Black uplift and integration rather than colonization. People of color, meanwhile, embraced uplift and integration while maintaining a cautious interest in emigration.[84]

Hopkins's efforts to promote African colonization benefitted from developments in Britain. In 1786, British reformers including Granville Sharp convinced the government to permit the creation of a settlement for Black loyalists (who had left America with the British army in 1783) and other free people of color in Sierra Leone, on the coast of West Africa. William Dillwyn followed the progress of the colony closely from London and kept his American correspondents informed about its many struggles. Much more enthusiastic about African colonization was William Thornton, a Quaker from the British Caribbean who traveled throughout the northern United States beginning in 1786, meeting with Quakers, Black leaders, and other abolitionists.[85]

Meanwhile, Prince Hall and seventy-two other Black men had submitted a colonization petition to the Massachusetts legislature in January 1787. They complained of living under "very disagreeable and disadvantageous circumstances," and wished "to return to Africa, our native country." They asked the legislature to support an expedition to procure a suitable tract of land for an African settlement, promising that future trade with the emigrants would "much more than overbalance all the expence which is now necessary in order to carry this plan into effect." The legislature simply tabled the petition without taking further action, but the Black delegation left with an expectation of future support. Although Black colonizationists sought white aid, they wanted to preserve control over any venture. Those in Boston and Philadelphia both rebuffed offers by Thornton to act on their behalf in planning an African settlement. He reported that they were "unwilling to be subject to any nation of whites" and would only emigrate to Africa if they could "be an independent people." African Americans would hold essentially the same position for decades; they were potentially interested in emigration to Africa or elsewhere, but only on their own terms.[86]

Much of the Black Pennsylvanians' hesitation stemmed from the progress they were making at home. In Philadelphia, Absalom Jones, Richard Allen, and several other free Black men and women established the Free African Society in the spring of 1787. The FAS served as a mutual aid organization, providing economic relief for members who fell on hard times, while also promoting religious and educational reform. It initially met in Allen's home, but when the group grew too large, it moved to a room in the Friends' Negro School. The group also chose Joseph Clark, a white Quaker PAS member who had taught at the school, as their first clerk and treasurer.[87] Although Black and white reform associations were largely segregated, they routinely collaborated. For example, Jupiter Hammon, an enslaved poet from New York, drew on connections to Edmund Prior of the New York Meeting for Sufferings to print an address to New York's Black community in 1787. Writing in a state where white politicians had failed to pass an abolition law, Hammon lamented, "I must say that I have hoped that God would open their eyes, when they were so much engaged for liberty, to think of the state of the poor blacks." Prior forwarded the pamphlet to James Pemberton, vouching that it was "the genuine production of a Slave." Philadelphia Quakers reprinted Hammon's pamphlet and distributed copies as far as London, where it was also reprinted.[88] During this time, John Pemberton was in London and sent copies of works by Black Britons (such as Ignatius Sancho) back to Philadelphia, where Quakers inserted them in newspapers and magazines.[89] In sum, the culture of Quaker abolitionism was increasingly interracial and collaborative.

Meanwhile, the most widely disseminated colonization proposal appeared in Thomas Jefferson's *Notes on the State of Virginia*, printed in the United States in early 1788 (after having been published in Paris and London). Intended originally for a French audience, the book discussed slavery in two chapters, nominally about "Laws" and "Manners." In the latter chapter, Jefferson conceded that slavery was a dangerous violation of God-given rights. In fact, he echoed the providentialist rhetoric of abolitionists:

> Indeed I tremble for my country when I reflect that God is just: that his justice cannot sleep forever: that considering numbers, nature and natural means only, a revolution of the wheel of fortune, an exchange of situation, is among possible events: that it may become probable by supernatural interference! The Almighty has no attribute which can take side with us in such a contest.

In other words, he acknowledged that a just God would side with rebel slaves and might even instigate slave revolts to punish American slaveholders for their sins. Jefferson concluded the chapter by expressing his hope that conditions were "preparing, under the auspices of heaven, for a total emancipation, and that this is disposed, in the order of events, to be with the consent the masters, rather than by their extirpation."[90] Given that Jefferson did not actually prioritize abolitionism in his political career, it seems that this providentialist rhetoric was in large part performative. Nonetheless, the passages indicate Jefferson's assumption that his intended audience of European intellectuals would find such rhetoric compelling.

Jefferson laid out his own proposal for emancipation—accompanied by colonization—in the chapter on "Laws." He proposed that enslaved people's future children be liberated at age eighteen (if female) or twenty-one (if male), and then colonized elsewhere as a "free and independent people." Anticipating objections to this deportation requirement, Jefferson responded by emphasizing his "suspicion" that Black people were innately "inferior to the whites in the endowments both of body and mind" to explain why they could not be integrated into free society. For instance, when belittling examples of Black accomplishment, he wrote: "Religion has indeed produced a Phillis Whately [i.e., Wheatley]; but it could not produce a poet. The compositions published under her name are below the dignity of criticism." In sum, he suggested that it was nature, not enslavement, that degraded Black people, thereby presenting "a powerful obstacle to the emancipation of these people." He also implied that because grief was allegedly only a "transient" emotion among Black people, emancipation was a less pressing matter than it would have been if the races were equal. Despite his belief in universal natural rights and his providentialist rhetoric about a just God, Jefferson lacked a sense of urgency and was clearly rationalizing inaction. Philadelphia's Quaker abolitionists were pleased by Jefferson's condemnation of slavery but disappointed by his racism. They had published a new edition of Phillis Wheatley's *Poems on Various Subjects* in 1786 and would do so again in 1789.[91] Despite Jefferson's aspersions, Quakers continued using Wheatley (who had died in late 1784 without fulfilling her plan to publish a second volume of poetry) as evidence of Africans' intellectual potential.

Meanwhile, Samuel Hopkins and the members of Newport's Free African Union Society remained enthusiastic about colonization, especially after news of improving conditions in Sierra Leone arrived in the summer of 1789. Newport's Black activists, who described themselves as "strangers and outcasts in a strange land," hoped that in Africa they "may be more happy . . . and promote the best good of our brethren in that country."[92] Black New Englanders' interest in African colonization reflected both push and pull factors.

Black Philadelphians, by contrast, appear to have generally felt less attraction to Africa as their status seemed to be improving in Pennsylvania. In October 1789, after the Black Newporters invited the Free African Society to join a venture to Africa, the Philadelphians expressed their best wishes for those who were inclined "to undertake such a long and perilous journey," but they had no interest in leaving themselves. Moreover, they celebrated that in Philadelphia there were some white people who followed the principle of "do unto men as we would they do unto us" and aided the "stranger and the fatherless."[93] Such optimism often proved well placed, and interracial activism increased among Philadelphians in the coming years.

In October 1789, the PAS implemented a new "Plan for Improving the Condition of the Free Blacks," creating a series of committees overseeing Black education and employment, guarding against kidnapping, and monitoring proper morals and conduct. Although clearly paternalistic, these efforts were based on white abolitionists' assumption that the apparent degradation of many free people of color reflected the effects of oppression rather than innate inferiority.[94] The abolitionists celebrated in 1790 when delegates at a convention amending Pennsylvania's constitution rejected a proposal to make being "white" a requirement to vote. James Pemberton proudly informed British abolitionists that "a free Black Man is to be put on the footing of a citizen of Pennsylvania."[95] This type of progress reduced Black

Pennsylvanians' interest in emigration and increased their commitment to fighting for further rights within the new nation.

* * *

During the Critical Period, abolitionist made considerable progress despite hostility or apathy from many white Americans. The 1787 Northwest Ordinance's ban on slavery was a major victory that originated with Quaker petitioning and lobbying. Quakers also organized across state, denominational, and racial lines to push for local antislavery reforms throughout the union, achieving significant victories, especially against slave trading. These achievements reflect the tenacity of abolitionists (the bulk of whom operated outside of secular antislavery groups) and the sophistication of their networks and tactics. Nonetheless, they still suffered defeats and setbacks, in the South as well as the North. Connecticut legislators willfully ignored masters who sold slaves and Black indentured servants out of the state into hereditary bondage, while New Jersey and New York still clung to slavery. Many Black Americans continued to doubt that they could ever be truly free in the United States. The limits of antislavery progress disappointed but did not surprise abolitionists, as they recognized the economic and social obstacles they faced. Warner Mifflin felt it was "instructive" to remember how Quakers themselves had long resisted antislavery pressure, and he noted that "we must not expect more from the worlds people, than those of our Society."[96] This realistic assessment did not discourage Mifflin; it merely led him to persist in his efforts, hoping that he could continue the progress begun by predecessors such as John Woolman and Anthony Benezet.

Epilogue

In 1770, hereditary slavery was considered legal in every British colony. Twenty years later, six states (counting Vermont) had taken steps to end slavery while Congress had forbidden it in the Northwest Territory. The population of free people of color in North America had risen from perhaps a few thousand to almost sixty thousand. This progress would not have occurred without the American Revolution. It is true that nearly seven hundred thousand African Americans remained enslaved, principally in the South, and that New York and New Jersey did not adopt gradual abolition laws until 1799 and 1804, respectively.[1] Still, if not for the Revolution, there is little reason to imagine that any British colony—with the possible exception of Massachusetts—would have ended slavery before the nineteenth century. The legislative reforms and judicial rulings that put northern slavery on the road to extinction were tied to the Revolution. Both the imperial crisis and the Revolutionary War undoubtedly facilitated and accelerated antislavery reform.

Although the Revolution's antislavery impact was deeply consequential, it was far from inevitable and did not reflect as much of a break with the past as scholars have commonly assumed. The patriots' natural rights rhetoric did not displace Quakers' older religious arguments and prove more effective; instead, the imperial crisis and war increased the persuasive power of traditional religious arguments. Abolitionists' biblicist arguments (that Christ's new covenant had rendered slavery sinful) and providentialist arguments (that the Lord punished nations for their sins) offered compelling explanations for the imperial crisis and the subsequent war. They also promised a means of regaining the Lord's blessing: Let the oppressed go free. The longer the war lasted, the more compelling these arguments seemed. Nonetheless, only a small minority of patriot politicians actively embraced the antislavery cause. Tenacious activism by dedicated abolitionists—mostly

Quakers and African Americans with a handful of white evangelical patriot allies—was necessary to overcome apathy, prejudice, and the obstructionist power of slaveholders in legislatures and courts. Antislavery reform thus depended on a confluence of three contingent factors: antislavery theology, moments of crisis, and concerted activism.

Abolitionists—even Quaker pacifists—recognized that the war aided their cause, and they presciently worried that peace would slow antislavery momentum. They shifted their providentialist arguments to warn that God would not allow the new nation to enjoy permanent peace and prosperity until Americans completed their antislavery reformation. By the 1780s, Quakers had also developed sophisticated institutional support for antislavery political activism. The Philadelphia Meeting for Sufferings coordinated with other Quaker groups throughout the nation, along with some key outside allies, to push through additional reforms at the state and federal levels. Still, peace and the stability brought by the U.S. Constitution did dampen the sense of antislavery urgency among many white Americans. Quakers were the only mainstream denomination of Christians to preserve policies against slaveholding. Efforts during the late 1780s and early 1790s to revive or initiate similar policies among the Presbyterians, Baptists, and Methodists all failed. Instead of seeking to purify themselves and the new nation from the sin of slavery, most white evangelicals prioritized spreading the Gospel.[2]

Even some individual ministers and politicians who had been prominent abolitionists during the revolutionary era lost their zeal. David Howell of Rhode Island remained active in the antislavery cause but found that the Reverend Jeremy Belknap of Massachusetts was ready to retire from the movement. In 1790, when Howell suggested creating an antislavery society in Massachusetts, Belknap responded: "I am of opinion that such an association is entirely needless here, as we have no slavery to abolish . . . but, alas! many of them are in a far worse condition than when they were slaves, being incapable of providing for themselves the means of subsistence." He also dismissed Howell's call for an antislavery petition to Congress, questioning the "prudence or propriety of such an application."[3] Many white northerners apparently shared the view that they had taken sufficient steps to end the sin of slavery within their own communities and felt little obligation to either aid the formerly enslaved people in their midst or promote emancipation elsewhere. Black people and Quakers thus remained the most dedicated abolitionists in the new nation.[4]

* * *

During the 1830s, amid the period of religious revival known as the Second Great Awakening, tens of thousands of white evangelicals embraced abolition as a means of purifying the nation from sin. Abolitionists such as William Lloyd Garrison, editor of *The Liberator* antislavery newspaper, advanced the same biblicist and providentialist arguments that abolitionists had long made. Indeed, Garrison routinely closed his letters by invoking Isaiah 58:6, writing, "Yours to break every yoke."[5] The growth of abolitionism, in turn, spurred a surge in proslavery publications that defended slavery on scriptural grounds, especially Noah's Curse (Genesis 9:25) and the permission to enslave heathen (Leviticus 25:44). Many of these publications were by northern ministers who opposed abolitionism, perceiving it as a misguided threat to national harmony that undermined efforts to evangelize in the South by alienating slaveholders.[6] Much of this posturing was undoubtedly cynical and opportunistic, based on economic interests. Still, the extent of biblicist debate regarding slavery in the northern press demonstrates how seriously many white Christians took the matter. Of course, theological debates were unable to solve the problem of slavery. After Abraham Lincoln was elected president in November 1860 on a platform promising to restrict slavery's further territorial spread, southern slaveholders organized secession, leading to the Civil War. Slavery's fate would largely be decided on the battlefield and through the actions of thousands of Black southerners who escaped from bondage during the war. Nonetheless, biblicist and providentialist arguments also helped ensure that the Civil War became a war for emancipation.[7]

The secession crisis provoked extensive biblicist debates in the northern press. In December 1860, the Reverend Henry J. Van Dyke of New York defended slavery in a sermon widely reprinted as *The Character and Influence of Abolitionism*. He quoted Bible passages and argued that slavery was "permitted and regulated by the Divine Law, under both the Jewish and Christian dispensations."[8] Van Dyke's proslavery sermon provoked numerous rebuttals, including an essay titled "Patriarchal and Jewish Servitude No Argument for American Slavery" by Tayler Lewis, a professor of Greek and Latin at Union College in Schenectady, New York. Lewis refuted all the common proslavery claims. Noah's curse on Canaan had already been fulfilled and was irrelevant because Africans were the "sons of Cush," not Canaan. Lewis also addressed the permission given to the Hebrews to enslave heathens in Leviticus 25, which he described as "the scriptural Gibraltar of the slavery cause." He argued (quoting Ephesians 2:14 without citation) that the central truth of Christianity "is that 'this wall of partition has been broken down.'" Considering Leviticus in light of Christ's New Covenant, Lewis maintained, "utterly sweeps away this stronghold of the pro-slavery cause." He concluded by addressing references to slavery in the New Testament, arguing that none should be interpreted as positive sanction any more than Jesus's injunction to turn the other cheek was intended to "justify the smiting and the smiter."[9] The central tenets of antislavery biblicism on the eve of the Civil War were essentially the same as in the late seventeenth century. Lewis's antislavery biblicism, including the central role of Ephesians 2:14, echoed the arguments first made by Quaker William Edmundson in 1676–1677 and Puritan Samuel Sewall in 1700, and subsequently developed by a host of revolutionary-era abolitionists (as well as those in the antebellum era).[10]

Once the Civil War began, days of fasting and prayer also echoed those of the Revolution and played an important role in persuading politicians and the northern public to support (or at least accept) emancipation as a war aim. Following the Union army's humiliating loss at the (First) Battle of Bull Run (Manassas), President Lincoln appointed September 26, 1861 as a national fast day (the first of several). He urged Americans "to recognize the hand of God in this terrible visitation" for "our own faults and crimes as a nation and as individuals." Frederick Douglass, the nation's most prominent Black abolitionist, denounced superficial fasts as "utterly repugnant to the Divine Mind." He called on Lincoln to follow the guidance of Isaiah and "let the oppressed go free." Numerous white ministers expressed similar sentiments on the ensuing fast day. In Massachusetts, the Reverend John Jay Dana based his fast sermon on Isaiah 58:6 and called on President Lincoln to use his powers as "Commander-in-Chief of the Army" to "break every yoke and say to the oppressed in every rebellious State, You are free." Of nineteen fast-day sermons summarized in the next day's issue of the *New York Times*, eight advocated emancipation while two more expressed moderate antislavery views.[11] Calls for emancipation became louder as the war progressed, based not only on practical considerations (such as military strategy and manpower shortages) but also because the war's unprecedented brutality and devastation lent renewed salience and urgency to abolitionists' claims that slavery was a God-provoking sin. In the summer of 1862, a delegation of ministers told Lincoln that "there can be no deliverance from divine judgments till slavery ceases in the land. We can not expect God to save a nation that clings to its sin."[12]

On September 22, 1862, Lincoln announced the Emancipation Proclamation, which would go into effect on New Year's Day. Lincoln's decision was of course shaped by "military necessity," but he also described it as an "act of justice" and invoked "the gracious favor of almighty God." Antislavery ministers immediately celebrated the proclamation in providentialist terms, predicting that God would now bless the Union cause.[13] Still, they also cautioned against any negotiated peace that did not involve complete emancipation. For example, the Reverend George B. Cheever of New York warned that if the North accepted reunification with slavery intact, God would conclude "that the Proclamation was only a gigantic sham" and punish the nation with renewed vigor. As with the American Revolution, the duration of the Civil War increased the likelihood of radical reform. Indeed, the Reverend Linus Shaw of Massachusetts concluded that the Union army's initial succession of "incompetent generals . . . one after another . . . showing an equal lack of the qualities of good generalship" was all part of God's plan to ensure that the war would not end until the North embraced emancipation as a goal.[14]

President Lincoln also began publicly describing emancipation in providentialist terms. "If slavery is not wrong, nothing is wrong," he wrote in a published letter to Kentucky Unionists in April 1864. He concluded by echoing the sentiments of countless antislavery sermons: "If God now wills the removal of a great wrong, and wills also that we of the North as well as you of the South, shall pay fairly for our complicity in that wrong, impartial history will find therein new cause to attest and revere the justness and goodness of God." In other words, he believed the entire nation deserved divine chastisement for allowing the sin of slavery to continue for so long. A succession of Union victories in the fall of 1864—including the capture of Atlanta and Mobile—seemed to confirm that the Lincoln administration's support for antislavery measures was paying providential dividends. The victories helped reelect Lincoln and enabled him to push the Thirteenth Amendment—permanently abolishing slavery—through a lame-duck session of Congress.[15]

In his second inaugural address of March 4, 1865, Lincoln reiterated his conviction that the war was God's means of punishing the nation and purging slavery from the land: "Fondly do we hope, fervently do we pray, that this mighty scourge of war may speedily pass away. Yet, if God wills that it continue until all the wealth piled by the bondsman's two hundred and fifty years of unrequited toil shall be sunk, and until every drop of blood drawn with the lash shall be paid by another drawn with the sword, as was said three thousand years ago, so still it must be said 'the judgments of the Lord are true and righteous altogether.' (Psalm 19:9)."[16]

Lincoln's providentialist interpretation had much in common with the ways in which abolitionists had interpreted the Revolutionary War and even, in the case of Quakers, the French and Indian War. Anthony Benezet, John Parrish, Warner Mifflin, Samuel Hopkins, and the other leading abolitionists of the eighteenth century would have shared Lincoln's view of the Civil War. And though they would have lamented the bloodshed, they would hardly have been surprised that slavery's end came through violence. The urgency of their antislavery impulse had always been inspired by fear of a righteous God who hated oppression.

ABBREVIATIONS

AHR	*American Historical Review*
CPW	Cox, Parrish, Wharton Papers, HSP
DHRC	*Documentary History of the Ratification of the Constitution: Digital Edition*, ed. John P. Kaminski et al.
EAS	*Early American Studies*
FAB	George F. Brookes, *Friend Anthony Benezet* (Philadelphia: University of Pennsylvania Press, 1937)
FO	Founders Online, National Archives, https://founders.archives.gov/
Haverford	Haverford College, Quaker & Special Collections Library
HSP	Historical Society of Pennsylvania
JAH	*Journal of American History*
JCC	*Journals of the Continental Congress*, 34 vols. (Washington DC: U.S. Government Printing Office, 1904–1937)
JCWE	*Journal of the Civil War Era*
JER	*Journal of the Early Republic*
JHRMA	*Journals of the House of Representatives of Massachusetts, 1715–1779*, 65 vols. (Boston: MHS, 1919–1990)
JSH	*Journal of Southern History*
LBRP	Letter Book of Robert Pleasants, 1754–1797 (at Haverford)
LCP	Library Company of Philadelphia
LOC	Library of Congress
LMS	London Meeting for Sufferings
LSF	Library of the Society of Friends (London)
LVA	Library of Virginia
MHS	Massachusetts Historical Society
NCSC	North Carolina Standing Committee (at Haverford)
NCYM	North Carolina Yearly Meeting (at Haverford)

NEMS	New England Meeting for Sufferings
NEQ	*New England Quarterly*
NEYM	New England Yearly Meeting
NYHS	New York Historical Society
N-YMS	New-York Manumission Society
Papers of the AST	Papers of the American Slave Trade: Series A, Selections from the Rhode Island Historical Society, ed. Jay Caughtry (microfilm) (Bethesda, MD: University Publications of America, 1996–)
PAS Papers	Pennsylvania Abolition Society Papers, HSP
PMHB	*Pennsylvania Magazine of History and Biography*
PMM	Philadelphia Monthly Meeting (at Haverford)
PMS	Philadelphia Meeting for Sufferings (at Haverford)
PQM	Philadelphia Quarterly Meeting (at Haverford)
PWL	Carl Prince et al., *Papers of William Livingston*, 5 vols. (New Brunswick, NJ: Rutgers University Press, 1978–1988)
PYM	Philadelphia Yearly Meeting (at Haverford)
VMS	Virginia Meeting for Sufferings (at Haverford)
VYM	Virginia Yearly Meeting (at Haverford)
VMHB	*Virginia Magazine of History and Biography*
WMQ	*William and Mary Quarterly* (Third Series)
WSH	*The Works of Samuel Hopkins, D.D., First Pastor of the Church in Great Barrington, Mass., Afterwards Pastor of the Congregational Church in Newport, RI . . .*, 3 vols. (Boston: Doctrinal Tract and Book Society, 1852)

NOTES

Introduction

1. [David Cooper], *A Serious Address to the Rulers of America, On the Inconsistency of Their Conduct Respecting Slavery: Forming a Contrast Between the Encroachments of England on American Liberty, and American Injustice in Tolerating Slavery* (Trenton, NJ: Isaac Collins, 1783), 4, 19, 12, 13; Patrick Rael, *Eighty-Eight Years: The Long Death of Slavery in the United States, 1777–1863* (Athens: University of Georgia Press, 2015), 63.

2. [Cooper], *Serious Address*, 16; PYM Minutes Vol. 2 (1747–1779), Haverford, 111–25, quotations from 121 (29 9mo 1758). (I have preserved the Quaker's traditional practice of numbering the dates, i.e., 9mo for September, rather than using their "pagan" names.) For information about Cooper, including the creation of his antislavery pamphlets, see the diary extracts and commentary in "David Cooper" and "Notices of David Cooper, [nos. I-XLV]" published in volumes 15 and 16 of the *Friends' Review* (Philadelphia, 1862–1863). See also Bill L. Smith, "Never Take Kinship Personally: Confronting Slavery, Masculinity, and Family in Revolutionary America," *Quaker History* 103 (Spring 2014): 17–35; and Jonathan D. Sassi, "The Legacies of James McCarty: The Story of How Quakers Secured One Family's Emancipation and Its Ramifications for Revolutionary-Era Antislavery," *EAS* 16 (Spring 2018): 282–316.

On Quakers' interpretation of the French and Indian War as divine retribution for slavery, see Thomas E. Drake, *Quakers and Slavery in America* (New Haven, CT: Yale University Press, 1950), 60–61; Sydney V. James, *A People Among Peoples: Quaker Benevolence in Eighteenth-Century America* (Cambridge, MA: University of Harvard Press, 1963), 134–38; David Brion Davis, *The Problem of Slavery in Western Culture* (Ithaca, NY: Cornell University Press, 1966), esp. 330–332; and Jack D. Marietta, *Reformation of American Quakerism, 1748–1783* (Philadelphia: University of Pennsylvania Press, 1984), 113–15.

3. [David Cooper], *A Mite Cast Into the Treasury: Or, Observations on Slave-Keeping* (Philadelphia: Joseph Crukshank, 1772), 5, 20, 19. [Cooper], *Serious Address*, 14, 17, 21–22.

4. John Coffey, *Exodus and Liberation: Deliverance Politics from John Calvin to Martin Luther King, Jr.* (New York: Oxford University Press, 2014), 87; Rael, *Eighty-Eight Years*, 46–47. Rael gives significant attention to abolitionists and African Americans but still tends to exaggerate the influence of natural rights rhetoric and widespread antislavery sentiment. For emphasis on patriot ideology as the primary inspiration for antislavery, see also Bernard Bailyn, *The Ideological Origins of the American Revolution* (Cambridge, MA: Harvard University Press, 1967), 237–40; Arthur Zilversmit, *The First Emancipation: The Abolition of Slavery in the North* (Chicago: University of Chicago Press, 1967), 93–138, 170, 226–28; Winthrop D. Jordan, *White Over Black: American Attitudes Toward the Negro, 1550–1812* (Chapel Hill: University of North Carolina Press, 1968), 279, 289–95; Duncan J. MacLeod, *Slavery, Race and the American Revolution* (New York: Cambridge University Press, 1974), 5–8, 14–20; Gary B. Nash, *Race and Revolution*

(Madison, WI: Madison House, 1990), 3–20; and Stanley Harrold, *American Abolitionism: Its Direct Political Impact from Colonial Times into Reconstruction* (Charlottesville: University of Virginia Press, 2019), 18. On providential thought, see also Nicholas Guyatt, *Providence and the Invention of the United States, 1607–1876* (New York: Cambridge University Press, 2007).

5. Landon Covington Bell, *The Old Free State: A Contribution to the History of Lunenburg County and Southside Virginia, Volume I* (Richmond, VA: William Byrd Press, 1927), 466. Such views were effectively refuted through the 1967 publications of Zilversmit, *First Emancipation*, and Bailyn, *Ideological Origins*.

6. Jordan, *White Over Black*, 342.

7. For population statistics, see Ira Berlin, *Many Thousands Gone: The First Two Centuries of Slavery in North America* (Cambridge, MA: Harvard University Press, 1998), 369–70. New York was an outlier in the North, with enslaved people making up about 12 percent of the population in 1770, while enslaved people made up only about 5 percent of the population in the "southern" colony of Delaware.

8. John P. Kaminski, ed., *Necessary Evil? Slavery and the Debate over the Constitution* (Madison, WI: Madison House, 1995), 243; Jordan, *White Over Black*, chap. 9; Nash, *Race and Revolution*, chap. 2; Paul Finkelman, *Slavery and the Founders: Race and Liberty in the Ave of Jefferson*, 3rd ed. (Armonk, NY: M. E. Sharpe, 2014). For critiques of this view, see Matthew Mason, "Necessary but Not Sufficient: Revolutionary Ideology and Antislavery Action in the Early Republic," in *Contesting Slavery: The Politics of Bondage and Freedom in the New Nation*, ed. John Craig Hammond and Matthew Masson (Charlottesville: University of Virginia Press, 2011), 11–31; Matthew Mason, "A Missed Opportunity? The Founding, Postcolonial Realities, and the Abolition of Slavery," *Slavery & Abolition* 35 (2014): 199–213; Christopher Leslie Brown, "The Problems of Slavery," in *Oxford Handbook of the American Revolution*, ed. Edward G. Gray and Jane Kamensky (New York: Oxford University Press, 2013), 427–46; John Craig Hammond, "Race, Slavery, Sectional Conflict, and National Politics, 1770–1820," in Jonathan Daniel Wells, ed., *The Routledge History of Nineteenth-Century America* (New York: Routledge, 2017), 11–32.

9. Robert G. Parkinson, *The Common Cause: Creating Race and Nation in the American Revolution* (Chapel Hill: University of North Carolina Press, 2016), 7; Robert G. Parkinson, *Thirteen Clocks: How Race United the Colonies and Made the Declaration of Independence* (Chapel Hill: University of North Carolina Press, 2021), 2, 178; Nikole Hannah-Jones, "Democracy," in *The 1619 Project: A New Origin Story*, ed. Nikole Hannah-Jones, Caitlin Roper, Ilena Silverman, and Jake Silverstein (New York: One World, 2021), 8–36, quotation from 16. For accounts of the Revolution that emphasize proslavery, see Gerald Horne, *The Counter-Revolution of 1776: Slave Resistance and the Origins of the United States of America* (New York: New York University Press, 2014), esp. 209–33; and Alfred W. Blumrosen and Ruth G. Blumrosen, *Slave Nation: How Slavery United the Colonies & Sparked the American Revolution* (Naperville, IL: Sourcebooks, 2005). For more balanced treatments, see David Waldstreicher, *Slavery's Constitution: From Revolution to Ratification* (New York: Hill and Wang, 2009), 39–41; and George William Van Cleve, *A Slaveholders' Union: Slavery, Politics, and the Constitution in the Early American Republic* (Chicago: University of Chicago Press, 2010), 31–45.

For accounts emphasizing hardening racism, see Leon F. Litwack, *North of Slavery: The Negro in the Free States* (Chicago: University of Chicago Press, 1961); Jordan, *White Over Black*, esp. chap. 9; Macleod, *Slavery, Race and Revolution*; Nash, *Race and Revolution*, chap. 2; James Brewer Stewart, "Modernizing 'Difference': The Political Meanings of Color in the Free States, 1776–1840," *Journal of the Early Republic* 19 (Winter 1999), 691–712; and Joanne Pope Melish,

Disowning Slavery: Gradual Emancipation and "Race" in New England (Ithaca, NY: Cornell University Press, 1998). For arguments that racism was virulent and prevalent from the start, see Jack P. Greene, "'Slavery or Independence': Some Reflections on the Relationship Among Liberty, Black Bondage, and Equality in Revolutionary South Carolina," *South Carolina Historical Magazine* 80 (July 1979):193–214; and F. Nwabueze Okoye, "Chattel Slavery as the Nightmare of the American Revolutionaries," *WMQ* 37 (1980): 3–28.

10. Gordon Wood's claims of antislavery declension caused by slave resistance are highly dubious, based on exaggerating white Virginians' "earlier enthusiasm for limiting slavery." Gordon S. Wood, *Power and Liberty: Constitutionalism in the American Revolution* (New York: Oxford University Press, 2021), 122–23. See also Gordon S. Wood, *The Radicalism of the American Revolution* (New York: Vintage Books, 1991), 186; Gordon S. Wood, *The Purpose of the Past: Reflections on the Uses of History* (New York: Penguin, 2008), 296; and Gordon S. Wood, *Empire of Liberty: A History of the Early Republic* (New York: Oxford University Press, 2009), 519–24.

Other scholars who are more critical of the founders nonetheless assert that many white Americans (especially northerners) naively believed slavery would simply "wither away" after slave importations ceased; see Mary Staughton Locke, *Anti-Slavery in America: From the Introduction of African Slaves to the Prohibition of the Slave Trade, 1619–1808* (Boston: Ginn, 1901), 155; James D. Essig, *The Bonds of Wickedness: American Evangelicals Against Slavery, 1770–1808* (Philadelphia: Temple University Press, 1982), 124; Van Cleve, *Slaveholder's Union*, 146, 189; Matthew Mason, *Slavery and Politics in the Early American Republic* (Chapel Hill: University of North Carolina Press, 2006), 3, 15–16, 28, 41; Edward E. Baptist, *The Half Has Never Been Told: Slavery and the Making of American Capitalism* (New York: Basic Books, 2014), 186; and Sean Wilentz, *No Property in Man: Slavery and Antislavery at the Founding* (Cambridge, MA: Harvard University Press, 2018), 134, 187.

For increasing attention to the role of Black activism, see Benjamin Quarles, *The Negro in the American Revolution* (Chapel Hill: University of North Carolina Press, 1961); Nash, *Race and Revolution*; Gary B. Nash, *The Forgotten Fifth: African Americans in the Age of Revolution* (Cambridge, MA: Harvard University Press, 2006); Douglas Egerton, *Death or Liberty: African Americans and Revolutionary America* (New York: Oxford University, 2009); Rael, *Eighty-Eight Years*; Manisha Sinha, *The Slave's Cause: A History of Abolition* (New Haven, CT: Yale University Press, 2016); and David Waldstreicher, *The Odyssey of Phillis Wheatley: A Poet's Journey Through American Slavery and Independence* (New York: Farrar, Strous and Giroux, 2023).

11. Christopher Leslie Brown, *Moral Capital: Foundations of British Abolitionism* (Chapel Hill: University of North Carolina Press, 2006), 461–62. For an emphasis on the extent rather than limits of antislavery progress in America, see also Sean Wilentz, "The Radicalism of Northern Abolition," *NEQ* 46 (March 2023): 8–26.

12. Christopher Leslie Brown, "Problems of Slavery," 437.

13. "Candidus," *Boston Gazette*, 14 October 1771; François Furstenberg, "Beyond Freedom and Slavery: Autonomy, Virtue, and Resistance in Early American Political Discourse," *JAH* 89 (March 2003): 1295–1330, quotations from 1303, 1305. On contemporaries' limited conceptions of rights, see also Michal Rozbicki, *Culture and Liberty in the Age of the American Revolution* (Charlottesville: University of Virginia Press, 2011).

14. My emphasis on the link between providentialist religious beliefs and antislavery seeks to revive an important but often overlooked aspect of David Brion Davis's work. In *Slavery in Western Culture*, he emphasizes that slavery had always presented an ideological problem, and he gives considerable attention to religious debates. In *The Problem of Slavery in the Age*

of Revolution, 1770–1823 (Ithaca, NY: Cornell University Press, 1975), Davis also gives significant attention to the role of Quakers and providentialist thought among antislavery patriots (while also arguing that antislavery faced insurmountable obstacles in the South). However, these themes and nuances have had less influence than Davis's discussions of natural rights and capitalism on subsequent historiography. See for example Wood, *Power and Liberty*, 100.

15. Bailyn, *Ideological Origins*, 236; Paul J. Polgar, *Standard-Bearers of Liberty and Equality: America's First Abolition Movement* (Chapel Hill: University of North Carolina Press, 2019), 4. For another account focusing on the postwar era, see Richard S. Newman, *The Transformation of American Abolitionism: Fighting Slavery in the Early Republic* (Chapel Hill: University of North Carolina Press, 2002). For studies that give greater attention to continuities between the colonial and national periods but still underestimate the extent of organized abolitionism before 1780, see Gary B. Nash and Jean R. Soderlund, *Freedom by Degrees: Emancipation in Pennsylvania and Its Aftermath* (New York: Oxford University Press, 1991); and Sinha, *Slave's Cause*. For overviews of the shifting historiography on abolitionism, see W. Caleb McDaniel, "The Bonds and Boundaries of Antislavery," *JCWE* 4 (March 2014): 84–105; and Corey M. Brooks, "Reconsidering Politics in the Study of American Abolitionists," *JCWE* 8 (June 2018): 291–317.

16. I have previously stressed the importance of John Parrish and the Philadelphia Meeting for Sufferings in Nicholas P. Wood, "A 'class of Citizens': The Earliest Black Petitioners to Congress and Their Quaker Allies," *WMQ* 74 (January 2017): 109–44. On Warner Mifflin, see Nicholas P. Wood, "Considerations of Humanity and Expediency: The Slave Trades and African Colonization in the Early National Antislavery Movement," (PhD diss., University of Virginia, 2013), chaps. 2–4; and Gary B. Nash, *Warner Mifflin: Unflinching Quaker Abolitionist* (Philadelphia: University of Pennsylvania Press, 2017). On Black activism in Massachusetts, see especially Christopher Cameron, *To Plead Our Own Cause: African Americans in Massachusetts and the Making of the Antislavery Movement* (Kent, OH: Kent State University Press, 2011).

17. William DeLoss Love, *The Fast and Thanksgiving Days of New England* (Boston: Houghton, Mifflin, 1895).

18. *Boston Evening-Post*, 2 May 1768, and reprinted in *Connecticut Gazette* (New London) 13 May 1768, *Providence Gazette* 14 May 1768, and *Connecticut Courant* (Hartford) 13 June 1768; *Boston Gazette*, 23 August 1773, cited in Waldstreicher, *Odyssey of Phillis Wheatley*, 199. On eighteenth-century Black Americans' use of the Bible for antislavery purposes, see especially John Saillant, "Origins of African American Biblical Hermeneutics in Eighteenth-Century Black Opposition to the Slave Trade and Slavery," in *African Americans and the Bible*, ed. Vincent Wimbush (New York: Continuum, 2001), 236–50; Christopher Cameron, "The Puritan Origins of Black Abolitionism in Massachusetts," *Historical Journal of Massachusetts* 39 (Summer 2011): 78–107; and Lisa M. Bowens, *African American Readings of Paul: Reception, Resistance, and Transformation* (Grand Rapids, MI: William B. Eerdmans, 2020), 15–58.

19. [Anthony Benezet], *Serious Considerations on Several Important Subjects; viz: On War and Its Inconsistency with the Gospel, Observations on Slavery, and Remarks on the Nature and Bad Effects of Spirituous Liquors* (Philadelphia: Joseph Crukshank, 1778), esp. 27–29. On the ways Quakers appropriated aspects of the Revolution to promote antislavery, see also Kristen Sword, "Remembering Dinah Nevil: Strategic Deceptions in Eighteenth-Century Antislavery," *JAH* 97 (September 2010): 315–43.

20. [Samuel Hopkins], *A Dialogue Concerning the Slavery of the Africans: Shewing It to be the Duty and Interest of the American States to Emancipate All Their African Slaves: With an Address to the Owners of Such Slaves: Dedicated to the Honourable Continental Congress*

(Norwich, CT: Judah P. Spooner, 1776), 5; [Jabez Huntington], *A Discourse on the Times*, 2nd ed. (Norwich, CT: Judah P. Spooner, 1776), 4, 5, 6.

21. [Cooper], *Serious Address*, 17.

Chapter 1

1. Thomas E. Drake, *Quakers and Slavery in America* (New Haven, CT: Yale University Press, 1950), 34; Manisha Sinha, *Slave's Cause: A History of Abolition* (New Haven, CT: Yale University Press, 2016), 9. The 1670s and 1680s also involved a surge in antislavery activism in Latin America, including by Capuchin missionaries and the African-born activist Lourenço da Silva Mendonça; see especially Richard Gray, "The Papacy and the Atlantic Slave Trade: Lourenço da Silva, the Capuchins and the Decisions of the Holy Office," *Past and Present* 115 (May 1987); José Lingna Nafafé, *Lourenço da Silva Mendonça and the Black Atlantic Abolitionist Movement in the Seventeenth Century* (New York: Cambridge University Press, 2022); and Christopher J. Kellerman, *All Oppression Shall Cease: A History of Slavery, Abolitionism, and the Catholic Church* (Maryknoll, NY: Orbis Books, 2022), 92–106.

2. Eran Shalev, *American Zion: The Old Testament as a Political Text from the Revolution to the Civil War* (New Haven, CT: Yale University Press, 2013), 151–84, quotation from 165. Mark Noll, perhaps the leading authority on religious debates over slavery in America, routinely portrays slaveholders as having stronger theological arguments than abolitionists. See for example Mark Noll, *America's God: From Jonathan Edwards to Abraham Lincoln* (New York: Oxford University Press, 2002), 386–421; Mark Noll, *The Civil War as Theological Crisis* (Chapel Hill: University of North Carolina Press, 2006); and Mark Noll, *In the Beginning Was the Word: The Bible in American Public Life, 1492–1783* (New York: Oxford University Press, 2016), 248.

3. When providing Bible verses, I quote from the King James Version (first published in 1611) as it was the most common version in the English colonies and the early United States. My understanding of the text is informed by the annotations in Adele Berlin and Marc Zvi Brettler, eds., *The Jewish Study Bible*, 2nd ed. (New York: Oxford University Press, 2014), and Bruce M. Metzger and Roland E. Murphy, eds., *The New Oxford Annotated Bible: With Apocryphal/Deuterocanonical Books* (New York: Oxford University Press, 1994).

For other overviews of the Bible verses most commonly used to justify slavery, see also David Brion Davis, *The Problem of Slavery in Western Culture* (Ithaca, NY: Cornell University Press, 1966), 1–4, 8–13, 63–66; Kenneth J. Zanca, ed., *American Catholics and Slavery: 1789–1866: An Anthology of Primary Documents* (Lanham, MD: University Press of America, 1994), 1–8; Kellerman, *All Oppression Shall Cease*, 1–15; and Noll, *Civil War as Theological Crisis*, chap. 3. On the Bible in early America, see Knoll, *In the Beginning Was the Word*; and Seth Perry, *Bible Culture and Authority in the Early United States* (Princeton, NJ: Princeton University Press, 2018).

4. "The 4th Homily of St. Gregory of Nyzza in the *Minge Patrology*," excerpted in Zanca, *American Catholics and Slavery*, 10–11. For early theological debates over slavery and servitude, see also Davis, *Slavery in Western Culture*, 62–121; and Kellerman, *All Oppression Shall Cease*, 16–46.

5. *Congressional Globe 37-1*, 1682 (12 April 1860). Theories abound regarding Ham's supposed sin, including the view that Ham slept with his mother while Noah was passed out and that Noah later cursed Canaan as the fruit of this incest. John Sietze Bergsma and Scott Walker Hahn, "Noah's Nakedness and the Curse on Canaan (Genesis 9:20–27)," *Journal of Biblical Literature* 124 (Spring 2005): 25–40. On the curse and slavery, see especially Stephen R. Haynes,

Noah's Curse: The Biblical Justification for American Slavery (New York: Oxford University Press, 2002); David M. Whitford, *The Curse of Ham in the Early Modern Era: The Bible and the Justification for Slavery* (Burlington, VT: Ashgate, 2009); and David M. Goldenberg, *Black and Slave: The Origins and History of the Curse of Ham* (Boston: De Gruyter, 2017). On the history of racism, see also Ibram X. Kendi, *Stamped from the Beginning: The Definitive History of Racist Ideas* (New York: Bold Type Books, 2016).

6. St. Augustine, *City of God* (413–426), excerpted in Zanca, *American Catholics and Slavery*, 14.

7. Keith Bradley, *Slavery and Society at Rome* (New York: Cambridge University Press, 1994); Katharine Gerbner, *Christian Slavery: Conversion and Race in the Protestant Atlantic World* (Philadelphia: University of Pennsylvania Press, 2018), 15–16.

8. Thomas Aquinas, *The "Summa Theologica" of St. Thomas Aquinas: Third Part (Supplement). Literally Translated by Fathers of the English Dominican Province* ([ca. 1265–1272], New York: Benzinger Brothers, 1922), 182 (query 52). "Title XXI: Concerning Slaves," *Las Siete Partidas, Volume 4, Family, Commerce, and the Sea: The Worlds of Women and Merchants (Partidas IV and V)*, ed. Robert I Burns, trans. Samuel Parsons Scott (Philadelphia: University of Pennsylvania Press, 2001), 977. On the transition from European forms of bondage to race-based slavery in the New World, see especially Davis, *Slavery in Western Culture*, 29–61; and Robin Blackburn, *The Making of New World Slavery: From the Baroque to the Modern, 1492–1800* (New York: Verso, 1997), 31–56.

9. Robin Blackburn, "The Old World Background to European Colonial Slavery," *WMQ* 54 (January 1997): 70.

10. Pope Nicholas V, "Dum Diversas" Papal Bull (1452), excerpted in *Changes in Official Catholic Moral Teachings*, ed. Charles E. Curran (New York: Paulist Press, 2003), 67 (quotation); Kellerman, *All Oppression Shall Cease*, 52–56.

11. Gomes Eannes de Azurara, *The Chronicle of the Discovery and Conquest of Guinea . . .*, ed. Charles Raymond Beazley and Edgar Prestage, 2 vols. (London: Hakluyt Society, 1896), 1:51 (quotation); A. J. R. Russell-Wood, "Iberian Expansion and the Issue of Black Slavery: Changing Portuguese Attitudes, 1440–1770," *AHR* 83 (February 1978): 16–42, esp. 20; A. J. R. Russell-Wood, "Before Columbus: Portugal's African Prelude to the Middle Passage and Contribution to Discourse on Race and Slavery," in *Race, Discourse, and the Origin of the Americas: A New World View*, ed. Vera Lawrence Hyatt and Rex Nettleford, (Washington, DC: Smithsonian Institution Press, 1995), 134–68; Blackburn, *Making of New World Slavery*, 97–123. On the development of the slave trade, see also Hugh Thomas, *The Slave Trade: The Story of the Atlantic Slave Trade, 1440–1870* (New York: Simon & Schuster, 1997).

12. Azurara, *Chronicle of the Discovery and Conquest of Guinea*, 1:54; James H. Sweet, "The Iberian Roots of American Racist Thought," *WMQ* 54 (January 1997): 143–66; Winthrop D. Jordan, *White Over Black: American Attitudes Toward the Negro, 1550–1812* (Chapel Hill: University of North Carolina Press, 1968), 56–98; Blackburn, *Making of New World Slavery*, 72–76; Kellerman, *All Oppression Shall Cease*, 47–67; Goldenberg, *Black and Slave*, 87–104, 134–36.

13. Estimates from the Trans-Atlantic Slave Trade Database: https://www.slavevoyages.org/assessment/estimates.

14. Older scholarship emphasizing the initial fluidity of Black bondage in colonial Virginia includes Edmund S. Morgan, *American Slavery, American Freedom: The Ordeal of Colonial Virginia* (New York: W. W. Norton, 1975); and T. H. Breen and Stephen Innes, *"Myne Own Ground": Race and Freedom on Virginia's Eastern Shore, 1640–1676* (New York: Oxford

University Press, 1980). For the more recent emphasis on slavery preceding codification, see John C. Coombs, "The Phases of Conversion: A New Chronology for the Rise of Slavery in Early Virginia," *WMQ* 68 (October 2011): 332–60; John C. Coombs, "'Others Not Christians in the Service of the English': Interpreting the Status of Africans and African Americans in Early Virginia," *VMHB* 127 (2019): 212–38; and Michael Guasco, *Slaves and Englishmen: Human Bondage in the Early Modern Atlantic World* (Philadelphia: University of Pennsylvania Press, 2014), 195–226.

On the centrality of religion to conceptions of race in Virginia, see Rebecca Anne Goetz, *The Baptism of Early Virginia: How Christianity Created Race* (Baltimore: Johns Hopkins University Press, 2012). On the broader context of conversion and slavery, see Travis Glasson, *Mastering Christianity: Missionary Anglicism and Slavery in the Atlantic World* (New York: Oxford University Press, 2017); and Gerbner, *Christian Slavery*.

15. Virginia's colonial slave codes are widely available online, including "Laws on Slavery," *Virtual Jamestown*: http://www.virtualjamestown.org/laws1.html. Note that the printed texts based on manuscript law codes printed "Free" and "Freedom" as "ffree" and "ffreedom." I have standardized the spellings for clarity.

16. "Laws on Slavery," *Virtual Jamestown*; Marcus W. Jernegan, "Slavery and Conversion in the American Colonies," *American Historical Review* 21 (April 1916): 504–27; William M. Wiecek, "The Statutory Law of Slavery and Race in the Thirteen Mainland Colonies of British America," *WMQ* 34 (April 1974): 258–80; Benjamin Joseph Klebaner, "American Manumission Laws and the Responsibility for Supporting Slaves," *VMHB* 63 (October 1995): 443–53.

17. The 1641 "Body of Liberties" appears in William Whetmore, ed., *The Colonial Laws of Massachusetts, Reprinted from the Edition of 1672* (Boston: Rockwell and Churchill, 1890), 32–61, quotations from 51.

18. Whetmore, *Colonial Laws of Massachusetts*, 53. On slavery in colonial Massachusetts, see George Henry Moore, *Notes on the History of Slavery in Massachusetts* (New York: D. Appleton, 1866); Lorenzo J. Greene, *The Negro in Colonial New England, 1620–1776* (New York: Columbia University Press, 1942); Robert C. Twomby and Robert H. Moore, "Black Puritan: The Negro in Seventeenth-Century Massachusetts," *WMQ* 24 (April 1967): 224–42, also 232 and 234 for slavery as punishment for white criminals; Margaret Ellen Newell, *Brethren by Nature: New England Indians, Colonists, and the Origins of American Slavery* (Ithaca, NY: Cornell University Press, 2015); Jared Ross Hardesty, *Unfreedom: Slavery and Dependence in Eighteenth-Century Boston* (New York: New York University Press, 2016); and Wendy Warren, *New England Bound: Slavery and Colonization in Early America* (New York: Liveright, 2016).

19. Wendy Anne Warren, "'The Cause of Her Grief': The Rape of a Slave in Early New England," *JAH* 93 (March 2007): 1031–49. Paul Baynes, *An Entire Commentary upon the Whole Epistle of the Apostle Paul to the Ephesians . . .* (London: M.F., 1645), 695; Deborah Colleen McNally, "To Secure Her Freedom: 'Dorcas ye blackmore,' Race, Redemption, and the Dorchester First Church," *NEQ* 89 (December 2016): 533–55.

20. Cotton Mather, *The Life and Death of the Reverend Mr. John Eliot, Who Was the First Preacher of the Gospel to the Indians in America . . .*, 3rd ed. (London: John Dunton, 1694), 150–68, quotations from 151, 163–64, 166. Cotton Mather, *A Good Master Well Served: A Brief Discourse on the Necessary Properties & Practices of a Good Servant in Every Kind of Servitude* (Boston: B. Green and J. Allen, 1696). Greene, *Negro in Colonial New England*, 263–67. On Mather and slavery, see also Jordan, *White Over Black*, 200–204; Bernard Rosenthal, "Puritan Conscience and New England Slavery," *NEQ* 46 (March 1973): 62–81, esp. 62–65; and Daniel K.

Richter, "'It Is God Who Has Caused Them to be Servants': Cotton Mather and Afro-American Slavery in New England," *Bulletin of the Congregational Library* 30 (1979): 4–15.

21. George Fox, "To Friends Beyond the Sea, That Have Blacks and Indian Slaves," in *Selections from the Writings of George Fox*, 2nd ed., ed. Samuel Tuke (London: Edward Marsh, 1848), 63; George Fox, *Gospel Family-Order: Being a Short Discourse Concerning the Ordering of Families, Both of Whites, Blacks and Indians* (1676) 7, 14, 16, 17,18, 19, reproduced in J. William Frost, ed., *The Quaker Origins of Antislavery* (Norwood, PA: Norwood Editions, 1980), 35–55. See also J. William Frost, "George Fox's Ambiguous Anti-slavery Legacy," in *New Light on George Fox (1624 to 1691)*, ed. Michael Mullett (York, UK: Ebor Press, 1993), 69–88; and Kenneth L. Carrol, "George Fox and Slavery," *Quaker History* 86 (Fall 1997) 16–25. Both Frost and Carroll note that manuscript accounts of Fox's 1671 address indicate that he stated Black people might be held in bondage for thirty years, which would have allowed enslavement virtually for life.

On early Quaker discussions of slavery, see also Drake, *Quakers and Slavery in America*; Davis, *Slavery in Western Culture*; 292–332; Jean R. Soderlund, *Quakers and Slavery: A Divided Spirit* (Princeton, NJ: Princeton University Press, 1985); Brycchan Carey, *From Peace to Freedom: Quaker Rhetoric and the Birth of American Antislavery, 1657–1761* (New Haven, CT: Yale University Press, 2012); and Jon R, Kershner, *"To Renew the Covenant": Religious Themes in Eighteenth Century Quaker Abolitionism* (Boston: Brill Publishers, 2018).

22. Richard Baxter, *A Christian Directory, or, A Summ of Practical Theologie and Cases of Conscience Directing Christians How to Use Their Knowledge and Faith . . .* (London: Robert White, 1673), 557–60; Morgan Godwyn, *The Negro's & Indians Advocate, Suing for Their Admission to the Church, or, A Persuasive to the Instructing and Baptizing of the Negro's and Indians in our Plantations . . .* (London: F.D., 1680). See also Alden T. Vaughan, *Roots of American Racism: Essays on the Colonial Experience* (New York: Oxford University Press, 1995), chap. 3; Philippe Rosenberg, "Thomas Tryon and the Seventeenth-Century Dimensions of Antislavery," *WQM* 61 (October 2004): 609–42, esp. 620–21; Christopher Leslie Brown, *Moral Capital: The Foundations of British Abolitionism* (Chapel Hill: University of North Carolina Press, 2006), 57–72; John Coffey, *Exodus and Liberation: Deliverance Politics from John Calvin to Martin Luther King, Jr.* (New York: Oxford University Press, 2014), 82; and Gerbner, *Christian Slavery*, 24.

23. Ruth Paley, Cristina Malcolmson, and Michael Hunter, "Parliament and Slavery, 1660–c. 1710," *Slavery & Abolition* 31 (June 2010): 268, 269.

24. David Humphreys, *An Historical Account of the Incorporated Society for the Propagation of the Gospel in Foreign Parts: Containing Their Foundation, Proceedings, and the Success of Their Missionaries in the British Colonies, to the Year 1728* (London: Joseph Downing, 1730), 257–72, quotation from 265. The Yorke-Talbot opinion is dated 14 January 1729, based on the Julian calendar in which January was the eleventh month and March was the first. Based on the modern Gregorian calendar (which England adopted in 1752), the Yorke-Talbot opinion is from January 1730, and it was published in the same year in the *Boston Gazette*, 7 September 1730. Travis Glasson, "'Baptism Doth Not Bestow Freedom': Missionary Anglicanism, Slavery, and the Yorke-Talbot Opinion, 1701–30," *WMQ* 67 (April 2010): 279–318. On missionaries' acceptance of slavery, see also Gerbner, *Christian Slavery*, 112–37.

25. Noll, *America's God*, 386–421; Noll, *Civil War as Theological Crisis*, chap. 3. See also David Brion Davis, *The Problem of Slavery in the Age of Revolution, 1770–1823* (Ithaca, NY: Cornell University Press, 1975), 523–56; and Shalev, *American Zion*, 151–84. Historians' tendency to portray proslavery writers as able to use the Bible more effectively than abolitionists is especially evident in scholarship on the 1700–1701 dispute between Samuel Sewall and John Saffin.

26. Mathew Poole et al., *Annotations Upon the Holy Bible . . . Being a Continuation of Mr. Poole's Work by Certain Judicious and Learned Divines*, 2 vols. (London, 1700), 2: [unpaginated annotations on Ephesians 2:13–14]. (Sewall would have read the first edition, published in Latin as *Synopsis Criticorim Aliorumqu Sacrae Scripturae Interpretum.*) By contrast, Baynes offered a more conservative reading of these passages, simply asserting that Christ ended the Jews' ceremonial laws (*Entire Commentary*, 291).

27. Ephesians 2:14 and the idea that Christ revolved past dispensations are crucial components of early abolitionists' writings. Historians, however, have given little attention to these themes, with Lawrence Towner as the main exception. He recognized that Ephesians 2:14 was central to Samuel Sewall's antislavery pamphlet. For another discussion of antislavery interpretations of Paul, see Lisa M. Bowers, *African American Readings of Paul: Reception, Resistance, and Transformation* (Grand Rapids, MI: William. B. Eerdmans, 2020).

28. William Edmundson, *A Journal of the Life, Travels, Sufferings, and Labour of Love in the Work of the Ministry, of that Worthy Elder, and Faithful Servant of Jesus Christ, William Edmundson, Who Departed This Life, the 31st of the 6th Month, 1712* (Dublin: Samuel Fairbrother, 1715), 69–102, quotation from 75; William Edmundson to Dear Friends, Newport, RI, 19 7mo 1676 (old style), in Frost, *Quaker Origins*, 68.

29. W[illiam] E[dmundson], "For Friends in Maryland, Virginia & Other Parts of America" [5 11mo 1676 (5 February 1677)], copy in "Epistles and Sermons of George Fox" (also known as the Richardson MSS), Haverford (HC.MC.975.07.117), 21–24. This letter is partially transcribed, with some altered spellings, in Frost, *Quaker Origins*, 66–67. For the date of Edmundson's letter, see Kenneth L. Carroll, "Maryland Quakers and Slavery," *Quaker History* 72 (Spring 1983): 28. Edmundson's use of Ephesians is central to his biblicist argument but has drawn little attention from scholars. Davis is a partial exception, referring to Edmundson's argument about the "wall of partition," though without identifying it as taken from Ephesians (*Slavery in Western Culture*, 307).

Brycchan Carey suggests that scholars have overstated Edmundson's antislavery sentiment, but he passes over Edmundson's use of Ephesians without comment, apparently missing the biblical paraphrase and its logical implications. Nor does Carey examine Edmundson's invocation of Isaiah 58:6 (*From Peace to Freedom*, 65). For other brief references to Edmundson that do not discuss his use of Ephesians, see Drake, *Quakers and Slavery in America*, 9–10; Sydney V. James, *A People Among Peoples: Quaker Benevolence in Eighteenth-Century America* (Cambridge, MA: University of Harvard Press, 1963), 105–7; Soderlund, *Quakers and Slavery*, 7; Carey, *From Peace to Freedom*, 65; and Sinha, *Slave's Cause*, 13.

30. Edmundson, "For Friends in Maryland." The material quoted in this paragraph is only available in "Epistles and Sermons of George Fox" and is not included in Frost's published excerpts, upon which most historians have relied.

31. "Germantown Friends' Protest Against Slavery," 1688, in Frost, *Quaker Origins*, 69; Katharine Gerbner, "'We are against the traffik of men-body': The Germantown Quaker Protest of 1688 and the Origins of American Abolitionism," *Pennsylvania History* 74 (2007), 149–72; Katharine Gerbner, "Antislavery in Print: The Germantown Protest, the 'Exhortation,' and the Seventeenth-Century Quaker Debate on Slavery," *EAS* 9 (Fall 2011): 552–75.

32. [George Keith et al.], *An Exhortation & Caution to Friends Concerning Buying or Keeping of Negroes* ([New York: William Bradford,] 1693), 1, 3, 6; John Hepburn, *The American Defence of the Golden Rule: Or, An Essay to Prove the Unlawfulness of Making Slaves of Men* ([New York?:] 1715), [preface, iii].

33. Nicholas P. Wood and Jean R. Soderlund, "'To Friends and All Whom It May Concerne': William Southeby's Rediscovered 1696 Antislavery Protest," *PMHB* (April 2017): 177–98, quotation from 195; Kenneth L. Carroll, "William Southeby, Early Quaker Antislavery Writer," *PMHB* 89 (1965): 416–27. For Edmondson's 1676 visit with "William Southerby," see Edmundson, *Journal of the Life*, 96.

34. Cadwalader Morgan to the Yearly Meeting, 1696, in Frost, *Quaker Origins*, 70; Robert Piles's essay on slavery, 71; "Germantown Friends' Protest Against Slavery," 69.

35. Gray's undated proslavery manuscript, believed to be from 1693 to 1700, is transcribed in Frost, "George Fox's Ambiguous Anti-slavery Legacy," 82–84. I follow Frost in emphasizing that Gray's primary objective was to defend slavery. However, the suggestion that Gray prepared his manuscript for the 1696 PYM meeting is my own. By contrast, Carey dates Gray's statement to 1700 and focuses on Gray's support for amelioration, ignoring his proslavery biblicism and racism (*From Peace to Freedom*, 103).

36. Gray copied two passages from the New Testament—Colossians 4:1 and Ephesians 6:9—about masters' obligations to treat their servants well. He did not provide any explanation, but presumably he intended them to indicate that slavery was defensible based on Christians principles as long as the masters treated their slaves well. Abolitionists such as Southeby could have responded by pointing out there was no evidence that the type of servitude described in Paul's letter was hereditary slavery rather than temporary slavery.

37. PYM Minutes Vol. 1 (1681–1746), Haverford, 57 (23 7mo 1696); Carey, *From Peace to Freedom*, 98; Drake, *Quakers and Slavery in America*, 19; Soderlund, *Quakers and Slavery*, 19, 34–35, 47–49; Frost, "George Fox's Ambiguous Anti-slavery Legacy," 79–82.

38. William A. Pettigrew, *Freedom's Debt: The Royal African Company and the Politics of the Atlantic Slave Trade, 1672–1752* (Chapel Hill: University of North Carolina Press, 2013).

39. Hardesty, *Unfreedom*, 104–35; Kerima Marie Lewis, "Fires of Discontent: Arson as a Weapon of Slave Resistance in Colonial New England, 1650 to 1775," (PhD diss., University of California, Berkeley, 2014).

40. M. Halsey Thomas, ed., *Diary of Samuel Sewall, 1674–1729: Newly Edited from the Manuscript at the Massachusetts Historical Society*, 2 vols. (New York: Farrar, Straus and Giroux, 1973), 1:432–33 (19 June 1700); Paul Bayne, *An Entire Commentary upon the Whole Epistle of the Apostle Paul to the Ephesians . . .* (London: M.F., 1645), 695. On Sewall's pamphlet, see also Mary Staughton Locke, *Anti-Slavery in America: From the Introduction of African Slaves to the Prohibition of the Slave Trade, 1619–1808* (Boston: Ginn, 1901), 17–20; Abner C. Goodell, "John Saffin and His Slave Adam," *Publications of the Colonial Society of Massachusetts, Volume I: Transactions, 1892–1894* (1895), 84–93; Lawrence W. Towner, "The Sewall-Saffin Dialogue on Slavery," *WMQ* 21 (January 1964): 40–52; Davis, *Slavery in Western Culture*, 343–48; Bernard Rosenthal, "Puritan Conscience and New England Slavery," *NEQ* 46 (March 1973): 62–81, esp. 68–69; Larry E. Tise, *Proslavery: A History of the Defense of Slavery in America, 1701–1840* (Athens: University of Georgia Press, 1987), 17–19; Albert J. Von Frank, "John Saffin: Slavery and Racism in Colonial Massachusetts," *Early American Literature* 29 (1994): 254–72; Mark A. Peterson, "The Selling of Joseph: Bostonians, Antislavery, and the Protestant International, 1689–1733," *Massachusetts Historical Review* 4 (2002): 1–22; Warren, *New England Bound*, 221–45; and Christopher Cameron, *To Plead Our Own Cause: African Americans in Massachusetts and the Making of the Antislavery Movement* (Kent, OH: Kent State University Press, 2011), 14–16.

41. [Samuel Sewall], *The Selling of Joseph: A Memorial* (Boston: Bartholomew Green and John Allen, 1700), 2. A clean digital version of the pamphlet, modeled after the original format,

is available at Digital Commons@University of Nebraska-Lincoln: https://digitalcommons.unl.edu/etas/26.

42. [Sewall], *Selling of Joseph*, 1, 3.

43. John Saffin, *A Brief and Candid Answer to a Late Printed Sheet, Entitled, the Selling of Joseph: Whereunto Is Annexed, a True and Particular Narrative by Way of Vindication of the Author's Dealing with and Prosecution of His Negro Man Servant* . . . (Boston, 1701), 1. It seems that no complete copy of Saffin's pamphlet survives. The first part, responding to Sewall's *Selling of Joseph*, is reproduced in the appendix of Moore, *Notes on the History of Slavery*, 251–56. Most of the second part, detailing Saffin's legal controversy with Adam, appears in Goodell, "John Saffin and His Slave Adam," 103–13 (missing a few lines at the end, where the manuscript was mutilated). Both republications include the original pagination, which I have used when citing the pamphlet.

44. Davis, *Slavery in Western Culture*, 345; Noll, *In the Beginning Was the Word*, 248. See also Rosenthal, "Puritan Conscience," 68; Richter, "'It Is God Who Has Caused Them to be Servants,'" 4; Hardesty, *Unfreedom*, 64; and Warren, *New England Bound*, 229, 236.

45. Mark Noll reports that Sewall "deployed fourteen scriptures specified by chapter and verse" but misses Sewall's paraphrase of Ephesians 2:14 (*In the Beginning Was the Word*, 247). The only previous scholar who recognized and understood the way Sewall used Ephesians was Lawrence Towner in "Sewall-Saffin Dialogue," 44–45. Davis follows Towner in acknowledging that Sewall's diary referred to reading Baynes's commentary on Ephesians but mischaracterizes Sewall as "develop[ing] Baynes's argument" rather than refuting it. Davis asserts that "the most striking characteristic of Sewall's writing is its mood of uncertainty" (*Slavery in Western Culture*, 345). Sewall may have equivocated on minor points, such as the extent of Noah's Curse or why it was permissible for Abraham to own slaves, but he viewed these points as moot as Christ had ended such distinctions between people. In an edited collection of primary sources, Cameron provides helpful annotations for many of Sewall's biblical references but misses the crucial reference to Ephesians: Christopher Cameron, *The Abolitionist Movement: Documents Decoded* [Santa Barbara, CA: ABC-CLIO, 2014], 7–12.

46. Saffin, *Brief and Candid Answer*, 3, 4, 2; Sewall to Nathaniel Byfield, 4 January 1704–1705, "Letter-Book of Samuel Sewall," *Collections of the Massachusetts Historical Society, Vol. I* (Boston: MHS, 1886), 322–23.

47. Thomas, *Diary of Samuel Sewall*, 1:456 (28 October 1701); Sewall memorandum of letter to Paul Dudley, 20 November 1700, in "Letter-Book of Samuel Sewal," 245; Moore, *Notes on the History of Slavery*, 52. The proposal, dated 26 May 1701, appears in "From the Boston Centinel," *Reporter* (Brattleboro, VT), 24 November 1818.

48. Goodell, "John Saffin and His Slave Adam," 88, 100.

49. *The Acts and Resolves, Public and Private, of the Province of the Massachusetts Bay: To Which are Prefixed the Charters of the Province with Historical and Explanatory Notes, and an Appendix, Volume 1, 1692–1714* (Boston: Wright & Porter, 1869), 519.

50. Moore, *Notes on the History of Slavery*, 53–55; Greene, *Negro in Colonial New England*, 138; Klebaner, "American Manumission Laws."

51. Sewall's opposition to the 1705 bill did not reflect support for interracial unions (which he treated as distasteful in *The Selling of Joseph*), but rather his view that such relations were largely inevitable among servants and that the marital ban would merely increase the frequency of abortions and infanticide in attempts to hide the crime. Thomas, *Diary of Samuel Sewall*, 1:532 (1 December 1705). Towner, "Sewall-Saffin Dialogue," 49–50.

52. *The Athenian Oracle, The Second Edition, Printed at London. 1704* (Boston: Bartholomew Green, 1705); Sewall to Nathaniel Byfield, 4 January 1705–1706, "Letter-Book of Samuel Sewall," 1:322–23;

53. Thomas, *Diary of Samuel Sewall*, 1:532 (1 December 1705); *Boston News-Letter*, 10 June 1706; Towner, "Sewall-Saffin Dialogue," 49–51; James J. Allegro, "'Increasing and Strengthening the Country': Law, Politics, and the Antislavery Movement in Early-Eighteenth-Century Massachusetts Bay," *NEQ* 75 (March 2002): 5–23.

54. Cotton Mather, *The Negro Christianized: An Essay to Excite and Assist that Good Work, the Instruction of Negro-Servants in Christianity* (Boston: B. Green, 1706), 2, 4, 15, 16. 26.

55. Cotton Mather, *Theopolis Americana: An Essay on the Golden Street of the Holy City: Publishing a Testimony Against the Corruptions of the Market-Place . . .* (Boston: B. Green, 1710), 15–16, 17, 25; Peterson, "Selling of Joseph," 10–11.

56. Soderlund, *Quakers and Slavery*, 32–53, esp. 34.

57. "New-York April 7th," *Boston News-Letter*, 14 April 1712; Ben Hughes, *When I Die, I Shall Return to My Own Land: The New York City Slave Revolt of 1712* (Yardley, PA: Westholme Publishing, 2021).

58. The legislative records are reproduced in Carey, *Peace to Freedom*, 109–10. See also: W.E. Burghardt Du Bois, *Suppression of the African Slave-Trade to the United States, 1638–1870* (New York: Longmans, Green, and Co, 1986), 22; Darold D. Wax, "Quaker Merchants and the Slave Trade in Colonial Pennsylvania," *PMHB* 86 (April 1962): 143–59; Wood and Soderlund, "To Friends and All Whom It May Concerne," 186.

59. John Hepburn, *The American Defence of the Christian Golden Rule, Or An Essay to Prove the Unlawfullness of Making Slaves of Men, By Him Who Loves the Souls and Bodies of All Men* ([William Bradford, New York?], 1715), [i], 11, 20, 36, 31, 34. Hepburn identified himself as a Quaker (and had previously been indentured to one), though historians have not found any records indicating that he was formally recognized as being in membership with the Society of Friends. It seems he published his essay without authorization but also without censure from the Quaker hierarchy. The pamphlet also contained several essays by Hepburn's father-in-law, Thomas Lowry, on baptism and predestination. Henry J. Cadbury, "John Hepburn and His Book Against Slavery, 1715, *Proceedings of the American Antiquarian Society* 59 (January 1949): 89–112; Davis, *lavery in Western Culture*, 316–19; Carey, *From Peace to Freedom*, 123–41.

60. William Southeby's ca. 1714 Paper Relating to Negroes, reproduced in Wood and Soderlund, "To Friends and All Whom It May Concerne," 198; PYM Minutes Vol. 1, 168 (18–22 7mo 1715), 176 (19 7mo 1716), 188; Carroll, "William Southeby," 426.

61. Kershner, *To Renew the Covenant*, 38.

62. For the importance of Ephesians 2:14 to nineteenth-century abolitionists, see the Epilogue.

Chapter 2

1. W[illiam] E[dmundson], "For Friends in Maryland, Virginia & Other Parts of America," [5 11mo 1676 (5 February 1677)], copy in "Epistles and Sermons of George Fox" (also known as the Richardson MSS), Haverford (HC.MC.975.07.117).

2. Guyatt also includes a third variety, "apocalyptic providentialism," the "belief that God was literally working out the narrative of Revelation in current events and had cast various nations in the leading roles." See Nicholas Guyatt, *Providence and the Invention of the United States, 1607–1876* (New York: Cambridge University Press, 2007), 6. See also Alexandra

Walsham, *Providence in Early Modern England* (New York: Oxford University Press, 1999; John Coffey, *Exodus and Liberation: Deliverance Politics from John Calvin to Martin Luther King, Jr.* (New York: Oxford University Press, 2014).

3. J. William Frost, "Why Quakers and Slavery? Why Not More Quakers?" in *Quakers and Abolition*, ed. Brycchan Carey and Geoffrey Plank (Urbana: University of Illinois Press, 2014), 29–42, quotation from 35; Thomas E. Drake, *Quakers and Slavery in America* (New Haven, CT: Yale University Press, 1950); Sydney V. James, *A People Among Peoples: Quaker Benevolence in Eighteenth-Century America* (Cambridge, MA: University of Harvard Press, 1963); David Brion Davis, *The Problem of Slavery in Western Culture* (Ithaca, NY: Cornell University Press, 1966), esp. 292–332, 483–86; David Brion Davis, *The Problem of Slavery in the Age of Revolution, 1770–1823* (Ithaca, NY: Cornell University Press, 1975), esp. 213–54; Darold W. Wax, "Reform and Revolution: The Movement Against Slavery and the Slave Trade in Revolutionary Pennsylvania," *Western Pennsylvania Historical Magazine* 57 (1974), 403–29; Jean R. Soderlund, *Quakers and Slavery: A Divided Spirit* (Princeton, NJ: Princeton University Press, 1985); Gary B. Nash and Jean R. Soderlund, *Freedom by Degrees: Emancipation in Pennsylvania and Its Aftermath* (New York: Oxford University Press, 1991), chap. 2; Brycchan Carey, *From Peace to Freedom: Quaker Rhetoric and the Birth of American Antislavery, 1657–1761* (New Haven, CT: Yale University Press, 2012). On the broader reformation, see especially Jack D. Marietta, *The Reformation of American Quakerism, 1748–1783* (Philadelphia: University of Pennsylvania Press, 1984).

4. PYM Women's Epistle (22 9mo 1755), Pemberton Papers, HSP, vol. 11; John Pemberton to John Churchman, Philadelphia, 4th Mo. 19th, 1754 (draft), Pemberton Papers, HSP, vol. 10:2.

5. Ralph Sandiford, *The Mystery of Iniquity in a Brief Examination of the Practice of the Times, by the Foregoing and the Present Dispensation . . . The Second Edition, with Additions* ([Philadelphia: Benjamin Franklin] 1730), 100, 54–55, 57, 27. Benjamin Franklin printed both editions but chose to leave his name off of such controversial publications. On Franklin's complex connections to slavery and abolitionism, see David Waldstreicher, *Runaway America: Benjamin Franklin, Slavery, and the American Revolution* (New York: Hill and Wang, 2004).

6. Sandiford, *Mystery of Iniquity*, 97–98, 107.

7. PYM Minutes Vol. 1 (1681–1746), Haverford, 349 (19 7mo 1730); Roberts Vaux, *Memoirs of the Lives of Benjamin Lay and Ralph Sandiford: Two of the Earliest Public Advocates for the Emancipation of the Enslaved Africans* (Philadelphia: Solomon W. Conrad, 1815); Drake, *Quakers and Slavery in America*, 41–43.

8. Elihu Coleman, *A Testimony Against That Antichristian Practice of Making Slaves of Men: Wherein It Is Shewed to be Contrary to the Dispensation of the Law and Time of the Gospel* ([Boston,] 1733), 13, ii, 3. Drake, *Quakers and Slavery in America*, 37–38; Carey, *From Peace to Freedom*, 163–64.

9. Benjamin Lay, *All Slave-Keepers That Keep the Innocent in Bondage, Apostates . . .* (Philadelphia: Benjamin Franklin], 1737 [*sic*, 1738]), 18, 92, 52, 114, 56, 54, 55. Lay reprinted Sewall's *The Selling of Joseph* on pages 199–207. On Lay, see especially Marcus Rediker, *The Fearless Benjamin Lay: The Quaker Dwarf Who Became the First Revolutionary Abolitionist* (Boston: Beacon Press, 2018).

10. *American Weekly Mercury* (Philadelphia), 24 August 1738 and 26 October 1738. Both the advertisements and the disavowal were printed in several issues. Drake, *Quakers and Slavery in America*, 22–47; Soderlund, *Quakers and Slavery*, 32–46; Carey, *From Peace to Freedom*, 105–77; Manisha Sinha, *The Slave's Cause: A History of Abolition* (New Haven, CT: Yale University Press, 2016), 13–19.

11. George Whitefield, *Three Letters from the Reverend Mr. G. Whitefield : viz. . . . Letter III. To the Inhabitants of Maryland, Virginia, North and South-Carolina, Concerning Their Negroes* (Philadelphia: B. Franklin, 1740), 13–16. On the limits of evangelical opposition to slavery in the colonial era, see also Davis, *Slavery in Western Culture*, 197–222; James D. Essig, *The Bonds of Wickedness: American Evangelicals Against Slavery, 1770–1808* (Philadelphia: Temple University Press, 1982), 1–14; Sylvia R. Fry and Betty Wood, *Come Shouting to Zion: African American Protestantism in the American South and British Caribbean to 1830* (Chapel Hill: University of North Carolina Press, 1998;); Katharine Gerbner, *Christian Slavery: Conversion and Race in the Protestant Atlantic World* (Philadelphia: University of Pennsylvania Press, 2018); Mark A. Noll, *In the Beginning Was the Word: The Bible in American Public Life, 1492–1783* (New York: Oxford University Press, 2016), 245–55.

12. To His Excellency General Oglethorpe, The Petition of the Inhabitants of New Inverness, in Harvey H. Jackson, "The Darien Antislavery Petition of 1739 and the Georgia Plan," *WMQ* 34 (October 1977): 619.

13. Whitefield, *Three Letters*), 13–16.

14. Whitefield quoted in Stephen J. Stein, "George Whitefield on Slavery: Some New Evidence," *Church History* 42 (June 1973): 245; Whitefield quoted in Philippa Koch, "Slavery, Mission, and the Perils of Providence in Eighteenth-Century Christianity: The Writings of Whitefield and the Halle Pietists," *Church History* 84 (June 2015): 390.

15. Justin James Pope, " Dangerous Spirit of Liberty: Slave Rebellion, Conspiracy, and the First Great Awakening, 1729–1746," (PhD diss., George Washington University, 2014), 372–78; Young Hwi Yoon, "The Spread of Antislavery Through Proslavery Tracts in the Transatlantic Evangelical Community, 1740s–1770s," *Church History* 81 (June 2012): 348–77.

16. Edwards quoted in Kenneth P. Minkema, "Jonathan Edwards's Defense of Slavery," *Massachusetts Historical Review* 4 (January 2002): 39. See also Heejoon Jeon, "Jonathan Edwards and the Anti-Slavery Movement," *Journal of the Evangelical Theology Society* 63 (December 2020): 773–88.

17. Kenneth P. Minkema, "Jonathan Edwards's Defense of Slavery," *Massachusetts Historical Review* 4 (January 2002): 23–59.

18. Kenneth P. Minkema, "Jonathan Edwards on Slavery and the Slave Trade," *WMQ* 54 (December 1997): 831, 832, 833.

19. Phillips P. Moulton, ed., *The Journal and Major Essays of John Woolman* (Richmond, IN: Friends United Press, 1971), 38, 45–47; Thomas Slaughter, *The Beautiful Soul of John Woolman, Apostle of Abolition* (New York: Hill and Wang, 2008); Geoffrey Plank, *John Woolman's Path to the Peaceable Kingdom: A Quaker in the British Empire* (Philadelphia: University of Pennsylvania Press, 2012).

20. PYM Minutes Vol. 2 (1747–1779), Haverford, 37–38 (19 9mo 1753). Soderlund, *Quakers and Slavery*, 43–46.

21. John Woolman, *Some Considerations on the Keeping of Negroes: Recommended to the Professors of Christianity of Every Denomination* (Philadelphia: James Chattin, 1754), [unpaginated Introduction,] 9, 6, 10, 18, 23

22. Drake, *Quakers and Slavery in America*, 58–67.

23. *Gentleman's Magazine* (London) Vol. 25 (December 1755), 570; William DeLoss Love, *The Fast and Thanksgiving Days of New England* (Boston: Houghton, Mifflin, 1895), 308–13; Guyatt, *Providence and the Invention of the United States*, 59–60, 66.

24. Samuel Davies, *The Crisis: Or, The Uncertain Doom of Kingdoms at Particular Times, Considered with Reference to Great-Britain and Her Colonies in Their Present Circumstances: A Sermon, Preached in Hanover, Virginia, October 28, 1756; A Day Appointed by the Synod of New-York, to be Observed as a General Fast, on Account of the Present War with France* (London: J. Buckland, 1757).

25. *Pennsylvania Gazette* (Philadelphia), 11 August 1763. Linda Colley, *Britons: Forging the Nation 1707–1837* (New Haven, CT: Yale University Press), 18, 52–54; Fred Anderson, *The Crucible of War: The Seven Years' War and the Fate of Empire in British America, 1754–1766* (New York: Knopf, 2000), 374–76; Noll, *In the Beginning Was the Word*, 150–51, 166–73.

26. John Lowell, *The Advantages of God's Presence with His People in an Expedition Against Their Enemies: A Sermon Preached at Newbury, May 22, 1755* . . . (Boston: J. Draper, 1755), 20.

27. Samuel Webster, *Soldiers, and Others, Directed and Encouraged, When Going on a Just and Important, Tho' Difficult, Enterprize, Against Their Enemies* . . . (Boston: Edes and Gill, 1756), 16. See also Arthur Browne, *The Necessity of Reformation, in Order to Avert Impending Judgments* . . . (Portsmouth, NH: Daniel Fowle, 1757), 14.

28. Matthias Harris, *A Sermon, Preached in the Church of St. Peters in Lewis, in Sussex County on Delaware, on July 8, 1757* . . . (Philadelphia: James Chattin, 1757), 43–44.

29. Rev. Philip Reading to Rev. Samuel Smith, Apoquiniminck [Delaware], October 10th, 1748, in John C. Van Horne, ed., *Religious Philanthropy and Colonial Slavery: The American Correspondence of the Associates of Dr. Bray, 1717–1777* (Urbana: University of Illinois Press, 1985), 99–100; Joseph Ottolenghe to [Rev. John Waring], [Savannah, 19 November 1753], ibid., 112. See also John C. Van Horne, "Impediments to the Christianization and Education of Blacks in Colonial America: Associates of Dr. Bray," *Historical Magazine of the Protestant Episcopal Church* 50 (September 1981): 243–69.

30. George William Pilcher, "Samuel Davies and the Instruction of Negroes in Virginia," *VMHB* 74 (July 1966): 292–300; Yoon, "Spread of Antislavery Sentiment," 348–77, esp. 364–68.

31. Samuel Davies, *Virginia's Danger, and Remedy: Two Discourses Occasioned by the Severe Drought in Sundry Parts of the Country; and the Defeat of General Braddock*, 2nd ed. (Glasgow: J. Bryce and D. Paterson, 1756), 5, 19, 24, 35. See also Samuel Davies, *The Crisis: Or, the Uncertain Doom*; Samuel Davies, *The Duty of Christians to Propagate Their Religion Among the Heathens, Earnestly Recommended to the Masters of Negroe Slaves in Virginia: A Sermon Preached in Hanover, January 8, 1757* (London: J. Oliver, 1758).

32. Samiel Davies, *Letters from the Rev. Samuel Davies, &c. Shewing the State of Religion in Virginia, Particularly Among the Negroes*, 2nd ed. (London: R. Pardon, 1757), 14, 21.

33. Benjamin Franklin to Rev. John Waring, Philad. December 17, 1763, in Van Horne, *Religious Philanthropy*, 204; John Waring to Fielding Lewis, [London, April 1769], ibid., 281. See also Grant Stanton and John C. Van Horne, "The Philadelphia Bray Schools: A Story of Black Education in early America, 1758–1845," *PMHB* 147 (October 2023): 75–104.

34. PYM Minutes Vol. 2, 44–45 (17 9mo 1754), 46 (19 9mo 1754). Geoffrey Plank, "Anthony Benezet, John Woolman, and Praise," in Marie-Jeanne Rossignol and Bertrand Van Ruymbeke, eds., *The Atlantic World of Anthony Benezet (1713–1784): From French Reformation to North American Quaker Antislavery Activism* (Leiden, Netherlands: Brill, 2016), 91–105, esp. 93–94. On Benezet, see George F. Brookes, *Friend Anthony Benezet* (Philadelphia: University of Pennsylvania Press, 1937) (hereafter cited as *FAB*); Maurice Jackson, *Let This Voice be Heard: Anthony Benezet, Father of Atlantic Abolitionism* (Philadelphia: University of Pennsylvania Press,

2009); Jonathan Sassi, "With a Little Help from the Friends: The Quaker and Tactical Contexts of Anthony Benezet's Abolitionist Publishing," *PMHB* 135 (January 2011): 33–71. My discussions of Benezet's various writings have benefited from the editorial commentary and annotations in David L. Crosby, ed., *The Complete Antislavery Writings of Anthony Benezet, 1754–1783: An Annotated Critical Edition* (Baton Rouge: Louisiana State University Press, 2014).

35. [Anthony Benezet], *An Epistle of Caution and Advice, Concerning the Buying and Keeping of Slaves* (Philadelphia: James Chattin, 1754), 3–4, 6, 7.

36. [Benezet], *An Epistle of Caution and Advice*, 3, 2; "The Watch-Tower, No. XXXIX," *New-York Mercury* (New York City), 18 August 1755 (and widely reprinted); PYM Minutes Vol. 2, 72 (22 9mo 1755); Soderlund, *Quakers and Slavery*, 27–28; Drake, *Quakers and Slavery in America*, 56–58.

37. "A Proclamation," *Pennsylvania Gazette* (Philadelphia), 15 April 1755.

38. James argues that Quakers' embrace of antislavery was in part a way to reclaim moral authority after withdrawing from politics, in *People Among Peoples*, esp. 216–22; on this context, see also Marietta, *The Reformation of American Quakerism*, 168–86. Carey and Plank both stress that the PYM's 1754 stance preceded the withdrawal from politics but probably underestimate the war's role in accelerating reform; see Carey, *From Peace to Freedom*, 182–95; and Plank, *John Woolman's Path*, 106–10.

39. John Churchman, *An Account of the Gospel Labours, and Christian Experiences of a Faithful Minister of Christ, John Churchman, Late of Nottingham, in Pennsylvania, Deceased* (Philadelphia: Joseph Crukshank, 1779), 68–69 (spring 1748), 175–76 (9mo 1757). On Churchman, see also Marietta, *Reformation of American Quakerism*, 119; Soderlund, *Quakers and Slavery*, 170–71.

40. Moulton, ed., *Journal of Woolman*, 51 (1755 or 1756), 66 ([28] 5mo 1757), 69 (29 5mo 1757),]), 71 ([after] 1 6mo 1757); VYM Minutes 1702–1835, Haverford, 96 (28 5mo 1757); Plank, *John Woolman's Path*, 69–70, 104–15; Sarah Crabtree, *Holy Nation: The Transatlantic Quaker Ministry in an Age of Revolution* (Chicago: University of Chicago Press, 2015).

41. Moulton, *Journal of Woolman*, 62–63 (11 5mo 1757).

42. James, *People Among Peoples*, 141–92, 216–20; Frederick B. Tolles, *Meeting House and Counting House: The Quaker Merchants of Colonial Philadelphia 1682–1763* (New York: W. W. Norton, 1963 [1948]), 230–43; Marietta, *Reformation of American Quakerism*, 136, 150–86; Carey, *From Peace to Freedom*, 28–29.

43. Despite its importance as an antislavery organization, the PMS has received little attention from scholars of slavery and abolitionism. The best discussion of the Philadelphia Meeting for Sufferings' antislavery activism remains Drake, *Quakers and Slavery in America*, esp. 84–113. Most recent treatments of Quaker antislavery have neglected the PMS. In *Quakers and Slavery*, Soderlund correctly emphasizes divisions within the PYM but gives little attention to the PMS, which was more uniformly antislavery. Carey's *From Peace to Freedom* focuses on antislavery discourse without discussing the PMS and ends in 1761. Plank mentions the creation of the PMS but does not examine its antislavery activism (*John Woolman's Path*, 125–26). Several historians of abolitionism have made effective use of the PMS's correspondence with the LMS but neglect the rest of the group's records; see for example Davis, *Slavery in Western Culture*, esp. 328–32; Davis, *Slavery in the Age of Revolution*, esp. 213–19; Betty Fladeland, *Men and Brothers: Anglo-American Antislavery Cooperation* (Chicago: University of Chicago Press, 1972), esp. 12–16; and Christopher Leslie Brown, *Moral Capital: Foundations of British Abolitionism* (Chapel Hill: University of North Carolina Press, 2006), esp. 401–32.

44. VYM Minutes (1702-1835), 90–92, 99 (28 5mo 1757); PMS Minutes Vol. 1 (1755–1775), 99 (19 9mo 1757); NCYM Minutes Vol. 1, 63 (16 10mo 1757), 66–67 (14 10mo 1758).

45. *Pennsylvania Gazette* (Philadelphia), 6 May 1756. For Quakers' use of Revelation 13:10 in an antislavery context, see [George Keith et al.], *An Exhortation & Caution to Friends Concerning Buying or Keeping of Negroes* ([New York: William Bradford,] 1693), 6; Sandiford, *Mystery of Iniquity*, epigraph on title page; Lay, *All Slave-Keepers*, 114.

46. George Fox, *A Warning from the Lord, to All Such as Hang Down the Head for a Day, and Pretend to Keep a Fast unto God, When They Smite with the Fist of Wickedness, and Suffers the Innocent to Lie Oppressed* (London: Giles Calvert, 1654), see esp. title page (Isaiah 58:6 epigraph), 1, 3, 6, 25; George Fox, *A Declaration Concerning Fasting, and Prayer . . .* (London: Thomas Simmons, 1656), 3–5; George Fox, *The Hypocrites Fast and Feast Not God's Holy Day* (London, 1677).

47. Philadelphia Meeting for Sufferings, *An Apology for the People Called Quakers: Containing Some Reasons for Their Not Complying with Human Injunctions . . .* ([Philadelphia,] 1757), 3, 6. PMS Minutes Vol. 1, 86–87 (28 6mo 1757).

48. PQM Minutes (1723–1772), 245 (6 2mo 1758), 250 (1 5mo 1758 and report from 28 3mo 1758), 254 (7 8mo 1758); Carey, *From Peace to Slavery*, 199 (Logan quotation), 201; Moulton, *Journal of Woolman*, 90–91 (8mo 1758); John Churchman to John Pemberton, E Nottingham, 8th mo 17th 1758, Pemberton Papers, HSP, vol. 12.

49. PYM Minutes Vol. 2, 112 (25 9mo 1758).

50. Moulton, *Journal of Woolman*, 92, 93 [29 9mo 1758].

51. PYM Minutes Vol. 2, 121 (29 9mo 1758).

52. Ibid. Vaux, *Memoirs of Lay and Sandiford*, 51. Some local meetings, such as in Shrewsbury, New Jersey, in 1757, had already begun disowning members who bought or sold slaves; see Soderlund, *Quakers and Slavery*, 28. Some scholars discuss the PYM's 1758 minute sanctions against Quakers who bought or sold slaves without acknowledging that it also called for manumission (albeit without coercion at this stage); for example, see Marietta, *Reformation of American Quakerism*, 116.

53. PYM Minutes Vol 2, 121–22 (29 9mo 1758), 130 (quotation, 25 9mo 1759); Churchman, *Account of the Gospel Labours*, 199–200 (1759); Moulton, *Journal of Woolman*, 97–98 (7mo 1759); Soderlund, *Quakers and Slavery*, 31, 61, 87–172; Marietta, *Reformation of American Quakerism*, 117; Wax, "Reform and Revolution," 405–12; Nash and Soderlund, *Freedom by Degrees*, 56–70.

54. [Anthony Benezet], *Observations on the Inslaving, Importing and Purchasing of Negroes, With Some Advice thereon extracted Form [sic] the Yearly Meeting Epistle of London for the Present Year* (Germantown, PA: Christopher Sower, 1759), 3–4. PYM Minutes Vol. 2,149–52 (28 9mo 1759 [out of place]); also in Moulton, *Journal of Woolman*, 98–101.

55. PYM Minutes Vol. 2, 138 (29 9mo 1760), 148 (2 10mo 1760), 160 (30 9mo 1761), 173 (1 10mo 1762).

56. Nash and Soderlund, *Freedom by Degrees*, 56–70.

57. Andrews also seems to have been concerned about a New Jersey law from 1713 that required manumitters to post a £200 bond in case their former slave required poverty relief. The Quaker circumvented this law by requiring Cato to contribute £5 per year, during his first five years of freedom, into an interest-bearing fund that would be held in trust for him to "use if he should live to want it, otherwise to be paid as he may Order at his Death." In other words, it was essentially a retirement savings plan designed to ensure that Cato's manumission did not

become a burden on Andrews or New Jersey taxpayers. Haddonfield Monthly Meeting Minutes Vol. 3 (1762–1781), 49–50 (10 9mo 1764).

58. Daniel Walton's manumission of James (17 6mo 1765), in "The Original Papers of Manumission by the Monthly Meetings Composing the Quarterly Meeting of Philadelphia," Haverford, available online through *Quakers & Slavery*: http://triptych.brynmawr.edu/cdm/ref/collection/HC_QuakSlav/id/9585. The vast majority of manumissions in this collection date from after 1776, when it became standard policy to preserve centralized records of manumissions. On the enforcement of Quakers' antislavery policies, see also Soderlund, *Quakers and Slavery*, 61, 87–172; Marietta, *Reformation of American Quakerism*, 117; Wax, "Reform and Revolution," 405–12; and Nash and Soderlund, *Freedom by Degrees*, 56–70.

59. Drake, *Quakers and Slavery in America*, 61–62; Judith Jennings, "Mid-Eighteenth Century British Quakerism and the Response to the Problem of Slavery," *Quaker History* 66 (Spring 1977): 23–40.

60. Brown, *Moral Capital*, 91. Soderlund similarly states that during the 1750s and 1760s, "Most reformers viewed slaveholding as sin to be banned from the Society [of Friends], not as a condition from which Afro-Americans must be delivered" (*Quakers and Slavery*, 177). Sinha portrays Woolman's ideas as "a bridge between the separatist Quaker attempt to rid their community of slavery and the revolutionary abolition movement," which she credits Benezet with pioneering in the 1770s; but she neglects 1760s antislavery activism by the PMS and other Quaker groups (*Slave's Cause*, 19–24). Carey emphasizes the radicalism of the PYM's 1758 policy but ends his study without examining the 1760s (*From Peace to Freedom*, 206–8).

61. Robert G. Parkinson, *Thirteen Clocks: How Race United the Colonies and Made the Declaration of Independence* (Chapel Hill: University of North Carolina Press, 2021), 52

62. Moulton, *Journal of Woolman*, 110 (summer 1760); PMS epistle to Fredericksburg [South Carolina] Monthly Meeting, Philad'a, 18th of 12th mo, 1760, in PMS Minutes Vol. 1, 183–86, quotation on 185. On Woolman's influence in New England, see Kevin Vrevich, "The Inner Light of Radical Abolitionism: Greater Rhode Island and the Emergence of Racial Justice," (PhD diss. Ohio State University, 2019), 32–33.

63. Benezet, *Observations on Inslaving*, 7; South Carolina legislator quoted in in W. E. Burghardt Du Bois, *Suppression of the African Slave-Trade to the United States of America, 1638–1870* (New York: Longmans, Green, 1896), 11. Edward B. Rugemer, *Slave Law and the Politics of Resistance in the Early Atlantic World* (Cambridge, MA: Harvard University Press, 2018), 160–69; Michael Craton, *Testing the Chains: Resistance to Slavery in the British West Indies* (Ithaca, NY: Cornell University Press, 1982).

64. PMS epistle to LMS, 24 3mo 1761, in PMS Minutes Vol. 1, 188–91, quotation from 190; Petition of the Merchants of Philadelphia, 1 March 1761, in Elizabeth Donnan, ed., *Documents Illustrative of the Slave Trade*, 4 vols. (Washington, DC: Carnegie Institution of Washington, 1930–1935), 3:453–54; Du Bois, *Suppression of the African Slave-Trade*, 23–25; Nash and Soderlund, *Freedom by Degrees*, 71–72.

65. John Woolman, *Some Considerations on the Keeping of Negroes, Recommended to the Professors of Christianity of Every Denomination: Part Second* (Philadelphia: B. Franklin and D. Hall, 1762), 20–2; *Pennsylvania Gazette*, 15 April 1762; Plank, *John Woolman's Path*, 153. For earlier use of Jeremiah 34, see Elihu Coleman, *Antichristian Practice of Making Slaves of Men* ([Boston], 1733), 7.

66. [Anthony Benezet,] *A Short Account of That Part of Africa, Inhabited by the Negroes . . .*, 2nd ed. (Philadelphia: John Dunlap, 1762), 7, 31, 34, 52, 65, 70. For an introduction to this text,

see David Brion Davis, "New Sidelights on Early Antislavery Radicalism," *WMQ* 28 (October 1971): 585–94; Crosby, *Antislavery Writings of Benezet*, 25–27, 238–40; Jackson, *Let This Voice be Heard*, 212–13.

67. [Benezet,] *Short Account*, 69–72.

68. PMS epistle to LMS, 24 3mo 1761, in PMS Minutes Vol. 1, 188–91, quotation from 190–91.

69. *Pennsylvania Gazette* (Philadelphia), 6 May 1762, cited in Darold W. Wax, "Africans on the Delaware: The Pennsylvania Slave Trade, 1759–1765," *Pennsylvania History* 50 (January 1983): 38–49, 44; Du Bois, *Suppression of the African Slave-Trade*, 11, 23–25.

70. [Benezet], *Short Account*, 72; Benezet to Joseph Phipps, Philad 28th 5th mo 1763, in Roger Bruns, ed., *Am I Not a Man and a Brother: The Antislavery Crusade of Revolutionary America, 1688–1788* (New York: Chelsea·House, 1977), 97–99; Sassi, "With a Little Help from the Friends," 45–46. On the expansion of slavery as a result of the Seven Years' War, see Jack P. Greene, *Evaluating Empire and Confronting Colonialism in Eighteenth-Century Britain* (New York: Cambridge University Press, 2013), 166; Anderson, *Crucible of War*, 505–6; and John Craig Hammond, "Slavery, Sovereignty, and Empires: North American Borderlands and the American Civil War, 1660–1860," *Journal of the Civil War Era* 4 (June 2014): 264–98, 275–76.

71. Brown, *Moral Capital*, 213–22, 267, 274–75; S. Max Edelson, *The New Map of Empire: How Britain Imagined America Before Independence* (Cambridge, MA: Harvard University Press, 2017), 65, 76–78, 85–93, 141–44, 153–59.

72. Morgan Godwyn, *The Negro's & Indians Advocate, Suing for Admission into the Church . . .* (London: F.D., 1680), 43–56, quotations from 43, 47; David M. Goldenberg, *Black and Slave: The Origins and History of the Curse of Ham* (Boston: De Gruyter, 2017), 146–47; David M. Whitford, *The Curse of Ham in the Early Modern Era: The Bible and the Justification for Slavery* (Burlington, VT: Ashgate, 2009), 141–61.

73. Thomas Newton, *Dissertations on the Prophecies, Which Have Remarkably Been Fulfilled, and at This Time Are Fulfilling in the World: Volume the First* (London: J. and R. Tonson and S. Draper, 1754), 9–36, quotations from 21, 29. Whitford asserts that "more than any other figure in the early modern era, Thomas Newton helped solidify the belief that Genesis 9:25 ought to be read primarily as a prophecy and that the prophecy was a direct curse upon Ham [rather than Canaan]" (*Curse of Ham*, 160).

74. "Imported from London," *Boston Post-Boy*, 6 August 1761.

75. See for example William Green, *A New Translation of the Psalms, To Which Is Added, a Dissertation on the Last Prophetick Words of Noah* (Cambridge, UK: Joseph Bentham, 1762), 233, cited in Whitford, *Curse of Ham*, 159.

Chapter 3

1. [John Dickinson], *Letters from a Farmer in Pennsylvania, to the Inhabitants of the British Colonies* (Philadelphia: David Hall, 1768), 38; James Otis, *The Rights of the British Colonies Asserted and Proved* (Boston: Edes and Gill, 1764), 29 (quotation), 37. On the slavery metaphor, see especially Bernard Bailyn, *The Ideological Origins of the American Revolution* (Cambridge, MA: Harvard University Press, 1967), 94–102, 232–38; Patricia Bradley, *Slavery, Propaganda, and the American Revolution* (Jackson: University Press of Mississippi, 1998), 1–24; and Peter Dorsey, *Common Bondage: Slavery as Metaphor in Revolutionary America* (Knoxville: University of Tennessee Press, 2009).

2. Bailyn, *Ideological Origins*, 235–36; Arthur Zilversmit, *The First Emancipation: The Abolition of Slavery in the North* (Chicago: University of Chicago Press, 1967), 93–138, 170, 226–28; Winthrop D. Jordan, *White Over Black: American Attitudes Toward the Negro, 1550–1812* (Chapel Hill: University of North Carolina Press, 1968), 279, 289–95; Duncan J. MacLeod, *Slavery, Race and the American Revolution* (New York: Cambridge University Press, 1974), 5–8, 14–20; Gary B. Nash, *Race and Revolution* (Madison, WI: Madison House, 1990), 3–20; Mark Somos, *American States of Nature: The Origins of Independence, 1761–1775* (New York: Oxford University Press, 2019), 63–65, 92, 314–19; C. Bradley Thompson, *America's Revolutionary Mind: A Moral History of the American Revolution and the Declaration That Defined It* (New York: Encounter Books, 2019), chap. 5; Stanley Harrold, *American Abolitionism: Its Direct Political Impact from Colonial Times into Reconstruction* (Charlottesville: University of Virginia Press, 2019), 18.

3. [Samuel Webster], "An Earnest Address to My Country, Upon Slavery," *Boston Chronicle*, 27 February to 2 March 1769. For Webster's authorship, see Joshua Coffin, *A Sketch of the History of Newbury, Newburyport, and West Newbury, from 1635 to 1845* (Boston: S. G. Drake, 1845), 338. David Brion Davis's work gives significant attention to providentialism, but scholars more commonly give it only brief attention compared to their focus on natural rights ideology; see Davis, *The Problem of Slavery in the Age of Revolution, 1770–1823* (Ithaca, NY: Cornell University Press, 1975), esp. 213–54, 284–99; Jordan, *White Over Black*, 298–300; Bailyn, *Ideological Origins*, 242–43; Nash, *Race and Revolution*, 10; and Manisha Sinha, *The Slave's Cause: A History of Abolition* (New Haven, CT: Yale University Press, 2016), 28. John Coffey gives considerable attention to antislavery providentialism during the Revolutionary War but largely neglects the period before 1773; see Coffey, *Exodus and Liberation: Deliverance Politics from John Calvin to Martin Luther King, Jr.* (New York: Oxford University Press, 2014), 79–106. Nicholas Guyatt demonstrates the importance of providentialist during the American Revolution but gives little attention to slavery until the postwar period; see Guyatt, *Providence and the Invention of the United States, 1607–1876* (New York: Cambridge University Press, 2007), 106, 131.

4. *By the Honorable Thomas Fitch, Esq; Governor of His Majesty's English Colony of Connecticut, in New-England, in America: A Proclamation for a Day of Public Fasting and Prayer* [25 November 1765, for a fast day on 18 December 1765] (New-London, CT: Timothy Green, 1765); *By the Honorable Thomas Fitch, Esq; Governor of His Majesty's English Colony of Connecticut, in New-England, in America: A Proclamation for a Day of Public Fasting and Prayer* [10 March 1766, for a fast day on 16 April 1766] (New-London, CT: Timothy Green, 1766); William DeLoss Love, *The Fast and Thanksgiving Days of New England* (Boston: Houghton, Mifflin, 1895).

5. PMS epistle to LMS, 20 2mo 1766, in PMS Minutes Vol. 1 (1755–1775), 261–62 (quotation from 261); PMS epistle to several meetings belonging to the PYM, ibid., 262–63; Jack D. Marietta, *The Reformation of American Quakerism, 1748–1783* (Philadelphia: University of Pennsylvania Press, 1984), 207–8.

6. When explaining the abolition of slavery in Massachusetts, scholars often point to a series of judicial decisions in 1781–1783, asserting judges and juries declared that slavery violated the state constitution of 1780. Yet specialists have increasingly challenged this narrative by demonstrating, on the one hand, that Massachusetts slavery was already collapsing by the mid-1770s and, on the other hand, that it persisted long past 1783. Abolition in Massachusetts is best understood, in the words of Jared Hardesty, as "a relatively long-term process lasting from the 1760s until the early 1800s"; see Hardesty, "Disappearing from Abolitionism's Heartland:

The Legacy of Slavery and Emancipation in Boston," *International Review of Social History* 65 (February 2020): 145–68, 151.

For other recent accounts arguing that emancipation in Massachusetts began before 1780, see Jeanne M. Pickering, "Suing Slavery: The Essex County Freedom Suits, 1765–1783," (master's thesis, Salem State University, 2018); Gloria McCahon Whiting, "Emancipation Without the Courts or Constitution: The Case of Revolutionary Massachusetts," *Slavery & Abolition* 41 (2020): 458–78; and Edward L. Bell, *Persistence of Memories of Slavery and Emancipation in Historical Andover: The Massachusetts Woman Enumerated as a "Slave" in the 1830 U.S. Census and the Family of Rosanna Coburn from the Enslavement to Contingent Freedom* (Boston: Shawsheen Press, 2021), esp. 6–7, 26–27, 117–36, 187–205.

7. Anthony Benezet, *A Caution and Warning to Great Britain and Her Colonies . . .* (Philadelphia: Henry Miller, 1766), 3.

8. "Humphrey Ploughjogger to the *Boston Gazette*, 14 October 1765," *FO*, https://founders.archives.gov/documents/Adams/06-01-02-0057. On the ways that white patriot rhetoric could implicitly justify Black slavery, see François Furstenberg, "Beyond Slavery and Freedom: Autonomy, Agency, and Resistance in Early American Political Discourse." *JAH* 89 (March 2003), 1295–1330.

9. Leon F. Litwack, *North of Slavery: The Negro in the Free States* (Chicago: University of Chicago Press, 1961), 10. Litwack's assertion about Adams supporting freedom suits, which other historians have repeated, is based on a 1795 letter in which Adams stated, "I was concerned in several causes in which negroes sued for their freedom, before the Revolution." However, Adams's legal papers reveal he always served on the side of slaveholding defendants; see "Editorial Note," *FO*, https://founders.archives.gov/documents/Adams/05-02-02-0004-0001. On Adams's role defending slaveholders against freedom suits, see also Hiller B. Zobel, "Jonathan Sewall: A Lawyer in Conflict," *Proceedings of the Cambridge Historical Society* 40 (1964–1966): 123–136. On Adam's racism and lack of antislavery sentiment, see John R. Howe, "John Adams's Views of Slavery," *Journal of Negro History* 49 (July 1964): 201–16; and Arthur Scherr, *John Adams, Slavery, and Race: Ideas, Politics, and Diplomacy in an Age of Crisis* (Santa Barbara, CA: Praeger, 2018). For a list of books (including the 17758 edition of Thomas Newton's *Dissertations on the Prophecies Which Have Remarkably Been Fulfilled, and at This Time Are Fulfilling in the World*) owned by John Adams, see https://www.bpl.org/archival_post/adams-john-1735-1826-library/.

10. Stephen Johnson, *Some Important Observations, Occasioned by, and Adapted to, the Publick Fast, Ordered by Authority, December 18th, A.D. 1765 . . .* (Newport, RI: Samuel Hall, 1766), 3, 5, 45. On patriot ideas about providentialism and deliverance see Guyatt, *Providence and Invention*, 76–103; Coffey, *Exodus and Liberation*, 66–75.

11. Benezet, *Caution and Warning*, 4, 9, 35.

12. PMS Minutes Vol. 1, 265 (18 9mo 1766), 266 (17 10mo 1766), 266–67 (20 11mo 1766), 269 (18 12mo 1766); PMS Committee to LMS, [ca. 12mo 1766], PMS Miscellaneous Papers, 1766:7; LMS Acc't: of the Charge of Reprinting & distributing the Caution ag't enslaving the Africans &c. in London 12mo: 1768, PMS Miscellaneous Papers, 1768:7. See also Jonathan Sassi, "With a Little Help from the Friends: The Quaker and Tactical Contexts of Anthony Benezet's Abolitionist Publishing," *PMHB* 135, (January 2011): 33–71, esp. 33, 47–48.

13. *Journals of the House of Representatives of Massachusetts: Volume 43, 1766–1767* (Boston: MHS, 1975), xii–xiii, 110 (20 June 1766). It is somewhat ambiguous whether the bill (which does not fully survive) sought to end slavery or merely slave importations; for the latter view, see

George Henry Moore, *Notes on the History of Slavery in Massachusetts* (New York: D. Appleton, 1866), 124.

14. Christopher Cameron notes that Appleton's father was a minister, in Cameron, *To Plead Our Own Cause: African Americans in Massachusetts and the Making of the Antislavery Movement* (Kent, OH: Kent State University Press, 2011), 52–53. However, most scholars ignore this connection and downplay the prominent religious themes in Appleton's pamphlet. For example, Bradley asserts that he "eschewed religious argument;" in *Slavery, Propaganda, and Revolution*, 99; see also MacLeod, *Slavery, Race and Revolution*, 18; Emily Blanck, *Tyrannicide: Forging an American Law of Slavery in Revolutionary South Carolina and Massachusetts* (Athens: University of Georgia Press, 2015), 32.

15. Nathaniel Appleton, *A Thanksgiving Sermon on the Total Repeal of the Stamp-Act . . .* (Boston: Edes and Gill, 1766), 21. In May 1766, Massachusetts ministers held unofficial days of thanksgiving because the royal governor would not authorize an official one. The governor of Connecticut formally proclaimed a day of thanksgiving, explicitly crediting repeal to the interposition of "*our most gracious God.*" See *By the Honorable William Pitkin, Esq; Governor of His Majesty's English Colony of Connecticut, in New England, in America: A Proclamation*, [12 June 1766, for a day of thanksgiving on 26 June 1766] (Hartford: Thomas Green, 1766).

16. [Nathaniel Appleton Jr.], *Considerations on Slavery in a Letter to a Friend* (Boston: Edes and Gills, 1767), 8, 9, 10, 11.

17. [Appleton], *Considerations on Slavery*, 13, 14, 19, 20. For distribution of the pamphlet, see Samuel Eliot to Robert Treat Paine, Feby. 26. 1767, *Robert Treat Paine Papers*, ed. Stephen Riley and Edward W. Hanson, 5 vols. to date (Charlottesville: University of Virginia Press, 1992), 2:395.

18. *JHRMA* 43: 110 (20 June 1766), 353 (4 March 1767), 358 (5 March 1767), 387 (13 March 1767), 390 (14 March 1767), 393 (16 March 1767), 408 (17 March 1767), 409 (18 March 1767), 420 (20 March 1767). Two versions of the bill, which placed a prohibitive duty of £40 on each slave imported into the colony from April 1767 to April 1768, survive: "Act for imposing a duty on the importation of slaves into Massachusetts (draft), [20 March?] 1767," MHS Online: https://www.masshist.org/database/viewer.php?item_id=809 (quotation); and "Act for imposing a duty on the importation of slaves into Massachusetts (draft), [April 1767]," MHS Online: https://www.masshist.org/database/viewer.php?item_id=810 (accessed 9 July 2019). For newspaper responses, see *Boston Gazette*, 16 March 1767; *Boston Gazette*, 30 March 1767 (quotation); and *Massachusetts Gazette*, 2 April 1767; *Massachusetts Gazette*, 31 December 1767. See also Moore, *Notes on the History of Slavery*,126–128; Zilversmit, *First Emancipation*, 100–101; Bradley, *Slavery, Propaganda, and Revolution*, 53; Cameron, *To Plead Our Own Cause*, 53.

19. Jonathan Edwards Jr., "Question," May 1767 (in private collection, transcript courtesy of the Jonathan Edwards Center, Yale University), 1, 5, 7, 9, 12, 17. Edwards indicated that he delivered the sermon in New Haven, CT, in April 1767, revised it at Princeton, NJ, in May, and delivered it in Kingston, RI, on 14 June 1767, before he settled into a permanent ministerial position in New Haven. On this sermon and Edwards's evolving views on slavery, see John Ericson, "When God Ceased Winking: Jonathan Edwards the Younger's Evolution on the Problem of Slavery," *Connecticut History Review* 57 (Spring 2018): 7–32.

20. Nash, *Race and Revolution*, 11 (see 91–96 for the text of Lee's essay). There are no copies of the 19 March 1767 issue of *Virginia Gazette* (Williamsburg, ed. William Rind), and scholars have relied on a manuscript copy of Lee's first Philanthropos essay held at the College of William

& Mary's Swem Library and reproduced in Richard K. MacMaster, "Arthur Lee's 'Address on Slavery': An Aspect of Virginia's Struggle to End the Slave Trade, 1765–1774," *VMHB* 80 (April 1972), 141–57 (document on 153–57). MacMaster explains that there were two rival *Virginia Gazettes* in Williamsburg at the time and that both refused to print the second "suppressed" Philanthropos essay. He states without evidence that Benezet reprinted the first Philanthropos essay as a pamphlet in 1767. The first Philanthropos essay also appeared in the *Pennsylvania Chronicle* (Philadelphia) on 11 May 1767.

21. "Philanthropos [Part 2]," *Pennsylvania Chronicle* (Philadelphia), 7 September 1767. The text, which provoked additional newspaper debate, is reproduced and analyzed in: Eva Sheppard Wolf, "The Second Installment of Arthur Lee's 'Suppressed' Antislavery Essay and the Fractured Public Sphere of Pre-Revolutionary America," *WMQ* 81 (July 2024):567–96.

22. "Philanthropos [Part 2]," *Pennsylvania Chronicle*, 7 September 1767.

23. Wolf, "Second Installment of Lee's Essay." Scholars and archival databases previously had indicated that Anthony Benezet and others printed lengthy extracts of Lee's essay (excising some of the material about slave revolt) in 1767, but this appears incorrect. The pagination of these pamphlets suggests they were actually copies printed in 1771 or later (but sometimes stitched together with earlier publications). Benezet does not refer to the Philanthropos essay in his surviving correspondence until 1773, when he states, "I reprinted Doctr. Lee's Address & added it to my last Book." See Benezet to Robert Pleasants, Philadelphia, ye 8th 4th Month 1773, in *FAB*, 298–302 (quotation on 301). Writing in 1773, Benezet's "last book" would have been *Some Historical Account of Guinea . . . With an Inquiry Into the Rise and Progress of the Slave Trade* (Philadelphia: Joseph Crukshank, 1771). As discussed, this volume was actually several books in one, as Benezet noted on its title page and table of contents.

24. Samuel Pleasants to Edward Stabler, Philad'a, 7, 5mo, 1767 (copy), CPW, box 14; Edward Stabler to [Israel Pemberton], Petersburg, 3mo: 19th. 1767, CPW, box 15; VYM Minutes, 134 (8 6mo 1767), 143 (23 5mo 1768); Edward Stabler to [Israel Pemberton], Petersburg, 5mo: 26th. 1768, CPW, box 15. See also William Fernandez Hardin, "Litigating the Lash: Quaker Emancipator Robert Pleasants, the Law of Slavery, and the Meaning of Manumission in Revolutionary and Early National Virginia," (PhD diss., Vanderbilt University, 2013), 37–38.

25. Thomas Nicholson's Open Letter to North Carolina Friends, 6 mo. 1st: 1767, in Michael J. Crawford, ed., *The Having of Negroes Is Becoming a Burden: The Quaker Struggle to Free Slaves in Revolutionary North Carolina* (Gainesville: University of Florida Press, 2010), 73–75; 1768 NCYM Minutes, ibid., 76.

26. Merrill Jensen, *Founding of a Nation: A History of the American Revolution, 1763–1776* (New York: Oxford University Press, 1968), 239–64; Alan Taylor, *American Revolutions: A Continental History, 1750–1804* (New York: W. W. Norton, 2016), 107–12.

27. Benezet released his second edition of *Caution and Warning* in April 1767 but did not advertise it for sale in Boston until September. *Pennsylvania Chronicle*, 30 March 1767, 13 April 1767; *Boston Gazette*, 21 September 1767.

28. "K. A True Son of Liberty," *Newport Mercury*, 11 January 1768; "The Slave Trade . . . ," *Boston Evening-Post*, 2 May 1768 (widely reprinted); "An Earnest Address to My Country, Upon Slavery," *Boston Chronicle*, 2 March 1769. On providentialism, see Perry Miller, *The New England Mind: From Colony to Province* ([1953,] Boston: Beacon Press, 1968); Guyatt, *Providence and Invention*, 11–94.

29. John Lathrop, *Innocent Blood Crying to God from the Streets of Boston: A Sermon Occasioned by the Horrid Murder . . . on the Fifth of March, 1770 and Preached the Lord's Day*

Following (Boston: Edes and Gill, 1771), 9, 17; Serena Zabin, *The Boston Massacre: A Family History* (Boston: Mariner Books, 2020).

30. Nathaniel Appleton, *The Right Method of Addressing the Divine Majesty in Prayer; So as to Support and Strengthen Our Faith in Dark and Troublesome Times, Set Forth in Two Discourses on April 5, 1770, Being the Day of General Fasting and Prayer . . .* (Boston: Edes and Gill, 1770), 34, 36, 55–56, 60, 61, 62. For Appleton's appointment as chaplain, see *JHRMA* 46: 106 (27 March 1770).

31. Samuel Cooke, *A Sermon Preached at Cambridge, in the Audience of His Honor Thomas Hutchinson . . . May 30th, 1770* (Boston: Edes and Gill), 41, 42; *Essex Gazette* (Salem), 19 June 1770. Bradley, *Slavery, Propaganda, and Revolution*, 100.

32. *Massachusetts Spy*, 8 January 1771, and published repeatedly in the following weeks. Cited in David Waldstreicher, *Odyssey of Phillis Wheatley: A Poet's Journeys Through American Slavery and Independence* (New York: Farrar, Straus and Giroux, 2023), 108.

33. Thomas Hutchinson to Lord Hillsborough, Boston, 1 May 1771, quoted in Moore, *Notes on the History of Slavery*, 131–32; *JHRMA* 47: 240, 242–43 (24 April 1771).

34. Jensen, *Founding of a Nation*, 329, 354–76. For examples of scholars who cite Cooke's 1770 sermon and then jump to 1773 without acknowledging the relative absence of patriot antislavery voices in between, see Bailyn, *Ideological Origins*, 239; Nash, *Race and Revolution*, 9; and Dorsey, *Common Bondage*, 110. Scholars often conflate the 1771 slave trade bill with a 1777 draft bill for emancipation, thereby overstating the level of prewar antislavery sentiment. This confusion seems to have begun with Patricia Bradley, who quotes a letter from Joseph Warren to John Adams about the 1777 bill as if it occurred in 1771. Other scholars have echoed Bradley, conflating the two bills; see: Bradley, *Slavery, Propaganda, and Revolution*, 64; *Gary B.* Nash, *Unknown American Revolution: The Unruly Birth of Democracy and the Struggle to Create America* (New York: Penguin, 2005), 121, Taylor, *American Revolutions*, 117–18.

35. *Massachusetts Spy*, 7 November 1771, 26 March 1772, 9 April 1772 (quotation), 19 November 1772; *Providence Gazette*, 28 March 1772; *Essex Gazette* (Salem), 31 March 1772; *Boston Post Boy/Massachusetts Gazette*, 16 November 1772.

36. For the role of mid-Atlantic Quakers in freedom suits, see Jonathan D. Sassi, "The Legacies of James McCarty: The Story of How Quakers Secured One Family's Emancipation and Its Ramifications for Revolutionary-Era Antislavery," *Early American Studies* 16 (Spring 2018): 282–316; and Amy C. Schutt and Judith L. Van Buskirk, "Gideon Moor's Road to Freedom, 1764–1777," *PMHB* 144 (January 2020): 1–28. For Quakers in New England, see Catherine Adams and Elizabeth H. Pleck, *Love of Freedom: Black Women in Colonial and Revolutionary New England* (New York: Oxford University Press, 2010),130, 135; and John Wood Sweet, *Bodies Politic: Negotiating Race in the American North, 1730–1830* (Baltimore: Johns Hopkins University Press, 2003), 238.

37. *Slew v. Whipple*, "[John] Adams' Minutes of the Argument: Essex Superior Court, Salem, November 1766," *FO*: https://founders.archives.gov/documents/Adams/05-02-02-0004-0002-0002; A. Leon Higginbotham, *In the Matter of Color: Race and the American Legal Process: The Colonial Period* (New York: Oxford University Press, 1978), 84; Adams and Pleck, *Love of Freedom*, 137–38; Pickering, "Suing Slavery," 22–27.

38. My discussion of the Essex County freedoms suits is indebted to Jean Pickering's master's thesis, "Suing Slavery," and her related website, www.northshoreslavery.org, which includes images of original sources and transcripts for many of the cases. A handful of Massachusetts freedom suits have garnered extensive attention (such as the cases of Quock Walker

and Elizabeth "Mum Bett" Freeman during the early 1780s), but there has been little collective analysis of freedom suits. For the most comprehensive list of freedom suits that have been identified to date, see Edward L. Bell, "Research Summaries of Massachusetts Freedom Suits 1660–1784" (unpublished draft manuscript last revised 18 April 18 2022 and available at https://www.academia.edu/76814209), which currently identifies more than seventy freedom suits and similar legal actions. Bell, who is the deputy state historic preservation officer at the Massachusetts Historical Commission in Boston, notes that "there are undoubtedly many more undiscovered Massachusetts 'freedom suits' in the judicial archives and other records" ("Research Summaries," 7). I discuss antislavery essays by Essex County writers in Chapter 4.

39. Pickering, "Suing Slavery," 28–32; http://www.northshoreslavery.com/freedomcases/participants.php; Nina Sankovitch, *The Lowells of Massachusetts: An American Family* (New York: St. Marton's Press, 2017), 41–94 (quotation from the Reverend Charles Lowell about his father on 93).

40. Zobel, "Jonathan Sewall," 131; "Writ and Pleadings: Middlesex Inferior Court, Cambridge, May 1768," *FO*, https://founders.archives.gov/documents/Adams/05-02-02-0004-0004-0001; Deposition of Jacob Green, Stafford, Connecticut, 17 March 1768, in Suffolk Files Collection, file #147830 (in vol. 1013): https://www.familysearch.org/ark:/61903/3:1:3Q9M-CSVR-639S-9?i=270&cat=240378. My understanding of *Margaret v. Muzzy* is informed by the summary and primary sources citations in Bell, "Research Summaries," 83–85.

41. When *James v. Lechmere* went before the Superior Court of Judicature in October; Lechmere failed to appear, and James received his freedom and was awarded £2 in damages plus court costs. It is likely that James and Lechmere negotiated a settlement out of court, presumably because Lechmere expected to lose based on the evidence that James's mother was free. *James v. Lechmere* [25 October 1769], SCJ Suffolk: https://www.familysearch.org/ark:/61903/3:1:3Q9M-CSZV-HB93?i=245&cat=301381. For the evidence that James was Margaret's son, see Zobel, "Jonathan Sewall," 134–35. Several scholars, unaware of the connection between James and Margaret, have assumed that *James v. Lechmere* lacked legal merit based on existing precedent; they therefore imbue James's victory with undue significance. This trend began in the antebellum era. A history of Salem published in 1849 reported, "In 1769, a slave, named James, sued his master Richard Lechmere, of Cambridge, for his liberty, and gained his cause. This was prior to the noted decision in the King's Bench, which liberated James Somersett." See Joseph Barlow Felt, *Annals of Salem*, 2 vols. (Salem, MA: W. & S. B. Ives, 1840), 2:416. It seems that Felt conflated some elements of the 1769 case of *James v. Lechmere* with the 1773 case of *Caesar v. Greenleaf* (which I discuss in Chapter 4).

Some modern scholars also overstate the significance of the 1769 case. Emily Blanck does not portray *James v. Lechmere* as a decisive judicial precedent, but she assumes that James's victory reflected "growing popular sentiment against slavery, compelling the jury to rule in favor of freedom" despite his lawyer's "weak legal argument"; see *Tyrannicide*, 35 (also 45). Hardesty does not examine the legal merits of James's case but assumes that Lechmere settled out of court because he expected to lose; see Hardesty, "Disappearing from Abolitionism's Heartland," 154. These scholars are likely correct that antislavery sentiment was growing, but James also had a much stronger legal case than they recognize. See also Higginbotham, *In the Matter of Color*, 85.

42. For the relevant court records, see Hampshire County Court of Common Pleas Records, November 1766, 16, https://archive.org/details/hampshirecountyc6670mass/page/16/mode/2up?view=theater; and Hampshire County Court of Common Pleas Records, February 1767, 29, https://archive.org/details/hampshirecountyc6670mass/page/28/mode/2up?view=theater. I

thank Edward L. Bell for helping me locate these sources. On this case, see also Moore, *Notes on the History of Slavery*, 22–23n1; and Emily Blanck, "The Legal Emancipations of Leander and Caesar: Manumission and the Law in Revolutionary South Carolina and Massachusetts," *Slavery & Abolition* 28 (August 2007): 235–54, 246–47. (Blanck mistakenly identifies Daniel Bliss rather than Moses Bliss as the lawyer.)

On Bliss and other lawyers involved in this and other freedom suits discussed in this chapter, see Charles R. McKirdy, "Massachusetts Lawyers on the Eve of the American Revolution: The State of the Profession," in *Law in Colonial Massachusetts, 1630–1800*, ed. Daniel R. Coquillette (Boston: The Colonial Society of Massachusetts, 1984), 313–58. On Amos Newport and a freedom suit initiated by his son, Dan, see Eric W. Weber, "'His Own Proper Negro Slave': Amos Newport & His Descendants in Hatfield, Williamsburg & Amherst" (revised 4 April 2014), Freedom Stories of the Pioneer Valley: https://freedomstoriespv.wordpress.com/newport-family/.

43. "Adams' Minutes of the Trial: Hampshire Superior Court, Springfield, September 1768," *FO*, https://founders.archives.gov/documents/Adams/05-02-02-0004-0003-0001. The editorial annotation indicates the reference to "Dr. Newton" referred to the Reverend John Newton (a former slave trader who later became an abolitionist), but he did not have a doctoral degree, and the placement next to "Noah's Curse" makes it clear that it was actually referring to Dr. Thomas Newton's *Dissertations on the Prophecies Which Have Remarkably Been Fulfilled, and at This Time Are Fulfilling in the World*.

44. "Wetmore's Minutes of the Trial: Essex Inferior Court, Newburyport, September 1771," *FO*, https://founders.archives.gov/documents/Adams/05-02-02-0004-0005-0001; "Wetmore's Minutes of the Argument: Essex Superior Court, Salem, November 1771," *FO*, https://founders.archives.gov/documents/Adams/05-02-02-0004-0005-0004. On this case, see also "Editorial Note," *FO*, https://founders.archives.gov/documents/Adams/05-02-02-0004-0001; Blanck, "Legal Emancipations of Leander and Caesar," esp. 235–39, 244–48; Cameron, *Plead Our Own Cause*, 73; and Pickering, "Suing Slavery," 38–55. Pickering has posted related primary sources, "Casar v. Samuel Taylor (1772)," at https://northshoreslavery.org/freedomcases/case.php?id=11. For the date of Caesar's baptism, see Bell, *Persistence of Memories of Slavery*, 292.

45. John Locke, *Two Treatises of Government*, ed. Peter Laslett ([1690] New York: Cambridge University Press, 1988), 383 (book 2, chap. 15, par. 172). It is possible Locke's doctrine regarding slavery and contracts may also have been used in the 1703 case of *Adam v. Saffin*.

46. "Wetmore's Minutes of the Trial: Essex Inferior Court, Newburyport, September 1771," *FO:* https://founders.archives.gov/documents/Adams/05-02-02-0004-0005-0001.

47. "Wetmore's Minutes of the Argument," https://founders.archives.gov/documents/Adams/05-02-02-0004-0005-0004.

48. *Essex Gazette*, 1 September 1772. Historians have not previously recognized that this essay was excerpted from Wallace's book or discussed its possible connection to *Caesar v. Taylor*. Bradley mentions it briefly but mistakenly assumes it was written in response to the *Somerset* decision, an account of which also appeared in the same issue; see Bradley, *Slavery, Propaganda, and Revolution*, 71. For the original text, see George Wallace, *A System of the Principles of the Law of Scotland Vol. I* (Edinburgh: 1760), 95–96. Anthony Benezet had recently reprinted part of Wallace's chapter on slavery in several publications; however, the first two sentences of the version in the *Essex Journal* paraphrase parts of Wallace's text that Benezet had not included, indicating that whoever submitted the excerpt to the newspaper had the original source in front of them. For Benezet's extracts of Wallace (misspelled "Wallis"), see *Some Historical Account*, appendix, 36–39.

49. *Essex Gazette*, 1 September 1772. For a broader argument about shifting public opinion, see T. H. Breen, "Making History: The Force of Public opinion and the Last Years of Slavery in Massachusetts," in *Through the Glass Darkly: Reflections on Personal Identity in Early America*, ed. Ronald Hoffman, Mechal Sobel, and Fredrika J. Tuete, (Chapel Hill: University of North Carolina Press, 1997), 67–95.

50. Vincent Carretta, *Phillis Wheatley: Biography of a Genius in Bondage* (Athens: University of Georgia Press, 2011); Waldstreicher, *Odyssey of Phillis Wheatley*; Wendy Raphael Roberts, "'On the Death of Love Rotch,' a New Poem Attributed to Phillis Wheatley (Peters): And a Speculative Attribution," *Early American Literature* 58 (2023): 155–84, esp. 162–66.

51. Phillis Wheatley, *Poems on Various Subjects, Religious and Moral* (London: A. Bell, 1773), 18; Phillis Wheatley to Obour [Tanner], Providence Feby 14, 1776, in Vincent Carretta, ed., *The Writings of Phillis Wheatley* (New York: Oxford University Press, 2019), 131. See also David Waldstreicher, "The Wheatleyan Moment," *EAS* 9 (Fall 2011): 522–51; David Waldstreicher, "Ancients, Moderns, and Africans: Phillis Wheatley and the Politics of Empire and Slavery in the American Revolution," *JER* 37 (Fall 2017): 701–33. On contemporaries' view that slavery might be part of God's providential plan, see also John Saillant, "Slavery and Divine Providence in New England Calvinism: The New Divinity and a Black Protest, 1775–1805," *NEQ* 68 (December 1995): 584–608.

52. *Boston Censor*, 29 February 1772; Carretta, *Phillis Wheatley*, 80–87, 95–108.

53. *Connecticut Gazette*, 1 May 1772, cited in Bradley, *Slavery, Propaganda, and Revolution*, 106.

54. Zilversmit provides a solid overview of the various legislative debates over slavery while noting Benezet's central role in coordinating antislavery activism, in *First Emancipation*, 85–97. Yet his historiographic framing—challenging Progressive historians who attributed abolition to economic factors by highlighting the role of revolutionary ideology—leads him to understate the evidence demonstrating the essential role of Quakers. Detailed studies of Quakers in Pennsylvania and New Jersey have begun establishing the sophistication of their activism; see especially Sassi, "With a Little Help from the Friends," and Bruce A. Bender "Discharging Their Duty: Salem Quakers and Slavery, 1730–1780," in *The American Revolution in New Jersey: Where the Battlefront Meets the Home Front*, ed. James J. Gigantino II (New Brunswick, NJ: Rutgers University Press, 2015), 121-47; and Bruce A. Bendler, "'Love to Justice, and a Wish to Promote It': The Politics of Slavery in New Jersey 1770–1775," *New Jersey Studies* (Winter 2017): 23–47.

55. Thomas E. Drake, *Quakers and Slavery in America* (New Haven, CT: Yale University Press, 1950), 48–89; Kevin Vrevich, "The Inner Light of Radical Abolitionism: Greater Rhode Island and the Emergence of Racial Justice," (PhD diss., Ohio State University, 2019), 33–36.

56. 1772 NCYM Minutes, in Crawford, *Having of Negroes*, 77; PYM Minutes Vol. 2 (1747–1779), 285 (28 9mo 1772); VYM Minutes, 138 (5mo 1769), 141 (6mo 1770), 143 (6mo 1772). See also Soderlund, *Quakers and Slavery*, 98–103. Drake, *Quakers and Slavery in America*, 71; A. Glenn Crothers, *Quakers Living in the Lion's Mouth: The Society of Friends in Northern Virginia, 1730–1865* (Gainesville: University Press of Florida), 45; and Hardin, "Litigating the Lash," 40–41.

57. PMM Negro School Minutes Vol. 1, 1–2 (23 2mo 1770), 23 (3 2mo and 6 3mo 1773), quotations from 38 (25 12mo 1773); Anthony Benezet, *Short Observations on Slavery: Introductory to Some Extracts from the Writing of the Abbe Raynal, on That Important Subject* ([Philadelphia, 1783]), 11–12. See also Sydney V. James, *A People Among Peoples: Quaker Benevolence in Eighteenth-Century America* (Cambridge, MA: University of Harvard Press, 1963), 294–95;

Gary B. Nash, *Forging Freedom: The Formation of Philadelphia's Free Black Community, 1720–1840* (Cambridge, MA: Harvard University Press, 1988), 29–31, 51, 68, 98–113, 130–33, 202–3; Maurice Jackson, *Let This Voice be Heard: Anthony Benezet, Father of Atlantic Abolitionism* (Philadelphia: University of Pennsylvania Press, 2009), 22–23.

58. Anthony Benezet, *Some Historical Account of Guinea . . . Also A Re-Publication of the Sentiments of Several Authors of Note, on This Interesting Subject; Particularly an Extract of a Treatise, by Granville Sharp* (Philadelphia: Joseph Crukshank, 1771), I, 51, 55, 65, 92, 131, 139. On this publication, see especially Davis, *Slavery in the Age of Revolution*, 196; David L. Crosby, ed., *The Complete Antislavery Writings of Anthony Benezet, 1754–1783: An Annotated Critical Edition* (Baton Rouge: Louisiana State University Press, 2014), 112–16, 240–41; Jonathan D. Sassi, "Africans in the Quaker Image: Anthony Benezet, African Travel Narratives, and Revolutionary-Era Antislavery," Journal of Early Modern History 10 (2006): 95–130; Sassi, "With a Little Help from the Friends," 51–54.

59. Granville Sharp, *A Representation of the Injustice and Dangerous Tendency of Tolerating Slavery . . .* (London: printed for Benjamin White and Robert Horsfield, 1769), 72, 73, 152; Benezet, *Some Historical Account* [Part 2], 13–14, 33–35. On Sharp's pamphlet, see David Brion Davis, *The Problem of Slavery in Western Culture* (Ithaca, NY: Cornell University Press, 1966), 487; Christopher Leslie Brown, *Moral Capital: Foundations of British Abolitionism* (Chapel Hill: University of North Carolina Press, 2006), 99; Jack P. Greene, *Evaluating Empire and Confronting Colonialism in Eighteenth-Century Britain* (New York: Cambridge University Press, 2013), 171–76.

60. *Pennsylvania Gazette*, 24 October 1771; *Boston Gazette*, 13 January 1772.

61. Benezet to Granville Sharp, Philadelphia, 5th Month 14th, 1772, in *FAB*, 290–93.

62. Robert Pleasants to Colonel Richard Bland, Curles [Virginia], 3d. mo. 15, 1770, LBRP, 124. For references to antislavery lobbying, see VYM Minutes, 138 (5mo 1769), 141 (6mo 1770), 143 (6mo 1772). Unfortunately, the VYM minutes from 1771 and 1773–1777 were destroyed in a fire at the home of clerk John Crew, as is explained at the start of the minute book. William H. Browne et al., eds., *Archives of Maryland*, 95 vols. (Baltimore, 1883–2000), 63:20 (1 November 1771), cited in an editorial note in "To Benjamin Franklin from Anthony Benezet, 27 April 1772," *FO*, https://founders.archives.gov/documents/Franklin/01-19-02-0083. See also Crothers, *Quakers Living in the Lion's Mouth*, 45; Hardin, "Litigating the Lash," 40–41.

63. Benezet to John and Henry Gurney, Philadelphia, First Mo. 10th, 1772, in *FAB*, 283–87; *Journal of the House of Burgesses of Virginia, 1770–1772* (Richmond: Colonial Press, 1906), 240 (12 March 1772), 256–57 (20 March 1772), 283–84 (quotations, 1 April 1772); *The Justice and Necessity of Taxing the American Colonies, Demonstrated*, quoted in Staughton Lynd and David Waldstreicher, "Free Trade Sovereignty, and Slavery: Toward and Economic Interpretation of American Independence," *WMQ* 68 (October 2011): 597–630, 601. See also Eva Sheppard Wolf, *Race and Liberty in the New Nation: Emancipation in Virginia from the Revolution to Nat Turner's Rebellion* (Baton Rouge: Louisiana State University, 2006), 23.

64. LMS Minutes Extract (5 2mo 1773), in PMS Miscellaneous Papers, 1773:6; Benezet to Granville Sharp, (18h February 1773), in Prince Hoare, ed., *Memoirs of Granville Sharp, Esq., Composed from His Own Manuscripts and Other Authentic Documents . . .* (London: Henry Colburn, 1820), 112–13. The House of Burgesses petition appeared in many newspapers; for examples, see *South-Carolina Gazette* (Charleston), 25 August 1772; *Massachusetts Gazette and Boston News-Letter*, 8 October 1772 supplement; *Connecticut Gazette* (New London), 9 October

1772; *Massachusetts Spy*, 22 October 1772; *Providence Gazette*, 24 October 1772; *Philadelphia Gazette*, 3 January 1773; *New-York Journal*, 18 February 1773.

65. Petition of the North Carolina Standing Committee, 11 7mo 1772, NCYM Standing Committee Minutes, 7–11, also available in Crawford, *Having of Negroes*, 77–78; NCSC Minutes, Haverford, 12–13 (28 8mo 1772), 17–18 (25 9mo 1773).

66. John [*sic*—Thomas] Knox Gordon to [Anthony Benezet], 1772 (copy), appended to Anthony Benezet to Granville Sharp, Philad.a ye 2oth. May 1773, "Copies of Letters to Granville Sharp, 1763–1773," NYHS; Anthony Benezet to Granville Sharp, Philadelphia ye. 1st. 5th mo April [*sic*—May] 1773 (copy), ibid.

67. Benezet to Sharp, Philadelphia, 5th Month 14th, 1772, in *FAB*, 287–90.

68. Granville Sharp, *An Appendix to the Representation, (Printed in the Year 1769,) of the Injustice and Dangerous Tendency of Tolerating Slavery . . .* (London: Benjamin White, 1772), 28. On Benezet's influence on the *Somerset* case, see also Jackson, *Let This Voice be Heard*, 145; and Kirsten Sword, "Remembering Dinah Nevil: Strategic Deceptions in Eighteenth-Century Antislavery," *JAH* (September 2010): 315–343, esp. 326–27.

69. Sharp to Dr. John Fothergill, [before 7 February 1772] and 8 February 1772, in Hoare, *Memoirs of Granville Sharp*, 81.

70. Sharp to Lord North, Old Jewry, 18th February, 1772, in Hoare, *Memoirs of Granville Sharp*, 78–80.

71. Granville Sharp to Benezet, Old Jewry, London, August 21, 1772, in *FAB*, 418–22 (quotations from 419). On the *Somerset* case, see Davis, *Slavery in the Age of Revolution*, 480–501; Higginbotham, *In the Matter of Color*, 333–55; William M. Wiecek, *Sources of Antislavery Constitutionalism in America, 1760–1848* (Ithaca, NY: Cornell University Press, 1977), 20–39; Steven M. Wise, *Though the Heavens May Fall: The Landmark Trial That Led to the End of Human Slavery* (Cambridge, MA: Da Capo Press, 2005), 179–91; Brown, *Moral Capital*, 93–98; George Van Cleve, "Somerset's Case and Its Antecedents in Imperial Perspective," *Law and History Review* 24 (2006): 601–45; George William Van Cleve, *A Slaveholders' Union: Slavery, Politics, and the Constitution in the Early American Republic* (Chicago: University of Chicago Press, 2010), 31–40.

72. *Caledonian Mercury* (Edinburgh), 24 August 1772, quoted in Matthew Mason, "North American Calm, West Indian Storm: The Politics of the Somerset Decision in the British Atlantic," *Slavery & Abolition* 41 (April 2020): 723–47. On the metropolitan view of slavery as a colonial aberration, see Eliga Gould, "Zones of Law, Zones of Violence: The Legal Geography of the British Atlantic, circa 1772," *WMQ* 60 (July 2003): 471–510; Green, *Evaluating Empire*, 178–79. See also Brown's broader discussion of Anglo-American jockeying for the moral high ground in *Moral Capital*.

73. [Benjamin Franklin], "The Sommersett Case and the Slave Trade, 18–20 June 1772," *FO*, https://founders.archives.gov/documents/Franklin/01-19-02-0128. See also "From Benjamin Franklin to Anthony Benezet, 22 August 1772," FO, https://founders.archives.gov/documents/Franklin/01-19-02-0173; *Massachusetts Spy*, 17 September 1772; David Waldstreicher, *Runaway America: Benjamin Franklin, Slavery, and the American Revolution* (New York: Hill and Wang, 2004), 195–99; and Bradley, *Slavery, Propaganda, and Revolution*, 77.

74. *Massachusetts Gazette* (Boston), 10 September 1772. On newspaper response in America, see Mason, "North American Calm, West Indian Storm"; Bradley, *Slavery, Propaganda, and Revolution*, 66–80; and Thea K. Hunter, "Publishing Freedom, Winning Arguments: Somerset,

Natural Rights and Massachusetts Freedom Cases, 1772–1836," (PhD diss., Columbia University, 2005), 108–24.

75. "John Marsham," *Boston Evening-Post*, 7 September 1772.

76. "Commiserator Africanorum," *Boston Evening-Post*, 21 September 1772; "John Marsham," ibid.; "M. Cato," *Boston Evening-Post*, 28 September 1772; "Manetho," *Massachusetts Spy*, 1 October 1772; "John Marsham," *Boston Evening-Post*, 12 October 1772; "John Marsham," *Boston Evening-Post*, 19 October 1772; "Manetho," *Massachusetts Spy*, 22 October 1772; "Commiserator Africanorum," *Boston Evening-Post*, 26 October 1772; "M. Cato," ibid.

77. James Swan, *A Dissuasion to Great-Britain and the Colonies, from the Slave-Trade to Africa . . .* (Boston: E. Russell, 1772), xi, 28, 29, 40, 44, 68, 69, 70. For the publication date, see *Boston Post Boy/Massachusetts Gazette*, 16 November 1772. For a proslavery essay from an English paper, perhaps reprinted in response to Swan's pamphlet, see *Boston Post-Boy*, 4 January 1773.

Chapter 4

1. Robert Middlekauf, *The Glorious Cause: The American Revolution, 1763–1789* (New York: Oxford University Press, 1985), 213–20; Alan Taylor, *American Revolutions: A Continental History, 1750–1804* (New York: W. W. Norton, 2016), 112–28.

2. Robert Parkinson represents a common assumption when he states, "Influenced in part by the considerable discussions of political slavery and a deepening discourse of natural rights, by the end of 1774, there was an almost rapturous feeling of expectation that slavery might disappear from America, and soon." Robert G. Parkinson, *Thirteen Clocks: How Race United the Colonies and Made the Declaration of Independence* (Chapel Hill: University of North Carolina Press, 2021), 56. See also Gordon S. Wood, *Power and Liberty: Constitutionalism in the American Revolution* (New York: Oxford University Press, 2021), 110; Edmund S. Morgan, *The Birth of the Republic, 1763–1789*, 3rd ed. (Chicago: University of Chicago Press, 1992), 96–97; Steven C. Pincus, *Heart of the Declaration: The Founders' Case for an Activist Government* (New Haven, CT: Yale University Press, 2016), 126; and Gary B. Nash, *Race and Revolution* (Madison, WI: Madison House, 1990), 9–10. My emphasis on the role of activism by marginalized groups is more in line with Manisha Sinha, *The Slave's Cause: A History of Abolition* (New Haven, CT: Yale University Press, 2016), 41–47.

3. [Anthony Benezet?], "A Copy of a Letter to a Pennsylvania Assembly-man, 1774," CPW, box 14:27. The handwriting appears to be Benezet's.

4. Benezet to Granville Sharp, Philadelphia, 5th Month 14th, 1772, *FAB*, 290–93; Granville Sharp to Anthony Benezet, Old Jewry, London, August 21, 1772 (copy), Allinson Papers, Haverford, box 10. Sharp's description of the Spanish regulations, which was later extracted in colonial newspapers, is missing from the version of his letter included in *FAB* (418–22) but is available in Roger Bruns, ed., *Am I Not a Man and a Brother: The Antislavery Crusade of Revolutionary America, 1688–1788* (New York: Chelsea House, 1977), 196–99. Extracts of various lengths appears in *Pennsylvania Gazette*, 13 January 1773; *Connecticut Gazette* (New London), 22 January 1773; *Essex Gazette* (Salem), 9 February 1773; and *Massachusetts Spy* (Boston), 11 February 1773. On Quaker antislavery activism during this time, see also Thomas E. Drake, *Quakers and Slavery in America* (New Haven, CT: Yale University Press, 1950), 85–89; and Arthur Zilversmit, *The First Emancipation: The Abolition of Slavery in the North* (Chicago: University of Chicago Press, 1967), 88–98.

5. These petitions do not appear extant, and this episode has received little scholarly notice. Allinson stated that one of the three petitions was directed to House of Lords and indicated that

each subscriber would sign all three, suggesting that the other two were directed to the House of Commons and the king, as Sharp had suggested. Samuel Allinson to Benezet, Burlington, 19th 11th mo. 1772, *FAB*, 422–23. On Pemberton's role, see Benezet to Allinson, Philadelphia, Eleventh Month, 30th, 1772, *FAB*, 297. On Allinson's legal aid to African Americans, see Jonathan D. Sassi, "The Legacies of James McCarty: The Story of How Quakers Secured One Family's Emancipation and Its Ramifications for Revolutionary-Era Antislavery," *Early American Studies* 16 (Spring 2018): 282–316.

6. The petition and the description of its signers appears in Granville Sharp, *The Law of Retribution: Or, a Serious Warning to Great Britain and Her Colonies, Founded on Unquestionable Examples of God's Temporal Vengeance Against Tyrants, Slave-holders, and Oppressors* (London: W. Richardson, 1776), 312–13; *Pennsylvania Packet* (Philadelphia), 4 October 1773.

7. Anthony Benezet to Sharp (18 February 1773), in Prince Hoare, ed., *Memoirs of Granville Sharp, Esq., Composed from His Own Manuscripts and Other Authentic Documents . . .* (London: Henry Colburn, 1820), 112–13; PMS epistle to the LMS in PMS Minutes Vol. 1, 381 (22 4mo 1773); LMS Minutes (25 6mo 1773) in LMS Minute Extracts, PMS Miscellaneous Papers, 1773:6.

8. [David Cooper], *A Mite Cast into the Treasury: Or, Observations on Slave-Keeping* (Philadelphia: Joseph Crukshank, 1772), 3, 4, 6, 13, 19, 20, 24. See also Bill L. Smith, "Never Take Kinship Personally: Confronting Slavery, Masculinity, and Family in Revolutionary America," *Quaker History* 103 (Spring 2014): 17–35.

9. Rush did not name the Somerset case, but he referred to "a late decision in favor of a Virginia slave in Westminster-Hall." [Benjamin Rush], *An Address to the Inhabitants of the British Settlements in America, Upon Slave-Keeping* (Philadelphia: John Dunlap, 1773), 19, 20, 28. *Pennsylvania Packet*, 18 January 1773. Rush's pamphlet was widely excerpted in newspapers and fully reprinted by John Boyles (for John Langdon) in Boston (1773), Hodges and Shober in New York (1773), and Judah P. Spooner in Norwich, CT (1775). See also Gary B. Nash and Jean R. Soderlund, *Freedom by Degrees: Emancipation in Pennsylvania and Its Aftermath* (New York: Oxford University Press, 1991), 77–79; Maurice Jackson, *Let This Voice be Heard: Anthony Benezet, Father of Atlantic Abolitionism* (Philadelphia: University of Pennsylvania Press, 2009), 117–26.

10. [John Peter Demarin], *A Treatise upon the Trade from Great-Britain to Africa: Humbly Recommended to the Attention of Government, by an African Merchant* (London: R. Baldwin, 1772), appendix, 30. Anthony Benezet to Granville Sharp, Philad.a ye 20th. May 1773 (copy), "Copies of Letters to Granville Sharp, 1763–1773," NYHS; Thomas Thompson, *The African Trade for Negro Slaves, Shewn to Be Consistent with Principles of Humanity, and with the Laws of Revealed Religion* (London: Simmons and Kirkby, 1772), 11, 15, 24. A facsimile of Benezet's copy with his marginalia, held at Rutgers University, New Brunswick, NJ, is reproduced in Bruns, *Am I Not a Man*, 217–20, quotation from 218. See also David Brion Davis, *The Problem of Slavery in the Age of Revolution, 1770–1823* (Ithaca, NY: Cornell University Press, 1975), 531–32; Larry E. Tise, *Proslavery: A History of the Defense of Slavery in America, 1701–1840* (Athens: University of Georgia Press, 1987), 25–28; and Jack P. Greene, *Evaluating Empire and Confronting Colonialism in Eighteenth-Century Britain* (New York: Cambridge University Press, 2013), 180.

11. [Richard Nisbet], *Slavery Not Forbidden by Scripture; Or a Defence of the West-India Planters, from the Aspersions Thrown Out Against Them, by the Author of a Pamphlet, Entitled, "An Address to the Inhabitants of the British Settlements in American, Upon Slave-Keeping," by a West-Indian* (Philadelphia, 1773), 8, 22–23, 28–29. See also Tise, *Proslavery*, 28–29. Ironically,

Richard Nisbet later ended up impoverished and mentally deranged, with Quaker abolitionist John Parrish helping to care for his family while Nisbet was locked up in an asylum under the supervision of Dr. Rush. See materials from 1794–1798 in CPW, box 1, and Benjamin Rush Family Papers, LCP, box 4.

12. [Benjamin Rush], *An Address . . . The Second Edition, to Which Is Added, a Vindication of the Address, in Answer to a Pamphlet Entitled, "Slavery not Forbidden in Scripture; Or, a Defence of the West India Planters," by a Pennsylvanian* (John Dunlap: Philadelphia, 1773), 22–23 (publication announced in *Pennsylvania Packet*, 20 September 1773); "Onesimus," *Pennsylvania Packet*, 25 October 1773.

13. *Pennsylvania Packet*, 15 November 1773 (also in *Connecticut Journal* [New Haven], 31 December 1773), reproduced and discussed in Winthrop Jordan, "An Antislavery Proslavery Document?," *Journal of Negro History* 47 (January 1962): 54–56.

14. *Personal Slavery Established, by the Suffrages of Custom and Right Reason, Being a Full Answer to the Gloomy and Visionary Reveries, of all the Fanatical and Enthusiastical Writers on that Subject* (Philadelphia: John Dunlap, 1773), 3, 26; Anthony Benezet to Robert Pleasants, Philad'a, ye [1st or 5th mo?] 1774, American Friends Letters, Swarthmore, folder 14. See also Lester B. Scherer, "A New Look at *Personal Slavery Established*," *William and Mary Quarterly* 30 (October 1973):645–652. Some scholars have been confused by the satirical nature of *Personal Slavery Established*; see for example Winthrop D. Jordan, *White Over Black: American Attitudes Toward the Negro, 1550–1812* (Chapel Hill: University of North Carolina Press, 1968), 305–8, 484–85; and Tise, *Proslavery*, 29.

15. Anthony Benezet to Robert Pleasants, Philad'a, ye [1st or 5th mo?] 1774, American Friends Letters, Swarthmore College, folder 14.

16. Benezet to Sharp, Philadia ye. 29th-March 1773, in Bruns, *Am I Not a Man*, 262–67; Benezet to Robert Pleasants, Philadelphia ye 8th. 4th. Month 1773, *FAD*, 298–302. Benezet wrote that he also sent the "substance" of this letter to Benjamin Berry of Maryland. This tactic represented a reversal for Benezet, who had previously minimized references to slave revolt.

17. Benezet to Sharp, Philadia ye. 29th-March 1773, in Bruns, *Am I Not a Man*, 262–67; *Maryland Gazette* (Annapolis), 1 April 1773; *Maryland Gazette*, 8 April 1773, 29 April 1773, 22 July 1773, 30 September 1773, 23 December 1773; Taylor, *American Revolutions*, 116.

18. The Salem petition, held at Swarthmore College, is available through *Quakers & Slavery*, triptych.brynmawr.edu/cdm/compoundobject/collection/HC_QuakSlav/id/10007/rec/5; Elias Boudinot to Samuel Allinson, [G?] Town, Jany. 29, 1774, Allinson Papers, box 6. Petitions from Essex and Somerset counties are included in Sharp, *Law of Retribution*, 309–11. For the total number of petitions, see Jonathan D. Sassi, "Anthony Benezet as Intermediary Between the Transatlantic and Provincial: New Jersey's Antislavery Campaign on the Eve of the American Revolution," in *The Atlantic World of Anthony Benezet (1713–1784): From French Reformation to North American Quaker Antislavery Activism*, ed. Marie-Jeanne Rossignol and Bertrand Van Ruymbeke (Boston: Brill, 2016), 129–46, esp. 138. See also Zilversmit, *First Emancipation*, 91–93; James J. Gigantino II, *The Ragged Road to Abolition: Slavery and Freedom in New Jersey, 1775–1865* (Philadelphia: University of Pennsylvania Press, 2025), 24–26; and Bruce A. Bender, "'Love to Justice, and a Wish to Promote It': The Politics of Slavery in New Jersey 1770–1775," *New Jersey Studies* 3 (Winter 2017): 23–47.

19. [William Dillwyn], *Brief Considerations on Slavery, and the Expediency of Its Abolition. With Some Hints on the Means Whereby It May Be Gradually Effected. Recommended to the Serious Attention of All, and Especially of Those Entrusted with the Powers of Legislation* (Burlington, NJ:

Isaac Collins 1773), 8. The pamphlet appeared in November; see *Pennsylvania Gazette*, 10 November 1773. On Dillwyn, see Benjamin L. Carp, "'Fix'd almost amongst Strangers': Charleston's Quaker Merchants and the Limits of Cosmopolitanism," *WMQ* 74 (January 2017): 77–108

20. Granville Sharp, *An Essay on Slavery: Proving from Scripture Its Inconsistency with Humanity and Religion; In Answer to a Late Publication . . .*, [ed. Samuel Allinson] (Burlington, NJ: Isaac Collins, 1773), vi, xiv, xv, 21, 24. On the publication of this essay, see Sassi, "Anthony Benezet as Intermediary."

21. *Pennsylvania Packet* (Philadelphia), 17 January 1774; *Pennsylvania Gazette*, 2 February 1774; *Pennsylvania Packet*, 7 February 1774.

22. Samuel Allison to Granville Sharp, Burl[ington], 10th: 5th mo: 1774, Allinson Family Papers, Haverford, box 3; Bender, "'Love to Justice,'" 33–38; Sassi, "Anthony Benezet as Intermediary," 142–46; Gigantino, *Ragged Road to Abolition*, 25–36.

23. Anthony Benezet to Sharp, 18 February 1773, in Hoare, *Memoirs of Granville Sharp*, 112–13; *New-York Journal*, 18 February 1773; Anthony Benezet to Granville Sharp, Philadelphia ye. 1st 5th mo April [*sic*] 1773 (copy), "Copies of Letters to Granville Sharp, 1763–1773," NYHS, http://digitalcollections.nyhistory.org/items/299650-granville-sharp-copies-letters-received-anthony-benezet-letter-granville-sharp-april-1; Zilversmit, *First Emancipation*, 90–91.

24. Scholars typically date the rise of the first abolition "movement" to the rise of secular abolition societies in the 1780s while acknowledging Benezet and his allies as important precursors. Sinha, *Slave's Cause*, 20–24; Paul J. Polgar, *Standard-Bearers of Liberty and Equality: America's First Abolition Movement* (Chapel Hill: University of North Carolina Press, 2019), 4–5, 14–15.

25. John Woolman, *Serious Considerations on Various Subjects of Importance by John Woolman, of Mount Holly, in the Jerseys, North America, Deceased; With Some of His Dying Expressions* (London: Mary Hinde, 1773), 9–10, 102–13, quotation from 105. Geoffrey Plank, *John Woolman's Path to the Peaceable Kingdom: A Quaker in the British Empire* (Philadelphia: University of Pennsylvania Press, 2012), 202–24.

26. John Wesley, *Thoughts upon Slavery: Reprinted with Notes* (Philadelphia: Joseph Crukshank, 1774); Jackson, *Let This Voice be Heard*, 154. On Methodists' partial embrace of antislavery, see Dee Andrews, *The Methodists and Revolutionary America, 1760–1800: The Shaping of an Evangelical Culture* (Princeton, NJ: Princeton University Press, 2000), 123–50.

27. Granville Sharp to Anthony Benezet, London, 7th Janry 1774, in Bruns, *Am I Not a Man*, 302–6, quotation from 305; Anthony Benezet to Granville Sharp (16 3mo 1774), in Hoare, *Memoirs of Granville Sharp*, 114–15; Benezet to Samuel Allinson, Philadelphia Third Month, 30th, 1774, *FAB*, 311. See also Kirsten Sword, "Remembering Dinah Nevil: Strategic Deceptions in Eighteenth-Century Antislavery," *JAH* 97 (September 2010): 315–43, esp. 330.

28. Recent scholarship has begun recognizing the level of coordination between white and Black activists in Massachusetts; see David Waldstreicher, *Odyssey of Phillis Wheatley: A Poet's Journeys Through American Slavery and Independence* (New York: Farrar, Straus and Giroux, 2023), 138–22; Grant Stanton, "The Freedom Petitions: Black Patriotism, Black Politics, and the Abolition of Slavery in Massachusetts, 1773–1783," *EAS* (Spring 2024) 262–304.

29. *The Votes and Proceedings of the Freeholders and Other Inhabitants of the Town of Boston, in Town Meeting Assembled, According to Law* (Boston: Edes and Gill, 1773), 30, 2, 13, 20, 34; Petersham resolutions quoted in *Massachusetts Spy*, 14 January 1773. See also *JHRMA* 49, x-xv; Robert Middlekauff, *The Glorious Cause: The American Revolution, 1763–1789* (New York: Oxford University Press, 1985), 215–18.

30. *Massachusetts Spy*, 14 January 1773; *Boston Evening-Post*, 25 January 1773; Nicholas Guyatt, *Providence and the Invention of the United States, 1607–1876* (New York: Cambridge University Press, 2007), 82–94; Mark Knoll, *In the Beginning Was the Word: The Bible in American Life* (New York: Oxford University Press, 2016), 297.

31. Felix [Holbrook], "To His Excellency Thomas Hutchinson, Esq; Governor; To The Honorable His Majesty's Council, and To the Honorable House of Representatives in General Court assembled at Boston, the 6th Day of January, 1773," printed in *The Appendix: Or, Some Observations on the Expediency of the Petition of the Africans Compiled by a Lover of Constitutional Liberty* (Boston: E. Russell, 1773), 9–10, and widely available, for example in Nash, *Race and Revolution*, 171–73, and online: http://www.historyisaweapon.com/defcon1/fourpetitionsagainstslavery.html.

On the Black petitioners in Massachusetts, see especially Thomas J. Davis, "Emancipation Rhetoric, Natural Rights, and Revolutionary New England: A Note on Four Black Petitions in Massachusetts, 1773–1777," *NEQ* 62 (June 1989): 248–63; Manish Sinha, "To 'Cast Obliquy' on Oppressors: Black Radicalism in the Age of Revolution," *WMQ* 64 (January 2007): 149–60, esp. 150–54; Chernoh M. Sesay Jr., "The Revolutionary Black Roots of Slavery's Abolition in Massachusetts," *NEQ* 87 (March 2014): 99–131; Grant Stanton, "Language of Liberty: Petitioning for Freedom in Revolutionary Massachusetts, 1773–1777," (master's thesis, University of Chicago, 2017); and Stanton, "Freedom Petitions."

On the broader context of Black activism, see also Douglas R. Egerton, *Death or Liberty: African Americans and Revolutionary America* (New York: Oxford University Press, 2009), 55–60; Christopher Cameron, *To Plead Our Own Cause: African Americans in Massachusetts and the Making of the Antislavery Movement* (Kent, OH: Kent State University Press, 2011), 55–65; and Sinha, *Slave's Cause*, 42–47. On antislavery debates in Massachusetts newspapers, see also Patricia Bradley, *Slavery, Propaganda, and the American Revolution* (Jackson: University Press of Mississippi, 1998), 80–130.

32. *Massachusetts Spy*, 28 January 1773.

33. *JHRMA* 49, 195 (28 January 1773), [203 (quotation)] (2 February 1773).

34. *Appendix*, 4,5, 7, 12–15. Advertised for sale in *Massachusetts Spy*, 4 February 1773. *JHRMA* 49, 208 (4 February 1773), 225 (12 February 1773), 252 (22 February 1773), 259 (25 February 1773), 287 (5 March 1773).

35. James Swan, *A Dissuasion to Great-Britain and the Colonies, from the Slave-Trade to Africa. Shewing the Injustice Thereof, &c: Revised and Abridged* (Boston: J. Greenleaf, 1773), ix; Peter Bestes, Felix Holbrook, Sambo Freeman, and Chester Joie, "For the Representative of the Town of _____," Boston April 20th, 1773 [Boston: Ezekiel Russell or J. Greenleaf?, 1773]. Scholars often refer to this single-page publication as if it were a second petition, but its form is actually that of a circular letter addressed to legislators and town hall meetings. The printed text is simply address to "Sir" at the top and "For the Representative of the town of __________" at the bottom. For example, the copy held at the MHS is addressed by hand to "The Clerk of the Town of Taunton for the use of the present Representatives": https://www.masshist.org/database/viewer.php?item_id=443.

John Allen also reported that this circular letter "accompanied with Mr. *Swan's* Piece, entitled a Dissuasion to *Great-Britain* . . . were lately presented to the Gentlemen who are chosen *Representatives* for this Province." [John Allen], *An Oration on the Beauties of Liberty, or the Essential Rights of the Americans . . . The Fourth Edition . . . And Remarks on the Rights and Liberties of Africans, inserted by particular Desire*, 4th ed. (Boston: E. Russell, 1773), 78.

36. Bestes et al., "For the Representative of the Town"; Samuel Dexter to Jeremy Belknap, Weston, Feb. 26, 1795, in "Letters and Documents Relating to Slavery in Massachusetts," *Collections of the Massachusetts Historical Society* 3 (1887), 387–88. For Sharp's reference to Spanish manumission practices, see Granville Sharp to Anthony Benezet, Old Jewry, London, August 21, 1772, in Bruns, *Am I Not a Man*, 196–99 (esp. 199); extracts of various lengths also appear in *Pennsylvania Gazette*, 13 January 1773; *Connecticut Gazette* (New London), 22 January 1773; *Essex Gazette* (Salem), 9 February 1773; and *Massachusetts Spy* (Boston), 11 February 1773.

37. [Allen], *Oration on the Beauties of Liberty*, 73–80, quotations from 73, 74, 75. For the release of the fourth edition of Allen's pamphlet, see *Massachusetts Spy*, 13 May 1773. On this pamphlet, see also Davis, *Slavery in the Age of Revolution*, 277.

38. Instructions from Salem (18 May 1773), Medford (n.d.), Leicester (19 May 1773), and Sandwich (18 May 1773) are quoted in George Henry Moore, *Notes on the History of Slavery in Massachusetts* (New York: D. Appleton, 1866), 133–34. Moore was apparently unaware of the slaves' April circular letter and thus does not indicate any connection, but the timing suggests that the circular letter was likely the catalyst. Moreover, the Pembroke instructions explicitly refer to the petition; "At a Town-Meeting held at Pembroke," *Supplement to the Boston Gazette*, 14 June 1773, cited in Sesay, "Revolutionary Black Roots," 115.

39. *JHRMA* 50, 17 (29 May 1773); *Massachusetts Spy*, 3 June 1773; *Essex Gazette*, 8 June 1773.

40. The petition is printed in *Massachusetts Spy*, 29 July 1773; and *Essex Gazette*, 3 August 1773. For the legislative response, see *JHRMA* 50, 85 (25 June 1773), 94 (28 June 1773). No manuscript versions of the petition of January 1773 or the circular letter of April 1773 appear extant, but manuscript copies of petitions dated June 1773, 25 May 1774, and June 1774 are held in the Jeremy Belknap Papers at the MHS and have been widely reprinted. As an editorial note in the *Proceedings of the Massachusetts Historical Society* explains, the manuscript petitions at the MHS appear to be later copies (presented to Jeremy Belknap in 1795, likely by Black activist Prince Hall); this explains why they lack signatures. "Letters and Documents Relating to Slavery in Massachusetts," *Collections of the Massachusetts Historical Society* 3 (Boston: MHS, 1877), 395–96n (see 432–437 for transcripts of the petitions). For the incomplete manuscript copy of the 25 June 1773 petition held at the MHS: https://www.masshist.org/database/viewer.php?item_id=558.

41. [Theodore Parsons and Eliphalet Pearson], *A Forensic Dispute on the Legality of Enslaving the Africans, Held at the Public Commencement in Cambridge, New-England, July 21st, 1773* (Boston: John Boyle, 1773), 3–4, 5, 26, 36–39, 48. The published pamphlet simply referred to Parsons and Pearson as "A" and "B," and archivists and scholars have long mistakenly identified Pearson as taking the side of antislavery. However, Peter Galison recently corrected this error through the use of Pearson's manuscript notes; see Galison, "21 July 1773: Disputation, Poetry, Slavery," *Critical Inquiry* 45 (Winter 2019): 351–79, 355. Larry Tise is among those who mistakenly attributed the proslavery side to Parsons and suggests the debate was a "public airing of an ongoing private feud," noting that Parsons's father had been criticized by a parishioner (Deacon Benjamin Colman) for holding slaves. However, that dispute came to a head in 1780, and there is no evidence that it began "[j]ust before" the debate, as Tise asserts (*Proslavery*, 30).

A memoir published by Theophilus Parsons Jr. asserts that his grandfather, the Reverend Moses Parsons, manumitted two enslaved men but that Violet, the subject of the 1780 controversy, declined the offer of freedom, expressing her desire to be taken care of during her elderly years. Theophilus Parsons [Jr.], *Memoir of Theophilus Parsons: Chief Justice of the Supreme*

Judicial Court of Massachusetts (Boston: Ticknor and Fields, 1859), 16–19. For Theophilus Parson's involvement in freedom suits, see Chapters 5 and 6 in this book and the materials compiled by Jeanne Pickering at http://northshoreslavery.org/freedomcases/participants.php.

42. *Boston Gazette*, 23 August 1773, cited in Waldstreicher's *Odyssey of Phillis Wheatley*, 199–200.

43. Moore, *Notes on the History of Slavery*, 209–23; William O'Brien, "Did the Jennison Case Outlaw Slavery in Massachusetts?" *WMQ* 17 (April 1960): 219–41; John D. Cushing, "The Cushing Court and the Abolition of Slavery in Massachusetts: More Notes on the 'Quock Walker Case,'" *American Journal of Legal History* 5 (April 1961): 118–44; Robert M. Spector, "The Quock Walker Cases (1781–83): Slavery, its Abolition, and Negro Citizenship in Early Massachusetts," *Journal of Negro History* 53 (January 1968): 12–32; Arthur Zilversmit, "Quok Walker, Mumbet, and the Abolition of Slavery in Massachusetts," *WMQ* 25 (December 1968): 614–24; Robert M. Cover, *Justice Accused: Antislavery and the Judicial Process* (New Haven, CT: Yale University Press, 1975), 43–50; A. Leon Higginbotham, *In the Matter of Color: Race and the American Legal Process: The Colonial Period* (New York: Oxford University Press, 1978), 91–99; T. H. Breen, "Making History: The Force of Public Opinion and the Last Years of Slavery in Massachusetts," in *Through the Glass Darkly: Reflections on Personal Identity in Early America*, ed. Ronald Hoffman, Mechal Sobel, and Fredrika J. Tuete (Chapel Hill: University of North Carolina Press, 1997), 67–95; Emily Blanck, "Seventeen Eighty-Three: The Turning Point in the Law of Slavery and Freedom in Massachusetts," *NEQ* 75 (2002): 24–51.

William Wiecek was among the few scholars in the twentieth century to challenge the emphasis that scholars often place on the Quock Walker cases of 1781–1783. He notes, "At most, Walker's was the most famous of a number of freedom suits brought after 1769." William Wiecek, *Sources of Antislavery Constitutionalism, 1760–1848* (Ithaca, NY: Cornell University Press, 1977), 47. On the longer process of emancipation in Massachusetts, see also Jared Ross Hardesty, "Disappearing from Abolitionism's Heartland: The Legacy of Slavery and Emancipation in Boston," *International Review of Social History* 56 (February 2020): 145–68, esp. 151.

44. Jeanne M. Pickering, "Suing Slavery: The Essex County Freedom Suits, 1765–1783," (master's thesis, Salem State University, 2018). Pickering's work has greatly shaped my thinking, though I differ with her in placing greater weight on the role of both the *Somerset* decision and religious arguments (relative to secular natural rights ideology) in explaining the shift in jury behavior. See also Edward L. Bell, *Persistence of Memories of Slavery and Emancipation in Historical Andover* (Boston: Shawsheen Press, 2021), 203. Bell highlights the persistence of unfreedom after the Quock Walker cases but also acknowledges that the process of emancipation was already underway before 1780; see also Bell's "Research Summaries of Massachusetts Freedom Suits, 1660–1784," unpublished draft manuscript last revised 18 April 2022 and available at https://www.academia.edu/76814209. Gloria McCahon Whiting, "Emancipation Without the Courts or Constitution: The Case of Revolutionary Massachusetts," *Slavery & Abolition* 41 (September 2020): 458–78, esp. 459, 465, 470. Whiting has shown a precipitous decline in slaveholding by the start of the Revolutionary War in 1775; however, her article neglects the essential role of earlier court decisions.

45. Bill of Sale of "molatto slave" Casar, 16 years old, from Joseph Woodbridge, boat builder, to Richard Greenleaf, Gentleman, Caesar vs Greenleaf Esq, Essex County Court of Common Pleas, September 1773, 29, available through http://www.northshoreslavery.com/freedomcases/case.php?id=13. On the case and its significance, see: Pickering, "Suing Slavery," 56–63. For the

pamphlet on *Somerset*, see Francis Hargrave, *An Argument in the Case of James Sommersett a Negro: Lately Determined by the Court of King's Bench . . .* (London: W. Otridge, 1772).

46. "Wetmore's Minutes of the Trial: Essex Inferior Court, Newburyport, October 1773," *FO*, https://founders.archives.gov/documents/Adams/05-02-02-0004-0006-0001.

47. Anthony Benezet to Granville Sharp, Philadelphia ye. 1st 5th mo April [*sic*] 1773 (copy), "Copies of Letters to Granville Sharp, 1763–1773," NYHS, http://digitalcollections.nyhistory.org/items/299650-granville-sharp-copies-letters-received-anthony-benezet-letter-granville-sharp-april-1, http://digitalcollections.nyhistory.org/islandora/object/islandora%3A153422#page/1/mode/1up; *Boston Post-Boy*, 18 October 1773; *Massachusetts Spy*, 21 October 1773; Joshua Coffin, *A Sketch of the History of Newbury, Newburyport, and West Newbury, from 1635 to 1845* (Boston: S. G. Drake, 1845), 330. Moore downplays the significance of *Caesar [Hendrick] v. Greenleaf* and similar cases, writing "the fact remains that . . . the legal effects of such verdicts reached none but the parties immediately concerned; and the institution of slavery continued to be recognized by law in Massachusetts, defying all direct attempts to destroy it" (*Notes on the History of Slavery*, 124).

By contrast, Pickering makes a persuasive argument about the importance of *Caesar [Hendrick] v. Greenleaf* as a watershed moment. However, she likely overstates the importance of natural rights ideology while underestimating the importance of the *Somerset* principle when she suggests that Lowell and jurors prioritized "natural rights" over "property rights." She largely neglects the distinction between enslavement-for-life (based on statute law) and hereditary slavery (usage only) that was likely a crucial to case's outcome. Pickering, "Suing Slavery," 61–63.

48. "Queries Respecting the Slavery and Emancipation of Negroes in Massachusetts, Proposed by the Hon. Judge Tucker of Virginia, and Answered by the Reverend Dr. Belknap," *Collections of the Massachusetts Historical Society* [1795] ([Boston: John H. Eastburn, 1835]), 191–211, quotations from 201, 202, 203.

49. T. H. Breen similarly emphasizes the shift in public opinion, though with less emphasis on religious sentiment, in "Making History," 67–95. Gloria McCahon Whiting also emphasizes public opinion but gives little attention to either religious sentiment or freedom suits in "Emancipation Without the Courts or Constitution," 458–78.

50. *Essex Gazette* (Salem), 26 October 1773. The providentialist language of "Justin" is similar to that of Samuel Webster in "An Earnest Address to My Country, Upon Slavery," *Boston Chronicle*, 27 February 1769, and in *A Sermon Preached Before the Honorable Council . . . May 28, 1777* (Boston: Edes and Gill, 1777), esp. 37.

51. *Boston Evening-Post*, 20 September 1773; Phillis Wheatley, *Poems on Various Subjects, Religious and Moral* (London: A Bell, 1773), 74. Vincent Carretta, *Phillis Wheatley: Biography of a Genius in Bondage* (Athens: University of Georgia Press, 2011), 95–138; Waldstreicher, *Odyssey of Phillis Wheatley*, 199–222.

52. Samuel Hopkins and Ezra Stiles, "Circular," Newport, Rhode Island, August 31, 1773, *WSH*, 1:131–32; Phillis Wheatley to the Rev. Samuel Hopkins, Boston, Feb. 9, 1774, in *The Writings of Phillis Wheatley*, ed. Vincent Carretta (New York: Oxford University Press, 2019), 38–39. On the African missionary scheme, see Floyd John Miller, *The Search for a Black Nationality: Black Emigration and Colonization, 1787–1863* (Urbana: University of Illinois Press, 1975), 3–15.

53. *Connecticut Gazette* (New London), 11 March 1774. See also Carretta, *Phillis Wheatley*, 165; Waldstreicher, *Odyssey of Phillis Wheatley*, 256–59. On the biblical theme of deliverance in Black protest in the revolutionary era, see John Coffey, *Exodus and Liberation: Deliverance*

Politics from John Calvin to Martin Luther King, Jr. (New York: Oxford University Press, 2014), 95–101.

54. Samuel Adams to John Pickering Jr., Boston, Jany. 8, 1774, quoted in Moore, *Notes on the History of Slavery*, 136; "Address of the Africans, to the Council and house of Representatives . . . the 20th day of January, 1774," *Massachusetts Spy*, 1 September 1774; *JHRMA* 50, 104 (26 January 1774).

55. "A Son of Africa," *Massachusetts Spy*, 10 February 1774.

56. *Massachusetts Spy*, 10 February 1774. For the pamphlet, see Hargrave, *Case of James Sommersett.*

57. *Massachusetts Spy*, 10 February 1774. The advertisement referred to "the trial of *Abraham Stockbridge*," which must have been a garbled reference to Abraham Colden, who sued his enslaver, Dr. Benjamin Stockbridge of Plymouth County. In April 1772 a jury had ruled in favor of the slaveholding defendant, but Colden had appealed. Russell must have been referring to the appeal, which was repeatedly postponed (in part due to the outbreak of war in 1775) and was eventually decided in Colden's favor through Stockbridge's default in 1777. For a brief summary and citations to the legal records, see Bell, "Research Summaries," 99–100.

58. [John Allen], *The Watchman's Alarm to Lord N—-H; Or, The British Parliamentary Boston Port-Bill Unwrapped* . . . (Salem, MA: E. Russell, 1774), 28n. Allen did not name Sampson but referred to the case between "Mr. Caleb Dodge, of Beverly and his negro servant." Although he reported a "verdict" in the enslaved plaintiff's favor, the court records indicate that the case of *Sampson v. Caleb Dodge and Josiah Batchelder* was simply referred to arbitration in July 1774 (likely because Dodge and Batchelder anticipated the jury would side with Sampson). See Pickering, "Suing Slavery," 93; and Bell, "Research Summaries," 91–93.

59. *Massachusetts Spy*, 3 March 1774 (cited in draft of Waldstreicher's *Odyssey of Phillis Wheatley*).

60. *JHRMA* 50, 221 (2 March 1774), 224 (3 March 1774), 226 (4 March 1774), 228 (5 March 1774), 237 (7 March 1774), 243 (9 March 1774). The initial bill included a provision (struck from the final bill) stating: "*And be it further Enacted and declared that nothing in this act contained shall extend or be construed to extend for retaining or holding in perpetual servitude any Negro or other Person or Persons now inslaved within this Province but that every such Negro or other Person or Persons shall be intituled to all the Benefits such Negro or other Person or Persons might by Law have been intituled to, in case this act had not been made.*" Moore, who reprinted the bill's text, observes that the passage indicated "indirect legislative approval of some of the doctrines maintained by Counsel for the negroes in the 'freedom suits'" (*Notes on the History of Slavery*, 138–40).

61. "Petition for Freedom to Massachusetts Governor Thomas Gage, His Majesty's Council, and the House of Representatives, 25 May 1774," MHS Online: https://www.masshist.org/database/viewer.php?item_id=549 (accessed 10 July 2019); *JHRMA* 50, [247] (25 May 1774), [253] (26 May 1774).

62. Grant Stanton has recently located a printed version of this petition, which refers to the legislature's relocation to Salem and thanks the petitioners' legislative allies, in *Massachusetts Spy*, 8 September 1774. It described this "petition" as "the third of us Subscribers," confirming that the same core group of activists led by Felix Holbrook was involved throughout. The description of it as the "third" also indicates that the draft dated 25 May 1774 had not been formally submitted (and, as Stanton notes, the address from January 1774 was a "memorial" intended to revive consideration of the two formal petitions from January and June 1773, rather

than being a third formal petition itself); Stanton, "Freedom Petitions." A partially damaged manuscript version of the June 1774 petition held at the MHS requested freedom, full privileges and immunities, and land grants. "Petition for Freedom to Massachusetts Governor Thomas Gage, His Majesty's Council, and the House of Representatives, June 1774" (partially damaged ms), MHS Online: https://www.masshist.org/database/550.

63. *JHRMA* 50, [271] (10 June 1774), 285 (16 June 1774).

64. *JHRMA* 50, [290] (17 June 1774). For the slavery metaphor in fast-day sermons, see for example Nathan Fisk, *The Importance of Righteousness to the Happiness, and the Tendency of Oppression to the Misery of a People, Illustrated in Two Discourses Delivered at Brookfield, July [1]4. 1774* . . . (Boston: John Kneeland, 1774), 10; Timothy Hilliard, *The Duty of a People Under the Oppression of Man, To Seek Deliverance From God: The Substance of Two Sermons, Delivered at Barnstable, July 14th, 1774* . . . (Boston: Greenleaf's Printing Office, 1774), 25. Based on published fast-day sermons, it seems only a small number of ministers took the opportunity to encourage antislavery reform. The Reverend Samuel Webster may have done so implicitly when he called on his congregation to "break off from all our iniquities by righteousness, and from our transgressions, by *shewing mercy to those who are poor and oppressed among us*." Samuel Webster, *The Misery and Duty of an Oppress'd and Enslav'd People, Represented in a Sermon Delivered at Salisbury, July 14, 1774, On a Day Set Apart for Fasting and Prayer, On Account of Approaching Calamities* (Boston: Edes and Gill, 1774), 30 (emphasis added).

65. Jeremy Belknap, *On Account of the Difficulties of the King*, 14 July 1774, excerpted in George Burley Spalding, *The Dover Pulpit During the Revolutionary War: A Discourse Commemorative of the Distinguished Service Rendered by Rev. Jeremy Belknap* . . . (Dover, NH: Morning Star Steam Job Printing House, 1876), 17; *Essex Journal* (Newburyport), 20 July 1774; [Allen], *Watchman's Alarm*, 27.

66. *Essex Journal* (Newburyport), 17 August 1774. Sarter's essay is also reprinted in Nash, *Race and Revolution*, 167–70. See also Cameron, *Plead Our Own Cause*, 41–44.

67. Nathaniel Niles, *Two Discourses on Liberty; Delivered at the North Church, in Newburyport, on Lord's-Day, June 5th, 1774* . . . (Newbury-port, MA: I. Thomas and H. W. Tinges, 1774), 37, 38, cited in James D. Essig, *The Bonds of Wickedness: American Evangelicals Against Slavery, 1770–1808* (Philadelphia: Temple University Press, 1982), 23.

68. *Boston Evening-Post*, 24 October 1774; *Boston Gazette*, 24 October 1774; William Lincoln, ed., *The Journals of Each Provincial Congress of Massachusetts in 1774 and 1775* . . . (Boston: Dutton and Wentworth, 1838), 26 (21 October 1774), 27–28 (22 October 1774), 29 (26 October 1774).

69. "Abigail Adams to John Adams, Boston Garison Sepbr. 22 1774," *FO*: https://founders.archives.gov/documents/Adams/04-01-02-0107, cited in Bradley, *Slavery Propaganda, and Revolution*, 132.

70. It is unclear whether the "Negro's memorial" was composed by or merely about Black people, and the legislative records simply reference postponing any discussion. However, an essay by "Freeman" in New London's *Connecticut Gazette* (9 September 1773) refers to an emancipation bill proposed in May. It seems likely that the bill had been submitted with the petition rather than drafted by legislators in response. Charles J. Hoadly, ed., *The Public Records of the Colony of Connecticut, Vol. 14: From October, 1772, to April, 1775, Inclusive* (Hartford: 1887), 155 (13 May 1773). See also Zilversmit, *First Emancipation*, 108. For the role of religion in shaping slavery debates in Connecticut, see also John Saillant, "Slavery and Divine Providence in New England Calvinism: The New Divinity and a Black Protest, 1775–1805," *NEQ* 68 (December

1995): 584–608); Kenneth P. Minkema and Harry Stout, "The Edwardsean Tradition and the Antislavery Debate, 1740–1865," *JAH* 92 (June 2005): 47–74; John Ericson, "When God Ceased Winking: Jonathan Edwards the Younger's Evolution on the Problem of Slavery," *Connecticut History Review* 57 (Spring 2018): 7–32.

71. "Philander," *Supplement to the Connecticut Journal* (New Haven), 16 September 1774. See also Ericson, "When God Ceased Winking."

72. Jonathan Edwards Jr., *The Injustice and Impolicy of the Slave Trade, and of the Slavery of the Africans: Illustrated in a Sermon Preached Before the Connecticut Society for the Promotion of Freedom, and for the Relief of Persons Unlawfully Holden in Bondage, at Their Annual Meeting in New-Haven, September 15, 1791* ([New Haven:] Thomas and Samuel Green, 1791), 25, 27; "Philander" *Connecticut Journal* (New Haven), 11 February 1774. Edwards and Baldwin wrote several multipart essays in the *Connecticut Gazette* and the *Connecticut Journal* in 1773 and 1774 under the pseudonyms or titles "Freeman," "Antidoulious," Philander," and "Some Observations upon the Slavery of Negroes." Other writers authored additional pieces. For the role of Edwards and Baldwin, see Jonathan Edwards [Jr] to Ebenezer Baldwin, New Haven, Jan. 5. 1774 and Jan. 17, 1774 (with postscript from Feb. 2. 1774), in Jonathan Edwards Papers, Beinecke Library, box 26 (available online at https://collections.library.yale.edu/catalog/10956664), cited in Kenneth Pieter Minkema, "The Edwardses: A Ministerial Family in Eighteenth-Century New England," (PhD diss., University of Connecticut, 1988), 522n110. See also Ericson, "When God Ceased Winking."

73. "Philemon," *Connecticut Journal* (New Haven), 7 January 1774 to 7 February 1774 (the final installment included two separate pieces, one directed specifically to "Antidoulious"); Jonathan Edwards [Jr] to Ebenezer Baldwin, New Haven, Jan. 17. 1774 (postscript from Feb. 2. 1774), Jonathan Edwards Papers, Beinecke Library, box 26.

74. The Connecticut petition, which shares much of the language from the Massachusetts petitions from June 1773, appears in *Providence Gazette*, 22 October 1774. The law of slavery in Connecticut involved the same ambiguities as in Massachusetts; see Margaret Ellen Newell, *Brethren by Nature: New England Indians, Colonists, and the Origins of American Slavery* (Ithaca, NY: Cornell University Press, 2015), 247–53.

75. "Liberty," *Connecticut Gazette*, 28 October 1774; "Antidoulios," *Connecticut Courant* (Hartford), 12 September 1774; "Philander," *Supplement to the Connecticut Journal* (New Haven), 16 September 1774; "Philander," *Supplement to the Connecticut Journal*, 23 September 1774; "Antidoulios," *Connecticut Courant* (Hartford), 10 October 1774. "An Act for Prohibiting the Importation of Indian, Negro or Molatto Slaves," in Hoadly, *Public Records Connecticut*, 329 (October 1774); *Connecticut Gazette*, 2 December 1774.

76. John Saillant, "'Some Thoughts on the Subject of Freeing the Negro Slaves in the Colony of Connecticut, Humbly Offered to the Consideration of All Friends of Liberty and Justice,' by Levi Hart, with a Response from Samuel Hopkins," *NEQ* 57 (March 2002): 107–28 (quotations from 115, bracketed insertion by Saillant).

77. The preamble is extracted in W. E. Burghardt Du Bois, *Suppression of the African Slave-Trade to the United States of America, 1638–1870* (New York: Longmans, Green, 1896), appendix A, 222; Morgan, *Birth of the Republic*, 96; Nash, *Race and Revolution*, 11.

78. "At a Town-Meeting Held at Providence," *Providence Gazette*, 21 May 1774. On Moses Brown's role and the limitations of law, see DuBois, *Suppression of the African Slave-Trade*, 36, 222; Drake, *Quakers and Slavery in America*, 89; Mack Thompson, *Moses Brown: Reluctant Reformer* (Chapel Hill: University of North Carolina Press, 1962), 97–98; John Wood Sweet,

Bodies Politic: Negotiating Race in the American North, 1730–1830 (Baltimore: Johns Hopkins University Press, 2003), 243–45. On slavery in Rhode Island, see Christy Clark-Pujara, *Dark Work: The Business of Slavery in Rhode Island* (New York: New York University Press, 2016).

79. Samuel Hopkins to Levi Hart, Newport, 25 January 1775, excerpted in Saillant, "'Some Thoughts on Freeing the Negro Slaves,'" 127–28. Hopkins's letter was referring to Connecticut, but his logic must have applied to Rhode Island as well.

80. *Journals of the Continental Congress* (hereafter *JCC*, [vol. #]), vol. 1:71 (14 October 1774); Taylor, *American Revolutions*, 128; [Richard Wells], *A Few Political Reflections Submitted to the Consideration of the British Colonies, by a Citizen of Philadelphia* (Philadelphia: John Dunlap, 1774), 83. For similar hopes, see also *Connecticut Gazette* (New London), 9 September 1774.

81. [Thomas Jefferson], *A Summary View of the Rights of British America* . . . (Philadelphia: John Dunlap, 1774), 16.

82. Wood, *Power and Liberty*, 108. As evidence for the claim that many Virginia patriots hoped independence would facilitate manumission reform, Wood cites an article by James H. Kettner about Robert Pleasants. However, Pleasants was a Quaker pacifist who initially opposed independence and hoped for manumission reform within the British Empire; he was hardly reflective of typical Virginia patriots. See Kettner, "Persons or Property? The Pleasants Slaves in Virginia Courts, 1792–1799," in *Launching the "Extended Republic": The Federalist Era*, ed. Ronald Hoffman and Peter J. Albert (Charlottesville: University of Virginia Press, 1996), 136–55.

83. Staughton Lynd and David Waldstreicher, "Free Trade, Sovereignty, and Slavery: Toward an Economic Interpretation of American Independence," *WMQ* 68 (October 2011): 597–630, 618. (Lynd and Waldstreicher refer to Jefferson's rough draft of the Declaration of Independence, but their assessment can also be applied to *A Summary View*.) On patriots' antislavery posturing, see also Davis, *Slavery in the Age of Revolution*, 169–84; and Peter A. Dorsey, "To 'Corroborate Our Own Claims': Public Positioning and the Slavery Metaphor in Revolutionary America," *American Quarterly* 55 (September 2003): 353–86, esp. 372–73. On Jefferson and slavery, see especially Peter S. Onuf, *The Mind of Thomas Jefferson* (Charlottesville: University of Virginia Press, 2007); and Christa Dierksheide, "'The Great Improvement and Civilization of That Race': Jefferson and the 'Amelioration' of Slavery, ca. 1770–1826," *Early American Studies* 6, (Spring 2008): 165–97.

84. William Allen, *The American Crisis: A Letter, Addressed by Permission to the Earl Gower, Lord President of the Council* . . . (London: T. Cadell, 1774), 13; Granville Sharp, *A Declaration of the People's Natural Right to a Share in the Legislature, Which is the Fundamental Principle of the British Constitution of State* (Philadelphia: reprinted by John Dunlap, 1774), 18n25. Although it is unlikely that Jefferson had read Sharp's pamphlet—which Benjamin Franklin sent to the colonies on 27 July 1774—he was clearly aware of similar criticism. Benjamin Franklin to Thomas Cushing, 27 July 1774," *FO*: https://founders.archives.gov/documents/Franklin/01-21-02-0135.

85. Rush to Granville Sharp, 1 November 1774, in John A. Woods, "The Correspondence of Benjamin Rush and Granville Sharp 1773–1809," *Journal of American Studies* 1 (April 1967):1–38, quotation from 13;Wood, *Power and Liberty*, 110; Robert G. Parkinson, *The Common Cause: Creating Race and Nation in the American Revolution* (Chapel Hill: University of North Carolina Press, 2016), 7. See also Morgan, *Birth of the Republic*, 96–97; Sean Wilentz, *No Property in Man: Slavery and Antislavery at the Founding* (Cambridge, MA: Harvard University Press, 2018), 125; Nash, *Race and Revolution*, 9–10; Parkinson, *Thirteen Clocks*, 56.

86. Sharp, *People's Natural Right to a Share in the Legislature*, 18n25. Previously, Sharp had mocked patriots for their "shameless prostitution" of natural rights language. Granville Sharp,

A Representation of the Injustice and Dangerous Tendency of Tolerating Slavery . . . (London: printed for Benjamin White and Robert Horsfield, 1769), 87.

87. Rush to Granville Sharp, 1 November 1774, in Woods, "Correspondence of Benjamin Rush," 13. Rush did acknowledge that Georgia was not involved in the decision. Georgia's stance on the slave trade was complex, perhaps reflecting the fact that slavery had been forbidden in the earliest years of the colony. Some residents of Darien, Georgia, issued a statement condemning slavery and calling for manumissions in January 1775, but others resisted the Continental Congress's slave trade ban. See Du Bois, *Suppression of the African Slave-Trade*, 45–4; Dorsey, "To 'Corroborate Our Own Claims,'" 379.

88. Benezet to Samuel Allinson, Philadelphia, Tenth Month, 23rd, 1774, *FAB*, 321.

89. Benezet to Sharp, 18 November 1774, quoted in Bruns, *Am I Not a Man*, 351; Anthony Benezet to Granville Sharp, Philadelphia ye. 1st 5th mo April [*sic*—May] 1773 (copy), "Copies of Letters to Granville Sharp, 1763–1773," NYHS, cited in Darold W. Wax, "Reform and Revolution: The Movement Against Slavery and the Slave Trade in Revolutionary Pennsylvania," *Western Pennsylvania Historical Magazine* 57 (October 1974), 409. Benezet's comment suggests that the scale of domestic slave had warranted public notice significantly earlier than most scholars have realized. Scholars often point to a 1798 letter by Quaker Warner Mifflin as the earliest evidence of abolitionists' concern about the domestic slave trade, see: Steven Deyle, "The Irony of Liberty: The Origins of the Domestic Slave Trade," *Journal of the Early Republic*, 12 (Spring 1992), 37–62.

90. "Extract of a Letter from the Author, to a Gentleman at Philadelphia [Benjamin Rush?]" (18 July 1775), in Granville Sharp, *The Just Limitation of Slavery in the Laws of God, Compared with the Unbounded Claims of the African Traders and British American Slaveholders* (London: B. White, 1776), appendix 6, 56.

91. *Pennsylvania Packet* (Philadelphia), 9 January 1775; reprinted in *Connecticut Gazette* (New London), 3 February 1775.

92. *Essex Gazette* (Newbury-Port), 31 January 1775.

93. Dorsey, "To 'Corroborate Our Own Claims,'" 365. Patrick Rael, *Eighty-Eight Years: The Long Death of Slavery in the United States, 1777–1863* (Athens: University of Georgia Press, 2015), 56; Sinha, *Slave's Cause*, 36 (noting the essay is "often attributed to Paine").

94. [Samuel Hopkins], "African Slavery in America," *Postscript to the Pennsylvania Journal and Weekly Advertiser* (Philadelphia), 8 March 1775, in *The Writings of Thomas Paine: Vol. I, 1774–1779*, ed. Moncure Daniel Conway (New York: G. P. Putnam's Sons, 1894), 4–9 (quotation from 7–8). Conway explained that he attributed this piece to Paine based on a letter by Benjamin Rush in 1809 that referred to an unspecified antislavery essay Paine published in 1775. Paine was likely the author of a shorter antislavery piece, "A Thought" by "Humanus," which appeared in the *Pennsylvania Journal* on 18 October 1775, but not of the "African Slavery in America" essay.

The Thomas Paine National Historical Society has concluded from software analysis of the writings that the Reverend Samuel Hopkins of Rhode Island was the most likely author (with Hopkins far ahead of Benezet, the second most likely author). The society also notes there is no evidence for Conway's claim that Paine was a member of the PAS. "African Slavery in America," *Thomas Paine National Historical Association*: http://thomaspaine.org/questionable-authorship/african-slavery-in-america.html. For other scholars who have questioned Paine's authorship, see James V. Lynch, "The Limits of Revolutionary Radicalism: Tom Paine and Slavery," *PMHB* 123 (July 1999): 177–99, esp. 183.

95. [Hopkins], "African Slavery in America." Hopkins had clearly read Benezet's work; in addition to the similarities in the emancipation plan, Hopkins included a footnote citing various authors whom Benezet had anthologized in his *Some Historical Account of Guinea*. It is possible that Hopkins sent his essay to Benezet after being inspired by his book (which was available in New England), though little of Benezet's correspondence survives from the mid-1770s.

96. Wood, *Power and Liberty*, 100. See also Gordon S. Wood, *The Radicalism of the American Revolution* (New York: Random House, 1991), 186. Paul J. Polgar gives more attention to Quaker antecedents but also stresses the PAS connection to the revolution's rhetoric of natural rights and republicanism, in *Standard-Bearers of Liberty and Equality: America's First Abolition Movement* (Chapel Hill: University of North Carolina Press, 2019), esp. 11, 31–32, 36–38. My thinking about the PAS's creation and its complicated connection to Quakerism and the revolution has been strongly influenced by Sword, "Remembering Dinah Nevil," 318–33.

97. Sassi, "Legacies of James McCarty"; Amy C. Schutt and Judith L. Van Buskirk, "Gideon Moor's Road to Freedom, 1764–1777," *PMHB* 144 (January 2020): 1–28.

98. Thomas Harrison to the Committee Appointed on My Application to the Abolition Society, [after June 1784], PAS Correspondence (misfiled with letters from 1794), quotation; Samuel Allinson to [Israel] Pemberton, Burlington, 7th: 9th: mo: 1773, Parrish and Pemberton Family Papers, HSP, box 1, folder 1; PAS Minutes, 1775 April 14th, 1775 November 27. The original manuscript of the PAS meeting minutes from 1775 is held in CPW box 19 and also available on PAS microfilm. Theodore Thayer, *Israel Pemberton: King of the Quakers* (Philadelphia: Historical Society of Pennsylvania, 1943), 200; Wayne J. Eberly, "The Pennsylvania Abolition Society, 1775–1830," (PhD diss., Pennsylvania State University, 1973), 22–24.

99. Christopher Brown also suggests that New England was the only region where slavery might have still ended in the eighteenth century even if the imperial crisis had not let to war and independence. See Christopher Leslie Brown, *Moral Capital: Foundations of British Abolitionism* (Chapel Hill: University of North Carolina Press, 2006), 454.

100. Elhanan Winchester, *The Reigning Abominations, Especially the Slave Trade, Considered as Causes of Lamentation; Being the Substance of a Discourse Delivered in Fairfax County, Virginia, December 30, 1774* (London: H. Trapp, 1788), 31.

101. Robert Walker quoted in "Journal of John Hunt, 5th of the 11th mo: 1774," in *Friends' Miscellany*, Sixth Month 1831, 98. The scriptural basis of Walker's speech was likely Isaiah 28:18: "And your covenant with death shall be disannulled, and your agreement with hell shall not stand; when the overflowing scourge shall pass through, then ye shall be trodden down by it." Antebellum abolitionists such as James W. C. Pennington and William Lloyd Garrison later drew on Isaiah 28 to describe the United States Constitution as a "covenant with death and an agreement with hell." Sinha, *Slave's Cause*, 471.

Chapter 5

1. Robert Middlekauff, *The Glorious Cause: The American Revolution, 1763–1789* (New York: Oxford University Press, 1985), 274–581; Alan Taylor, *American Revolutions: A Continental History, 1750–1804* (New York: W. W. Norton, 2016), 131–311.

2. Patrick Rael, *Eighty-Eight Years: The Long Death of Slavery in the United States, 1777–1863* (Athens: University of Georgia Press, 2015), 46–69 (quotation from 48); Benjamin Quarles, *The Negro in the American Revolution* (Chapel Hill: University of North Carolina Press, 1961); Gary B. Nash, *Race and Revolution* (Madison, WI: Madison House, 1990), 57–71; Douglas Egerton, *Death or Liberty: African Americans and Revolutionary America* (New York: Oxford

University Press, 2009); 93–121; Manisha Sinha, *The Slave's Cause: A History of Abolition* (New Haven, CT: Yale University Press, 2016), 41–53; Judith L. Van Buskirk, *Standing in Their Own Light: African American Patriots in the American Revolution* (Norman: University of Oklahoma Press, 2017); Karen Cook Bell, *Running from Bondage: Enslaved Women and Their Remarkable Fight for Freedom in Revolutionary America* (New York: Cambridge University Press, 2021).

3. Bernard Bailyn, *The Ideological Origins of the American Revolution* (Cambridge, MA: Harvard University Press, 1967), 235; Gordon S. Wood, *Power and Liberty: Constitutionalism in the American Revolution* (New York: Oxford University Press, 2021), 112. Rael gives more attention than Wood does to white abolitionists and Black activism, but he similarly highlights the role of enlightened legislators, writing: "The process of general emancipation began in the midst of the Revolutionary War itself, as political leaders in select northern state began seriously to doubt the ethics and utility of seeking to liberate themselves while holding others as slaves." Rael, *Eighty-Eight Years*, 62.

4. Sinha, *Slave's Cause*, 34–53, quotation from 35.

5. Robert G. Parkinson, *Thirteen Clocks: How Race United the Colonies and Made the Declaration of Independence* (Chapel Hill: University of North Carolina Press, 2021), 2, 57, 173. See also Robert G. Parkinson, *The Common Cause: Creating Race and Nation in the American Revolution* (Chapel Hill: University of North Carolina Press, 2016), 172, 471–73, 529–533.

6. Parkinson mistakenly asserts that Samuel Hopkins's *Dialogue Concerning the Slavery of the Africans* (1776) was the "only" antislavery pamphlet published from 1775 until 1778 (*Common Cause*, 471; *Thirteen Clocks*, 57). This statement neglects antislavery pamphlets by Jabez Huntington, Isaac Foster, and others, discussed later in this chapter. Moreover, the decline of antislavery activism by Quakers has been overstated, even by specialists. For instance, Thomas Drake reports that during the Revolutionary War, "Friends turned inward, and concentrated on reforming their own Society." He treats the "few individual Quakers," like Anthony Benezet, who persisted in their activism as outliers. Thomas E. Drake, *Quakers and Slavery in America* (New Haven, CT: Yale University Press, 1950), 90; see also Arthur Zilversmit, *The First Emancipation: The Abolition of Slavery in the North* (Chicago: University of Chicago Press, 1967), 92–93.

7. John Coffey, *Exodus and Liberation: Deliverance Politics from John Calvin to Martin Luther King, Jr.* (New York: Oxford University Press, 2014), 69–70. On religion and providentialist beliefs during the war, see Perry Miller, *Nature's Nation* (Cambridge, MA: Harvard University Press, 1967), esp. 90–106; Edmund S. Morgan, "The Puritan Ethic and the American Revolution," *WMQ* 24 (January 1967): 3–43; Gordon S. Wood, *Creation of the American Republic, 1776–1787* (Chapel Hill: University of North Carolina Press, 1968), 114–18; Nicholas Guyatt, *Providence and the Invention of the United States, 1607–1876* (New York: Cambridge University Press, 2007), 95–133; Thomas S. Kidd, *God of Liberty: A Religious History of the American Revolution* (New York: Basic Books, 2010); James P. Byrd, *Sacred Scripture, Sacred War: The Bible and the American Revolution* (New York: Oxford University Press, 2013); Eran Shalev, *American Zion: The Old Testament as a Political Text from the Revolution to the Civil War* (New Haven, CT: Yale University Press, 2013), 1–6, 19; and Mark Knoll, *In the Beginning Was the Word: The Bible in American Life* (New York: Oxford University Press, 2016), 271–88.

The connection between antislavery and providentialism during the revolution has received less attention than "secular" natural rights ideology, but it is discussed in Winthrop D. Jordan, *White Over Black: American Attitudes Toward the Negro, 1550–1812* (Chapel Hill: University of North Carolina Press, 1968), 298–300; David Brion Davis *The Problem of Slavery in the Age of Revolution, 1770–1823* (Ithaca, NY: Cornell University Press, 1975), 285–98; James D. Essig, *The*

Bonds of Wickedness: American Evangelicals Against Slavery, 1770–1808 (Philadelphia: Temple University Press, 1982); Nash, *Race and Revolution*, 10; Guyatt, *Providence and Invention*, 106, 132; Christopher Leslie Brown, *Moral Capital: Foundations of British Abolitionism* (Chapel Hill: University of North Carolina Press, 2006), 167; Kidd, *God of Liberty*, 152–54; Coffey, *Exodus and Liberation*, 87–94; Byrd, *Sacred Scripture, Sacred War*, 55–62; Anthony Di Lorenzo, "A Higher Law: Transatlantic Revolution and Antislavery Radicalism in Early America," (PhD diss., Loyola University of Chicago, 2016), 83–148; and Ben Wright, *Bonds of Salvation: How Christianity Inspired and Limited American Abolitionism* (Baton Rouge: Louisiana State University Press, 2020), 22–55.

8. Elisha Rich, *A Poem upon the Bloody Engagement That Was Fought on Bunker's-Hill, at Charlestown, (in New England.) on the 17th of June 1775* ([Newburyport, MA: E. Lunt and H. W. Tinges, 1775]). The broadside poem was also printed, with several typographical errors, in Chelmsford, MA, by N. Coverly. See also Byrd, *Sacred Scripture, Sacred War*, 62; and Di Lorenzo, "Higher Law," 121.

9. William Foster, *True Fortitude Delineated: A Sermon Preached at Fags Manor, to Captain Taylor's Company of Recruits . . .* (Philadelphia: John Dunlap, 1776), 5, 6, 24. As I discuss in Chapter 6, Foster was the likely author of a proslavery petition in 1780.

10. "A Hearty Friend to All the Northern Colonies," *Connecticut Gazette* (New London), 10 September 1773 (see also 9 September 1774); [Jabez Huntington], *A Discourse on the Times* (Norwich, CT: Judah P. Spooner, 1776), 12–13. This pamphlet, attributed to Jabez Huntington by the LCP and other archives, appeared under the pseudonym "A Hearty Friend to All the Colonies" and is similar in substance to the earlier essays in the *Connecticut Gazette* by "A Hearty Friend to All the Northern Colonies." Despite going through three editions, the pamphlet has drawn little notice from scholars, but see Kidd, *God of Liberty*, 154; and Thomas N. Ingersoll, *The Loyalist Problem in Revolutionary New England* (New York: Cambridge University Press, 2016), 229.

11. Brown, *Moral Capital*, 2. Davis also emphasizes the difficulty facing abolitionists, even in the North, in *Slavery in the Age of Revolution*, 87–89, 163–69, 255–57, 262, 285–86, 299–319.

12. Abiel Leonard, *A Prayer, Composed for the Benefit of the Soldiery, in the American Army, to Assist Them in Their Private Devotions; and Recommended to Their Particular Use* (Cambridge, MA: S. & E. Hall, 1775), 7; *New-England Chronicle* (Cambridge, MA), 13 July 1775 (and widely republished); John Locke, *Two Treatises of Government*, ed. Peter Laslett ([1690] New York: Cambridge University Press, 1988), 386 (book 2, chap. 16, par. 176), see also 427 (book 2, chap. 19, par. 241–42); *Connecticut Courant* (Hartford), 27 February 1775. See also *New-York Journal*, 12 January 1775.

13. *JCC*, 2:87–88 (12 June 1775, establishing a fast on 20 July 1775). The proclamations were published in handbills and in newspapers throughout the colonies; see for example *Pennsylvania Evening Post* (Philadelphia), 16 June 1776; *Massachusetts Spy* (Boston), 28 June 1775.

14. Antislavery sermons on fast days were rare enough that most scholarship on wartime fast days ignores them entirely. Scholars of antislavery, meanwhile, have discussed some of sources cited with little reference to state and national fast days, context that helps elucidate the role of providentialism in abolitionist thought. On the wartime fast days, see William DeLoss Love, *The Fast and Thanksgiving Days of New England* (Boston: Houghton, Mifflin, 1895), 328–46; and Guyatt, *Providence and Invention*, 96–104.

Historians have noted that these proclamations helped the Continental Congress promote national unity while expanding its own influence and authority, but they have given little attention to the potential antislavery connection. David Waldstreicher, *In the Midst of Perpetual Fetes: The Making of American Nationalism, 1776–1820* (Chapel Hill: University of North Carolina Press, 1997), 34–35; Benjamin H. Irvin, *Clothed in the Robes of Sovereignty: The Continental Congress and the People Out of Doors* (New York: Oxford University Press, 2011), 109–14; Spencer W. McBride, *Pulpit and Nation: Clergymen and the Politics of Revolutionary America* (Charlottesville: University of Virginia Press, 2016), 11–37.

15. Jacob Duché, *The Duty of Standing Fast in Our Spiritual and Temporal Liberties, a Sermon, Preached in Christ-Church, July 7th, 1775. Before the First Battalion of the City and Liberties of Philadelphia* . . . (Philadelphia: James Humphreys Jr., 1775), 16–17; Jacob Duché, *The American Vine, a Sermon, Preached in Christ-Church, Philadelphia, Before the Honourable Continental Congress, July 20th, 1775. Being the Day Recommended by Them for a General Fast* . . . (Philadelphia: James Humphreys Jr., 1775), iii, 32. For Duché's anti-Quaker sentiments, see Edward Duffield Neill, "Rev. Jacob Duché: The First Chaplain of Congress," *PMHB* 2 (1878): 58–73.

16. P. P. Sandiford, *Memoirs of Mr. Wesley's Missionaries to America: Compiled from Authentic Sources* (New York: G. Lane & P. P. Sandiford, 1843), 233; Samuel Andrews, *A Discourse, Shewing the Necessity of Joining Internal Repentance, with the External Profession of It. Delivered upon the General Fast, July 20th. 1775* (New Haven, CT: Thomas and Samuel Green, 1775), 14. Essig, *Bonds of Wickedness*, 22.

17. Abigail Adams to John Adams, October 25, 1775, *FO*: https://founders.archives.gov/documents/Adams/04-01-02-0206.

18. Freeborn Garrettson, *The Experience and Travels of Mr. Freeborn Garrettson, Minister of the Methodist-Episcopal Church in North-America* (Philadelphia: Crukshank, 1791), 25, 31, 33–34, 70. John Wesley, *Thoughts upon Slavery: Reprinted in Philadelphia, with Notes,* [ed. Anthony Benezet] (Philadelphia: Joseph Crukshank, 1774). On Garrettson, see also Donald G. Matthews, *Slavery and Methodism: A Chapter in American Morality, 1780–1845* (Princeton, NJ: Princeton University Press, 1965), 26, 54–55; Essig, *Bonds of Wickedness*, 55–56, 71–72; Christopher Cannon Jones, "Freeborn Garrettson's Revolution: Religion and the American War for Independence," in *A Companion to American Religious History*, ed. Benjamin E. Park (New York: Wiley-Blackwell, 2021), 71–86.

19. Richard Allen, *The Life, Experience, and Gospel Labours of the Rt. Rev. Richard Allen* . . . (Philadelphia: Martin & Boden: 1833), 7–8; Richard S. Newman, *Freedom's Prophet: Bishop Richard Allen, the AME Church, and the Black Founding Fathers* (New York: New York University Press, 2008).

20. "A Serious Thought," *Pennsylvania Journal and Weekly Advertiser* (Philadelphia), 18 October 1775, in *The Writings of Thomas Paine: Vol I, 1774–1779*, ed. Moncure Daniel Conway (New York: G. P. Putnam's Sons, 1894), 65–66. As noted in the previous chapter, specialists no longer believe that Paine authored an earlier antislavery piece, "African Slavery in America," but think his authorship of "A Serious Thought" is more likely. See James V. Lynch, "The Limits of Revolutionary Radicalism: Tom Paine and Slavery," *PMHB* 123 (July 1999): 177–99, esp. 186–88.

21. PYM to VYM, Philadelphia, 30th of the 9th month 1775 (draft), PYM Miscellaneous 1775:20; PYM Minutes Vol. 2, 331 (29 9m 1775), 354 (27 9mo 1776). In 1774, the PYM had appointed a committee to revisit the 1758 policy against buying or selling slaves and calling for manumissions. The revised policy strengthened the punishment for buying or selling a slave to full disownment; it also encouraged monthly meeting committees to put more pressure on the remaining slaveholding members to liberate their bondspeople. PYM Minutes Vol. 2, 315

(1 10mo 1774); Drake, *Quakers and Slavery in America*, 72; Jean R. Soderlund, *Quakers and Slavery: A Divided Spirit* (Princeton, NJ: Princeton University Press, 1985), 102–103.

22. Statistics from Gary B. Nash and Jean R. Soderlund, *Freedom by Degrees: Emancipation in Pennsylvania and Its Aftermath* (New York: Oxford University Press, 1991), 64, 81. When the monthly meetings compiled manumission books beginning in 1776, they included many manumissions from 1775 but few from the earlier years. The pre-1775 manumissions entered into the PQM's book dealt with special circumstances that had attracted or required the attention of monthly meetings at the time (such as Quakers who had purchased slaves after 1758 and were thus required to free them in order to remain in good standing). The manumissions collected by Philadelphia Quakers are available through PMM, Philadelphia Manumission Book [1772–1786], Haverford and online through Quakers and Slavery at https://digitalcollections.tricolib.brynmawr.edu/object/hc135523#page/1/mode/1up; and PQM, "The Original Papers of Manumission by the Monthly Meetings Composing the Quarterly Meeting of Philadelphia," Haverford and online through Quakers and Slavery at http://triptych.brynmawr.edu/cdm/ref/collection/HC_QuakSlav/id/9585.

23. In two other cases, Waln expedited the manumissions of slaves whose masters had died. For example, after his wife inherited a Black youth named Peter who was scheduled to be liberated at age thirty-one, Waln enacted a new manumission in 1774 liberating him at age twenty-one. PMM, Philadelphia Manumission Book, 163 (for Waln's manumission of Peter); PQM, "Original Papers of Manumission."

24. Petition of the Inhabitants of Chesterfield to the New Jersey Legislature, November 9th 1775, in Clement Price, ed. *Freedom Not Far Distant: A Documentary History of Afro-Americans in New Jersey* (Newark: New Jersey Historical Society, 1980), 56. The manuscript petition is reproduced in Sue Kozel, "Black Lives Matter in the Past and Present," *NJEA Review* (October 2020): 32–35, 34. For legislative inaction, see *Minutes of the Provincial Congress and the Council of Safety of the State of New Jersey* (Trenton, NJ: Naar, Day & Naar, 1879), 287 (20 November 1775), 294–95 (23 November 1775), 308 (30 November 1775); *The Ancient Testimony and Principles of the People Called Quakers . . . Touching the Commotions Now Prevailing in These and Other Parts of America . . .* ([Philadelphia, 1776]), 1–2. See also PMS Minutes Vol 2, 19–21 (31 8mo 1775), 53 (19 January 1776); *The Epistle from the Meeting for Sufferings in London, To Friends and Brethren in New-England* ([Philadelphia, 1775]), 2. On resistance to antislavery agitation in New Jersey, see James J. Gigantino II, *The Ragged Road to Abolition: Slavery and Freedom in New Jersey, 1775–1865* (Philadelphia: University of Pennsylvania Press, 2025), 25–63.

25. Neither PMS nor PYM records refer to the petition, so it is unclear if Quakers were involved. The petition was presumably in favor of emancipation, though without the text we cannot be sure (it is possible for example, that it was from slaveholders complaining about the rise in Quaker manumissions). Pennsylvania's legislative journals simply indicate that the petition was signed by "a considerable Number of Inhabitants of the City of *Philadelphia*." *Votes and Proceedings of the House of Representatives of the Province of Pennsylvania, January 7, 1771—September 26, 1776*, vol. 8 of Pennsylvania Archives, 8th Series, ed. Charles F. Hoban (1935), 7471 (3 April 1776), 7510 (6 April 1776).

26. *Essex Journal* (Middlebury-Port), 8 March 1776, also transcribed in Joshua Coffin, *A Sketch of the History of Newbury, Newburyport, and West Newbury, from 1635 to 1845* (Boston: S. G. Drake, 1845), 340–42.

27. The bill and the essay by "A Friend to America" appear in *Providence Gazette*, 9 September 1775; "A Sincere Friend to the Community," *Newport Mercury*, 18 September 1775; Zilversmit, *First Emancipation*, 106–7.

28. Samuel Hopkins to Thomas Cushing, 29 December 1775, *FO*: https://founders.archives.gov/documents/Adams/06-03-02-0196.

29. [Jabez Huntington], *A Discourse on the Times*, 2nd ed. (Norwich, CT: Judah P. Spooner, 1776), 5, 2, 4, 13, 15, 16. (The reference to the defeat at Quebec was not included in the first edition; otherwise the text was largely the same.) See also Kidd, *God of Liberty*, 154.

30. Van Buskirk, *Standing in Their Own Light*, 53–54; Peter Maslowski, "National Policy Toward the Use of Black Troops in the Revolution," *South Carolina Historical Magazine* 73 (January 1972): 1–17, esp. 3–5; Eric G. Grundset, et al., eds., *Forgotten Patriots: African American and American Indian Patriots in the Revolutionary War: A Guide to Service, Sources and Studies* (Daughters of the American Revolution, 2008), available online at https://www.dar.org/library/forgotten-patriots/forgotten-patriots-book; Alan Taylor, *The Internal Enemy: Slavery and War in Virginia, 1772–1832* (New York: W. W. Norton, 2013). On the ubiquity of patriot propaganda stoking racial fear of nonwhite British proxies, see Parkinson, *Common Cause*; Parkinson, *Thirteen Clocks*.

31. *JCC*, 4:208–9 (emphasis added, 16 March 1776, establishing a fast day on 17 May 1776); *An Apology for the People Called Quakers, Containing Some Reasons, for Their not Complying with Human Injunctions and Institutions in Matters Relative to the Worship of God* (Philadelphia: Joseph Crukshank, 1776), 3; PMS Minutes Vol. 2, 79–80 (27 4mo 1776); Jack D. Marietta, *Reformation of American Quakerism, 1748–1783* (Philadelphia: University of Pennsylvania Press, 1984), 231.

32. Ezra Stiles and Samuel Hopkins, *To the Public . . . Newport, April 10, 1776* ([Newport, RI, 1776]), 8; also in *Massachusetts Spy*, 10 and 17 July 1776.

33. [Samuel Hopkins], *A Dialogue Concerning the Slavery of the Africans: Shewing It to Be the Duty and Interest of the American States to Emancipate All Their African Slaves: With an Address to the Owners of Such Slaves: Dedicated to the Honourable Continental Congress* (Norwich, CT: Judah P. Spooner, 1776), iii, iv, 6, 36, 45, 50, 53, 63. The *Connecticut Gazette* (New-London) described Hopkin's *Dialogue* as "just published" on 16 August 1776, but it appears that he wrote it before the Declaration of Independence, as the pamphlet makes no mention of it. A later edition of Hopkins's pamphlet states it was first published "early in the year 1776." Samuel Hopkins, *A Dialogue Concerning the Slavery of the Africans . . .*, 2nd ed. (New York: Robert Hodge, 1785), 8.

34. [Hopkins], *Dialogue*, 21, 23, 24, 54. The continuity of antislavery biblicism has been obscured by scholars who fail to recognize the way Samuel Sewall and other early abolitionists used the New Testament—especially Ephesians 2:14—to universalize the Old Testament's protections for Hebrew servants. For example, Eran Shalev asserts that "abolitionists such as New Divinity theologian Samuel Hopkins could transcend earlier reliance on the Old Testament (evident in Samuel Sewall's *The Selling of Joseph* [1700]) and emphasize Jesus—and the New Testament—in revolutionary-era attacks on slavery" (*American Zion*, 153). Hopkins's providentialist arguments used contemporary examples, but the biblicist and providentialist basis of his abolitionism was far from new.

35. Duché recanted his support for independence and returned to Britain after the British captured Philadelphia in 1777; Rankin returned there in 1778; and Andrews was put under house arrest after being deemed "*unfriendly to his country*" and moved to Canada after the war.

See Neill, "Rev. Jacob Duché"; Franklin Bowditch Dexter, *Biographical Sketches of the Graduates of Yale College with Annals of the College History, Vol. II: May 1745-May 1763* (New York: Henry Holt, 1896), 568–69; and Sandiford, *Memoirs of Wesley's Missionaries*, 238.

36. "A Lover and Friend of Mankind," *An Affectionate Address to the Inhabitants of the British Colonies* ([Philadelphia], 1776), iv, 40, 44. The author also praised Congress for banning stage plays in Philadelphia.

37. "Declaration of Independence: A Transcription," LOC: https://www.archives.gov/founding-docs/declaration-transcript.

38. On the purpose and limitations of the declaration, see also John Phillip Reid, "The Irrelevance of the Declaration," in *Law in the American Revolution and the Revolution in the Law*, ed. Hendrik Hartog (New York: New York University Press, 1981), 46–89; Peter S. Onuf, "A Declaration of Independence for Diplomatic Historians," in *The Mind of Thomas Jefferson* (Charlottesville: University of Virginia Press, 2007), 65–81; Eric Slauter, "Rights," in *Oxford Handbook of the American Revolution*, ed. Edward G. Gray and Jane Kamensky (New York: Oxford University Press, 2013), 447–64, esp. 458. In *White Over Black* (esp. 279–90, 310, 342–52, 482–569), Jordan argues thar only the growth of racist ideologies can explain the failure of the revolution's natural rights principles to lead to abolition. By contrast, Davis has stressed that there was "no automatic connection between a defense of natural rights [in the American Revolution] and the imperative that slavery be abolished." Davis, *Slavery in the Age of Revolution*, 262. For Davis's critique of Jordan's overemphasis on racism, see ibid., 14, 255–56.

39. Virginian Declaration of Rights, quoted, with emphasis added, in Eva Sheppard Wolf, *Race and Liberty in the New Nation: Emancipation in Virginia from the Revolution to Nat Turner* (Baton Rouge: Louisiana State University Press, 2006), 4–5.

40. *Minutes of the Provincial Congress and the Council of Safety of the State of New Jersey*, 572 (11 August 1775).

41. François Furstenberg, "Beyond Slavery and Freedom: Autonomy, Agency, and Resistance in Early American Political Discourse," *JAH* 89 (March 2003), 1295–1330, quotation from 1297.

42. Woody Holton, *Forced Founders: Indians, Debtors, Slaves, and the Making of the American Revolution* (Chapel Hill: University of North Carolina Press, 1999) 158; David Waldstreicher, *Slavery's Constitution: From Revolution to Ratification* (New York: Hill and Wang, 2009), 46–47; Parkinson, *Common Cause*, 244–63.

43. [John Dickinson], *An Essay of a Frame of Government for Pennsylvania* (Philadelphia: James Humphreys Jr., 1776), 16; Jane E. Calvert, "An Expansive Conception of Rights: The Quakerly Abolitionism of John Dickinson," in *"When in the Course of Human Events": 1776 at Home, Abroad, and in American Memory*, ed. Will R. Jordan (Macon, GA: Mercer University Press, 2018), 21–54, 38.

44. Constitution of Pennsylvania, September 28, 1776, Avalon Project: https://avalon.law.yale.edu/18th_century/pa08.asp. Although Parkinson does not specifically discuss the Pennsylvania Constitution, its preamble supports his argument in *Common Cause* and *Thirteen Clocks* about the role of racialized fear in promoting white patriot unity.

45. *JCC*, 4:258 (6 April 1776).

46. *JCC*, 5:549 (12 July 1776).

47. Woody Holton notes these revisions in *Liberty Is Sweet: The Hidden History of the American Revolution* (New York: Simon & Schuster, 2021), 247; however, his discussion of antislavery progress during the revolution largely neglects the role of religion.

48. George Henry Moore, *Notes on the History of Slavery in Massachusetts* (New York: D. Appleton, 1866), 148–53; *Journals of the House of Representatives of Massachusetts*, 52: 105 (13 September 1776), 106 (14 September 1776), 127 (19 October 1776).

49. *Independent Chronicle* (Boston), 10 October 1776; "A Son of Liberty," *Independent Chronicle* (Boston), 28 November 1776; Moore, *Notes on the History of Slavery*, 177.

50. Jonathan D. Sassi, "'This Whole Country Have Their Hands Full of Blood This Day': Transcription and Introduction of an Antislavery Sermon Manuscript Attributed to the Reverend Samuel Hopkins," *Proceedings of the American Antiquarian Society* 112 (June 2004): 29–92, quotations from 63, 66, 71, 90, 91. Sassi suggests that this sermon was most likely delivered sometime between August and early December 1776 based on events to which the sermon referred. I conclude it was a fast-day sermon based on its style and substance, and the November fast day (announced in the *Providence Gazette*, 9 November 1776) fits the timing.

51. Ruth Bogin, "'The Battle of Lexington': A Patriotic Ballad by Lemuel Haynes," *WMQ* 42 (October 1985):499–606, quotations from 501, 502, 505, 506. On Haynes, see also John Saillant, *Black Puritan, Black Republican: The Life and Thought of Lemuel Haynes, 1753–1833* (New York: Oxford University Press, 2002), esp. 15–40; Sinha, *Slave's Cause*, 44–46.

52. Ruth Bogin, "'Liberty Further Extended': A 1776 Antislavery Manuscript by Lemuel Haynes," *WMQ* 40 (January 1983): 85–105, quotations from 100, 102, 103, 104. Bogin suggest that Haynes initially drafted his manuscript before the Declaration of Independence and added the epitaph later.

53. Benezet to Henry Laurens, [Philadelphia] 12th mo. 1776, *FAB*, 324–25; [Benjamin Rush], *An Address to the Inhabitants of the British Colonies in America, Upon Slave-Keeping* (Norwich, CT: Judah P. Spooner, 1775), 24 (for advertisements see New London's *Connecticut Gazette*, 25 October 1776, 1 November 1776); *The Strange and Remarkable Swansey Vision; Or, a Dream That Was Dreamed Above Forty Years Ago . . .* (Salem, MA: E. Russell, 1776), 5, cited in Jennifer Egloff, "Revelation and the American Revolution: Understanding and Justifying War with Britain through Personal Prophecy and Biblical Exegesis," American Philosophical Society and David Center for the American Revolution Seminar, 24 January 2024 (cited with permission). The unnamed author of the *Swansey Vision* was likely a Quaker, based on the reference to the vision occurring during the "eleventh month."

54. [Jabez Huntington], *A Discourse on the Times*, 3rd ed. (Norwich, CT: Trumbull, 1777), 3. Huntington preserved his anonymity but added a brief preface to the pamphlet (referring now to "states") while leaving the rest of the text unchanged. For an advertisement, see *Norwich Packet*, 3 March 1777.

55. Elam Potter, *A Second Warning to America* (Hartford: Hannah Watson, 1777), 13. I thank Jennifer Egloff for pointing me to this source.

56. *Connecticut Courant* (Hartford), 19 May 1777; *Massachusetts Spy* (Worcester), 9 January 1777.

57. Granville Sharp, *The Just Limitation of Slavery in the Laws of God, Compared with the Unbounded Claims of the African Traders and British American Slaveholders* (London: B. White, 1776); Granville Sharp, *The Law of Liberty, or, Royal Law, by Which All Mankind Will Certainly Be Judged! Earnestdly Recommended to the Serious Consideration of All Slaveholders and Slave-dealers* (London: B. White, 1776); Granville Sharp, *The Law of Passive Obedience: Or Christian Submission to Personal Injuries: Wherein Is Shewn, That the Several Texts of Scripture, Which Command the Entire Submission of Servants or Slaves to Their Masters, Cannot Authorize the*

Latter to Exact and Involuntary Servitude, nor, in the Least Degree, Justify the Claims of Modern Slaveholders ([London: B. White], 1776).

58. Granville Sharp, *The Law of Retribution: Or, a Serious Warning to Great Britain and Her Colonies, Founded on Unquestionable Examples of God's Temporal Vengeance Against Tyrants, Slave-holders, and Oppressors* (London: W. Richardson, 1776), 3, 7, 19–20. Davis, *Slavery in the Age of Revolution*, 393; Brown, *Moral Capital*, 177–82.

59. Sharp, *Law of Retribution*, 305, for Jeremiah 34 see 16–20, 169–84, 202–4.

60. James Oglethorpe to Granville Sharp, Cranham Hall, [September 1776], in Prince Hoare, ed., *Memoirs of Granville Sharp, Esq., Composed from His Own Manuscripts and Other Authentic Documents . . .* (London: Henry Colburn, 1820), 155–56; Oglethorpe to Sharp, Cranham Hall, Oct. 13, 1776, ibid., 157–59; John Fletcher, *The Bible and the Sword, or, The Appointment of the General Fast Vindicated* (London: R. Hawes, 1776), 8–9, 21. See also Byrd, *Sacred Scripture, Sacred War*, 118–20; Brown, *Moral Capital*, 194–200, 294, 308–11.

61. Isaac Foster, *Discourse Upon Extortion: Wherein It Is Shewn . . . That by Enslaving the Negroes, the American States Are Become Guilty of the Worst Kind of Extortion* (Hartford: Ebenezer Watson, 1777), 3, 4, 5, 11, 13. Only a single copy of this pamphlet survives, and of its ten sections, two are damaged and four are missing. Thus it has largely escaped the notice of most historians; for exceptions, see Monica C. Reed, "They Are Men, and Not Beasts: Religion and Slavery in Colonial New England," (PhD diss. Florida State University, 2013), 156–58; Ingersoll, *Loyalist Problem*, 229. On the conditions of POWs during the war, see T. Cole Jones, *Captives of Liberty: Prisoners of War and the Politics of Vengeance in the American Revolution* (Philadelphia: University of Pennsylvania Press, 2019).

62. "Antibiastes," *Observations on the Slaves and the Indented Servants, Inlisted in the Army, and in the Navy of the United States* (Philadelphia: Styner and Cist, 1777). *Observations* was advertised in the *Pennsylvania Evening Post* (Philadelphia), 4 September 1777, and its text was reprinted in the *Maryland Journal* (Baltimore), 7 October 1777, and the *Boston Gazette*, 13 October 1777. See also Parkinson, *Common Cause*, 366–67.

63. Marietta, *Reformation of American Quakerism*, 215–48; PMS Minutes Vol. 2, 174–83 (16 9mo 1778).

64. *An Address to the Inhabitants of Pennsylvania, by Those Freemen, of the City of Philadelphia, Who Are Now Confined in the Mason's Lodge . . .* (Philadelphia: Robert Bell, 1777), 6. This pamphlet, published by Quakers, contained the relevant official documents and the Quakers' petitions complaining of their treatment. Spanktown was a nickname for Rahway, NJ—referring to when an early settler had publicly disciplined his wife—and Quakers would not have used the slang, as they pointed out in their response to the forgery. See also PMS Minutes Vol. 2, 128–29 (8 9mo 1777); Paige L. Whidbee, "The Quaker Exiles: 'The Cause of Every Inhabitant,'" *Pennsylvania History* 83 (Winter 2016): 28–57; Marietta, *Reformation of American Quakerism*, 240–43, 253–54; Sydney V. James, *A People Among Peoples: Quaker Benevolence in Eighteenth-Century America* (Cambridge, MA: University of Harvard Press, 1963), 242–46.

65. Theodore G. Tappert, ed., *The Notebook of a Colonial Clergyman: Condensed from the Journals of Henry Melchior Muhlenberg* (Philadelphia: Fortress Press, 1975), 179 (16 September 1777), 180 (20 September 1777); and John Pemberton, *The Life and Travels of John Pemberton: Minister of the Gospel of Christ*, ed. W. H., Jun (London: Harles Gilpin, 1844), 76 (7 9mo 1777).

66. Henry Drinker to Elizabeth Drinker, Winchester, 10 mo. 12, 1777 and 11 mo. 20, 1777, Henry Drinker Correspondence, 1777–1778, Haverford. On the Drinkers, see also Richard

Godbeer, *World of Trouble: A Philadelphia Quaker Family's Journey Through the American Revolution* (New York: New York University Press, 2019).

67. Jeanne M. Pickering, "Suing Slavery: The Essex County Freedom Suits, 1765–1783," (master's thesis, Salem State University: 2018), 65–77. Parsons later became chief justice and explained the history of freedom suits as part of an 1808 ruling: "Several negroes, born in this country, of imported slaves, demanded their freedom of their masters by suit at law, and obtained it by a judgment of court. The defence of the master was faintly made, for such was the temper of the times, that a restless, discontented slave was worth little; and when his freedom was obtained, in a course of legal proceedings, the master was not holden for his future support, if he became poor." As Parsons noted, freedom suits contained a silver lining for slaveholders by exempting them from the security bond established by the 1703 manumission law. "The Inhabitants of Winchendon, Plaintiffs in Error, Versus the Inhabitants of Hatfield," in Dudley Atkins Tyng, ed., *Reports of Cases Argued and Determined in the Supreme Judicial Court of the Commonwealth of Massachusetts, Vol. IV.* (Boston: Charles C. Little and James Brown, 1851),127, cited in Pickering, "Suing Slavery," 69.

68. Thomas Pemberton to Belknap, Boston, March 12, 1795, "Letters and Documents Relating to Slavery in Massachusetts," *Collections of the Massachusetts Historical Society Vol. III—Fifth Series* (Boston: MHS, 1877), 392–93. The town of Wilmington (in Middlesex County), for example, voted to waive (at least temporarily) the bond requirement for manumissions in March 1777; see Edward L. Bell, *Persistence of Memories of Slavery and Emancipation in Historical Andover* (Boston: Shawsheen Press, 2021), 148.

69. Elaine MacEachern, "Emancipation of Slavery in Massachusetts: A Reexamination 1770–1790," *Journal of Negro History* 55 (October 1970): 289–306, esp. 299; Gloria McCahon Whiting, "Emancipation Without the Courts or Constitution: The Case of Revolutionary Massachusetts," *Slavery & Abolition* 41 (November 2020): 458–78, esp. 464 (quotation), 465, 467.

70. Bestes's name appeared on the printed circular letter from 20 April 1773, discussed in Chapter 4. Unfortunately, the extant copies of the petitions submitted by black activists from 1773 to 1775 do not contain the subscribers' names, so we cannot determine if any more of the eight subscribers in 1777 endorsed an earlier petition. For the 1777 petition submitted to the legislature with signatures (or marks), see Lancaster Hill, Peter Bess [i.e., Bestes, who made his mark], Bruster Slenfen, Prince Hall, Jack Peirpint, Nero Funelo, Newport Summer, and Job Look, "To the Honourable Council & House of Representatives for the State of Massachusetts . . . January 13th, 1777," Massachusetts Anti-Slavery and Anti-Segregation Petitions; Massachusetts Archives Collection: http://nrs.harvard.edu/urn-3:FHCL:13906064. Although the petition was written in January, the legislature did not consider it until March. See also Chernoh M. Sesay Jr., "The Revolutionary Black Roots of Slavery's Abolition in Massachusetts," *NEQ* 87 (March 2014): 99–131, esp. 126, 128–29; Christopher Cameron, *To Plead Our Own Cause: African Americans in Massachusetts and the Making of the Antislavery Movement* (Kent, OH: Kent State University Press, 2011), 64–65; and Grant Stanton, "The Freedom Petitions: Black Patriotism, Black Politics, and the Abolition of Slavery in Massachusetts, 1773–1783," *EAS* (Spring 2024): 262–304, esp. 295–99.

71. Samuel Webster, *A Sermon Preached Before the Honorable Council, and the Honorable House of Representatives, of the State of Massachusetts-Bay, in New-England. At Boston, May 28, 1777 . . .* (Boston: Edes and Gill, 1777), 37; William Gordon, *Independent Chronicle* (Boston), 15 May 1777; Timothy Pickering Sr. to My Brethren in the 13 United American Colonies or

States, Salem N.E. June 4, 1777, *Proceedings of the Massachusetts Historical Society*, Vol. 53 (Boston: MHS, 1920), 22–23, cited in Stanton, "Freedom Petitions," 286.

72. The two bills are reproduced in Moore, *Notes on the History of Slavery*,182–85; for legislative proceedings, see *JHRM* 52:274 (18 March 1777) and *JHRM* 53: 19 (9 June 1777), 25 (13 June 1777).

73. James Warren to John Adams, Boston June 22d: 1777, *FO*, https://founders.archives.gov/documents/Adams/06-05-02-0139; John Adams to James Warren, Phyladelphia July 7. 1777, *FO*, https://founders.archives.gov/documents/Adams/06-05-02-0145; Zilversmit, *First Emancipation*, 111; Stanton, "Freedom Petitions," 297.

74. Joseph Prout of Scarborough in the County of Cumberland, 19th Septr Anno Domini 1777, Massachusetts Anti-Slavery and Anti-Segregation Petitions Dataverse, Harvard: https://iiif.lib.harvard.edu/manifests/view/drs:50257741$1i. *JHRMA* 53:86.

75. "Vermont Constitution," in Roger Bruns, ed., *Am I Not a Man and a Brother: The Anti-slavery Crusade of Revolutionary America, 1688–1788* (New York: Chelsea House, 1977), 429–32; Rael, *Eighty-Eight Years*, 64. See also John H. Watson, "In Re Vermont Constitution of 1777, As Regards Its Adoption, and Its Declaration Forbidding Slavery; and Subsequent Existence of Slavery Within the Territory of the Sovereign State," *Proceedings of the Vermont Historical Society for the Years 1920–1921* (Barre, VT: Vermont Historical Society, 1921), 227–56; Harvey Amani Whitfield, *The Problem of Slavery in Early Vermont, 1777–1810* (Barre, VT: Vermont Historical Society, 2014); and Peter S. Onuf, "State-Making in Revolutionary America: Vermont as a Case Study," *JAH* 67 (March 1981): 797–815.

76. *JCC*, 9:854–55 (1 November 1777, establishing a day of thanksgiving on 18 December 1777); David Avery, *The Lord Is to Be Praised for the Triumphs of His Power: A Sermon Preached at Greenwich, in Connecticut, on the 18th of December 1777, Being a General Thanksgiving Through the United American States* (Norwich, CT: Green & Spooner, 1778), 12. For typical sermons without reference to actual slavery, see Timothy Dwight, *A Sermon Preached at Stamford, in Connecticut, upon the General Thanksgiving, December 18th, 1777* (Hartford: Watson and Goodwin, 1778); Samuel Spring, *A Sermon Delivered at the North Congregational Church in Newbury-Port, on a Day of Public Thanksgiving*... (Newburyport: John Mycall, 1778); and Love, *Fast and Thanksgiving Days*, 344.

77. *The Public Records of the State of Connecticut*, 23 vols. to date (Hartford: Connecticut State Library, 1894-), 1: 415–16 (October 1777); Bernard Christian Steiner, *History of Slavery in Connecticut* (Baltimore: Johns Hopkins University Press, 1893), 25–26; Zilversmit, *First Emancipation*, 122–23.

78. Van Buskirk, *Standing in Their Own Light*, 95–141.

79. *JCC*, 10:229 (12 March 1778, establishing a fast day on 22 April 1778).

80. Jacob Green, *A Sermon Delivered at Hanover, (in New-Jersey) April 22d, 1778. Being the Day of Public Fasting and Prayer Throughout the United States of America* (Chatham, NJ, 1779), 6, 14, 15, 16, 23. The pamphlet is excerpted with an introduction in Bruns, *Am I Not a Man*, 432–40. For his early support of independence, and a brief reference to the sin of slavery, see [Jacob Green], *Observations on the Reconciliation of Great-Britain, and the Colonies; In Which Are Exhibited, Arguments for, and Against, That Measure. By a Friend of American Liberty* (Philadelphia: Robert Bell, 1776), 29n. See also: Gigantino, *Ragged Road*, 27–28; S. Scott Rohrer, *Jacob Green's Revolution: Radical Religion and Reform in a Revolutionary Age* (University Park: Pennsylvania State University Press, 2014), 210–22.

81. William Livingston, "Address to the Assembly," Princeton, May 29, 1778, *PWL* 2:343–55, quotations from 343–44, 346.

82. Samuel Allinson to William Livingston, 7th Mo: 13th 1778, *PWL* 2:380–90, (quotations from 380, 382, 387); William Livingston to Samuel Allinson, Morristown, 25th July 1778, *PWL* 2:399–404; Samuel Allinson to William Livingston, Burn [Burlington], 8th Mo 12th. 1778, PWL 2:407–14, esp. 408. This correspondence is partially excerpted in Bruns, *Am I Not a Man*, 440–43. Allinson also sent Livingston a copy of Anthony Benezet's *Serious Considerations on Important Subjects*, discussed later in this chapter.

83. *JCC*, 12:1139 (17 November 1778, establishing a thanksgiving day on 30 December 1778).

84. [Anthony Benezet], *Serious Considerations on Several Important Subjects; viz: On War and Its Inconsistency with the Gospel, Observations on Slavery, and Remarks on the Nature and Bad Effects of Spirituous Liquors* (Philadelphia: Joseph Crukshank, 1778), 28–29, 30; Benezet to John Jay, Chestnut Street, [7?] 2d. mo. Feb. 1779, in *FAB*, 330–31. The second half of Benezet's antislavery essay consisted primarily of excerpts from John Wesley's *Thoughts upon Slavery*. Several years later, Benezet again reprinted the excerpts from Wesley as *Notes on the Slave Trade* ([Philadelphia, ca. 1780]). In 1780 he also reprinted antislavery statements by George Wallace, Arthur Lee, and others whom he had previously excerpted, in Benezet, *An Extract from a Treatise on the Spirit of Prayer . . . And Considerations on Slavery* (Philadelphia: Crukshank, 1780), 79–84.

85. *JCC*, 13:343–44 (20 March 1779, establishing a fast day on 6 May 1779). On Jay's nascent antislavery beliefs at this time, including his disappointment that New York's 1777 constitutional convention declined to take a stance against slavery, see David Gellman, *Liberty's Chain: The Jay Family, Slavery, and Emancipation, 1685–1912* (Ithaca, NY: Cornell University Press, 2022), 33–49.

86. John Jay to Egbert Benson, 20 September 1780, quoted in Rael, *Eighty-Eight Years*, 45. Despite quoting Jay and naming his chapter on the revolution "Impious Prayers," Rael neglects to explore the importance of providential thinking. He instead argues that Revolution popularized antislavery sentiment by secularizing what had been a religious movement.

87. James Francis Armstrong, "Righteousness Exalteth a Nation," in Marian B. McLeod, ed., *Light My Path: Sermons by the Rev. James F. Armstrong, Revolutionary Chaplain* (Trenton, NJ: First Presbyterian Church, 1976), 10–19 (quotations from 10, 17). See also William Harrison Taylor, "'Made of One Flesh?': Revisiting the 1787 Slavery Policy of the Synod of New York and New Jersey," *Faith and Slavery in the Presbyterian Diaspora*, ed. William Harrison Taylor and Peter C. Messer (Cranbury, PA: Lehigh University Press, 2016), 71–94, esp. 82–83.

88. Henry Laurens to John Laurens, Charles Town So Carolina 14 Aug 1776, excerpted in Bruns, *Am I not a Man*, 427–28; *Fragment of an Original Letter on the Slavery of the Negroes, Written in the year 1776. By Thomas Day, Esq.* (Philadelphia: Francis Bailey, 1784). Day indicates that he wrote the letter to someone whom John Laurens had introduced to him.

89. William Whipple quoted in Egerton, *Death or Liberty*, 83.

90. *JCC*, 13:386–87 (29 March 1779); Maslowski, "National Policy Toward Black Troops," 11; Van Buskirk, *Standing in Their Own Light*, 143–72; Gregory D. Massey, "The Limits of Antislavery Thought in the Revolutionary Lower South: John Laurens and Henry Laurens," *JSH* 63 (August 1997), 495–530. On the confiscation and distribution of loyalists' slaves in New Jersey, see Gigantino, *Ragged Road*, 57–60; and Maslowski, "National Policy Toward Black Troops," 11–15.

91. *Royal Gazette* (New York), 3 July 1779; Bell, *Running from Bondage*, 12, 91–93; Holton, *Liberty Is Sweet*, 370–71.

92. "From the New-Jersey Journal," *Independent Ledger* (Boston), 9 August 1779; ["From the New-York Packet"], *Norwich Packet*, 16 November 1779. Parkinson suggests that these sources instead reflected patriot racism (*Common Cause*, 465, 473).

93. John Murray, *Nehemiah, or The Struggle for Liberty Never in Vain, When Managed with Virtue and Perseverance. A Discourse Delivered at the Presbyterian Church in Newbury-Port, Nov. 4th, 1779. Being the Day Appointed by Government to be Observed as a Day of Solemn Fasting and Prayer*... (Newbury, MA: John Mycall, 1779), 4, 9. Massachusetts, like other New England states, routinely held additional fast days on top of those proclaimed by Congress.

94. PYM Minutes Vol 2, 389–90 (4 10mo 1777); LMS to PMS, 2nd: of the 4th: Mo: 1779, in PMS Minutes Vol. 2, 224–31 (quotation from 229); PYM Minutes Vol. 2, 439 (1 10mo 1779). See also *The Epistle from the Meeting for Sufferings in London, To Friends and Brethren in New-England* ([Philadelphia, 1775]), 2. PMS Minutes Vol 2, 21 (31 8mo 1775).

95. Although I doubt any colonial legislature would have ended slavery during the 1770s or 1780s if not for the American Revolution, it is possible that Black activists in Massachusetts might still have succeeded in ending slavery through the court system by relying on the *Somerset* principle. However, this tactic still required sympathetic lawyers and jurors, which might have been harder to find if the imperial crisis had been resolved peacefully.

96. Rael, *Eighty-Eight Years*, 60.

Chapter 6

1. Benjamin Colman, "Declaration and Testimony," 7 November 1780, in Roger Bruns, ed., *Am I Not a Man and a Brother: The Antislavery Crusade of Revolutionary America, 1688–1788* (New York: Chelsea House, 1977), 460–65, quotation from 462–63.

2. Arthur Zilversmit, *The First Emancipation: The Abolition of Slavery in the North* (Chicago: University of Chicago Press, 1967), 138. Robert Parkinson, one of the most recent scholars to discuss the passage of Pennsylvania's abolition law, correctly emphasizes that the war provided crucial context. However, whereas he argues that the war undermined support for the bill, I argue it was war and providentialist beliefs that inspired abolitionists and created the political context in which the bill could pass. Robert G. Parkinson, *The Common Cause: Creating Race and Nation in the American Revolution* (Chapel Hill: University of North Carolina Press, 2016), 471–73, 480–81; Robert G. Parkinson, *Thirteen Clocks: How Race United the Colonies and Made the Declaration of Independence* (Chapel Hill: University of North Carolina Press, 2021), 173–74. My interpretation of the passage of Pennsylvania's Gradual Abolition Act of 1780 builds on that of Nash and Soderlund while placing greater emphasis on the role of providentialist thought and the likely connection to the Quaker exiles; see Gary B. Nash and Jean R. Soderlund, *Freedom by Degrees: Emancipation in Pennsylvania and Its Aftermath* (New York: Oxford University Press, 1991), 102–5. On the political aspect, with emphasis on natural rights ideology, see also Burton Alva Konkle, *George Bryan and the Constitution of Pennsylvania, 1731–1791* (Philadelphia: William J. Campbell, 1922), 164–65, 168–70, 182–83, 189–98; Zilversmit, *First Emancipation*, 126–32; George William Van Cleve, *A Slaveholders' Union: Slavery, Politics, and the Constitution in the Early American Republic* (Chicago: University of Chicago Press, 2010), 62–66; Douglas Egerton, *Death or Liberty: African Americans and Revolutionary America* (New York: Oxford University Press, 2009), 97–101; Paul J. Polgar, *Standard-Bearers of Liberty and Equality: America's First Abolition Movement* (Chapel Hill: University of North Carolina Press,

2019), 92–93n16–17; and Beverly C. Tomek, *Slavery and Abolition in Pennsylvania* (Philadelphia: Temple University Press, 201), 42–44.

3. Presbyterian General Assembly, *Records of the Presbyterian Church in the United States of America, 1706–1788* (New York: Arno Press, 1969 [1904]), 481 (21 May 1778). Although Davis does not examine the passage of Pennsylvania's 1780 Gradual Abolition Act in detail, he concisely encapsulates the main influences: "The Philadelphia radicals, though politically opposed to Quakers, fulfilled the Quakers' goal as proof of their own revolutionary sincerity, as a means of winning divine favor, and as an expression of gratitude to God for the British evacuation from their city, an event which had incidentally led also the exodus of many Negro slaves." See David Brion Davis, *The Problem of Slavery in the Age of Revolution, 1770–1823* (Ithaca, NY: Cornell University Press, 1975), 87–88). George Bancroft (who himself believed that God had a providentialist plan for the United States) also recognized the role of contemporaries' providentialist beliefs in inspiring abolition in Pennsylvania: "The retreat of the British from Philadelphia, and the restoration to Pennsylvania of peace within ins border, called forth in its people a sentiment of devout gratitude." George Bancroft, *History of the United States of America, from the Discovery of the Continent* (6 vols. Centenary Edition, Boston: Little, Brown and Company, 1876), VI:306.

4. The relevant official documents and Quaker petitions were published in *An Address to the Inhabitants of Pennsylvania, by Those Freemen, of the City of Philadelphia, Who Are Now Confined in the Mason's Lodge* . . . (Philadelphia: Robert Bell, 1777), 6, 9, 13, 14, 22, 24, 49, 52.

5. Robert Middlekauf, *The Glorious Cause: The American Revolution, 1763–1789* (New York: Oxford University Press, 1985), 386–89; Paige L. Whidbee, "The Quaker Exiles: 'The Cause of Every Inhabitant,'" *Pennsylvania History* 83 (Winter 2016): 39–40.

6. [Anthony Benezet], *Serious Considerations on Several Important Subjects; viz: On War and Its Inconsistency with the Gospel, Observations on Slavery, and Remarks on the Nature and Bad Effects of Spirituous Liquors* (Philadelphia: Joseph Crukshank, 1778), 31. David Crosby interprets this passage similarly in *The Complete Antislavery Writings of Anthony Benezet, 1754–1783: An Annotated Critical Edition* (Baton Rouge: Louisiana State University Press, 2014), 221.

7. "Address of the Supreme Executive Council to the General Assembly," *Pennsylvania Packet*, 28 November 1778; "A Proclamation," *Pennsylvania Packet*, 10 December 1778. In August 1778, the legislature briefly considered the proposal but instead passed a different bill designed to collect money from Pennsylvanians who had brought enslaved Africans into the state without paying the import duty. *Journals of the House of Representatives of the Commonwealth of Pennsylvania, 1776–1781* (Philadelphia: John Dunlap), 213 (8 August 1778), 217 (18 August 1778), 218 (21 August 1778), 222 (31 August 1778), 229 (11 September 1778).

8. *Journal of the House*, 304 (5 February 1779), 305–7, quotation from 307 (7 February 1779 [letter dated 5 February 1779]), 311 (13 February 1779), 317 (19 February 1779), 319 (23 February 1779); Nash and Soderlund, *Freedom by Degrees*, 102; Konkle, *George Bryan*, 170n.

9. "An Act for the Gradual Abolition of Slavery," *Pennsylvania Packet*, 4 March 1779. The final phrasing of the preamble was modified slightly but kept the providentialist theme. The final law also dropped a prohibition on interracial marriage and fornication contained in the initial bill.

10. "A Citizen," *Pennsylvania Packet*, 13 March 1779; *Journal of the House*, 392 (3 November 1779), 394 (8 November 1779), 365 (9 September 1779), 398 (17 November 1779), 399 (18 November 1779); "An Act," *Pennsylvania Packet*, 23 December 1779; Nash and Soderlund, *Freedom by Degrees*, 34.

11. In 1780, William Foster registered three enslaved people. By 1789, the Reverend Alexander Mitchell of Sadsbury, who became the pastor of Upper Octorara Church in 1785, owned at least one enslaved woman and registered births in 1789 and 1793. The only other Chester County slaveholder identified as "Rev[d]" in 1780 was James Anderson of Middeltown (now Delaware County), farther to the east. "A Census of the Slaves in Chester County, Pennsylvania, 1780–1815," Slavery and Miscellaneous Manuscripts Collection, Yale University, [part 1] 7, 25, [part 2] 1, 7. For the ministers of Upper Octorara Church, see "Register of Pastors," Upper Octorara Presbyterian Church, in U.S., Presbyterian Church Records, 1701–1790: https://www.ancestrylibrary.com/discoveryui-content/view/443904:61048.

12 "Reverend and Dear Sir," *Pennsylvania Packet*, 25 December 1779; Konkle, *George Bryan*, 109–94; Nash and Soderlund, *Freedom by Degrees*, 104, 160–63.

13. "Another Letter to a Clergyman," *Pennsylvania Packet*, 1 January 1780; Bryan to Samuel Adams quoted in Bancroft, *History of the United States*, VI:307.

14. Samuel Allinson to William Livingston, Burn [Burlington] 8th Mo 12th. 1778, *PWL* 2:407–14, quotation from 408.

15. "Phileleutheros," *Pennsylvania Gazette*, 2 February 1780. Nash and Soderlund suggest Benezet's authorship; see *Freedom by Degrees*, 223n23. For Benezet's lobbying, see Roberts Vaux, *Memoirs of Anthony Benezet* (Philadelphia: James P. Parke, 1817), 92.

16. *Journal of the House*, 412 (27 January 1780), 424 (15 February 1780), 435 (1 March 1780, quotation). Twenty of the twenty-one legislators who voted against the bill signed the "Dissentient," along with three others who had either abstained or missed the vote; see ibid., 436 (1 March 1780). For the "Dissentient" and a critique by "Liberal," see *Pennsylvania Packet*, 25 March 1780.

17. *Freeman's Journal*, 21 September 1781. Benezet later wrote that he received "frequent solicitations to assist" African Americans and that "Lewis the lawyer has undertook to plead the cause of several." Anthony Benezet to John Pemberton, Philadelph'a y'e 10th 8th mo 1783, Pemberton Papers, HSP, vol. 39:109. For petitions criticizing the 1780 abolition law, see *Journal of the House*, 537, 540, 547, 562, 570, 573, 574, 586, 591, 595, 601, 607, 679. The 1781 bill would have extended the registration period until 1 January 1782. A less controversial feature of the 1781 bill allowed slaveholders living in a region that Virginia had recently ceded to Pennsylvania additional time to register their slaves. *Freeman's Journal*, 13 June 1781; Nash, *Forging Freedom: The Formation of Philadelphia's Free Black Community, 1720–1840* (Cambridge, MA: Harvard University Press, 1988), 63–65; Nash and Soderlund, *Freedom by Degrees*, 112.

18. *Freeman's Journal*, 21 September 1781. For other criticism of the proposed extension, see *Freeman's Journal*, 13 June 1781 and 26 September 1781. For legislative references to the petitions, see *Journal of the House*, 607 (4 April 1781) and 690 (21 and 22 September 1781). On the importance of the 1780 law's registration clause, see Richard S. Newman, *The Transformation of American Abolitionism: Fighting Slavery in the Early Republic* (Chapel Hill: University of North Carolina Press, 2002), 60–85; Richard S. Newman, "'Lucky to Be Born in Pennsylvania': Free Soil, Fugitive Slaves and the Making of Pennsylvania's Anti-Slavery Borderland," *Slavery & Abolition* 32 (September 2011): 413–30; and Polgar, *Standard-Bearers of Equality*, 81–85, 91–103.

19. Nash and Soderlund, *Freedom by Degrees*, 111. For an emphasis on the radicalism of the Pennsylvania law, see Sean Wilentz, "The Radicalism of Northern Abolition," *NEQ* 96 (March 2023): 8–26. For an emphasis on its conservative basis and implementation, see Cory James Young, "For Life or Otherwise: Abolition and Slavery in South Central Pennsylvania, 1780–1847," (PhD diss., Georgetown University, 2021).

20. John Cooper, "To the Publick," *New-Jersey Gazette*, 20 September 1780, in Bruns, *Am I Not a Man*, 456–59.

21. *Votes and Proceedings of the [4th] General Assembly of the State of New-Jersey, At a Session Begun at Trenton the 26th day of October 1779* (Trenton, NJ: Isaac Collins, 1780), 262 (18 November 1780). For the text of the petitions, which were apparently the same, see *New-Jersey Gazette*, 21 March 1781. See also S. Scott Rohrer, *Jacob Green's Revolution: Radical Religion and Reform in a Revolutionary Age* (University Park: Pennsylvania State University Press, 2014), 213–16.

22. John Cooper, "To the Publick," *New-Jersey Gazette* (Newark) 20 September 1780. This essay and several published in response are transcribed and annotated in Larry R. Gerlach, ed., *New Jersey in the American Revolution, 1763–1783: A Documentary History* (Trenton, NJ: New Jersey Historical Commission, 1975), 437–52. Additional essays debating slavery were published in the *New Jersey Journal.*

23. *New-Jersey Gazette* (Trenton), 4 October 1780, 8 November 1780. James J. Gigantino II, *The Ragged Road to Abolition: Slavery and Freedom in New Jersey, 1775–1865* (Philadelphia: University of Pennsylvania Press, 2025), 27–30; Parkinson, *Common Cause*, 506; Parkinson, *Thirteen Clocks*, 174; Polgar, *Standard-Bearers of Equality*, 42–43. Jonathan Sassi emphasizes the religious context in "Religion, Race, and the Founders," in *Faith and Founders of the American Republic*, ed. Daniel L. Dreisbach and Mark David Hall (New York: Oxford University Press, 2014), 174–200, esp. 186–89.

24. *Votes and Proceedings of the [5th] General Assembly of the State of New-Jersey, At a Session Begun at Trenton on the 24th Day of October, 1780* (Trenton, NJ: Isaac Collins, 1780), 11 (30 October 1780), 20 (6 November 1780), 27 (14 November 1780); *Minutes and Proceedings of the Council and General Assembly of the State of New-Jersey, in Joint-Meeting, from August 30, 1776 to May, 1780* (Trenton, NJ: Isaac Collins, 1780), 57 (30 December 1780).

25. *New-Jersey Gazette*, 14 February 1781, 14 March 1781, 21 March 1781, 11 April 1781, 27 June 1781.

26. For the argument that the war undermined antislavery progress, see Parkinson, *Common Cause*, 473, 480–82, 506; and Parkinson, *Thirteen Clocks*, 174.

27. *Massachusetts Spy*, 21 June 1775; George Henry Moore, *Notes on the History of Slavery in Massachusetts* (New York: D. Appleton, 1866), 145.

28. Jeanne M. Pickering, "Suing Slavery: The Essex County Freedom Suits, 1765–1783," (master's thesis, Salem State University, 2018); Jared Ross Hardesty, "Disappearing from Abolitionism's Heartland: The Legacy of Slavery and Emancipation in Boston," *International Review of Social History* 56 (February 2020): 145–68; Gloria McCahon Whiting, "Emancipation Without the Courts or Constitution: The Case of Revolutionary Massachusetts," *Slavery & Abolition* 41 (November 2020): 458–78.

29. "The Rejected Constitution of 1778," in *The Popular Sources of Political Authority: Documents on the Massachusetts Constitution of 1780*, ed. Oscar Handlin and Mary Handlin (Cambridge, MA: Harvard University Press, 1966), 190–200, quotation from 192–93.

30. *Independent Chronicle* (Boston), 8 January 1778, 29 January 1778, 12 February 1778. For a final racist rejoinder, see *Independent Chronicle*, 19 February 1778. See also Moore, *Notes on the History of Slavery*, 186; David Waldstreicher, "Racism, Black Voices, Emancipation, and Constitution-Making in Massachusetts, 1778," *Journal of Constitutional History* 2 (Spring 2024): 325–54.

31. *Independent Chronicle* (Boston), 23 September 1779, also available in Moore, *Notes on the History of Slavery*, 187–91; "Journal of the Convention," in Handlin and Handlin, *Popular*

Sources of Political Authority, 186 (12 February 1778). On Bacon, see also Ronald Lettieri, "John Bacon," *American National Biography Online*, February 2000: http://www.anb.org/articles/01/01-00042.html.

32. "To the Freemen of Massachusetts-Bay," *Continental Journal* (Boston), 2 April 1778; "Letter II," *Continental Journal*, 9 April 1778 (quotation); Moore, *Notes on the History of Slavery*, 192–94.

33. "Essex Result," in Handlin and Handlin, *Popular Sources of Political Authority*, 325–65, quotations from 339, 341; "Returns of the Towns on the Constitution of 1778," ibid., 202–382. Most of the 177 town returns compiled by Handlin and Handlin do not explain why the town voted for or against the constitution. Of those that explained their votes, twenty identified Article V as a point of contention. Of these twenty towns, nine specifically complained about the racial restriction; seven complained about another provision that added a property requirement of £60 to vote for the state senate, governor, and executive governor; and four other towns did not clarify which part(s) of Article V they opposed. The nine town returns collected by Handlin and Handlin that specifically objected to racist language are Blandford (Hampton County), Boothbay (Maine), Charlemont (Hampshire County) Georgetown (Maine), Hardwick (Worcester County), Spencer (Worcester County), Sutton (Worcester County), Upton (Worcester County), and Westminster (Worcester County). A tenth town, Dartmouth, did not offer an explanation in its return, but the townspeople later explained that one of their objections was that Article V's discrimination against people of color "deprives them of the natural right all men have to make their own laws, and dispose of their own property." *Continental Journal* (Boston), 18 June 1788, cited in Moore, *Notes on the History of Slavery*, 196.

Scholars have interpreted the significance of the towns' reactions to Article V in different ways, with some emphasizing the extent of antiracist statements and others stressing that only a small minority of towns issued such statements. My approach is more in line with David Waldstreicher, who asserts that "the question is not why 'only' eight (or ten) of the written returns from towns did so, but why *any* did so at all—and its relationship to the results" ("Constitution-Making in Massachusetts," 345). Black activism and religious inspiration appear central in inspiring white Bay Staters to oppose the 1778 constitution's racist provisions.

34. "Returns of the Towns on the Constitution of 1778," in Handlin and Handlin, *Popular Sources of Political Authority*, 216 (Hardwick), 231 (Sutton), 245 (Boothbay), 312 (Westminster).

35. George Washington to Phillis Wheatley, 28 February 1776," *FO*, https://founders.archives.gov/documents/Washington/03-03-02-0281; Wheatley to Obour Tanner, Providence, feb[y] 14, 1776, *The Writings of Phillis Wheatley*, ed. Vincent Carretta (New York: Oxford University Press, 2019), 131; Mukkhtar Ali Isani, "'On the Death of General Wooster': An Unpublished Poem by Phillis Wheatley," *Modern Philology* 77 (1980): 306–09, quotation from 308 Vincent Carretta, *Phillis Wheatley: Biography of a Genius in Bondage* (Athens: University of Georgia Press, 2011), 155–57; David Waldstreicher, *Odyssey of Phillis Wheatley: A Poet's Journeys Through American Slavery and Independence* (New York: Farrar, Straus and Giroux, 2023), 294–99.

36. Samuel Stillman, *A Sermon Preached Before the Honorable Council, and the Honorable House of Representatives of the State of Massachusetts-Bay, in New-England, at Boston, May 26, 1779 . . .* (Boston: T. and J. Fleet, 1779), 34, 35; J. Murray, *Nehemiah, or The Struggle for Liberty Never in Vain, When Managed with Virtue and Perseverance. A Discourse Delivered at the Presbyterian Church in Newbury-Port, Nov. 4th, 1779 . . .* (Newbury, MA: John Mycall, 1779), 12, 51, 9; Handlin and Handlin, *Popular Sources of Political Authority*, 411.

37. "The Constitution of 1780," in Handlin and Handlin, *Popular Sources of Political Authority*, 441–72, quotations from 442, 455, 471; Hardwick town meeting quoted in Margot Minardi, *Making Slavery History: Abolitionism and the Politics of Memory in Massachusetts* (New York: Oxford University Press, 2010), 16. Braintree and Petersham focused on forbidding the importation of slaves in the future. It may be they feared that enslaved Africans might still be imported and held in lifelong (though not hereditary) bondage in Massachusetts. As discussed later in this chapter, the status of African-born slaves remained unclear even after the freedom suits of 1781–1783. See Handlin and Handlin, *Popular Sources of Political Authority*, 707 (Rochester), 765 (Braintree), 860 (Petersham). "The Declaration and Testimony of Benjamin Colman," in Joshua Coffin, *A Sketch of the History of Newbury, Newburyport, and West Newbury, from 1635 to 1845* (Boston: S. G. Drake, 1845), 340.

38. Harriet Martineau, *Retrospect of Western Travels*, 2 vols. (New York: Harper & Brothers, 1838), 1:246–47. Martineau's account was informed by conversation with Theodore Sedgwick Jr. and Catherine Sedgwick. The ruling in *Brom and Bett v. Ashley* is transcribed in James M. Rosenthal, "Free Soil in Berkshire County, 1781," *NEQ* 10 (December 1937): 781–85; and also available at https://elizabethfreeman.mumbet.com/who-is-mumbet/mumbet-court-records/. See also Richard E. Welch, "Mumbet and Judge Sedgwick: A Footnote to the Early History of Massachusetts Justice," *Boston Bar Journal* 8 (1964): 12–19; Christopher Cameron, *To Plead Our Own Cause: African Americans in Massachusetts and the Making of the Antislavery Movement* (Kent, OH: Kent State University Press, 2011), 73–76.

39. Theodore Sedgwick [Jr.], *The Practicability of the Abolition of Slavery: A Lecture, Delivered at the Lyceum in Stockbridge, Massachusetts, February, 1831* (New York: J. Seymour, 1832), 14–20, quotations from 18; Cameron, *To Plead Our Own Cause*, 76.

40. Sedgwick [Jr.], *Practicability of the Abolition of Slavery*, 16. Cameron notes, "It is not clear whether Freeman's case was decided on these constitutional arguments or a on a more specific point of law" (*To Plead Our Own Cause*, 75).

41. Nathaniel Jenison signed his name with a single *n*, as it also appears in census records, but court proceedings and scholars generally spell it *Jennison*. The Quock Walker cases have been treated most extensively in William O'Brien, "Did the Jennison Case Outlaw Slavery in Massachusetts?" *WMQ* 17 (April 1960): 219–41; John D. Cushing, "The Cushing Court and the Abolition of Slavery in Massachusetts: More Notes on the 'Quock Walker Case,'" *American Journal of Legal History* 5 (April 1961): 118–44; Arthur Zilversmit, "Quok Walker, Mumbet, and the Abolition of Slavery in Massachusetts," *WMQ* 25 (December 1968): 614–24; Robert M. Spector, "The Quock Walker Cases (1781–83): Slavery, Its Abolition, and Negro Citizenship in Early Massachusetts," *Journal of Negro History* 53 (January 1968): 12–32; Emily Blanck, "Seventeen Eighty-Three: The Turning Point in the Law of Slavery and Freedom in Massachusetts," *NEQ* 75 (2002): 24–51; William Wiecek, *The Sources of Antislavery Constitutionalism in America, 1760–1848* (Ithaca, NY: Cornell University Press, 1977), 45–48; Robert M. Cover, *Justice Accused: Antislavery and the Judicial Process* (New Haven, CT: Yale University Press, 1975), 43–50; A. Leon. *In the Matter of Color: Race and the American Legal Process: The Colonial Period* (New York: Oxford University Press, 1978), 91–99; Phillip Hamburger, *Law and Judicial Duty* (Cambridge, MA: Harvard University Press, 2008), 476–84; and Cameron, *To Plead Our Own Cause*, 76–78.

42. Minardi, *Making Slavery History*, 17. For the order of the various suits and excerpts of the court documents, see O'Brien, "Did the Jennison Case Outlaw Slavery?" 225–35. See also *History of Worcester County, Massachusetts, Embracing a Comprehensive History of the County*

from Its First Settlement to the Present Time, with a History and Description of Its Cities and Towns, 2 vols. (Boston: C. F. Jewett, 1879), 1:66–69.

43. "Brief of Levi Lincoln in the Slave Case Tried in 1781," *Collections of the MHS, Volume III* (Boston: MHS, 1877), 438–42.

44. "Brief of Levi Lincoln"; Petition of Nathaniel Jenison [before 18 June 1782], Massachusetts Anti-Slavery and Anti-Segregation Petitions Dataverse, Harvard: http://nrs.harvard.edu/urn-3:FHCL:13448114. Extracts of Jenison's petition are included in Moore, *Notes on the History of Slavery*, 217–18. See also O'Brien, "Did the Jennison Case Outlaw Slavery?" 233; Edward L. Bell, *Persistence of Memories of Slavery and Emancipation in Historical Andover* (Boston: Shawsheen Press, 2021), 204–5.

45. Wetmore's Minutes of the Trial: Essex Inferior Court, Newburyport, September 1771," *FO*: https://founders.archives.gov/documents/Adams/05-02-02-0004-0005-0001. For Sargeant's involvement in freedom suits (including on behalf of a slaveholder in the first instance), see Pickering, "Suing Slavery," 92. In addition to Sargeant, the two other judges present—David Sewall and James Sullivan—had also been delegates at the 1779–1780 constitutional convention.

46. Petition of Nathaniel Jenison.

47. Ibid. For the earlier petitions, see Petition of Nathaniel Jenison to the Honorable Senate & the Honorable House of Representatives of the Commonwealth of Massachusetts, [before 28 January 1782], Massachusetts Petitions Dataverse, https://doi.org/10.7910/DVN/DQ7QF; Petition of Quork Walker, April the 9th, 1782, Massachusetts Petitions Dataverse, https://doi.org/10.7910/DVN/7UTVP.

48. Massachusetts House Journal, vol. 3: 99 (18 June 1782), 436 (7 February 1783), 444 (8 February 1783), SC1/series 532, Massachusetts Archives. My thanks to Caitlin Jones at the Massachusetts Archives for supplying pictures of the relevant pages of this journal, which only exists in manuscript form for the years 1782–1783. Moore reprints the resolutions but without indicating the revision to the first one, in *Notes on the History*, 220.

49. Landon Covington Bell, *The Old Free State: A Contribution to the History of Lunenburg County and Southside Virginia*, 2 vols. (Richmond, VA: William Byrd Press, 1927), 1:461; Moore, *Notes on the History of Slavery*, 220–21. For scholars who assume "indemnifying" meant compensating rather than protecting from liability, see Van Cleve, *Slaveholders' Union*, 66; and Egerton, *Death or Liberty*, 107. The provision is correctly characterized in Zilversmit, *First Emancipation*, 114; and Hamburger, *Law and Judicial Duty*, 438n15.

50. Since 1781, the legislature had already been responding on a case-by-case basis to individual petitions from estate managers about the status of Black dependents who were either children or elderly; see Petition of Samuel Curtis, May 31st 1781, Massachusetts Petitions Dataverse, https://doi.org/10.7910/DVN/VFV5N; Petition of Jesse Putnam, [before 25 September 1781], Massachusetts Petitions Dataverse, https://doi.org/10.7910/DVN/SUPHGS. Because the legislature failed to establish a formal policy, town governments disputed with one another and with the state well into the nineteenth century over who was financially responsible for the maintenance of Black paupers. In 1847 a report by a gubernatorial commission determined that paupers who had formerly been enslaved would be maintained at the expense of the state rather than local towns. Bell, *Persistence of Memories of Slavery*, esp. 21–26. See also Moore, *Notes on the History of Slavery*, 122n1; Kunal Parker, "Making Blacks Foreigners: The Legal Construction of Former Slaves in Post-Revolutionary Massachusetts," *Utah Law Review* 75 (2001): 75–124.

51. "Mentor," *Boston Evening-Post*, 3 May 1783; O'Brien, "Did the Jennison Case Outlaw Slavery?" 240.

52. Two versions of Cushing's charge to the jury exist in manuscript form. Cushing's rough notes, in his hand, are held at the MHS and are transcribed in [Gray], *The Case of Nathaniel Jennison*, 5 (quotations). The originals can be viewed online through the MHS: https://www.masshist.org/database/viewer.php?item_id=630. A slightly more polished version, recorded in another hand and held at the Harvard Law Library, is transcribed in Cushing, "Cushing Court," 132–33.

53. Scholars who emphasize that Cushing's jury charge did *not* rest on judicial review and who highlight the role of public opinion include Cover, *Justice Accused*, 44–46; and Hamburger, *Law and Judicial Duty*, 476–84.

54. Scholars have identified numerous Black people who were held in servitude into the 1790s; often these were minors or were at least under the age of twenty-eight. For example, a 1777 agreement that was reaffirmed by a probate judge in 1786 required a "Negro Boy Chance" to labor until 1789, when he would have been twenty-seven. See Bell, *Persistence of Memories of Slavery*, 129. Bell also notes runaway ads from 1793 referring to a twenty-year-old "Negro Boy" named Felix; although Felix was clearly considered unfree, it is not clear whether he was considered enslaved-for-life (ibid., 132).

55. The census worker appears to have made several errors when recording Walker's information, misspelling his name and placing the three residents in the column for "Free white females" rather than the neighboring column for "All other free persons" (where free people of color were normally recorded). It seems unlikely that there was a white woman with nearly the same name as Quock Walker in the same town living with two other white females. 1790 U.S. Census for Barre, MA, available at https://www.ancestrylibrary.com/discoveryui-content/view/93438:5058. For the marriage of Quock Walker and Elizabeth Harvey, "negroes," on 6 February 1786, see https://www.ancestrylibrary.com/discoveryui-content/view/81400160:2495

56. S. [Samuel] Hopkins to Anthony Benezet, Newport, December 8, 1783, CPW, box 11. This letter is filed under "L. Hopkins," but that appears to be a misreading of Hopkins's first initial.

57. Curiously, the petition was not printed until after the legislature concluded its public hearing. It appears, with a few errors such as missing words, in *New Hampshire Gazette* (Portsmouth), 15 July 1780. Images of the manuscript are reproduced in Robert B. Dishman, "Jeremy Belknap and Jonathan Mitchell Sewall as Abolitionists: Defining the Extent of New Hampshire's Bill of Rights," *Historical New Hampshire* 10 (Winter 2010): 66–92, 73–76. Dishman suggests that Jonathan Mitchell Sewall (from the same ancestral family as Judge Samuel Sewall and who later authored New Hampshire's bill of rights), was the "primary candidate to have been the slave petitioners' legal advocate" (78).

58. *New Hampshire Gazette* (Portsmouth), 20 May 1780. The legislative records are excerpted in Isaac W. Hammond, "Slavery in New Hampshire," *Magazine of American History* 21 (1889): 62–65. See also Robert B. Dishman, "'Natives of Africa, Now Forcibly Detained': The Slave Petitioners of Revolutionary Portsmouth," *Historical New Hampshire* 61 (Spring 2007): 6–27; Zilversmit, *First Emancipation*, 118; Mark J. Sammons and Valerie Cunningham, *Black Portsmouth: Three Centuries of African-American Heritage* (Durham: University of New Hampshire Press, 2004), 62–74; and Patrick Rael, *Eighty-Eight Years: The Long Death of Slavery in the United States, 1777–1863* (Athens: University of Georgia Press, 2015), 48, 65.

59. Jeremy Belknap, "Queries Respecting the Slavery and Emancipation of Negroes in Massachusetts, Proposed by the Hon. Judge Tucker of Virginia, and Answered by the Rev. Dr. Belknap," *Collections of the Massachusetts Historical Society for the Year M,DCC,XCV* (Boston: Samuel Hall, 1975), 204. See also Dishman, "Jeremy Belknap and Jonathan Mitchell Sewall";

and Ben Leubsdorf, "234 Years Later, N.H. Legislature Might Answer Slaves Plea for Freedom," *Concord Monitor*, 28 February 2013.

60. The 1779 and 1780 petitions are transcribed in Vincent J. Rosivach, "Three Petitions by Connecticut Negroes for the Abolition of Slavery in Connecticut," *Connecticut Review* 17 (Fall 1995), 79–85, quotations from 80, 84. See also Isabelle Laskaris, "'Thousands Now Unhappy': Slave Petitions in Eighteenth-Century Connecticut," *Slavery & Abolition* 44 (2023): 26–47. For the assertion that the legislature considered an antislavery bill in 1780, see Zilversmit, *First Emancipation*, 123.

61. [Thomas Jefferson], *A Summary View of the Rights of British America* (Williamsburg, VA: Clementina Rind, [1774]), 16–17.

62. Robert McColley, *Slavery in Jeffersonian Virginia* (Urbana: University of Illinois Press, 1964); Duncan J. MacLeod, *Slavery, Race and the American Revolution* (New York: Cambridge University Press, 1974), 31–34; Eva Sheppard Wolf, *Race and Liberty in the New Nation: Emancipation in Virginia from the Revolution to Nat Turner's Rebellion* (Baton Rouge: Louisiana State University, 2006); Michael A. McDonnell, *The Politics of War: Race, Class, and Conflict in Revolutionary Virginia* (Chapel Hill: University of North Carolina Press, 2010).

63. Rael, *Eighty-Eight Years*, 68 (quotations). See also Edmund S. Morgan, *The Birth of the Republic, 1763–1789*, 3rd ed. (Chicago: University of Chicago Press, 1992), 97; Gary B. Nash, *Race and Revolution* (Madison, WI: Madison House, 1990), 17; and Gordon S. Wood, *Power and Liberty: Constitutionalism in the American Revolution* (New York: Oxford University Press, 2021), 108, 112, 117.

64. Wolf's *Race and Liberty in the New Nation* challenges the traditional focus on the revolutionary impulse, noting that Quakers and a minority of evangelical Methodists and Baptists were responsible for most of a short-lived burst of manumissions. Other scholars have increasingly highlighted the roles of Quakers in pushing the law; see for example Gary B. Nash, *Warner Mifflin: Unflinching Quaker Abolitionist* (Philadelphia: University of Pennsylvania Press, 2017), esp. 120–25; and Manisha Sinha, *The Slave's Cause: A History of Abolition* (New Haven, CT: Yale University Press, 2016), 85.

65. Robert Pleasants to Patrick Henry, Curles, 5 mo. 28. 1777, American Friends Letters, box 14, Haverford (original at Virginia Historical Society, Henry Family Papers, 1723–1801, MSSS 1/H3968/a 1–30). Pleasants explains that he and Edward Stabler met with Patrick Henry in Robert Pleasants to Israel Pemberton, Curles, 4mo. 21st. 1777, LBRP, 44–45. See also James H. Kettner, "Persons or Property? The Pleasants Slaves in Virginia Courts, 1792–1799," in *Launching the "Extended Republic": The Federalist Era*, ed. Ronald Hoffman and Peter J. Albert (Charlottesville: University of Virginia Press, 1996), 136–55, esp. 141; William Fernandez Hardin, "Litigating the Lash: Quaker Emancipator Robert Pleasants, the Law of Slavery, and the Meaning of Manumission in Revolutionary and Early National Virginia," (PhD diss., Vanderbilt University, 2013), 90.

66. Edward Stabler to John Pemberton, Petersburg, 9mo 8th. 1778, Pemberton Papers, HSP, vol. 32. The 1778 law that prohibited bringing slaves into the state did liberate slaves brought into the state illegally, but this provision reflected legislators' commitment to preventing slave importations—especially in the midst of war, when the British were arming runaway slaves—rather than their support for general emancipation. Wolf, *Race and Liberty in the New Nation*, 24–26, 29–30; McDonnell, *Politics of War*, 330–31.

67. VYM Minutes 1702–1835, 144–45 (5mo 1779). Quakers in Northern Virginia were still under the jurisdiction of the Philadelphia Yearly Meeting (and would be until 1790), and

thus had been subject to disownment for slaveholding since 1776. See also: A. Glenn Crothers, *Quakers Living in the Lion's Mouth: The Society of Friends in Northern Virginia, 1730–1865* (Gainesville: University Press of Florida, 2012), 43–46.

68. Francis Asbury, *The Journal of Rev. Francis Asbury: Bishop of the Methodist Episcopal Church* (3 vols., New York: Eaton & Mains, 1900–1904), I:280 (10 June 1778); *Minutes of the Annual Conferences of the Methodist Episcopal Church* (New York: T. Mason and G. Lane, 1840), 12 (24 April 1780), 24 (1785); Mathews, *Slavery and Methodists*, 8–10. See also Donald G. Mathews, *Slavery and Methodism: A Chapter in American Morality, 1780–1845* (Princeton: Princeton University Press, 1965), 3–10; Dee Andrews, *The Methodists and Revolutionary America, 1760–1800: The Shaping of an Evangelical Culture* (Princeton: Princeton University Press, 2001).

69. VYM Extracts, 20 5mo 1780, 23 5mo 1781; Edward Stabler to John Pemberton, Petersburg, 8th mo; 26th, 1780, Pemberton Papers, vol 35.

70. "The Humble Petition of Sundry Members of the Society of People Called Quakers, on Behalf of Themselves, and Those Who May Not Have the Ability or Opportunity to Plead Their Own Cause," 29 November 1780, LVA, Legislative Petitions of the General Assembly, 1776–1865, accession no. 36121, box 289, folder 107, available online through http://www.virginiamemory.com/collections/petitions); Robert Pleasants to Benezet, Curles, 2d mo. 1781, *FAB*, 436–37. Wolf, *Race and Liberty in the New Nation*, 32.

71. *JCC*, 21:1074–76 (26 October 1781, establishing a day of thanksgiving on 13 December 1781); PMS Minutes Vol. 2: 326 (16 11mo 1781), 327–32 (22 11mo 1781).

72. James Francis Armstrong, "The Lord Was on Our Side," in Marian B. McLeod, ed., *Light My Path: Sermons by the Rev. James F. Armstrong, Revolutionary Chaplain* (Trenton, NJ: First Presbyterian Church, 1976), 20–27, quotations from 26, 27. See also William Harrison Taylor, "'Made of One Flesh?': Revisiting the 1787 Slavery Policy of the Synod of New York and New Jersey," *Faith and Slavery in the Presbyterian Diaspora*, ed. William Harrison Taylor and Peter C. Messer (Cranbury, PA: Lehigh University Press, 2016), 71–94, esp. 82–83; William DeLoss Love, *The Fast and Thanksgiving Days of New England* (Boston: Houghton, Mifflin, 1895), 551.

73. Warner Mifflin, *The Defence of Warner Mifflin Against Aspersions Cast on Him on Account of His Endeavours to Promote Righteousness, Mercy, and Peace, Among Mankind* (Philadelphia: Samuel Sansom, 1796), 11, 17; Warner Mifflin to John Pemberton, Kent, 12mo: ye 5th Day 1781, vol 36. Since the completion of my research, most of Mifflin's correspondence has been published in Gary B. Nash and Michael R. McDowell, eds., *Writings of Warner Mifflin: Forgotten Quaker Abolitionist of the Revolutionary Era* (Newark: University of Delaware Press, 2021). On Quaker involvement, see also Nash, *Warner Mifflin*, 28–42, 121–24; Crothers, *Quakers Living in the Lion's Mouth*, 58–60; and Hardin, "Litigating the Lash," 57–128.

74. John Parrish, "Notes on a Journey to Virginia" (unpaginated), Small Collections, Swarthmore. My quotations are from the original manuscript, but Parrish's journal has also been recently published with modernized spelling and annotations in Gary B. Nash and Michael R. McDowell, eds., "Notes on a Journey to Virginia," *Quaker History* 111 (Spring 2022): 1–50.

75. VYM Extracts, 21 5mo 1782.

76. "Memorial of a Committee of the People called Quakers," 29 May 1782, LVA, Legislative Petitions of the General Assembly, 1776–1865, accession no. 36121, box 290, folder 23, available online: http://www.virginiamemory.com/collections/petitions.

77. Parrish, "Notes on a Journey to Virginia"; Warner Mifflin to John Parrish, Kent, ye 9th of 2 mo. 1787, CPW, box 1. Unfortunately, the VMS minutes before 1811 do not appear extant. In Parrish's journal, he recorded that the VMS appointed a committee "to lay before the Assembly the many distrest cases of the poor blacks in our society on account of the inequity of the Laws." Wolf notes that the "legislative journal for 1782 was never printed and has not been found" (*Race and Liberty in the New Nation*, 34n). Parrish's journal refers to the support of "P.H.," who must have been Patrick Henry.

78. "To the Honorable the Speaker and Gentlemen of the House of Delegates, the Petition of the Subscribers Inhabitants of the County of Accomack" (received and referred on 3 June 1782), LVA, Legislative Petitions of the General Assembly, 1776–1865, accession no. 36121, box 1, folder 10, available online: http://www.virginiamemory.com/collections/petitions. The Henrico petitioners' primary concern was opposing the practice of slaveholders hiring out their slaves (which reduced oversight). Henrico Co. Proslavery Petition (8 June 1782), LVA, Legislative Petitions of the General Assembly, 1776–1865, accession no. 36121, box 116, folder 13, available online: http://www.virginiamemory.com/collections/petitions. On Daniel Mifflin's manumissions (performed in 1775 and filed officially in 1782), see Wolf, *Race and Liberty in the New Nation*, 45, 55–56, 239.

79. Parrish, "Notes on a Journey to Virginia." Stabler agreed that the presence of Mifflin and Parrish was "instrumental" in passing the law. Edward Stabler to ?, Petersburg, Sixth mo., 26th, 1782, in "Relics of the Past: Warner Mifflin, No. 6," *The Friend* 17 (1844), 172. On the passage of the law and its text, see Wolf, *Race and Liberty in the New Nation*, 33–35. The text of the law is reproduced in Nash, *Race and Revolution*, 115–16.

80. Wood, *Power and Liberty*, 112; Edward Stabler to ?, Petersburg, Sixth mo., 26th, 1782, in "Relics of the Past: Warner Mifflin, No. 6," *The Friend* 17 (1844), 172; VYM Extracts, 17–18 5mo 1784; John Pemberton to John Parrish, F———g, 7th [9th?]mo; 29th. 1782, CPW box 1:8.

81. Freeborn Garrettson, *The Experience and Travels of Mr. Freeborn Garrettson, Minister of the Methodist-Episcopal Church in North-America* (Philadelphia: Crukshank, 1791), 187 (14 March 1781); *Minutes of the Annual Conferences of the Methodist Episcopal Church*, 24 (1785); Donald G. Matthews, *Slavery and Methodism: A Chapter in American Morality, 1780–1845* (Princeton, NJ: Princeton University Press, 1965), 8–10.

82. Wolf estimates that 8,500 to 11,000 Virginia slaves were manumitted between 1782 and 1806. Wolf, *Race and Liberty in the New Nation*, 39–84, esp. 43.

83. NCYM Minutes, 28 10mo 1776, in Michael J. Crawford, ed., *The Having of Negroes Is Becoming a Burden: The Quaker Struggle to Free Slaves in Revolutionary North Carolina* (Gainesville: University of Florida Press, 2010), 92, 93. Crawford's book contains an overview of the North Carolina manumission controversy and many relevant primary sources; see also Nicholas P. Wood, "A 'Class of Citizens': The Earliest Black Petitioners to Congress and Their Quakers Allies," *WMQ* 74 (January 2017): 105–55, esp. 110–12, 116–17.

84. [David Cooper], *A Serious Address to the Rulers of America, On the Inconsistency of Their Conduct Respecting Slavery . . .* (Trenton, NJ: Isaac Collins, 1783), 17, 22, 23; "Justice," *Freeman's Journal* (Philadelphia) 24 September 1783. Crawford reprinted this letter in Charles Crawford, *Observations Upon Negro Slavery* (Philadelphia: Joseph Crukshank, 1784), 24. See also Lewis Leary, "Charles Crawford: A Forgotten Poet of Early Philadelphia," *PMHB* 83 (July 1959): 293–306.

85. Anthony Benezet to Benjamin Franklin, Philadelpa the 8th 5th mo 1783, https://founders.archives.gov/documents/Franklin/01-39-02-0374; [Anthony Benezet], *Short Observations on Slavery: Introductory to Some Extracts from the Writing of the Abbe Raynal, on That Important Subject* ([Philadelphia, 1783]), 4, 6–7.

Chapter 7

1. For the concept of a critical period, see John Fiske, *The Critical Period of American History, 1783–1789* (Boston: Houghton Mifflin, 1916). For a recent reevaluation of the period, see Douglas Bradburn and Christopher R. Pearl, *From Independence to the U.S. Constitution: Reconsidering the Critical Period of American History* (Charlottesville: University of Virginia Press, 2022).

2. Patrick Rael, *Eighty-Eight Years: The Long Death of Slavery in the United States, 1777–1863* (Athens: University of Georgia Press, 2015), 62–63; Edward Baptist, *The Half Has Never Been Told: Slavery and the Making of American Capitalism* (New York: Basic Books, 2014), 4. While overstating the strength of the abolitionist movement, Baptist correctly emphasizes that economic trends caused slavery to expand in the South more rapidly than it declined in the North.

3. My emphasis on Quaker activism builds on Thomas E. Drake, *Quakers and Slavery in America* (New Haven, CT: Yale University Press, 1950), 95–99; and Arthur Zilversmit, *The First Emancipation: The Abolition of Slavery in the North* (Chicago: University of Chicago Press, 1967), 156–62. For debates over slavery within other denominations, see also James D. Essig, *The Bonds of Wickedness: American Evangelicals Against Slavery, 1770–1808* (Philadelphia: Temple University Press, 1982); Donald G. Mathews, *Slavery and Methodism: A Chapter in American Morality, 1780–1845* (Princeton, NJ: Princeton University Press, 1965); and Ben Wright, *Bonds of Salvation: How Christianity Inspired and Limited American Abolitionism* (Baton Rouge: Louisiana State University, 2020).

4. *The Constitution of the Pennsylvania Society for Promoting the Abolition of Slavery and the Relief of Free Negroes, Unlawfully Held in Bondage: Begun in the Year 1774 and Enlarged on the Twenty-third of April 1787 . . .* (Philadelphia: Joseph James, 1787); Kirsten Sword, "Remembering Dinah Nevil: Strategic Deceptions in Eighteenth-Century Antislavery," *JAH* (September 2010): 315–343, esp. 318–33; Richard S. Newman, *The Transformation of American Abolitionism: Fighting Slavery in the Early Republic* (Chapel Hill: University of North Carolina Press, 2002); Paul J. Polgar, *Standard-Bearers of Liberty and Equality: America's First Abolition Movement* (Chapel Hill: University of North Carolina Press, 2019); Sarah L. H. Gronningsater, *The Rising Generation: Gradual Abolition, Black Legal Culture, and the Making of National Freedom* (Philadelphia: University of Pennsylvania Press, 2024), 47–127.

On secular antislavery groups, see Thomas Robert Mosely, "A History of the New-York Manumission Society, 1785–1849" (PhD diss., New York University, 1963); Gary B. Nash and Jean R. Soderlund, *Freedom by Degrees: Emancipation in Pennsylvania and Its Aftermath* (New York: Oxford University Press, 1991); Shane White, *Somewhat More Independent: The End of Slavery in New York City* (Athens: University of Georgia Press, 1991), 81–88; David N. Gellman, *Emancipating New York: The Politics of Slavery and Freedom* (Baton Rouge: Louisiana State University), 56–77; and Manisha Sinha, *The Slave's Cause: A History of Abolition* (New Haven, CT: Yale University Press, 2016), 72–74, 77–79.

5. PAS Minute Book 2, 7–8 (23 4mo 1787); David Waldstreicher, *Runaway America: Benjamin Franklin, Slavery, and the American Revolution* (New York: Hill and Wang, 2004), 236. Most

of Pemberton's antislavery correspondence before 1790 is housed in the Pemberton Papers, while most of it from after 1790 is in the PAS Papers, both at the HSP. Throughout this time he remained active in the PMS, often drafting or signing its correspondence and documents in the PMS Minutes and Miscellaneous Papers (at Haverford). Some scholars, unaware of the PMS's antislavery activities, have portrayed Pemberton's membership in the PAS as the start of his activism and assumed that his main contribution was his high social status. For example see J. R. Oldfield, *Transatlantic Abolitionism in the Age of Revolution: An International History, c. 1787–1820* (New York: Cambridge University Press, 2013), 30–31. Although largely unaware of the Quaker precedents, Oldfield provides an excellent discussion of transatlantic antislavery networks; see also Betty Fladeland, *Men and Brothers: Anglo-American Antislavery Cooperation* (Urbana: University of Illinois Press, 1972); W. Caleb McDaniels, "Philadelphia Abolitionists and Antislavery Cosmopolitanism," in *Antislavery and Abolition in Philadelphia: Emancipation and the Long Struggle for Racial Justice in the City of Brother of Love*, ed. Richard Newman and James Mueller, (Baton Rouge: Louisiana State University Press, 2011), 149–73.

6. Samuel Hopkins, *A Dialogue Concerning the Slavery of the Africans . . .* (2 ed., New York: Robert Hodges, 1785), 69–71, quotations from appendix to 2nd edition. Scholars who neglect providentialism and focus on natural rights and republicanism as the main impulse for antislavery reform have not realized the degree to which war facilitated reform while peace led to malaise among much of the public.

7. George William Van Cleve, *We Have Not a Government: The Articles of Confederation and the Road to the Constitution* (Chicago: University of Chicago Press, 2017); Robert Allison, *The Crescent Obscured: The United States and the Muslim World, 1776–1815* (New York: Oxford University Press, 1995); Lawrence Peskin, *Captives and Countrymen: Barbary Slavery and the American Public, 1785–1816* (Baltimore: Johns Hopkins University Press, 2009).

8. PMS to New York Meeting for Sufferings, Philada, 20th: day of the 11th: mo: 1783, PMS Minutes Vol. 2, 410–11: http://slavevoyages.org/voyages/0IIgVvvk. James A. McMillin, *The Final Victims: Foreign Slave Trade to North America, 1783–1810* (Charleston: University of South Carolina Press, 2004).

9. PMS to LMS, Philada., 8th. mo: 1782, PMS Minutes Vol. 2, 360–64; PMS to LMS, 17th: day of 7th: mo: 1783, ibid., 399–403; Anthony Benezet to George Dillwyn, [Philad'a Anno 1783], *FAB*, 372–75; Christopher Leslie Brown, *Moral Capital: Foundations of British Abolitionism* (Chapel Hill: University of North Carolina Press, 2006); John Coffey, "'Tremble Britannia!': Fear, Providence and the Abolition of the Slave Trade, 1758–1807," *English Historical Review* (August 2012): 844–81. See also Seymour Drescher, *Econocide: British Slavery in the Era of Abolition* (Chapel Hill: University of North Carolina Press, 1977).

10. William Dillwyn Diaries, 1774–1790, transcribed by Richard Morris, 177 (11 4mo 1783), available online at https://www.swansea.ac.uk/crew/research-projects/dillwyn/diaries/william-dillwyn-diaries/ (original ms held at National Library of Wales, Abersystwyth). Dillwyn served on both the LMS slave trade committee and a similar one established later in 1783 by the London Yearly Meeting. Quaker Slave Trade Committee Minutes, 1783, in Thompson-Clarkson Scrapbook vol. 2, LSF, London; London Meeting for Sufferings Committee on the Slave Trade, 1783–1792, transcript, LSF, 2 (29 8mo 1783) (I thank Lisa McQuillan of the LSF for providing this transcript). On Dillwyn, see also Judi Jennings, *The Business of Abolishing the Slave Trade, 1783–1807* (London: F. Case, 1997); and Benjamin L. Carp, "'Fix'd Almost amongst Strangers': Charleston's Quaker Merchants and the Limits of Cosmopolitanism," *WMQ* 74 (January 2017): 77–107.

11. James Pemberton to John Pemberton, Philad. 7th mo. 19th: 1783, Pemberton Papers, HSP, vol. 39.

12. David Barclay to James Pemberton, London, Red Lion Square, 2d: of 7th: mo: 1783, Pemberton Papers, HSP, vol. 39. The LYM decided to petition Parliament rather than the king when it learned that Parliament was in the midst of considering a bill that dealt with the Royal African Company. See also James Phillips to James Pemberton, London, 30th. 6mo 1783, ibid. On the transatlantic Quaker connection, see also David Brion Davis, *The Problem of Slavery in the Age of Revolution, 1770–1823* (Ithaca, NY: Cornell University Press, 1975); Roger Anstey, *The Atlantic Slave Trade and British Abolition, 1760–1810* (New York: Macmillan, 1975); 213–54; Fladeland, *Men and Brothers*, 30–32; Brown, *Moral Capital*, 402, 412–424; Oldfield, *Transatlantic Abolitionism*, 17–99; W. Caleb McDaniels, "Philadelphia Abolitionists and Antislavery Cosmopolitanism," in *Antislavery and Abolition in Philadelphia: Emancipation and the Long Struggle for Racial Justice in the City of Brother of Love*, ed. Richard Newman and James Mueller (Baton Rouge: Louisiana State University Press, 2011), 149–73.

13. The LYM petition of 16 6mo 1783 is reproduced in *The Case of Our Fellow-Creatures, the Oppressed Africans, Respectfully Recommended to the Serious Consideration of the Legislature of Great Britain, by the People Called Quakers* (Philadelphia: Joseph Crukshank, 1784), 6; and *Cobbet's Parliamentary History of England* 23:1026 (17 June 1783).

14. LMS to PMS, London, 4th: of the 4th: mo 1783, PMS Minutes Vol. 2, 394–95; John Pemberton to James Pemberton, York, 6th mo; 27th, 1783, Pemberton Papers, HSP, vol. 39; David Barclay to James Pemberton, London, Red Lion Square, 2d: of 7th: mo: 1783, ibid.

15. James Pemberton to John Pemberton, Philad'a., 9mo: 21st: 1783, Pemberton Papers, HSP, vol. 39; Benezet to George Dillwyn, [Philad'a Anno 1783], *FAB*, 372–75; Anthony Benezet to the Queen [Charlotte], Philadelphia, 25th 8th m (August) 1783 (draft), Thompson-Clarkson vol. 2, LSF (Benezet's letter was delivered two years later by the painter Benjamin West; see William Dillwyn to John Pemberton, Clapton, Middlesex, 1mo. 31, 1785, Pemberton Papers, HSP, vol. 42); LYM, Quaker Slave Trade Committee Minutes, 1783, in Thompson-Clarkson Scrapbook vol. 2; LMS Committee on the Slave Trade, 1783–1792; William Dillwyn to John Pemberton (c/o Daniel Mildred), London, 12th mo; 6th: 1783, Pemberton Papers, HSP, vol. 40, 5. For the antislavery items and the newspapers in which they were published, see Quaker Slave Trade Committee Minutes, 1783, 1–7 (7 7mo 1783 to 6 7mo 1784).

16. *The Case of Our Fellow-Creatures, the Oppressed Africans* (London: James Phillips, 1783), 4, 6. See also Patrick C. Lipscomb III and Edward C. Mulligan, "A Note on the Authorship of 'The Case of Our Fellow-Creatures' (1784)," *Quaker History* 55 (Spring 1966): 47–51.

17. Anthony Benezet, *A Caution and Warning to Great Britain and Her Colonies, in a Short Representation of the Calamitous State of the Enslaved Negroes in the British Dominions . . .* (London: James Phillips, 1784); Thomas Clarkson, *An Essay on the Slavery and Commerce of the Human Species . . .* (Philadelphia: Joseph Crukshank, 1786), v, 110–12, chap. 10, chap. 11. Brown, *Moral Capital*, 442–50.

18. PYM, "To the United States in Congress Assembled, the Address of the People Called Quakers," fourth day of the tenth Month 1783, in *A Necessary Evil? Slavery and the Debate over the Constitution*, ed. John P. Kaminski (Madison, WI: Madison House, 1995), 26–27. A facsimile of the petition and signatures is available in Roger Bruns, ed., *Am I Not a Man and a Brother: The Antislavery Crusade of Revolutionary America, 1688–1788* (New York: Chelsea House, 1977), 493–503. The original can be viewed at www.fold3.com/image/184860/ (accessed 6 January 2016).

19. James Pemberton to John Pemberton, Philad'a: 11th mon: 28th: 1783, Pemberton Papers, HSP, vol. 39; *JCC*, 25:654 (7 October 1783), 660 (8 October 1783), 699–700 (18 October 1783). Drake, *Quakers and Slavery in America*, 90–94.

20. Moses Brown to James Pemberton, Providence, 22d, 5th mo. 1782, Pemberton Papers, HSP, vol. 36; *JCC*, 25:660n (18 December 1783); *JCC*, 26:13–14 (8 January 1784).

21. *JCC*, 26:13–14 (8 January 1784).

22. *JCC*, 26:119 (1 March 1784). The role of Quaker abolitionism is absent in most scholarship on the 1784 Land Ordinance (and the 1787 Northwest Ordinance), but it is highlighted in "Relics of the Past No. 7," *The Friend* (1844), 181–82. For typical accounts that highlight Jefferson's role while neglecting Howell, see Duncan J. MacLeod, *Slavery, Race and the American Revolution* (New York: Cambridge University Press, 1974), 46; Peter S. Onuf, *The Origins of the Federal Republic: Jurisdictional Controversies in the United States, 1775–1787* (Philadelphia: University of Pennsylvania Press, 1983), 149–67; William G. Merkel, "Jefferson's Failed Anti-Slavery Proviso of 1784 and the Nascence of Free Soil Constitutionalism," *Seton Hall Law Review* 38 (April 2008): 555–603; and Baptist, *Half Has Never Been Told*, 7–8.

23. Moses Brown to David Howell (3 5mo 1784), excerpted in Davis, *Slavery in the Age of Revolution*, 153–54n74; James Pemberton to Moses Brown, Philad:, 4mo. 9th: 1784 (draft), Pemberton Papers, HSP, vol. 40; Moses Brown to James Pemberton, Providence, 2nd: 5th: Mo: 1784, ibid. Davis is unusual in acknowledging Howell's role (if only in a footnote), though without realizing how Quakers had spurred him to act. On Howell's role, see also Robert F. Berkhofer Jr., "Jefferson, the Ordinance of 1784, and the Origins of the American Territorial System," *WMQ* 29 (April 1972): 231–62, esp. 248. For typical accounts that highlight Jefferson's role while neglecting Howell, see Duncan J. MacLeod, *Slavery, Race and the American Revolution* (New York: Cambridge University Press, 1974), 46; Peter S. Onuf, *The Origins of the Federal Republic: Jurisdictional Controversies in the United States, 1775–1787* (Philadelphia: University of Pennsylvania Press, 1983), 149–67; Peter S. Onuf, *Statehood and Union: A History of the Northwest Ordinance* (Bloomington: Indiana University Press, 1987); and Merkel, "Jefferson's Failed Anti-Slavery Proviso," 555–603. The role of Quaker abolitionism is absent in most scholarship on the 1784 Land Ordinance (or the 1787 Northwest Ordinance) but is highlighted in "Relics of the Past No. 7," 181–82.

24. *JCC*, 26:247 (19 April 1784), 277 (23 April 1784); James Pemberton to John Pemberton, 6mo 14 1784, Pemberton Papers, HSP, vol. 41; *JCC*, 26:625 (2 August 1784), 627–28 (3 August 1784).

25. PMS Minutes Vol. 2, 429–30 (19 8mo 1784); *The Case of Our Fellow-Creatures, the Oppressed Africans, Respectfully Recommended to the Serious Consideration of the Legislature of Great-Britain, by the People Called Quakers* (Philadelphia: Joseph Crukshank, 1784), 5. For excerpts from the *Case of Our Fellow-Creatures*, and Ramsey's *Essay on the Treatment and Conversion of African Slaves*, see *Pennsylvania Mercury* (Philadelphia), 10 September 1784; *Political Intelligencer* (New Brunswick, NJ), 21 September 1784; *United States Chronicle* (Providence, RI), 27 October 1784; and *Pennsylvania Mercury*, 15 October 1784 and 22 October 1784.

26. *Pennsylvania Mercury*, 22 October 1784; *New-York Journal*, 16 September 1784 and 14 October 1784; *Providence Gazette*, 6 November 1784; *Massachusetts Spy*, 14 October 1784; *Essex Journal*, 27 October 1784; *New-York Packet*, 15 November 1784; *New-Haven Gazette*, 18 November 1784; *Newport Mercury*, 27 November 1784. For other antislavery pieces from this time, see also *Connecticut Courant* (Hartford), 9 November 1784; and *American Mercury* (Hartford), 29 November 1784.

27. Howell to James Pemberton, Trenton, Dec. 22d, 1784, PMS Miscellaneous, 1784:24. PMS Minutes Vol. 2, 437 (16 12mo 1784); James Pemberton to David Howell (in Congress at Trenton), Phiad: 12mo: 21st: 1784 (copy), Pemberton Papers, HSP, vol. 42.

28. PMS to Richard Henry Lee and Congress, Philadelphia, 26th of First mo., 1785, Papers of Continental Congress, reel 57, Remonstrances and Addresses to Congress, 1776–88, 347, available at http://www.fold3.com/image/184874/ (accessed 11 June 2014). The letter to Lee and the Congress was forwarded in James Pemberton to David Howell (in NYk), Philad 26. 1mo. 1785 (2 drafts), Pemberton Papers, HSP, vol. 42. Manuscript notations on the back of the Quakers' address indicate that their address was read in Congress, but the body made no official record of the episode (though an editor added a mention in a footnote: *JCC*, 28:19n). PMS Minutes Vol. 2, 457–58 (24 9mo 1784); Drake, *Quakers and Slavery in America*, 94–95; George William Van Cleve, *A Slaveholders' Union: Slavery, Politics, and the Constitution in the Early American Republic* (Chicago: University of Chicago Press, 2010), 104.

29. *JCC*, 28:164–65 (16 March 1785), 239 (6 April 1785). *The committee consisting of, &c. to whom was referred a motion of Mr. King, for the exclusion of involuntary servitude in the states described in the resolve of Congress of the 23d day of April, 1784* . . . [New York: 1785].

30. PMS to Congress, 20th of the 10mo: 1786, PMS Minutes Vol. 3, 38–39; New York Meeting for Sufferings Minutes Vol. 1, 176–77 (14 11mo 1786); James Pemberton to John Pemberton, Philad: 29th: 11thth mo. 1786, Pemberton Papers, HSP, vol. 47; PMS Minutes Vol. 3, p. 41–42 (21 12mo 1786); Edmund Prior to James Pemberton, New York, 3 M 15, 1787, Pemberton Papers, HSP, vol. 47; John Murray Jr. to James Pemberton, New York, 12 Mo. 8. 1786, ibid.

31. Edmund Prior to James Pemberton, New York, 3M 18, 1787, Pemberton Papers, HSP, vol. 47.

32. PAS Petition to the Honourable Convention of the United States Now Assembled in the City of Philadelphia, June 2d: 1787, PAS Papers, reel 25. The PAS published the petition in the press and shared it with British abolitionists who printed it as well; see *Pennsylvania Packet* (Philadelphia), 14 February 1788; *Independent Gazette* (Philadelphia), 7 March 1788; *Massachusetts Centinel* (Boston), 19 March 1788; *American Museum* (May 1788), 404–5; *Edinburgh Magazine or Literary Miscellany* (appendix to vol. 6 [1787]), 453; *Gentleman's Magazine* 2 (London, 1787) 925; and *Scots Magazine* 49 (Edinburgh, 1787) 564.

33. Waldstreicher, *Runaway America*, 234. The New-York Manumission Society papers indicate that John Jay, president of the N-YMS, helped draft the petition to the Federal Convention on 16 August 1787. The next day Hamilton arrived, having left the Federal Convention early. The N-YMS minutes recorded that "the Committee appointed last Evening to draw a Memorial to the federal Convention reported that they had prepared one which was read and approved, but the Society being informed that it was probable the Convention would not take up the Business, resolved not to send the same." Given that Hamilton had just returned, it appears most likely that he was the one who convinced the N-YMS not to submit the petition. See N-YMS Vol. 6: Meeting Minutes, 69–73.

Ron Chernow mistakenly assumed that the N-YMS petition *was* delivered to the convention and—completely misrepresenting the historical record—suggests that Hamilton deserves credit for proposing the petition; see Chernow, *Alexander Hamilton* (New York: Penguin Press, 2004), 239. More recent scholarship on Hamilton and slavery has undermined the notion that he was a committed abolitionist; see for example Jessie Serfilippi, "'As Odious and Immoral a Thing': Alexander Hamilton's Hidden History as an Enslaver," Schuyler Mansion State Historic Site research paper (2020); Arthur Scherr, "Alexander Hamilton and Slavery: A Closer

Look at the Founder," *Historian* 83 (2021), 130–70; and Andrew J. Fagal, "*The United States vs. The Young Ralph* (1802): Initial Attempts by the Jefferson Administration to Suppress the Slave Trade," *JER* (forthcoming).

34. *JCC*, 32:342 (13 July 1787).

35. Nathan Dane to Rufus King, New York, July 16, 1787, in Paul H. Smith and Ronald M. Gephart, eds., *Letters of Delegates to Congress, 1774–1789*, 26 vols. (Washington DC: Library of Congress, 1976–2000), 24:358.

36. On the Northwest Ordinance, see Staughton Lynd, *Class Conflict, Slavery, and the United States Constitution* (New York: Bobbs-Merrill, 1967), 185–213; Paul Finkelman, "Slavery and the Northwest Ordinance: A Study in Ambiguity," *JER* 6 (Winter 1986): 343–70; Onuf, *Statehood and Union*; David Brion Davis, "The Significance of Excluding Slavery from the Old Northwest in 1787," *Indiana Magazine of History* 84 (March 1988): 75–89; Van Cleve, *Slaveholders' Union*, 153–59; Baptist, *Half Has Never Been Told*, 7–8; Sean Wilentz, *No Property in Man: Slavery and Antislavery at the Founding* (Cambridge, MA: Harvard University Press, 2018),103–5.

On the tendency of slavery's nineteenth-century opponents to connect the 1787 restriction to Jefferson, see Merrill D. Peterson, *The Jefferson Image in the American Mind* (New York: Oxford University Press, 1962 [1960]), 189–94; and Nicholas P. Wood, "Jefferson's Legacy, Race Science, and Righteous Violence in Jabez Hammond's Abolitionist Fiction," *EAS* (Summer 2016): 568–609. Nathan Dane himself believed that Howell likely deserved more credit than Jefferson for the 1784 antislavery provision; see "Northwest Territory: Letter of Nathan Dane Concerning the Ordinance of 1787," *Indiana Historical Society Publications Volume 1* (Indianapolis: Bowen-Merrill, 1897), 69–74. Disputes over slavery in federal territories were central to nineteenth-century abolitionism and politics; see for example John Craig Hammond, *Slavery, Freedom, and Expansion in the Early American West* (Charlottesville: University of Virginia Press, 2007); and Michael A. Morrison, *Slavery and the American West: The Eclipse of Manifest Destiny and the Coming of the Civil War* (Chapel Hill: University of North Carolina Press, 1997).

37. James Pemberton to Daniel Mildred, Philad: 6mo. 20: 1786 (draft), Pemberton Papers, HSP, vol. 46.

38. Samuel Hopkins to Moses Brown, Newport, April 29, 1784, *WSH*, 119–20; Hopkins to Brown, Nov. 17, 1784, ibid., 120; New England Yearly Meeting Minutes Vol. 1, 391 (14 6mo 1784); Elizabeth Donnan, "Agitation Against the Slave Trade in Rhode Island, 1784–1790" in *Persecution and Liberty: Essays in Honor of George Lincoln Burr* (New York: Century Co., 1931), 473–482; Mack Thompson, *Moses Brown: Reluctant Reformer* (Chapel Hill: University of North Carolina Press, 1962), 177–80; Zilversmit, *First Emancipation*, 118–22; Kevin Vrevich, "The Inner Light of Radical Abolitionism: Greater Rhode Island and the Emergence of Racial Justice," (PhD dissertation, Ohio State University, 2019), 42–43, 53–55.

39. *Public Records of the State of Connecticut*, 5:122 (May 1783), 5:281–82 (January 1784), 8:xviii; The Memorial of Charles, Cato, Frank, Jack, Cuff, Yarrow, and Abel to the Hon[ble.] Generable Assembly of the Governor & Company of the State of Connecticut (9 October 1783), New Haven Museum, MSS 119, box 1, folder H. This petition had previously escaped historians' notice, and I thank Isabelle Laskaris for sharing images of it with me. See also Isabelle Laskaris, "'Thousands Now Unhappy': Slave Petitions in Eighteenth-Century Connecticut," *Slavery & Abolition* 44 (2023): 26–47, 36–36, 40.

40. *Acts and Laws of the State of Connecticut in America* (New London: Timothy Green, 1784), 233–35. Historians have debated whether Connecticut legislators realized when they approved the

346-page law compilation in January 1784 that it included the gradual abolition provision; see: Zilversmit, *First Emancipation*, 123–24; and Menschel, "Abolition Without Deliverance: The Law of Connecticut Slavery 1784–1848," *Yale Law Review* 11 (Septe,ber 2001), 183–222, esp. 187–89. The petition from the Black activists (of which neither Zilversmit nor Mencshel was aware) increases the likelihood that legislators were paying attention and supported gradual abolition.

41. Moses Brown to James Pemberton, Providence, 20th, 3d. mo. 1784, Pemberton papers, HSP, vol. 40; Isaac Hillard, *To the Honorable the General Assembly of the State of Connecticut, to Be Holden at Hartford, on the Second Thursday of May Next: The Memorial of Harry, Cuff, and Cato, Black Men, Now in Slavery in Connecticut, in Behalf of Ourselves and the Poor Black People of Our Nation in Like Circumstances* ([New Haven?], CT, [ca. 1796]), 2, 5.

42. Edmund Prior to James Pemberton, New York, 2M 26, 1784, Pemberton Papers, HSP, vol. 40; New York Meeting for Sufferings Minutes, Vol. 1, 114 (5 3mo 1784), 129–30 (14 12mo 1784), 135 (21 4mo 1785); New York Meeting for Sufferings to PMS (21 4mo 1785), in PMS Minutes Vol. 2, 449–50. The council of revisions vetoed the gradual abolition law ostensibly because it denied free Black people the right of suffrage. Zilversmit, *First Emancipation*, 146–52; Gellman, *Emancipating New York*, 45–55; Polgar, *Standard-Bearers of Equality*, 122–23; Gronningsater, *Rising Generation*, 44–47.

43. Hopkins, *Dialogue*, 69–70, quotations from appendix to 2nd edition; New York Meeting for Sufferings Minutes Vol. 1, 154–55 (15 2mo 1786); "To the Honorable Senate and Assembly of the State of New York," *Daily Advertiser* (New York) 16 March 1786 quotation; N-YMS Minutes Vol. 1, 34–38 (8 February 1786), 38–44 (11 May 1786), 52–58 (11 November 1786), 58–62 (15 February 1787), 64–68 (17 May 1787).

44. "Notices of David Cooper No. XXV," *Friends Review* 16 (1863), 21–22; Zilversmit, *First Emancipation*, 152–53; James J. Gigantino II, *The Ragged Road to Abolition: Slavery and Freedom in New Jersey, 1775–1865* (Philadelphia: University of Pennsylvania Press, 2025), 66; Bruce A. Bender, "'Love to Justice, and a Wish to Promote It': The Politics of Slavery in New Jersey 1770–1775," *New Jersey Studies* 3 (Winter 2017): 23–47.

45. Hanover Co. proslavery petition (16 November 1784), available through the Library of Virginia's petition database: https://lva-virginia.libguides.com/petitions. Mathews, *Slavery and Methodism*, 9–10.

46. *Minutes of Several Conversations Between the Rev. Thomas Coke, LL.D. the Rev. Francis Asbury and Others . . . Composing a Form of Discipline for the Ministers, Preachers and Other Members of the Methodist Episcopal Church in America* (Philadelphia: Charles Cist, 1785), 15–17; also in Mathews, *Slavery and Methodism*, 296–98.

47. *Extracts of the Journals of the Late Rev. Thomas Coke, L. L. D.: Comprising Several Visits to North America and the West-Indies . . .* (Dublin: R. Napper 1816), 63 (9 April 1785), 64 (11 April 1785).

48. For the creation of the Quaker petition, see NCSC Minutes, 64 (9 9mo 1785), 66–67 (31 12mo 1785). In response to the Quaker petition, the House of Commons passed "a bill, for permitting the emancipation of slaves under certain restrictions," which the Senate rejected. *Journals of the General Assembly of the State of North-Carolina [November to December 1785]* (New Bern, NC: Arnett & Hodges), [Part 2: House of Commons,] 15 (5 December 1785), [Part 1: Senate,] 16 (6 December 1785).

49. *Journal of the Rev. Francis Asbury: Bishop of the Methodist Episcopal Church* (3 vols., New York: Eaton & Mains, 1900–1904), 1:494–95 (30 April 1785); *Journals of the Late Rev. Thomas Coke*, 67–68 (1–4 May 1785), 69 (13 May 1785), 73 (26 May 1785).

50. *Minutes of the Annual Conferences of the Methodist Episcopal Church*, 24 (April-June 1785); *Journals of the Late Rev. Thomas Coke*, 74 (1 June 1785). See also Mathews, *Slavery and Methodism*, 10; Dee Andrews, *The Methodists and Revolutionary America, 1760–1800: The Shaping of an Evangelical Culture* (Princeton, NJ: Princeton University Press, 2000), 126; Charles F. Irons, *Origins of Proslavery Christianity: White and Black Evangelicals in Colonial and Antebellum Virginia* (Chapel Hill: University of North Carolina Press, 2008), 73–74; Wright, *Bonds of Salvation*, 47–48, 50–51.

51. Methodist Petition Against Slavery, November 8, 1785, in Kaminsky, *Necessary Evil?* 33–34. Eight of the original manuscripts are available through the Library of Virginia's petition database: https://lva-virginia.libguides.com/petitions. See also Richard K. MacMaster, "Liberty or Property? The Methodist Petition for Emancipation in Virginia, 1785," *Methodist History* 10 (1971): 44–55; Eva Sheppard Wolf, *Race and Liberty in the New Nation: Emancipation in Virginia from the Revolution to Nat Turner's Rebellion* (Baton Rouge: Louisiana State University, 2006), 88–96; Andrews, *Methodists and Revolutionary America*, 123–30.

52. Remonstrance and Petition of the Free Inhabitants of Amelia County, in Fredrika Teute Schmidt and Barbara Ripel Wilhelm, "Early Proslavery Petitions in Virginia," *WMQ* 30 (January 1973): 133–46, quotations from 139.

53. Madison to GW, Richmond Novr. 11. 1785, http://founders.archives.gov/documents/Madison/01-08-02-0208; James Madison to Ambrose Madison, Richmond Decr. 15—1785, *FO*, http://founders.archives.gov/documents/Madison/01-08-02-0231; Madison to Jefferson, Richmond Jan. 22d. 1786, *FO*, http://founders.archives.gov/documents/Madison/01-08-02-0249; *Journal of Rev. Francis Asbury*, 1:502 (15 November 1785).

54. Robert Pleasants to George Washington, Curles 12 mo. 11. 1785, *FO*, https://founders.archives.gov/documents/Washington/04-03-02-0384; Rosemarie Zagarri, ed., *David Humphreys' "Life of General Washington": With George Washington's "Remarks"* (Athens: University of Georgia Press, 1991), 78. For scholarly commentary on Washington and slavery, see Kenneth Morgan, "George Washington and the Problem of Slavery," *Journal of American Studies* 34 (August 2000): 279–301; Dorothy Twohig, "'That Species of Property': Washington's Role in the Controversy Over Slavery," in *George Washington Reconsidered*, ed. Don Higginbotham (Charlottesville: University of Virginia Pres, 2001), 114–38; Henry Wiencek, *An Imperfect God: George Washington, His Slaves, and the Creation of America* (New York: Farrar, Straus and Giroux, 2005); Philip D. Morgan, "'To Get Quit of Negroes': George Washington and Slavery," *Journal of American Studies* 39 (December 2005): 403–29; Nicholas P. Wood, "George Washington's Contested Antislavery Legacy," *Mount Vernon Magazine* (Winter 2016): 42–43; and Mary V. Thompson, *"The Only Unavoidable Subject of Regret": George Washington, Slavery, and the Enslaved Community at Mount Vernon* (Charlottesville: University of Virginia Press, 2019).

55. Irons, *Origins of Proslavery Christianity*, 68–70; Monica Najar, "'Meddling with Emancipation': Baptists, Authority, and the Rift over Slavery in the Upper South," *JER* 25 (July 2005): 157-86, esp. 162–63.

56. Robert Holliday to [James Pemberton], Duck Creek, 12mo 12—1785, PMS Miscellaneous, 1792 (filed out of order); [John Parrish] to Robert Holliday, Philad:, 12mo: 17: 1785, ibid.; PMS Minutes Vol. 3, 7–8 (17 12mo 1785 and 19 1mo 1786). For the text of the petition, see ibid., 17–18, and "Relics of the Past [Warner Mifflin] No. 8," *The Friend* (1844), 189. Statistics for 1783 through 1786: http://slavevoyages.org/voyages/Db11FiOR. Patrick S. Brady, "The Slave Trade and Sectionalism in South Carolina, 1787–1808," *JSH* 38 (November 1972): 601–20.

57. For scholarship emphasizing the proslavery aspect of the Constitution, see especially Lynd, *Class Conflict*; Gary B. Nash, *Race and Revolution* (New York: Rowman & Littlefield, 1990), 25–56; Paul Finkelman, *Slavery and the Founders: Race and Liberty in the Ave of Jefferson*, 3rd ed. (Armonk, NY: M. E. Sharpe, 2014); David Waldstreicher, *Slavery's Constitution: From Revolution to Ratification* (New York: Hill and Wang, 2009); and Van Cleve, *Slaveholders' Union*. An important body of scholarship rejects or qualifies the proslavery interpretation of the Constitution while generally acknowledging that the implementation of federal power increasingly benefited slaveholders through the 1850s. See for example William Wiecek, *The Sources of Antislavery Constitutionalism in America, 1760–1848* (Ithaca, NY: Cornell University Press, 1977); Howard A. Ohline, "Slavery, Economics, and Congressional Politics, 1790," *JSH* 46 (August 1980):335–60; Earl M. Maltz, "The Idea of a Proslavery Constitution," *JER* 17 (April 1997): 37–59; Don E. Fehrenbacher, *The Slaveholding Republic: An Account of the United States Government's Relations to Slavery* (New York: Oxford University Press, 2002); and Wilentz, *No Property in Man*.

58. William Rotch Sr. to Moses Brown, Nantucket, 8 November 1787, *DHRC*; James Thornton, Sr. to Moses Brown, Byberry, Philadelphia County, 17 December [1787], *DHRC*; James Phillips to James Pemberton, Lond'n, 28th 2d month 1788, Pemberton Papers, HSP, vol. 49. See also the letters collected in "Quaker Opposition to the Constitution's Provisions Concerning Slavery" at the University of Wisconsin-Madison, Center for the Study of the American Constitution: https://csac.history.wisc.edu/document-collections/religion-and-the-ratification/quaker-opposition/.

59. [Hugh Hughes], "A Countryman II," *New York Journal*, 23 November 1787, *DHRC*; [DeWitt Clinton], "A Countryman II," *New York Journal*, 13 December 1787, *DHRC*. On the issue of slavery during ratification debates, see Kaminski, *Necessary Evil?*; Waldstreicher, *Slavery's Constitution*, 107–51, esp. 127–33; Van Cleve, *Slaveholders' Union*, 134–39, 172–78; John Craig Hammond, "'We Are to Be Reduced to the Level of Slaves': Slavery, Planters, Taxes, Aristocrats, and Massachusetts Antifederalists, 1787–1788," *Historical Journal of Massachusetts* 31 (Summer 2003): 172–98; and Mark Boonshoft, "Doughfaces at the Founding: Federalists, Anti-Federalists, Slavery, and the Ratification of the Constitution in New York," *New York History* (Summer 2012): 187–218.

60. Benjamin Rush to Jeremy Belknap, Philadelphia, 28 February 1788, *DHRC*; James Pemberton to Moses Brown, Philad:a, 11mon: 16, 1787 (draft), Pemberton Papers, HSP, vol. 49. See also Robert Waln to Richard Waln, Philadelphia, October 3, 1787, in Kaminski, *Necessary Evil*, 118. Wilentz also argues that abolitionists correctly recognized the Constitution's antislavery potential. However, he exaggerates their naiveté, suggesting they "believed that slavery would still require additional importation of Africans to flourish; and it followed that permanently ending the slave trade would hasten slavery's doom." Wilentz, *No Property in Man*, 134.

61. Moses Brown to James Pemberton, Providence, 17 October [1787], *DHRC*; Granville Sharp, *The Just Limitation of Slavery in the Laws of God, Compared with the Unbounded Claims of the African Traders and British American Slaveholders* (London: B. White, 1776), 55; Benezet to Samuel Allinson, Philadelphia Third Month, 30th, 1774, *FAB*, 311; Anthony Benezet to John Pemberton, Philadelph'a y'e 10th 8th mo 1783, *FAB*, 395–99.

62. PYM Minutes Vol. 3, 119 (29 9mo 1787).

63. PMS epistle to the New England Meeting for Sufferings, 21 12mo 1786, in PMS Minutes Vol. 3, 43–45. According to the available data, from 1780 through 1785, American slavers made nineteen voyages serving the domestic market and four to foreign markets; from 1786

through 1789, they made ten serving the domestic market and thirty to foreign markets: http://slavevoyages.org/voyages/eQSWS8FS. On the American slave trade to foreign markets, see Jay Coughtry, *The Notorious Triangle: Rhode Island and the African Slave Trade, 1700–1807* (Philadelphia: Temple University Press, 1981); and Leonardo Marquez, *The United States and the Transatlantic Slave Trade to the Americas, 1776–1867* (New Haven, CT: Yale University Press, 2016). On kidnapping and the domestic slave trade, see Carol Wilson, *Freedom At Risk: The Kidnapping of Free Blacks in America, 1780–1865* (Lexington: University of Kentucky, 1994); and Richard Bell, *Stolen: The Astonishing Odyssey of Five Boys Along the Reverse Underground Railroad* (New York: Simon & Schuster, 2019).

64. Warner Mifflin to James Pemberton, Kent ye 3th Day of 2mo: 1787, Pemberton Papers, HSP, vol. 47; Warner Mifflin to John Parrish, Kent ye 9th of 2 mo. 1787, CPW, box 1. "An Act to Prevent the Exportation of Slaves, and for Other Purposes," chap. CXLV, *Laws of the State of Delaware: from the Fourteenth Day of October, [1700], to the eighteenth day of August, [1797]*, 384–88 (3 February 1787). See also Patience Essah, *A House Divided: Slavery and Emancipation in Delaware, 1638–1865* (Charlottesville: University of Virginia Press, 1996), 40–41; Gary B. Nash, *Warner Mifflin: Unflinching Quaker Abolitionist* (Philadelphia: University of Pennsylvania Press, 2017).

65. PMS Minutes Vol. 3, 51–52 (15 3mo 1787), 53–54 (27 3mo 1787); Warner Mifflin to John Parrish, 19th of 6 mo: 1787, CPW, box 1; James Pemberton to John Pemberton, Philad:a, 8th 6th mo: 1787, Pemberton Papers, HSP, vol. 48; George Churchman to James Pemberton, E. Nottingham, 12mo. 14th. 1787, ibid., vol. 49. PMS members later recorded their disappointment "that Discouragement had too easily taken place on the Appearance of warm opposition [in 1787]." PMS Minutes Vol. 3, 78–79 (20 3mo 1788).

66. NCSC Minutes, 69–73 (6 9mo 1787); Warner Mifflin to John Parrish, Accomack in Virginia the 13th Day of 12 mo: 1787, CPW, box 1; Warner Mifflin to James Pemberton, Kent, ye 21th of 12mo: 1787, Pemberton Papers, HSP, vol. 49; Warner Mifflin to Moses Brown, Portsmouth in Virginia ye 3th [*sic*] of 12mo. 1787, Papers of the American Slave Trade: Series A: Selections from the Rhode Island Historical Society: Part 1, Brown Family Collection, reel 18; Michael J. Crawford, ed., *The Having of Negroes Is Becoming a Burden: The Quaker Struggle to Free Slaves in Revolutionary North Carolina* (Gainesville: University of Florida Press, 2010), 135.

67. William Welsh Harrison, *Harrison, Waples and Allied Families: Being the Ancestry of George Leib Harrison of Philadelphia and of His Wife Sarah Ann Waples* (Philadelphia: Printed for Private Circulation Only, 1910), 11. See also "Memoirs of the Life and Travels of Sarah Harrison, Late of Philadelphia, Deceased," *Friend's Miscellany* (Philadelphia), vol. 11 (third month 1838), 97–216.

68. Edmund Prior to James Pemberton, New York, 6M 3, 1787, Pemberton Papers, HSP, vol. 48; William Savery to James Pemberton, Newport, 6 mo. 14th. 1787, Pemberton Papers, HSP, 48; Moses Brown to [John Pemberton?], Providence, 21st, 6th mo. 1787 (updated and sent on 4 10mo 1787), CPW, box 9; NEYM, *To the General Assembly of the State of Rhode-Island. Respectfully Sheweth, the Religious Society of the People Called Quakers, in New England, Met Together in Their annual Assembly on Rhode-Island . . .* ([Providence?], [1787]). Hopkins to Moses Brown, August 13, 1787, *WSH*, 121–22; Hopkins to Moses Brown, October 22, 1787, *WSH*, 122; Moses Brown to James Pemberton, Providence, 17th. 10th, mo, 1787, Pemberton Papers, HSP, vol. 48 (excerpted in *DHRC*: http://rotunda.upress.virginia.edu/founders/RNCN-03-14-03-0003-0004). Moses Brown was undoubtedly the most active abolitionists among the New England Quakers, but his biographers tend to exaggerate his personal initiative by ignoring

the larger efforts of the various Quaker meetings for sufferings. Thompson, *Moses Brown*, 189–92; Charles Rappleye, *Sons of Providence: The Brown Brothers, the Slave Trade and the Revolution* (New York: Simon & Schuster, 2007), 246–49.

69. "Crito," *Providence Gazette*, 6 and 13 October 1787; "An Act to Prevent the Slave Trade, and to Encourage the Abolition of Slavery," 1787, in Elizabeth Donnan, ed., *Documents Illustrative of the Slave Trade*, 4 vols. (Washington, DC: Carnegie Institution of Washington, 1930–1935), 3:343–44.

70. Moses Brown to [John Pemberton?], Providence, 21st, 6th mo. 1787 [updated and sent on 4 10mo 1787], CPW, box 9; Jeremy Belknap to Benjamin Rush, Boston, Sep'r 29 1787, Rush Papers, vol. 30; Moses Brown to the Committee of the Assembly & Senate of the State of Massachusetts on the Memorial of the People called Quakers, Providence, 1st, 11th mo, 1787, Massachusetts Anti-Slavery and Anti-Segregation Petitions Dataverse, Harvard, http://nrs.harvard.edu/urn-3:FHCL:10935256.

71. Petition of Prince Hall et al., (27 February 1788), Massachusetts Petitions Dataverse: http://nrs.harvard.edu/urn-3:FHCL:12176678. The signers included Lancaster Hill, who had also signed Hall's 1777 petition calling for emancipation. Moses Brown to James Pemberton, Providence, 5th. 5th Mo. 1788, Pemberton Papers, HSP, vol. 50. Cameron, *To Plead Our Own Cause*, 79–82.

72. Jeremy Belknap to Benjamin Rush, Boston, 16[?] Aug't 1788, Rush Papers, vol. 30, 5. Rush had extracts of this letter printed, which other newspapers then reproduced; see for example *Pennsylvania Mercury* (Philadelphia), 23 August 1788, republished in *New-Haven Gazette*, 4 September 1788; *Freeman's Oracle* (Exeter, NH), 13 September 1788; and *Cumberland Gazette* (Portland, ME), 18 September 1788. Jeremy Belknap to Benjamin Rush, Boston, Sep'r 1788, Rush Papers, vol. 30; NEMS to New York Meeting for Sufferings (25 2mo 1788) in New York Meeting for Sufferings Minutes Vol. 1, 212 (13 5mo 1788).

73. PAS Minutes, 21–25 (7 1mo 1788), 26–28 (21 1mo 1788); PMS Minutes Vol. 3, 74–75 (17 1mo 1788); "The Fathers of African Emancipation in the State of Pennsylvania," *Genius of Universal Emancipation (Jonesboro, TN), 18 7th Month 1823* (I thank Michael Crowder for this source); *Minutes of the . . . Twelfth General Assembly of the Commonwealth of Pennsylvania* (Philadelphia: Sellers and Hall, 1788), 104–5 (23 February 1788), 108 (25 February 1788), 109 (26 February 1788), 128 (7 March 1788), 133–35 (10 March 1788), 137 (12 March 1788). On the antislavery lobbying, see James Pemberton to John Pemberton, Philad:a, 30th: 3d mon, 1788, Pemberton Papers, HSP, vol. 49; James Pemberton to Moses Brown, Philad:, 3: 4mo, 1788 (draft), ibid.; and PAS Minutes, 28–31 (7 4mo 1788), 39 (7 7mo 1788). The report was printed in *Pennsylvania Packet* (Philadelphia), 13 March 1788; *The Constitution of the Pennsylvania Society, for Promoting the Abolition of Slavery, and the Relief of Free Negroes, Unlawfully Held in Bondage . . . to Which Are Added, the Acts of the General Assembly of Pennsylvania, for the Gradual Abolition of Slavery* (Philadelphia: Francis Bailey, 1788).

74. "Fathers of African Emancipation," 178–79 (28 March 1788); *Proceedings and Debates of the General Assembly of Pennsylvania, Taken in Short Hand by Thomas Lloyd: Volume the Third [February 19—March 29, 1788]* (Philadelphia: printed for the editor, 1788), 219–25 (28 March 1788); James Pemberton to William Dillwyn, Philad:a, 21st 4th mo 1788 (draft by secretary), Pemberton Papers, HSP, vol. 50. See also Nash and Soderlund, *Freedom by Degrees*, 127; Newman, *Transformation of American Abolitionism*, 72–85; Richard S. Newman, "'Lucky to Be Born in Pennsylvania': Free Soil, Fugitive Slaves and the Making of Pennsylvania's Anti-Slavery Borderland," *Slavery & Abolition* (September 2011): 413–30; Dee E. Andrews, "Reconsidering

the First Emancipation: Evidence from the Pennsylvania Abolition Society Correspondence, 1785–1810," *Pennsylvania History* 64 (July 1997): 230–49, esp. 235–36; Polgar, *Standard-Bearers of Equality*, 99–102; and Michael Crowder, "Human Capital: The Moral and Political Economy of Northeastern Abolitionism, 1763–1833," (PhD diss., CUNY Graduate Center, 2019), 1–2, 145–46.

75. PMS Minutes Vol. 3, 83 (15 5mo 1788); Warner Mifflin to James Pemberton, Kent in Maryland, ye 28 Day of 5mo: 1788, Pemberton Papers, HSP, vol. 50; Warner Mifflin to John Parrish, 19 Day of 11mo: 1788, CPW, box 1; Warner Mifflin to John Parrish & Evan Williams, Annapolis, Seventh day morning, 29th of 11 mo: 1788, ibid.; Warner Mifflin to James Pemberton, Kent ye 29th of 12mo: 1788., Pemberton Papers, HSP, vol. 51. A year later, James Pemberton attended the Baltimore Yearly Meeting, which again petitioned the legislature, but revived antislavery debates failed to result in legislation. James Pemberton to Sarah & Mary S. Pemberton, Baltimore, 12: 6mon. 1789, Pemberton Papers, HSP, vol. 52. James Pemberton to William Dillwyn (draft), ibid.

76. James Pemberton to John Pemberton, Philad:a, 29th: 6th mon: 1788, Pemberton Papers, HSP, vol. 50; Edward Miller to James Pemberton, Dover, Feby 2d, 1789, Pemberton Papers, HSP, vol. 51; James Pemberton to Edward Miller (Dover), 18 6mo 1789 (copy), Pemberton Papers, HSP, vol. 52; PMS Minutes Vol. 3, 86–87 (17 7mo 1788), 94 (16 10mo 1788), 99 (15 1mo 1789), 100 (19 2mo 1789). "An Additional Supplementary Act to an Act, Intituled An Act to Prevent the Exportation of Saves . . . ," chap. CXIV, *Laws of the State of Delaware: from the Fourteenth Day of October, [1700], to the Eighteenth Day of August, [1797]*, 942–44 (3 February 1789). Other legislatures, motivated by fears of slave insurrection, banned the domestic slave trade *into* their states, but Delaware was the only slave state to restrain sales *out* of the state. This was among the factors that increased the rate of manumissions there, so that a majority of the state's Black inhabitants were free by the early nineteenth century.

77. David Cooper's diary (16 11mo 1788), excerpted in "Notices of David Cooper No. XXXII," *Friends Review* 16 (1863), 135; William Livingston to James Pemberton, Elizabeth Town, 20 Oct 1788, *PWL* 5:357–59; Livingston to Pemberton, Elizabeth Town, 21st December 1788, ibid., 365–68. PMS Minutes Vol. 3, 92–93 (16 10mo 1788), 94–95 (20 11mo 1788), 95–98 (18 12mo 1788); James Pemberton to John Pemberton, Philad:a, 11th mon: 12th 1788, Pemberton Papers, HSP, vol. 51; James Pemberton to William Dillwyn, Philad:, 4mon: 25th, 1789 (copy), Pemberton Papers, HSP, vol. 51. Zilversmit, *First Emancipation*, 159–60; Gigantino, *Ragged Road*, 72–73. Gigantino demonstrates slaveholder opposition to abolitionism in New Jersey but also exaggerates the conservatism and racism of abolitionists; see especially *Ragged Road*, 98.

78. Edmund Prior to James Pemberton, New York, 3M 16, 1788, Pemberton Papers, HSP, vol. 49. The following year, Prior reported that "party spirit runs so high in our Assembly that I fear there is no room for any relief to the poor Africans this year." Edmund Prior to James Pemberton, New York, 1M 26, 1789, Pemberton Papers, HSP, vol. 51. Zilversmit, *First Emancipation*, 149–50.

79. White, *Somewhat More Independent*, 85. For more balanced accounts of the N-YMS, see Robert J. Swan, "John Teasman: African-American Educator and the Emergence of Community in Early Black New York City, 1787–1815," *JER* 12 (Autumn 1992): 331–56; Gellman, *Emancipating New York*; Sinha, *Slave's Cause*, 77–79, 81–83; Gronningsater, *Rising Generation*; and Polgar, *Standard-Bearers of Equality*.

80. Edmund Prior to James Pemberton, New York, 3M 16, 1788, Pemberton Papers, HSP, vol. 49; New York Meeting for Sufferings Minutes Vol. 1, 215 (13 5mo 1788), 216 (10 6mo 1788),

218 (12 8mo 1788), 223 (9 12mo 1788). "The Following Is Extracted from a Late Publication on the Slave Trade," *New-Haven Gazette*, 22 May 1788; "Extract from . . . Thoughts on the African Slave Trade," ibid., 29 May 1788; "A Late British Paper . . . Infamous African Slave Trade," ibid., 5 June 1788; "A Letter to the Society Instituted (in England) for the Purpose of Effecting the Abolition of the Slave Trade," ibid., 23 October 1788; "The Memorial and the Petition of the . . . Quakers," ibid.

81. Moses Brown to Samuel Hopkins, Providence, 24th 10th Mo 1788, (copy), Papers of AST, reel 18; "The Representatives of the Religious Society of the People Call'd Quakers in the State of New York and Western Parts of Connecticut . . . to the General Assembly of the State of Connecticut," in New York Meeting for Sufferings Vol. 1, 221–22 (29 9mo 1788).

82. "Negroes Memorial Oct'r 1788," in Vincent J. Rosivach, "Three Petitions by Connecticut Negroes for the Abolition of Slavery in Connecticut," *Connecticut Review* 17 (Fall 1995): 79–92, quotation from 87; "A.Z." [Moses Brown?], *Providence Gazette*, 1 November 1788 (the writer forwarded a copy of the Connecticut law and clearly had knowledge of the proceedings in New Haven, suggesting that A.Z. was Moses Brown); Edmund Prior to James Pemberton, New York, 10 M 19, 1788, Pemberton Papers, HSP, vol. 51; Moses Brown to Samuel Hopkins, Providence, 24th 10th Mo 1788 (copy), Papers of AST, reel 18.

83. Edmund Prior to James Pemberton, New York, 11M 20 1788, Pemberton Papers, HSP, vol. 51; Jonathan Edwards to Moses Brown, New Haven, Oct. 20, 1788, in Elizabeth Donnan, ed., *Documents Illustrative of the Slave Trade*, 4 vols. (Washington, DC: Carnegie Institution of Washington, 1930–1935), 3:345; James Pemberton to John Pemberton, Philad:a, 11th mon: 12th 1788, Pemberton Papers, HSP, vol. 51; James Pemberton to William Dillwyn, Philad;, 3. 12mo: 1788 (copy), Pemberton Papers, HSP, vol. 51. See also PMS epistle to LMS, 18 12mo 1788, in PMS Minutes Vol. 3, 95–98. On efforts to evade gradual abolition laws, see Robert William Fogel and Stanley Engerman, "Philanthropy at Bargain Prices: Notes on the Economics of Gradual Emancipation," *Journal of Legal Studies* 3 (June 1974): 377–401; and John Wood Sweet, *Bodies Politic: Negotiating Race in the American North, 1730–1830* (Baltimore: Johns Hopkins University Press, 2003), 260.

84. Moses Brown to Samuel Hopkins (draft), Providence 14th. 5mo. 1784, Papers of AST, reel 4; Hopkins to Dr. Levi Hart, June 10, 1791, *WSH*, 1:136–37; William H. Robinson, ed., *The Proceedings of the Free African Union Society and the African Benevolent Society: Newport, Rhode Island 1780–1824* (Providence: Urban League of Rhode Island, 1976). For early national debates over Black emigration, see especially John Floyd Miller, *The Search for a Black Nationality: Black Emigration and Colonization, 1787–1863* (Urbana: University of Illinois Press, 1975); and Samantha Seeley, *Race, Removal, and the Right to Remain: Migration and the Making of the United States* (Chapel Hill: University of North Carolina Press, 2021).

85. See for example William Dillwyn to John Pemberton, London, 9mo 25. 1784, Pemberton Papers, HSP, vol. 42; William Dillwyn to [James Pemberton], Clapton near Hackney, Middlesex, 2mo 23d. 1785, Pemberton Papers, HSP, vol. 43; William Dillwyn to Moses Brown, London, 11mo. 29. 1786, Papers of AST, reel 18; C. M. Harris and Daniel Preston, eds., *The Papers of William Thornton: Volume One, 1871–1802* (Charlottesville: University of Virginia Press, 1995), 1:xlii-xliii. 101–3. See also Seeley, *Race, Removal, and the Right to Remain*, 177–84; Christopher Leslie Brown, *Moral Capital: The Foundations of British Abolitionism* (Chapel Hill: University of North Carolina Press, 2006), 315–21; Cassandra Pybus, *Epic Journeys of Freedom: Runaway Slaves of the American Revolution and Their Global Quest for Liberty* (Boston: Beacon Press, 2006).

86. Samuel Stevens, Prince Hall, et al. (4 January 1787), Massachusetts Petitions Dataverse, http://nrs.harvard.edu/urn-3:FHCL:10935255; Thornton to Jacques Pierre Brissot de Warville, Philadelphia 29th of the 11th month 1788, in Harris and Preston, *Papers of William Thornton*, 1:80–84, quotation from 82. See also Samuel Stevens to Anthony Tiller [Taylor] of Newport, June 1, in the year 1787 [Boston, Massachusetts,] in Robinson, *Proceedings of the Free African Union*, 17–18. Miller, *Search for Black Nationality*, 12–15. On Black Americans' insistence on self-determination, see also Gary B. Nash, *Forging Freedom: The Formation of Philadelphia's Free Black Community, 1720–1840*, (Cambridge, MA: Harvard University Press, 1988), 100–103; Julie Winch, *A Gentleman of Color: The Life of James Forten* (New York: Oxford University Press, 2002), 177–206; James Sidbury, *Becoming African in America: Race and Nation in the Early Black Atlantic* (New York: Oxford University Press, 2007), 67–130; Richard S. Newman, *Freedom's Prophet: Bishop Richard Allen, the AME Church, and the Black Founding Fathers* (New York: New York University Press, 2008), 183–208; and Samantha Seely, *Race, Removal, and the Right to Remain: Migration and the Making of the United States* (Chapel Hill: University of North Carolina Press, 2021), 3, 174–80.

87. Unfortunately, few records survive for the men's branch of the FAS and none survive for the women's group. Joseph Clark explained that there were "two societies held in Philadelphia of free Africans, and their descendants; one of Men, and the other of Women." See "Joseph Clark's Acco. of an Association of Free Negroes in Philad for Care of Their Poor," 19th 9mo, 1787, PAS Papers, box 7, folder 5 (Series IV: Manumission and Indentures, in a folder titled "Miscellaneous papers"). For early records of the FAS (kept using Quaker dating style), noting Clark's role, and the changes in location, see William Douglass, ed., *Annals of the First African Church, in the United States of America . . .* (Philadelphia, 1862), 15 (12 4mo 1787), 15–17(17 5mo 1787), 18. See also Nash, *Forging Freedom*, 100–103; Newman, *Freedom's Prophet*; and Sinha, *Slave's Cause*, 136.

88. Jupiter Hammon, *An Address to the Negroes, in the State of New York* (Philadelphia: Daniel Humphreys, 1787), 10 (the pamphlet was first printed in New York by Carrol and Patterson); Edmund Prior to James Pemberton, New York, 6M 19. 1787, Pemberton Papers, HSP, vol. 48. For the London republication, see Capel Loft to Samuel Hoare Junr., Trostonhall, 23. Dec: [17]87, Papers of Thomas Clarkson, Huntington Library, San Marino, CA. On Hammon, see also Gellman, *Emancipating New York*, 105–7; and Dickson D. Bruce, *Origins of African American Literature, 1680–1865* (Charlottesville: University of Virginia Press, 2001), 37–39, 50, 80, and passim. The New York African Society was a group of Black Episcopalians; see Kyle T. Bulthius, *Four Steeples over the City Streets: Religion and Society in New York's Early Republic Congregations* (New York: New York University Press, 2014), 67–69.

89. John Pemberton to James Pemberton, London, 7th mo: 18th. 1787, Pemberton Papers, HSP, vol. 48; "Letter of a Negro," *Pennsylvania Mercury* (Philadelphia), 29 April 1788; *Freeman's Journal* (Philadelphia), 14 May 1788; "Letter on Slavery. By a Negro," *American Museum* (Philadelphia) 6 (July 1789), 77–80.

90. Thomas Jefferson, *Notes on the State of Virginia* (Philadelphia: Richard and Hall, 1788), 173–74 (Query 18: Manners). My page citations are to the Philadelphia edition that contemporaries would have read, but I have benefited from the annotations in Thomas Jefferson, *Notes on the State of Virginia: An Annotated Edition*, ed. Robert Forbes (New Haven, CT: Yale University Press, 2022).

91. Jefferson, *Notes on the State of Virginia*, 147, 150, 154 (Query 14: Laws). For Quakers' republication of Phillis Wheatley's *Poems on Various Subjects, Religious and Moral*, see the 1786

and 1789 editions printed by Joseph Crukshank in Philadelphia. On Jefferson's complex views on slavery, emancipation, and colonization, see especially William W. Freehling, "The Founding Fathers, Conditional Antislavery, and the Nonradicalism of the American Revolution," in *The Reintegration of American History: Slavery and the Civil War* (New York: Oxford University Press, 1994), 12–28; Peter S. Onuf, "'To Declare Them a Free and Independent People': Race, Slavery, and National Identity in Jefferson's Thought," *JER* 18 (Spring 1998): 1–46; Ari Helo and Peter S. Onuf, "Jefferson, Morality, and the Problem of Slavery," *WMQ* 60 (July 2003): 583–614; Peter S. Onuf, *The Mind of Thomas Jefferson* (Charlottesville: University of Virginia Press, 2007); Christa Dierksheide, "'The Great Improvement and Civilization of That Race': Jefferson and the 'Amelioration' of Slavery, ca. 1770–1826," *Early American Studies* 6, (Spring 2008):165–97.

92. Union Society of Africans to the Free African Society, Newport, Sep. 1st, 1789, Douglass ed., *Annals of the First African Church*, 25–28, quotation; Prince Hall to Free African Society, Boston, Sep. 16th, 1789, ibid., 30–31. See also the correspondence of the Newport society in Robinson, *Proceedings*, 19–32. See also Christy Clark-Pujara, *Dark Work: The Business of Slavery in Rhode Island* (New York: New York University Press, 2016), 117–21.

93. Free African Union Society to Union Society of Africans, [Philadelphia], [17th, 10th mo., 1789], Douglass, *Annals of the First African Church*, 28–29; Nash, *Forging Freedom*, 103.

94. *American Museum* 6 (November 1789), 383–85; Nash and Soderlund, *Freedom by Degrees*, 128; Polgar, *Standard-Bearers of Equality*, 83, 139–41.

95. James Pemberton to the London Society, May 3, 1790, PAS Letterbook, 1:32–35, PAS Papers. It seems that Black voting remained rare in Philadelphia but was more common in rural areas; see Nicholas Wood, "'A Sacrifice on the Altar of Slavery': Doughface Politics and Black Disenfranchisement in Pennsylvania, 1837–1838," *JER* 31 (Spring 2011): 75–105; and Van Gosse, *The First Reconstruction: Black Politics in America from the Revolution to the Civil War* (Chapel Hill: University of North Carolina Press, 2021), 94–141.

96. Warner Mifflin to James Pemberton, Kent ye 3th [*sic*] Day of 2mo: 1787, Pemberton Papers, HSP, box 47.

Epilogue

1. Ira Berlin, *Many Thousands Gone: The First Two Centuries of Slavery in North America* (Cambridge, MA: Harvard University Press, 1998), 370, 372.

2. James D. Essig, *The Bonds of Wickedness: American Evangelicals Against Slavery, 1770–1808* (Philadelphia: Temple University Press, 1982), 115–66; Ben Wright, *Bonds of Salvation: How Christianity Inspired and Limited American Abolitionism* (Baton Rouge: Louisiana State University, 2020), 47–54.

3. Jeremy Belknap to David Howell, Boston, June 14th, 1790, in *Life of Jeremy Belknap, D. D.: The Historian of New Hampshire: With Selections from His Correspondence and Other Writings . . .* (New York: Harper and Brothers, 1847), 169–70. On the lack of enthusiasm for abolitionist agitation in Massachusetts at this time, see also Richard S. Newman, *The Transformation of American Abolitionism: Fighting Slavery in the Early Republic* (Chapel Hill: University of North Carolina Press, 2002), 35.

4. Thomas E. Drake, *Quakers and Slavery in America* (New Haven, CT: Yale University Press, 1950); Christopher Cameron, *To Plead Our Own Cause: African Americans in Massachusetts and the Making of the Antislavery Movement* (Kent, OH: Kent State University Press, 2011); Patrick Rael, *Eighty-Eight Years: The Long Death of Slavery in the United States, 1777–1863* (Athens: University of Georgia Press, 2015); Manisha Sinha, *The Slave's Cause: A History*

of Abolition (New Haven, CT: Yale University Press, 2016); Gary B. Nash, *Warner Mifflin: Unflinching Quaker Abolitionist* (Philadelphia: University of Pennsylvania Press, 2017); Paul J. Polgar, *Standard-Bearers of Liberty and Equality: America's First Abolition Movement* (Chapel Hill: University of North Carolina Press, 2019); Nicholas P. Wood, "A 'Class of Citizens': The Earliest Black Petitioners to Congress and Their Quaker Allies," *WMQ* 74 (January 2017): 109–44; Nicholas P. Wood, "Abolitionists, Congress, and the Atlantic Slave Trade: Before and After Ratification," in *From Independence to the U.S. Constitution: Reconsidering the Critical Period of American History*, ed. Douglass Bradburn and Christopher Pearl (Charlottesville: University of Virginia Press, 2022), 93–125.

5. John Coffey, *Exodus and Liberation: Deliverance Politics from John Calvin to Martin Luther King, Jr.* (New York: Oxford University Press, 2014), 126.

6. John R. McKivigan, *The War Against Proslavery Religion: Abolitionists and the Northern Churches, 1830–1865* (Ithaca, NY: Cornell University Press, 1984; Larry E. Tise, *Proslavery: A History of the Defense of Slavery in America, 1701–1840* (Athens: University of Georgia Press, 1987); Mitchell Snay, *Gospel of Disunion: Religion and Separatism in the Antebellum South* (Chapel Hill: University of North Carolina Press, 1997); Mark Noll, *The Civil War as Theological Crisis* (Chapel Hill: University of North Carolina Press, 2006); Jordan Watkins, *Slavery and Sacred Texts: The Bible, the Constitution, and Historical Consciousness in Antebellum America* (New York: Cambridge University Press, 2021).

7. Nicholas Guyatt, *Providence and the Invention of the United States, 1607–1876* (New York: Cambridge University Press, 2007), 256–98; Coffey, *Exodus and Liberation*, 134–44, 165–67. For an account of the Civil War that gives considerable attention to providentialist beliefs and rhetoric, see Elizabeth Varon, *Armies of Deliverance: A New History of the Civil War* (New York: Oxford University Press, 2019). For an account stressing the limits of antislavery sentiment among white northerners, see Gary Gallagher, *The Union War* (Cambridge, MA: Harvard University Press, 2011). For accounts highlighting abolitionists' influence, see James Oakes, *Freedom National: The Destruction of Slavery in the United States, 1861–1865* (New York: W. W. Norton, 2013); and Frank J Cirillo, *The Abolitionist Civil War: Immediatist and the Struggle to Transform the Union* (Baton Rouge: Louisiana University Press, 2023).

8. Henry J. Van Dyke, "The Character and Influence of Abolitionism," 9 December 1860, in *Fast Day Sermons: Or, The Pulpit on the State of the Country* (New York: Rudd & Carleton, 1861), 127–76, esp. 139, 152. Van Dyke's sermon was also published in December 1860 in New York by D. Appleton and in Baltimore by Henry Taylor. See also Sean A. Scott, "The Character and Influence of Abolitionism: A Sermon that Gripped a Nation and Defined a Man," *American Nineteenth Century History* 16 (September 2015): 193–211.

9. Tayler Lewis, "Patriarchal and Jewish Servitude No Argument for American Slavery," (originally published in *The World* in December 1860), in *Fast Day Sermons: Or, The Pulpit on the State of the Country* (New York: Rudd & Carleton, 1861), 177–226, quotations from 191, 204, 209, 222. See also James Renwick Wilson, *Review of Rev. Henry J. Van Dyke's Discourse on "The Character and Influence of Abolitionism," a Sermon Preached in the Third Reformed Presbyterian Church, Twenty-third Street, New York, on Sabbath Evening, December 23, 1860* (New York: William Erving, 1861); William H. Boole, *Antidote to Rev. H. J. Van Dyke's Pro-slavery Discourse . . .* (New York: E. Jones, 1861).

10. For Edmundson and Sewall, see Chapter 1. For other antebellum abolitionists' use of Ephesians 2:14, see for example Theodore Dwight Weld, *The Bible Against Slavery: An Inquiry Into the Patriarchal and Mosaic Systems on the Subject of Human Rights*, 4th ed. (New York:

American Anti-Slavery Society, 1838), 75; J. Blanchard and N. L. Rice, *A Debate on Slavery Held in the City of Cincinnati, on the First, Second, Third, and Sixth Days of October, 1845 . . .* (Cincinnati: Wm. H. Moore, 1846), 461; and Harriet Beecher Stowe, *A Key to Uncle Tom's Cabin: Presenting the Original Facts and Documents Upon Which the Story is Founded . . .* (Boston: John P. Jewett, 1853), 31, 33.

11. "Proclamation of President Lincoln," *New York Times*, 16 August 1861; "Our National Fast," *Douglass' Monthly* (Rochester, NY), October 1861, 531–32; John Jay Dana, *The Acceptable Fast: A Sermon Delivered in the Village Church in Cummington, Mass., on the Day of the National Fast, September 26, 1861* (Northampton, MA: Metcalf, 1861), 15, 16; "The National Fast Day: How It Was Observed . . . ," *New York Times*, 27 September 1861.

12. Joseph E. Roy, *Pilgrim's Letters: Bits of Current History* (Boston and Chicago: Congregational Sunday-School and Publishing Society, 1888), 26–30. "The President and Emancipation: An Interview with a Delegation from Chicago," *New York Times*, 26 September 1862; Varon, *Armies of Deliverance*, 110, 154–55.

13. Emancipation Proclamation, 1 January 1863, in William E. Gienapp, ed., *This Fiery Trial: The Speeches and Writings of Abraham Lincoln* (New York: Oxford University Press, 2002), 151–52; Chauncey Giles, *The Problem of American Nationality, and the Evils Which Hinder Its Solution: A Discourse Delivered on the Day of the National Fast, April 30, 1863* (Cincinnati: Published by Request, 1863), 24. See also "Sermon of Rev. Henry Ward Beecher," *New York Times*, 1 May 1863.

14. "The National Fast: Its Local Observance . . . Sermon of Rev. Dr. G. B. Cheever," *New York Times*, 1 May 1863 (see also the sermons of Henry Ward Beecher, Dr. Bellows, S. H. Tyng, I. S. Kalloch, and J. R. W. Sloane in the same issue); Linus H. Shaw, *The Black Man and the War: A Sermon, Preached at Sudbury, Mass., on Thanksgiving Day, Nov. 24, 1864 . . .* (Waltham, [MA]: Hastings's 'Sentinel' Office, 1864), 8, 10. See also William Lamson, *God Hiding Himself in Times of Trouble: A Sermon Preached on the Day of the State Fast, April 2, 1863, in the Baptist Church, Brookline, Mass.* (Boston: Gould and Lincoln, 1863), 17, 24.

15. Lincoln to A. G. Hodges, April 4, 1864, in Gienapp, *This Fiery Trial*, 194–95; Varon, *Armies of Deliverance*, 356–403.

16. Lincoln, Second Inaugural Address, in Gienapp, *This Fiery Trial*, 220–22.

INDEX

ACKNOWLEDGMENTS

This book has taken me a very long time to complete, in part because it is not the book I intended to write but rather a prequel. In 2013, I completed a dissertation that, like this book, was seven chapters long. Looking back, I now realize that this entire book grew out of the first chapter of that dissertation. Initially, I assumed that I could cover the American Revolution in a few pages to set up my actual focus, antislavery politics in the early republic. However, I eventually determined that both the Revolution and the religious component of antislavery were far more complex and deserved more space than I had initially granted them. Then I realized I could not understand them without going back earlier, first to the French and Indian War, then to the seventeenth century, and even back to biblical times. Hopefully, the resulting book provides a more thorough but not exhausting explanation of the interplay between religion, the Revolution, and the antislavery movement. I should perhaps mention that most of the people thanked below have not actually seen the material in this volume but have helped me on the larger project and commented on material that will appear in a sequel. I am grateful for their support in my intellectual endeavors.

The genesis of this project dates back to the last millennium, when I randomly took a class on slavery in world history at Rutgers University, New Brunswick, because it fit well with the rest of my schedule. In that class, Christopher Leslie Brown planted the seed that led to my honors thesis and eventually to this book. As an undergraduate, I also benefited from the coursework and guidance of Herman Bennett and Jennifer Morgan. When I was getting my master's degree at Rutgers, Camden, Andrew Shankman was an excellent mentor. Much of this book is an answer to Andy's pushing me to explain the perpetuation of slavery after the American Revolution in a more nuanced form than my initial response that "they knew it was wrong but did it anyway." I also thank Wayne Glasker, Howard Gillette, Lorrin Thomas, the late Andy Lees, and the other history department faculty.

At the University of Virginia, Peter Onuf lived up to his reputation as a wonderful advisor. His encouragement, scholarly rigor, and good cheer made my time in Charlottesville exceptionally rewarding. My other committee members at UVA, Max Edelson, Elizabeth Varon, and Jennifer Greeson, also helped me develop as a scholar through their courses and feedback. I also benefited from two bonus committee members. Matthew Mason generously offered to serve on my committee after I got to know him through the Society of Historians of the Early American Republic. Alan Taylor, as the incoming Thomas Jefferson Foundation Professor at UVA, graciously agreed to add my dissertation defense to his schedule while in town for a book talk. At UVA I also benefited from coursework and conversations with Gary Gallagher, Patrick Griffin, Paul Halliday, and the late Joe Miller. I had a great cohort of graduate student colleagues, especially Mike "Kettle Bell" Caires, Carli Conklin, Jason Farr, David Flaherty, Randi Lewis Flaherty, Jon Grinspan, and Will Kurtz. I also benefited from the camaraderie and constructive criticism of other participants in the Early American Seminar with whom I overlapped, especially Asaf Almog, Jim Ambuske, Kate Brown, Christa Dierksheide, Lawrence Hatter, Jim Hrdlicka, Whitney Martinko, Martin Öhman, R. S. T. Stoermer, George Van Cleve, Gaye Wilson, and Jeff Zvengrowski. During my time in Charlottesville, I also received important funding from the Robert H. Smith International Center for Jefferson Studies and employment as a research assistant at Monticello. Thanks to Anna Berkes, Ellen Hickman, Andrew Jackson O'Shaughnessy, Mary Scott-Fleming, Leni Sorensen, and Cinder Stanton for making these experiences enriching and fun.

Short-term fellowships at the Library Company of Philadelphia (LCP) and the Historical Society of Pennsylvania (HSP), followed by a dissertation fellowship at the McNeil Center for Early American Studies, were crucial for my research. Thanks to all the archivists, especially James Green and Connie King at the LCP and Steve Smith at the HSP. My time at the MCEAS was both productive and fun, thanks to Dan Richter, Amy Baxter-Bellamy, and the fellows of 2011–2012, especially the other members of the Suds of Liberty Brewing Club along with Sari Altschuler, Cassie Good, Rachel Hermann, Matt Karp, Dael Norwood, Ed Pompeian, and Jessica Roney. A fellowship at the Huntington Library provided access to some rare sources and an excuse for a cross-country road trip with my wife; thanks to Liz and Dennis Kneier for hosting us. Thanks to Ted O'Reilly and Tammy Kitter for helping me navigate the New York Historical Society during a fellowship funded by the

Gilder Lehrman Institute of American History. A National Endowment for the Humanities postdoctoral fellowship at the LCP allowed me to revisit my favorite archives. Randy Browne, Aston Gonzalez, Jessica Linker, Brian Luskey, Rachel Walker, and other fellows helped enliven the reading room and the Cassatt House. A fellowship at the Fred W. Smith National Library for the Study of George Washington provided important access to online databases that have been key to my continued research. Thanks to Doug Bradburn and Stephen McLeod, along with my fellow fellows Cole Jones and Lydia Brandt. A fellowship at Haverford College, along with trips to Swarthmore College, allowed me to dive deep into Quaker sources. Thanks to Mary Crauderueff, Christopher Densmore, Sarah Horowitz, and Ann Upton for help navigating the records.

A two-year Cassius M. Clay postdoctoral fellowship at Yale University provided time to expand my project. I benefited from the seminars hosted by the Yale Early America Historians and the Race and Slavery Working Group. Thanks to Michael Blaakman, David Blight, Zach Conn, Rob Forbes, Joanne Freeman, Michael Hattem, Josh Lynn, Steve Pincus, Brad Proctor, Ariel Ron, Ed Rugemer, Thomas Thurston, Connor Williams, and the other participants. It was a great treat to be able to invite Rich Newman and James Brewer Stewart to participate in a book manuscript workshop (even if most of the material they read will be saved for my next book). Thanks to Sarah Gronningsater for joining as well, as a bonus commenter.

I have received valuable feedback from commentators and copanelists at various conferences and seminars hosted by organizations such as the MCEAS, the Omohundro Institute of Early American History and Culture, and SHEAR. Thanks to Dee Andrews, Rick Bell, Richard Blackett, David Blight, Chris Bonner, John Brooke, Corey Brooks, Chris Brown, Kathleen Brown, Jane Calvert, Frank Cogliano, Catherine Clinton, Aaron Crawford, David Crosby, Michael Crowder, Lo Faber, Paul Finkelman, David Gellman, Teresa Goddu, Sally Gordon, Annette Gordon-Reed, Sarah Gronningsater, Nick Guyatt, Craig Hammond, Scot Heerman, Matthew Hetrick, Sue Kozel, Jane Landers, Matt Mason, Evelyn McCollin, Margot Minardi, Johann Neem, Richard Newman, Dael Norwood, Anthony Parent, Rob Parkinson, Lawrence Peskin, Marcus Rediker, Jonathan Sassi, Samantha Seeley, Jason Sharples, Manisha Sinha, Matt Spooner, Grant Stanton, Beverly Tomek, Matt White, Eva Sheppard Wolf, and Mike Zuckerman. Among established scholars, Craig Hammond, Matt Mason, and Rich Newman have been especially supportive over the years. Among those whom I first knew as fellow graduate students, special thanks to Andrew Diemer, Andrew Fagal, Craig Hollander, Paul Polgar, and Paddy Riley, for sharing sources, feedback, meals, and drinks.

My research on Quakers brought me into contact with Jean Soderlund, whose work I have always admired, and I thank her for coauthoring an article with me and helping me become comfortable in the seventeenth century. The late Gary Nash was another scholarly idol, and I enjoyed our many discussions about Warner Mifflin and John Parrish. I regret that I did not finish this book in time for him to see it or to coauthor an article we had planned. My interest in Massachusetts has been a relatively recent development; special thanks to Edward Bell and Jeanne Pickering for sharing their unpublished work with me and helping me understand the eighteenth-century legal system and its records. Thanks also to Emily Blanck for answering email queries about freedom suits.

I am pleased to have found a scholarly home at Spring Hill College. Thanks to my colleagues (including some whom have left) for making SHC and Mobile, Alabama, a great place to live and work (and for listening to me talk about this project for eight years), especially Shane Dillingham, Harold (and Dorothy) Dorton, Sarah Duncan, Tom Hoffman, Vlad Kravstov, Wyndi Ludwikowski, Kathleen Orange, Alex Ruble, Tom Ward, and the rest of the Social Sciences Division, along with Matthew Bagot, Ryan Noble, and Fr. Chris Viscardi, SJ. Teaching four classes each semester has slowed my writing, but my students have also helped me (largely unknowingly) formulate and hone much of the material in this book. Thanks to all the students, especially those in my "Slavery and the Bible" and my "Black Lives in Early America classes," along with Claire Witt, who read a draft of the manuscript and gave me feedback from the perspective of an undergraduate honors student. A Mitchell Faculty Scholarship Grant funded a summer research trip, Provost Rebecca Cantor found some funds for conference travel another summer, and Bret Heim has helped stretch a tight library budget. Thanks to Duncan James for serving as a volunteer research assistant one summer. Thanks to my history friends over at the University of South Alabama—Claire Cage, Tim Lombardo (and his partner, Beca Venter-Lombardo), and Kelly Urban—for workshopping chapter drafts over drinks.

I am thrilled to have this book published by Penn Press and appreciate Bob Lockhart's long patience with me as I missed deadlines, added new chapters that no one asked for, and ultimately split my project in two. I appreciate his faith in me and his willingness to give me the time and space to try to figure out how exactly the Revolution fit into my narrative of abolitionism.

Having David Waldstreicher as a series editor was a key consideration that brought me to Penn Press, as I have long admired his scholarship. I am grateful for David's support and insightful feedback over the years, even after I took so long to finish that he is no longer a formal editor of the Early American Studies series. I was also very pleased that Penn Press selected Craig Hammond as one of the external readers; his detailed comments have been extremely helpful. Thanks also to the anonymous other reader for their helpful feedback. Thanks to Noreen O'Connor-Abel and Jon Dertien for overseeing the final production of the book, and to Amaranth Tupelo and the rest of the Twin Oaks Community for compiling the index and making my favorite tofu. The final completion of this book was facilitated by grants from the Friends Historical Association and the Fellowship in Memory of Kenneth R. LaVoy Jr., established by the Society of Colonial Wars in the state of Florida and administered by Florida Atlantic University.

Thanks to many friends and family who have housed and fed me on various research trips over the years—especially the Deppens, my in-laws Lew and Martha Gay, Kurt Kesedar (and filetmignonathons), Pete Mastriano, Ryan and Jaimie Sholinsky, Dave and Tara Strohmeier, Tim Wood and Megan Olsen, my Aunt Eleanor, and my late Uncle Jerry. My love and thanks to my parents, my late stepmom Monika, my stepmom Holly, and all the other family members who have supported me over the years.

No one has been more patient with this project than Alison, the love of my life. Thank you for all of the support, encouragement, and love over the last twenty years, and for reading drafts and allowing me to give impromptu lectures on abolitionism over dinner. Our children, Felix and Leona, have mostly found ways of lending support other than observing the claims of the sanctity of my study (I have been interrupted more times than I can count while trying to finish these acknowledgments), but their challenge and delight is the best contribution of all.